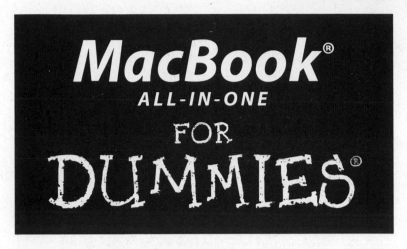

# MacBook®
## ALL-IN-ONE
## FOR
# DUMMIES®

## by Mark L. Chambers

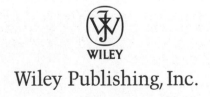

WILEY

Wiley Publishing, Inc.

**MacBook® All-in-One For Dummies®**

Published by
**Wiley Publishing, Inc.**
111 River Street
Hoboken, NJ 07030-5774

www.wiley.com

Copyright © 2010 by Wiley Publishing, Inc., Indianapolis, Indiana

Published by Wiley Publishing, Inc., Indianapolis, Indiana

Published simultaneously in Canada

For general information on our other products and services, please contact our Customer Care Department within the U.S. at 877-762-2974, outside the U.S. at 317-572-3993, or fax 317-572-4002.

For technical support, please visit www.wiley.com/techsupport.

Wiley also publishes its books in a variety of electronic formats. Some content that appears in print may not be available in electronic books.

Library of Congress Control Number: 2009937842

ISBN: 978-0-470-47568-3

Manufactured in the United States of America

10 9 8 7 6 5 4 3 2 1

WILEY

# About the Author

**Mark L. Chambers** has been an author, computer consultant, BBS sysop, programmer, and hardware technician for more than 25 years — pushing computers and their uses far beyond "normal" performance limits for decades now. His first love affair with a computer peripheral blossomed in 1984 when he bought his lightning-fast 300 BPS modem for his Atari 400. Now he spends entirely too much time on the Internet and drinks far too much caffeine-laden soda.

With a degree in journalism and creative writing from Louisiana State University, Mark took the logical career choice: programming computers. However, after five years as a COBOL programmer for a hospital system, he decided there must be a better way to earn a living, and he became the Documentation Manager for Datastorm Technologies, a well-known communications software developer. Somewhere in between writing software manuals, Mark began writing computer how-to books. His first book, *Running a Perfect BBS*, was published in 1994 — and after a short fifteen years of fun (disguised as hard work), Mark is one of the most productive and best-selling technology authors on the planet.

Along with writing several books a year and editing whatever his publishers throw at him, Mark has also branched out into Web-based education, designing and teaching a number of online classes — called *WebClinics* — for Hewlett-Packard.

His favorite pastimes include collecting gargoyles, watching St. Louis Cardinals baseball, playing his three pinball machines and the latest computer games, supercharging computers, and rendering 3D flights of fancy with *TrueSpace* — and during all that, he listens to just about every type of music imaginable. Mark's worldwide Internet radio station, *MLC Radio* (at www.mlcbooks.com), plays only CD-quality classics from 1970 to 1979, including everything from Rush to Billy Joel to the *Rocky Horror Picture Show*.

Mark's rapidly expanding list of books includes *MacBook For Dummies*, 2nd Edition; *Mac OS X Snow Leopard All-in-One For Dummies*; *Macs for Seniors For Dummies*; *iMac For Dummies*, 5th Edition; *Build Your Own PC Do-It-Yourself For Dummies*; *Building a PC For Dummies*, 5th Edition; *Scanners For Dummies*, 2nd Edition; *CD & DVD Recording For Dummies*, 2nd Edition; *PCs All-in-One Desk Reference For Dummies*, 4th Edition; *Mac OS X Tiger: Top 100 Simplified Tips & Tricks*; *Microsoft Office v. X Power User's Guide*; *BURN IT! Creating Your Own Great DVDs and CDs*; *The Hewlett-Packard Official Printer Handbook*; *The Hewlett-Packard Official Recordable CD Handbook*; *The Hewlett-Packard Official Digital Photography Handbook*; *Computer Gamer's Bible*; *Recordable CD Bible*; *Teach Yourself the iMac Visually*; *Running a Perfect BBS*; *Official Netscape Guide to Web Animation*; and *Windows 98 Troubleshooting and Optimizing Little Black Book*.

His books have been translated into 15 different languages so far — his favorites are German, Polish, Dutch, and French. Although he can't read them, he enjoys the pictures a great deal.

Mark welcomes all comments about his books. You can reach him at mark@mlcbooks.com, or visit MLC Books Online, his Web site, at www.mlcbooks.com.

# Dedication

This book is dedicated with all my love to my aunt and uncle, Ruby and Tuffy Chambers, and their masterpiece: the grand mansion that is the White Elephant!

# Author's Acknowledgments

Yes, I've written yet another Macintosh book — but this title is another in the hefty All-in-One series, which demands more work from everyone at Wiley Publishing! Now that the tome is ready for the shelves, I'd like to thank everyone who pitched in to make this project such a success.

As with all my books, I'd like to first thank my wife, Anne; and my children, Erin, Chelsea, and Rose, for their support and love — and for letting me follow my dream!

The Composition Services team is in charge of the figures, artwork and layout for each of my books — they turn a plain document into printed pages that are informative, easy to read, and attractive! Thanks to each of the team members for a beautiful book.

Next, I again send my heartfelt thanks and appreciation to my superb technical editor Dennis Cohen, who once again took on the challenge of checking the technical accuracy of every word contained herein! His comprehensive knowledge of everything Apple (including the beta features tucked into the crannies of Snow Leopard) was invaluable throughout.

Finally, hats off to my project editor Susan Christophersen, who patiently managed the entire title from beginning to end, and my acquisitions editor Bob Woerner, who once again provided guidance throughout. Folks like Susan and Bob are the perfect example of why I'm proud (and lucky) to call Wiley my publisher!

## Publisher's Acknowledgments

We're proud of this book; please send us your comments through our online registration form located at http://dummies.custhelp.com. For other comments, please contact our Customer Care Department within the U.S. at 877-762-2974, outside the U.S. at 317-572-3993, or fax 317-572-4002.

Some of the people who helped bring this book to market include the following:

### Acquisitions and Editorial

**Project and Copy Editor:** Susan Christophersen

**Executive Editor:** Bob Woerner

**Technical Editor:** Dennis Cohen

**Editorial Manager:** Jodi Jensen

**Sr. Editorial Assistant:** Cherie Case

**Cartoons:** Rich Tennant (www.the5thwave.com)

### Composition Services

**Project Coordinator:** Patrick Redmond

**Layout and Graphics:** Ana Carrillo, Christin Swinford, Ronald Terry, Christine Williams

**Proofreaders:** Evelyn C. Gibson, Rob Springer

**Indexer:** BIM Indexing & Proofreading Services

---

**Publishing and Editorial for Technology Dummies**

**Richard Swadley,** Vice President and Executive Group Publisher

**Andy Cummings,** Vice President and Publisher

**Mary Bednarek,** Executive Acquisitions Director

**Mary C. Corder,** Editorial Director

**Publishing for Consumer Dummies**

**Diane Graves Steele,** Vice President and Publisher

**Composition Services**

**Debbie Stailey,** Director of Composition Services

# Contents at a Glance

*Introduction* ..................................................................... 1

*Book I: Say Hello to Your MacBook* .............................. 7

Chapter 1: Exploring MacBook Basics ................................................. 9

Chapter 2: MacBook Models Compared ............................................. 21

Chapter 3: Setting Up and Taking Care of Your MacBook .................. 29

Chapter 4: Extra Stuff You'll Likely Want .......................................... 39

*Book II: Using Mac OS X with Your MacBook* ............... 45

Chapter 1: Shaking Hands with Mac OS X .......................................... 47

Chapter 2: Navigating and Running Programs .................................... 61

Chapter 3: Basic OS X Housekeeping ................................................. 87

Chapter 4: Searching Everything with Spotlight ............................... 115

Chapter 5: Fun with Photo Booth and Front Row ............................. 125

Chapter 6: Keeping Track with the Address Book ............................. 133

Chapter 7: The Joys of Maintenance ................................................ 145

Chapter 8: Getting Help for the Big X .............................................. 167

Chapter 9: Troubleshooting the X .................................................... 175

*Book III: MacBook Customizing and Sharing* .............. 185

Chapter 1: Building the Finder of Your Dreams ............................... 187

Chapter 2: Giving Your Desktop the Personal Touch ....................... 207

Chapter 3: Delving under the Hood with System Preferences .......... 221

Chapter 4: You Mean Others Can Use My MacBook, Too? ............... 261

Chapter 5: Setting Up Multiuser Accounts ...................................... 269

Chapter 6: Sharing Documents for Fun and Profit ........................... 283

Chapter 7: Common-Sense Laptop Security ..................................... 291

*Book IV: Going Mobile with iLife* ............................... 297

Chapter 1: The World According to Apple ....................................... 299

Chapter 2: Jamming with iTunes and iPod ...................................... 309

Chapter 3: Focusing on iPhoto ....................................................... 333

Chapter 4: Making Magic with iMovie ............................................. 357

Chapter 5: Burn Those DVDs! Using iDVD ....................................... 375

Chapter 6: Becoming a Superstar with GarageBand ..................................... 395
Chapter 7: Crafting a Web Site with iWeb .................................................... 417
Chapter 8: No, It's Not Called iQuickTime ................................................... 429
Chapter 9: Turning Your MacBook into a DVD Theater ............................. 435

## Book V: iWork for the Road Warrior .......................... 445

Chapter 1: Desktop Publishing with Pages ................................................. 447
Chapter 2: Creating Spreadsheets with Numbers ...................................... 461
Chapter 3: Building Presentations with Keynote ....................................... 475

## Book VI: The Typical Internet Stuff .......................... 487

Chapter 1: Getting on the Internet .............................................................. 489
Chapter 2: Using Apple Mail ........................................................................ 497
Chapter 3: Staying in Touch with iChat ...................................................... 521
Chapter 4: Expanding Your Horizons with iDisk ....................................... 535
Chapter 5: Surfing with Safari ..................................................................... 541
Chapter 6: Staying Secure Online ............................................................... 557

## Book VII: Networking in Mac OS X .......................... 567

Chapter 1: Setting Up a Small Network ...................................................... 569
Chapter 2: Using Your Network ................................................................... 585
Chapter 3: Going Wireless ........................................................................... 599
Chapter 4: Sharing That Precious Internet Thing ..................................... 611

## Book VIII: Expanding Your System .......................... 623

Chapter 1: Hardware That Will Make You Giddy ....................................... 625
Chapter 2: Add RAM, Hard Drive Space, and Stir ..................................... 637
Chapter 3: Port-o-Rama: Using USB and FireWire .................................... 649
Chapter 4: I'm Okay, You're a Printer ......................................................... 655
Chapter 5: Applications That You've (Probably) Gotta Have ................... 663
Chapter 6: Putting Bluetooth to Work ........................................................ 679

## Book IX: Advanced Mac OS X .......................... 687

Chapter 1: Using UNIX on Your MacBook ................................................... 689
Chapter 2: AppleScript Just Plain Rocks .................................................... 711
Chapter 3: Writing and Conversing with Your MacBook .......................... 725

## Index .................................................. 739

# Table of Contents

*Introduction* ......................................................................... *1*

    What's Really Required..........................................................2

    About This Book .....................................................................3

    Conventions Used in This Book............................................3

        Stuff you type .................................................................3

        Menu commands............................................................3

        Display messages ..........................................................4

        In case you're curious about computers ....................4

    How This Book Is Organized ................................................4

        Book I: Say Hello to Your MacBook ............................4

        Book II: Using Mac OS X with Your MacBook............4

        Book III: MacBook Customizing and Sharing.............5

        Book IV: Going Mobile with iLife................................5

        Book V: iWork for the Road Warrior ..........................5

        Book VI: The Typical Internet Stuff............................5

        Book VII: Networking in Mac OS X ............................5

        Book VIII: Expanding Your System .............................6

        Book IX: Advanced Mac OS X ......................................6

    Icons Used in This Book ........................................................6

*Book I: Say Hello to Your MacBook*.................................. *7*

    **Chapter 1: Exploring MacBook Basics** ...........................**9**

    "One Uses a Battery!"............................................................9

        The "absolute" need for mobility................................10

        Space saving is a good thing ......................................10

        Enclosed and constrained ..........................................11

        Paying the laptop price................................................11

        Repairs may cause dizziness ......................................12

    So, Are You Ready for a MacBook? ....................................12

    Looking Over Your Laptop...................................................13

        The parts you probably recognize ............................13

        The holes called ports................................................17

        Don't forget the parts you can't see..........................18

    **Chapter 2: MacBook Models Compared** ........................**21**

    Your Entry-Level Mac Laptop .............................................21

    The Power User's Toolbox....................................................22

Meet the MacBook Air...........................................................................23
   Comparing MacBooks ...............................................................23
   Look, Ma, no moving parts! The magic of solid-state drives..........26
   What if I need that pesky optical drive? .....................................27

**Chapter 3: Setting Up and Taking Care of Your MacBook . . . . . . . . .29**
   Location, Location, Location!.....................................................29
   Unpacking and Connecting Your Laptop.....................................30
      Unpacking for the road warrior ..........................................30
      Connecting cables 101.......................................................31
   Fire That Puppy Up ..................................................................32
   Mark's Favorite Signs of a Healthy MacBook ..............................33
   A Primer in MacBook Handling and Care ....................................34
      Great, a lecture about handling my laptop ..........................34
      Keeping things clean .........................................................35
      More about batteries than you likely thought possible ...............35

**Chapter 4: Extra Stuff You'll Likely Want. . . . . . . . . . . . . . . . . . . . .39**
   An Overview of MacBook Software Goodness...............................39
      What comes with my laptop? .............................................39
      Connecting to the Internet from your lap ............................40
      Applications that rock........................................................40
      Boot Camp for Dummies ...................................................41
      Applications you'll end up getting.......................................41
   Other Stuff That Nearly Everyone Wants .....................................42

*Book II: Using Mac OS X with Your MacBook ............... 45*

**Chapter 1: Shaking Hands with Mac OS X . . . . . . . . . . . . . . . . . . . .47**
   Convince Me: Why Mac OS X?....................................................48
      Pretty to behold ..............................................................48
      Stable, stable, stable.........................................................52
      Multitasking and multithreading for normal human beings...........54
      The definition of Internet savvy.........................................55
      Lots of free goodies .........................................................56
   What Do I Really Need to Run the Big X?.....................................57
   Upgrading from Earlier Versions of Mac OS .................................58
      Back up — PLEASE back up.................................................58
      Snuff out disk errors ........................................................58
      Plug it, road warrior ........................................................58
   Personalizing the Big X .............................................................59

**Chapter 2: Navigating and Running Programs . . . . . . . . . . . . . . . . . .61**
   Restarting, Sleeping, and Shutting Down.....................................61
      Living the Trackpad Lifestyle .............................................64

A Window Is Much More Than a Frame...................................................65
    Opening and closing windows ................................................65
    Scrolling windows ..................................................................66
    Minimizing and restoring windows ......................................67
    Zooming windows ..................................................................68
    Toggling toolbars ...................................................................68
    Moving windows ....................................................................69
    Resizing windows...................................................................69
    Switching windows ................................................................69
Menu Mysteries Explained .........................................................71
Icons 'R Us ...................................................................................72
    Hardware.................................................................................72
    Programs and applications....................................................74
    Files.........................................................................................74
    Folders....................................................................................75
    Aliases ....................................................................................76
Selecting Icons for Fun and Profit.............................................77
    Selecting a single icon ..........................................................77
    Selecting multiple icons .......................................................78
Keyboard Shortcuts for the True Power User ...........................79
Houston, We're Go to Launch Programs ....................................80
    Running applications from your hard drive.........................80
    Running applications from a CD-ROM or DVD-ROM ...........81
Switching 'Twixt Programs with Aplomb ...................................82
Opening and Saving Your Stuff in an Application ......................84
    Opening a document .............................................................84
    Saving a document.................................................................86
Quitting Programs ........................................................................86

**Chapter 3: Basic OS X Housekeeping............................87**

The Finder: It's the Wind beneath Your Wings.........................87
Copying and Moving Files and Folders .....................................89
Cloning Your Items — It's Happening Now! ...............................90
Deleting That Which Should Not Be............................................91
    Dragging unruly files against their will................................91
    Deleting with the menus and the keyboard.........................91
Emptying That Wastepaper Basket.............................................91
WAIT! I Need That After All! ........................................................92
Renaming Your Items....................................................................93
Adding a Dash of Color ................................................................93
Displaying the Facts on Files and Folders .................................93
    Adding Spotlight comments..................................................95
    Displaying extensions............................................................95
    Choosing the application with which to launch a file.......96
    Locking files against evildoers ............................................97
Creating an Alias............................................................................98
Using the Apple Menu...................................................................98
    Using Recent Items ...............................................................98
    Playing with the Dock............................................................100

Bad program! Quit!.................................................................100
Tracking down your version ..............................................102
Specifying a location..........................................................102
Availing Yourself of Mac OS X Services ......................................103
Get Thee Hence: Using the Go Menu.........................................104
Monkeying with the Menu Bar ....................................................105
Using menu bar icons .........................................................105
Doing timely things with the Clock.....................................107
Eject, Tex, Eject!.........................................................................108
Common Tasks Aplenty...............................................................109
Opening and editing text files.............................................109
Listening to an audio CD.....................................................110
Recording — nay, burning — a data CD ............................111
All You Really Need to Know about Printing ...........................111

**Chapter 4: Searching Everything with Spotlight** . . . . . . . . . . . . . . . .**115**
Basic Searching 101...................................................................115
Is Spotlight Really That Cool? ...................................................117
Expanding Your Search Horizons...............................................120
Customizing Spotlight to Your Taste ........................................121

**Chapter 5: Fun with Photo Booth and Front Row** . . . . . . . . . . . . . . . .**125**
Capturing the Moment with iSight and Photo Booth..............126
Producing Video on the Spot with iMovie................................128
Controlling Your MacBook Remotely with Front Row.............129

**Chapter 6: Keeping Track with the Address Book** . . . . . . . . . . . . . . . .**133**
Hey, Isn't the Address Book Just a Part of Mail?......................133
Entering Contact Information ....................................................135
Using Contact Information ........................................................137
Arranging Your Contact Cards...................................................139
Using Network Directories ........................................................140
Printing Contacts with Flair ......................................................142
Swapping Bytes with vCards.....................................................143

**Chapter 7: The Joys of Maintenance** . . . . . . . . . . . . . . . . . . . . . . . . . . .**145**
Deleting Applications the Common Sense Way.........................145
Popping the Hood: Using the System Profiler..........................147
Tracking Performance with Activity Monitor ..........................148
Fixing Things with the Disk Utility ...........................................151
Displaying the goods on your disks .....................................151
Playing doctor with First Aid...............................................153
Erasing without seriously screwing up ................................154
Partitioning the right way.....................................................156
RAID has nothing to do with insects ...................................158
Updating Mac OS X....................................................................160

I Demand That You Back Up Your Hard Drive.............................161
    Hitching a ride on the Time Machine.............................161
    Using other backup solutions .............................163
I Further Demand That You Defragment .............................164
Special Start-Up Keys for Those Special Times .............................164
Crave the Newest Drivers .............................165

**Chapter 8: Getting Help for the Big X .............................167**

Displaying the Help Viewer Window.............................167
Searching for Specific Stuff.............................169
Prodding Apple for the Latest Gossip.............................170
Calling for Help Deep in the Heart of X.............................171
Other Resources to Chew On.............................171
    Voice support.............................172
    Mac publications and resource sites .............................172
    Local Mac outlets and user groups .............................173

**Chapter 9: Troubleshooting the X .............................175**

Don't Panic! .............................175
The Troubleshooting Process.............................176
    Step 1: Always try a simple shutdown .............................177
    Step 2: Check all cable connections .............................177
    Step 3: Retrace your steps.............................177
    Step 4: Run Disk Utility.............................178
    Step 5: Run antivirus software .............................178
    Step 6: Check the Trash .............................178
    Step 7: Check online connections .............................179
    Step 8: Disable troublesome Login Items.............................179
    Step 9: Turn off your screen saver.............................180
    Step 10: Check for write protection.............................180
    Step 11: Check your System Profiler .............................181
    Step 12: Reboot with the Mac OS X Installation disc.............................181
Do I Need to Reinstall Mac OS X? .............................181
It's Still Not Moving: Troubleshooting Resources.............................182
    The Mac OS X Help Viewer .............................182
    The Apple Mac OS X Support site.............................183
    Your local Apple dealer .............................183

**Book III: MacBook Customizing and Sharing .............. 185**

**Chapter 1: Building the Finder of Your Dreams .............................187**

Will That Be Icons or Lists or Columns . . . or Even a Flow?.............................188
Doing the Toolbar Dance.............................191
    Hiding and showing the toolbar.............................191
    Hiding and showing the status bar.............................191
    Giving your toolbar big tires and a loud exhaust .............................192
Searching for Files from the Toolbar .............................194

Searching for Files from the Find Dialog...................................195
Configuring the View Options ........................................197
    Setting icon view options.......................................197
    Setting list view options........................................200
    Setting column view options .................................202
    Setting Cover Flow view options.............................204
Setting Finder Preferences ..........................................204

## Chapter 2: Giving Your Desktop the Personal Touch..............207

Changing the Background .............................................207
    Picking something Apple .......................................208
    I just gotta have lavender ......................................210
    Selecting your own photo......................................210
Changing the Screen Saver..........................................211
Changing Colors in Mac OS X.......................................212
Adding Stickies........................................................212
Customizing the Dock ...............................................214
    Adding applications and extras to the Dock ...............215
    Keeping track(s) with Stacks.................................216
    Resizing the Dock...............................................217
Stick It on the Dashboard ...........................................218
Arranging Your Precious Desktop..................................220

## Chapter 3: Delving under the Hood with System Preferences......221

The Preferred Way to Display the Preferences ..................221
Saving Your Preferences.............................................222
Searching for Specific Settings.....................................223
Getting Personal .....................................................223
    Appearance preferences .......................................223
    Desktop and screen saver preferences......................225
    Dock preferences................................................226
    Exposé and Spaces preferences..............................228
    Language & Text preferences.................................230
    Security preferences............................................232
    Spotlight preferences ..........................................234
It's All about the Hardware ..........................................235
    CDs and DVDs preferences...................................235
    Displays preferences...........................................235
    Energy Saver preferences .....................................236
    Keyboard preferences..........................................238
    Mouse preferences.............................................239
    Trackpad preferences..........................................240
    Printing and fax preferences.................................240
    Sound preferences..............................................242
Sharing the Joy: Internet and Network ...........................243
    MobileMe preferences.........................................243
    Network preferences ...........................................244
    Bluetooth preferences..........................................248
    Sharing preferences............................................249

Tweaking the System ...................................................................250
   Accounts preferences ...........................................................250
   Date and time preferences....................................................252
   Parental Controls preferences ..............................................253
   Software Update preferences ...............................................254
   Speech preferences ..............................................................254
   Startup Disk preferences .....................................................256
   Time Machine preferences ...................................................257
   Universal Access preferences ..............................................258

**Chapter 4: You Mean Others Can Use My MacBook, Too?** ........**261**

How Multiuser Works on Mac OS X .........................................261
Configuring Your Login Screen ...............................................263
Locking Things Down................................................................266
Starting Applications Automatically after Login .....................267

**Chapter 5: Setting Up Multiuser Accounts** .......................**269**

Adding, Editing, and Deleting Users........................................269
   Adding a new user account ..................................................270
   Editing an existing account ..................................................272
   Deleting an existing account ................................................273
Tightening Your Security Belt...................................................274
   Setting Parental Controls.....................................................275
   Assigning the Simple Finder ................................................278
Using Keychains — NOT...........................................................279

**Chapter 6: Sharing Documents for Fun and Profit** ...............**283**

Sharing over a Network versus Sharing on a Single Mac .......283
   No network is required .........................................................284
   Relying on a guaranteed lock ..............................................284
   Most places are off-limits ....................................................284
Permissions: Law Enforcement for Your Files.........................285
Permission and Sharing Do's and Don'ts................................287
Sharing Stuff in Office 2008.....................................................288
   Document-sharing features ..................................................289
   File-level sharing features ....................................................289

**Chapter 7: Common-Sense Laptop Security** ....................**291**

MacBook Security 101................................................................291
   Mark your MacBook .............................................................291
   Use those doggone passwords.............................................292
   Screen saver hot corners equal instant privacy.................292
   Buy a security cable, and use it ..........................................292
   Avoid the Obvious Laptop Case ..........................................293
   Encryption is your friend......................................................293
   Unsecured Wireless is . . . unsecured ................................294
Using a Security Application.....................................................295

# Book IV: Going Mobile with iLife ............................... 297

## Chapter 1: The World According to Apple.....................299

First, Sliced Bread . . . and Now, the Digital Hub....................299
What Does Digital Mean, Anyway? ....................................300
What Can I Digitize?........................................................301
    Photographs ..........................................................301
    Music ....................................................................302
    Video......................................................................302
    DVD........................................................................302
The Software That Drives the Hub ....................................302
    iPhoto ....................................................................303
    iTunes ....................................................................304
    iMovie ....................................................................304
    iDVD ......................................................................306
    GarageBand ..........................................................306
    iWeb ......................................................................306
Can I Use All This Stuff at One Time?................................307

## Chapter 2: Jamming with iTunes and iPod .....................309

What Can I Play on iTunes?..............................................310
Playing an Audio CD ......................................................311
Playing Digital Audio and Video ......................................312
    Browsing the Library..............................................314
    Finding songs in your Music Library........................315
    Removing old music from the Library ....................316
    Watching video ....................................................316
Keeping Slim Whitman and Slim Shady Apart:
   Organizing with Playlists ............................................316
Know Your Songs............................................................318
    Setting the song information automatically ............319
    Setting or changing the song information manually ....319
Ripping Audio Files........................................................321
Tweaking the Audio for Your Ears ....................................322
A New Kind of Radio Station ............................................323
    iTunes Radio..........................................................324
    Tuning in your own stations....................................324
    Radio stations in your playlists ..............................325
iSending iStuff to iPod ....................................................326
Sharing Your Media across Your Network..........................327
Burning Music to Shiny Plastic Circles..............................328
Feasting on iTunes Visuals..............................................329
Buying Digital Media the Apple Way..................................330

## Chapter 3: Focusing on iPhoto . . . . . . . . . . . . . . . . . . . . . . . . . . . . . . .333

Delving into iPhoto . . . . . . . . . . . . . . . . . . . . . . . . . . . . . . . . . . . . . . . . . . . . . . . . . . . 333
Working with Images in iPhoto . . . . . . . . . . . . . . . . . . . . . . . . . . . . . . . . . . . . . 335
  Import Images 101 . . . . . . . . . . . . . . . . . . . . . . . . . . . . . . . . . . . . . . . . . . . . . 335
  Organize mode: Organizing and sorting your images . . . . . . . . . . . . . . 337
  Edit mode: Removing and fixing stuff the right way . . . . . . . . . . . . . . . . 346
Producing Your Own Coffee-Table Masterpiece . . . . . . . . . . . . . . . . . . . . . 349
You'll Love MobileMe Gallery! . . . . . . . . . . . . . . . . . . . . . . . . . . . . . . . . . . . . . . 352
Mailing Photos to Aunt Mildred . . . . . . . . . . . . . . . . . . . . . . . . . . . . . . . . . . . . . 354

## Chapter 4: Making Magic with iMovie . . . . . . . . . . . . . . . . . . . . .357

The iMovie Window . . . . . . . . . . . . . . . . . . . . . . . . . . . . . . . . . . . . . . . . . . . . . . . . 357
A Bird's-Eye View of Moviemaking . . . . . . . . . . . . . . . . . . . . . . . . . . . . . . . . . . 360
Importing the Building Blocks . . . . . . . . . . . . . . . . . . . . . . . . . . . . . . . . . . . . . . 361
  Pulling in video clips . . . . . . . . . . . . . . . . . . . . . . . . . . . . . . . . . . . . . . . . . . 361
  Making use of still images . . . . . . . . . . . . . . . . . . . . . . . . . . . . . . . . . . . . . 363
  Importing and adding audio from all sorts of places . . . . . . . . . . . . . . . 364
Building the Cinematic Basics . . . . . . . . . . . . . . . . . . . . . . . . . . . . . . . . . . . . . . 367
  Adding clips to your movie . . . . . . . . . . . . . . . . . . . . . . . . . . . . . . . . . . . . . 367
  Removing clips from your movie . . . . . . . . . . . . . . . . . . . . . . . . . . . . . . . . 368
  Reordering clips in your movie . . . . . . . . . . . . . . . . . . . . . . . . . . . . . . . . . . 369
  Editing clips in iMovie . . . . . . . . . . . . . . . . . . . . . . . . . . . . . . . . . . . . . . . . . 369
  Transitions for the masses . . . . . . . . . . . . . . . . . . . . . . . . . . . . . . . . . . . . . 370
  Even Gone with the Wind had titles . . . . . . . . . . . . . . . . . . . . . . . . . . . . . 370
Sharing Your Finished Classic with Others . . . . . . . . . . . . . . . . . . . . . . . . . . 372

## Chapter 5: Burn Those DVDs! Using iDVD . . . . . . . . . . . . . . . . . . .375

Introducing Your Mac to iDVD . . . . . . . . . . . . . . . . . . . . . . . . . . . . . . . . . . . . . . 375
Starting a New DVD Project . . . . . . . . . . . . . . . . . . . . . . . . . . . . . . . . . . . . . . . . 378
  Creating a new project . . . . . . . . . . . . . . . . . . . . . . . . . . . . . . . . . . . . . . . . . 379
  Opening an existing project . . . . . . . . . . . . . . . . . . . . . . . . . . . . . . . . . . . . 379
  Automating the whole darn process . . . . . . . . . . . . . . . . . . . . . . . . . . . . . 379
Creating a DVD from Scratch . . . . . . . . . . . . . . . . . . . . . . . . . . . . . . . . . . . . . . . 380
  Choosing just the right theme . . . . . . . . . . . . . . . . . . . . . . . . . . . . . . . . . . 380
  Adding movies . . . . . . . . . . . . . . . . . . . . . . . . . . . . . . . . . . . . . . . . . . . . . . . . 381
  Great, now my audience demands a slideshow . . . . . . . . . . . . . . . . . . . 385
  Now for the music . . . . . . . . . . . . . . . . . . . . . . . . . . . . . . . . . . . . . . . . . . . . 386
Giving Your DVD the Personal Touch . . . . . . . . . . . . . . . . . . . . . . . . . . . . . . . . 387
  Using Uncle Morty for your DVD Menu background . . . . . . . . . . . . . . . . 387
  Adding your own titles . . . . . . . . . . . . . . . . . . . . . . . . . . . . . . . . . . . . . . . . . 388
  Changing buttons like a highly paid professional . . . . . . . . . . . . . . . . . 388
  Give my creation motion! . . . . . . . . . . . . . . . . . . . . . . . . . . . . . . . . . . . . . . . 389
Previewing Your Masterpiece . . . . . . . . . . . . . . . . . . . . . . . . . . . . . . . . . . . . . . 390
A Word about Automation . . . . . . . . . . . . . . . . . . . . . . . . . . . . . . . . . . . . . . . . . . 391
  One-click paradise with OneStep DVD . . . . . . . . . . . . . . . . . . . . . . . . . . . 391
  Exercising control with Magic iDVD . . . . . . . . . . . . . . . . . . . . . . . . . . . . . 392
Recording a Finished Project to a Shiny Disc . . . . . . . . . . . . . . . . . . . . . . . . 394

## Chapter 6: Becoming a Superstar with GarageBand . . . . . . . . . . . .395

Shaking Hands with Your Band ............................................... 396
Composing and Podcasting Made Easy ................................... 398
    Adding tracks ......................................................... 399
    Choosing loops ...................................................... 402
    Resizing, repeating, and moving loops ................. 406
    Using the Arrange track ......................................... 408
    Tweaking the settings for a track .......................... 409
Automatic Composition with Magic GarageBand ................... 411
Sharing Your Songs and Podcasts .......................................... 413
    Creating MP3 and AAC files and ringtones .......... 413
    Sending a podcast to iWeb or iTunes .................... 415
    Burning an audio CD .............................................. 415

## Chapter 7: Crafting a Web Site with iWeb . . . . . . . . . . . . . . . . . . .417

Looking around the iWeb Window ........................................ 417
Planning Your Pages ............................................................... 419
Adding a New Site ................................................................... 420
Adding a New Page .................................................................. 421
Editing a Page .......................................................................... 421
    Modifying text ........................................................ 422
    Replacing images ................................................... 423
    Adding new elements ............................................. 425
Tweaking with the Inspector .................................................. 426
Publishing Your Web Site ....................................................... 427

## Chapter 8: No, It's Not Called iQuickTime . . . . . . . . . . . . . . . . . . .429

QuickTime Can Do That? ........................................................ 429
Playing Media with QuickTime ............................................... 430
    Opening QuickTime movies ................................... 430
    Operating QuickTime Player .................................. 431

## Chapter 9: Turning Your MacBook into a DVD Theater . . . . . . . . . . .435

The DVD Hardware .................................................................. 435
The DVD Player: It's Truly Shiny ............................................ 435
    Using the controller ............................................... 436
    Keeping your eyes on the Viewer .......................... 438
Taking Advantage of Additional DVD Features ..................... 438
    Controller extras ................................................... 439
    DVD Player preferences ......................................... 440

# *Book V: iWork for the Road Warrior* .......................... 445

## Chapter 1: Desktop Publishing with Pages . . . . . . . . . . . . . . . . . . .447

Creating a New Pages Document ............................................ 447
Open an Existing Pages Document .......................................... 448

Saving Your Work ..................................................................449
Touring the Pages Window .....................................................449
Entering and Editing Text ......................................................451
Using Text and Graphics Boxes ..............................................451
The Three Amigos: Cut, Copy, and Paste ...............................452
 Cutting stuff .................................................................452
 Copying text and images...............................................453
 Pasting from the Clipboard ..........................................453
Formatting Text the Easy Way ................................................453
Adding a Spiffy Table .............................................................454
Adding Alluring Photos ..........................................................455
Adding a Background Shape ...................................................457
Are You Sure about That Spelling?..........................................457
Printing Your Pages Documents ..............................................458
Sharing That Poster with Others .............................................459

**Chapter 2: Creating Spreadsheets with Numbers** ...............**461**

Before We Launch Numbers . . . ..............................................461
Creating a New Numbers Document .......................................462
Opening an Existing Spreadsheet File.....................................462
Save Those Spreadsheets!.......................................................464
Exploring the Numbers Window.............................................464
Navigate and Select Cells in a Spreadsheet............................465
Entering and Editing Data in a Spreadsheet...........................466
Selecting the Right Number Format .......................................467
Aligning Cell Text Just So .......................................................467
Format with Shading ..............................................................469
Insert and Delete Rows and Columns .....................................470
The Formula Is Your Friend ....................................................471
Adding Visual Punch with a Chart..........................................472

**Chapter 3: Building Presentations with Keynote** ...............**475**

Creating a New Keynote Project..............................................476
Opening a Keynote Presentation .............................................477
Saving Your Presentation ........................................................477
Putting Keynote to Work .........................................................478
Adding Slides...........................................................................479
Working with Text and Graphics Boxes ...................................479
Adding and Editing Slide Text.................................................481
Formatting Slide Text for the Perfect Look .............................481
Using Presenter's Notes in Your Project ..................................482
Every Good Presentation Needs Media ...................................482
Adding a Background Shape ...................................................482
Creating Your Keynote Slideshow ...........................................483
Printing Your Slides and Notes................................................484

# Book VI: The Typical Internet Stuff .......................... 487

## Chapter 1: Getting on the Internet ...........................489
Shopping for an ISP ..................................................489
Investigating Various Types of Connections ...................491
Setting Up Your Internet Connection...........................493
Using an internal or external modem........................493
Using Ethernet hardware......................................494

## Chapter 2: Using Apple Mail ...............................497
Know Thy Mail Window.............................................497
Setting Up Your Account ...........................................499
Adding an account..............................................500
Editing an existing account ...................................503
Deleting an account .............................................503
Receiving and Reading E-Mail Wisdom.........................503
Reading and deleting your messages .......................504
Replying to mail ................................................505
Raise the Little Flag: Sending E-Mail...........................509
What? You Get Junk Mail, Too? .................................513
Attachments on Parade ...........................................514
Fine-Tuning Your Post Office ....................................515
Adding sound ...................................................516
Checking Mail automatically ..................................516
Automating junk mail and message deletion ...............516
Adding signatures ..............................................516
Changing the status of an account ..........................517
Automating Your Mail with Rules...............................517

## Chapter 3: Staying in Touch with iChat ...................521
Configuring iChat..................................................522
Changing Modes in iChat..........................................524
Will You Be My Buddy?............................................525
Chat! Chat, I Say!..................................................527
Sharing Screens and iChat Theater ............................530
Sending Files with iChat...........................................531
Eliminating the Riffraff ...........................................532
Adding Visual Effects .............................................532

## Chapter 4: Expanding Your Horizons with iDisk.............535
Grabbing Internet Storage for Your MacBook .................536
Understanding What's on Your iDisk...........................538
Opening and Using iDisk..........................................539

**Chapter 5: Surfing with Safari** . . . . . . . . . . . . . . . . . . . . . . . . . . .**541**

Pretend You've Never Used This Thing.........................542
Visiting Web Sites.................................................543
Navigating the Web.............................................544
Setting Up Your Home Page...................................547
Adding and Using Bookmarks.................................548
Downloading Files...............................................550
Using Subscriptions and History.............................551
Tabs Are Your Browsing Friends..............................552
Saving Web Pages...............................................553
Protecting Your Privacy.......................................554
    Yes, there are such things as bad cookies..............554
    Cleaning your cache....................................555
    Handling ancient history...............................555
    Avoiding those @*!^%$ pop-up ads.....................556

**Chapter 6: Staying Secure Online** . . . . . . . . . . . . . . . . . . . . . . . . . .**557**

What Can Really Happen?......................................557
"Shields Up, Chekov!"..........................................560
    Firewall basics..........................................561
    Antivirus basics.........................................563
A Dose of Common Sense: Things Not to Do Online...........564

**Book VII: Networking in Mac OS X** . . . . . . . . . . . . . . . . . . . . . . **567**

**Chapter 1: Setting Up a Small Network** . . . . . . . . . . . . . . . . . . . . . .**569**

What Do I Need to Set Up My Network? ...........................569
    Something to network...................................570
    Network interface card (NIC)............................570
    Switch.....................................................570
    Cables.....................................................572
Setting Up Your Network.......................................573
Understanding the Basics of Network Configuration............574
    TCP/IP.....................................................574
    Software applications...................................576
Configuring Network System Preferences........................576
    Using DHCP for automatic IP address assignment......577
    Manually choosing an IP address range.................578
Verifying Connectivity.........................................580
Troubleshooting Your New Network..............................582
    Physical problems with your network...................582
    Network configuration problems........................583

## Chapter 2: Using Your Network . . . . . . . . . . . . . . . . . . . . . . . . . . . . .585

It's All about (File) Sharing....................................................................585
    Creating an account.........................................................................585
    Enabling file sharing ........................................................................587
    Connecting to a shared resource.....................................................587
Sharing a Connected Printer ...................................................................588
Sharing Files with Windows Computers...................................................588
Accessing File Shares on Windows Computers.........................................589
Using FTP to Access Files .......................................................................590
    Using the Mac OS X built-in FTP to share files.................................591
    Using FTP from Terminal to transfer files.........................................592
Using the Built-in Firewall......................................................................593
Remote Control of Your MacBook...........................................................595
    Using Screen Sharing.......................................................................595
    Remotely control your MacBook (for free, no less!) .....................596
    How VNC works..............................................................................596
    Remote control of another computer from your MacBook..........597

## Chapter 3: Going Wireless . . . . . . . . . . . . . . . . . . . . . . . . . . . . . . . . . .599

Speaking the Wireless Lingo ..................................................................599
Figuring Out the Different Flavors of Wireless Ethernet .........................601
    Basic Wi-Fi: 802.11b ........................................................................601
    Let's get Extreme: 802.11g ...............................................................602
    Raising the bar to 802.11n................................................................602
    The guy with the turquoise teeth ....................................................603
Keeping Your Wireless Network Secure....................................................603
    WPA and WPA2 ..............................................................................604
    WEP..................................................................................................605
    The LEAP security standard..............................................................605
Setting Up Your Wireless Network...........................................................606
    Setting up an Ad Hoc wireless network ...........................................606
    Setting up wireless networks with an AirPort Base Station .........608

## Chapter 4: Sharing That Precious Internet Thing. . . . . . . . . . . . . . . . .611

Sharing the Internet................................................................................611
Using Network Address Translation .........................................................612
Ways to Share Your Internet Connection..................................................614
    Using hardware for sharing an Internet connection .....................614
    Using software for sharing an Internet connection......................616
Connecting Everything for Wired Sharing.................................................617
    Using the software method................................................................617
    Using the hardware method ..............................................................618
Adding Wireless Support.........................................................................620
    If you already have a cable/DSL router or
        are using software Internet sharing.........................................620
    If you do not have a cable/DSL router or
        an AirPort Extreme Base Station.............................................621

*Book VIII: Expanding Your System* ............................... 623

**Chapter 1: Hardware That Will Make You Giddy** ...............**625**

Parading Pixels: Digital Cameras, DV Camcorders, and Scanners ........626
   Digital cameras ...................................................626
   DV camcorders ...................................................627
   Scanners ...........................................................628
Incredible Input: Keyboards, Trackballs,
   Joysticks, and Drawing Tablets .....................................629
   Keyboards ..........................................................630
   Trackballs ..........................................................630
   Joysticks ...........................................................632
   Drawing tablets ...................................................633
Sublime Storage: DVD/Blu-Ray Recorders.............................634
Awesome Audio: Subwoofer Systems and MP3 Hardware..................635
   Subwoofer speaker systems .......................................635
   MP3 players (well, actually, just the iPod) .....................636

**Chapter 2: Add RAM, Hard Drive Space, and Stir** ...............**637**

Adding Memory: Reasons for More RAM ...............................637
Shopping for a RAM Upgrade.........................................639
   Finding out the current memory in your MacBook..................639
   Determining the exact model of your laptop ......................640
The Tao of Hard Drive Territory .....................................641
Internal versus External Storage ....................................642
   External drives ...................................................642
   Internal drives ...................................................644
Determining How Much Space You Need...............................644
Shopping for a Hard Drive...........................................645
Installing Your New Stuff ...........................................646
   The easy way ......................................................646
   The hard way ......................................................646

**Chapter 3: Port-o-Rama: Using USB and FireWire** ...............**649**

Appreciating the Advantage of a FireWire Connection ...............649
Understanding USB and the Tale of Two Point Oh ....................651
Hey, You Need a Hub!...............................................652
Uh, It's Just Sitting There...........................................652
   Common FireWire and USB headaches..............................652
   Check those drivers ...............................................654

**Chapter 4: I'm Okay, You're a Printer** ........................**655**

Meet the Printer Browser ...........................................655
Adding a Funky Printer .............................................657
Managing Your Printing Jobs .......................................659
Sharing a Printer across That There Network ........................661

**Chapter 5: Applications That You've (Probably) Gotta Have** . . . . . . .663

The Trundling Microsoft Mammoth ........................................... 664
Your Mac OS X Toolbox: TechTool Pro ..................................... 666
Image Editing for the Masses .................................................. 667
The Morass of Digital Video ................................................... 668
Yes, It's Really Called "Toast" ................................................ 669
If You Positively Have to Run Windows . . . ............................. 670
All Hail FileMaker Pro ........................................................... 672
Utilities That Rock ................................................................. 673
    StuffIt .................................................................................. 673
    QuicKeys X3 ........................................................................ 673
    BBEdit ................................................................................. 674
    REALbasic ............................................................................ 675
At Least One Game ................................................................. 676
    Mac OS X Chess ................................................................... 676
    World of WarCraft ............................................................... 677

**Chapter 6: Putting Bluetooth to Work** . . . . . . . . . . . . . . . . . . . . . . . .679

Bluetooth: What a Silly Name for Such Cool Technology ........... 679
    A little Danish history .......................................................... 680
    Is your MacBook Bluetooth-ready? ....................................... 680
    Snow Leopard and Bluetooth, together forever ...................... 681
Adding Wireless Keyboards and Mice to Your MacBook ............. 683
Getting Everything in iSync .................................................... 684
The Magic of Wireless Printing ............................................... 685

*Book IX: Advanced Mac OS X* . . . . . . . . . . . . . . . . . . . . . . . . . . . *687*

**Chapter 1: Using UNIX on Your MacBook** . . . . . . . . . . . . . . . . . . . . .689

Why Use the Keyboard? ........................................................... 689
    UNIX keyboarding is fast ..................................................... 690
    The UNIX keyboard is a powerful beast ................................ 690
    Go where no trackpad has gone before ................................. 691
    Automate to elevate ............................................................. 692
    Remote control .................................................................... 692
Uncovering the Terminal ......................................................... 693
    What's a prompt? ................................................................ 693
    A few commands to get started ............................................ 694
    Using the skills you already have ......................................... 695
UNIX Commands 101 ............................................................... 696
    Anatomy of a UNIX command .............................................. 696
    Command-line gotchas ........................................................ 697
    Help is on the way! .............................................................. 698
    Autocompletion .................................................................. 698

Working with Files ........................................................................... 699
    Paths ........................................................................................... 699
    Copying, moving, renaming, and deleting files ..................... 701
    Opening documents and launching applications .................. 702
Useful Commands ........................................................................... 703
    Calendar .................................................................................... 703
    Processes ................................................................................... 704
UNIX Cadillac Commands .............................................................. 705
    Finding files .............................................................................. 706
    Using pipes ................................................................................ 706
UNIX Programs That Come in Handy ........................................... 707
    Text editors ............................................................................... 707
    Creating a new document ....................................................... 707
    Networking with the Terminal ............................................... 708

**Chapter 2: AppleScript Just Plain Rocks........................711**

What's So Great about AppleScript? .............................................. 711
    Automate common tasks in the Finder ................................. 711
    Automate tasks in other applications ................................... 712
Running a Script .............................................................................. 713
    Identifying scripts in the field .............................................. 713
    The AppleScript Editor application ....................................... 714
    Executing a script .................................................................... 714
Writing Your Own Simple Scripts ................................................. 716
    Create a script without touching a key ................................ 716
    Building your own scripts ....................................................... 717
One Step Beyond: AppleScript Programming ............................... 718
    Grab the Dictionary ................................................................. 718
    Anatomy of a simple script ..................................................... 720
I Summon Automator — the Silicon Programmer! ....................... 721
Help Is at Your Fingertips .............................................................. 723
    Built-in AppleScript Help ........................................................ 724
    AppleScript on the Web ........................................................... 724

**Chapter 3: Writing and Conversing with Your MacBook ..........725**

Using Ink with a Tablet ................................................................... 726
Computer, Can You Hear Me? ......................................................... 727
    The Speech Recognition tab .................................................... 727
    The Feedback window ............................................................... 731
    The Speech Command window ................................................ 731
Your Mac Talks Back! ...................................................................... 732
    The Text to Speech panel ........................................................ 733
    The Date & Time pane .............................................................. 735
    Configuring VoiceOver within the Universal Access pane ........... 735
    Speaking text through applications ....................................... 736
    Speaking text through services ............................................... 737

*Index* ............................................................................. 739

# Introduction

o you feel it, too? The lure of freedom? The open road?

Since the early days of the so-called "portable" computer — which was easily the size of a modern carry-on suitcase — some computer owners have lived the mobile lifestyle. Back then, a mobile computer was generally considered to be too expensive, with far fewer features than a desktop computer. Only those business travelers and on-site professionals that really needed a mobile computer would possibly buy one, and they'd pay top dollar for it. The mantra was simple: a *real* computer is tied to your desk; a portable computer is practically a toy.

Those portable computers were just the beginning, of course — today's laptops are easily carried to a coffee shop, a meeting room, or out in the middle of the ocean! (Just keep it below decks.) An Apple MacBook offers the same processing power, holds the same RAM, and has the same hard drive capacity as one of Apple's desktop iMac systems. A MacBook hums contentedly as you run Apple's latest operating system, Mac OS X Snow Leopard. Heck, you can even connect the same external devices and access the same networks as a desktop!

So now, the mantra has changed irrevocably from the old days: The important thing is to compute (and if you're in range of a wireless network, to communicate) wherever *you* want to work today! In fact, I've written a good chunk of this book from my backyard, using my MacBook Pro . . . while flinging bread crumbs at our resident cardinals.

The book that you hold in your hands uses the classic *For Dummies* design; it provides you with the step-by-step instruction (plenty of which my editors grudgingly agree is somewhat humorous) on every major feature of both your MacBook and Mac OS X Snow Leopard. It also goes a step further from time to time, delving into why something works the way that it does or what's going on behind the scenes. You can chalk that up to my sincere admiration for everyone in Cupertino and what they've perfected.

What you *won't* find in this *All-in-One* is wasted space. Your MacBook is covered from front to back, including the latest hardware that Apple has added to the MacBook line. Snow Leopard's new features are here too, including improvements to Apple Mail, Safari, the latest versions of all the "iApps '09" (including iWeb), and the new incarnation of iWork '09. Everything's explained from the ground up, just in case you've never touched a MacBook before. By the time you reach the final pages, you'll have covered advanced topics, such as networking, AppleScript, Internet security . . . and yes, even an introduction to the powerful world of UNIX that exists underneath.

I sincerely hope that you enjoy this book and that it will act as your guide while you discover all the wonderful features of the MacBook and Mac OS X Snow Leopard that I use every day. Remember, if a Windows-enslaved acquaintance still titters about your Mac laptop, I'll understand if you're tempted to drop this weighty tome on his foot. (Of course, because you're using an Intel-based MacBook, you can also boot into Windows and watch him turn purple.)

The official name of the latest version of your operating system is (portentous pause here, please) Mac OS X version 10.6 Snow Leopard. But who wants to spit out that mouthful every time? Throughout this book, I refer to the operating system as *Mac OS X,* and when I discuss something that's particular to the latest version, I call it *Snow Leopard.*

## What's Really Required

If you have a MacBook that's either running Mac OS X version 10.6 (Snow Leopard) or is ready to be upgraded to it, you're set to go. Despite what you might have heard, you *won't* require any of the following:

✦ **A degree in computer science:** Apple designed the MacBook for regular people, and I designed this book for people of every experience level. Even if you've never used a Mac before, you'll find no hostile waters here.

✦ **A fortune in software:** I do describe additional software that you can buy to expand the functionality of your MacBook; however, that section is only a few pages long. *Everything else* covered in this book is included with Mac OS X Snow Leopard — and by the size of this volume, you get a rough idea of just how complete Mac OS X is! Heck, many folks buy Macs just because of the free software you get, such as iMovie and iPhoto. (Tough cookies to the vast Unwashed Windows Horde.)

✦ **An Internet connection:** Granted, you're not going to do much with Apple Mail without an Internet connection, but computers *did* exist before the Internet (and not every spot on Earth has wireless network access yet). You can still be productive with your MacBook and Mac OS X without the Internet.

Oh, you will need a Mac OS X version 10.6 installation disc, unless Snow Leopard came pre-installed on your MacBook. Go figure.

## About This Book

Although this book is an *All-in-One*, you can also read it in a linear fashion (straight through) — probably not in one session, mind you. (Then again, Diet Coke is cheap, so it *is* possible.) The material is divided into nine minibooks, each of which covers an entire area of MacBook or Mac OS X knowledge. For example, you'll find minibooks on upgrading your hardware, networking, the Apple Digital Hub suite of applications known as iLife, Apple's iWork office productivity suite, customizing your Desktop, and Internet-related applications.

Each self-contained chapter discusses a specific feature, application, connection, or cool thing about either your MacBook or Mac OS X. Feel free to begin reading anywhere or skip chapters at will. For example, if you're already using an Internet connection, you won't need the chapter on adding an Internet connection. However, I recommend that you read this book from the front to the back, as you do any good mystery novel. (Spoiler alert: For those who want to know right now, Bill Gates did it.)

## Conventions Used in This Book

Even *For Dummies* books have to get technical from time to time, usually involving commands that you have to type and menu items that you have to click. If you've read any of my other *For Dummies* books, you know that a helpful set of conventions is used to indicate what needs to be done or what you see on-screen.

### Stuff you type

When I ask you to type a command or enter something in a text field (such as your name or phone number), the text appears like this: **Type me.**

Press the Return key to process the command or enter the text.

### Menu commands

When I give you a specific set of menu commands to use, they appear in the following format: Edit⇨Copy.

In this example, you should click the Edit menu and then choose the Copy menu item.

## Display messages

If I mention a specific message that you see on your screen, it looks like this on the page: This is a message displayed by an application.

## In case you're curious about computers

No one expects a book in the *For Dummies* series to contain techno-jargon or ridiculous computer science semantics — especially a book about the MacBook! (Horrible pun unavoidable.) Apple has always strived for simplicity and user friendliness. I hereby promise that I've done my absolute best to avoid unnecessary techno-talk. For those who are interested in what's happening under the hood, I provide sidebars that explain a little more about what's doing what to whom. If you'd rather just have fun and ignore the digital dirty work, please feel free to disregard these additions (but don't tear sidebars out of the book, because there's likely to be important stuff on the opposite side of the page).

# How This Book Is Organized

I've done my best to emulate the elegant design of your laptop by organizing this book into nine minibooks, with cross-references where appropriate.

## Book I: Say Hello to Your MacBook

This minibook is an introduction to your Mac laptop — even if you need a little convincing about actually *buying* a new MacBook! I compare desktop Macs to the MacBook line and provide you with a hardware overview of just what exactly resides beneath your MacBook's sleek exterior. If you're comparing the different MacBook models before deciding on which to buy, you'll find the chapter that discusses each of the three MacBook models useful. Also in this minibook, I provide tips on unpacking and setting up your new laptop and a guide to maintaining your MacBook in tip-top shape. You'll also find a chapter on additional stuff that most MacBook owners covet. (You can even buy most of it before Apple ships your new Mac!)

## Book II: Using Mac OS X with Your MacBook

This minibook begins with an invigorating chapter explaining exactly why you should be so happy to be a Mac OS X owner. Then I provide an introduction to the basic tasks that you'll perform — copying files, running programs, and the like. You also find coverage of Snow Leopard's Spotlight search engine, tips on using your MacBook's built-in camera, a guide to normal Mac OS X maintenance and troubleshooting, and instructions on using the Mac OS X Help system.

## Book III: MacBook Customizing and Sharing

Who wants to stick with the defaults? The material in this minibook leads you through the steps that you need to customize both your MacBook and Snow Leopard to your specific needs and desires . . . everything from a tweak to your background or screen saver to a description of how to set up and administer multiple accounts on a single MacBook. You also find comprehensive coverage of the different settings you can change in System Preferences, which is an important place in Mac OS X — including the MacBook-specific settings that only laptop owners can use. Finally, I discuss tips and important rules you should follow to help keep your MacBook and your private information safe online.

## Book IV: Going Mobile with iLife

*Sweet!* This minibook jumps right in among the crown jewels of the Digital Hub: iTunes, iPhoto, iDVD, iMovie, iWeb, GarageBand, QuickTime Player, and the DVD Player. Taken as a suite, those first six applications make up iLife '09, and they allow you to plug in and use all sorts of electronic gadgets while you're on the road, including digital cameras, digital video (DV) camcorders, and MP3 players. Plus, you can edit or create your own DVDs, audio CDs, and movies — from the comfort of your favorite coffee shop!

## Book V: iWork for the Road Warrior

iWork '09 is rapidly becoming the favorite office productivity suite among the Apple Faithful, and the suite runs beautifully on a MacBook — I recommend a bench at the park! You'll find a chapter devoted to each application: Pages for desktop publishing, Numbers for spreadsheets, and Keynote for presentation projects. Who needs that other productivity suite? (I forget the name.)

## Book VI: The Typical Internet Stuff

This minibook contains just what it says. But then again, it's easy to get enthusiastic about Apple Mail, the latest version of Apple's instant messaging application (iChat), and the online storage provided by iDisk. I also cover Safari, Apple's hot-rod Web browser. Finally, you discover more about the built-in Internet firewall and how you can use it to safeguard your MacBook from Internet undesirables.

## Book VII: Networking in Mac OS X

Wired and wireless Ethernet lurk in this minibook. I explain them step by step, in language that a normal human being can understand. Find out how to use wireless networks such as AirPort Extreme from Apple as well as how to share an Internet connection with other computers in a local network.

## Book VIII: Expanding Your System

Time to take things up a notch. In this minibook, I discuss the hardware and software that you can add to your MacBook and why you might (or might not) need such toys. Memory (RAM), hard drives, printers, USB, and FireWire 800 . . . they're all discussed here in detail. Consider this a banquet of expansion information.

## Book IX: Advanced Mac OS X

I know that I told you earlier that I was going to avoid techno-talk whenever possible, yet I also mentioned the advanced things that you find in this minibook, such as using UNIX within Mac OS X and using Automator to build your own custom workflow applications that handle repetitive tasks. If you don't mind immersing yourself in all that's technical, read here for the skinny on communicating with Mac OS X by using your voice and your handwriting.

# Icons Used in This Book

The icons in this book are more than just attractive — they're also important visual cues for stuff that you don't want to miss.

Mark's Maxims represent way-important stuff, so I call your attention to these nuggets in bold, like this:

**Something *Really* Important Is Being Said that will likely affect your person in the near future. Pay attention, commit those Maxims to memory, and you'll avoid the pitfalls that the rest of us have hit along the way.**

The Tip icons flag snippets of information that will save you time or trouble (and, in some cases, even cash).

These icons highlight optional technical information for folks like me. If you also used to disassemble alarm clocks for fun when you were six years old, you'll love this stuff.

*Always* read the information next to this icon first! Something looms ahead that could put your hardware or software at risk.

Look to the Remember icons for those tidbits that you need to file away in your mind. Just remember to remember.

# Book I

# Say Hello to Your MacBook

# Contents at a Glance

**Chapter 1: Exploring MacBook Basics** ..........................9

    "One Uses a Battery!" ...................................................................9

    So, Are You Ready for a MacBook? ...........................................12

    Looking Over Your Laptop ..........................................................13

**Chapter 2: MacBook Models Compared** ......................21

    Your Entry-Level Mac Laptop .....................................................21

    The Power User's Toolbox ..........................................................22

    Meet the MacBook Air................................................................23

**Chapter 3: Setting Up and Taking Care of Your MacBook** .........29

    Location, Location, Location!......................................................29

    Unpacking and Connecting Your Laptop....................................30

    Fire That Puppy Up ....................................................................32

    Mark's Favorite Signs of a Healthy MacBook............................33

    A Primer in MacBook Handling and Care ..................................34

**Chapter 4: Extra Stuff You'll Likely Want**.........................39

    An Overview of MacBook Software Goodness............................39

    Other Stuff That Nearly Everyone Wants ..................................42

# Chapter 1: Exploring MacBook Basics

## In This Chapter

- ✔ Comparing MacBooks to desktop Macs
- ✔ Deciding on a laptop
- ✔ Identifying the external parts of your Mac laptop
- ✔ Understanding the important hidden components

Most of my readers who pick up this book are already MacBook owners, happy with their mobile Mac and yearning to know more about how it works and how to use it. Folks, I salute you, but I'll be honest: You don't really need to read the first part of this chapter! You've already made your decision betwixt laptop and desktop.

It's true, however, that not every computer owner needs a laptop. (I'm no heretic — just pointing out that mobility isn't of primary importance to many people.) Because laptops are generally more expensive than desktop systems of similar power and capabilities, you should consider a laptop only if you really need the unique features it offers.

If you haven't yet made up your mind about whether to replace your desktop computer with a laptop — or whether you need to add a MacBook to your present collection of desktop computers — then this chapter is especially for you. I compare laptop and desktop configurations, and ask you the three important questions you should consider before making the decision to buy a MacBook. Next, I give you a quick tour of the basics of a MacBook.

## "One Uses a Battery!"

That's a quote from one of my family members — I won't say who — concerning the main difference between my MacBook laptop and my iMac desktop. And you know, many Mac owners would probably agree with my youngest daughter on that point. (Whoops, what a giveaway!)

However, there's a surprising number of pros and cons to owning a laptop compared to a stationary Mac desktop computer. In this section, I cover those pros and cons — just so that you'll have the whole picture.

## The "absolute" need for mobility

Many Mac owners just plain need the portability of a MacBook — either they need to run their applications on-site, or they're constantly traveling as part of their career or lifestyle. If you fit into this group, you really have no choice other than to have a laptop. Students, business travelers, and those who need their applications wherever they are, look no further than a MacBook.

But what about those folks who travel only occasionally, or people who like a change of scenery from time to time (such as downstairs, the backyard, or the library)? Or folks who simply want a computer they can put away easily when it's not in use? Although a MacBook is less of a "sure thing" purchase for those who aren't born nomads, that versatility can still be *very* tempting! Oh, and don't forget that you also carry all your data and those all-important applications with you whenever you lug your MacBook from one spot to another.

Therefore, if you feel that you'd prefer to work away from your home (or office or dorm) at least once or twice a week, you should also consider the MacBook alternative.

## Space saving is a good thing

Do you operate in a minimum of space? The MacBook is a good choice for those looking to achieve the smallest *footprint* possible (that's a term that technowizards use to describe the amount of space a computer takes up on your desk). The other obvious choices are the iMac and the Mac mini, which are both desktops.

The Mac mini is a computer that takes up very little desktop space — in fact, the mini is about the size of a ham sandwich (with two slices of cheese and a tomato or two). However, it doesn't include a monitor, keyboard, or mouse, so you have to add those things (with the space they demand), so the footprint you're left with is really not much better than a typical PC in a "pizza box" case.

The iMac includes an internal monitor, but it's a minimum of 20 inches, which increases the footprint of the entire computer. As with the Mac mini, you have to add a keyboard and mouse.

So we're left with the MacBook, which takes up about 13 x 9 inches of desk space with its built-in display panel, keyboard, and trackpad. It's no accident that many corporations now supply laptops to employees as standard equipment — even to those office-bound workers who don't take business trips. Laptops offer the full computing experience, no matter how small your cubicle!

## Enclosed and constrained

Sometimes it's easy for many Mac owners to forget that MacBooks aren't as expandable as a Mac Pro desktop. (In fact, this limitation also applies to the Apple iMac and the Mac mini, which are — same as a MacBook — highly integrated, with no room for hardware expansion.)

Although you can hang plenty of peripherals off a modern MacBook (using USB and FireWire ports), full-size desktops are just plain easier to expand and upgrade with internal hardware. The prime examples of this are the internal graphics, sound, and wireless networking cards on a full-size Mac Pro, which on a MacBook are impossible to upgrade.

Adding a second or even a third hard drive to a Mac Pro is a fairly simple operation: The case has plenty of room, and the Mac Pro already sports the internal connectors and power cabling for all those new drives. With a MacBook, however, you can upgrade the internal hard drive only with another high-capacity drive, and the procedure is best performed by an Apple technician. Adding a second drive to a MacBook can be done only with an external USB or FireWire drive (which adds more stuff to carry with you . . . which cuts down on that mobility you prize so highly as a laptop user).

In a nutshell, those Mac power users who will want to upgrade their computers with the latest technologies in the future (such as hard-core gamers) should consider a Mac Pro desktop system first.

## Paying the laptop price

Dear readers, I cannot lie: You pay dearly for the portability of a MacBook. As an example, compare an iMac desktop computer and a MacBook Pro laptop computer with these (roughly) similar components:

✦ **Processor:** The iMac sports a 2.66GHz Intel Core 2 Duo processor, whereas the MacBook Pro has a slightly faster 2.8GHz Core 2 Duo CPU.

✦ **RAM:** Both computers have 4GB of RAM installed.

✦ **Hard drive capacity:** The MacBook Pro sports a 500GB hard drive, whereas the iMac offers a larger 640GB hard drive.

✦ **Screen size:** Our MacBook Pro has a 17-inch widescreen display, and the iMac has a 20-inch widescreen monitor.

Now for the tale of the register tape: At the time of this writing, the iMac will set you back $1,374, whereas the MacBook Pro runs a hefty $2,499! Portability comes at a premium for road warriors.

### Repairs may cause dizziness

There's another high-dollar headache for all laptop owners (both Mac and PC). Compared to a desktop computer, repairs on your laptop are harder to perform, the components cost more, and the repairs are almost certain to take longer. Also, depending on use, a MacBook's battery is almost certain to require replacement in four to five years.

Consider this typical scenario: If the graphics card fails in your Mac Pro desktop, you can easily replace it yourself with a new (and likely even more powerful) graphics adapter card. You simply open the case, unscrew the old card, and replace it with a new one.

However, if the sound hardware fails in your MacBook (or iMac, or Mac mini), it's time to pull out your wallet. Why? As I mention earlier, the hardware on these three systems is all integrated onto the motherboard, so you can't fix it yourself. Therein lies the rub. The entire motherboard probably needs to be replaced, and ordering parts and performing the necessary surgery take time.

Here's an important Mark's Maxim that I practice myself:

**If you invest in a MacBook, you should also invest in AppleCare coverage for your laptop.**

Although AppleCare is pricey ($249 extends your technical support and warranty coverage for a full three years), it's worth every penny if a hardware component breaks!

## So, Are You Ready for a MacBook?

Now that you've absorbed all the pros and cons of a laptop computer, it's time to make the decision on which system you should buy. If you answer "yes" to each of these three questions, a MacBook should be in your future!

✦ **Is mobility important?** If you need your computing on the go (or you'd like the freedom to be able to move from place to place), I recommend that you jump to the MacBook side of the fence.

✦ **Is a laptop in your price range?** As I prove earlier, you'll pay considerably more for a MacBook (as well as for repairs later, if you should need them). If you can afford the higher price point, you've cleared another hurdle.

✦ **Are you comfortable with the upgrade limitations of a laptop?** If your MacBook will probably run your applications acceptably for at least four years (or more), hardware upgrades are likely to be less of a concern and you can buy a MacBook with confidence.

After you've chosen the Way of the Laptop, you also have to select the MacBook model that's right for you — and it's no small coincidence that Chapter 2 of this minibook is devoted to helping you with that choice if you haven't already. The rest of this chapter, meanwhile, is devoted to familiarizing you with the basic parts of the MacBook you have or are considering.

# Looking Over Your Laptop

Most action films have one scene in common: I call it the "gear up" scene, where the good guys strap on their equipment in preparation for battle. (It doesn't matter what era: You see "gear up" scenes in *Gladiator, Aliens,* and virtually every movie Arnold has made.) You're sure to see lots of clicking straps and equipping of offensive weapons (and sometimes even a dash of war paint). The process usually takes a minute or so, all told with whiplash camera work and stirring martial music in the background.

Well, fellow Macintosh Road Warrior, it takes only *two seconds* and *one move* for you to gear up: closing the lid! That's because your MacBook is a self-contained world, providing virtually everything you'll find on a desktop iMac or Mac Pro. This is indeed the decade of the laptop, meshing nicely with your cell phone and that wireless connection at your local coffee shop. You have selected the right companion for the open road.

Unlike some of Apple's other designs, such as the Mac Mini or the iMac, your MacBook looks similar to a PC laptop running Windows. (In fact, a MacBook can run Windows, if you absolutely must.) But your laptop holds a number of pleasant surprises that no PC laptop can offer — and, in the case of the MacBook Air, you'll lose pounds and inches from your chassis! Sure, your MacBook Pro might be but an inch thin (and a MacBook Air, which I cover in Chapter 2 of this minibook, is even more svelte than that), but a lot of superb design lives inside, and you'll encounter the same parts that you'd find in a desktop machine. In this section, I discuss those important parts — both the stuff you can see and the stuff that's shoehorned within. Welcome to your Mac laptop, good reader. Gear up!

## The parts you probably recognize

All laptops require some of the same gizmos. Figure 1-1 helps you track them down. Of course, as you'd expect, a computer has a body of sorts in which all the innards and brains are stored. It also sports a display screen, a keyboard, a trackpad or other pointing device, and ports for powering and exchanging data with outside toys.

iSight camera

LCD screen

**Figure 1-1:**
The
charismatic
form of a
typical Mac
laptop.

Keyboard          Trackpad

# Feeling outdated? Never!

Are you using an older iBook or PowerBook? It seems that Apple's product line changes every time you tear a page from your 12-month calendar, and every new generation of laptops includes new whiz-bang features. Sometimes you can add those features — such as an external iSight camera or an AirPort Extreme card — separately to your older machine, but you can't update some things, such as your iBook motherboard. Sigh.

Here's my take on this situation: If your older laptop does what you need at a pace you can accept, there is *no need* to upgrade it.

Skeptical? Here's the proof: Before my recent upgrade to a MacBook Pro, yours truly was lugging a pristine iBook G3, which booted Mac OS X Tiger and did absolutely everything that I demanded. (A little more patience was required, certainly, but technology authors are simply *brimming* with patience.) The moral: Avoid the upgrade fever unless you really need a new companion!

If your laptop bears the iBook or PowerBook logo, you can still enjoy this book and discover new tips and tricks from it! (Remember, however, that features that are specific to Snow Leopard require an Intel-based MacBook.) Unless today's breed of Intel-based Mac laptops has a feature that you absolutely can't use on your iBook (such as booting directly into Windows or using Multi-touch trackpad motions), you can sail on with your current computer, fiercely proud of The Bitten Apple that appears on the cover. Although this book was written with the MacBook, MacBook Air, and MacBook Pro lines in mind, much of what you read here still applies to your older laptop. Unless it's steam driven, of course.

### That magnificent screen

What a view you have! Today's Mac laptops feature a 13", 15", or 17" LCD or LED display (depending on the model you choose). Today's displays are available in glossy finish (a good choice for the brightest colors and deepest blacks).

LCD screens use far less electricity than their antique CRT ancestors do, and they emit practically no radiation.

Apple's laptop screens offer a *widescreen* aspect ratio (the screen is considerably wider than it is tall), which augurs well for those who enjoy watching DVD movies. (A favorite editor of mine loves it when I use the antique word *augur,* meaning *to predict or foretell.*)

That reminds me: Throw away your printed dictionary! You won't need it, because Mac OS X Snow Leopard includes the fantastic Dictionary widget, which uses the Internet to retrieve definitions from the online Oxford American Dictionary site. More on widgets in general in Book III, Chapter 2 . . . and yes, the Dictionary widget does contain *augur.*

### The keyboard and trackpad

Hey, here's something novel for your laptop. Whereas a standard desktop computer has external input devices, your Mac has a built-in keyboard and trackpad (which does the job of a mouse). The keyboard is a particular favorite of mine for a few reasons:

✦ You can either control the sound volume or mute all that noise completely.

✦ You can use illuminated keyboards (at least on high-end Mac laptops), which are perfect for darkened dorm rooms and airplane flights.

✦ A handy-dandy Media Eject key lets you eject a CD or DVD.

### The disc slot

You'll notice a long groove at the bottom-right corner of your MacBook or MacBook Pro. (No, it's not for your credit card.) This slot accepts CDs and DVDs into your optical drive. If the drive is empty, loading a disc is as simple as sliding it in an inch or so; the drive sucks in the disc automatically. (And we don't need a stinkin' floppy. Macs haven't had floppy drives for years now, and the PC types are finally following suit.)

A MacBook Air doesn't sport any internal optical drive. You use either the CD & DVD Sharing feature in Snow Leopard to read discs remotely (from another Mac or PC on your network), or you can pick up an external optical drive from Apple for about $100. (Such is the price you pay for super-thin and super-light.) I discuss the MacBook Air in detail in Chapter 2 of this very minibook.

"Luke, the printed label side of the disc should always be *facing you* when you load a disc. Always."

### Food for your ears

A machine this nice had better have great sound, and the MacBook doesn't disappoint. You have a couple of options for Mac laptop audio:

✦ All Mac laptops sport built-in speakers (and a microphone to boot). The MacBook Air has a single speaker, and MacBook and MacBook Pro models have stereo speakers.

✦ The built-in audio Line Out jacks connect your MacBook's audio to a pair of headphones, or a more powerful (and expensive) external speaker system, or a home stereo system.

### The power cable

Sorry, can't get a wireless power system . . . yet. (Apple's working hard on that one.) However, the MacBook Pro was the first major release of a laptop with a magnetic power connector; the MacBook and MacBook Air followed suit soon after. The MagSafe connector reduces the chances of your pride and joy being yanked off a desk when someone trips over the power cord, because the magnetic closure pops off under significant strain. Now that's *sassy.*

### The power button

Yep, you have one of these, too. It's on the upper right, next to the keyboard, bearing the familiar "circle with a vertical line" logo.

---

## Hey, where's my remote?

If this isn't your first Mac laptop, you're probably looking for the Apple Remote amongst all the styrofoam. Unfortunately, the latest crop of MacBooks doesn't come with a remote. This once-standard device, which looks like an iPod Shuffle, allowed you to control your laptop wireless from across the room. Think DVD viewings, presentations, and lazy iTunes listening.

If you've picked up a used MacBook or MacBook Pro, you might have a remote already. Otherwise, you can always buy one directly from Apple for about $20. However, you can't use an Apple Remote with the MacBook Air, which doesn't have an IR (infrared) receiver.

### The iSight camera

Check out that tiny square lens above your screen. That's a built-in iSight camera, which allows you to chat with others in a videoconferencing environment using Snow Leopard's iChat feature. You can even take photos with it, using the Photo Booth software that comes with your laptop, or set up a travelin' Webcam.

### The battery compartment

Owners of a MacBook or MacBook Pro can open the cover on the bottom of your laptop to switch batteries. Many road warriors who constantly use their laptops for extended periods swear by extra batteries, especially if they're on-site in the middle of nowhere and there's not an AC outlet to be found.

Of course, your laptop automatically charges the battery while it's plugged in, so you shouldn't have to remove the battery unless you're replacing it or switching it with another battery.

If you're using a MacBook Air, your battery is sealed inside the case and can't be swapped. Only an Apple technician can replace a dead battery in a MacBook Air laptop.

## The holes called ports

The next stop on your tour of Planet Laptop is Port Central — those rows of holes on the sides of your computer. Each port connects a different type of cable or device, allowing you to easily add all sorts of functionality to your computer.

Each of these stellar holes is identified by an icon to help you identify it. Here's a list of what you'll find and a quick rundown on what these ports do.

Connections for external devices and networking:

✦ **FireWire:** These ports are the standard in the Apple universe for connecting external hard drives and DVD recorders, but they do double-duty as the connector of choice for peripherals such as mini-DV camcorders. (A *peripheral* is another silly techno-nerd term that means a separate device you connect to your computer.) Depending on the model of laptop you chose, you may have one of the older FireWire 400 ports or you may have a much faster FireWire 800 port. Current MacBooks (except the MacBook Air) have at least one FireWire port; the MacBook Air, on the other hand, offers only USB. Speaking of which . . .

✦ **USB:** Short for *Universal Serial Bus,* the familiar USB port is the jack-of-all-trades in today's world of computer add-ons. Most external devices that you want to connect to your laptop (such as portable hard drives, scanners, and digital cameras) use a USB port, including the iPod. Depending on the model of laptop, you'll have either two or three USB 2.0 ports available. USB 2.0 connections are much faster than the old USB 1.1 standard, but they still accept USB 1.1 devices running at the slower speed.

Get the lowdown on FireWire and USB ports in Book VIII, Chapter 3.

✦ **Ethernet:** Today's Mac laptops include a standard 10/100/1000 Ethernet port, so the laptop is ready to join your existing wired Ethernet network. (Alternatively, you can go wireless for your network connection; more on that in Book VII.) Because the MacBook Air is designed to be completely wireless, it doesn't have a wired Ethernet port, but if necessary, you can add a USB Ethernet adapter to add a wired network port to your Air.

✦ **ExpressCard/34 or SD memory:** When you need the absolute fastest performance possible from an external device, you can connect that device to your laptop using the ExpressCard slot. These cards are the descendants of the popular PCMCIA (or PC Card) cards, which many models of older Mac PowerBooks used. Currently, only the 17-inch MacBook Pro offers an ExpressCard slot, but the 13- and 15-inch MacBook Pro models include a standard SD memory card slot (a treat for digital photographers because it allows iPhoto to import photos directly from an SD memory card).

Connections for external video and audio are

✦ **VGA/DVI connector:** In case that splendid screen isn't big enough, you can buy an adapter for this port that allows you to send the video signal from your laptop to another VGA or DVI monitor, or even S-Video output for your TV and VCR.

✦ **Headphone/Optical Output:** You can send the high-quality audio from your rectangular beast to a set of standard headphones or an optical digital audio device such as a high-end home theater system.

✦ **Optical Line In:** Last (but certainly not least) is the optical audio Line In jack, which allows you to pipe the signal from another audio device into your laptop. This one comes in particularly handy when you record MP3 files from your old vinyl albums or when you want to record loops in GarageBand. (The MacBook Air doesn't have a Line In jack.)

## Don't forget the parts you can't see

When you bought your new digital pride and joy, you probably noticed a number of subtle differences between the low-end MacBook and the uber-expensive, top-end MacBook Pro and MacBook Air models. I call these differences the Important Hidden Stuff (or IHS, for those of you addicted to acronyms), and they're just as important as the parts and ports that you can see.

Internal storage devices:

✦ **CPU:** Today's Mac laptops feature — gasp! — Intel processors, which run faster and cooler than the old Motorola processors that powered the iBook and PowerBook models. Of course, the faster the processor, the better. (Definitely *not* rocket science.)

✦ **Hard drive:** MacBook laptops use the current standard in hard drive technology: namely, serial ATA hard drives. As you might expect, the MacBook Pro laptop line has a larger capacity hard drive as standard equipment, but you can special-order a MacBook from Apple with a larger hard drive.

The MacBook Pro and MacBook Air have two storage options: You can choose serial ATA hard drive or opt for the much more expensive (and much more technically impressive) solid-state drive. Hold on to your chair — there are no moving parts with a solid-state drive, and it offers better performance than a standard hard drive. Think of the solid-state drive as an internal USB flash drive, which uses RAM chips instead of magnetic platters to hold your data! Pricey, but *super-sweet*, and Apple once again introduces the latest in computer hardware.

✦ **Optical drive:** Okay, I'm cheating a little here. I mention the optical drive in an earlier section, but all you can see is the slot, so it qualifies as an IHS item. Depending on your MacBook, your computer includes one of the following:

• *No built-in optical drive:* The MacBook Air can be equipped with an external SuperDrive, or you can use another computer's drive remotely over your wireless network.

• *A DVD-R/CD-RW SuperDrive:* This drive can play and record both CDs and DVDs.

Wireless communications devices:

✦ **Wireless Ethernet:** "Look, Ma, no wires!" As I mention earlier, you can connect your laptop to an existing wireless Ethernet network. All current MacBooks have built-in AirPort Extreme hardware. With wireless connectivity, you can share documents with another computer in another room, share a single high-speed Internet connection betwixt several computers, or enjoy wireless printing. Truly *sassy!*

Although Apple would want you to build your wireless wonderland with an Apple AirPort Extreme Base Station (go figure), you can use your MacBook with any standard 802.11 wireless network. And yes, PCs and Macs can intermingle on the same wireless network without a hitch. (Scandalous, ain't it?)

+ **Bluetooth:** Let's get the old "digital pirate" joke out of the way: "Arrgh, matey, I needs me a wireless parrot." (Engineers again . . . sheesh.) Although strangely named, Bluetooth is another form of wireless connectivity. This time, however, the standard was designed for accessories such as your keyboard and mouse, and devices such as a personal digital assistant (PDA) and a cell phone.

Video display device:

+ **Video card:** If your applications rely heavily on high-speed 3-D graphics, you'll be pleased as punch to learn that today's MacBook Pro line of laptops come equipped with muscle-bound GeForce cards from nVIDIA. These cards are well suited to 3-D modeling, video editing, and well, honestly, blasting the enemy into small smoking pieces with aplomb. As of this writing, the MacBook and MacBook Air laptops use an integrated video card, so they're not a good choice for hard-core gaming or 3-D design.

# Chapter 2: MacBook Models Compared

*In This Chapter*

✔ **Choosing a MacBook**

✔ **Selecting a MacBook Pro**

✔ **Introducing the MacBook Air**

**C**hoices, choices! After you've made the decision that a laptop is the right destination, you still need to choose the model that's best suited for your applications and your computing lifestyle. Apple's MacBook line can fit anyone from a student to a digital media professional, so it's important to select the model that best fits your needs and price range.

In this chapter, I outline the differences between each MacBook model.

## Your Entry-Level Mac Laptop

In both price and features, Apple's MacBook is designed for students and Mac users with typical needs, including office applications (such as iWork or Microsoft Office), Internet applications, the iLife suite, and the majority of games on the market. The default configuration includes 2GB of RAM, but the MacBook can accept up to 4GB total.

The MacBook is equipped with a 13.3-inch widescreen LCD screen, and the standard hard drive capacity is 160GB. (You can special-order up to 500GB for extra elbow room.) MacBooks come standard with a SuperDrive, so they can read and write DVDs. Of course, AirPort Extreme 802.11n and Bluetooth wireless networking are both built in.

At the time of this writing, the MacBook carries the following ports:

✦ **Gigabit Ethernet:** You can connect your MacBook to a wired Ethernet network with ease.

✦ **Mini-DVI:** This port allows you to connect your MacBook to an external monitor or flat-panel TV.

✦ **FireWire 400:** This port is a standard one for connecting external devices such as hard drives and cameras.

✦ **USB 2.0:** These two ports are the most popular ports for connecting external devices.

✦ **Audio In and Out:** You can connect an external microphone, a pair of headphones, or external speakers to your MacBook using these jacks.

Your MacBook also comes equipped with a built-in iSight video camera (for taking both still images and digital video), an on-board microphone, and built-in stereo speakers.

At the base price of $999, a MacBook is the perfect ticket for mobile computing for the typical Mac user.

# The Power User's Toolbox

You know the old saw about two scoops of ice cream in a cone? Folks used to say, "You get everything you get with one scoop, only more." In effect, the MacBook Pro builds on the basic equipment provided with an entry-level MacBook, providing serious users with faster performance and storage capacity. The MacBook Pro is meant for those using processor-intensive behemoths such as Photoshop and Final Cut Pro (think digital media professionals), as well as computer users who want to play the latest games or run the most demanding applications.

To support the faster processors in the MacBook Pro, Apple also provides 4GB of RAM as a standard; the laptop can accept a maximum of 8GB, which I highly recommend if you're looking for the best possible performance from your MacBook Pro. The MacBook Pro also sports a backlit keyboard, which glows in a darkened room or airplane to allow you to continue working while everyone around you snoozes (lucky you!).

Currently, your MacBook Pro can be ordered with three different LED screen sizes: 13.3 inches, 15.4 inches, and the super-glorious 17-inch display (all in widescreen format). Storage capacity is 500GB for the traditional magnetic Serial ATA hard drive, or you can opt for up to 256GB of solid-state storage. (More on solid-state drives later in this chapter.) A SuperDrive, AirPort Extreme 802.11n, and Bluetooth wireless networking are all on board. The MacBook's iSight camera, built-in microphone, and stereo speakers are also included.

The MacBook Pro naturally offers a wider range of ports and connectors than a MacBook. The ports include:

✦ **Gigabit Ethernet**

✦ **Mini-DVI**

✦ **FireWire 800:** At double the speed of the older FireWire 400 ports, your FireWire 800 port is the fastest connection you can make to external devices. (Note, however, that you'll need an adapter to use an older FireWire 400 device with this FireWire 800 port.)

✦ **USB 2.0:** The 17-inch MacBook Pro carries three ports instead of the two offered on the 13-inch and 15-inch MacBook Pro models.

✦ **SD card slot:** The 13- and 15-inch MacBook Pro models have a built-in SD memory card slot (a great choice for digital photographers).

✦ **ExpressCard/34 slot:** If you opt for the 17-inch model, this slot allows you to add peripheral cards that provide additional functions for your MacBook Pro, such as an eSATA connection. (In the Windows world, these are called PC cards.)

✦ **Audio In and Out**

The least-expensive MacBook Pro runs $1,199, which is a steal for the computing professional who needs a laptop on the road with the same processing power as a desktop Mac.

# Meet the MacBook Air

Here's a corker of a conundrum: The MacBook Air is a revolutionary laptop, unique for both its size and weight, and yet the Air is just like the MacBook and the MacBook Pro. Well, mostly.

"Hold on, Mark. How can it be so singular and yet share so much with its road-warrior siblings?" That's what I show you in this section, which discusses both the many similarities and the handful of very striking differences among the three laptops in the MacBook line. If you're considering buying an Air, this section can help you decide whether you'd like to go ultra-thin or stick with the conventional laptop crowd.

One thing's for sure — Apple *never* does things in a mundane manner!

## Comparing MacBooks

Do you remember when Apple introduced those first iMacs? Although they shared the same basic components as any computer — a monitor, keyboard, ports, speakers, and cables — the iMac was revolutionary because it was completely self-contained. And it came in colors. And it didn't have a floppy drive. In fact, Apple had redesigned the common computer with the focus on *style* and *ease of use*, and had scrapped the floppy (and rightly so, seeing as how floppies had become practically useless and were unreliable, to boot).

I consider the MacBook Air to be an extension of the iMac revolution. With this new design, Apple has focused this time on *physical dimensions* and *weight,* and has tossed anything that isn't absolutely necessary for the lecture hall, board room, or city park. However, I'm happy to note that the Air is no toy, nor is it a bare-bones subnotebook. You'll find the Air as powerful as the MacBook, and the Air even shares some of the features of the MacBook Pro.

### What are the MacBook similarities?

Consider the similarities between the Air and the other MacBooks:

✦ **Widescreen display:** The Air has the same size display as the other MacBook models. Same display resolution, same gorgeous graphics.

✦ **Intel Core 2 Duo processor:** The Air is powered by the same type of CPU as its siblings.

✦ **Keyboard and trackpad:** The Air has a full-size keyboard, and it's even backlit, just like the MacBook Pro. The Air's trackpad includes support for Multi-Touch control, too.

✦ **Snow Leopard:** The Air runs the latest version of Mac OS X with aplomb.

✦ **iSight and microphone:** Every MacBook Air is video ready, using the same iSight camera. You can record audio with the built-in microphone as well.

✦ **Wireless support:** As do the other MacBooks, the Air has both built-in AirPort Extreme hardware (802.11n) and built-in Bluetooth hardware.

I think most Apple laptop owners would agree that this list covers the major features to look for in a MacBook, so we can all agree that the MacBook Air is no underpowered pushover.

### So what's so flippin' radical?

I'm glad you asked! Here's the checklist of striking differences that set the Air apart from the MacBook and MacBook Pro:

✦ **Physical dimensions:** Apple doesn't call this machine the Air for nothing! The current Air laptop measures a mere 0.76" in height (at its tallest point) when closed, 12.8" in width, and 8.94" in depth. Oh, and hold on to your chair for this one: Our champ weighs in at a lightweight three pounds! (That's a couple of pounds you won't be carrying around all day at that expo. Take it from this traveler: You *will* feel the refreshing difference in just an hour or two.)

✦ **Cost:** At the time of this writing, there are two versions of the Air laptop. An entry-level MacBook Air will set you back $1,499, and the top-of-the-line Air is a very reasonable $1,799. The more expensive Air is equipped with a solid-state drive and a faster CPU. (Don't miss the upcoming coverage on why solid-state is worth every penny.)

✦ **Ports:** The Air offers only three ports: a USB 2.0 port, an audio out jack, and a Micro-DVI for connecting an external monitor or video device. Notice that I don't mention a FireWire port, which can be a problem for Apple old-timers like me. I have a huge collection of FireWire devices. The Air also doesn't have an infrared port, so it's not compatible with the Apple Remote. Rats.

✦ **Sealed battery:** You can't swap batteries with a MacBook Air because the battery is sealed inside the laptop. (Think iPod.)

✦ **Sealed case:** You can't add or replace RAM modules. However, a MacBook Air comes equipped with 2GB of RAM, so you should be good to go. Comparatively, the MacBook can hold a maximum of 4GB, and MacBook Pro models can be upgraded to 8GB of RAM.

✦ **Speaker(s):** The MacBook Air includes but one speaker.

✦ **Solid-state drive:** Now we're talkin', Buck Rogers! I discuss the solid-state drive option in the next section. The MacBook Pro also offers a solid-state drive option.

✦ **No built-in optical drive:** *Whoa, Nellie!* This is a big one. Apple decided that a typical Air owner is likely to use a wireless connection for transferring files and media. But what if you have to re-install Snow Leopard or new applications? If you need to read or burn discs, a separate external USB SuperDrive is available for about $100, or you can use the Remote Disc feature and share the drive on another computer. (More on Remote Disc later in this section.)

As you can see, these striking differences make the choice between a MacBook Air and a MacBook/MacBook Pro very easy indeed. To wit: The Air is designed for the traveler who appreciates minimum weight and size but doesn't want to sacrifice the power, full-size screen, and full-size keyboard of a typical MacBook. These folks see the MacBook Air as a racecar: nimble, with reduced weight and no unnecessary frills. (Think of a typical NASCAR entry: Who needs an expensive stereo or air-conditioning?)

If you prefer instead the additional versatility of a MacBook or MacBook Pro — including the standard set of ports, the ability to swap batteries, and a built-in optical drive — and can live with carrying a few more pounds, I highly recommend that you stick with the more conventional MacBook or MacBook Pro.

## Look, Ma, no moving parts!
## The magic of solid-state drives

You're probably familiar with the common species of *usbius flashimus* — more commonly called the USB flash drive. With one of these tiny devices, you get the equivalent of a 2–128GB hard drive that plugs into a USB 2.0 port, allowing you to pack your data with you as you jet across the continents. But have you ever asked yourself, "Self, why don't they make internal hard drives that use this same technology?"

Actually, dear reader, solid-state drives have been around for a number of years now (think iPod Shuffle). Unfortunately, however, the solid-state memory used in today's flash drives gets pretty expensive as capacity increases. In fact, the cost has been the limiting factor, because a solid-state drive offers a number of advantages that really set it apart from a conventional magnetic hard drive:

✦ **No moving parts:** Unlike a typical magnetic hard drive, there's no read-write heads, no magnetic platter — just gobs of happy silicon memory chips. In effect, a solid-state drive works along the same lines as your MacBook's system RAM. Unlike your Mac's RAM, though, a solid-state drive doesn't lose the data it stores when you turn off your laptop. As you can imagine, no moving parts on a computer in motion is superior on two levels:

  • The solid-state drive never wears out or needs replacing.

  • If your laptop is accidentally abused (think getting knocked off your desk), it's far less likely that you'll lose a hard drive's worth of priceless data when it hits the ground.

✦ **Speed:** Oh, my goodness, is this thing fast! Your MacBook will boot/restart/awake in far less time than computers with magnetic drives can, and everything you do on your laptop will benefit from the speed boost. A solid-state drive can read data far faster than a conventional magnetic hard drive.

✦ **Power usage:** Forget your hard drive spinning up from sleep mode. The solid-state drive uses far less power than a conventional hard drive, resulting in significantly longer battery life.

✦ **Blessed silence:** The solid-state drive is completely silent. (No more of that gargling noise while the disk is accessed. *Sweet.*)

So do you need the solid-state drive option for your MacBook Air? The answer lies in your bank account (as well as your need for elbow room). If you can afford the extra expense of the solid-state drive and you can fit all your applications and data into 128 or 256GB, I heartily recommend that you consider joining Buck Rogers with the storage device of the future.

If you'd rather save that coin for something else, or you need a larger internal hard drive to hold things like digital video and a massive collection of digital images, stick with the tried-and-true magnetic hard drive.

## What if I need that pesky optical drive?

Can a laptop survive in the jungle that is Real Life without a DVD drive? The terse answer is *no*. I'll be honest here: Ripping an audio CD or burning an iDVD slideshow disc without an optical drive is impossible. (Rather like a cheap tank of gas.) And the wonders of digital media are a big part of the iWorld. So what was Apple thinking?

First, a bit of explanation. Today's DVD drives are thin, but not Air thin. In order to create the stunning Air design with truly revolutionary dimensions, Apple's engineers had to leave out the drive. However, if you own a MacBook Air, you have two choices when it comes to reading the contents of a CD or DVD: Go external, or learn to share.

### The external USB route

This is my choice. Personally, I have no problem at all toting around an external USB DVD burner with a MacBook Air. Heck, half the time, you're likely to leave it at home because most of us don't install software every day. The folks at Cupertino want you to download your movies from the iTunes Store, so if you follow the Apple Path, you still don't need an optical drive!

A USB SuperDrive from Apple costs a mere $100, and it can read and write DVDs as well as the built-in SuperDrive you'll find in the MacBook and MacBook Pro.

You can also use any third-party USB DVD drive that's compatible with Apple's laptops and Mac OS X Snow Leopard (they're easy to find on any online store that sells Mac external hardware).

### Sharing a CD or DVD drive

The other option for installing software or reading a DVD on the MacBook Air is Snow Leopard's built-in CD/DVD Sharing feature. Sharing is an option if you have a wired or wireless network with at least one of the following:

✦ **A Macintosh running Mac OS X Tiger, Leopard, or Snow Leopard**

✦ **A PC running Windows XP or Vista**

   This requires you to install a Windows application supplied by Apple with your MacBook Air.

You can ***only read from a shared optical drive.*** You can't write data to the remote drive, even if that drive is a DVD recorder.

To enable sharing, open System Preferences on the Macintosh with the optical drive, click the Sharing icon and then select the DVD or CD Sharing check box. Note that you can set whether the Mac will request your permission when another computer attempts to share the drive.

On a PC, display Control Panel, click the DVD or CD Sharing icon, and then select the Enable DVD or CD Sharing check box. Again, you can specify that permission is required, in case security is a concern.

After you set up the shared drive, just load the disc and select the Remote Disc item in any Finder Sidebar. (Remote Disc appears under the Devices heading in the Sidebar.) Now you can access the drive as if it were directly connected to your MacBook Air. Ah, technology!

# Chapter 3: Setting Up and Taking Care of Your MacBook

## In This Chapter

- ✓ Locating the right home for your computer
- ✓ Plugging in stuff and getting hooked up
- ✓ Starting the beast for the first time
- ✓ Handling your MacBook properly
- ✓ Cleaning your portable powerhouse
- ✓ Recharging and maintaining your battery

*C*onfiguration is not a dirty word. In fact, this chapter contains a set of procedures that are a snap to learn: unpacking your new MacBook; finding just the right place to park it (when you're not scampering around the world, that is); and connecting sundry cables. Oh, and don't forget starting up your MacBook. I wouldn't leave out the best part!

Nor would I leave out a *really* important aspect of owning a MacBook — that is, taking care of it. Although laptops are meant for the road, they still need regular maintenance (especially the battery, screen, and keyboard).

## Location, Location, Location!

If you choose the wrong spot to park your new laptop, I can *guarantee* that you'll regret it. Some domiciles and office cubicles don't offer a choice — you have one desk at work, for example, and nobody's going to hand over another one — but if you can select a home for your MacBook, consider the important placement points in this section:

- ✦ **Keep things cool.** Your new laptop is silent, but that super fast Intel Core 2 Duo processor generates heat. Make sure the location you choose is far from heating vents and shielded from direct sunlight. I also recommend a laptop cooling pad, which elevates the base of your laptop to allow air to circulate underneath.

- ✦ **Outlets are key!** Your computer needs a minimum of at least one nearby outlet, and perhaps as many as three:

- *A standard AC outlet:* Make sure to use an appropriate current adapter if you're traveling abroad.

You can always add a surge protector (for basic protection against lightning). It's not really necessary to use a Uninterruptible Power Supply (or UPS) because your MacBook's battery will kick in automatically in case of a power failure.

- *A telephone jack:* You'll need this if you have an Apple modem for connecting to the Internet or sending and receiving faxes.

- *A nearby Ethernet jack:* This might be needed if you use the MacBook or MacBook Pro's built-in Ethernet port for connecting to a wired Ethernet network, or if you buy a USB Ethernet port adapter for your MacBook Air.

If you prefer to send your data over the airwaves, consider wireless networking for your MacBook.

✦ **Don't forget the lighting.** Let me act as your mom. (I know that's a stretch, but bear with me.) She'd say, "You can't possibly expect to work without decent lighting! You'll go blind!" She's right, you know. You need a desk or floor lamp, at a minimum — something to illuminate your work.

✦ **Plan to expand.** If your laptop hangs out on a desk, allow an additional foot of space on each side. That way, you have room for external peripherals, more powerful speakers, and an external keyboard and mouse if you need one.

If you want to keep an external keyboard handy, consider using a laptop shelf. These Plexiglas or metal stands elevate your laptop several inches above the desk, putting the screen at a better ergonomic position and allowing you to park your keyboard and external mouse underneath.

# Unpacking and Connecting Your Laptop

You're going to love this section. It's short and sweet because the hardware configuration of a laptop is a piece of cake. (Sorry about the cliché overload, but this really *is* easy.)

## Unpacking for the road warrior

Follow these guidelines when unpacking your system:

✦ **Check for damage.** I've never had a box arrive from Apple with shipping damage, but I've heard horror stories from others (who claim that King Kong must have been working for That Shipping Company).

Check all sides of your box before you open it. If you find significant damage, take a photograph (just in case).

✦ **Search for all the parts.** When you're removing those chunks o' foam, make certain that you've checked all sides of each foam block for parts snuggled therein or taped for shipment.

✦ **Keep all packing materials.** Do *not* head for the trash can with the box and packing materials. Keep your box and all packing materials for at least a year, until the standard Apple warranty runs out. If you have to ship the laptop to an Apple service center, the box and the original packing is the only way for your machine to fly.

And now, a dramatic Mark's Maxim about cardboard containers:

**Smart computer owners keep their boxes far longer than a year. If you sell your laptop or move across the country, for example, you'll want that box.** *Trust me on this one.*

✦ **Store the invoice for safekeeping.** Your invoice is a valuable piece of paper, indeed.

Save your original invoice in a plastic bag, along with your computer's manuals, original software, and other assorted hoo-hah. Keep the bag on your shelf or stored safely in your desk, and enjoy a little peace of mind.

✦ **Read the MacBook's manual.** "Hey, wait a minute, Mark. Why do I have to read the manual from Apple along with this tome?" Good question, and here's the answer: The documentation from Apple might contain new and updated instructions that override what I tell you here. (For example, *"Never* cut the red wire. Cut the blue wire instead." Or something to that effect.) Besides, Apple manuals are rarely thicker than a restaurant menu.

You can always download the latest updated manuals for Apple computers in electronic format from Apple's Web site. (Adobe's PDF format is the standard for reading documents on your computer, and Snow Leopard can open and display any PDF document using the Preview application or Snow Leopard's Quick Look feature.) I always keep a copy of the PDF manual for my MacBook Pro on my hard drive, just in case.

## Connecting cables 101

Apple makes all your laptop's connections simple, but your computer depends on *you* to get the outside wires and thingamabobs where they go.

### The absolutely essential connection

After your new MacBook is resting comfortably in its assigned spot (a traditional desktop or otherwise), you need to make just one required connection: the power cable! Plug the cable into the corresponding socket on the Mac first and then plug 'er into that handy AC outlet. (After your battery is completely charged, of course, you can go mobile at a moment's notice.)

### Adding the Internet to the mix

If you have Internet access or a local computer network, you need to make at least one of the following connections in this section.

If you get on the Internet by dialing a standard phone number and your laptop has an external USB modem, just make two more connections:

1. **Plug one of the telephone cable's connectors into your external modem.**

2. **Plug the other telephone cable connector into your telephone line's wall jack.**

After you get your account information from your ISP, check out Book VI, Chapter 1 for the details on configuring your modem and Internet settings for dial-up access.

If you have high-speed Internet service, or if you're in an office or school with a local computer network, you can probably connect through your MacBook or MacBook Pro's built-in Ethernet port (or an external USB Ethernet adapter connected to your MacBook Air). You make two connections:

1. **Plug one end of the Ethernet cable into the Ethernet port on the MacBook.**

2. **Plug the other end of the Ethernet cable into the Ethernet port from your network.**

   Your network port is probably one of the following: an Ethernet wall jack, an Ethernet hub or switch, or a cable or DSL Internet router (or sharing device).

 Will you be joining a wireless network? If so, you'll find the information you need on configuring Snow Leopard for wireless networking in Book VII, Chapter 3.

## Fire That Puppy Up

Your MacBook's power switch is located on the right side of the keyboard. Press it now to turn on your laptop, and you will hear the pleasant startup tone that's been a hallmark of Apple computers for many years. Don't be alarmed if you don't immediately see anything on-screen; it takes a few seconds for the initial Apple logo to appear.

In my experience, sometimes a quick press of the power button on some Mac laptop models just doesn't do it. Rather, you actually have to hold the button down for a count of two or so before the computer turns on. However, if your Mac laptop ever locks up (and you can't quit an application), the power button gives you another option: Hold it down for a count of five to ten (depending on your counting speed) and your MacBook shuts off — even if your laptop is locked up tight.

As the Apple logo appears, you see a twirling, circular, high-tech progress indicator that looks like something from a James Bond movie. That's the sign that your MacBook is loading Snow Leopard and checking your internal drive for problems. Sometimes the twirling circle can take a bit longer to disappear. As long as it's twirling, though, something good is happening — your MacBook is loading some file-sharing, networking, and printing components (and such).

At last, your patience of a whole 10 seconds is rewarded, and after a short (but neat) video, you see the Snow Leopard Setup Assistant appear. (You can find out more about personalizing your MacBook with the Setup Assistant in Chapter 1 of Book II.)

## Mark's Favorite Signs of a Healthy MacBook

Before you jump into the fun stuff, don't forget an important step — a quick prelim check of the signs that your new mobile Mac survived shipment intact and happy.

If you can answer "yes" to each of these questions, your MacBook likely made the trip without serious damage:

1. **Does the computer's chassis appear undamaged?**

   It's pretty easy to spot damage to your MacBook's svelte design. Look for scratches and puncture damage.

2. **Does the screen work, and is it undamaged?**

   Does the cover open smoothly? Are any individual dots (or *pixels*) on your monitor obviously malfunctioning? Bad pixels appear black or in a different color from everything surrounding them. (Techs call these irritating anarchists *dead pixels.*) A 13" MacBook screen has literally hundreds of thousands of pixels, and unfortunately, some screens include one or two dead ones.

*3.* **Do the keyboard and trackpad work?**

Check your MacBook's built-in trackpad by moving your finger across its surface; the cursor should move on your screen. To check the keyboard, press the Caps Lock key on the left and observe whether the Caps Lock light turns on and off.

If you do notice a problem with your laptop (and you can use your Safari browser and reach the Web), you can make the connection to an Apple support technician at www.apple.com. If your MacBook Pro remains dead — like an expensive paperweight — and you can't get to the Internet, you can check your phone book for a local Apple service center, or call the AppleCare toll-free number at 1-800-275-2273.

# A Primer in MacBook Handling and Care

When I first started with computers, a "luggable" computer like my TRS-80 Model IV was the size of a portable sewing machine or a large manual typewriter (yes, I still have it, although I keep it only as a museum piece). These behemoths were built like tanks — and they weighed as much, too. Portable computers were designed to take considerable punishment, and batteries were a dream for the future.

Today's laptops, however, are a different matter entirely than the luggable computers of old: trim, lightweight, and battery-powered, but unfortunately much easier to damage while traveling. In this section, I provide you with a crash course on proper MacBook handling and battery maintenance.

## Great, a lecture about handling my laptop

Proper handling of your MacBook is important, so take a moment to cover the Rules of Proper Laptop Deportment. Okay, perhaps I'm lecturing a bit, but a little common sense goes a long way when handling any computer equipment, and your laptop is no different. (Scolding mode off.)

Keep these rules in mind while opening and carrying your MacBook:

✦ **The cover is your friend.** Open your laptop's cover slowly, without jerking or bending it.

✦ **Close it before you move it.** By closing your laptop, you put your Mac OS X operating system into sleep mode. If your MacBook has a typical magnetic hard drive with moving parts, the hard drive automatically spins down, making it safer to move. (Naturally, if your MacBook uses a solid-state drive with no moving parts, this isn't a concern.) The laptop is still on and will spring back to life after you open the cover.

✦ **Be nice to your keyboard.** Don't press too hard on those keys! Use the same amount of pressure that you use with a desktop computer keyboard.

✦ **Keep food and drinks far away.** Care to turn your laptop into a very expensive doorstop? Then go ahead and park your soda next to it. (Oh, and crumbs are perfect if you're interested in buying replacement keyboards.)

✦ **Keep your laptop as level as possible.** Using your laptop while it's tilted too far in any direction can eventually cause problems with your hard drive. I kid you not.

## Keeping things clean

Like any desktop computer, your MacBook should receive basic care to banish dust and dirt. Although you can't completely open the case to dust (as you can on a Mac Pro), follow these guidelines to keep your MacBook's external surfaces clean:

✦ **Wipe your laptop's case every week.** I use a soft cloth, but there are cleaning wipes specifically made for cleaning computer cases.

✦ **Consider a laptop sleeve.** You can protect your MacBook from dust without constantly dragging around a laptop bag or case — invest in a cloth or leather sleeve, which simply slides on over the laptop. Easy on, easy off!

✦ **Clean the screen the right way.** I always recommend either a photographer's lens cloth or monitor cleaning wipes for use on your MacBook's display panel. (This is *not* a job for a soft cloth.)

✦ **Don't forget the vents.** If your MacBook uses a fan or the case sports cooling vents, use either compressed air or a computer mini-vacuum to clean them every three months or so (or more often if you're using your MacBook in a particularly dusty environment).

✦ **Your keyboard needs attention, too.** In contrast to how you can treat a traditional keyboard, it's never a good idea to turn your Mac laptop upside down and shake it! Instead, use the aforementioned computer mini-vacuum to clean any crumbs, dust, or other detritus from your keyboard.

## More about batteries than you likely thought possible

Your MacBook's battery might appear to be maintenance free, but unfortunately that's not the case. Consider these tips as your rules of the road for monitoring and charging your battery:

✦ **Recharge in sleep mode or when powered off.** Your battery recharges faster when your laptop is off or in sleep mode. (I go into more detail on sleep mode in Book II, Chapter 2.)

✦ **Keep your laptop plugged into an AC socket when possible.** I take every opportunity to top off my laptop's battery, and so should you.

If you don't have much time to charge your battery before you're away from an AC socket — say, half an hour — don't use your MacBook whilst it's plugged in and charging.

**Save your juice.** For the most juice you can scavenge, here are some easy tricks:

• *Turn off your laptop or leave it in sleep mode.*

• *Turn off unnecessary hardware.* To conserve battery power as much as possible, disconnect any USB or FireWire devices, and turn off your AirPort and Bluetooth wireless hardware if you're not connected to a network. (I cover AirPort wireless networking in Book VII, Chapter 3. Bluetooth comes into focus in Book VIII, Chapter 6.)

• *Reduce the brightness of your display from your laptop's keyboard, using the F1 key.*

• *Remove CDs and DVDs from the optical drive. (MacBook Air owners, don't go hunting for a built-in optical drive, because your laptop doesn't have one.)*

✦ **Monitor your battery level from the Finder menu.** I love Snow Leopard's battery-monitoring system! Your laptop's battery life can be displayed in the Finder menu in several different views; my personal favorite is as a percentage of power remaining (with a fully charged battery registering at 100%). To display the percentage, click the battery icon in the Finder menu and choose Show⟳Percentage.

Keep in mind that the percentage shown is estimated using your current System Preference settings and power usage, so if you change your Energy Saver settings or remove a USB device that draws power from your laptop, you'll see that change reflected in the battery meter. Figure 3-1 illustrates the battery meter in Percentage view.

**Figure 3-1:**
Monitor your MacBook's juice from the Finder menu.

✦ **Calibrate your battery.** You can "train" your battery to provide the maximum charge by calibrating it, which Apple recommends doing monthly. It's a snap:

a. *Charge your battery until the Finder menu battery meter indicates that the unit is fully charged at 100%.*

b. *Keep your laptop connected to an AC socket for another two hours to ensure a maximum charge.*

c. *Disconnect the power cord and use your laptop on battery power until it's fully discharged and it automatically switches to sleep mode.*

Make sure that you close all your applications when you see the low battery warning dialog box so that you don't lose anything.

d. *Allow your laptop to sleep (or turn it off) for a full five hours.*

e. *Reconnect the AC cord and fully charge your battery.*

If your battery is no longer holding a charge — in other words, if you fully charge it and unplug the AC adapter, only to discover that you have only a few minutes of battery life — it's time to invest in a replacement battery. MacBook and MacBook Pro owners can buy a new battery themselves (from Apple or any one of a number of online vendors), but owners of MacBook Air laptops must take their computers in for servicing. The Air is a sealed unit, and you can't replace the battery yourself.

# Hot patootie, is my laptop steam powered?

Laptops generate heat. Today's super-fast multicore processors can work up a head of steam — pun intended — while you're using them, and even though most MacBooks have a fan, some of that heat is simply radiated from the bottom of the computer.

What you might not realize, however, is just how *much* heat your MacBook, MacBook Air, or MacBook Pro can produce! No, you won't be scalded if you shift your MacBook from a desk to your lap (Apple dislikes lawsuits as much as the next company), but if you've been using that laptop for hours, it will be uncomfortably hot!

To avoid that burning sensation, buy a laptop stand or cooling pad for your desk. These nifty metal or Plexiglas pedestals raise your laptop off your desk, allowing air to flow under the bottom of the computer for better cooling. Also, a laptop stand elevates the screen to a more ergonomic position. (The keyboard might suddenly be harder to use, naturally, but that's yet another reason that I recommend an external keyboard when you're using your Mac laptop at a semipermanent desk location; it saves wear and tear on your laptop keyboard, and you get a full-size keyboard.)

# Chapter 4: Extra Stuff You'll Likely Want

### In This Chapter

✔ Playing with your bundled software

✔ Buying additional stuff that you might need

Okay, I know that I've been harping on how self-sufficient and all-inclusive you are as a MacBook road warrior — and believe me, it's true! Everything you need to compute just about anywhere on the planet is included when you close your laptop's cover and go mobile. If you're in a bohemian mood and you want nothing but your MacBook, it's ready.

But is there other stuff that will make that mobile computing even more productive? And convenient? Well, of course — every MacBook power owner has extra stuff, and in this chapter I cover the software and hardware that most mobile veterans tote along with their laptops.

## An Overview of MacBook Software Goodness

This section answers the most common of all novice computer questions: "What the heck will I *do* with this thing?" Here, you find details and exciting factoids about the software that you get for free, software you'll want to buy, and stuff you can do on the Internet.

### What comes with my laptop?

Currently, Apple laptops ship with the following major software applications installed and ready to use:

✦ **The iLife '09 suite:** You know you want these applications! They turn your MacBook into a digital hub for practically every kind of high-tech device on the planet, including DV camcorders, digital cameras, portable music players, PDAs, and even cell phones.

Book IV focuses on the major applications that make up iLife: iTunes, iPhoto, iWeb, iMovie, iDVD, and GarageBand.

✦ **Photo Booth and Front Row:** You can discover more about these applications in Book II, Chapter 5. For now, suffice it to say that Photo Booth works with your laptop's iSight camera, and Front Row is the remote-control software you'll use with your Apple Remote (if you have one).

The installed software on your MacBook might change as new programs become available.

## Connecting to the Internet from your lap

What is a modern computer without the Internet? Apple gives you great tools to take full advantage of every road sign and off-ramp on the Information Superhighway right out of the box:

✦ **Web surfing:** I use Snow Leopard's Apple Safari Web browser every single day. It's faster and better designed than Internet Explorer, with unique features such as tabbed browsing and built-in RSS feeds.

If *tabbed browsing* and *RSS feeds* sound like ancient Aztec to you, don't worry. Book VI, Chapter 5 is devoted entirely to Safari.

✦ **Web searches:** Dashboard widgets can search the entire Internet for stocks, movie listings, airline schedules, dictionaries, and foreign language translations. I explain Dashboard in Chapter 2 of Book III.

✦ **Chat:** iChat lets you use your MacBook to chat with others around the world for free using the Internet — by keyboard, voice, or full-color video. This is awesome stuff straight out of Dick Tracy and Buck Rogers. If you've never seen a video chat, you'll be surprised by just how good your friends and family look!

Always wear a shirt when videoconferencing.

✦ **E-mail:** Soldier, Apple's got you covered. The Mail application is a full-featured e-mail system, complete with defenses against the torrent of junk mail awaiting you. (Imagine a hungry digital saber-toothed tiger with an appetite for spam.) Send pictures and attached files to everyone on the planet, and look doggone good doing it.

## Applications that rock

Dozens of small applications are built into Mac OS X. I mention them in later chapters, but here are four good examples to whet your appetite:

✦ **Safari:** Apple's Web browser of choice — it's fast, simple, and easily customized. See how to navigate the Web in style in Book VI, Chapter 5.

✦ **DVD Player:** Put all that widescreen beauty to work and watch your favorite DVD movies with DVD Player! You have all the features of today's most expensive standalone DVD players, too, including a spiffy on-screen control that looks like a remote.

✦ **Address Book:** Throw away that well-thumbed collection of fading addresses. Use the Snow Leopard Address Book to store, search, and recall just about any piece of information on your friends, family, and acquaintances.

✦ **Chess:** Ah, but this isn't the chessboard your Dad used! Play the game of kings against a tough (and configurable) opponent — your MacBook — on a beautiful 3-D board. Heck, your laptop even narrates the game by speaking the moves!

You can use the data you store in your Address Book in other Apple applications included with Snow Leopard, such as Apple Mail and iChat.

## Boot Camp for Dummies

Mac OS X Leopard introduced one particularly exciting feature for Windows switchers: You can use the Apple Boot Camp utility and your licensed copy of Windows XP to install and boot Windows on your Intel-based Mac laptop! Snow Leopard adds Vista support as well as faster operation.

Boot Camp creates a Windows-friendly *partition* (or section) on your hard drive and stores all your Windows files in that partition. Other than the slightly strange key assignments you'll have to remember, early adopters of Boot Camp report that it's surprisingly reliable and easy to use. However, I strongly urge that you back up your laptop on a regular basis; inviting Windows to your Mac laptop also invites potential viruses and spyware as well.

Apple's Boot Camp Assistant provides step-by-step instructions, making it easy to configure your laptop for Windows. To run the Boot Camp Assistant, open your Applications folder and double-click the Utilities folder; then double-click the Boot Camp Assistant application icon.

## Applications you'll end up getting

Although I cover my favorite must-have applications and utilities in Book VIII, Chapter 5, I mention the categories here:

✦ **A productivity suite:** Whether it be Microsoft Office, iWork, or a free alternative such as Google's online applications or OpenOffice.org 3, you'll likely want a quality word processor, spreadsheet, and presentation application.

✦ **Image and video editors:** Most MacBook owners need a bit more image editing versatility than the basic tools provided by iPhoto and Preview — and if iMovie isn't enough to handle your video-editing chores, Apple offers more robust tools.

✦ **Utilities:** Monitor your hard drives and defragment them using tools that aren't included in Snow Leopard's Disk Utility, such as TechTool Pro from Micromat. You can also burn all sorts of data and music discs using a third-party application such as Roxio's Toast Titanium.

✦ **Games:** Your MacBook is powerful enough to run today's latest games, such as Blizzard's World of Warcraft or Harry Potter and the Half-Blood Prince from Electronic Arts.

## Other Stuff That Nearly Everyone Wants

No man is an island and no computer is, either. I always recommend the same set of stuff for new PC and Mac owners. These extras help keep your new computer clean and healthy (and some make sure you're happy as well):

✦ **Surge suppressor:** Even an all-in-one computer like your laptop can fall prey to a power surge. I recommend using one of these:

- *A basic surge suppressor* with a fuse can help protect your Mac from an overload.

- *A UPS (uninterruptible power supply)* costs a little more, but it does a better job of filtering your AC line voltage to prevent brownouts or line interference from reaching your computer.

Of course, your laptop's battery immediately kicks in if you experience a blackout, so a UPS is less important for your computer. However, any computer tech will tell you that filtered AC current is far better for your laptop, and your UPS will also provide power for external devices that *don't* have a battery.

✦ **Screen wipes:** Invest in a box of premoistened screen wipes to keep your screen pristine. Your MacBook's screen can pick up dirt, fingerprints, and other unmentionables faster than you think.

Make sure your wipes are especially meant for LCD or laptop computer screens.

✦ **Blank CDs and DVDs:** Depending on the type of optical drive installed in your laptop — and the type of media you're recording, such as computer data CDs, DVD movies, or audio CDs — you'll want blank discs for

- CD-R (record once)

- CD-RW (record multiple times)

- DVD-R (record once)

✦ **Cables:** Depending on the external devices and wired network connectivity you'll be using, these are

  • A standard Ethernet cable (for wired networks or high-speed Internet)

  • FireWire or USB cables for devices you already have

✦ **A restraining cable:** For those who are a little more security-conscious or tend to use their laptops in public places, a standard Kensington laptop lock slot is provided on the MacBook and MacBook Pro case. (Sorry, MacBook Air owners, but your case is too thin to sport a lock slot.) The principle is the same as a bicycle cable lock: If your laptop is secured by a cable to a sturdy fixture, it's nearly impossible for it to walk off with someone else.

✦ **A wrist rest:** You might have many reasons to buy a new Mac laptop, but I know that acquiring a bad case of carpal tunnel syndrome is not one of them. Take care of your wrists by carrying a keyboard wrist rest in your laptop bag.

# Book II

# Using Mac OS X with Your MacBook

You can select a gaggle of icons to copy or move files around.

# Contents at a Glance

**Chapter 1: Shaking Hands with Mac OS X**..................... 47

Convince Me: Why Mac OS X? ......... 48
What Do I Really Need
to Run the Big X? ........................... 57
Upgrading from Earlier
Versions of Mac OS ...................... 58
Personalizing the Big X..................... 59

**Chapter 2: Navigating and Running Programs** ..................... 61

Restarting, Sleeping, and
Shutting Down................................ 61
A Window Is Much More
Than a Frame ................................. 65
Menu Mysteries Explained.............. 71
Icons 'R Us...................................... 72
And more...

**Chapter 3: Basic OS X Housekeeping**..................... 87

The Finder: It's the Wind
beneath Your Wings..................... 87
Copying and Moving Files
and Folders..................................... 89
Cloning Your Items — It's
Happening Now!.............................. 90
Deleting That Which
Should Not Be ............................... 91
And more...

**Chapter 4: Searching Everything with Spotlight** ..................... 115

Basic Searching 101 ........................ 115
Is Spotlight Really That Cool?........ 117
Expanding Your Search
Horizons......................................... 120
Customizing Spotlight
to Your Taste ............................... 121

**Chapter 5: Fun with Photo Booth and Front Row**...................... 125

Capturing the Moment with
iSight and Photo Booth.............. 126
Producing Video on the Spot
with iMovie..................................... 128
Controlling Your MacBook
Remotely with Front Row .......... 129

**Chapter 6: Keeping Track with the Address Book** ..................... 133

Hey, Isn't the Address Book
Just a Part of Mail? ...................... 133
Entering Contact Information........ 135
Using Contact Information............. 137
Arranging Your Contact Cards ...... 139
And more...

**Chapter 7: The Joys of Maintenance**..................................... 145

Deleting Applications the
Common Sense Way.................... 145
Popping the Hood: Using
the System Profiler ...................... 147
Tracking Performance with
Activity Monitor........................... 148
Fixing Things with the
Disk Utility .................................... 151
And more...

**Chapter 8: Getting Help for the Big X**............................... 167

Displaying the Help
Viewer Window............................. 167
Searching for Specific Stuff ............ 169
Prodding Apple for the
Latest Gossip................................. 170
Calling for Help Deep in
the Heart of X ............................... 171
Other Resources to Chew On ........ 171

**Chapter 9: Troubleshooting the X**.... 175

Don't Panic!...................................... 175
The Troubleshooting Process ........ 176
Do I Need to Reinstall
Mac OS X?...................................... 181
It's Still Not Moving:
Troubleshooting Resources........ 182

# Chapter 1: Shaking Hands with Mac OS X

---

## In This Chapter

✔ **Understanding the advantages of Mac OS X**

✔ **Checking your system requirements**

✔ **Upgrading from earlier versions of Mac OS**

✔ **Installing Mac OS X**

✔ **Running Mac OS X for the first time**

---

It's human nature to require instant gratification from your software. I've seen it countless times: Someone runs a program, immediately feels comfortable with it, and then spends the rest of his days using that program religiously. Or another person plays with the same program for 120 seconds and dismisses it as too difficult or too confusing. It's rather like watching a fancy fashion show runway in Rome or Paris: There had better be eye appeal pretty quickly or the bucks won't flow.

Ditto for modern computer operating systems. An *operating system* is the basic software that determines the look and feel of your entire computer and usually extends to the programs that you run as well. Microsoft felt the pinch of an old-fashioned operating system when Windows 98 and Windows Me were starting to appear rather plain looking. Then came Windows XP, where menus fade in and out like fireflies on a summer night, little puppies help you find files, and other animation abounds. With Windows Vista, Microsoft attempted to match some of the elegance and power of Mac OS X in the PC world . . . but to be honest, updating a PC by upgrading to Windows Vista is a little like putting on a polyester sports coat over the same tired old leisure suit — most of what changes is on the *outside*. (And from what I've seen so far, Windows 7 is more of the same.)

Apple doesn't work that way. Sure, Mac OS X looks doggone good. Forget the minimum requirement of shirt and shoes because this operating system is wearing an Armani suit. What's really exciting for Macintosh owners around the world, however, is the heart that beats *beneath* the pretty form. At its introduction, Mac OS X was quite literally an operating system revolution, and it still delivers some of the most advanced features available on any personal computer in use today while remaining as easy to use as the first Macintosh. (And yes, I do own, use, and enjoy both PCs and Macs — what's important to me is which computer does the best job the fastest in the easiest manner.)

Now, I'm not going to just haul off and proclaim that Mac OS X can run rings around — well . . . you know, the *W* word — without solid proof. In this chapter, I introduce you to the advantages of using Mac OS X on your laptop and why it's such a step ahead for those running Windows. I also cover the hardware requirements for running Mac OS X version 10.6 (Snow Leopard) as well as guidelines on switching from Windows. Finally, I familiarize you with the steps that you'll encounter the first time you fire up the Big X.

## Convince Me: Why Mac OS X?

Apple was one of the first to pioneer the graphical approach to computing with the appearance of the first Macintosh, so you'd expect Mac OS X to be simple to use — and indeed it is. For many folks, that's Job One. If you're one of those people, you can happily skip this section without need of further evidence because Mac OS X is undoubtedly the easiest operating system on the planet to use. (And believe me, I'm not knocking simplicity. Computers are supposed to be getting easier to use, and techno-nerds like me are supposed to be rendered unnecessary as computers advance.) Here is the mantra of the Mac — and the first of Mark's Maxims for this volume:

**Make it *easy*.**

Still with me? Need more testimony? Or perhaps you're just curious about the engine under the hood. Then read on — and if you're a MacBook owner, feel free to gloat! (If you're a PC owner, there's always eBay.)

### Pretty to behold

Let me illustrate with a screenshot or two. Figure 1-1 illustrates a typical screen from a day spent in Mac OS v. 9.2, the capable — albeit rather old-fashioned — version of the Mac OS operating system that shipped in the days before Mac OS X.

Compare that screen with a similar screen from the latest version of the Big X, as shown in Figure 1-2. As you can see, everything's streamlined in appearance, with maximum efficiency in mind. Tasteful 3-D abounds, from the drop-shadowed windows to the liquid-look scroll bars. Icons look like miniature works of art. Macintosh owners appreciate outstanding design — and can recognize the value of a great computer. After all, many MacBook owners are professionals in the graphic arts, and Apple provides the hardware that they need — like the top-of-the-line, light-emitting diode (LED) used with the 17-inch MacBook Pro.

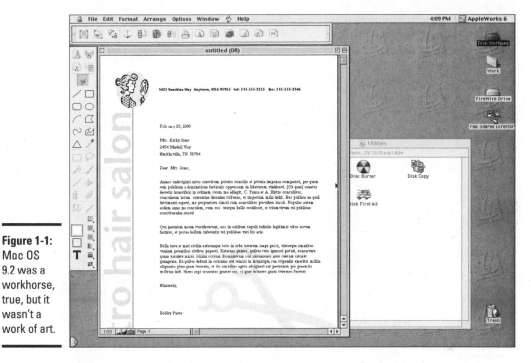

**Figure 1-1:**
Mac OS
9.2 was a
workhorse,
true, but it
wasn't a
work of art.

**Figure 1-2:**
Eye-
catching?
You bet!
Mac OS
X Snow
Leopard is a
knockout.

Take a look at what's going on behind the curtain — the Great Oz is actually pretty busy back there.

### The allure of Aqua

The Apple software developers who introduced us to Mac OS X designed this "liquid" look from the ground up. They call it *Aqua,* and it's Snow Leopard's standard user interface.

Whoops, I just realized that I slipped a ten-cent example of techno-babble into that previous paragraph. Let me explain: A *user interface design* determines how things look throughout both the operating system itself and all applications that are written to run under an operating system (OS). This includes the buttons that you push, the controls that you click or move, and even the appearance of the windows and menus themselves. For example, if you've already begun to use Mac OS X, you've probably stopped right in the middle of a task and exclaimed to yourself, "Why, Self, look at that cool 3-D contour effect on that menu bar!" That shapely contour is a tiny part of the Aqua user interface design.

Aqua also extends to the placement of controls and how they're shown to you. For example:

✦ Mac OS X uses Aqua *sheets* (which are attached to their parent windows) to prompt you for input, such as confirming when you're about to close a document without saving it. In contrast to Windows, multiple programs can have multiple sheets open, so you can continue to work in other applications without being rudely forced to answer the query immediately.

✦ Aqua's file selection controls, such as the one in Figure 1-3, make it much easier to navigate quickly to a specific file or folder from within an application — as a matter of fact, they look much like Finder windows, to keep things consistent and easier to use.

**Figure 1-3:**
A typical file selection dialog (done right in Aqua).

✦ The *Dock* is another Aqua favorite. The Dock launches your favorite applications, indicates what's running on your MacBook, and allows you to switch between those programs — and all in a strip that you can relocate and customize at will. I talk about the Dock in greater detail in Book III, Chapter 2.

Consider Aqua as the *look-and-feel* of Mac OS X and virtually all applications that it runs; you can discover how to use these Aqua controls in the pages to come. Of course, MacBook owners really don't have to worry about Aqua itself; the Aqua guidelines are a roadmap for those writing applications for Mac OS X. Programs written to the common Aqua interface standard will be easier for you to use, and you'll become a proficient power user of that program much faster.

## The quality of Quartz

The second ingredient in the visual feast that is Mac OS X is *Quartz Extreme* — and I must ask your forgiveness, good reader, because I have to get a tad technical again. Quartz Extreme is a *graphics engine:* It's the portion of Mac OS X that draws what you see on the screen (in the Aqua interface, natch). Think of the engine in your car, which is responsible for making your car move. Whether your MacBook is running Microsoft Word or simply idling at the Desktop waiting for you to finish your soda, Quartz Extreme is at work displaying icons, drawing shapes, exhibiting the Finder, and animating things in the Dock.

What sets Quartz Extreme apart from the ho-hum graphics engine that Windows uses? It's all about international programming standards . . . you know, those things that Microsoft would much rather you forget. To wit:

✦ **PDF:** The Quartz Extreme engine is built around the Acrobat Portable Document Format (*PDF* for short) developed by Adobe. If you've been spending any time at all on the Internet in the last ten or so years, you know that PDF files have emerged as the standard for displaying and printing the highest-quality electronic documents. Plus, Adobe has released a version of the free Acrobat Reader (www.adobe.com) for just about every computer on this green Earth. This means that text and graphics displayed in Quartz Extreme are razor sharp, resizable, and easily portable from one computer to another. In fact, Mac OS X displays PDF files without even requiring Acrobat, using the built-in Preview application. Figure 1-4 shows a complex PDF document that I opened in Mac OS X.

✦ **OpenGL:** Gamers will get really excited about this one: Quartz Extreme also uses the OpenGL graphics acceleration standard, which delivers the fastest 3-D graphics on the planet. (Think photo-realistic, high-resolution graphics drawn in the blink of an eye.) In fact — and this is a really cool trick — OpenGL is even used to produce the Desktop in Mac OS X Snow Leopard.

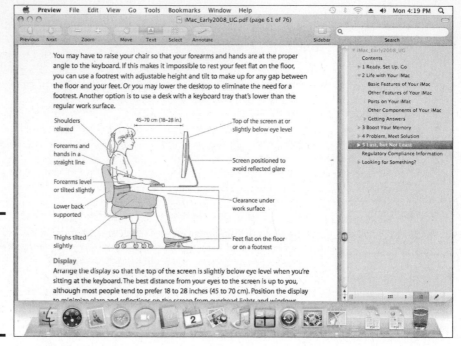

**Figure 1-4:** Yep, that's a PDF document, not a scanned image!

In English, that means that today's top-of-the-line, 3-D gaming and 3-D graphics acceleration can take care of drawing *everything;* forget about waiting for windows to close or menus to appear, even when you're creating the world's biggest honking spreadsheet or building a presentation the size of Baltimore. As the Chairman of the Board would say, "We're talkin' fast, baby, like a rocket ship to the moon!"

✦ **Core Animation:** Snow Leopard includes functionality that Apple calls Core Animation, which makes it much easier for programmers to animate backgrounds and objects within their programs. Text, 3-D animation, and video now work seamlessly side-by-side, and eye-catching animations within applications, such as Time Machine, are the norm for MacBook owners.

## Stable, stable, stable

"So it's elegant in design. That's great, Mark, but what if Mac OS X crashes? Aqua and Quartz Extreme aren't worth a plug nickel if my cursor doesn't move and I lose my document!" Believe me, I couldn't agree more; I make my living from computers, and every time that a misbehaving program locks up one of my machines, I throw a tantrum that would make Godzilla back off. Lockups shouldn't be tolerated in this day and age.

Luckily, the folks who designed Mac OS X were just as interested in producing a rock-solid operating system as they were in designing an attractive look. (Think of Tom Cruise's face on The Rock's body.)

Mac OS X is as hard to crash as the legendary UNIX operating system — that's right, the same reliable workhorse that techno-wizards around the world use to power the Internet, where stability is all-important. In fact, Mac OS X is actually built on top of a UNIX base. It's just well hidden underneath, allowing you and me to focus on our programs and zip around with our trackpads without knowing any of those obscure, arcane keyboard commands. You get the benefits of UNIX without a pair of suspenders, a pocket protector, or the hassle of growing a beard. (Not to mention years of computer programming experience.)

Apple calls this UNIX foundation at the heart of Mac OS X by another nifty title: *Darwin*. I could tell you that Darwin provides the latest in 64-bit memory support and CPU management, but if you're a normal human being, your eyes will glaze over. Suffice it to say that Darwin makes the best use of your laptop's memory (RAM) and your computer's brain (CPU) — Snow Leopard has been fine-tuned for processors with multiple cores, such as the Core 2 Duo CPU from Intel. Rest assured that your Web server will stay up even if your misbehaving Virtual Birdcalling simulation decides to run amok. (Emus running amok . . . how dreadful.)

# Don't forget QuickTime X!

If you've recorded or edited digital video (DV), you're probably already familiar with Apple's QuickTime MOV format. QuickTime movies are typically high resolution, relatively small in size, and easily created with iMovie, which I discuss in Book IV, Chapter 4. Although QuickTime X isn't "on stage" all the time as is Aqua or Quartz Extreme, it's still an important part of Mac OS X: Every time you display a video clip that you've recorded or watch a streaming TV broadcast from a Web site, you use QuickTime X. (Note, however, that you don't use QuickTime X to watch DVD movies — that job is reserved for the Apple DVD Player.) QuickTime X includes support for AVC (Advanced Video Codec) for the best possible display of the latest HD (High Definition) video signals from the expensive hardware that's now appearing at your local electronics Maze o' Wires chain store.

QuickTime is actually not a new Mac OS X feature — it's been around since the early 1990s — but the latest versions of Mac OS X include the free QuickTime Player, which provides support for the latest broadcast and Web video. In fact, you can set up your own TV station on the Web with the tools included in the Professional QuickTime package.

Yes, yet another standard is at work here — uh-oh, Overlord Gates is truly angry now! For those who *do* have a beard and are curious about such things, Darwin uses a FreeBSD kernel, so it also inherits all the protocol standards that have made UNIX the foundation of today's Internet. You can find more about FreeBSD at www.freebsd.org. Because Mac OS X is developed as an open source project, software engineers outside Apple can actually contribute ideas and code, just as UNIX continues to evolve over time. (And yes, you'll even discover how to access the powerful UNIX command prompt from Mac OS X in Book IX, Chapter 1!)

To get an idea of just how well armored Mac OS X is, consider Figure 1-5. See how one program, which I call Titanic 1.0, has locked up like San Quentin. Under Mac OS 9 and older versions of Windows, your only chance at recovering anything would involve divine intervention. However, in Mac OS X, my Pages application is unaffected because it has a completely protected area of system memory to play in. (I show you how to force a misbehaving application to go away in Book II, Chapter 3.)

**Figure 1-5:**
Mac OS X keeps applications separate for a reason.

By the way, Darwin makes it easy for UNIX software developers to quickly and easily *port* (or modify) all sorts of UNIX applications to work under Mac OS X. I think you'll agree that a wider selection of applications is a good thing.

## Multitasking and multithreading for normal human beings

And now, for your entertainment, a short one-act play. (Yes, really.)

### A Shakespearean Moment of Multitasking and Multithreading

Our play opens with Julius Caesar shaking his head in disgust at his Mac OS 9 Desktop.

**Caesar:** Anon, I am only one mortal, yet my Desktop doth abound with portals to applications of all different mien. Tell me, foul beast, why thy spirit seems slow and sluggish, and my Excel spreadsheet doth crawl on its belly!

[Enter Romeo, a cocky and rather brash young Apple software developer.]

**Romeo:** Dude, the problem is, like, your operating system. Y'see, older versions of both Mac OS and Windows ended up constantly, like, shifting your computer's attention from one app to another — Excel has to cooperate with everything else that's running in the background, like a good little corporate boy. It's less efficient and very, very '90s. Upgrade to Mac OS X, and you get *pre-emptive multitasking* — the app you're actually using, like, gets the lion's share of the processing time, and everything runs smoother when you need it. That's the way UNIX works.

**Caesar:** Verily, your strange tongue doth annoy me. Guards, behead him — then obtain for me this Mac OS X.

**Romeo:** I'm outta here — I've got a hot date — but don't forget, like, Mac OS X also uses *multithreaded processing,* so your MacBook can handle different operating system tasks at the same time. It's kind of like your computer can both walk and chew gum at the same time: fast, fast, fast!

[Exit Romeo — rather swiftly — stage right.]

**Fin**

When the play closes, we can only hope that Romeo is fast as well. (I told you it was a short play.)

## The definition of Internet savvy

Remember the classic iMac advertisements that touted the one-plug approach to the Internet? That entire campaign was centered on one idea: that the Internet was *supposed* to be easy to use. The folks at Microsoft sat up and took notice when the iMac proved so incredibly successful, and Windows Vista actually reduced some of the overwhelming folderol that you had to encounter just to connect to the Internet — but Mac OS X still wipes the floor with Vista when it comes to easy and complete Internet connectivity. For example:

✦ **Easy configuration:** Mac OS X sets up your entire Internet connection with a simple assistant (Windows users, think "wizard") of four screens. As long as you've got the right information handy (which your Internet service provider [ISP] should supply), it's a snap to set up.

✦ **iDisk:** What if I told you that for a reasonable yearly subscription fee, Apple can provide you with a chunk of Internet-accessible, private hard drive space — and that you can access this hard drive space from anywhere on Earth with an Internet connection? Absolutely, unbelievably, massively cool. This neat trick is called *iDisk,* and I cover it in detail in Book VI, Chapter 4.

✦ **All the Internet behind-the-scenes stuff:** The Internet is basically built on a number of *protocols* (read that as *rules for exchanging all sorts of data*) — and, as I mention earlier, UNIX machines dominate the Internet. Ergo, Mac OS X on your MacBook also provides you with support for just about every Internet protocol on the planet. Even if you don't know them by name or write your own software, the applications that you buy can use them.

✦ **A gaggle of great Internet applications:** Mac OS X ships with all sorts of Internet magic built in. For example, you'll get instant Internet and local network communication with iChat (which I cover in Book VI, Chapter 3), Safari (covered in Book VI, Chapter 5), and Apple Mail, a standard-issue, battle-ready e-mail program (which I discuss in Book VI, Chapter 2). Yup, it's all free.

## Lots of free goodies

You don't just get Internet applications when you latch your fingers onto a box o' Mac OS X — you can start doing all sorts of neat stuff without investing one extra dollar in more software!

Remember, what you receive along with Mac OS X depends on whether you're buying a boxed copy, upgrading from an older version of Mac OS, or receiving the Big X already installed on a new MacBook. With that in mind, check out the possibilities.

✦ **This is the iLife:** This suite of easy-to-use integrated programs is included with a new MacBook, and it's practically as well known as the computer itself these days: iDVD, iPhoto, iTunes, GarageBand, iMovie, and iWeb. Each of these stellar programs is covered in full in Book IV. If you've got a digital camera, an MP3 player, a USB musical keyboard, or a DV camcorder, you'll be a very happy individual. I promise.

✦ **iWork to the rescue:** If you've bought a new MacBook with Mac OS X pre-installed, you probably also received a test drive version of *iWork* (Apple's answer to Microsoft Office). Good stuff, indeed. If you don't want to spend the bucks on Office 2008 and you don't need the complex gewgaws and baroque architecture of Word, Excel, and PowerPoint, I can guarantee you that Pages, Numbers, and Keynote are powerful enough to satisfy your office document and presentation yearnings. I discuss iWork '09 in Book V.

✦ **The obligatory games:** Apple typically chooses new games to bundle with MacBooks every three or four months — typically, games are selected that show off your laptop's 3-D power, as well as finger-exercising arcade challenges. Because this book isn't a game guide, I leave you to explore these games at your leisure.

# What Do I Really Need to Run the Big X?

I've written ten other *For Dummies* books — I know, it's getting to be a habit (and a career) — and I always find the "Hardware Requirements" section a hard one to write. Why? Well, I know what Apple claims as the minimum hardware requirements necessary to run Mac OS X. But, on the other hand, I know what *I* would consider the minimum hardware requirements, and they're substantially different. Oh, well, let me list the bare bones and then I'll give you my take on what you really need. (Naturally, if Mac OS X Snow Leopard is pre-installed on your MacBook, feel free to tear out this page and create a handful of celebratory confetti.)

From *The World According to Jobs*, the minimum requirements are as follows:

✦ **Hardware:** You'll need any MacBook with an Intel processor. This means that just about any recent laptop Mac is *technically* eligible to play (although you might find the performance of a first-generation single-core MacBook running Snow Leopard to be unacceptable). Again, note that you'll need a DVD drive to install Snow Leopard (although it can be installed on the MacBook Air using the remote DVD feature).

✦ **RAM:** You'll need at least 1GB of memory (RAM). At today's low prices, that's like buying a pizza.

✦ **Hard drive territory:** Although svelte by Windows standards, Mac OS X still needs about 8GB of free space on your hard drive.

From *The World According to Chambers*, the minimum requirements are

✦ **Hardware:** I recommend a MacBook with at least an Intel Core 2 Duo processor. Remember, this is *my* take on what you'll need to really take advantage of Mac OS X Snow Leopard, and again, I have to say that I don't think it performs well enough on Intel single-core computers.

✦ **RAM:** Don't settle for anything less than 2GB. Again, with memory as cheap as it is these days, this is like adding extra cheese to that pizza.

Time for a Mark's Maxim:

**Any techno-nerd worth the title will tell you that the *single most important key* to performance in today's operating systems is RAM — yep, it's actually more effective than a faster processor!**

If you've got any extra spending cash in between your sofa cushions, spend it on RAM. (Up to an earth-shaking 8GB of RAM on the latest MacBook Pro racehorses!)

✦ Hard drive territory: I'd recommend having the following:

  • 10GB free for just the operating system

  • A minimum of an additional 40 to 60GB for any digital video clips, photographs, and songs you'll be collecting

# Upgrading from Earlier Versions of Mac OS

Because the installation of Mac OS is as simple as loading a DVD and double-clicking an icon, there's not much to tell. What's important is the steps that you should take care of *before* you start the installation. I cover those in the next section. Pay heed, or pay later. I won't go into detail about the actual installation because there really aren't any details to speak of — you'll answer a question or two and then hop up to get another cup of coffee or another caffeine-laden soda while the installer does the rest. Would anyone expect any different from Apple?

## Back up — PLEASE back up

I know you're anxious to join the In crowd, and Apple makes the upgrade process as noninvasive and as safe as possible, but SNAFUs such as power loss and hard drive failures do happen. With a full backup of your system on CD or DVD (or to an external hard drive using Time Machine), you can rest assured that you'll get your precious files and folders back in pristine shape if tragedy strikes. To be honest, you need to back up your system on a regular basis anyway. Promise me **now** that you'll back up your system, won't you?

## Snuff out disk errors

Before you upgrade, I recommend that you check that hard drive for errors one last time — upgrading a disk with directory errors takes longer. If you're upgrading from an older version of Mac OS X, use *Disk Utility,* which I cover in Book II, Chapter 7. Ain't technology grand?

## Plug it, road warrior

You're on the road with your MacBook Pro, and you've just bought your copy of Mac OS X Snow Leopard. You're thinking of installing your brand-spanking-new operating system. . . . Stop! NOW.

Before you decide to upgrade your laptop, consider what will happen if that magical vessel containing all your files should flicker and . . . No, on second thought, don't even *visualize* it. (Even if the battery is fully charged.) If you're installing a Mac OS X upgrade on a MacBook, MacBook Air, or MacBook Pro, make sure that it's plugged in and receiving its share of good, clean AC power from a handy, nearby wall socket. The installation process could take an hour, and there'll be constant hard drive and DVD drive activity — think "Attack of the Energy-Draining Installation from Planet Lithium." You *don't* want to try this while your MacBook is operating on battery power.

## Pet peeve number 1 . . .

The round object that you load into your CD-ROM or DVD-ROM drive is a *disc,* not a *disk,* like your hard drive or that flimsy floppy that some of the Windows horde still uses.

Anyone who pretends to talk oh-so-knowingly about a *CD-ROM disk* or *DVD disk* is likely a dweeb, and you should steer as far away from that dweeb as possible in the future.

Heck, a techno-purist would probably recommend that you attach your MacBook to an uninterruptible power supply (UPS) for the installation process, but I'm not quite *that* paranoid about power outages.

Keep one thing in mind while installing Mac OS X: If you format the *destination drive* — the drive where you'll install Mac OS X — you'll lose everything that it stored. No big surprise there, and the installation program will warn you profusely about this beforehand. There's really no reason to do so unless you just crave a *clean* installation (an installation of a new operating system on a newly formatted drive, compared with an upgrade of your existing Mac OS System files). Oh, and don't forget to use Mac OS Extended (Journaled) format.

## Personalizing the Big X

After the installation is complete and you have rebooted the beast, stand back and watch those beautiful rounded edges, brushed stainless-steel surfaces, and liquid colors appear. But wait — you're not quite done yet! Mac OS X needs to be personalized for you, just like your toothbrush or your SUV's six-way power seat; therefore, use the Setup Assistant that automatically appears the first time you boot Mac OS X Snow Leopard.

These assistant screens change periodically — and they're completely self-explanatory — so I won't march you through each one step by step. However, here are a few tips that provide a bit of additional over-the-shoulder help while you're setting things up.

✦ **How rude!** If you're outside the United States or other English-speaking countries, you should know that Mac OS X defaults to U.S. formats and keyboard layouts. Rest assured, though, because Mac OS X does indeed provide full support for other languages and keyboard configurations.

To display these options in the list boxes, click the Show All button at the bottom of the assistant screen.

✦ **Accounts are important.** When Mac OS X asks you to create your account, don't forget your password — oh, and they're case sensitive, too, so *THIS* is different from *this* or *ThiS*. It's a good idea to enter a password hint, but don't make that hint too easy to guess. For example, *My first dog's name* is probably preferable to *Plays Seinfeld on TV*. Mac OS X uses the name and password that you enter to create your account, which you use to log in if you set up a multiuser system for several people. (More on this in Book III, Chapter 4.) *Never* write down your passwords, either; such crib sheets work just as well for others as for you.

✦ **I need to fix that.** You can click the Back button any time to return to previous assistant screens. Mac OS X, being the bright child that it is, automatically saves your choices for you, so when you click Continue to return, everything is as you left it.

✦ **Extra stuff.** Whether you decide to accept the news, offers, and related-product information from Apple is your decision. However, it's only right that I point out that you can find this same information on the Apple Web site, so there's no need to engorge your e-mail Inbox unless you so desire. (In other words, I turned this off.)

✦ **Local area network (LAN) connections.** If you're connecting your MacBook to a Transmission Control Protocol/Internet Protocol (TCP/IP) network (or you're using an Internet router that uses Dynamic Host Configuration Protocol [DHCP]), it's a good idea to click Yes when you're asked whether you should use the configuration supplied by the existing server.

DHCP automatically provides the computers on the network with all the settings that they need to connect. If that sounds like ancient Sumerian, find out more in Book VII, Chapter 1.

✦ **Do create your MobileMe account!** Apple's MobileMe service just plain rocks — especially the iDisk storage that you receive. Again, more on this in Book VI, Chapter 4, but take my word for it. Join up, trooper. (The trial subscription is free, and it's easy to upgrade to a full membership if you decide that you like the MobileMe benefits. Check Amazon.com for discount pricing on your MobileMe subscription.)

✦ **Have your Mail settings handy.** If you set up your trial MobileMe account, you can set up your @me.com address without any bother — again, this is A Good Thing. However, if you're setting up an existing account, make sure you have all those silly settings and numbers and names that your ISP supplied you with when you signed up. This stuff includes your e-mail address, mail server variety, user account ID, password, and outgoing mail server.

# Chapter 2: Navigating and Running Programs

## In This Chapter

- ✔ Restarting, sleeping, and shutting down Mac OS X
- ✔ Using windows
- ✔ Using menus
- ✔ Recognizing and selecting icons
- ✔ Using the keyboard
- ✔ Running applications
- ✔ Switching between programs
- ✔ Opening, saving, and quitting within an application

A s the folks in Cupertino will tell you, "It's all about the graphics." They're right, of course — Mac OS X is a highly visual operating system, and using it without a trackpad or mouse is like building Hoover Dam with a pocketknife. (And not a particularly sharp pocketknife, either.) Therefore, most of this chapter requires you to exercise your trackpad finger — I introduce you to little graphical bits such as icons and menus, and you discover how to open windows that can display anything from the contents of a document to the contents of your hard drive.

On the other hand, any true MacBook power user will tell you that the keyboard is still a useful piece of hardware. Because I want you to be a bona fide, well-rounded Mac OS X power user, I also demonstrate those key combinations that can save you time, effort, and possible tennis elbow from all that pointer-wrangling.

Finally, I lead you through the basic training that you need to run your programs: how to start them, how to open and save documents, and how to quit an application as gracefully as Fred Astaire on his best day.

## Restarting, Sleeping, and Shutting Down

First things first. As the guy on the rocket sled probably yelled, "This is neat, but how do you stop it?" Call 'em The Big Three — Sleep, Restart, and Shut Down are the Mac OS X commands that you use when you need to take care of business away from your computer. All three appear on the friendly Apple menu (🍎) at the top-left corner of your Desktop (as shown in friendly Figure 2-1).

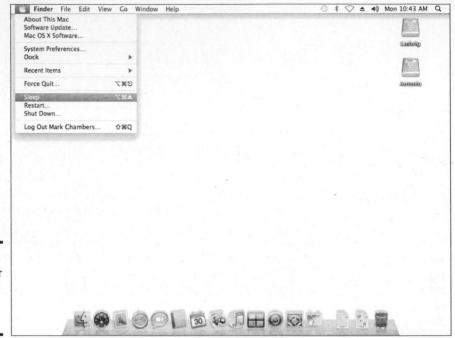

**Figure 2-1:**
Choose your
path from
the Apple
menu.

Each of these options produces a different reaction from your MacBook:

✦ **Sleep:** You don't need a glass of water or a bedtime story when you put
Mac OS X to *Sleep,* which is a power-saving mode that allows you to
quickly return to your work later. (Waking your laptop up from Sleep
mode is much faster than booting or restarting it, and Sleep mode can
conserve battery power on your MacBook.) Depending on the settings
that you choose in System Preferences — which I discuss in Book III,
Chapter 3 — your MacBook can power-down the monitor and spin-down
the hard drives to save wear and tear on your hardware. You can set
Mac OS X to automatically enter Sleep mode after a certain amount of
trackpad and keyboard inactivity. To awaken your slumbering super-
computer, just poke the trackpad or press any key on the keyboard. And
talk about convenience: Savvy MacBook owners like you can put their
laptops to sleep by simply closing the computer, and wake the beast by
opening it back up again.

✦ **Restart:** Use Restart if your MacBook has suddenly decided to work
"outside the box" and begins acting strangely — for instance, if your
Universal Serial Bus (USB) ports suddenly lock up or your FireWire
drive no longer responds. Naturally, you first need to save any work
that's open (unless your computer has locked up altogether). You also
elect to restart Mac OS X when you switch start-up volumes, or switch
a MacBook to a Windows XP or Vista partition using Boot Camp. (Many

applications and Apple software updates require a restart after you install them.)

✦ **Shut Down:** When you're ready to return to the humdrum, real world and you're done with your MacBook for the time being, use the Shut Down option. Well-behaved Mac applications automatically prompt you to save any changes that you've made to open documents before the computer actually turns itself off (or restarts itself). If you've configured your MacBook with multiple accounts — and you use the default login security settings in the Accounts pane in System Preferences — you can shut down Mac OS X from the login screen as well.

Besides the Apple menu command, all MacBooks have a Power key on the keyboard that you can press to display the dialog that you see in Figure 2-2. If you change your mind and decide to tie up loose ends before you leave, click the Cancel button to return to Mac OS X.

**Book II
Chapter 2**

**Navigating and
Running Programs**

**Figure 2-2:**
Will that
be Restart,
Sleep, or
Shut Down?

Are you sure you want to shut down your computer now?

Restart    Sleep    Cancel    **Shut Down**

*TIP*

Your MacBook has a Drive Eject key that you can use to load and eject discs. You can hold down the Control key and press the Drive Eject key to display the same restart/sleep/shutdown options.

---

# Actually, we're not finished just yet . . .

I should probably also mention the other guys: the Log Out command (which you can find under the Apple menu) and the User Switch menu (at the right side of the Finder menu).

✔ Choose Log Out when you're running your MacBook with multiple users and you want to completely pass control over to another person. All your programs will quit, and the other person can take over by logging in with his/her account. Mac OS X then reconfigures with the other user's preferences.

✔ If you've enabled Fast User Switching, another user can log in from the User Switch menu. However, your applications don't quit, you don't have to formally log out, and you can take control back when the other user is finished. (Hence the words *Fast* and *Switching* in the name.) To turn on this feature, log in with an administrator account, display the Accounts pane in System Preferences, click Login Options, and then select the Enable Fast User Switching check box. (More on Fast User Switching appears in Book III, Chapter 4.)

# Doing the Multi-Touch thing

The latest crop of MacBooks have the smartest trackpads on the planet! That's because Apple now includes a feature called *Multi-Touch,* which allows you to control the view of a document by using specific finger motions on the trackpad. At the time of this writing, here's the rundown:

↙ **Two-finger zooming:** Pinching your thumb and first fingertip toward each on the trackpad other zooms in on a document or image. The reverse (moving your fingertips away from each other) zooms out. You can also enable zooming with a modifier key — see the description of the Trackpad pane in Book III, Chapter 3 for more information.

↙ **Two-finger rotating:** Rotate your thumb and first fingertip in a circle on the trackpad to rotate an image or document in the corresponding direction.

↙ **Three-finger paging:** Move your thumb and first two fingertips to the left or right across your trackpad to page through a document or move to the next or previous image in a set.

Unfortunately, Multi-Touch doesn't work with every application, but support for this neat feature is rapidly being added by Apple software developers. (For now, I recommend you try out your fingertips in iPhoto and Pages!)

## Living the trackpad lifestyle

As a MacBook owner, the *trackpad* is your primary navigational tool. You move your finger over the surface of the trackpad, and the pointer follows like an obedient pup. The faster you move your finger, the farther the pointer goes. You click an item by tapping once on the trackpad — it opens, you do your thing, and life is good.

However, you can always customize how your trackpad operates! For example, click the System Preferences icon in the Dock, then click the Trackpad icon. From here you can:

✦ **Enable the Clicking check box.** Now, when you tap the trackpad quickly, your Mac laptop counts that as a click, and two fast taps act as a double-click.

✦ **Enable the Tap Trackpad Using Two Fingers for Secondary Click check box.** Suddenly a single tap with two fingers displays the right-click menu (which I cover in more detail in a paragraph or two).

✦ **Adjust your tracking speed.** Click and drag the Tracking speed slider to speed up or slow down the rate at which your pointer moves.

# A Window Is Much More Than a Frame

"And in the beginning, there was the window." As with older Mac operating systems, most of what you'll do in Mac OS X occurs within these fancy frames. And, as you might imagine, a number of controls are at your disposal, which you can use to control the size, shape, and appearance of these potent portals. In this section, I — well, to be blunt, I do windows. (No squeegee jokes, if you please.)

## Opening and closing windows

Windows are generally opened automatically. Usually, a window gets opened by an application (when you first run it or it needs to display a document) or by Mac OS X itself (when the Finder opens a window to display the contents of your hard drive). The *Finder,* by the way, is the application that Mac OS X runs to display the operating system's menus and windows.

Some programs even let you open new windows on the fly; for example, Figure 2-3 illustrates a window in its purest form: a new Finder window. To display this window on your own MacBook, choose File⇨New Finder Window or press ⌘+N. From here, you can reach any file on your MacBook or even venture to the Internet.

Book II
Chapter 2

Navigating and
Running Programs

Close button

**Figure 2-3:** You're ready to navigate with this Finder window.

The Command key usually has both an Apple ( ) and a rather strange-looking symbol (⌘) on it that I often call the Spirograph.

When you're finished with a document or you no longer need a window open, you can close it to free that space on your Desktop. To close a window in Mac OS X, move your pointer over the Close button; it's the red circular button at the top-left corner of the window (see Figure 2-3). An X appears on the button when you're in the zone. When the X appears, just tap the trackpad.

If you've been living the life of a hermit in a cave for the last decade or so, pressing the button on a mouse or trackpad is called *clicking.* In fact, today's MacBooks don't have any buttons at all! (You tap the trackpad with one finger to click.) If you're using an external pointing device (like an Apple Mighty Mouse, a trackball, or any pointing device with a right button), a right-click usually acts the same as holding down the Control key while you click with an older one-button Apple mouse or trackpad.

**Never use any object other than your finger on the trackpad!** That means no pencils (no, not even the eraser end), pens, or chopsticks; they can damage your trackpad in no time at all.

Most Mac applications don't want you closing a window willy-nilly if you've changed the contents without saving them. For example, try to close a document window in Word or Pages without saving the file first. The program asks you for confirmation before it closes the window containing your Great American Novel. Most programs also have a Close command on their File menu. (Here's another indicator: Most programs display a black dot in the center of the program's Close button to indicate that there are unsaved changes.)

To close all windows that are displayed by a particular program, hold down the Option key while you click the Close button on one of the windows. Whoosh! They're all gone.

## Scrolling windows

Often, more stuff is in a document or more files are on your hard drive than you can see in the space available for a window. Guess that means it's time to delete stuff. No, no, *just joking!* You don't have to take such drastic measures to see more in a window.

Just use the scroll bars that you see in Figure 2-4 to move through the contents of the window. You can click the scroll bar and drag it — for the uninitiated, that means clicking the bar and holding down your finger on the trackpad while you move your finger in the desired direction. Alternatively, you can click in the empty area above or below the bar to scroll pages one at a time. If you've enabled two-finger scrolling in the Trackpad pane within System Preferences, you can scroll by dragging two fingers across the trackpad.

Minimize button   Zoom button

**Figure 2-4:**
You can use the scroll bars to boldly go — well — anywhere in a window.

Scroll bars

Book II
Chapter 2

Navigating and
Running Programs

Depending on the type of application that you're using, you might be able to scroll a window with your arrow keys as well — or perhaps use the Page Up and Page Down keys to move through a window.

## Minimizing and restoring windows

The multitalented Figure 2-4 also displays another control that you can use with a window: the Minimize button. When you *minimize* a window, you eliminate it from your Desktop and store it safely in the *Dock* — that strip of icons that appears along the bottom (or the side) of your Mac OS X Desktop. In fact, a minimized window appears as a miniature icon in the Dock, so you can actually keep an eye on it (so to speak). Figure 2-5 illustrates a minimized window from Safari, which is actually displaying my Web site at www. mlcbooks.com. To minimize a window, move your pointer over the yellow Minimize button at the top-left corner of the window — a minus sign appears on the button — and then click.

You're gonna love this "Easter egg" hidden in Mac OS X — if you hold down the Shift key whilst you minimize, the window shrinks in *cool* slow motion. (Who says operating systems have to be totally serious, anyway?)

**Figure 2-5:**
Note the
miniature
Web page in
the Dock —
minimizing
at work.

When you're ready to display the window again on your Desktop — a process called *restoring* the window — simply click the thumbnail icon representing the window in the Dock, and Mac OS X automagically returns it to its former size and location.

By the way, some — note that I said *some* — applications continue to run when minimized, whereas others simply stop or pause until you return them to the Desktop. Such is the crazy world we live in.

## Zooming windows

Zooming windows has a kind of Flash Gordon sound to it, don't you think? It's nothing quite that exciting — no red tights or laser guns — still, when you're trying to view a larger portion of a document, *zooming* is a good thing because it expands the window to the maximum practical size for the application that you're using (and the content being displayed). In some cases, zooming a window fills the entire screen; in others, the extra space would be wasted, so the application zooms the window to the maximum size that shows as much content as possible (without any unnecessary white space). In fact, the Zoom button can even be disabled by an application that doesn't want you to muck about with the window; for example, I own some games that don't allow zooming.

To zoom a window, move your pointer over the green Zoom button at the top-left corner of the window. Again, Figure 2-4 (a couple of sections back) struts its stuff and illustrates the position. (Man, that is one versatile figure.) A plus sign appears on the Zoom button. Click to expand your horizons.

After you've finished with a zoomed window, you can return it to its previous dimensions by clicking the Zoom button again.

## Toggling toolbars

If you're wondering what that little lozenge-shaped button is at the right corner of many Mac OS X application windows, I won't leave you in suspense: This button toggles the display of the window's toolbar on and off. A *toolbar* is a strip of icons that appears across the top of a window that you can click to perform common commands, such as changing the display format or printing the current document. (The toolbar in Figure 2-4, for example, features icons to move Back and Forward, among others.) You'll encounter more toolbar technology throughout the book.

## Moving windows

In contrast to the rather permanent windows in your home, you can pick a window and cart it to another portion of the Desktop. Typically, you do this when you're using more than one application at a time and you need to see the contents of multiple windows. To grab a window and make off with it, click the window's *title bar* — the strip at the top of the window that usually bears a document or application name — and drag your finger (and the window) to the new location. (Don't click the icon in the title bar, however — you want to click the title bar itself.) Then release your finger to plant the window firmly in the new location.

By the way, some applications allow you to arrange multiple windows in a graceful swoop with a single click of a menu. Click the Window menu and choose Arrange All to perform this magic.

I talk about Exposé and Spaces later, in the section "Switching 'Twixt Programs with Aplomb." Exposé helps you organize a large number of open windows on your Desktop. You can use it to display all open application windows so that you can pick the one you want . . . or even display all the windows opened by a specific application. Spaces allows you to create entire custom virtual desktops. (Truly *cool*.) Each of your Spaces desktops can contain a different set of application windows that you use for different tasks!

## Resizing windows

Next, consider how to change the width or height of your window. To change the dimensions of a window to your exact specifications, move your pointer over the lower-right corner of the window (which is usually marked with a number of slashed lines to indicate its status as a control), click, and drag until the window is the size that you prefer.

## Switching windows

Before I move on to other graphical wonders of Mac OS X, it's important that you master how to switch between windows on your Desktop. First, remember this old Norwegian saying (or is it one of Mark's Maxims?):

**Only *one* can be active at one time.**

What our Oslo friends are communicating is that only one window can be active at any time. The active window appears on top of other windows, and it's the one that you can edit by typing or by moving your pointer. (It also sports Close, Minimize, and Zoom buttons in color.) Other windows that

Book II
Chapter 2

Navigating and
Running Programs

you have opened might be minimized, as I describe earlier, in the section "Minimizing and restoring windows," or they can be inactive (mere ghosts of themselves) and remain on your Desktop. Mac OS X dims the controls for inactive windows so that you can tell they're hanging around . . . but you can't use them at the moment. Figure 2-6 illustrates a number of open windows, with the iTunes window active.

I know you're going to get tired of hearing me say this, but here I go again: Certain applications continue to run while their windows are inactive, such as File Transfer Protocol (FTP) clients and others. Most programs, however, stop or pause until you make their window active.

And how do you switch to — *activate* — a different window in Mac OS X? Again, Exposé allows you to activate another window, but if the window is currently visible, you can simply click any part of that window. I generally click the window's title bar if it's visible, but any part of the inactive window will do. (You can also right-click the application's icon in the Dock and choose the desired window from the menu.) The window that you click leaps like a proud stallion to the fore, and the previously active window now skulks in the background.

You can still use a window's Close, Minimize, and Zoom buttons even when the window is inactive.

**Figure 2-6:** Many are open, but only one is active.

# Menu Mysteries Explained

Next, I move on to menu control in Mac OS X. *Menus* are handy drop-down controls that allow you to select commands that are grouped together logically. For example, an application's File menu usually allows you to create or open a document, save a document to disk, or print a document. To pull down a menu, click the desired menu group name on the bar at the top of the screen and then click the desired menu option from the extended menu.

Figure 2-7 illustrates the Safari menu: Note the submenus designated by right-arrow icons. When you move your pointer over a submenu command, you get another set of even more specific menu commands — in this case, the Services submenu command displays commands, such as Mail and Grab.

Some applications allow you to create your own custom menus; naturally, configuring a new menu system takes some time to figure out, but imagine the productivity gains that you'll enjoy! For example, my menus in Microsoft Word 2008 for Mac feature only the commands that I use often — they're sleeker and easier to navigate. (However, you have to stop short of claiming that you wrote the application. And yes, I already checked with Microsoft, which got downright snippy about it.)

**Figure 2-7:**
Drilling
deeper into
Safari's
Services
menu.

Mac OS X also provides another type of menu: contextual. A *contextual menu* appears when you hold down the Control key and click certain items on the screen, revealing commands that relate specifically to that item. (Unfortunately, the items that sport contextual menus vary from application to application, so it's best to check the documentation for a program before you spend countless hours Control-clicking everything on-screen.) The same items in the Control-click menu appear when you select an item and then click the Action pop-up menu, which looks like a mechanical gear.

As I mention earlier, Apple's current crop of desktop and laptop pointing devices all have methods (such as a *right-click*) of activating a contextual menu. Many manufacturers sell mice, trackballs, and other pointing things that include a secondary button. Generally, if you have a pointing device with multiple buttons, the device displays contextual menus when you click the secondary button. Then again, you might launch Aunt Harriet into a geo-synchronous orbit, so double-check the manual for your pointing thing on the default button assignment (and how to change it, if necessary).

You'll note that many commands in menus have keyboard shortcuts. Because I hold forth on this subject in the upcoming section, "Keyboard Shortcuts for the True Power User," I hold off describing those shortcuts here.

# Icons 'R Us

Icons are more than little pictures. They're . . . well . . . actually, I guess they're little pictures. However, these graphical WUDs (that's short for *Wonderful User Devices*) are really representations of the components of your Mac OS X system, and therefore they deserve a section of their own.

For complete details on what any icon is, what it represents, and what it does, click the icon once to highlight it and then press ⌘+I. This displays the Info dialog that you see in Figure 2-8, which tells you what kind of icon it is, where the item it represents is actually located, and how big it is. You also see a version number for applications — a handy way of quickly checking the version of a program you're running — and when the file was created and last modified. The Info dialog also offers other settings and options that you can display by clicking in the General section, and I cover them in other parts of the book.

## Hardware

Mac OS X uses icons to represent the various hardware devices of your MacBook, including your

✦ Hard drive or solid-state drive

✦ DVD drive (if a disc is loaded)

✦ iPod

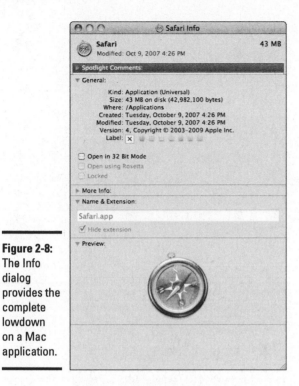

**Figure 2-8:**
The Info dialog provides the complete lowdown on a Mac application.

You get the idea. Just double-click a hardware icon to display the folders and files that it contains, as you do with your hard drive and a disc loaded in your DVD drive.

Generally, you'll encounter hardware icons only on your Desktop or in Finder windows, or within a device or source list in applications such as iTunes and iPhoto. Figure 2-9 illustrates some of the hardware icons that live in my system.

**Figure 2-9:**
A wealth of different hardware icons.

## Programs and applications

These are the fancy icons, folks. Most applications have their own custom icons, and double-clicking one typically whisks you on your way. Mac OS X also includes a generic icon or two for applications that don't include their own custom icon. Figure 2-10 illustrates a number of my favorite program icons from all sorts of Mac OS X applications.

Running a program in Mac OS X can be as simple as double-clicking the application icon — more on this later, in the section "Houston, We're Go to Launch Programs."

**Figure 2-10:**
Most Snow Leopard applications are represented by custom icons.

## Files

Your hard drive will contain many thousands of individual files, and the Big X tries to make it as easy as possible to identify visually which application owns which file. Therefore, most applications use a special icon to indicate their data files. For example, Figure 2-11 illustrates several documents and data files created by a range of applications: Microsoft Word, Pages, QuickTime, Safari, and Adobe Acrobat. Some cheeky applications even use more than one icon to differentiate among different file types, such as documents and templates in Microsoft Word.

A number of generic file icons indicate text files, including RTF (short for rich text format) documents and PDF (Portable Document Format) documents, which use the Adobe Acrobat format.

**Figure 2-11:**
File icons generally give you a visual clue about their origin.

You can open most documents and data files by double-clicking them, which automatically launches the proper application and loads the document.

I also recommend Quick Look (the toolbar button is visible in the middle of the toolbar in Figure 2-11) for a lightning-fast peek at the contents of a file. Click the file once to select it; then click the Quick Look button to view the document — all without opening any applications!

## Folders

Folders have a 3-D look in Mac OS X — and, as you can see in Figure 2-12, some applications even customize their folder icon!

**Figure 2-12:**
A selection of different generic and custom folder icons.

Major system folders — including Applications, Library, System, Users, Downloads, and Utilities — sport distinctive folder icons in Snow Leopard that help identify their contents.

To open a folder within Mac OS X, just double-click it. (Alternatively, you can click it once to select it and then press ⌘+O or ⌘+↓.) Discover more about how to control the look of folder contents in Book III, Chapter 1.

## Aliases

An *alias* is a strange beast. Although it might look like a standard icon, upon closer examination, you'll notice that an alias icon sports a tiny curved arrow at the base, and the tag `alias` often appears at the end of the icon name. Figure 2-13 has roped in a variety of aliases for your enjoyment, along with one or two actual icons for comparison.

**Figure 2-13:** An alias is a pointer to another application, file, or folder.

Essentially, an alias is a link to something else on your system. For example, a Photoshop alias can run Photoshop just as the actual program icon can, but it takes up only a scant few bytes on your hard drive. (If you're a Switcher who's just crossed over from the Windows Wilderness, think *shortcut* — Windows shortcuts work in a similar manner.) The alias file is just big enough to hold the location of the actual file or folder, allowing it to yell at Mac OS X: "Hey, the Human actually wants you to run *this* or open *that thing* over there!"

Aliases come in handy for a number of reasons:

✦ **They allow you to launch applications and open files and folders from anywhere in your system.** For example, you might want an alias icon in your MP3 folder that runs the DVD-burning application Toast Titanium. With an alias icon, you can launch the application and burn a data DVD without laboriously navigating to the Toast Titanium folder, which could be nested in goodness-knows-how-many layers of subfolders.

✦ **They can be easily deleted when no longer needed without wreaking havoc on the original application, file, or folder.** If you decide that you'd rather use iTunes to burn audio CDs, you can simply delete the Toast Titanium alias without trashing the application itself.

✦ **Their tiny size allows you to add multiple aliases (and mucho convenience) for a single application without gulping down hard drive space.**

You might be wondering, "Why use aliases when I can just copy the actual application, file, or folder to the desired spot?" Well, indeed you can do that. However, the application might not work in its new location because you didn't copy any of the supporting files that most applications need to run. (An alias actually runs the original application or opens the original file or folder, so things should work just as if you'd double-clicked the original icon.) Additionally, remember that copying applications willy-nilly throughout your hard drive eats up territory like a horde of angry Vikings.

If you dislike the `alias` hanging off the end of the icon name, feel free to rename it (as I show you in Chapter 3 of this minibook). The alias continues to function nicely no matter what moniker you give it. (If you create an alias by holding down ⌘+Option whilst dragging the original icon to a new location, the alias name won't include the `alias` appendage.)

If the original file no longer exists, an alias naturally no longer works, either. However, Mac OS X is sharp enough to automatically "fix" an alias if you rename or move the original file, pointing it to the new location (as long as it remains on the same volume). *Slick!*

**Book II
Chapter 2**

**Navigating and
Running Programs**

# Selecting Icons for Fun and Profit

You'll often find yourself performing different actions on one icon — or a number of icons at one time. For example, you can copy or move files from one location on your hard drive to another, or delete a group of files that you no longer need. (The idea of drag-and-drop file management using icons originated on the Macintosh, and in Chapter 3 of this minibook, I describe these operations in detail.) In this section, I focus on the basics of selecting one or more icons to specify the files and folders you want to use for whatever you're going to do next.

## Selecting a single icon

First, here are the various ways that you can select a single icon for an impending action:

✦ **Place your pointer over the file and click once.** Mac OS X darkens the icon to indicate that it's selected — a mysterious process called *highlighting*.

✦ **Type the first few letter of the icon's name.** After you type a letter, Mac OS X highlights the first icon that matches that character.

✦ **If an icon in a window is already highlighted, you can move the highlight to the next icon across by pressing the right-arrow key.** Likewise, the other three directional arrow keys move the highlight in the other directions. To move through the icons alphabetically, press Tab to go forward and Shift+Tab to go backward.

## Selecting multiple icons

To select a gaggle of icons for an action, use one of these methods:

✦ If the icons are next to each other, click and drag within the window (and not directly on a specific item) to highlight them all. While you drag, Mac OS X displays a selection box, and any icons you touch with that box are highlighted when you lift your finger (as shown in Figure 2-14). Think "lasso" and you'll get the picture.

**Figure 2-14:** Dragging a selection box in Mac OS X.

✦ You can also select multiple adjacent icons by clicking the first item to highlight it and then holding down the Shift key while clicking the last icon in the series that you want to select.

If the icons are *not* next to each other, you can hold down the ⌘ key while you click each item that you want to select.

Just selecting an icon doesn't launch or do anything . . . you're just marking your territory.

# Keyboard Shortcuts for the True Power User

Virtually all Mac OS X applications have their own *keyboard shortcuts* — a ten-cent term for a key combination that performs the same operation as a menu command or a toolbar button. Although the trackpad might seem the easier path when controlling your MacBook, it's not always the fastest. Those hardy souls who venture to learn common keyboard shortcuts can zip through a spreadsheet or warp through a complex outline at speeds that no mere trackpad-wrangler could ever hope to attain.

With that in mind — and with the goal of "pumping you up" into a power user — I hereby present the most common keyboard shortcuts for the Big X in Table 2-1. I've also sprinkled other keyboard shortcuts liberally through the book when I discuss other applications, but these combinations are the classics that appear virtually everywhere.

**Book II
Chapter 2**

**Navigating and
Running Programs**

| Table 2-1 | Common Mac OS X Keyboard Shortcuts | |
|---|---|---|
| *Combination Key* | *Location* | *Action* |
| ⌘+A | Edit menu | Selects all (works in the Finder, too) |
| ⌘+C | Edit menu | Copies the highlighted item to the Clipboard |
| ⌘+H | Application menu | Hides the application |
| ⌘+M | Window menu | Minimizes the active window to the Dock (works in the Finder, too) |
| ⌘+O | File menu | Opens an existing document, file, or folder (works in the Finder, too) |
| ⌘+P | File menu | Prints the current document |
| ⌘+Q | Application menu | Exits the application |
| ⌘+V | Edit menu | Pastes the contents of the Clipboard at the current cursor position |
| ⌘+X | Edit menu | Cuts the highlighted item to the Clipboard |
| ⌘+Z | Edit menu | Reverses the effect of the last action you took |
| ⌘+? | Help menu | Displays the Help system (works in the Finder, too) |
| ⌘+Tab | Finder | Switches between open applications |
| ⌘+Option+M | Finder | Minimizes all Finder windows to the Dock |
| ⌘+Option+W | Finder | Closes all Finder windows |

By the way, I should mention that many keyboard combinations use three different keys instead of just two (and a few even use four). When these shortcuts appear in a menu, they look something akin to Egyptian hiero-glyphics, but you need only hold down the first two keys simultaneously and press the third key. Common "strange" key symbols that you'll see in both the Finder and most applications are shown in Table 2-2.

| Table 2-2 | Arcane Key Symbols |
| --- | --- |
| *Action* | *Symbol* |
| Control | C |
| Command | ⌘ |
| Del | d |
| Option | O |
| Shift | S |

# Houston, We're Go to Launch Programs

The next stop on your introductory tour of Mac OS X is the launch pad for your applications. Although the Finder is useful, you'll likely want to actually do something with your Mac as well.

## Running applications from your hard drive

You can launch an application from your hard drive by

- ✦ Navigating to the corresponding application folder — by either clicking or double-clicking drive and folder icons — and double-clicking (tapping twice) on the application icon.

- ✦ Double-clicking a document or data file that's owned by the application. For example, double-clicking an MP3 audio file runs iTunes.

- ✦ Double-clicking an alias that you've created for the application. (Get the skinny on aliases in the earlier section, "Aliases." I'll wait.)

- ✦ Double-clicking an Automator workflow or compiled AppleScript. (More on Automator and AppleScript in Book IX, Chapter 2.)

- ✦ Clicking the application's icon in the Dock. (More on adding items to the Dock in Book III, Chapter 2.)

✦ Selecting the application icon and pressing the ⌘+O keyboard shortcut.

✦ Clicking the Menu button on an Apple Remote to display the Front Row menu. From here, you can choose to watch a DVD movie (using Apple's DVD Player), peruse your collection of digital images (using iPhoto), watch a video you've created (using iMovie), or listen to music (using iTunes). The applications are launched automatically when you select the media you want to play. (You can find more on Front Row in Chapter 5 of this minibook.)

✦ Adding the application to your Login Items list. (I cover the Login Items list in more detail in Book III, Chapter 3.)

## Running applications from a CD-ROM or DVD-ROM

After you load a CD-ROM or DVD-ROM, you can display its contents by double-clicking the disc icon that appears on your Desktop. A Finder window opens and shows the files that reside on the disc. (See Figure 2-15.)

**Book II
Chapter 2**

Navigating and
Running Programs

**Figure 2-15:**
The Finder window shows the contents of a disc when you double-click the icon.

After you locate the application you want to run on the disc, you can launch it by double-clicking it or selecting it and pressing ⌘+O.

## Switching 'Twixt Programs with Aplomb

You might think that juggling multiple applications will lead to confusion, fatigue, and dry mouth, but luckily Mac OS X makes it easy to jump between programs that are running on your MacBook. Use any of these methods to jump from open application to application:

✦ **Click anywhere in the desired window to make it the active window.**

✦ **Click the application icon in the Dock**. All applications that are running have an icon in the Dock, and the icon has a shiny dot beneath it to indicate that the application is open.

✦ **Press ⌘+Tab.** If you have a dozen windows open, this can get a bit tedious, which leads us to one of Snow Leopard's sassiest features, brazenly named Exposé and shown in Figure 2-16. (Am I stretching things a bit?)

✦ **Press F9 (or F3, depending on your keyboard) to show all open application windows using Exposé; then click the one you want.** Figure 2-16 illustrates the tiled window display on my Mac after I press F3. The cursor changes into the traditional (and highly elegant) gloved hand. Move the cursor on top of the window you want to activate — the window turns blue when it's selected — and click once to switch to that window. You can specify which keys you want to use to control Exposé within System Preferences.

✦ **Press F10 (or Control+F3, depending on your keyboard) to show all open windows from the application that you're currently using; then click the one that you want to activate.** This Exposé function is great for choosing from all the images that you've opened in Photoshop or all the Safari Web pages littering your Desktop!

Along with the window switch, an astute observer will notice that the application menu bar also changes to match the now-active application.

Besides the F9/F3 and F10/Control+F3 hot keys that I just discussed, Exposé provides one more nifty function: Press F11 (or ⌘+F3), and all your open windows scurry to the side of the screen. (Much like a herd of zebras if you dropped a lioness in the middle.) Now you can work with drives, files, and aliases on your Desktop — and when you're ready to confront those dozen application windows again, just press the keyboard shortcut a second time.

Ah, but what if you want to switch to an entirely different set of applications? For example, let's suppose that you're slaving away at your pixel-pushing job — designing a magazine cover with Pages. Your page design desktop also includes Photoshop and Aperture, which you switch between often using one of the techniques I just described. Suddenly, however, you realize you need to schedule a meeting with others in your office using iCal, and you want to check your e-mail in Apple Mail. What to do?

**Figure 2-16:**
Exotic
Exposé
displays
thumbnails
on all open
windows in
your current
desktop.

Well, you could certainly launch those two applications on top of your
graphics applications, and then minimize or close them . . . but with
Snow Leopard's *Spaces* feature, you can press the Control+Left Arrow or
Control+Right Arrow sequences to switch to a completely different "communications" desktop, with iCal and Apple Mail windows already open and
in your favorite positions! (Figure 2-17 illustrates the Spaces screen, showing
two available desktops.)

After you're done setting up your meeting and answering any important e-mail,
simply press Control+Left Arrow or Control+Right Arrow again to switch back to
your "graphics" desktop, where all your work is exactly as you left it!

Now imagine that you've also created a custom "music" desktop for
GarageBand and iTunes . . . or perhaps you paired iWeb, MobileMe, and
iPhoto together as a "Webmaster" desktop. See why everyone's so excited?
(Let's see Windows Vista do *that* out of the box.)

In contrast to Exposé, Spaces has to be enabled and configured before you
can use it. You can create new desktops, customize your desktops, and
even choose a different set of key sequences to activate Spaces from within
System Preferences. For the complete story on configuring Spaces, see Book
III, Chapter 3.

**Figure 2-17:**
With
Spaces,
I can
instantly
switch
between
multiple
desktops!

# Opening and Saving Your Stuff in an Application

Almost all Mac OS X applications open and save documents in the same way,
whether you're creating a presentation with Keynote or expressing your cinematic side with iMovie. Therefore, I take a moment to outline the common
procedures for opening and saving documents. Believe me, you'll perform
these two rituals dozens of times a week, so no nodding off.

## Opening a document

First, the simple way to load a document: Double-click that document in a
Finder window, and . . . well, that's it. (This is my preferred method because
I'm an ALT — short for *Admitted Lazy Techno-wizard* — who would rather
use complex hand movements to pour myself another Diet Coke.)

To open a document the hard way — from inside an application — here's
the plan:

*1.* **Choose File⇨Open or press that handy ⌘+O key combination.**

Your Mac OS X program is likely to display the attractive Open dialog
that you see in Figure 2-18.

**Figure 2-18:**
The soon-
to-be-quite-
familiar
Open dialog.

2. **Navigate to the location of the document that you want to open.**

   The pop-up menu allows you to jump directly to common locations —
   such as the Desktop, your Home folder, and your iDisk — as well as
   places that you've recently accessed (Recent Places).

   If the target folder isn't in your pop-up menu, move the slider at the
   bottom of the dialog to the far left to display your hard drives, DVD
   drives, and network locations.

3. **Click the habitat where the file will be found.**

   You'll note that the right column(s) changes to show you the contents
   of the item that you just clicked. In this way, you can cruise through
   successive folders to find that elusive document. (This time-consuming
   process is somewhat derisively called *drilling* — hence, the importance
   of using Recent Items, or dragging files, locations, and applications into
   the sidebar at the left of the Finder.)

4. **When you sight the document that you want to load, either double-
   click it or click once to highlight the filename and then click Open.**

"Hey, the Open dialog can be resized!" That's right, good buddy — you can
expand the Open dialog to show more columns and find things more easily.
Click and drag the bottom-right corner of the Open dialog to resize it. (You
can also switch from column view to list view or icon view, just as you can in
a Finder window, using the buttons to the left of the pop-up location menu.)

## Saving a document

To save a document, follow these steps:

**1. Choose File⇨Save.**

If you've previously saved this document, your application should immediately overwrite the existing document with the new copy, and you get to return to work . . . end of story. If you *haven't* previously saved this document, the program displays a Save dialog that's usually very similar to the Open dialog; it generally has a few more options, however, so stay frosty.

**2. Navigate to the location where you'd like to save the document and then type a filename.**

Often, you can use a default name that's already provided by the thoughtful folks who developed the software. Note that you might be given the chance to save the document in several different formats. For example, a word processing application might allow you to save a document in RTF, HyperText Markup Language (HTML), and even bargain-basement text format.

**3. Click Save (or OK, depending on the application).**

If an application offers a Save As menu option in the File menu, you can in effect copy the document by saving a new version of the document under another name. Save As comes in particularly handy when you want to retain the original version of a document.

# Quitting Programs

If I had a twisted and warped sense of humor, I'd simply tell you to quit applications by pulling your MacBook's power cord from the wall socket. (Luckily, I don't. Besides, it wouldn't work anyway, because your laptop's battery would automatically kick in!) There are, however, more sane ways to exit a program — use one of these methods instead:

✦ Press the ⌘+Q keyboard shortcut.

✦ Choose the Application's named menu and then click Quit.

✦ Right-click the application icon in the Dock and click Quit on the pop-up menu that appears.

You can also click the Close button on the application window. Note, however, that this doesn't always completely close down the application. For example, Safari stays running even if you close the browser window. In general, if the application works within a single window (such as System Preferences), closing the window also quits the application.

# Chapter 3: Basic OS X Housekeeping

## In This Chapter

- ✓ Copying, moving, and duplicating files
- ✓ Deleting and recovering files
- ✓ Renaming files
- ✓ Finding specific files
- ✓ Locking files
- ✓ Using Apple menu commands
- ✓ Using Services, the Go menu, and menu icons
- ✓ Listening to audio discs and recording data discs
- ✓ Printing within Mac OS X applications

A fter you master basic Mac spell-casting — things like selecting items, using menus, opening and saving documents, working with windows, and launching an application or two — it's time to delve deeper into Mac OS X. (Can you tell I'm a Dungeons & Dragons old-timer?)

In this chapter, I discuss file management, showing you the hidden power behind the friendly Apple menu. I also discuss some of the more advanced menu commands, how to print within most applications, and how to listen to an audio CD on your MacBook. (It makes a doggone good stereo.) Finally, I introduce you to the built-in CD/DVD recording features within the Big X and adding a standard USB printer to your system.

## The Finder: It's the Wind beneath Your Wings

So what exactly is the Finder, anyway? It's a rather nebulous term, but in essence, the *Finder* gives Mac OS X the basic functions that you use for the procedures I outline in this chapter. This multitasking uber OS has been around in one guise or another since the days of System 6 — the creaking old days when a Mac was an all-in-one, toteable computer with a built-in screen. Come to think of it, some things never change.

The Finder is always running, so it's always available — and you can always switch to it, even when several other applications are open and chugging away. Figure 3-1 illustrates the Dock with the rather perspective-crazy Finder icon at the far-left side.

Action button

**Figure 3-1:**
The Finder
is always
there,
supporting
you with
a unique
smile.

Finder icon

Is that icon supposed to be one face or two faces? I'm still confused, and I've been using the Mac now since 1989.

Don't forget that Mac OS X gives you a second method of doing everything I cover in this chapter: You can use Terminal to uncover the UNIX core of Mac OS X, employing your blazing typing speed to take care of things from the command line. Of course, that's not the focus of this book, but for those who want to boldly go where no Mac operating system has ever gone before, you'll find more in Book IX, Chapter 1. Despite what you might have been led to believe, power and amazing speed are to be found in character-based computing.

# Copying and Moving Files and Folders

Here's where drag-and-drop makes things about as easy as computing can get:

+ **To copy a file or folder from one window to another location on the same drive:** Hold down the Option key and click and drag the icon from its current home to the new location. (*Note:* You can drop files and folders on top of other folders, which puts the copy inside that folder.) If you're copying multiple items, select them first (read how in Book II, Chapter 2) and then drag and drop the entire crew.

"Is the Desktop a valid target location for a file or folder?" You're darn tootin'! I recommend, though, that you avoid cluttering up your Desktop with more than a handful of files. Instead, create a folder or two on your Desktop and then store those items within those folders. If you work with the contents of a specific folder often, drag it into the Places heading in the Sidebar (the column at the left side of any Finder window), and you can open that folder from the Finder with a single click — no matter where you are! (Alternatively, drag the folder to the Dock and drop it there, and you can open it with a single click from anywhere.)

+ **To copy items from one window to a location on another drive:** Click and drag the icon from the window to a window displaying the contents of the target drive. Or, in the spirit of drag-and-drop, you can simply drag the items to the drive icon, which places them in the root folder of that drive.

+ **To move items from one window to a location on another drive:** Hold down the ⌘ key while you drag the items to the target drive icon (placing them in the root folder of that drive) or to a window displaying the contents of the target drive.

+ **To move items from one window to another location on the same drive:** Simply drag the icon to the new location, whether it be a window or a folder.

Mac OS X provides you with a number of visual cues to let you know what's being copied or moved. For example, dragging one or more items displays a ghost image of the items, and when you've positioned the pointer over the target, Mac OS X highlights that location to let you know that you're in the zone. If you're moving or copying items into another Finder window, the window border is highlighted to let you know that Mac OS X understands the game plan.

In case you move the wrong thing or you port it to the wrong location, press ⌘+Z to undo the previous action.

If the item that you're dragging already exists in the target location, you get a confirmation dialog like the one you see in Figure 3-2. You can choose to replace the file, leave the existing file alone, or stop the entire shooting match.

**Figure 3-2:**
To replace
or not to
replace —
the choice
is yours.

## Cloning Your Items — It's Happening Now!

No need for sci-fi equipment or billions in cash — you can create an exact duplicate of any item within the same folder. (This is often handy when you need a simple backup of the same file in the same folder or when you plan to edit a document but you want to keep the original intact.)

Click the item to select it and then choose File⇨Duplicate (or use the keyboard shortcut and press ⌘+D). To distinguish the duplicate from the original, Mac OS X adds the word *copy* to the end of the duplicate's icon name; additional copies have a number added to the name as well.

Alternatively, drag-and-drop aficionados can hold down the Option key and drag the original item to another spot in the same window. When you release the button, the duplicate appears. You can create a clone in another location (such as another window or folder) by holding down the Option key while dragging the original item to its new location.

Heck, if you prefer the Control key, you can hold it down while clicking the item and then choose Duplicate from the contextual menu that appears. Decisions, decisions. . . .

Oh, and don't forget that Action button (it looks like a little gear with a downward-pointing arrow) on the Finder toolbar (refer to Figure 3-1). You can also click the Action button and choose Duplicate from the pop-up menu.

When you duplicate a folder, Mac OS X automatically duplicates all the contents of the folder as well. Remember that this could take some time if the folder contains a large number of small files (or a small number of large files). Groucho would've loved computers!

# Deleting That Which Should Not Be

Even Leonardo da Vinci made the occasional design mistake — his trash can was likely full of bunched-up pieces of parchment. Luckily, no trees will be wasted when you decide to toss your unneeded files and folders; this section shows you how to delete items from your system.

By the way, as you'll soon witness for yourself, moving items to the Trash doesn't necessarily mean that they're immediately history.

## Dragging unruly files against their will

In Mac OS X, the familiar Macintosh Trash can has been moved to the right edge of the Dock — in fact, it's now a spiffy-looking wire can instead of the old clunker that the Mac faithful remember. You can click and drag the items that you've selected to the Trash and drop them on top of the wire can icon to delete them. When the Trash contains at least one item, the wire can icon changes to appear as if it were full of trash.

You can also add a Delete icon to your Finder toolbar. For all the details, see Book III, Chapter 1.

## Deleting with the menus and the keyboard

It isn't absolutely necessary to drag a file to the Trash to delete it. Your other options for scrapping selected files include

✦ Choosing File from the Finder menu and choosing the Move to Trash menu item

✦ Pressing the ⌘+Delete keyboard shortcut

✦ Clicking the Action button on the Finder toolbar and selecting Move to Trash from the pop-up menu

✦ Right-clicking the item to display the contextual menu and then choosing Move to Trash from that menu

# Emptying That Wastepaper Basket

As I mention earlier, moving items to the Trash doesn't actually delete them immediately from your system. Believe me, this fail-safe measure comes in handy when you've been banging away at the keyboard for several hours and you stop paying close attention to what you're doing. (I usually also blame lack of Diet Coke.) More on how to rescue files from the Trash in the next section.

As you can with any folder, you can check the contents of the Trash by clicking its icon in the Dock.

After you double-check the Trash contents and you're indeed absolutely sure that you want to delete its contents, use one of the following methods to nuke the digital Bit Bucket:

✦ Choose the Empty Trash menu item from the Finder menu.

✦ Choose Secure Empty Trash from the Finder menu.

Believe it or not, if you use the standard Empty Trash command, you *still* haven't completely zapped that refuse! Some third-party hard drive repair and recovery programs will allow an uncool person to restore items from the Trash. Use the Secure Empty Trash method for those sensitive files and folders that you want to immediately and irrevocably delete — the data is overwritten with random characters, making it impossible to recover. (A great idea for that Mac you want to sell on eBay, no? In fact, if you like, you can reinstall Mac OS X before you ship the Mac, leaving the Setup Assistant ready-to-run for the new owner.)

✦ Press the ⌘+Shift+Delete keyboard shortcut.

✦ Click the Trash icon in the Dock and hold your finger down on the trackpad until the menu appears, then choose Empty Trash.

✦ Right-click the Trash icon in the Dock and then choose Empty Trash from the contextual menu that appears.

Depending on the method you select and the settings you choose in System Preferences (which I cover in Book III, Chapter 3), Mac OS X might present you with a confirmation dialog to make sure that you actually want the Trash emptied.

## WAIT! I Need That After All!

In the adrenaline-inducing event that you need to rescue something that shouldn't have ended up in the scrap pile, first click the Trash icon in the Dock to display the contents of the Trash. Then rescue the items that you want to save by dragging them to the Desktop or a folder on your hard drive. (This is roughly analogous to rescuing your old baseball glove from the family garage sale.)

Feel free to gloat. If someone else is nearby, ask her to pat you on the back and call you a lifesaver.

# Renaming Your Items

You wouldn't get far in today's spacious virtual world without being able to change a moniker for a file or folder. To rename an item in Mac OS X, use one of these two methods:

✦ **With the trackpad:** Click an icon's name once (or just press Return). Mac OS X highlights the text in an edit box. Type the new name and then press Return.

You want to wait a few seconds between clicks, as opposed to doing a rapid-fire double-click.

✦ **From the Info dialog:** Select the item and press ⌘+I to display the Info dialog; then click the triangle next to Name & Extension. Click in the name field, drag to highlight the text that you want to change, and type the replacement text.

Naturally, the first method is the easiest, and it's the one that I use most often.

**Book II
Chapter 3**

**Basic OS X
Housekeeping**

# Adding a Dash of Color

Snow Leopard also provides the ability to *color-code* files and folders to help you organize and recognize your data in a hurry. For example, why not assign the green label color to the files and folders that make up your current project? Or, if you need to mark a file for immediate attention, assign it the red label color.

To assign a label color to selected files and folders, you have three options:

✦ Click the Action button on the Finder toolbar and then click the desired color.

✦ Right-click the selection and then choose the color from the pop-up menu.

✦ Click File and choose that perfect shade from the menu.

# Displaying the Facts on Files and Folders

The Finder's Info dialog is the place to view the specifics on any highlighted item (including drives and aliases). Select an item and press ⌘+I, click the Action toolbar button and then select Get Info from the menu, right-click and choose Get Info, or choose the Finder's File menu and then choose Get Info (see the results in Figure 3-3). If you select more than one item (up to ten items), Snow Leopard opens a separate Info dialog for each item.

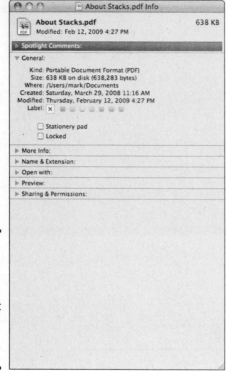

**Figure 3-3:**
The General information panel appears first when you display the Info dialog.

Mac OS X displays the General information panel when you first open the Info dialog, but other panels are usually available (depending on the type of selected items). To display the other panels, click the panel that you want to see.

For most types of files and folders, the Info dialog can tell you

+ **Kind:** What type of item it is — for example, whether it's a file, folder, drive, or alias

+ **Open with:** What program launches automatically when you open the selected item

+ **Size:** The total size of the item (or items, if there are more than ten) that you select

+ **Where:** The actual path on your hard drive where the item is located

✦ **Dates:** The date when the item was created and was last modified

✦ **Version:** The application version number

✦ **Sharing & Permissions:** The privileges that control who can do what to the file (more on this later, in Book II, Chapter 6) and whether a file is locked in read-only mode

Some of this information you can change, and some can only be displayed. To banish the Info dialog from your Desktop, click the dialog's Close button.

You can hide or display various parts of the Info dialog by clicking the triangles next to each section heading.

For the rest of this section, I describe a number of tasks that you can accomplish from the Info dialog.

If you use a specific document over and over as a basis for different revisions, you can enable the Stationery Pad check box on the General information panel to use the file as stationery. Opening a stationery file automatically creates a new, untitled version of the file in the linked application; this can save you steps compared with duplicating the file or using the Save As procedure that I show you in Book II, Chapter 2.

## Adding Spotlight comments

Mac OS X provides you with a Spotlight Comments field, where you can add more text about the file (and can be matched with Spotlight). I use this feature to record the version number of manuscript chapters and programs that I create during the course of writing books.

To add a comment, follow these steps:

*1.* **Display the Info dialog for the item by pressing ⌘+I or choosing File⇨ Get Info.**

*2.* **Click in the Spotlight Comments box and type the comment text.**

If you need to expand the Spotlight Comments section of the Info dialog, click the triangle next to the Spotlight Comments heading. The arrow rotates and the Spotlight Comments box appears.

*3.* **Close the Info dialog to save the comment.**

## Displaying extensions

Extensions are alien creatures to most Mac owners. However, these (usually) three- or four-character add-ons that follow a period at the end of a filename have been a mainstay in the Windows and UNIX environments for years. An *extension* identifies what program owns a specific file, and therefore which application launches automatically when you double-click that file's icon. Examples of common extensions (and the applications that own them) include

✦ **.pdf:** Preview or Adobe Acrobat

✦ **.doc:** Microsoft Word

✦ **.pages:** Apple Pages

✦ **.key:** Apple Keynote

✦ **.psd:** Adobe Photoshop or Photoshop Elements

✦ **.jpeg or .jpg:** Preview, QuickTime, or your image editor

✦ **.tiff or .tif:** Preview or your image editor

✦ **.htm or .html:** Safari or your Web browser of choice

Why would someone want to see a file's extension? It comes in handy when a number of different types of files are linked to the same application. For example, if you install Adobe Photoshop, both JPEG and TIFF images have virtually the same icon, so it's sometimes very hard to tell one from the other. With extensions displayed, it's easy to tell what type of file you're looking at.

Follow this procedure to hide or display extensions with your filenames:

1. **Display the Info dialog for the item by pressing ⌘+I or choosing File⇨ Get Info.**

2. **If you need to expand the Name & Extension section of the Info dialog, click the triangle next to the Name & Extension heading.**

3. **To display the extension for the selected file, clear the Hide Extension check box to disable it.**

4. **Close the Info dialog to save your changes.**

## Choosing the application with which to launch a file

So what's the plan if the wrong application launches when you double-click a file? Not a problem: You can also change the linked application from the Info dialog as well. (I told you this was a handy toybox, didn't I?) Follow these steps to choose another application to pair with a selected file:

1. **Click the Action button on the Finder toolbar and click Get Info to display the Info dialog for the item.**

2. **Click the triangle next to the Open With heading to expand it.**

3. **Click the pop-up menu button.**

   Mac OS X displays the applications that it feels are best suited to open this type of document.

4. **Select the application that should open the file.**

   To go completely hog-wild and choose a different application, select Other from the pop-up menu. Mac OS X opens a Choose Other Application dialog, where you can navigate to and select the application you want. (If the application isn't recognized as *recommended,* click the Enable pop-up menu and choose All Applications.) After you highlight the application, click Add.

5. **To globally update all the documents of the same type to launch the application that you chose, click the Change All button.**

   Mac OS X displays a confirmation dialog asking whether you're sure about making this drastic change. Click Continue to update the other files of the same type or click Cancel to return to the Info dialog.

6. **Close the Info dialog to save your changes.**

## Locking files against evildoers

"Holy Item Insurance, Batman!" That's right, Boy Wonder: Before I leave the friendly land of the Info dialog, every MacBook owner needs to know how to protect files and folders from accidental deletion or editing. By *locking* a file, you allow it to be opened and copied — but not changed, renamed, or sent to the Trash. Locked items appear in the Finder with a small padlock attached to the icon.

To lock or unlock a file, you have to have ownership of the file. I cover privileges in Book III, but on a MacBook where you've configured only one administrator account, you should already have ownership.

If you're considering changing the ownership of a system-owned file, *don't do it.* You could throw a serious monkey wrench into your Snow Leopard system.

To lock a file, follow this procedure:

1. **Display the Info dialog for the item.**

2. **Select the Locked check box to enable it.**

   The Locked check box is in the General section of the dialog.

3. **Close the Info dialog to save your changes.**

# Creating an Alias

I mention aliases in Book II, Chapter 2. As I discuss in that chapter, an *alias* acts as a link to an application or document that actually exists elsewhere on your system (a handy trick to use when organizing items on your hard drive). You have a number of different ways to conjure an alias after you select an item:

✦ Choose File from the Finder menu and choose the Make Alias menu item. (You have to move the alias yourself.)

✦ Press the ⌘+L keyboard shortcut. (Again, you have to move the new alias to its new location.)

✦ Click the Action button on the Finder toolbar and then click Make Alias.

✦ Right-click the selected item and then choose Make Alias from the contextual menu that appears.

In addition, you can hold down the ⌘+Option key combination and drag the item to the location where you want the alias.

Although Mac OS X does a great job in tracking the movements of an original and updating an alias, some actions can break the link. For example, if you delete the original, the alias is left wandering in search of a home. However, all is not lost — when you double-click a broken alias, Mac OS X offers to help you fix the alias. This involves browsing through your system to locate a new original.

# Using the Apple Menu

The Apple menu is a familiar sight to any Mac owner. Although Apple contemplated removing it during the original development and beta cycle for Mac OS X version 10.0, the ruckus and cry from beta-testers ensured that it remains today. It's amazing how reassuring that little fellow can be when you boot the Big X for the first time.

In this section, I cover the important things that are parked under the Apple menu.

## Using Recent Items

If you're like most of us — and I think I'm safe in assuming that you are — you tend to work on the same set of applications and files (and use the same network servers) during the day. Normally, this would be somewhat of a pain because each time you sit down in front of the keyboard, you have to drill down through at least one layer of folders to actually reach the stuff that you need. To make things easier on yourself, you could create a set of aliases on your Desktop that link to those servers, files, and applications . . . but as you moved from project to project, you'd find yourself constantly updating the aliases. As Blackbeard the Pirate was wont to exclaim, "Arrgh!"

Ah, but Mac OS X is a right-smart operating system, and several years ago, Apple created the Recent Items menu to save you the trouble of drilling for applications and files (and even network servers as well). Figure 3-4 illustrates the Recent Items menu from my system. Note that the menu is thoughtfully divided into Applications, Documents, and Servers. When you open documents or launch applications, they're added to the list. (Accountants will revel in this First In, First Out technology.) To launch an application or document from the Recent Items menu — or connect to a network server — just click it.

To wipe the contents of the Recent Items menu — for example, if you've just finished a project and want to turn over a new digital leaf — click Recent Items and choose the Clear Menu item.

**Book II
Chapter 3**

**Basic OS X
Housekeeping**

**Figure 3-4:**
Use the
Recent
Items
menu to
access files,
applications,
and servers
you've been
using.

You can specify the number of recent items that will appear in the menu from System Preferences; display the Appearance pane and click the Applications, Documents, and Servers list boxes in the Number of Recent Items field. (More on this in Book III, Chapter 3.)

Also, remember the trick that I mention earlier: You can drag any folder or server into the Sidebar column at the left of a Finder window, adding it to that exclusive club that includes your Home folder and Applications folder.

## Playing with the Dock

You know how Air Force One acts as the mobile nerve center for the president? And how The Chief can jet all around the world and take all his stuff along with him? Well, the Dock is kind of like that. Sort of.

If you want your Dock to go mobile as well, click the Apple menu and choose the Dock item to display the submenu. Here's a rundown of the options that you'll find:

✦ **Hiding:** Click Turn Hiding On/Off to toggle the automatic hiding of the Dock. With hiding on, the Dock disappears off the edge of the screen until you move the pointer to that edge. (This is great for those who want to make use of as much Desktop territory as possible for their applications.)

You can press ⌘+Option+D to toggle Dock hiding on and off from the keyboard.

✦ **Magnification:** Click Turn Magnification On/Off to toggle icon magnification when your pointer is selecting an icon from the Dock. With magnification on, the icons in the Dock get really, *really* big . . . a good thing for Mr. Magoo or those with grandiose schemes to take over the world. Check out the rather oversized icons in Figure 3-5. (The amount of magnification can be controlled from the System Preferences Dock settings, which I explain in Book III, Chapter 3.)

✦ **Position:** Click one of three choices (Position on Left, Bottom, or Right) to make the Dock appear on the left, bottom, or right of the screen, respectively.

✦ **Dock Preferences:** Click this to display the System Preferences Dock settings, which I explain in Book III, Chapter 3.

## Bad program! Quit!

Once in a while, you'll encounter a stubborn application that locks up, slows to a crawl, or gets stuck in an endless loop. Although Mac OS X is a highly advanced operating system, it can still fall prey to bad programming or corrupted data.

**Figure 3-5:**
Now those,
my friend,
are some
pumped-up
icons.

Luckily, you can easily shut down these troublemakers from the Apple menu. Just choose Force Quit to display the Force Quit Applications dialog that you see in Figure 3-6. (Keyboard types can press ⌘+Option+Esc.) Select the application that you want to banish and then click the Force Quit button; Mac OS X requests confirmation, after which you click the Force Quit button again.

**Figure 3-6:**
Forcing an
application
to take a
hike.

If you select Finder in the Force Quit Applications dialog, the button changes to Relaunch. This allows you to restart the Finder, which comes in handy if your system appears to be unstable. (This is much faster than actually restarting your MacBook.)

Forcing an application to quit will also quit any open documents that you were working with in that application, so *save your work* (if the program will allow you to save anything). If you relaunch the Finder, some programs might restart as well.

### Tracking down your version

This isn't a big deal, but if you choose About This Mac from the Apple menu, Mac OS X displays the About This Mac dialog that you see in Figure 3-7. In case you need to check the amount of memory or the processor in an unfamiliar Mac, the About This Mac dialog can display these facts in a twinkling. However, I primarily use it to check the Mac OS X version and build number as well as to launch the Apple System Profiler (which I discuss in full in Chapter 7 of this minibook). Click the More Info button to launch the Profiler.

**Figure 3-7:**
Display
your Mac's
memory,
processor,
startup disk,
and Big X
version.

Apple allows you to launch Software Update from both the About This Mac dialog and the Apple menu . . . sheesh, they must really want you to keep your Big X up to date, I guess.

### Specifying a location

Mac OS X allows you to create multiple network locations. Think of a location as a separate configuration that you use when you connect to a different network from a different locale. For instance, if you travel to a branch office, you'd assign a location for your desk and a location for the remote branch. A student might assign one location for her home network and another for the college computer lab network.

A location saves all the specific values that you've entered in the System Preferences Network settings, including IP address, DNS servers, proxy servers, and the like. If all this means diddly squat to you, don't worry — I explain this in Book VII, Chapter 1. For now, just remember that you can switch between locations by choosing Location from the Apple menu, which displays a submenu of locations that you can choose from. (You must create at least a second location for the Location menu item to appear in the Apple menu.)

# Availing Yourself of Mac OS X Services

In Mac OS X, Services allow you to merge information from one application with another. To Mac old-timers, that might sound suspiciously like the Clipboard; however, Services can also include functionality from an application, so you can create new documents or complete tasks without running another program! Services can be used in both the Finder and Mac OS X applications.

**Book II
Chapter 3**

**Basic OS X
Housekeeping**

To illustrate, here's a fun example:

1.  **Launch TextEdit (you'll find it in your Applications folder) and type your name.**

2.  **Highlight your name.**

3.  **Click the TextEdit menu — don't switch to the Finder; use the TextEdit Application menu — and choose Services.**

4.  **From the Services submenu, choose Search in Google.**

After you've shaken your head at all the sites devoted to people with the same name, consider what you just did — you ran the Safari application from within TextEdit, using selected words! Pretty slick, eh?

A glance at the other Services that show up within most applications gives you an idea of just how convenient and powerful Mac OS X Services can be. I often use Services to take care of things such as

✦ Sending an e-mail message from an e-mail address in a text file or the Address Book (via the Mail Service)

✦ Capturing a screen snapshot within an application (using the Grab Service)

✦ Sending a file to a Bluetooth-equipped PDA or cell phone within an application (using the Send File to Bluetooth Device service)

Remember, you can access the Services menu from a Mac OS X application by picking that program's Application menu (sometimes called the *named menu*). For instance, in the demonstration earlier, I use the TextEdit menu that appears on the TextEdit menu bar. In Microsoft Word, I would click the Word menu.

Geez, I think the computing world needs another word for *menu* — don't you?

Many third-party applications that you install under Mac OS X can add their own commands under the Services menu, so be sure to read the documentation for a new application to see what Service functionality it adds.

## Get Thee Hence: Using the Go Menu

Remember the transporter from "Star Trek"? Step on the little platform, assume a brave pose, and whoosh! — you're transported instantaneously to another ship or (more likely) to a badly designed planet exterior built inside a soundstage. Talk about convenience . . . that is, as long as the doggone thing didn't malfunction.

The Finder's Go menu gives you the chance to play Captain Kirk: You can jump immediately to specific spots, both within the confines of your own system as well as external environments, such as your network or the Internet. (You can leave your phaser and tricorder in your cabin.)

The destinations that you can travel to using the Go menu and the iDisk submenu include the following:

✦ **Back/Forward/Enclosing Folder:** I lump these three commands together because they're all basic navigation commands. For example, Back and Forward operate just as they do in Safari or your favorite Web browser. If you're currently inside a folder, you can return to the parent folder by clicking Enclosing Folder.

✦ **Computer:** This window includes your hard drives, CD and DVD drives, and your network — the same places that appear when you open a new Finder window with the ⌘+N key shortcut.

✦ **Home:** This window displays the home directory for the user currently logged in.

✦ **Desktop:** This window displays the files and folders that you've stored on your Snow Leopard desktop.

✦ **Network:** Did you guess that this displays a window with all your network's servers? Dead giveaway, that.

✦ **iDisk:** This window displays the contents of your Internet iDisk storage (or someone else's). (More on the coolness that is iDisk in Book VI, Chapter 4.)

✦ **Applications:** This window includes all the applications that appear in your Mac OS X Applications folder (a neat *Just the programs, ma'am* arrangement that really comes in handy).

✦ **Documents:** Yep, you guessed it: This window displays the contents of your Documents folder.

✦ **Utilities:** This window displays the contents of your Mac OS X Utilities folder.

✦ **Recent Folders:** This window displays a submenu that allows you to choose from the folders that you've recently opened.

You can also type the path for a specific folder (use the Go to Folder command) or connect to a specific network server (use the Connect to Server command).

Note that most of the Go menu commands include keyboard shortcuts, proving once again that the fingers are quicker than the trackpad.

# Monkeying with the Menu Bar

Ever stared at a menu bar for inspiration? Fortunately for MacBook owners like you and me, people in Cupertino are paid to do just that, and these designers get the big bucks to make the Mac OS X menu bar the best that it can be. Thus were born menu bar icons, which add useful controls in what would otherwise be a wasted expanse of white.

## Using menu bar icons

Depending on your hardware, Mac OS X might install several menu bar icons. The Volume icon is always there by default, along with the Clock display, which is actually an icon in disguise. Figure 3-8 illustrates these standard icons, along with a couple of others.

Some icons won't appear unless you turn them on. For instance, the Displays icon won't appear unless you enable the Show Displays in Menu Bar check box within the Displays pane in System Preferences. The Displays menu bar icon, which looks like a monitor, allows you to choose the recommended resolutions and color depth settings for your graphics card and monitor. For example, the recommended settings for my MacBook Pro's LCD monitor include 1024 x 768, 1280 x 800, and 1440 x 900 resolutions, and my display can be set to thousands or millions of colors. Typically, it's a good idea to choose the highest resolution and the highest color depth. You can also jump directly to the System Preferences Display settings by clicking Displays Preferences in the menu.

**Figure 3-8:**
Adjust your
Mac with
a click of
these menu
icons.

To quickly change the audio volume level within Mac OS X, click the Sound
Volume icon (it looks like a speaker with emanating sound waves) once to
display its slider control; then click and drag the slider to adjust the level
up or down. After you select a level by lifting your finger from the trackpad,
your MacBook thoughtfully plays the default system sound to help you
gauge the new volume level.

Depending on the functionality that you're using with Mac OS X, these other
menu bar icons might also appear:

✦ **Modem status:** You can turn on the display of the Modem status icon
  from the corresponding modem panel on the Network pane in System
  Preferences, which I discuss in Book III, Chapter 3. The icon can be set
  to show the time that you've been connected to the Internet as well as
  the status of the connection procedure. (Naturally, your MacBook will
  need an external USB modem to use this status icon.)

✦ **AirPort:** Because your MacBook is equipped with AirPort Extreme
  hardware, you can enable the Show AirPort Status in Menu Bar check
  box within System Preferences. To do so, click the Network icon and
  then choose your AirPort connection in the column at the left. The
  AirPort status icon displays the status of the AirPort connection; click
  the AirPort icon to toggle AirPort on or off. The icon displays the relative strength of your AirPort signal, whether you're connected to a
  Base Station or a peer-to-peer computer network, or whether AirPort is

turned off. You can also switch between multiple AirPort networks from the menu.

✦ **Bluetooth:** You can toggle Bluetooth networking on or off. You can also make your MacBook discoverable or hidden to other Bluetooth devices, send a file to a Bluetooth device, or browse for new Bluetooth devices in your vicinity. Additionally, you can set up a Bluetooth device that's already recognized or open the Bluetooth pane within System Preferences.

✦ **Time Machine:** If you're using Time Machine to back up your MacBook automatically, this icon displays the date of your last backup. You can also manually start a backup from the menu bar icon. To display the icon, open System Preferences and click the Time Machine icon; then click the Show Time Machine Status in the Menu Bar check box to select it.

✦ **PPoE:** The display of this icon is controlled from the PPoE settings on the Network pane within System Preferences. Click this icon to connect to or disconnect from the Internet using *Point-to-Point over Ethernet* (PPoE), which is a type of Internet connection offered by some digital subscriber line (DSL) providers.

**Book II
Chapter 3**

**Basic OS X
Housekeeping**

## Doing timely things with the Clock

Even the Clock itself isn't static eye candy on the Mac OS X menu bar (I told you this was a hardworking operating system, didn't I?). Click the Clock display to toggle the icon between the default text display and a miniature analog clock. You'll also find the complete day and date at the top of the menu.

## Mark's totally unnecessary Computer Trivia 1.0

"Where the heck did *mounting* come from, anyway? Sounds like a line from a John Wayne Western!" Well, pardner, the term dates back to the heyday of Big Iron — the Mainframe Age, when giant IBM dinosaurs populated the computing world. (And, coincidentally, I was a COBOL programmer.) Sherman, set the WayBack Machine....

At the time, disks were big, heavy, removable cartridges the diameter of dinner plates (and about as tall as a 100-count spindle of CD-Rs). The acolytes of the mainframe, called computer *operators,* would have to trudge over to a cabinet and swap disk cartridges whenever the program stopped and asked for them.

That's right, those mainframes would actually stop calculating and print, "I need you to mount cartridge 12-A-34, or I can't go any further. Have a nice day." (Can you imagine what it'd be like loading and unloading a hard drive every time you needed to open a folder?)

Anyway, even though eons passed and mini-computers appeared — which were only the size of a washing machine — the terms *mounting* and *unmounting* still commonly appeared in programs. This time, the removable volumes were 8-inch floppy disks and tape cartridges. Because UNIX (and its offspring Linux) date from the Minicomputer Age, these operating systems still use the terms.

In fact, you can even open the System Preferences Date & Time settings from the icon. From within the Date & Time settings, you can choose whether the seconds or day of the week are included, whether the separators should flash, or whether Mac OS X should display the time in 24-hour (military) format. More on this in Book III, Chapter 3.

# Eject, Tex, Eject!

Mac OS X makes use of both static volumes (your MacBook's hard drive, which remains mummified inside your computer's case) and removable volumes (such as USB Flash drives, your iPod, and CDs/DVD-ROMs). Mac OS X calls the process of loading and unloading a removable volume by old-fashioned terms — *mounting* and *unmounting* — but you and I call the procedure *loading* and *ejecting*.

Just to keep things clear, I should point out that we're talking hardware devices here, so static and removable volumes have nothing to do with the *sound* volume control on your menu bar.

I won't discuss loading/mounting a removable volume — the process differs depending on the computer because some MacBooks need a button pushed on the keyboard, others have buttons on the drive itself, and some drives have just a slot, with no button at all. However, there are a number of standard ways of unloading/unmounting/ejecting a removable volume:

 ✦ **Drag the Volume's icon from the Desktop to the Trash,** which displays an Eject pop-up label to help underline the fact that you are *not* deleting the contents of the drive. Let me underline that with a Mark's Maxim because Switchers from the Windows world are usually scared to death by the concept of dragging a volume to the Trash.

 **Have no fear — in the Apple universe, you *can* drag removable volumes to the Trash with aplomb.**

 ✦ **Click the Volume's icon and use the ⌘+E keyboard shortcut.**

 ✦ **With the volume open in a Finder window, click the Action button and choose Eject from the pop-up menu.**

 ✦ **Click the File menu and choose Eject.**

 ✦ **Click the Eject button next to the device in the Finder window sidebar.**

 ✦ **Right-click the Volume's icon to display the contextual menu; then choose Eject.**

 ✦ **Press your MacBook's keyboard Eject key to eject a CD or DVD from your built-in optical drive. (If you're using an external keyboard without a Media Eject key, you may be able to press and hold F12 instead.)**

You can't unmount a static volume from the Desktop — you have to use the Disk Utility application — so your internal hard drive icon will stay where it is.

# Common Tasks Aplenty

Okay, I admit it — this section is kind of a grab bag of three very common tasks. However, I want to walk you through these three procedures early in the book. Most MacBook owners want to listen to and record CDs as soon as they start using Snow Leopard, and you'd be amazed how much information still flows across the Internet in plain, simple text.

Therefore, hang around and take care of business.

## Opening and editing text files

Text files would seem to be another anachronism in this age of formatted Web pages, rich-text format (RTF) documents, and word processors galore. However, virtually every computer ever built can read and write in standard text, so text files are often used for

✦ **Information files on the Internet,** such as FAQs (Frequently Asked Questions files)

✦ **README and update** information by software developers

✦ **Swapping data between programs,** such as comma- and tab-delimited database files

Here's the quick skinny on opening, editing, and saving an existing text file:

*1.* **Navigate to your Applications folder and launch TextEdit.**

*2.* **Press ⌘+O to display the Open dialog.**

*3.* **Navigate to the desired text file and double-click the filename to load it.**

You can also open an existing text file by dragging its icon from the Finder window to the TextEdit icon.

*4.* **Click the insertion cursor anywhere in the file and begin typing. Or, to edit existing text, drag the insertion cursor across the characters to highlight them and type the replacement text.**

TextEdit automatically replaces the existing characters with those that you type. To simply delete text, highlight the characters and press Delete.

*5.* **After you finish editing the document, you can overwrite the original by pressing ⌘+S (which is the same as choosing File⇨Save), or you can save a new version by choosing File⇨Save As and typing a new, unique filename.**

*6.* **To exit TextEdit, press ⌘+Q.**

## Listening to an audio CD

By default, Snow Leopard uses iTunes to play an audio CD. Although I cover iTunes in complete detail in Book IV, Chapter 2, take a moment to see how to master the common task of playing an audio CD (just in case you want to jam while reading these early chapters). Follow these steps:

1. **Load the audio CD into your MacBook's optical drive. (Remember, MacBook Air owners, you can add an external USB optical drive at any time.)**

   A CD volume icon appears on your Desktop, and then Mac OS X automatically loads iTunes and displays its spiffy window.

2. **If you have iTunes set up to start playing by default, it automatically begins playing the disc; however, if you have to manually start the music, click the Play button at the upper left of the iTunes window to begin playing the disc at the beginning. To play an individual track, double-click the track name in the iTunes window.**

3. **To adjust the volume from within iTunes, drag the Volume slider to the left or right — it's to the right of the Play and Fast Forward buttons.**

4. **To eject the disc and load another audio CD, press ⌘+E, click the Eject icon next to the CD entry in the Source list, or click Controls⇨Eject Disc.**

5. **To exit iTunes, press ⌘+Q.**

The first time you run iTunes, you're asked to configure the program and specify whether Mac OS X should automatically connect to the Internet to download the track titles for the disc you've loaded. I recommend that you accept all the default settings and that you allow automatic connection. Is simple, no?

---

# Adding the perfect font with Font Book

Need to install a font in Mac OS X, or perhaps you'd like to organize your fonts into collections based on their theme or their designer? If so, you're talking about *Font Book,* which is the font organizer that ships with Snow Leopard. To open Font Book, visit your Applications folder and double-click the Font Book icon.

Press ⌘+O (or choose File⇨Add Fonts) to import a new font into your system, or simply drag the font file from a Finder window into the Font Book window. Snow Leopard can accept TrueType, OpenType, and PostScript Type 1 fonts. When it's been added, your new font can be categorized by dragging it into one of your *collections,* thus making that font easier to locate and display. Individual fonts and entire collections can be enabled or disabled (by using the Enable and Disable items on the Edit menu) so that you can "turn on" only those fonts that you need for a specific application or project. The Font Book window also comes fully equipped with a Search box, so you can find any font by name.

### Recording — nay, burning — a data CD

Mac OS X offers a built-in CD recording feature that allows you to burn the simplest form of CD: a standard data CD-ROM that can hold up to approximately 660MB of files and folders, and can be read on both Macs and PCs running Windows, UNIX, and Linux. (To burn an audio CD, use iTunes, as I show you in Book IV, Chapter 2.)

Back to the story! To record a data disc, follow these steps:

1. **Load a blank CD-R, CD-RW, DVD-R, or DVD-RW into your drive.**

   I assume for this demonstration that you're using a write-once CD-R.

2. **In the dialog that appears and prompts you for an action to take, choose the default, Open Finder, for this demonstration.**

   Mac OS X displays an Untitled CD volume icon on your Desktop. (It's marked with the letters CDR so that you know that the disc is recordable.)

3. **Double-click the Untitled CD icon to display the contents. (It'll be empty, naturally.)**

4. **Click and drag files and folders to the CD window as you normally do.**

5. **Rename any files or folders as necessary.**

   Remember, after you've started recording, this stuff is etched in stone, so your disc window should look the same as the volume window looks on the finished CD-ROM.

6. **Click File on the Finder menu and choose Burn Disc, or click the Burn button in the CD window.**

   The Big X displays a confirmation dialog.

7. **If you've forgotten something, you can click the Cancel or Eject button. Otherwise, click the Burn button and sit back and watch the fun.**

Unfortunately, Mac OS X doesn't support recording from the Finder for some external and third-party drives available for the Macintosh. If you can't burn from the Finder (or you're willing to pay for extra features), I recommend that you buy a copy of Roxio Toast Titanium recording software (www.roxio.com).

## All You Really Need to Know about Printing

To close out this chapter, I turn your attention to another task that most MacBook owners need to tackle soon after buying their laptop or installing Snow Leopard: printing documents. Because basic printing is so important (and in most cases, so simple), allow me to use this final section to demonstrate how to print a document.

Most of us have a Universal Serial Bus (USB) printer — USB being the favored hardware connection within Mac OS X — so, as long as your printer is supported by Mac OS X, setting it up is as easy as plugging it into one of your Mac's USB ports. The Big X does the rest of the work, selecting the proper printer software driver from the Library/Printers folder and setting your printer as the default power of the universe.

Before you print, *preview!* Would you jump from an airplane without a parachute? Then why would you print a document without double-checking it first? Click Preview, and Mac OS X opens the Preview application to show you what the printed document will look like. (Once again, some upstart applications have their own built-in Print Preview mode thumbnails within the Print dialog, so previewing may not be necessary.) When you're done examining your handiwork, close the Preview application to return to your document.

To print from within any application using the default page characteristics — standard 8½-x-11-inch paper, portrait mode, no scaling — follow these steps:

*1.* **Within your application, click File and choose Print — or press the ⌘+P keyboard shortcut.**

Mac OS X displays the simple version of the Print dialog. (To display all the fields that you see in Figure 3-9, click the button with the down arrow next to the Printer pop-up menu.)

**Figure 3-9:**
The Print dialog is available from any application with any real guts.

Some applications use their own custom Print dialogs, but you should see the same general settings.

2. **Click in the Copies field and enter the number of copies that you need.**

   You can also enable or disable collation, just as you can with those oh-so-fancy copiers.

3. **Decide what you want to print.**

   - *The whole shootin' match:* To print the entire document, use the default Pages radio button setting of All.

   - *Anything less:* To print a range of selected pages, select the From radio button and enter the physical starting and ending pages.

4. **(Optional) Choose application-specific printing parameters.**

   Each Mac OS X application provides different panes so that you can configure settings specific to that application. You don't have to display any of these extra settings to print a default document, but the power is there to change the look dramatically when necessary. To display these settings, click the pop-up menu in the center of the Print dialog and choose one of these panes. For example, if you're printing from the Address Book, you can choose the Address Book entry from the pop-up menu and elect to print a phone list or an e-mail list.

5. **When everything is go for launch, click the Print button.**

Of course, there are more settings and more functionality to the printing system within Mac OS X, and I cover more complex printing topics in much more detail in Book VIII, Chapter 4. However, I can tell you from my experiences as a consultant and hardware technician that this short introduction to printing will likely suffice for 90 percent of the MacBook owners on Earth. 'Nuff said.

# Chapter 4: Searching Everything with Spotlight

## In This Chapter

✔ Mastering basic Spotlight searching skills

✔ Selecting text and keywords for best results

✔ Displaying results in the Spotlight window

✔ Customizing Spotlight settings in System Preferences

*Spotlight* is Apple's desktop search technology that you can use to find anything on your laptop as quickly as you can type. (Yep, that includes all the documents, Address Book contacts, Mail messages, folders, and drives that your MacBook can access.) In fact, the version of Spotlight included with Snow Leopard can even search folders shared on other Macs across your network! Yes, you read right: If the information is on your MacBook's hard drive, a CD, your network, or even *another Mac* in your network, consider it located.

This chapter is your ticket to using this new search technology like a professional techno-wizard from day one. I discuss how Spotlight works and how you can use it to locate exactly what you want (and present those results as proudly as a wine steward showing off a fine vintage).

## Basic Searching 101

Figure 4-1 illustrates the Spotlight search field, which is always available from the Finder menu bar. Click the magnifying glass icon once (or press ⌘+Spacebar), and the Spotlight search box appears.

To run a search, simply click in the Spotlight box and begin typing. You see matching items appear as soon as you type, and the search results are continually refined while you type the rest of your search criteria. As with the Search box in earlier Finder window toolbars, you don't need to press Return to begin the search.

**Figure 4-1:**
A lot of
power is
behind
this single
Spotlight
search box.

The results of your Spotlight search are presented in the Spotlight menu, which is updated automatically in real time while you continue to type. The top 20 most-relevant items are grouped into categories right on the Spotlight menu, including Messages, Definitions, Documents, Folders, Images, Contacts, and so on. Spotlight takes a guess at the item that's most likely the match you're looking for (based on your Search Results list in System Preferences, which I cover later in the chapter) and presents it in the special Top Hit category that always appears first.

To open the Top Hit item like a true Snow Leopard power user, just press Return. (My brothers and sisters, it just doesn't get any easier than that.)

Literally any text string is acceptable as a Spotlight search. However, here's a short list of the common search criteria I use every day:

✦ **Names and addresses:** Because Spotlight has access to Snow Leopard's Address Book, you can immediately display contact information using any portion of a name or address.

✦ **E-mail message text:** Need to open a specific e-mail message, but you'd rather not launch Mail and spend time digging through the message list? Enter the person's e-mail address or any text string contained in the message you're looking for.

✦ **File and folder names:** This is the classic search favorite. Spotlight searches your entire system for that one file or folder in the blink of an eye.

✦ **Events & To Do items:** Yep, Spotlight gives you access to your iCal calendars and those all-important To Do lists you've created.

✦ **System Preferences:** Now things start to get *really* interesting! Try typing the word **background** in the Spotlight field. Some of the results will actually be System Preference panes! That's right, every setting in System Preferences is referenced in Spotlight. (For example, the Software Update pane contains the word *background* while the desktop background setting is on the Desktop & Screen Saver pane in System Preferences.)

✦ **Web pages:** *Whoa.* Stand back, Google. You can use Spotlight to search the Web pages you've recently displayed in Safari! (Note, however, that this feature doesn't let you search through all the Internet as Google does . . . only the pages stored in your Safari Web cache and any HTML files you've saved to your MacBook's hard drive.)

✦ **Metadata:** That's a pretty broad category, but it fits. For example, I like to locate Word documents on my system using the same metadata that's stored in the file, such as the contents of the Comments field in a Word document. Other supported applications include Photoshop images, Excel spreadsheets, Keynote presentations, and other third-party applications that offer a Spotlight plug-in.

**Book II
Chapter 4**

To reset the Spotlight search and try another text string, click the X icon that appears at the right side of the Spotlight box. (Of course, you can also backspace to the beginning of the field, but that's a little less elegant.)

After you find the item that you're looking for, you can click it once to

✦ Launch it (if the item is an application)

✦ Open it in System Preferences (if it's a setting or description on a Preferences pane)

✦ Open it within the associated application (if the item is a document or a data item)

✦ Display it within a Finder window (if the item is a folder)

Here's another favorite timesaver: You can display all the files of a particular type on your system by using the file type as the keyword. For example, to provide a list of all images on your system, just use *images* as your keyword — the same goes for *movies* and *audio,* too.

In fact, you can display the same search results from the Snow Leopard Sidebar, which includes a Search For heading! You can display All Images, All Movies, and All Documents with a single click of your mouse button, from any Finder window.

# Is Spotlight Really That Cool?

Don't get fooled into simply using Spotlight as another file-'n-folder-name search tool. Sure, it can do that, but Spotlight can also search inside PDF,

Word, Pages and HTML files, finding matching text that doesn't appear in the name of the file! To wit: A search for *Snow Leopard* on my system pulls up all sorts of items with Snow Leopard in their names, but also files with Snow Leopard *in* them:

✦ *Apple Store SF.ppt:* A PowerPoint presentation that contains several slides containing the text Snow Leopard

✦ *bk01ch03.doc:* A rather cryptically named Word file chapter of this book that mentions Snow Leopard in several spots

✦ *Conference Call with Bob:* An iCal event pointing to a conference call with my editor about upcoming Snow Leopard book projects

Notice that not one of these three examples actually has the words *Snow Leopard* occurring anywhere in the title or filename, yet Spotlight found them because they all contain the text *Snow Leopard* therein. That, dear reader, is the true power of Spotlight, and how it can literally guarantee you that you'll never lose another piece of information in the hundreds of thousands of files and folders on your hard drive!

Heck, suppose that all you remember about a file is that you received it in your mail last week or last month. To find it, you can actually type in time periods, such as *yesterday, last week,* or *last month,* to see every item that you saved or received within that period. (Boy, howdy, I *love* writing about truly good ideas.)

Again, the Sidebar also allows you to search for files by time period, using the links under the Search For heading.

---

# Is Spotlight secure?

So how about all those files, folders, contacts, and events that you *don't* want to appear in Spotlight? What if you're sharing your MacBook as a multiuser computer, or accessing other Macs remotely? Can others search for and access your personal information through Spotlight?

**Definitely not!** The results displayed by Spotlight are controlled by file and folder permissions as well as your account login, just as the applications that create and display your personal data are. For example, you can't access other users' calendars using iCal,

and they can't see your Mail messages. Only *you* have access to your data, and only after you've logged in with your username and password. Spotlight works the same way. If a user doesn't normally have access to an item, the item simply doesn't appear when that user performs a Spotlight search. (In other words, only you get to see your stuff.)

However, you can even hide certain folders and disks from your own Spotlight searches if necessary. Check out the final section of this chapter for details on setting private locations on your system.

Be careful, however, when you're considering a search string. Don't forget that (by default) Spotlight matches only those items that have *all* the words you enter in the Spotlight box. To return the highest number of possible matches, use the fewest number of words to identify the item; for example, use *horse* rather than *horse image,* and you're certain to be rewarded with more hits. (On the other hand, if you're looking specifically for a picture of a knight on horseback, a series of keywords, such as *horse knight image,* shortens your search considerably. It all depends on what you're looking for and how widely you want to cast your Spotlight net.)

To allow greater flexibility in searches, Apple also includes those helpful Boolean friends that you may already be familiar with: AND, OR, and NOT. For example, you can perform Spotlight searches, such as

Book II
Chapter 4

Searching
Everything
with Spotlight

✦ *Horse* AND *cow* (which collects all references to both those barnyard animals into one search)

✦ *Batman* OR *Robin* (which returns all references to either Batman or Robin, but not both)

✦ *Apple* NOT *PC* (which displays all references to Apple that don't include any information on dastardly PCs)

Because Spotlight functions are a core technology of Mac OS X Snow Leopard — in other words, all sorts of applications can make use of Spotlight throughout the operating system, including the Finder — the Finder window's Search box now shares many of the capabilities of Spotlight. In fact, you can use the time period trick that I mention earlier (entering *yesterday* as a keyword) in the Finder window Search box.

Okay, parents, listen closely: Here's a (somewhat sneaky) tip that might help you monitor your kid's computer time as well as what your kids are typing/reading in iChat:

1. **Enable the iChat transcript feature.**

   a. *From within iChat, choose iChat⇨Preferences.*

   b. *Click Messages.*

   c. *Select the Save Chat Transcripts To check box and choose a destination folder in a location you can access.*

2. **Click OK to return to iChat.**

   Now you can use Spotlight to search for questionable words, phrases, and names within those iChat transcripts. (For more on iChat, turn to Book VI, Chapter 3.)

# Expanding Your Search Horizons

I can just hear the announcer's voice now: "But wait, there's more! If you click the Show All menu item at the beginning of your search results, we'll expand your Spotlight menu into the Spotlight Results window!" (Fortunately, you don't have to buy some ridiculous household doodad.)

Keyboard mavens will appreciate the Spotlight window shortcut key, and I show you where to specify this shortcut in the final section of this chapter.

Figure 4-2 illustrates the Results window (which is actually a Finder window with extras). To further filter the search, click one of the buttons on the Spotlight Results window toolbar or create your own custom filter. Click the button with the plus sign to display the search criteria bar and then click the pop-up menus to choose from criteria, such as the type of file, the text content, or the location on your system (for example, your hard drive, your Home folder, or a network server). You can also filter your results listing by the date the items were created or last saved. To add or delete criteria, click the plus and minus buttons at the right side of the search criteria bar. To save a custom filter that you've created, click the Save button.

**Figure 4-2:** The spacious borders of the Spotlight Results window.

Images appear as thumbnail icons, so you can use that most sophisticated search tool — the human eye — to find the picture you're looking for. (If you don't see thumbnail images, click the Icon view button on the toolbar.) Don't forget that you can increase or decrease the size of the icons by dragging the slider at the bottom right of the window.

To display the contents item in the list (without leaving the comfortable confines of the Results window), click. the icon to select it and click the Quick Look icon in the toolbar (or press the spacebar) for a better view.

Again, when you're ready to open an item, just double-click it in the Results window.

As I mention earlier, Spotlight can look for matching items on other Macs on your network — but only if those remote Macs are configured correctly. To allow another Mac running Mac OS X Tiger, Leopard, or Snow Leopard to be visible to Spotlight on your system, enable File Sharing on the other Mac. (Oh, and remember that you need an admin-level account on that Mac — or access to a good friend who has an admin-level account on that Mac.)

Follow these steps to enable File Sharing on the other Mac:

**Book II
Chapter 4**

Searching
Everything
with Spotlight

1. **Click the System Preferences icon in the Dock.**

2. **Click the Sharing pane.**

3. **Select the On check box next to the File Sharing item in the service list to enable it.**

4. **Click the Close button on the System Preferences window.**

Remember, you can search only items that you have rights and permissions to view on the remote Mac (such as the contents of the Public folders on that computer). I discuss more about these limitations earlier in this chapter, in the "Is Spotlight secure?" sidebar.

# Customizing Spotlight to Your Taste

You might wonder whether such an awesome Mac OS X feature has its own pane within System Preferences — and you'd be right again. Figure 4-3 shows off the Spotlight pane within System Preferences: Click the System Preferences icon (look for the gears) in the Dock and then click the Spotlight icon (under Personal) to display these settings.

Click the Search Results tab to

✦ **Determine which categories appear in the Spotlight menu and Results window.** For example, if you don't use any presentation software on your MacBook, you can clear the check box next to Presentations to disable this category (thereby making more room for other categories that you *will* use).

✦ **Determine the order that categories appear in the Spotlight menu and Results window.** Drag the categories to the order in which you want them to appear in the Spotlight menu and window. For example, I like the Documents and System Preferences categories to appear higher in the list because I use them most often.

✦ **Specify the Spotlight menu and Spotlight Results window keyboard shortcuts.** You can enable or disable either keyboard shortcut and choose the key combination from the pop-up menu.

**Figure 4-3:** Fine-tune your Spotlight menu and Results window from within System Preferences.

Click the Privacy tab (as shown in Figure 4-4) to specify disks and folders that should never be listed as results in a Spotlight search. I know, I know, I said earlier that Spotlight respected your security, and it does. However, the disks and folders that you add on this list won't appear even if *you* are the one performing the search. (This is a great idea for folders and removable hard drives that you use to store sensitive information, such as medical records.)

To add locations that you want to keep private, click the Add button (bearing a plus sign) and navigate to the desired location. Click the location to select it and then click Choose. (Alternatively, you can drag folders or disks directly from a Finder window and drop them into the pane.)

**Figure 4-4:**
When certain folders and disks must remain private (even from you!), add them to this list.

# Chapter 5: Fun with Photo Booth and Front Row

## In This Chapter

- Using Photo Booth to take photos
- Capturing video with iMovie
- Working with the Apple Remote
- Using Front Row

Many Apple switchers and first-time owners quickly notice the unusual feature that accompanies the latest MacBooks: a tiny square lens and LED light at the top of the laptop's screen. That square is the lens of your MacBook's built-in iSight camera, which allows video chatting in iChat or a quick, fun series of photos or video clips via Snow Leopard's Photo Booth and iMovie applications. (Some third-party applications can use your MacBook's camera for things like reading bar codes.) Heck, you can even take your user account photo with your iSight camera (in the System Preferences window)!

Ah, but there's more. You can also buy an Apple Remote, which appears to be a stick of chewing gum with buttons (or an old-style iPod Shuffle). You can use an Apple Remote to control your MacBook from the comfort of your lounge chair or breakfast nook via Snow Leopard's Front Row software (as well as other third-party applications with Apple Remote support). What's that you say? Your last computer didn't have a remote control? You've never used a computer video camera? Well then, good reader, you've come to the right place!

In this chapter, I show you how to use your MacBook's remote to dazzle your friends and family with all sorts of digital media; then, I demonstrate how easy it is to produce photos and video with your iSight camera. *Sassy!*

# Capturing the Moment with iSight and Photo Booth

Does your MacBook have that tiny lens at the top of the screen? Then you're in business with your built-in iSight camera . . . pat yourself on the back and do the Technology dance.

Figure 5-1 illustrates a typical MacBook iSight camera. With iChat, you can videoconference in style, and you'll find everything you need to join the ranks of the iChat elite in Book VI, Chapter 3. Photo Booth allows you to snap digital pictures just as you did in the old automatic photo booth at your local arcade, but Photo Book comes complete with visual effects to add pizzazz and punch to your photos.

Camera
indicator light

iSight
camera lens

**Figure 5-1:** Your Mac may already pack its own camera punch.

The iSight camera's indicator light glows green whenever you're taking a snapshot or recording video . . . which, when you think about it, is A Good Thing (especially if you prefer chatting at home in Leisure Mode).

TIP

Need to quickly get a picture of yourself for use on your Web page? Or perhaps your iChat icon needs an update to show off your new haircut. Photo Booth can capture images at 640 x 480 resolution and 32-bit color — and although today's digital cameras produce a much higher-quality photo, you can't beat the built-in convenience of Photo Booth for that quick snapshot! To snap an image in Photo Booth, follow these steps:

*1.* **Launch Photo Booth from the Applications folder.**

Figure 5-2 illustrates the application window that appears. (Ignore the rather silly gentleman who wandered into the frame. I doubt he'll be in your Photo Booth window!)

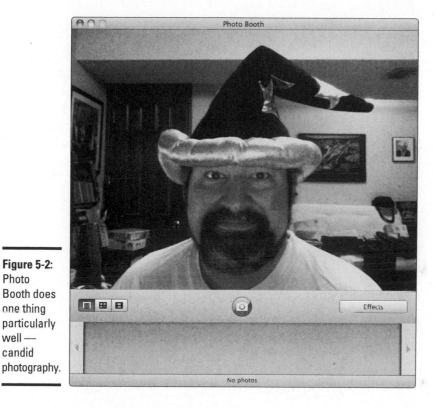

**Figure 5-2:**
Photo
Booth does
one thing
particularly
well —
candid
photography.

2. **(Optional) Click the Effects button to choose an effect you'd like to apply to your image.**

   Photo Booth displays a screen of thumbnail preview images so that you can see how each effect changes the photo. You can produce some of the simple effects you may be familiar with from Photoshop, such as a black-and-white image or a fancy color-pencil filter, but Photo Booth can also deliver some mind-blowing distortion effects, and even an Andy Warhol–style pop-art image!

   To return the display to normal without choosing an effect, click the Normal thumbnail, which appears in the center. (Paul Lynde's spot, for those of you old enough to remember "Hollywood Squares.")

   Of course, you can always launch your favorite image editor afterward to use a filter or effect on a photo — for example, the effects available in iPhoto. Photo Booth can apply these effects automatically as soon as you take the picture.

3. **(Optional) Click a thumbnail to select the desired effect.**

   When you choose an effect, Photo Booth automatically closes the Effects display.

4. **Click the Camera button.**

You'll notice that the image appears in the filmstrip at the bottom of the window. Photo Booth keeps a copy of all the images you take in the filmstrip so that you can use them later. After you click a photo in the filmstrip, a series of buttons appears, including

+ Sending the photo in an e-mail message

+ Saving the photo directly to iPhoto

+ Using the image as your Snow Leopard user account icon

+ Using the image as your iChat Buddy icon

To delete an image from the Photo Booth filmstrip, click the offending photo and then click the X button that appears underneath.

## Producing Video on the Spot with iMovie

"Mark, am I limited to capturing still images with my MacBook's camera?" Oh, pshaw on limitations . . . you're a MacBook owner, after all! You can also use your iSight camera to snag video clips (complete with audio) in iMovie.

You don't need an expensive digital camcorder to produce video clips for use in iMovie! Your MacBook's camera can capture those clips for you — think of the party possibilities! (And the opportunity for practical jokes. But then again, you're not that kind of person, now *are* you?) To capture video directly from your iSight camera into iMovie, follow these steps:

1. **Launch iMovie from the Dock or from the Applications folder.**

2. **Click the Open Camera Import Window button to switch to Import Video mode.**

   The button is located at the far left of the toolbar running down the center of the iMovie window, and it sports a camera icon.

3. **Click the Camera pop-up menu at the bottom of the Import window and click Built-in iSight.**

4. **When you're ready to start recording video, click the Capture button.**

   iMovie displays a sheet allowing you to select the location for the movie clip (including the approximate amount of time you can record). You can also choose to add the video to an existing iMovie Event or a brand-new Event. To help keep things steady in your clip, click the Analyze for Stabilization after Import check box to enable it — but note that the stabilization process significantly adds to the time it takes for iMovie to save your clip to disk. (Also, the stabilization data that's created during this step isn't actually applied to the video until the clip is added to a project, so your clip may still look shaky in the Event browser.)

5. **When you're ready to start recording video, click the Capture button.**

   iMovie automatically displays the incoming video in the monitor window while it's recorded. (As you might expect, the goofy behavior on the part of the distinguished cast usually starts at about this moment.)

6. **Click the Stop button to stop recording.**

   After you've ended the recording, iMovie creates the video clip and adds it to your Clips pane.

I go into much more detail on iMovie in Chapter 4 of Book IV, but that's the gist of recording video clips.

# *Controlling Your MacBook Remotely with Front Row*

Okay, you've seen some neat stuff so far, but things get *really* cool about now! With Apple's Front Row software, you can turn your MacBook into a multimedia presentation center that can show off all your digital media to your adoring public (and friends and family to boot). In fact, with the Apple Remote, you don't even have to leave the comfort of the couch to start the show.

The Front Row application performs four different functions:

✦ **Watching DVD movies with DVD Player:** If you already loaded a DVD into your optical drive, you can watch it. (Sorry, your MacBook doesn't load the DVD for you. I guess *some* things have to remain manually driven for a few years yet.)

✦ **Viewing photos and slideshows:** Front Row calls upon iPhoto so that you can see your albums, film rolls, and slideshows.

✦ **Displaying TV shows, movies, videos, and movie trailers:** You can choose most types of video you download from the iTunes Music Store or save to your Movies folder. If your laptop has a high-speed broadband connection to the Internet, you can also watch movie trailers straight from the Apple Web site.

✦ **Coaxing your favorite music and podcasts from your iTunes library:** Find your songs and playlists available from Front Row.

All this is accomplished with the awesome infrared Apple remote you see in Figure 5-3. It's as simple to use as an iPod Shuffle!

Volume/menu up

Previous/rewind

Volume/menu down

IR window

Next/fast forward

Select/play/pause

Menu

**Figure 5-3:**
Is it an antique iPod Shuffle? No, it's the Apple Remote!

To launch the application, press the Menu button on the remote. As long as your MacBook is on, Front Row runs automatically. To put your laptop to sleep after a night of fun, press and hold the Select/play/pause button.

Table 5-1 includes the important functions of the Apple remote in Front Row.

| Table 5-1 | Using the Apple Remote in Front Row |
|---|---|
| *Action* | *Purpose* |
| Menu | Press to launch Front Row or to return to the previous menu. |
| Volume/menu down | Press to navigate down through menu options or to lower the volume while media is playing. |
| Volume/menu up | Press to navigate up through menu options or to raise the volume while media is playing. |
| Select/play/pause | Press to select a menu item, or play or pause media from within iTunes, DVD Player, QuickTime, or iPhoto. |
| Next/fast forward | Press to skip to the next song or DVD chapter or hold down to fast-forward through a song. |
| Previous/rewind | Press to skip to the previous song or DVD chapter, or hold down to rewind a song. |

You can also go the mundane route and use keyboard shortcuts to control Front Row. (But it's nowhere near as cool.) Table 5-2 explains the keyboard shortcuts.

| Table 5-2 | Using the Keyboard in Front Row |
| --- | --- |
| *Action* | *Keyboard Equivalent* |
| Menu | ⌘+Esc to enter the menu; Esc to exit it |
| Volume/menu down | Down arrow |
| Volume/menu up | Up arrow |
| Select/play/pause | Space or Return |
| Next/fast forward | Right arrow |
| Previous/rewind | Left arrow |

Your Apple remote is supported by only a handful of applications at the time of this writing — for example, you can't use it as a presentation aide in PowerPoint or as a playback controller in GarageBand. However, Apple may continue to add functionality to the Apple remote in the future, so check the Apple remote section of Snow Leopard's online help system to keep tabs on what's happening!

**Book II
Chapter 5**

**Fun with Photo
Booth and
Front Row**

# Chapter 6: Keeping Track with the Address Book

## In This Chapter

✔ Adding contact cards

✔ Editing contacts

✔ Using contact information throughout Mac OS X

✔ Creating and e-mailing groups

✔ Printing contacts

✔ Importing and exporting vCards

**D**o you have a well-thumbed address book stuck in a drawer of your office desk? Or do you have a wallet or purse stuffed with sticky notes and odd scraps of paper, each of which bears an invaluable e-mail address or phone number? If so, you can finally set yourself free and enjoy the "Paperless Lifestyle" of the new millennium with the revolutionary new Rauncho Digital Address Book! As seen on TV! Only $29.95 — and it doubles as an indestructible garden hose! But wait! If you order now, we'll also send you . . . .

Of course, you and I would tune that stuff out as soon as we heard, "As seen on TV" — but, believe it or not, the Rauncho Digital Address Book does exist (after a fashion), and you already have one on your MacBook. It's called the *Address Book,* and in this chapter, I show you how to store and retrieve all your contact data, including iChat information, photographs, and much more.

(And before you ask, operators are *not* standing by.)

## Hey, Isn't the Address Book Just a Part of Mail?

It's true that in early versions of Mac OS X, Address Book was relegated to the minor leagues and usually appeared only when you asked for it within Mail. Although it could be run as a separate application, there was no convenient route to the Address Book from the Desktop, so most Mac owners never launched it as a standalone.

Now, however, the Address Book appears in the limelight, earning a default location in the Dock and available whenever you need it. Although the Address Book can still walk through a meadow hand-in-hand with Mail, it also flirts with other Mac OS X applications and can even handle some basic telephony chores all by itself through the use of Services.

Figure 6-1 illustrates the default face of the Address Book, complete with a personal address card: your own contact information, which you enter within the Setup Assistant that I mention in Book II, Chapter 1. This card carries a special me tag on your thumbnail image (indicating that it's your personal card) as well as a suave-looking silhouette next to your name in the Name column. Other Mac OS X applications use the data in your card to automatically fill out your personal information in all sorts of documents. (In Figure 6-1, I added a number of well-known friends as well . . . a few TV characters, a composer or two. You know the drill.)

Click to show and hide Group and Name columns

**Figure 6-1:**
Greetings
from the
Mac OS X
Address
Book!

Drag to resize columns

Note that when you move your mouse cursor over the Group and Name column dividers, the cursor changes to a double arrow. This indicates that when you click and drag the divider, you can resize the Group and Name columns as well as the display pane on the right. Plus, you can click the two buttons at the upper-left corner (underneath the window controls) to hide or show the Group and Name columns.

# Entering Contact Information

Unless you actually meet and hire a group of DataElves — see the sidebar, "I gotta type (or retype) that stuff?" — you have to add contacts to your Address Book manually. Allow me to demonstrate here how to create a new contact within your Address Book:

*1.* **Launch Address Book from the Dock by clicking its icon.**

   The icon looks like an old-fashioned paper Address Book with an @ symbol on the cover.

*2.* **Press the ⌘+N shortcut to create a new contact. Alternatively, choose File⇨New Card or click the Add a New Person button at the bottom of the Name column.**

   Address Book displays the template that you see in Figure 6-2, with the First name field highlighted and ready for you to type.

*3.* **Enter the contact's first name and press Tab to move to the Last name field.**

*4.* **Continue entering the corresponding information in each field, pressing Tab to move through the fields.**

   If a field isn't applicable (for example, if a person has no home page), just press Tab again to skip it. You can press Return to add extra lines to the Address field.

**Book II
Chapter 6**

**Keeping Track with
the Address Book**

**Figure 6-2:**
"Hey, I don't know anyone named *First Last!*"

> ○ ○ ○               Address Book
>
> | Group | Name | |
> |---|---|---|
> | All Contacts | No Name | First Last |
> | | Antonio Vivaldi | Company |
> | | Apple Inc. | ☐ Company |
> | | Bruce Wayne | |
> | | Dick Grayson | |
> | | Gomez Addams | work ▾ phone |
> | | Hawkeye Pierce | mobile ▾ phone |
> | | Mark Chambers | work ▾ email |
> | | Wolfgang Mozart | friend ▾ name |
> | | | assistant ▾ name |
> | | | work ▾ user name AIM ▾ |
> | | | work ▾ Street |
> | | | City State ZIP |
> | | | Country |
> | | | Note: |
> | + | + | Edit          9 cards |

Click to add a new person

When you complete certain fields — such as the Address field — a green plus sign pops up to the left of the field. That's the Address Book telling you that there are additional versions of the field that you can enter as well. (Think home and work addresses.) Click this plus sign, and you can enter the other version. For example, if you enter an iChat address for the contact at home, the plus sign appears; click it and then you can enter the contact's work iChat address, too.

You can also add new fields to a card, such as Web addresses, birthdays, maiden names, and the like. To add a new field, click Card⇨Add Field and choose the field you want to add from the menu that appears.

5. **To add a photograph to the card, click Card⇨Choose Custom Image (or drag an image from a Finder window on top of the thumbnail square).**

Address Book displays a sheet that you can use to select the image. Click Choose to display our old friend the Open dialog.

Click the Capture a picture from a video camera button (which bears a snazzy camera icon) to use your MacBook's built-in iSight camera for a quick snapshot.

6. **When you're done, click the Edit button (bottom center) to save the card.**

You can edit the contents of a card at any time by displaying it and clicking the Edit button at the bottom (or by pressing ⌘+L, or even by clicking Edit and choosing the Edit Card menu item).

No need to edit a card to add information to the Note field — just click and type.

You can also add contact cards directly to your Address Book from the Mac OS X Mail application — go figure. Within Mail, click the message (to highlight it) from the person whom you want to add, click the friendly Message menu, and then click Add Sender to Address Book, or press ⌘+Y. Naturally, adding people this way doesn't add their supporting information — just their name and e-mail address (and, if they used Mail on their end to send the message and they have a photo attached to their personal card, their photo gets imported as well). Once again, your nimble fingers have to manually enter the rest. For more on Mail, see Book VI, Chapter 2.

Don't forget to add those fax numbers! If you have an external analog modem, Snow Leopard can fax from any application — just click File and choose Print (or press ⌘+P) as you always have, and then click the PDF button at the bottom of the Print dialog and choose Fax PDF. Mac OS X automatically fills in the address for you, but only if the contact has a fax number entered as part of the contact card.

## "I gotta type (or retype) that stuff?"

In my two-and-a-half decades of travel through the personal computing world, I've noticed one lovely recurring fantasy shared by computer users that keeps cropping up over and over: I call it the *DataElf Phenomenon.* You see, *DataElves* are the hard-working, silicon-based gnomes in tiny green suspenders who magically enter all the information that you want to track into your database (or Address Book, or Quicken, or whatever). They burrow into your papers and presto! — out pops all that data, neatly typed and . . . whoa, Nellie! Let's stop there.

For some reason, computer users seem to forget that *there are no DataElves.* I wish I had a dime for every time I've heard a heartbroken computer user say, "You mean I have to *type* all that stuff *in?*" (My usual retort is, "Affirmative . . . unless you want to pay me a hideous amount to do it for you.") Make no mistake — adding a lifetime's worth of contact information into your Address Book can be several hours of monotonous and mind-bendingly boring work, which is another reason that many computer owners still depend on paper to store all those addresses. But take my word for it, dear reader, your effort is worth it — the next time that you sit down to prepare a batch of Christmas cards or you have to find Uncle Milton's telephone number in a hurry, you *will* appreciate the effort that you made to enter contact information into your Address Book. (Just make sure that you — say it with me — **back up your hard drive.**)

By the way, if you've already entered contact information into another PIM (short for Personal Information Manager), you can reuse that data without retyping everything — that is, as long as your old program can export contacts in vCard format. After you export the records, just drag the vCards into the Address Book window to add them, or import them by pressing ⌘+I. (More on this at the end of this chapter.) Address Book can also import old-fashioned tab-delimited text.

If someone sends you a vCard (look for an attachment with a `.vcf` extension), consider yourself lucky. Just drag the vCard from the attachment window in Mail and drop it in your Address Book; any information that the person wants you to have is added automatically!

To delete a card, click the unlucky name to display the card, click Edit, and then choose Delete Card. Alternatively, press Delete and then Return to confirm the deletion.

## *Using Contact Information*

Okay, after you have your contact information in Address Book, what can you actually *do* with it? Often, all you really need is a quick glance at an address. To display the card for any contact within Address Book, just click the desired entry in the Name column. You can move to the next and previous cards by using the up- and down-arrow keys on your keyboard.

(Oh, and don't forget that you can right-click many items within a card to display menu commands specific to those items.)

But wait, there's more! You can also

✦ **Copy and paste.** The old favorites are still around. You can copy any data from a card (press ⌘+C) and paste it into another open application (press ⌘+V).

✦ **Visit a contact's home page.** Click the contact entry to select it, and click the page link displayed within the card. Safari dutifully answers the call, and next thing you know, you're online and at the home page specified in the entry.

✦ **Send an e-mail message.** If you've already read through Chapter 3 of this minibook, you'll remember the Mac OS X Services feature that I tell you about. Click and drag to select any e-mail address on a card; then click the Address Book menu, click the Services menu, and choose Send To. Bingo! Depending on the information that you select, other services might also be available.

✦ **Add an iChat buddy.** From within iChat, click the Buddies menu and then click Add a Buddy. From the dialog that appears, you can select a contact card that has an Instant Messenger address and add it to your Buddy List.

✦ **Export contacts.** From within the Address Book, select the contacts that you want to export, click File, and then choose Export vCards from the Export submenu. Address Book displays a Save sheet. Navigate to the location where you want to save the cards and click Save.

✦ **Search amongst your contacts.** If you're searching for a specific person and all you have is a phone number or a fragment of an address, click in the Search field at the top right of the Address Book window and type the text. While you continue to enter characters, Address Book shows you how many contacts contain matching characters and displays just those entries in the Name column. Now that's *sassy!* (And convenient. And fast as all get-out.) Check out Figure 6-3, where many of the characters from my favorite TV show are gathered — note that a number of very familiar folks share the same address in Gotham City, and I found them by using the Search field.

Speaking of searching using a contact in the Address Book, Spotlight is also at your beck and call — click a contact to select it, then click the Edit menu and choose Spotlight. *Whoosh!* Snow Leopard searches your entire system for everything related to that contact and displays it in the familiar Spotlight window.

**Figure 6-3:**
Holy Text
Match,
Batman!

# Arranging Your Contact Cards

Address Book also provides you with a method of organizing your cards into groups. A *group* usually consists of folks with a common link, such as your family, friends, co-workers, and others who enjoy yodeling. For example, you could set up a Cell Phone group that you can use when syncing data with your Bluetooth cell phone.

To create a group, choose File⇨New Group or press ⌘+Shift+N. (Using the Hollywood method, click the plus sign button at the bottom of the Group column.) Address Book creates a new entry in the Group column, with a highlighted text box so that you can type the group name. After you type the group name, press Return to save it, and then click and drag the entries that you want to add to the New Group icon.

If you already selected the entries for those contacts that you want to add to the group, choose File⇨New Group from Selection instead. This saves you a step because the group is created and the members are added automatically.

After you create a New Group, you can instantly display members of that group by clicking its icon in the Group column. To return to the display of all your contacts, click the All Groups button.

To further organize your groups, you can drag and drop a group on top of another group. It becomes a subgroup, which is handy for things like branch offices within your company or perhaps relatives to whom you're not speaking at the moment.

Need an even harder-working group? Create a *Smart Group,* which — get this — automatically adds new contacts you create to the proper group, depending on the criteria you specify! To create a Smart Group, follow these steps:

*1.* **Click File and click New Smart Group.**

*2.* **Type a name for the new Smart Group.**

*3.* **Click the Card pop-up menu and choose the item that will trigger the action.**

For example, you can choose to automate a Smart Group according to the contents of each new card, a company name, or a particular city or state.

*4.* **Click the Contains pop-up menu and choose the criteria for the item.**

An item might contain (or not contain) a specific string of characters, or it might have changed in a certain amount of time. To illustrate, one of my hardest-working Smart Groups automatically checks the Company field in every new card for my publisher's company name and adds that contact card to my Wiley Publishing group if a match occurs.

*5.* **To add another criteria line, click the button with the plus sign at the end of the first text field.**

If you decide you have one criteria line too many, click the button with the minus sign next to the offending rule.

*6.* **After your Smart Group criteria are correct, click OK.**

The Smart Group name appears in your group list, complete with a gear icon to indicate its intelligent status. *Voilà!*

Here's another handy feature of an Address Book group: You can send all the members of a group the same e-mail message at one time. Within Mail, simply enter the Group name in the To field in the Compose window, and the same message is sent to everyone. Even Gandalf couldn't do that (but my copy editor bets that Dumbledore could).

## Using Network Directories

I know, I know, I said earlier that you'd have to enter all your contacts yourself — but I was talking about your personal contacts! You can also access three types of external directories from within Address Book:

✦ Mac users working in a Windows network environment can use Exchange 2007 network directories.

✦ If you're a member of a company NetInfo network — and if you don't know, ask your wizened network administrator — you can search network directory servers from within Address Book. These servers are available automatically, so no configuration is necessary. *Sweet.*

✦ You can search Internet-based LDAP directories. Sorry, folks, I know that's pretty cryptic, but others have written entire books on this technology. Again, suffice it to say that your network guru can tell you whether LDAP servers are available to you. (In another blazing display of techno-nerd acronym addiction, LDAP stands for *Lightweight Directory Access Protocol.*) With LDAP, you can search a central company directory from anywhere in the world as long as you have an Internet connection. To configure this feature, click Address Book from the menu and choose Preferences; click the LDAP tab and then click the + (plus sign) button to enter the specific settings for the server that you want to access. Your network administrator or the LDAP server administrator can supply you with these settings.

Book II
Chapter 6

Keeping Track with the Address Book

To search any network directory, you need to create a corresponding directory account. Follow these steps to add a directory account:

1. **Click Address Book⇨Preferences to display the Preferences window.**

2. **Click the Add button to launch the Add Account assistant.**

3. **Click the Account Type pop-up menu to choose the desired species of network directory.**

   Type the required information in the fields that appear. (Your network administrator should be able to provide you with the necessary values.)

4. **Click Create.**

   You'll see the blue network directory entry appear in the Group column.

The rest is easy! Click the Directories entry in the Group column and use the Search field as you normally would. Matching entries display the person's name, e-mail address, and phone number.

"But hey, Mark, what if I'm not online? My company's LDAP directory isn't much good then, right?" Normally, that's true. If you're a mobile user, LDAP information is available to you only when you're online and the LDAP server is available. Ah, but here's a rocking power user tip that'll do the trick for MacBook owners: To make a person's information always available, search the LDAP database and drag the resulting entry from the Directories window to the All group. You'll import the information to your local Address Book — and you'll see it even when you're not online!

## Printing Contacts with Flair

Consider how to print your contacts (for those moments when you need an archaic hard copy). Address Book offers two different formats.

By default, Address Book prints on standard U.S. letter-size paper (8½ x 11 inches) in portrait orientation. You can change these settings right from the Print dialog: Choose File and click Print or press ⌘+P. From the Print dialog, you can choose exotic settings, such as legal-size paper or landscape orientation.

Follow these steps to print your contacts:

*1.* **Press ⌘+P.**

Address Book displays the Print dialog. To show all the settings, click the Expand button next to the Printer field, which carries a downward-pointing triangle.

If you need more than one copy, click in the Copies field to specify the desired number.

Need labels? We've got 'em! Click the Style pop-up menu and choose Mailing Labels to specify what type of label stock you're using on the Layout panel. Click the Label button to sort your labels by name or postal code, choose a font, select a text color, and add an icon or image to your labels. To switch back to a standard contact list, click Style again and then click Lists. (You can also print envelopes and pocket address book pages in a similar manner — just choose the desired entry from the Style pop-up menu.)

*2.* **Select the desired Attributes check boxes to specify which contact card fields you want to appear in your list.**

The Attributes list appears only if you're printing contacts in Lists style.

*3.* **Click the Print button to send the job to the selected printer.**

Alternatively, you can create a PDF file in a specified location — a handy trick to use if you'd rather not be burdened with paper, but you still need to consult the list or give it to others. (*PDF files* are a special document display format developed by Adobe; they display like a printed document but take up minimal space.) To display the contents of a PDF file in Mac OS X, you need only double-click it in the Finder window, and the built-in Preview application is happy to oblige.

# Swapping Bytes with vCards

A *vCard* is a standard file format for exchanging contacts between programs such as Address Book, Microsoft Entourage, Eudora, and the Palm computer desktop. (Heck, if you're lucky enough to have an iPod or iPhone, you can even store vCard data there.) Think of a vCard as an electronic business card that you can attach to an e-mail message, send via File Transfer Protocol (FTP), or exchange with others by using your cellular phone and palmtop computer. vCard files end with the extension .vcf.

In Address Book, you can create a single vCard containing one or more selected entries by choosing File➪Export and choosing Export vCard. Then, as with any other Mac OS X Save dialog, just navigate to the spot where you want the file saved, give it a name, and click Save.

To import vCards into Address Book

+ Drag the vCard files that you've received to Address Book and drop them in the application window.

+ Alternatively, choose File➪Import (or press ⌘+O). From the Open dialog, navigate to the location of the vCard files that you want to add, select them, and then click Open.

# Chapter 7: The Joys of Maintenance

## In This Chapter

- ✔ Deleting applications
- ✔ Using Apple System Profiler
- ✔ Using Activity Monitor and Disk Utility
- ✔ Updating Mac OS X and your drivers
- ✔ Backing up your system
- ✔ Using a disk defragmenter and start-up keys

The title of this chapter really sounds like a contradiction in terms, doesn't it? The concepts of *joy* and *maintenance* are likely mutually exclusive to you — and it's true that most MacBook owners would rather work or play than spend time under the hood, getting all grimy. I understand completely; maintenance is far less sexy than a game like Sims 3 or even an exciting productivity application like Pages.

However, if you do want to work or play uninterrupted by lockups and crashes — yes, believe it or not, the Big X can indeed take a dive if it's not cared for — and you'd like your MacBook to perform like Lance Armstrong, you have to get your hands dirty. That means performing regular maintenance on your hardware, Mac OS X, and your all-important applications, documents, and folders.

As do most techno-types, I actually *enjoy* pushing my system to the limit and keeping it running in top form. And who knows — after you become a Snow Leopard power user, you could find yourself bitten by the maintenance bug as well. In this chapter, I cover how to take care of necessary tune-up chores, step by step.

## Deleting Applications the Common Sense Way

Nothing lasts forever, and that includes your applications. You might no longer need an application, or maybe you need to remove it to upgrade to a new version or to reinstall it. In contrast to Windows XP and Vista, Mac OS X doesn't have an Add or Remove Programs utility for uninstalling software — nor does it need one, because virtually all Macintosh applications are self-contained in a single folder or series of nested folders. (And not by accident . . . keeping everything related to an application within a single folder has always been a rule for Apple software developers since the first days of the Macintosh.) Therefore, removing an application is usually as easy as deleting the contents of the installation folder from your hard drive (for example, removing the Quicken folder to uninstall Quicken).

**Always check the application's README file and documentation for any special instructions before you delete any application's folder!** If you've created any documents in that folder that you want to keep, don't forget to move them before you trash the folder and its contents. In fact, some applications may come complete with their own uninstall utility, so checking the README and documentation may save you unnecessary steps.

Some applications can leave preference files, start-up applications, or driver files in other spots on your disk besides their home folder. When you're uninstalling a program that has support files in other areas, use the Search box in the Finder toolbar to locate other files that might have been created by the application. (I cover this feature in Book II, Chapter 1.) Again, don't forget to check whether an application has an uninstall utility (or an uninstall option available through the original setup application).

For example, Figure 7-1 illustrates a Spotlight search that I've run on Microsoft Office 2008. By searching for the word *office,* I found a number of files created in other folders, such as the Settings file that's in my Preferences folder. Typically, you want to delete the main application folder and then remove these orphans.

**Figure 7-1:** Use Spotlight to locate support files after uninstalling an application.

Spring Cleaning, from Smith Micro ($50; my.smithmicro.com), also has the ability to uninstall a program, as well as a feature that can find and remove orphaned files left from past applications.

# Popping the Hood: Using the System Profiler

Need hard information about your hardware? You might need to determine precisely what hardware is installed in your MacBook for the following reasons:

✦ **If you're working with a technical support person to solve a problem:** This person will usually request information about your system, such as what processor you're running and how much memory you have.

✦ **If you're evaluating an application before you buy it:** You'll want to check its minimum system requirements against the hardware on your laptop.

✦ **If you're considering an upgrade to your MacBook:** You'll likely need to determine how much memory you have, what type it is, and which memory slots are filled. (The same goes for your hard drive.) For more on upgrading your MacBook, thumb through Book VIII, Chapter 2.

Apple provides Mac OS X with an all-in-one hardware and software display tool, aptly named *System Profiler,* which you can find in the Utilities folder within your Applications folder. You can also reach the Profiler through the Apple menu (). Just click About This Mac and then click the More Info button.

As with the folders in a Finder window in List View mode, you can expand or collapse each major heading that appears in a Profiler screen. Just click the triangle that appears to the left of each Contents heading to expand or collapse that heading.

The System Profiler major headings include

✦ **Hardware:** This heading tells you volumes about your hard drives (forgive me, I couldn't help that) as well as specifics concerning your optical drives; modem; AirPort and Bluetooth hardware; graphics hardware; AC power settings; and any FireWire, CardBus, and USB devices connected to your system. Figure 7-2 illustrates the information from my USB screen, with many of the devices expanded so that you can see them. (The text you see at the bottom half of the window is the detailed information on the item that's selected.)

✦ **Network:** This heading shows a listing of your network configuration, active network connections, and other assorted network paraphernalia. You'll probably need this screen only when asked by a technical support person for the network protocols that you're using, but it's handy nonetheless. (You'll find details on your network connection here that you can't find anywhere else in Snow Leopard.)

**Book II
Chapter 7**

**The Joys of
Maintenance**

**Figure 7-2:**
Display information about your Mac's ports and connections.

+ **Software:** Okay, this heading shows something useful to the average human being! This screen lists all the applications, fonts, and preferences recognized on your start-up volume, along with their version numbers. If you're wondering whether you need to update an application with a *patch file* (to fix bugs in the software) or update a file from the developer, you can look here to check the current version number for the application. You also get a rather boring list of the *extensions* (or drivers) used by Mac OS X applications. Logs are usually valuable only to tech support personnel; they document recent lockups, application crashes, and even system crashes.

# Tracking Performance with Activity Monitor

Our next stop in Maintenance City is a useful little application dubbed *Activity Monitor,* which is specially designed to show you just how hard your CPU, hard drive, network equipment, and memory modules are working behind the scenes. To run Activity Monitor, open the Utilities folder in your Applications folder.

To display each different type of usage, click the tabs in the lower half of the window; the lower pane changes to reflect the desired type (see Figure 7-3). For example, if you click System Memory, you see the amount of unused memory; click CPU or Network to display real-time usage of your MacBook's CPU and network connections.

# Processes for dummies

"Mark, what's that arcane-looking list doing in the middle of the Activity Monitor window in Figure 7-3?" I'm glad you asked. A *process* is a discrete task (either visible or invisible) that Snow Leopard performs in order to run your applications. (Some processes are executed by Snow Leopard just to keep itself running.) For example, the Dock and Finder are actually processes, as are Adobe Acrobat and iPhoto.

You can quit a specific process within Activity Monitor. Just click the offending process in the

list and then click the Quit Process button on the Activity Monitor toolbar. But tread carefully, Mr. Holmes, for there's danger afoot. For example, deleting a system process (such as the Dock or Finder) can result in *all* of Mac OS X locking up! Therefore, delete a process *only if instructed to do so by a support technician.* If you need to terminate a misbehaving application, click the Apple menu and choose Force Quit instead.

**Figure 7-3:** Keep tabs on Snow Leopard and what you're running.

You can also display a separate window with your CPU usage; choose Window⇨CPU Usage or press ⌘+2. There are three different types of central processing unit (CPU, which is commonly called the "brain" of your MacBook) displays available from Activity Monitor:

✦ **Floating CPU window:** This is the smallest display of CPU usage; the higher the CPU usage, the higher the reading on the monitor. You can arrange the floating window in horizontal or vertical mode from the Window menu.

✦ **CPU Usage window:** This is the standard CPU monitoring window, which uses a blue thermometer-like display. The display works the same as the floating window.

✦ **CPU History window:** This scrolling display uses different colors to help indicate the percentage of CPU time being used by your applications (green) and what percentage is being used by Snow Leopard to keep things running (red). You can use the History window to view CPU usage over time.

The CPU usage and history displays can also be displayed in the Dock.

You have two bars in your CPU usage monitor because you're running one of Apple's multiple-core Intel processors in your MacBook. More than one engine is under the hood!

Whichever type of display you choose, you can drag the window anywhere that you like on your Mac OS X Desktop. Use the real-time feedback to determine how well your system CPU is performing when you're running applications or performing tasks in Mac OS X. If this meter stays peaked for long periods of time while you're using a range of applications, your processor(s) are running at full capacity.

You can even monitor CPU, network, hard drive, or memory usage right from the Dock! Choose View➪Dock Icon; then choose what type of real-time graph you want to display in your Dock. (Feeling like a Snow Leopard power user yet? I thought so.) When you're monitoring CPU usage from the Dock, the green portion of the bar indicates the amount of processor time used by application software, and the red portion of the bar indicates the CPU time given to the Mac OS X operating system (same as how this works in the CPU History window).

Note, however, that seeing your CPU capacity at its max doesn't necessarily mean that you need a faster CPU or a new computer. For example, when I'm running memory-ravenous applications, such as Photoshop or Word, the Activity Monitor on my MacBook Pro is often pegged (indicating maximum use) for several seconds at a time. The rest of the time, it barely moves. Whether a computer is actually fast enough for you and the applications that you run is more of a subjective call on your part.

# Fixing Things with the Disk Utility

Another important application in your maintenance toolbox is Disk Utility, which you find — no surprise here — in the Utilities folder within your Applications folder. When you first run this program, it looks something like Figure 7-4, displaying all the physical disks and volumes on your system.

The Disk Utility application has its own toolbar that you can toggle on and off. Click the lozenge-shaped button at the upper-right corner of the window to display or hide the toolbar.

**Book II**
**Chapter 7**

The Joys of
Maintenance

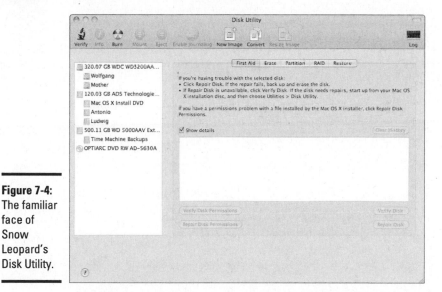

**Figure 7-4:**
The familiar face of Snow Leopard's Disk Utility.

## Displaying the goods on your disks

The volume tree structure on the left of the Disk Utility window lists both the physical disks and the partitions that you've set up. A *partition* is nothing more than another word for *volume,* which is the formatted section of a disk that contains data. A single physical hard drive can contain several partitions. The information display at the bottom of the Disk Utility window contains data about both the volumes and the partitions on your hard drive.

To illustrate: On my system, clicking the drive labeled 320.07 GB (the physical hard drive at the top of the tree) displays a description of the drive itself, including its total capacity, interface (connection type), and whether the drive is internal or external. (See Figure 7-5.)

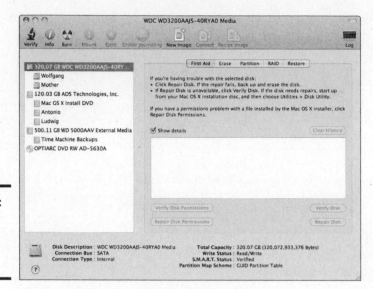

**Figure 7-5:**
Display
data on a
physical
drive.

Clicking the tree entry for Wolfgang, however — that's the name of the partition that I created when I formatted the drive — displays information about the type of formatting, the total capacity of the partition and how much of that is used, and the number of files and folders stored on the partition (as shown at the bottom of Figure 7-6).

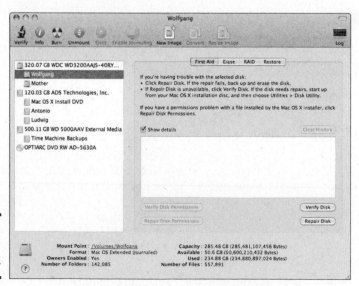

**Figure 7-6:**
Display data
on a volume.

# So what's a disk image?

You might have noticed the New Image button on the Disk Utility toolbar (or the image creation commands on the File⇨New submenu). If you're wondering what a *disk image* is, you've come to the right place. Think of a disk image as a file that looks (and acts) like an external storage device within Snow Leopard; for example, a mounted disk image operates much like a CD or DVD, and it can be ejected just as a disc can. Images can be read-only (same as a standard CD-ROM or DVD-ROM) or they can be created blank (same as an empty hard drive), ready to accept files and folders that you copy using the Finder.

So what are images used for? They're great for storing data that would normally have to be loaded from a CD or DVD (a great convenience if you don't want to lug optical media along with you during a vacation). Remember, a disk image acts just the same as removable storage media as far as Snow Leopard's concerned. Many Mac Web sites also offer images as download files because a simple double-click is all that's necessary to automatically mount a disk image. (Software developers like words such as *fast* and *simple* when offering their shareware and demo applications to the public.)

Finally, images are often used to create simple archives of little-used data: The images can be burned to CD/DVD or even copied to other hard drives. Oh, and don't forget the security aspect — you can choose to encrypt the data stored in an image, protecting it from prying eyes. (However, I don't recommend using disk images to create full backups of your MacBook's hard drives; more on this in the section "Hitching a ride on the Time Machine," later in the chapter.) To restore a disk image — to move the files back to your hard drive — you can use the Restore tab in Disk Utility.

If you're intrigued, I encourage you to click New Image on the Disk Utility toolbar (see Figure 7-5) and create a simple, unencrypted blank disk image on your Desktop. Then you can experiment with it. A disk image can be ejected to unmount it (same as with a CD/DVD, an iPod, or a USB Flash drive), and you can delete the image file at any time. (Just remember not to delete it if it contains anything you want to keep, of course . . . but you knew that already.)

## *Playing doctor with First Aid*

From the First Aid pane, you can use Disk Utility to *verify* (or check) any disk (well, *almost* any disk) for errors, as well as repair most errors that it finds. Here are the two exceptions when the buttons are disabled:

✦ **The start-up disk:** Disk Utility can't repair the *start-up disk* — that's Mac talk for the boot drive that contains the Mac OS X system you're using at the moment — which makes sense if you think about it, because that drive is currently being used!

If you have multiple operating systems on multiple disks, you can boot from another Mac OS X installation on another drive to check your current start-up disk. Or you can boot your system from the original Mac OS X installation DVD and run Disk Utility from the Installation menu.

✦ **Write-protected disks:** Although you can use the Disk Utility to verify CDs and DVDs, Disk Utility can't repair them. (Sound of my palm slapping my forehead.)

You usually can't repair a disk that has *open* files that are currently being used. If you're running an application from a drive or you've opened a document that's stored on that drive, you probably can't repair that drive.

You can also elect to verify and repair *permissions* (or *privileges*) on a disk; these are the read/write permissions that I discuss in detail in Book III, Chapter 6. If you can't save or move a file that you should be able to access, I recommend checking that drive for permissions problems. Although you can't fix disk errors on a boot drive, you can verify and repair permissions on any volume that contains a Mac OS X installation (whether it was used to boot your MacBook or not).

In order to verify or repair, you must be logged in as an admin-level user.

To verify or repair a drive, first select the target volume/partition in the list at the left. To check the contents of the drive and display any errors, click the Verify Disk button. Or, to verify the contents of the drive and fix any problems, click the Repair Disk button. (I usually just click Repair Disk because an error-free disk needs no repairs.) Disk Utility displays any status or error messages in the scrolling list; if you have eagle eyes, you'll note that the window can be resized so that you can expand it to display more messages. (You can also drag the dot between the left and right panes to expand the list.)

I generally check my disks once every two or three days. If your MacBook is caught by a power failure or Mac OS X locks up, however, it's a good idea to immediately check disks after you restart your laptop. (Don't forget that the start-up volume is automatically checked and repaired, if necessary.)

A number of very good commercial disk repair utilities are on the market. My favorite is Drive Genius 2 from Prosoft Engineering ($99; www.prosoft eng.com) — however, Disk Utility does a good job on its own, and it's free.

## Erasing without seriously screwing up

"Danger, Will Robinson! Danger!" That's right, Robot, it is indeed very easy to seriously screw up and get "Lost in Erase." (Man, I can't believe I actually typed such a bad pun. I have no shame.) Anyway, it's time for another of Mark's Maxims. To paraphrase the rules for handling a firearm responsibly:

*Never* **click the Erase tab unless you mean to use it.**

Figure 7-7 illustrates the Erase controls within Disk Utility. You need to erase a disk or volume only when you want to *completely wipe* the contents of that existing disk or volume. You can also erase a rewritable CD (CD-RW) or DVD (DVD-RW, DVD+RW, or DVD-RAM) from this pane.

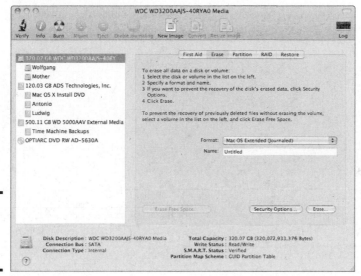

**Figure 7-7:**
The Disk Utility Erase controls.

✦ Erasing an *entire disk* deletes *all volumes* on the disk and creates a single new, empty volume.

✦ Erasing a *volume* wipes only the *contents of that specific volume,* leaving all other volumes on the physical disk untouched.

To erase, follow these steps:

*1.* **Click the disk or volume icon that you want to erase from the list on the left side of the screen.**

*2.* **Click the Erase tab.**

*3.* **Click the format that you want to use from the Format pop-up menu.**

   *Always* choose Mac OS Extended (Journaled) entry from the Format list unless you have a specific reason to use the MS-DOS File System (for compatibility with PCs running Windows) or the UNIX File System (for compatibility with UNIX/Linux machines). In some cases, Disk Utility will force you to choose the Mac OS Extended entry instead, but the end result is the same. Note that you do not need to format a disk or volume with the MS-DOS File System just to read a file from a PC system — Mac OS X recognizes MS-DOS removable media (such as a USB drive formatted under Windows) without a problem.

**4.** **In the Name field, type the name for the volume.**

If you're erasing an existing volume, the default is the existing name.

**5.** **If you're worried about security, click Security Options and specify the method you want to use.**

By default, this is set to Don't Erase Data, so Disk Utility doesn't actually overwrite any data while formatting; instead, it simply trashes the existing directory, rendering that data unreachable. *Or is it?* With some third-party disk utilities, some unscrupulous bum could actually recover your files if you choose, so you can specify alternative, more secure methods of erasing a disk or volume. Unfortunately, these more secure erasure methods can take a horrendous amount of time.

Therefore, it's okay to use the Don't Erase Data option unless you want to make sure that nothing can be recovered, or use the Zero Out Data to take a more secure route with the least amount of extra waiting. For example, you'd want to use the Zero Out Data option if you're selling your MacBook on eBay and you're formatting the drive for the new owner. If you're really set on the tightest, government-quality security, select either 7-Pass Erase or 35-Pass Erase . . . but make sure you have plenty of time to spare!

You can even click Erase Free Space to wipe the supposedly "clean" areas of your drive *before* you format. Man, talk about airtight security! Again, the Zero Out method is the fastest.

**6.** **Click the Erase button.**

In the sheet that appears, click Erase to confirm that you do actually want to do the deleterious deed.

## Partitioning the right way

From time to time, just about everyone wishes he or she had additional volumes handy for organizing files and folders, or at least a little extra space on a particular partition. If you find yourself needing another volume on a disk — or if you need to resize the total space on existing volumes on a disk — click the Partition tab within Disk Utility to display the controls that you see in Figure 7-8. (Make sure that you select a *disk* and not a volume.) From here, you can choose a volume scheme, creating anywhere from 1 to 16 volumes on a single disk.

You can't monkey around with the partitions on a start-up disk because Mac OS X is currently running on that disk. (Think about removing your own appendix, and you get the idea.) Also, if you resize an existing volume, you may lose files and folders on that volume — Disk Utility prompts you for permission, but it's always a good idea to back up a partition before you resize it!

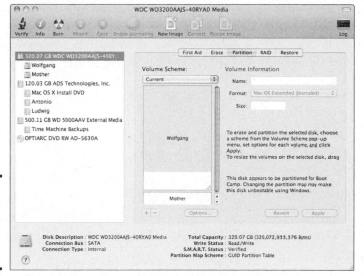

**Figure 7-8:**
The Disk
Utility
Partitioning
controls.

To set up the partitions on a disk, follow these steps:

*1.* **From the Partition pane within Disk Utility, click the disk icon (left side of the pane) that you want to partition.**

*2.* **Click the Volume Scheme pop-up menu and choose the total number of volumes that you want on the selected disk.**

*3.* **Click the first volume block in the partition list (under the Volume Scheme pop-up menu) to select it.**

I have two partitions set for this disk, as you can see.

*4.* **Click in the Name field and enter the name for the selected volume.**

*5.* **From the Format pop-up menu, choose a format for the volume.**

*Always* use Mac OS Extended or Mac OS Extended (Journaled) from the Format menu unless you have a specific reason to use the MS-DOS File System (for compatibility with PCs running Windows) or the UNIX File System (for compatibility with UNIX/Linux machines).

*6.* **Type a total size for this volume in the Size field.**

*7.* **After you set up your first volume partition, select the Locked for Editing check box to prevent any further changes to that volume.**

*8.* **If you're creating multiple volumes, click the next volume block to select it and repeat Steps 4–7.**

*9.* **To delete a partition from your new scheme, click the unwanted volume and then click the Delete button to remove it.**

If the partition is locked, clear the Locked for Editing check box before deleting it.

10. **To split a partition from your new scheme into two volumes, click the desired volume and then click the Split button.**

Some folks create multiple volumes so that they can boot from multiple versions of Snow Leopard — like us author types.

If the partition is locked, clear the Locked for Editing check box before splitting it.

11. **After everything is set to your liking, click the Apply button to begin the process.**

If you suddenly decide against a partition change, click the Revert button to return to the original existing partition scheme.

The Revert button is available only before you click the Partition button!

If you have more than one partition, check out the bar(s) with a handle separating the volumes in the partition list. If you leave all your partitions unlocked (by leaving the Locked for Editing check box disabled), you can click and drag these separator bars to dynamically resize the volumes. This makes it easy to adjust the individual volume sizes for the disk until you get precisely the arrangement you want. If a volume is locked, it can't be resized dynamically in this fashion.

## *RAID has nothing to do with insects*

The next stop on the Disk Utility hayride isn't for everyone — as a matter of fact, only a Mac OS X power user with a roomful of hardware is likely to use it. RAID, *Redundant Array of Independent/Inexpensive Disks,* is actually what it says. In normal human English, a *RAID set* is a group of multiple separate disks, working together as a team. RAID can

✦ **Improve the speed of your system**

✦ **Help prevent disk errors from compromising or corrupting your data**

The RAID controls within Disk Utility are illustrated in Figure 7-9. (Note that I've turned on the Disk Utility toolbar as well, just to show you what it looks like.) You need at least two additional hard drives on your system besides the start-up disk, which I don't recommend that you use in a RAID set.

To set up a RAID array in Mac OS X, follow these steps:

1. **From the RAID tab of Disk Utility, click and drag the disks from the list at the left to the Disk box at the right.**

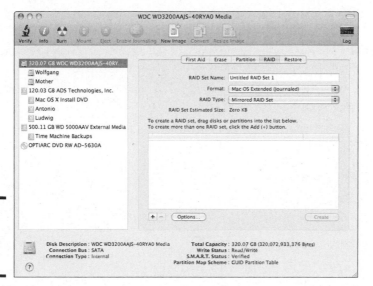

**Figure 7-9:**
The Disk
Utility RAID
controls.

2. **Click the RAID Type pop-up menu to specify the type of RAID that you need.**

   • *Striped RAID Set:* Choosing this can speed up your hard drive performance by splitting data between multiple disks.

   • *Concatenated RAID Set:* Choosing this allows several volumes (or even multiple disks) to appear as one volume within Snow Leopard.

   • *Mirrored RAID Set:* Choosing this increases the reliability of your storage by creating a mirror backup of that data across multiple disks.

3. **Click in the RAID Set Name field and type the name for your RAID set.**

4. **From the Volume Format pop-up menu, choose a format for the volumes.**

   *Always* use Mac OS Extended or Mac OS Extended (Journaled) from the Volume Format list unless you have a specific reason to use the MS-DOS File System (for compatibility with PCs running Windows) or the UNIX File System (for compatibility with UNIX/Linux machines). Journaling helps reduce the amount of disk fragmentation and also helps speed up your hard drive's performance.

5. **Click the Create button.**

# Updating Mac OS X

As any good software developer should, Apple constantly releases improvements to Mac OS X in the form of software updates. These updates can include all sorts of fun stuff, like

+ **Bug fixes**
+ **Improvements and new features**
+ **Enhanced drivers**
+ **Security upgrades**
+ **Firmware upgrades**

Apple makes it easy to keep Mac OS X up-to-date with the Software Update controls in System Preferences.

You don't even have to display the System Preferences window to check for new software updates manually. Click the Apple menu in the Finder menu bar and then choose Software Update to perform a manual check immediately.

To check for new updates periodically, display the Software Update pane in System Preferences and click the Scheduled Check tab. Select the Check for Updates check box and choose how often you want these updates from the pop-up menu. (I suggest at least weekly, if not daily.) For a manual check, make sure that you're connected to the Internet and then click the Check Now button.

To download updates automatically, mark the Download Important Updates in the Background check box to enable it; the Big X politely downloads the updates behind the scenes and then alerts you that they're ready to be installed. (With automatic downloading disabled, Mac OS X displays any available updates with short descriptions, and you can toggle the installation of a specific update by selecting or deselecting the check box next to it.)

I recommend installing all updates, even for hardware that you don't have yet. For example, I always install AirPort updates even though I don't use an AirPort connection at home. The reason? Often, the functionality covered by an update may include system software that you do use, so you still benefit from installing it. (Also, when I'm on the road with my MacBook and I do turn on AirPort, I'll have the latest software.)

After you specify the updates that you want to install, click the Install button to begin the update process. You might have to reboot after everything has been installed.

To see which updates you've installed already, click the Installed Updates tab on the Software Update pane in System Preferences.

# I Demand That You Back Up Your Hard Drive

I know we're friends, but there's no excuse for not backing up your data. The more valuable and irreplaceable your documents are, the more heinous it is to risk losing them. (I don't get to use the word *heinous* in many of my books, but it fits *really* well here.)

Although Apple does include the ability to create *disk images* and restore them in the Disk Utility (see the "So what's a disk image?" sidebar, earlier in this chapter), I don't recommend that you use disk images as your comprehensive backup solution. (Insert sound of stunned silence here.) That's because the restore process can be confusing, and the disk image method doesn't offer the level of control that you need when it comes to backing up and restoring individual files and folders (or selectively backing up by date or recent use).

**Book II
Chapter 7**

**The Joys of Maintenance**

If you do create backup datasets using disk images, you can restore them from the Restore tab in Disk Utility. You can also restore from a volume — typically, a volume you want to restore would be saved on a DVD or an external hard drive.

"Okay, Mark, what do I use to back up my valuable data?" Well, good citizen, only a bona fide backup application gives you such flexibility and convenience . . . and that's why Snow Leopard power users turn to *Time Machine,* a feature that makes restoring files as easy as pointing and clicking!

## Hitching a ride on the Time Machine

If you enable backups through Snow Leopard's Time Machine feature, you can literally move backward through the contents of your MacBook's hard drive, selecting and restoring all sorts of data. Files and folders are ridiculously easy to restore — and I mean easier than *any* restore you've ever performed, no matter what the operating system or backup program. Time Machine can even handle things like deleted Address Book entries and photos you've sent to the Trash from iPhoto!

Because Time Machine should be an important and integral part of every Mac owner's existence, the Time Machine icon is included in the Dock. (Apple is not messing around!)

Before you can use Time Machine, it must be enabled within the Time Machine pane in System Preferences. I cover these settings in detail in Chapter 3 of Book III. I also recommend that you invest in an external USB or FireWire hard drive to hold your Time Machine backups.

Here's how you can turn back time, step-by-step, to restore a file that you deleted or replaced in a folder:

*1.* **Open the folder that contained the file you want to restore.**

*2.* **In a separate window, open your Applications folder and launch the Time Machine application, or click the Time Machine icon in the Dock.**

The oh-so-ultra-cool Time Machine background appears behind your folder, complete with its own set of buttons at the bottom of the screen (as shown in Figure 7-10). On the right, you see a timeline that corresponds to the different days and months included in the backups that Snow Leopard has made.

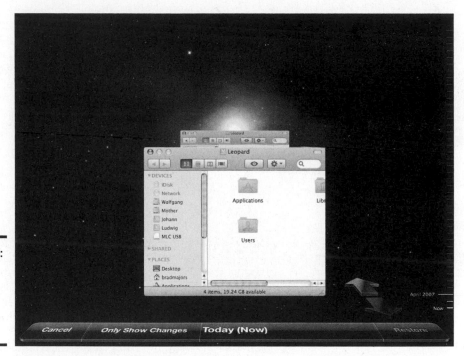

**Figure 7-10:** Yes, Time Machine really *does* look like this!

*3.* **Click within the timeline to jump directly to a date (displaying the folder's contents on that date).**

Alternatively, use the Forward and Back arrows at the right to move through the folder's contents through time. (You should see the faces of Windows users when you "riffle" through your folders to locate something you deleted several weeks ago!)

The backup date of the items you're viewing appears in the button bar at the bottom of the screen.

4. **After you locate the file you want to restore, click it to select it.**

5. **Click the Restore button at the right side of the Time Machine button bar.**

   If you want to restore all the contents of the folder, click the Restore All button instead.

Time Machine returns you to the Finder, with the newly restored file now appearing in the folder. *OUTstanding!*

To restore specific data from your Address Book or images from iPhoto, launch the desired application first and then launch Time Machine. Instead of riffling a Finder window, you can move through time within the application window.

For simple backup and restore protection, Time Machine is all that a typical MacBook owner at home is likely to ever need. Therefore, a very easy Mark's Maxim to predict:

**Connect an external hard drive and turn on Time Machine. *Do it now.* Don't make a heinous mistake.**

How about that? I got to use *heinous* twice in one chapter.

## Using other backup solutions

Time Machine is indeed awesome, but some MacBook owners prefer a more traditional automated backup and restore process — one that doesn't involve running the Time Machine application and navigating through the files and folders on a drive. For example, a person backing up a Mac acting as a Web server or iTunes media server would much rather restore the entire contents of a volume automatically, in bulk, or create a custom backup/restore schedule that safeguards only certain files and folders.

If you're dead-set against Time Machine, you can turn to a commercial backup application for your salvation — my personal recommendation is EMC Retrospect, from EMC (www.retrospect.com). This well-written "software bungee cord" has saved my posterior more than once.

Using EMC Retrospect is cheap security, but if you can't afford it at the moment, take a second to at least back up your most important documents by copying them to a rewriteable CD or DVD or a USB flash drive. With this poor man's backup, even if you lose your entire hard drive, you can still restore what matters the most.

# 1 Further Demand That You Defragment

Defragmenting your hard drive can significantly improve its performance. Using a defragmenter scans for little chunks of a file that are spread out across the surface of your hard drive and then arranges them to form a contiguous file. After a file has been optimized in this way, it's far easier and faster for Mac OS X to read than reassembling a fragmented file.

However, Apple dropped the ball on this one and didn't include a defragmenter with Mac OS X. Luckily, many third-party disk utilities (such as the aforementioned Drive Genius 2 from Prosoft Engineering) also include a defragmenting feature. If you have a defragmenter, I recommend that you use it once a month.

# Special Start-Up Keys for Those Special Times

Mac OS X includes a number of special keys that you can use during the boot process. These keys really come in handy when you need to force your operating system to do something that it normally wouldn't, such as boot from a CD instead of the hard drive.

✦ **To boot from a CD or DVD:** Restart your MacBook while pressing the C key. This is a great way to free your startup volume when you want to test it or optimize it using a commercial utility.

✦ **To eject a recalcitrant disc that doesn't show up on the Desktop:** Restart Mac OS X and press the Media Eject key as soon as you hear that magnificent startup chord.

✦ **To use your MacBook as an external hard drive (also known as Target mode):** Connect the two Macs using a FireWire cable and then hold down the T key on the MacBook keyboard while restarting or booting your laptop.

✦ **To force your Mac to boot in Mac OS X:** Hold down the X key while restarting or booting the MacBook.

✦ **To display a system boot menu:** Hold down the Option key while restarting or booting the MacBook, and you can choose which operating system you want to use.

✦ **To prevent start-up applications from running during login:** Hold down the Shift key while you click the Login button on the Login screen. If you don't see the Login screen during startup, just hold down Shift while Mac OS X boots until the Finder menu appears.

# Crave the Newest Drivers

No chapter on maintenance would be complete without a reminder to keep your hardware drivers current. *Drivers* are simply programs that allow your MacBook to control hardware devices, such as an external SATA (eSATA) card that you've added to your laptop. The Mac OS X Software Update feature that I discuss earlier, in the section "Updating Mac OS X," provides most of the drivers that you need for things like printers, USB and FireWire peripherals, and digital cameras, but it's still very important to check those manufacturer Web sites.

As can the software updates from Apple, updated drivers can fix bugs and even add new features to your existing hardware, which is my definition of getting something for nothing.

**Book II
Chapter 7**

**The Joys of
Maintenance**

# Chapter 8: Getting Help for the Big X

## In This Chapter

↙ **Using the Mac OS X Help Center**

↙ **Searching for specific help**

↙ **Getting help in applications**

↙ **Finding other help resources**

Whether the voice echoes from a living room, home office, or college computer lab, it's all too familiar: a call for help. No matter how well written the application or how well designed the operating system, sooner or later you're going to need support. That goes for everyone from the novice to the experienced MacBook owner to the occasional e-mail user to the most talented software developer.

In this short but oh-so-important chapter, I lead you through the various help resources available within Mac OS X as well as native Mac OS X applications. I show you how to tap additional resources from Apple, and I also point you to other suppliers of high-quality (as well as even questionable) assistance from sources on the Internet and in your local area.

## Displaying the Help Viewer Window

Your first line of defense is the Mac OS X Help Viewer, as shown in Figure 8-1. To display the Help Viewer from the Finder menu, click Help and choose Mac Help; or you can press the ⌘+? keyboard shortcut. This Help menu is context sensitive, so it contains different menu items when you're working inside an application.

As shown in Figure 8-1, the Help Viewer is divided into three sets of controls:

✦ **Toolbar:** The toolbar includes navigational controls (Back, Forward, and Home buttons), an Action button (where you can print a topic or change the text size), and the Ask a Question (or Search) text box. On the far right, you see an Index link; click it to display an alphabetical index of help topics.

✦ **Quick Clicks:** Clicking these links takes you directly to some of the most frequently asked Help topics for the Finder (or the application you're using), such as Connecting to the Internet and Switching from Windows. To use a Quick Click, just click once on the question that you want to pursue.

✦ **Apple Web site link:** Click this link to display the latest Mac OS X news and the latest Help topics from the Apple Web site.

Toolbar                                                        Quick Links

**Figure 8-1:**
The reservoir of Snow Leopard assistance: The Help Viewer.

Apple Web site link

I know that the Help Viewer looks a little sparse at first glance. However, when you realize how much information has to be covered to help someone with an operating system — check out the size of the book you're holding, for instance — you get an idea of why Mac OS X doesn't try to cover everything on one screen. Instead, you get the one tool that does it all: the Spotlight search box.

# Searching for Specific Stuff

To search for the Help topic you need, here are two paths to righteousness:

✦ **From the Finder Help menu:** Wowzers! In Snow Leopard, you don't even have to open the Help Viewer to search for assistance on a specific topic . . . just choose Help from the Finder menu, click in the Search field right there in the menu, and type a keyword or two. (Although you can ask a full-sentence question, I find that the shorter and more concise your search criteria are, the more relevant your results are.) As with the Spotlight search box, you don't need to press Return; just click the topic that sounds the most helpful.

✦ **From the Help Viewer:** Click in the Search text box at the right side of the toolbar, type one or two words that sum up your question, and press Return. Figure 8-2 illustrates a typical set of topics concerning DVD movies.

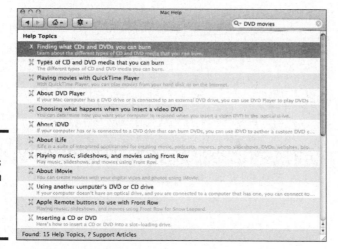

**Figure 8-2:**
The results
of a search
within
the Help
Viewer.

No matter which method you use, the topics are sorted by approximate relevance first. Within the Help Viewer, articles taken from the AppleCare Support section of the Apple Web site appear in the Support Articles portion of the window. (Because Web stuff is going on in the background, you don't see these articles unless your MacBook has an active Internet connection.)

You can double-click any topic to display the topic text, which looks like the text that you see in Figure 8-3.

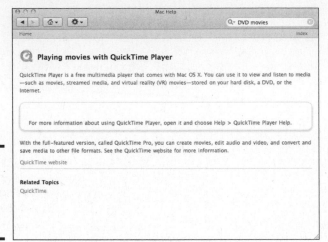

**Figure 8-3:**
A typical topic within the Help Viewer.

To move back to the previous topic that you chose, click the Back button on the Help Viewer toolbar.

## Prodding Apple for the Latest Gossip

As I mention in the earlier section, "Displaying the Help Viewer Window," in this chapter, I heartily recommend that you visit the Apple Web site at www.apple.com and surf wildly to and fro. You'll often pick up on news and reviews that you won't find anywhere else on the Internet.

From the opening Web screen, click the Hot News link on the Apple tab and the Support tab during every visit to the Apple site. These pages give you

✦ Articles about the latest news from Cupertino

✦ Downloads of the latest Mac OS X freeware, shareware, and demo-ware

✦ The *Knowledge Base* (an online searchable troubleshooting reference)

✦ News about upcoming versions of Mac OS X and Apple applications galore

You'll also find Mac OS X product manuals in Adobe Acrobat PDF format and online discussion forums that cover Mac OS X.

# *Calling for Help Deep in the Heart of X*

A number of different help avenues are available within Mac OS X applications as well. They include

✦ **The Help button:** A number of otherwise upstanding Mac OS X windows, dialogs, and System Preference panes include a Help button, as shown in the lower right of Figure 8-4. Click the button marked with ? to display the text for the settings in that dialog or window.

**Figure 8-4:**
Notice the
not-so-well-
camouflaged
Help button.

✦ **Pop-up help for fields and controls:** Most Mac OS X applications display a short line of help text when you hover the mouse pointer on top of a field or control. Sometimes it's just the name of the item; sometimes it's a full descriptive line. Them's the breaks.

✦ **Application-specific help:** Applications typically have their own Help system, which can use the Help Viewer, a separate Help display program, or a HyperText Markup Language (HTML; read that *Web-based*) Help system.

# *Other Resources to Chew On*

Although the Help Viewer can take care of just about any question that you might have about the basic controls and features of Mac OS X, you might also want to turn to other forms of help when the going gets a little rougher. In this last section, I cover resources that you can call on when the Help Viewer just isn't enough.

## Voice support

As of this writing, Apple provides voice technical support for Mac OS X. You can find the number to call in your MacBook's printed manuals or online in the Support section of the Apple Web site. However, exactly when you qualify for voice support and exactly how long it lasts depends on a number of different factors, such as whether you received Mac OS X when you bought a new machine, or whether you purchased a support plan from Apple.

You can also try the general online support site at www.info.apple.com — it's a great starting point for obtaining Mac OS X help.

## Mac publications and resource sites

You can refer to a number of great Mac-savvy publications and resources, both printed and online, for help. My favorites include

✦ **Macworld** (www.macworld.com) and **MacLife** (www.macaddict.com) magazines, both in archaic hard copy and oh-so-slick online versions

✦ **MacGamer** (www.macgamer.com), the online gaming resource for the Macintosh

✦ **VersionTracker** (www.versiontracker.com), an online resource for the latest updates on all sorts of Macintosh third-party applications

✦ **MacFixIt** (www.macfixit.com), a well-respected troubleshooting site devoted to the Mac that offers downloads, news, and discussion areas (a subscription is required for some of the more useful sections of the site)

In most of my books, I mention specific Internet newsgroups that cater to the topic I'm discussing; however, virtually all the Mac-specific newsgroups are devoted to illegally swapping pirated games and applications, so I don't cover them. Also, the help that you receive from individuals in newsgroups is sometimes misguided — and sometimes downright wrong — so take any claims with a grain of salt.

As a general rule, *never* identify yourself or provide your snail-mail or e-mail addresses in a newsgroup post! These messages are public, and they remain hanging around in cyberspace on newsgroup servers for years — you'll be a prime target for spam (or even worse).

## Local Mac outlets and user groups

Finally, you can find local resources in any medium-sized to large town or city: A shop that's authorized by Apple to sell and repair Macintosh computers can usually be counted upon to answer a quick question over the phone or provide more substantial support for a fee. (For example, my local Mac outlet sponsors inexpensive classes for new MacBook owners, and if you can reach an Apple Store, the Genius Bar is a great resource.)

You might also be lucky enough to have a local Macintosh user group that you can join — members can be counted on for free answers to your support questions at meetings and demonstrations. To find a group near you, visit the Apple User Group Support site at `www.apple.com/usergroups` and use the locator.

**Book II
Chapter 8**

**Getting Help for
the Big X**

# Chapter 9: Troubleshooting the X

## In This Chapter

✔ **Mastering the scientific approach**

✔ **Using troubleshooting techniques**

✔ **Performing the radical solutions**

✔ **Checking troubleshooting resources**

Mac OS X Snow Leopard is rugged, stable, and reliable — and as you can read in Chapter 7 of this minibook, practicing regular maintenance can help eliminate problems caused by everything from power failures to faulty software drivers to cats on the keyboard. However, sooner or later you *will* encounter what I like to call *The Dark Moments* . . . a blank screen, a locked MacBook, or an external device that sits there uselessly like an expensive paperweight.

How you handle The Dark Moments defines you as a true Mac OS X power user because most folks seem to fall into one of two categories: Either you panic and beat your head against the wall (which really has little effect on the computer, when you think about it), or you set your brow in grim determination and follow the troubleshooting models that I provide in this chapter to locate (and hopefully fix) the source of the problem.

## Don't Panic!

My friend, this is the first — and **most important** — rule of troubleshooting, and yet another of Mark's Maxims:

**Whatever the problem, you *can* fix it (or get it fixed).**

Most computer owners seem to forget the idea that a hardware or software error can be fixed because they panic — they simply see The Problem, and somehow they feel that they'll never be able to use their computer again.

Although the situation might look grim, don't ignore these facts:

✦ **You don't need to scrap your MacBook.** As long as you haven't taken a hammer or a chainsaw to your laptop, the problem is only temporary. Sure, individual components do fail over time — heck, so do *people* — but the problem is certainly something that can be tracked down and fixed without scrapping your entire computer.

✦ **Don't beat yourself up.** As long as you haven't installed a virus on purpose or deleted half your system files to spite yourself, the problem *isn't* your fault. Sure, it's possible that you might have done something by accident, but don't blame yourself — it happens to everybody.

✦ **Trust your Apple dealer.** As long as an Apple dealer is in your area, you can always get your computer repaired professionally if a component's gone south. (In some cases, professional help is a necessity: For example, swapping out a MacBook motherboard requires an Apple technician, unless you have copious experience.)

✦ **Rely on your backup.** As long as you've made a backup, you won't lose much (if any) work. (You *did* back up your hard drive, didn't you? I harp about backups further in Chapter 7 of this minibook.) I'm talking about a backup to an external hard drive here, using either an application such as Disk Utility or Snow Leopard's Time Machine feature.

Commit these facts to head and heart, and you can rest easy while you track down and attack the *real* enemy — whatever's causing the problem.

## The Troubleshooting Process

When I first conceived this chapter, I had originally decided to divide this section into separate hardware and software troubleshooting procedures. However, that turned out to be impractical because often you won't know whether a problem is caused by hardware or software until you're practically on top of it.

Therefore, here's the complete 12-step troubleshooting process that I designed while working as a consultant and Macintosh hardware technician for 15 years. Feel free to add your own embellishments in the margin or include reminders with sticky notes.

If you're not sure quite what's producing the error, this process is designed to be *linear* — meaning that you should follow it in order — but if you already know that you're having a problem with one specific peripheral or one specific application, feel free to jump to the steps that concern only hardware or software.

It's always a good idea to create a completely default user account for troubleshooting. Techs call this a *vanilla* or *clean* account. You can use the vanilla account to test whether a problem occurs system-wide or is limited to a single user account. For example, this is a great way to determine whether an application is misbehaving because of a corrupted preference file: If the same problem doesn't appear when you use the application with the vanilla account, the culprit is likely the user's copy of the application's preference file. (Follow the instructions provided by the application for resetting or deleting the preference file it creates.)

## Step 1: Always try a simple shutdown

You'd be amazed at how often a *reboot* (the process of shutting down and restarting) can cure a temporary problem. For example, this can fix the occasional lockup in Mac OS X or a keyboard that's not responding because of a power failure. If possible, make sure that you first close any open documents; otherwise, you might lose unsaved work. When troubleshooting, always do a shutdown instead of simply restarting the computer because when Mac OS X shuts down, all the hardware components that make up your system are reset.

If your MacBook is locked tight and you can't use the Shut Down command from the Apple menu ( ), press and hold the Power button on your laptop for a few seconds (which turns your computer off).

Book II
Chapter 9

Troubleshooting the X

## Step 2: Check all cable connections

Check all connections: the AC power cord, as well as any modem or network connections and all cable connections to external peripherals. Look for loose connectors — and if you have a cat or dog, don't forget to check for chew marks. (Yep, that's the voice of experience talking there.) If you've recently replaced a cable — especially a network, Universal Serial Bus (USB), or FireWire cable — replace it with a spare to see whether the problem still occurs.

## Step 3: Retrace your steps

If the problem continues to occur, the next step is to consider what you've done in the immediate past that could have affected your MacBook. Did you install any new software or have you connected a new peripheral? If your MacBook was working fine until you made the change to your system, the problem likely lies in the new hardware or software.

✦ **If you added an external device:** Turn off your MacBook and disconnect the peripheral. Then turn on the laptop to see whether all proceeds normally. If so, check the peripheral's documentation and make sure that you correctly installed the *driver* — the software provided by the device manufacturer — and that you connected it properly to the right port. (You can also use System Profiler, which I discuss later in this chapter, to check to see whether your MacBook recognizes the external device.) To verify that the cable works, substitute another cable of the same type or try the peripheral on another Mac.

Make it a practice to check the manufacturer's Web site for the latest driver when you get new hardware. The software that ships in the box with your new toy could have been on the shelf for months before being sold, and the manufacturer has probably fine-tuned the driver in the interim. You should also run Software Update to verify that the drivers that Apple supplies are up-to-date.

✦ **If you installed new software or applied an update/patch:** Follow the guidelines in Chapter 7 of this minibook to uninstall the application and search for any files that it might have created elsewhere. (Searching by date created and date modified can help you locate files that were recently created.) If this fixes the problem, it's time to contact the developer and request technical support for the recalcitrant program; you can always re-install the program after the problem has been solved by the developer.

Not all versions of Mac OS X are created equal. If you've recently upgraded to a major or minor new release of Mac OS X, some of the applications that you've been using without trouble for months can suddenly go on the warpath and refuse to work (or exhibit quirky behavior). If this happens, visit the developer's Web site often to look for a patch file that will update the application to work with the new version of Mac OS X.

✦ **If you recently made a change within System Preferences:** It's possible that you've inadvertently "bumped" something. For instance, you might have accidentally changed your modem or network settings or perhaps made a change to your login options. Verify the settings screens that you visited to make sure that everything looks okay.

## Step 4: Run Disk Utility

Next, run Disk Utility (as shown in Figure 9-1) to check for disk errors and permissions errors — especially permissions errors, which can wreak absolute havoc on just about any application on your hard drive. (Click the Disk Utility icon in the Utilities folder inside your Applications folder. Chapter 7 of this minibook provides all the details.)

## Step 5: Run antivirus software

Run your antivirus software and scan your entire system for viruses, including all system disks and removable disks. Although Mac OS X doesn't come with antivirus protection built in, Intego's VirusBarrier X5 (www.intego.com) can constantly scan each file that you open or download for infections.

If you haven't already set your antivirus application to automatically update itself, download the latest virus update — usually called a *signature file* or *data file* — to keep your virus protection current.

## Step 6: Check the Trash

Check the contents of your Trash to make sure that you haven't inadvertently tossed something important that could be causing trouble for an application. Click the Trash icon in the Dock to open the Trash window and peruse its contents. (To see the file types easier, switch to List mode.) To restore items to their rightful place, drag them from the Trash back to the correct folder on your hard drive.

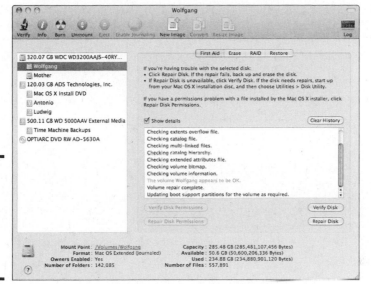

**Figure 9-1:**
Use Disk
Utility to
check the
integrity of
your drive
and files.

## Step 7: Check online connections

If you're connected to an Ethernet network, a cable modem, or a digital
subscriber line (DSL), check your equipment to make sure that you're
currently online and receiving packets normally. Your network system
administrator will be happy to help you with this, especially if you're blood
relatives.

## Step 8: Disable troublesome Login Items

Disable any *Login Items* that might be causing trouble. As you can read in
Book III, Chapter 3, Login Items are launched automatically as soon as you
log in. For example, an older application that doesn't fully support Snow
Leopard can cause problems if used as a Login Item (such as an older
version of a disk-scanning utility for use with Mac OS X Jaguar or Tiger).
You can do this from the Login Items settings in the System Preferences
Accounts pane (as shown in Figure 9-2); click the Apple menu, choose
System Preferences, click Accounts, and then click the Login Items tab.

Unfortunately, if a Login Item doesn't display an error message, your old
friend Trial-and-Error is just about the only sure-fire way to detect which
item (if any) is causing the problem. Click an item to select it, click the
Remove button (marked with a minus sign), and then press ⌘+Q to quit
System Preferences. Log out to see whether the problem's solved. (If not,
don't forget to add the item again to the Login Items list.)

**Figure 9-2:**
A misbehaving Login Item can cause you a world of grief.

You can also disable Login Items entirely when you reboot. If the login window appears when you reboot your computer, hold down the Shift key and then click the Login button. If you don't see the login window when you reboot, hold down the Shift key when you see the James Bond–style twirling progress indicator in the startup window and continue to hold down the key until the Finder appears.

## Step 9: Turn off your screen saver

Another candidate for intermittent lockups is your screen saver, especially if you're running a shareware effort written by a 12-year-old with a limited attention span. Display your System Preferences, choose Desktop & Screen Saver, and click the Screen Saver tab. You can deactivate the saver entirely (by moving the Start Screen Saver slider to Never) or choose the Computer Name saver (which is provided by Apple) from the Screen Savers list.

## Step 10: Check for write protection

If you're running a multiuser ship, check to make sure that another user with administrator access hasn't accidentally write-protected your documents, your application, or its support files. If possible, log in with an administrator account yourself (as I describe in Book III, Chapter 5) and then try running the application or opening the document that you were unable to access under your own ID.

Trying an application under the aforementioned "clean" account is also a great way to determine whether your user-specific preference file for that application has been corrupted. If you can run the application using your "clean" account, contact the software developer to see how you can repair or delete a preference file that's causing problems.

### Step 11: Check your System Profiler

If you've reached this point in the troubleshooting process and haven't found the culprit, you've probably experienced a hardware failure in your MacBook. If possible, display the Hardware category within the Apple System Profiler (see Figure 9-3) and make sure that it can recognize and use all the internal drives, ports, and external devices on your MacBook. To start the System Profiler, click the Apple menu, choose About This Mac, and then click the More Info button.

**Figure 9-3:**
Use System Profiler to check the devices and ports on your system.

### Step 12: Reboot with the Mac OS X Installation disc

In case your MacBook is in sad shape and won't even boot from its hard drive, here's a last step that you can take before you seek professional assistance: Reboot your laptop from the Mac OS X Snow Leopard Installation disc. Hold down the C key immediately after you hear the startup chord (which boots your system from the DVD-ROM drive) and then run Disk Utility from the Installation DVD's Apple menu that appears. Because you've booted the system from the installation disc, you can verify and repair problems with your startup hard drive. (Some new MacBook models also come with a diagnostic DVD that can help you pin down hardware problems.) After you're done, restart your system.

## Do I Need to Reinstall Mac OS X?

To be honest, this is a difficult question to answer. Technically, you should never *need* to reinstall the Big X, but there's also no reason why you *can't*.

I can think of only two scenarios where reinstalling the operating system will **likely** solve a problem. One, if your system files have been so heavily corrupted — by a faulty hard drive or a rampaging virus, for example — that you can't boot Mac OS X at all. Two, if the operating system encounters the death-dealing kernel panic on a regular basis. A *kernel panic* displays a dialog that instructs you to restart your MacBook (in multiple languages, no less), usually overwriting whatever's on the monitor at the time. (This is analogous to the infamous Windows Blue Screen of Death — I've grown to hate that shade of blue with a passion.)

If you receive kernel panics on an ongoing basis, something is really, *really* wrong. Make sure that your documents are copied to a rewriteable DVD or network drive, and don't overwrite any existing backup that you have with a new backup because the backup application is likely to lock up as well.

To reinstall, you must reboot from your Mac OS X Snow Leopard Installation disc. Hold down the C key immediately after you hear your MacBook's startup chord. (Read the earlier section, "Step 12: Reboot with the Mac OS X Installation disc.")

# It's Still Not Moving: Troubleshooting Resources

As I mention earlier in this chapter, you can pursue other avenues to get help when you can't solve a troubleshooting problem on your own. Mind you, I'm talking about professional help from sources that you can trust. Although you can find quite a bit of free advice on the Internet (usually on privately run Web sites and in the Internet newsgroups), most of it isn't worth your effort. In fact, some of it's downright wrong. That said, here are some sources that I *do* recommend.

## The Mac OS X Help Viewer

Although most Mac OS X owners tend to blow off the Help Viewer when the troubleshooting gets tough, that's never the best course of action. Always take a few moments to search the contents of the Help Viewer — click Help on the Finder menu — to see whether any mention is made of the problem that you've encountered.

## The Apple Mac OS X Support site

Home to all manner of support questions and answers, the Mac OS X Support section of the Apple Web site (www.apple.com/support) should be your next stop in case of trouble that you can't fix yourself. Topics include

✦ Startup issues

✦ Internet and networking problems

✦ Printing problems

You can search the Apple Knowledge Base, download the latest updates and electronic manuals, and participate in Apple-moderated discussion boards from this one central location.

## Your local Apple dealer

Naturally, an Apple dealer can provide just about any support that you're likely to need — for a price — but you can usually get the answers to important questions without any coinage changing hands. Your dealer is also well versed in the latest updates and patches that can fix those software incompatibility problems. Check your telephone book for your local dealer.

**Book II
Chapter 9**

Troubleshooting
the X

# Book III

# MacBook Customizing and Sharing

Wowsers! Check out the Flow view for Snow Leopard's Finder windows.

# Contents at a Glance

**Chapter 1: Building the Finder of Your Dreams** . . . . . . . . . . . . . . . .**187**

Will That Be Icons or Lists or Columns . . . or Even a Flow?................. 188
Doing the Toolbar Dance....................................................... 191
Searching for Files from the Toolbar ..................................... 194
Searching for Files from the Find Dialog................................ 195
Configuring the View Options .............................................. 197
Setting Finder Preferences .................................................. 204

**Chapter 2: Giving Your Desktop the Personal Touch**. . . . . . . . . . . . .**207**

Changing the Background ..................................................... 207
Changing the Screen Saver .................................................. 211
Changing Colors in Mac OS X................................................ 212
Adding Stickies.................................................................... 212
Customizing the Dock ......................................................... 214
Stick It on the Dashboard .................................................... 218
Arranging Your Precious Desktop ......................................... 220

**Chapter 3: Delving under the Hood with System Preferences**. . . . . .**221**

The Preferred Way to Display the Preferences .......................... 221
Saving Your Preferences....................................................... 222
Searching for Specific Settings............................................. 223
Getting Personal ................................................................. 223
It's All about the Hardware .................................................. 235
Sharing the Joy: Internet and Network ................................... 243
Tweaking the System .......................................................... 250

**Chapter 4: You Mean Others Can Use My MacBook, Too?** . . . . . . . .**261**

How Multiuser Works on Mac OS X ....................................... 261
Configuring Your Login Screen ............................................. 263
Locking Things Down .......................................................... 266
Starting Applications Automatically after Login ....................... 267

**Chapter 5: Setting Up Multiuser Accounts** . . . . . . . . . . . . . . . . . . . . .**269**

Adding, Editing, and Deleting Users....................................... 269
Tightening Your Security Belt................................................ 274
Using Keychains — NOT...................................................... 279

**Chapter 6: Sharing Documents for Fun and Profit** . . . . . . . . . . . . . . .**283**

Sharing over a Network versus Sharing on a Single Mac .............. 283
Permissions: Law Enforcement for Your Files........................... 285
Permission and Sharing Do's and Don'ts................................. 287
Sharing Stuff in Office 2008................................................. 288

**Chapter 7: Common-Sense Laptop Security** . . . . . . . . . . . . . . . . . . . .**291**

MacBook Security 101......................................................... 291
Using a Security Application................................................. 295

# Chapter 1: Building the Finder of Your Dreams

## In This Chapter

- ✔ Choosing a view mode
- ✔ Modifying the toolbar
- ✔ Searching for files from the toolbar
- ✔ Searching for files with the Find command
- ✔ Changing view options
- ✔ Changing Finder preferences

The Finder is the heart of Mac OS X — and we all know how heart surgeons like to tinker, don't we? (*Ouch.* Start again.)

The Finder is the heart of Mac OS X, and as you might expect, it's highly configurable. You can customize the Finder to present icons, or you can peruse folders with a column view that can pack much more information on-screen at one time. Some folks prefer the default Finder toolbar, and others like to customize it with the applications and features that they use most often.

Decisions like these can help you transform Snow Leopard into *Your Personal Operating System* — and every Mac OS X power user worth the title will take the time to apply these changes because an operating system that presents visual information the way that *you* want to see it is easier and more efficient to use.

No need for a hammer or saw — when you're building the Finder of your dreams, the only tool that you need is your finger!

## Will That Be Icons or Lists or Columns . . . or Even a Flow?

The default appearance of a window in Mac OS X uses the familiar large-format icons that have been a hallmark of the Macintosh operating system since Day One — but there's no reason you *have* to use them. (In fact, most Mac OS X power users I know consider the icon view mode rather inefficient and slow.) Besides the icon view, as shown in Figure 1-1, Mac OS X offers three other window view modes: *list, column,* and *flow.*

**Figure 1-1:**
A Finder window in icon view mode.

Mac OS X old-timers will thrill to the slider control at the bottom-right corner of Finder windows in icon view mode. Why? Drag this control to the right to expand the size of the icons within the window, and drag the control to the left to reduce the icon size! (This is A Big Thing for those who prefer icon view — and it makes quite a difference for those with less-than-perfect eyesight.)

✦ **List view:** *List view* displays the folders on the volume in a hierarchical fashion. To display the contents of a folder, you can either click the right-facing small triangle next to the folder name — it rotates downward to indicate that you've expanded the folder — or you can double-click the folder icon to display the contents in a Finder window. To collapse the contents of the folder, click the small triangle again; it rotates back to face the right. Figure 1-2 illustrates the same Finder window in list view.

You can resize a column by dragging the right edge of the column heading.

**Figure 1-2:**
The contents of a Finder window in list view mode.

✦ **Column view:** Figure 1-3 shows the same window in column view, in which the volumes on your Mac OS X system are displayed on the left. Each column on the right represents a lower level of subfolders. Click the volume in the Devices list and then click the desired folder in the first column on the right to display its contents, and so forth. (Personally, this is my favorite view — thanks, Apple! It's efficient and fast as all get-out.) When you drill deeper, the columns shift automatically to the left. When you click an item (instead of a folder), the Finder displays a preview and a quick summary of the selected item in the rightmost column.

**Figure 1-3:**
Snow Leopard's column view requires very little scrolling.

Each column has its own scroll bar (for those really, really big folders), and you can drag the column handle at the bottom of the separators to resize the column width to the left. When you hold down Option and drag a column handle, all the columns are adjusted at once.

✦ **Flow view:** When a new software feature or function turns out to be incredibly popular, a developer tries to use it wherever possible — hence the Flow view shown in Figure 1-4, which Apple took directly from the Cover Flow view that proved so successful in iTunes (as well as on the iPhone and iPod touch). Flow view still displays the sidebar, but each document or item is showcased in a preview pane (and with an accurate thumbnail, if possible). You can resize the preview pane by dragging the three-line handle on the bottom edge of the pane. The remainder of the Finder window in Flow view works very similarly to list view, complete with the rotating triangles. However, if you like, you can click the scroll buttons or drag the scroll bar under the preview pane to move through the contents of your drive in a very classy visual display!

**Figure 1-4:** Wowzers — check out the Flow view for Snow Leopard's Finder windows!

Another of my pet peeves is cluttered disks. If you're continually having problems locating files and folders, ask yourself, "Self, do I need to organize? Am I — gasp — *cluttered*?" If your answer is yes, take an hour and organize your files logically into new folders. (Remember, I'm talking your documents and such — not your applications, which are usually where they need to be — in your Applications folder.) Often, documents that you create end up as stragglers, usually located in the root folder of your hard drive, which sooner or later ends up looking like a biker bar after Ladies' Night. (The same can be said of many Mac OS X Desktops, too.) By keeping your root folder and Desktop clean and saving your files in organized folders, you waste less time searching for files and more time actually *using* them.

To switch between the four modes, click one of the four view mode buttons on the Finder window toolbar (the current view is highlighted) or click the View menu and choose As Icons, As List, As Columns, or As Cover Flow. Mac OS X places a helpful check mark next to the current view mode. (Keyboard lovers can hold down ⌘ and press the 1, 2, 3, or 4 keys to switch views.)

# Doing the Toolbar Dance

You can work your customization magic on the Finder toolbar as well! In this section, I show you how to customize that strip of icons across the top of the Finder window that's affectionately called the *toolbar*. Or, if you like, you'll discover how to dismiss it entirely to gain additional real estate for the contents of your Finder window.

## Hiding and showing the toolbar

You can toggle the display of the toolbar in an active Finder window in one of three ways:

✦ By clicking the toolbar button located at the upper-right corner of the Finder window

✦ By pressing ⌘+Option+T

✦ By choosing View from the Finder menu and then choosing Hide (or Show) Toolbar

Hiding the toolbar also hides the Sidebar, which many MacBook owners dislike — me included.

## Hiding and showing the status bar

The status bar at the bottom of the Finder window displays a number of helpful informational-type tidbits about the window's contents. Depending on what you've opened, the status bar can include

✦ **Statistics:** See the number of items in the window and the amount of free space remaining on the volume.

✦ **A write-protect icon:** This icon looks like a pencil with a line running through it, as shown in Figure 1-5. This indicates that you don't have write permissions for the contents of the window — or the volume where the contents reside. (Note that this doesn't necessarily mean that folders at a lower level are write-protected as well.) You'll typically see this icon when you're viewing the contents of a CD or DVD, where everything is write-protected.

**Figure 1-5:**
Check the
status bar
to scope out
your write
permissions.

✦ **The current automatic icon view setting:** For windows in icon view, the status bar can display either a grid icon (indicating that the icons are set to snap-to-grid) or four tiny icons (indicating that the icons are displayed in a sorted order). You'll discover more about these settings in the section "Configuring the View Options," later in this chapter.

TIP

To toggle the display of the status bar, choose View from the Finder menu and then choose Show/Hide Status Bar.

## Giving your toolbar big tires and a loud exhaust

The default icons on the toolbar include

✦ **Back and Forward:** As with a Web browser, clicking the Back button moves you to the previous window's contents. If you use the Back button, the Forward button appears. Click this to return to the contents that you had before clicking the Back button.

✦ **View:** Click this control to toggle between the four view modes (icon, list, column, or flow).

✦ **Quick Look:** Click this control to display a window with the contents of the selected file or document without launching the corresponding application. Quick Look works with all sorts of images, video, and documents, allowing you to efficiently peruse files on your system without the hassle of constantly launching and quitting applications. Quick Look works in any Finder window view mode, too. To activate Quick Look for a selected file from the keyboard, press the spacebar.

While Quick Look is active, a number of format-specific buttons appear at the bottom of the Quick Look window. For example, displaying an image file in Quick Look adds a button that can automatically import the image into iPhoto. These buttons vary with the format or type of document, but you'll always see a full-screen/exit full-screen button that toggles the Quick Look window between full-screen and regular size.

TIP

Pssst. Selecting a folder and pressing the spacebar displays a summary of its size and last modification date. Pass it on.

✦ **Action:** Click this pop-up menu to display context-sensitive commands for the selected items. In plain English, you'll see the commands that you'd see if you held down Control and clicked the selection.

✦ **Search:** Okay, I know it's not technically an icon, but the Search box is a member of the default toolbar family nonetheless. You can search for a file or folder using this box. More on this in the section "Searching for Files from the Toolbar," later in this chapter.

But, as one of my favorite bumper stickers so invitingly asks, "Why be normal?" Adding or deleting items from the toolbar is a great way to customize Mac OS X. Follow these steps:

*1.* **From the active Finder window menu, choose View⇨Customize Toolbar (or right-click the toolbar and choose Customize Toolbar) to display the sheet that you see in Figure 1-6.**

**Book III
Chapter 1**

**Building the Finder of Your Dreams**

**Figure 1-6:**
Changing the toolbar status quo in Mac OS X.

Along with controls such as Back, Forward, and View, you find a number of system functions, such as Eject and Burn.

2. **To add items to the toolbar, drag them from the Customize Toolbar dialog up to the toolbar at the top of the window.**

   To add an item between existing buttons, drop it between the buttons, and they obligingly move aside. If you get exuberant about your toolbar and you add more icons than it can hold, a double-right arrow appears at the right side of the toolbar. A click of the arrow displays a pop-up menu with the icons that won't fit.

   In fact, the Customize Toolbar dialog isn't necessary for some toolbar modifications: You can also drag files, folders, and disk volumes directly from the Desktop or other Finder windows and add them to your toolbar at any time. To remove a file, folder, or disk volume from the toolbar, hold down Control and click (or right-click) the icon on the toolbar; then click Remove Item from the shortcut menu — it vanishes like a CEO's ethics.

   You can also hold down ⌘ and drag any item off the toolbar, or hold down ⌘ and drag toolbar items to reorder them.

   You can always drag a file or folder into the Sidebar column at the left of the Finder window. (The Sidebar column is a separate entity entirely from the toolbar.)

3. **To remove an item from the toolbar, drag it off to the center of the window, amongst the other icons.**

4. **Naturally, you can swap item positions. Just click an item, drag it to its new spot, and then lift your finger from the trackpad.**

5. **To choose the default toolbar configuration or to start over, drag the default bar at the bottom of the window to the toolbar at the top.**

   This is the toolbar equivalent of tapping your ruby slippers together three times and repeating, "There's no place like home."

6. **To toggle between displaying the icons with accompanying text (the default), the icon only, or a text button only, click the Show pop-up menu at the bottom of the Customize Toolbar dialog.**

7. **After you arrange your toolbar as you like, click the Done button.**

## Searching for Files from the Toolbar

Need to find a file fast? The default toolbar has just what you need: the *Search field,* which offers the ability to perform a Spotlight search for a string of text within your files (including both filenames and contents). To locate a file with the Search field, follow these steps:

1. **Click in the Search box on the toolbar and type the text that you want to find.**

   It's the text box on the right with the magnifying glass. (The folks at Apple are really, *really* into Sherlock Holmes . . . as am I!) If you need to clear the field and start over, click the circular X button, which appears only when text is in the Search field.

   Hey, who needs to press Return? The Finder immediately displays the files with names (or contents) that include the text, as shown in Figure 1-7.

**Figure 1-7:** Locating a file or folder with the toolbar Search box.

2. **To display the location of a file, click it once. To launch it, double-click the entry.**

   Files can also be moved or copied from the Search results list with the standard drag and Option+drag methods.

3. **To perform a new search, click the circular X button and type new text in the Search field.**

   To return to your original location in the Finder window, click the Back button on the toolbar.

# Searching for Files from the Find Dialog

Although the Search box on the toolbar is all you usually need to find most files and folders, sometimes you need a little more flexibility and power to locate what you need on your system. To do so, add the Find controls, which you can use to create custom searches with more complex criteria. To locate a file by using the Find controls, follow these steps:

*1.* **With the Finder active, display the Find controls by pressing ⌘+F (or choose File from the Finder menu and then choose Find).**

Mac OS X displays the controls that you see in Figure 1-8.

**Figure 1-8:**
The Find controls add a bit of extra power to a search.

*2.* **Click the buttons at the top of the list to specify where you want to search.**

You can choose Computer (your entire system, including network volumes), a local volume, or your Home folder.

*3.* **To search for a specific filename, click the first pop-up menu in a row and choose Name; then type all or part of the filename in the Contains box.**

Snow Leopard automatically begins searching as soon as you type at least one character.

After you locate the file or folder that you need, click the entry name to reveal the location of the matching file or folder. You can also double-click it to launch (or display) it.

*4.* **If you want to search for a text string within the document itself, click the first pop-up menu in a row, choose Contents, and then type the string to match in the box.**

The text must appear just as you've typed it, so it's always a good idea to restrict what you're searching for to a minimum of words that you're fairly sure will cause a match. (Content searching is not case sensitive, though.) Content searching works only when you've generated an index, which I explain later in this section.

5. **To include additional search criteria lines, click the button with the plus sign next to the last criterion line.**

   You can limit your results based on all sorts of rules, including the date that the file or folder was last modified, when it was created, the file type, the size, the extension, or whether the file or folder is marked visible or hidden (such as a system file).

   You can also remove a search criterion line by clicking the button with the minus sign.

6. **To save the search criteria that you selected, click Save.**

   This creates a *Smart Folder*, which (you're gonna *love* this) Snow Leopard automatically updates (in real time) to contain whatever items match the criteria you've saved! You can specify the location for your Smart Folder, and you can choose to add it to your Finder Sidebar for the ultimate convenience. *Sweet.*

7. **When you're done canvassing your computer, click the Back button in the Find dialog to return to the Finder.**

## Configuring the View Options

As I discuss at the beginning of the chapter, you have a lot of control over how Mac OS X presents files and folders in the Finder. In this section, I cover how you can make further adjustments to the view from your windows. (Pardon me for the ghastly cliché posing as a pun.)

### Setting icon view options

First, allow me to provide a little detail on housekeeping in the Big X. After a few hours of work, a Finder window in icon mode can look something like a teenager's room: stuff strewn all over the place, as I demonstrate with my Applications folder in Figure 1-9. To restore order to your Desktop, right-click (by tapping two fingers on the trackpad) in any open area of the active window and then choose Clean Up. This command leaves the icons in approximately the same position but snaps them to an invisible grid so that they're aligned, as shown in Figure 1-10.

**Figure 1-9:**
Will
someone
please
clean up
this mess?

**Figure 1-10:**
Tidying up is
no problem
with the
Clean
Up menu
command.

After things are in alignment, work with the icon view options. (Naturally, you'll want the active Finder window in icon view first, so choose View⇨ As Icons or press ⌘+1.) From the Finder menu, choose View⇨Show View Options — or press that swingin' ⌘+J shortcut — to display the View Options dialog that you see in Figure 1-11. (Remember that these are the options available for icon view; I discuss the options for list, column, and Cover Flow view later in this chapter.)

**Figure 1-11:**
The settings available for icon view.

Of course, Mac OS X remembers the changes that you make within the View Options dialog, no matter which view mode you're configuring. Now, the changes that you can make from this dialog include

Book III
Chapter 1

**Building the Finder of Your Dreams**

✦ **Always Open in Icon View:** When you select this check box, each Finder window that you open automatically uses icon view. (If deselected, the new window uses the last view mode you used.)

✦ **Resizing your icons:** Click and drag the Icon Size slider to shrink or expand the icons within the window. The icon size is displayed in pixels above the slider. (Remember, however, that Snow Leopard offers an icon resizing slider at the lower-right corner of any Finder window that's currently using icon view mode; it's much easier and more convenient just to drag the slider to expand or reduce the size of icons in a window.)

✦ **Specifying grid spacing:** Click and drag the Grid Spacing slider to shrink or expand the size of the grid used to align icons within the window. The larger the grid, the more white space between icons.

✦ **Resizing icon label text:** Click the up and down arrows to the right of the Text Size pop-up menu to choose the font size (in points) for icon labels.

✦ **Moving icon label text:** Select either the Bottom (default) or the Right radio button to choose between displaying the text under your Desktop icons or to the right of the icons.

✦ **Show Item Info:** With this check box selected, Mac OS X displays the number of items within each folder in the window. Many filenames also display helpful information (such as the dimensions of a photo).

✦ **Show Icon Preview:** If you select this check box, the Finder displays icons for image files using a miniature of the actual picture. (A cool feature for those with digital cameras; however, this does take extra processing time because Mac OS X has to load each image file and shrink it down to create the icon.)

✦ **Arranging icons:** From this pop-up menu, you can automatically align icons to a grid within the window, just as if you had used the Clean Up menu command. You can also sort the display of icons in a window by choosing one of the following criteria from its pop-up menu: by name, date modified, date created, size, item type, or the icon label you've assigned.

✦ **Choosing a background:** To select a background for the window, select one of three radio buttons here:

  • *White:* This is the default.

  • *Color:* Click a color choice from the color block that appears if you make this selection.

  • *Picture:* Select this radio button and then click the Select button to display a standard Open dialog. Navigate to the location where the desired image is stored, click it once to select it, and then click Open.

✦ **Use as Defaults:** When you first open the View Options dialog, the changes you're making apply only to the Finder window that opens when you open the selected item — in other words, the item that appears in the window's title bar, such as a folder or drive.

  For example, any changes made to the settings in Figure 1-11 will affect only my Applications folder because it was the active Finder window when I pressed ⌘+J. (You might have noticed that the window name also appears as the title of the View Options dialog.)

  However, you can decide to apply the changes that you make to *all* Finder windows that you view in your current mode. Click the Use as Defaults button to make a global change.

After all your changes are made and you're ready to return to work, click the dialog's Close button to save your settings.

## Setting list view options

If you're viewing the active window in list view, choose View➪Show View Options to display the View Options dialog that you see in Figure 1-12.

**Figure 1-12:**
Here
are your
list view
settings.

As in icon view, changes you make in this dialog normally apply only to this window, but you can click Use as Defaults to assign these settings to all windows that you view in list mode. The other list view settings include

✦ **Always Open in List View:** Select this check box and Snow Leopard will open all Finder windows in list view. (If deselected, new windows use the last view mode you used.)

✦ **Resizing your icons:** You can choose from two sizes of icons.

✦ **Resizing icon label text:** Click the up and down arrows to the right of the Text Size pop-up menu to choose the font size (in points) for icon labels.

✦ **Show Columns:** Select the check boxes under this heading to display additional columns in list view, including the date that the item was modified, the creation date, the size, the item type, the version (supplied by most applications), the label color, and any comments you've added in the Info dialog for that item. (In my personal opinion, the more columns you add, the more unwieldy the Finder gets, so I advise disabling the display of columns that you won't use.)

✦ **Use Relative Dates:** Select this check box to display modification dates and creation dates with relative terms, such as *Today* or *Yesterday*. If this freaks you out, deselect this check box to force all dates to act like adults.

✦ **Calculate All Sizes:** Select this check box to have Mac OS X display the actual sizes of folders, including all the files and subfolders they contain. (Handy for figuring out where all your disk space went, no?) *Note:* Using this option takes processing time, so I recommend that you avoid using it unless you really need to see the size.

✦ **Show Icon Preview:** Select this check box to display preview icons for image files. (Again, this takes extra processing time, and the image preview icons are pretty doggone small in list view, so this feature may be of limited value to you.)

To save your settings, click the dialog's Close button.

## Setting column view options

To make changes to view options in column view mode, choose View⇨Show View Options to display the View Options dialog that you see in Figure 1-13.

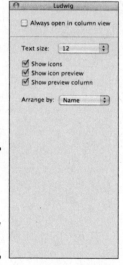

**Figure 1-13:**
Snow Leopard's glamorous column view settings.

You have only five column view options, and any changes that you make to this dialog are *always* reflected in **every** column view:

✦ **Always Open in Column View:** If this check box is selected, all Finder windows open in column view. (If deselected, new windows use the last view mode you used.)

✦ **Resizing icon label text:** Click the Text Size pop-up menu to choose the font size (in points) for icon labels.

✦ **Show Icons:** Select this check box to display icons in the columns. If this option is deselected, the icons don't appear and you'll gain a little space.

✦ **Show icon preview:** Click this check box to select it, and Snow Leopard displays preview icons for image files — taking a little extra time to perform this service, naturally. (As you find out in the next bullet, column mode can be set to automatically display a preview thumbnail in the last column when you click an image or video file, and even some documents to boot . . . . Therefore, the usefulness of tiny icon previews in column mode may be limited for you.)

✦ **Show Preview Column:** If this check box is selected, clicking a file in column mode displays a *thumbnail* (reduced image) and preview information in the right-most column, as shown in Figure 1-14.

**Figure 1-14:** The Preview column provides more information on the selected file.

**Book III Chapter 1**

**Building the Finder of Your Dreams**

If you store a slew of smaller QuickTime movies and digital images on your drive, the Preview column is great. (You can even play a QuickTime movie from the Preview column.) Of course, longer movies and larger photos take more time to load!

✦ **Arranging icons:** Click this pop-up menu to specify the sort criteria for the item names displayed in each column, using name, date modified, date created, size, item type, or the icon label.

Click the dialog's Close button to save your settings and return to the Finder.

## Setting Cover Flow view options

The View options for Cover Flow view are the same as those for list view that I covered earlier in this section except forAlways Open in Cover Flow. You select this check box to open all new Finder windows in Cover Flow view. (If deselected, new windows use the last view mode you used.)

# Setting Finder Preferences

Finally, you can change a number of settings to customize the Finder itself. From the Finder menu, click Finder and choose the Preferences menu item to display the Finder Preferences dialog that you see in Figure 1-15.

**Figure 1-15:** You can configure your Finder preferences here.

In the General section, the preference settings include

✦ **Displaying Icons on the Desktop:** Select these check boxes to display your hard disks, removable volumes (including CDs, DVDs, and iPods), and connected network servers.

✦ **New Finder Windows Open:** Click the pop-up menu to specify the spot where a new Finder window should open. By default, a new window displays the contents of your Home folder.

✦ **Always Open Folders in a New Window:** When this check box is selected, double-clicking a folder will open it in a new Finder window, as did earlier versions of Mac OS. (If deselected, the contents of the folder appear in the same Finder window, which makes it easier to focus on just the folder you need at the moment.)

✦ **Spring-Loaded Folders and Windows:** It sounds a little wacky, but using this feature can definitely speed up file copying! If this check box is selected, you can drag an item on top of a folder — *without* releasing the trackpad — and after a preset time (controlled by the Delay slider), a spring-loaded window appears to show you the folder's contents. At that point, you can either lift your finger from the trackpad to drop the file inside the folder (upon which the window disappears), or you can drag the icon on top of another subfolder to spring it forth and drill even deeper.

The Labels preference pane is a simple one — just click next to each label color to type your own text for that label. (I've gotta recommend red for deadlines and green for contracts . . . call me sentimental.)

From the Sidebar preferences pane, you can choose which default items should appear in the Finder window Sidebar column. Your choices include locations (such as your Home and Applications folders), network servers, removable media, the Desktop itself, and — naturally — your hard drives. To add a default item to the Sidebar column, click the corresponding check box to select it, or deselect the check box to banish that item forthwith.

The Advanced preference settings include

✦ **Show All File Extensions:** If this check box is selected, the Finder displays the file extensions at the end of filenames. This comes in handy for some applications, where everything from a document to a preference file to the application itself all share the same icon. However, I find extensions distasteful and leave things set with the default of extensions off.

✦ **Show Warning before Changing an Extension:** Also on by default, this setting forces Snow Leopard to display a confirmation dialog before allowing you to change the extension on a filename. Why? Well, changing an extension usually results in a "broken" file association, so the file's corresponding application may not launch automatically any longer when you double-click the item. Double-clicking a Word document, for example, might not launch Word automatically as it used to do. If you show file extensions and you often change them, click this check box to disable the warning.

✦ **Show Warning before Emptying the Trash:** By default, this check box is selected, and Mac OS X displays a confirmation dialog before allowing you to — in the words of Mac OS X patrons around the world — *toss the Bit Bucket.* If you're interested in speed and trust your judgment (and your trackpad finger), you can disable this setting.

✦ **Empty Trash Securely:** If you'd prefer to use the more secure method of emptying your Trash — where deleted items are far harder for anyone to recover — select this check box.

**Book III
Chapter 1**

**Building the Finder
of Your Dreams**

✦ **When Performing a Search:** Click this pop-up menu to specify whether the text you enter in the Finder window Search box should match everything on your Mac or be limited to the current folder only. Choose Use the Previous Search Scope to use the scope setting you used during your last search.

After you make the desired changes to the Finder Preferences, click the dialog's Close button to save your settings and return to the Finder.

# Chapter 2: Giving Your Desktop the Personal Touch

## In This Chapter

↙ **Picking your own background**

↙ **Adding and selecting a screen saver**

↙ **Choosing menu colors and highlights**

↙ **Keeping track of things with Stickies**

↙ **Customizing the Dock and using Dashboard**

↙ **Cleaning and sorting the Mac OS X Desktop**

"**T**weak! Tweak!" It's not the cry of some exotic bird — that's the call of the wild MacBook Power User. Power users like to tweak their Mac OS X Desktops just so, with *that* menu color, *this* background, and *those* applications in the Dock. Noncomputer types just can't understand the importance of the proper arrangement of your virtual workplace: When things are familiar and customized to your needs, you're more productive, and things get done faster. In fact, if you've set up multiple users on your computer under Mac OS X, the Big X automatically keeps track of each user's Desktop and restores it when that person logs in. (For example, when you use the MacBook, you get that background photo of Suzanne Sommers from the '70s whereas your daughter gets Avril Lavigne.)

In this chapter, I show you what you can do to produce a Desktop that's uniquely your own, including tweaks that you can make to the background and your Desktop icons. I also show you how to use Desktop Stickies instead of a forest of paper slips covering your monitor.

With your Mac OS X Desktop clad in the proper harmonious colors — yes, that can be your favorite photo of Elvis himself — and your new Dock icons ready for action, you're indeed prepared for whatever lies ahead in your computing world!

## Changing the Background

You might be asking, "Mark, do I really need a custom background?" That depends completely on your personal tastes, but I've yet to meet a computer owner who didn't change his or her background when presented with the opportunity. Favorite backgrounds usually include

✦ Humorous cartoons and photos that can bring a smile to your face (even during the worst workday)

✦ Scenic beauty

✦ Photos of family and friends (or the latest Hollywood heartthrob)

✦ The company logo (not sure it does much for morale, but it does impress the boss)

If you do decide to spruce up your background, you have three choices: You can select one of the default Mac OS X background images, choose a solid color, or specify your own image. All three backgrounds are chosen from the Desktop & Screen Saver pane, located within System Preferences (as illustrated in Figure 2-1).

**Figure 2-1:**
To select a background, get thee hence to System Preferences.

## Picking something Apple

To choose a background from one of the collections provided by Apple, click one of these groups from the list at the left:

✦ **Desktop Pictures:** These default backgrounds range from simple patterns to somewhat strange and ethereal flux shapes. (You have to see them to understand what I mean.)

✦ **Nature:** These backgrounds feature scenic beauty, such as blades of grass, sand dunes, snowy hills . . . that sort of thing.

✦ **Plants:** Close-up backgrounds of plant life — I especially recommend the autumn leaves.

✦ **Black & White:** Several truly stunning black-and-white backgrounds that look especially good on a widescreen display. These are my favorite images provided by Apple.

✦ **Abstract:** These backgrounds have even weirder twisting shapes in flux, this time with bright contrasting colors. Good for a psychiatrist's office.

✦ **Solid Colors:** This is for those who desire a soothing solid shade. More on this in the following section.

✦ **Pictures Folder:** This displays the images saved in the active user's Pictures folder.

✦ **Choose Folder:** You can open a folder containing images and display them instead. (I discuss this in more detail in a page or two.)

If you see something you like, click the thumbnail, and Mac OS X displays it in the well and automatically refreshes your background so that you can see what it looks like. (By the way, in the Apple universe, a *well* is a sunken square area that displays an image or color swatch — in this case, the background image that you select.)

Notice your iPhoto albums in the list? That's no accident — Snow Leopard automatically offers your iPhoto Photo Library so that you can choose images from your iPhoto collection!

Mac OS X automatically manipulates how the background appears on your Desktop. If an image conforms to your screen resolution, fine — otherwise, click the pop-up menu next to the well and you can choose to

✦ **Tile the background.** This repeats the image to cover the Desktop. (This is usually done with pattern images to produce a smooth, creamy, seamless look.)

✦ **Fill the screen.** This can be used with a solid color to get uniform coverage. The original aspect ratio of the image is preserved, so it's not stretched.

✦ **Stretch the background to fit the Desktop.** If your Desktop image is smaller than the Desktop acreage, this works, but be warned — if you try to stretch too small an image over too large a Desktop, the pixilated result can be pretty frightening. (Think of enlarging an old Kodak Instamatic negative to a 16 x 20 poster. Dots, dots, dots.) The original aspect ratio of the image isn't preserved, so you might end up with results that look like the funhouse mirrors at a carnival.

✦ **Center the image on the Desktop.** This is my favorite solution for Desktop images that are smaller than your resolution.

## How to annoy friends and confuse co-workers

Never let it be said that I can't dish out revenge when necessary. I don't know whether I should call this a *Tip* or a *Devilish Practical Joke That Will Drive People Nuts* — anyway, it's fun as all get-out. Right before you go to lunch, use the Grab utility in your Applications/Utilities folder to take a snapshot of your Desktop with a number of windows open (or an error dialog with an OK or a Close button) and then save the image to your Pictures folder. Select the image as your Desktop background and then watch others go crazy trying to click those faux windows, buttons, and icons. For an archenemy, try the same trick on *his* Mac! Arrange a slightly embarrassing Desktop on his computer, specify it as the background, and sit back while the fun begins. (Perhaps a Web browser that's open to a somewhat unusual Web site?)

Note that this pop-up menu appears only if the Desktop picture that you select isn't one of the standard Apple images. All the pictures in the Apple Desktop Pictures, Nature, Abstract, and Solid Colors categories are scaled automatically to the size of your screen.

To change your Desktop background automatically on a regular basis, select the Change Picture check box and then choose the delay period from the corresponding pop-up menu. To display the images in random order, select the Random Order check box; otherwise, Mac OS X displays them in the order that they appear in the folder. You can also select a translucent Finder menu bar, which (almost) blends in with your background. If you prefer a solid-color, matter-of-fact workman's menu bar, click the Translucent Menu Bar check box to deselect it.

### I just gotta have lavender

As I mention earlier, for those who want their favorite color without the distraction of an image, you can choose from a selection of solid colors. You can choose from these colors the same way that you'd pick a default Mac OS X background image (as I describe in the preceding section).

### Selecting your own photo

Finally, you can drag your own image into the well from a Finder window to add your own work of art. To view thumbnails of an entire folder, click the Pictures Folder (to display the contents of your personal Pictures folder) or click the Add button (bearing the plus sign) to specify any folder on your system. Click the desired thumbnail to embellish your Desktop.

# Changing the Screen Saver

Screen savers are another popular item. Because I cover the Screen Saver preferences in Chapter 3 of this minibook, I simply illustrate here how to choose one. Open System Preferences and click the Desktop & Screen Saver icon; then click the Screen Saver tab to display the settings that you see in Figure 2-2.

**Figure 2-2:** A good screen saver can cancel the effects of a bad boss.

**Book III Chapter 2**

**Giving Your Desktop the Personal Touch**

To add a third-party screen saver module so that everyone can use it on a multiuser system, copy it into the Screen Savers folder within the top-level Library folder. To selfishly keep that saver all to yourself, copy it into your user account's Screen Savers folder (which is located within the Library folder in your Home folder).

Click one of the entries in the Screen Savers column to display a thumbnail of the effect. Selecting the Use Random Screen Saver check box runs through 'em all, naturally. You can also test the appearance of the saver module by clicking the Test button; the screen saver runs until you move the mouse or press a key.

To keep tabs on the current time, click the Show with Clock check box to select it. Snow Leopard adds a clock display to any screen saver.

Many screen savers allow you to monkey with their settings. If the Options button is enabled (not grayed out), click it to see how you can change the effects.

## Changing Colors in Mac OS X

I can't understand it, but some people just don't appreciate menus with purple highlights! (You can tell a Louisiana State University graduate a mile away.) To specify your own colors for buttons, menus, and windows, follow these steps:

*1.* **Open System Preferences and click the Appearance icon to display the settings, as shown in Figure 2-3.**

**Figure 2-3:** Okay, then, set up your own school colors with the Appearance settings!

*2.* **Click the Appearance pop-up menu and choose the main color choice for your buttons and menus.**

*3.* **Click the Highlight Color pop-up menu and pick the highlight color that appears when you select text in an application or select an item from a list.**

*4.* **Press ⌘+Q to exit System Preferences and save your changes.**

## Adding Stickies

Stickies are interesting little beasts — I don't know their genus or phyla, but they're certainly handy to have around. To be technical for a moment, a *Sticky* is actually nothing more than a special type of application window, but these windows remain on your Desktop as long as the Stickies application is running.

I use Stickies for anything that a real-world sticky note can handle, including

✦ Reminders that you don't want to misplace

✦ Snippets of text that you want to temporarily store while your MacBook is turned off (without launching a behemoth like Word or digging for TextEdit)

✦ Boilerplate (repeated and standard) text that you're constantly including in your documents, such as your address

✦ A quick note that includes someone's e-mail address or phone number

✦ Today's Dilbert cartoon from www.dilbert.com

A Sticky can contain data pasted from the Clipboard, or you can simply type directly into the Stickies application window. Sticky windows can include graphics and different fonts and colors. You can even locate specific text from somewhere in your vast collection of Stickies by using the Find command within the Stickies application. Just press ⌘+F while the Stickies menu is active to display the Stickies Find dialog. (And you don't use up our bark-covered friends of the forest, either.)

In Book II, I discuss the Mac OS X Services menu. You can make a Sticky note from the Services menu in many applications as well.

Follow these steps to stick your way to success:

**1. Open your Applications folder and run the Stickies application to display the new window that you see in Figure 2-4.**

The text cursor is already idling in the new window.

**2. Type text in the window or press ⌘+V to paste the contents of the Clipboard into the window.**

You can also import the contents of an existing file into a Sticky. Just click File and then choose Import Text to display a standard Open dialog.

**3. (Optional) Add text formatting, change text font, and change font color from the Font menu.**

From the Note menu, you can also choose to make the Sticky translucent. (No pressing reason; they just look cool.)

**4. To change the Sticky color, click the Color menu and choose the appropriate hue.**

**5. Resize and drag the Sticky window to the desired location.**

Press ⌘+M to toggle between a *miniaturized* view (showing only the title bar) and the expanded view.

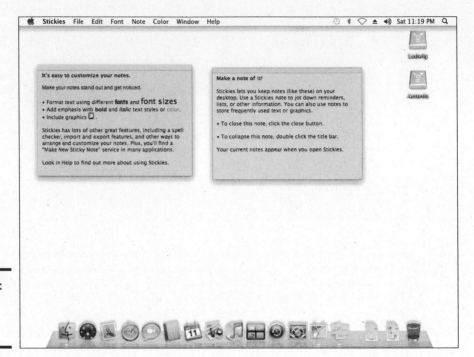

**Figure 2-4:**
"Look, Ma, it's a Sticky!"

To automatically run the Stickies application each time you log on, open the Accounts settings in System Preferences and click your account in the list. Click the Login Items button and add Stickies to the list by clicking the plus button.

To delete a Sticky, simply click the Close button at the upper-left corner of the Sticky window. Or click the Sticky to make it the active note and then click Close. Stickies displays a dialog to confirm that you want to close the note; click Save to save the contents in a file or click the Don't Save button to close the note and discard its contents.

To close the Stickies application completely, click any note and press ⌘+Q. The application remembers the position and contents of each note for when you launch it again.

## Customizing the Dock

In terms of importance, the *Dock* — the launch pad for applications and documents that appears on your Desktop — ranks right up there with the command center of a modern nuclear submarine. As such, it had better be easy to customize, and naturally, Mac OS X doesn't let you down.

## Adding applications and extras to the Dock

Why be satisfied with just the icons that Apple places in the Dock? You can add your own applications, files, and folders to the Dock as well.

✦ **Adding applications:** You can add any application to your Dock by simply dragging its icon into the area to the *left* side of the Dock (that's to the left side of the vertical dotted line that's visible in the Dock). You'll know when you're in the proper territory because the existing Dock icons obligingly move aside to make a space for it.

Attempting to place an application directly on the right side of the Dock sends it to the Trash (if the Trash icon is highlighted when you release the button), so beware. Note, however, that you can drop an application icon inside a Stack or a folder that already exists at the right side of the Dock.

Snow Leopard adds a new Exposé feature to the Dock: With Exposé active, click the Dock icon for any open application, and Exposé displays all the application's windows, allowing you to change to another window. Just click the Exposé window you want to work with. . . Convenience is King in Cupertino!

✦ **Adding individual files and volumes:** Individual files and volume icons can be added to the Dock by dragging the icon into the area to the *right* side of the Dock. (Attempting to place these to the left of the side of the Dock opens an application with the contents, which usually doesn't work.) Again, the existing Dock icons will move aside to create a space when you're in the right area.

To open the Dock item you've added in a Finder window, right-click the icon to display a Dock menu, where you can open documents, run applications, and have other assorted fun, depending on the item you choose.

✦ **Adding several files or a folder:** Snow Leopard uses a feature called Stacks, which I discuss in a few paragraphs, to handle multiple files or add an entire folder to the Dock.

✦ **Adding Web sites:** You can drag any URL from Safari directly into the area at the right of the Dock. Clicking that icon automatically opens your browser and displays that page. (Safari gets the treatment in Book VI, Chapter 5.) Now that, my friends, is genuine *sassy!*

To remove an icon from the Dock, just click and drag it off the Dock. You get a rather silly (but somehow, strangely satisfying) animated cloud of debris, and the icon is no more. Note, however, that the original application, folder, or volume is *not* deleted — just the Dock icon itself is permanently excused. If you like, you can delete *almost* any of the default icons that Mac OS X installs in the Dock; only the Finder and Trash icons must remain in the Dock.

To set up a Dock icon as a Login Item — without the hassle of opening the Accounts pane in System Preferences — just click a Dock icon and hold the mouse button down until the pop-up menu appears. Then select the Open at Login menu item.

If you can't delete items from the Dock, you're using a *managed* account — your account is configured with Parental Controls turned on, and your administrator has deselected the Can Modify the Dock check box in your account. In order to delete Dock items, you'll need an admin-level user to log in; then visit the Accounts pane in System Preferences and select the check box again. For more information on user accounts, see Chapter 5 of this minibook.

## Keeping track(s) with Stacks

I know, it's a horrible play on words, but my editors are doing me a favor.

Snow Leopard offers *Stacks,* which are groups of items (documents, applications, and folders) that you want to place in the Dock for convenience — perhaps the files needed for a project you're working on, or your favorite game applications. For example, I have a Stack named Wiley on my Dock that holds all the project files I need for the book I'm currently writing.

To create a Stack, just select and drag the items you want to include to the right side of the Dock. As always, the Dock opens a spot on the right side of the Dock to indicate you're in the zone.

To display the items in a Stack, just click it:

✦ **If the Stack holds relatively few items,** they're displayed in a really cool-looking arc that Apple calls a *fan* (as shown in Figure 2-5), and you can click the item you want to open or launch.

✦ **If the Stack is stuffed full of many items,** the Stack opens in a grid display, allowing you to scroll through the contents (and even open subfolders inside the Stack) to find what you need.

You can remove a Stack from the Dock by Control-clicking or right-clicking the Stack icon. To do so, choose Remove from Dock from the menu that appears. Alternatively, just drag that sucker right off the Dock.

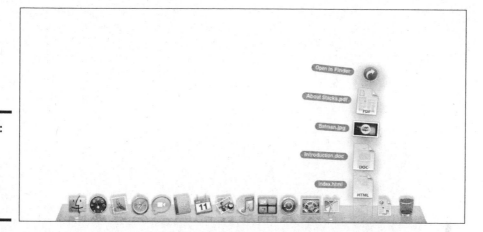

**Figure 2-5:**
Click a
Stack in
the Dock
to view its
contents.

If you add a folder full of items, the Stack is named after the folder; otherwise, Snow Leopard does the best job it can in figuring out what to name the Stack. (Although Apple makes a righteous attempt, I usually end up renaming the Stack. Right-click the Stack icon, or hold down Control while clicking the icon, and you'll see the Rename Stack menu item appear.)

Apple provides two Stacks already set up for you. One, the Download folder, situated next to the Trash, is the default location for any new files that you download using Safari or receive in your e-mail. Snow Leopard bounces the Download Stack icon to indicate that you've received a new item. Next to the Download Stack is the Documents Stack, which conveniently displays the contents of your Documents folder.

## Resizing the Dock

You can change the size of the Dock from the Dock settings in System Preferences — I explain this in more detail in Book III, Chapter 3 — but here's a simpler way to resize the Dock, right from the Desktop.

Move your cursor over the vertical dotted line that separates the left side of the Dock from the right side; the cursor turns into a funky line with arrows pointing up and down. This is your cue to click and drag while moving your finger up and down on the trackpad, which expands and shrinks the Dock, respectively.

**Book III
Chapter 2**

**Giving Your Desktop
the Personal Touch**

You can also right-click when the funky line cursor is visible to display a menu of Dock preferences. This allows you to change your Dock preferences without the hassle of opening System Preferences and displaying the Dock settings.

## Stick It on the Dashboard

One of Snow Leopard's most popular features is *Dashboard,* which you can use to hold widgets and display them with the press of a button. (Okay, I know that sounds a little wacky, but bear with me.) *Widgets* are small applications — dubbed *applets* — that typically provide only one function. For example, Dashboard comes complete with a calculator, a clock, a weather display, and a quick-and-simple calendar. You can display and use these widgets at any time by pressing the Dashboard key; by default, that's F4 on current MacBook keyboards, but you can modify the key on the Exposé & Spaces pane within System Preferences. Snow Leopard also includes a thoughtful Dashboard icon in the Dock, which you can click to display your widgets. (Geez, that sounds kind of racy. Best not to pursue it.)

Figure 2-6 illustrates Dashboard in action. Press the Dashboard key, and the widgets appear, ready for you to use. You can add widgets to or delete them from your Dashboard by clicking the Add button (which bears a plus sign, naturally) at the lower-left corner of the Dashboard screen. When you click the Add button, a scrolling menu strip appears at the bottom of the Dashboard display, and you can drag new widgets directly onto your Dashboard from this menu. It's also easy to rearrange the widgets that are already populating Dashboard by dragging them to the desired spot. Press the Dashboard key again to return to your Snow Leopard Desktop.

Most widgets have an option button that allows you to change things, such as borders, ZIP Codes, display columns, and the like; look for a tiny circle with a lowercase letter *i*. Click this information icon and you can tweak whatever options are available for that widget.

To remove a widget, just click the Add button to display the menu strip, and you'll notice a tiny X button appears next to each widget on your Dashboard. Click the X button next to the widget you want to remove, and it vanishes from the display. You can add it back again at any time from the strip.

While you're adding or deleting widgets, you can also click Manage Widgets, which displays a dialog where you can sort your widgets in a list by name or date added, disable any widget, and delete a widget (click the red minus icon next to the offending widget in the list). Click the More Widgets button to jump directly to the widget download area on the Apple Web site.

**Figure 2-6:**
Dashboard proudly displays its widgets.

Book III
Chapter 2

Giving Your Desktop
the Personal Touch

If you need to use a widget for only a second or two, press the Dashboard key and hold it. When you release the key, you're back to your Desktop.

Apple offers additional widgets that you can download on the Mac OS X download site (www.apple.com/macosx). Third-party software developers also provide both freeware and shareware widgets.

You can also modify the Dashboard key by turning it into a key sequence, which is a good thing if you're already using an application that thrives on F4. Visit the Exposé & Spaces pane in System Preferences, and use the Shift, Control, Option, and ⌘ keys in conjunction with the Dashboard key to specify a modifier.

Oh, did I mention that Snow Leopard allows you to create your own Dashboard widgets? That's right, this feature is sure to be a winner amongst the In Crowd. Follow these steps to create a new *WebClip* Dashboard widget from your favorite Web site:

*1.* **Run Safari and navigate to the site you want to view as a widget.**

*2.* **Click File➪Open in Dashboard.**

3. **Select the portion of the page you want to include in your widget and click Add.**

   Many Web pages use frames to organize and separate sections of a page, so this step allows you to choose the frame with the desired content.

4. **Drag the handles at the edges of the selection border to resize your widget frame to the right size and then click Add.**

   Bam! Snow Leopard displays your new WebClip widget within Dashboard.

A WebClip widget can include text, graphics, and links, which Dashboard updates every time you display your widgets. Think about that for a second: Dynamic displays, such as weather maps, cartoons, even the Free Music Download image from the iTunes Store, are all good sources of WebClip widgets! (That last one is a real timesaver.)

If you click a link in a WebClip widget, Dashboard loads the full Web page in Safari, so you can even use WebClips for surfing chores with sites you visit often.

## Arranging Your Precious Desktop

Consider the layout of the Desktop itself. You can set the options for icon placement from the Finder View menu. Just as you can with the options for Finder windows that I cover in Chapter 1 of this minibook, you can clean up and arrange your Desktop by name, date, size, or kind.

The View Options for the Desktop are different in two ways from the View Options for a Finder window in icon view (which I discuss in Chapter 1 of this minibook):

✦ You choose a background for the Finder from System Preferences.

✦ There's no Always Open check box. Your Desktop always opens in Icon view!

# Chapter 3: Delving under the Hood with System Preferences

## In This Chapter

✓ Displaying and customizing settings in System Preferences

✓ Saving your changes

✓ Changing settings

The System Preferences window is the place to practice behavior modification in Mac OS X. The settings that you specify in System Preferences affect the majority of the applications that you use as well as the hardware that you connect to your MacBook; your Internet and network traffic; the appearance and activity on your Desktop; and how Snow Leopard handles money, dates, and languages. Oh, and don't forget your screen saver — important stuff!

In this chapter, I discuss the many settings in System Preferences. You discover what does what and how you can customize the appearance and operation of Mac OS X.

## The Preferred Way to Display the Preferences

Apple has made it easy to open the System Preferences window. Just click the System Preferences icon (which looks like a number of gears) in the Dock, and the window shown in Figure 3-1 appears. You can also open the window by clicking the Apple menu and choosing the System Preferences item.

To display all the System Preferences icons at any time, click the Show All button. You can also use the Back and Forward buttons (in the toolbar's upper-left corner) to move backward and forward through the different panes you've accessed in System Preferences, just as you use the similar buttons in a Web browser (yes, just like Safari!).

**Figure 3-1:**
The System
Preferences
window is a
familiar face
to any Snow
Leopard
user.

Although the System Preferences panes are arranged by category when you first install Snow Leopard, you can also display the panes in alphabetical order — making it easier to choose a pane if you're unsure what group it's in. To do so, choose View⇨Organize Alphabetically. (Note that you can also select any pane directly from the View menu.)

In fact, you can right-click the System Preferences icon in the Dock to jump to any pane from the contextual menu. *Wowzers!*

## Saving Your Preferences

Note that the System Preferences window has no Save or Apply button. Illustrating the elegant design of Mac OS X, simply quitting System Preferences automatically saves all the changes that you make. (However, some panes in System Preferences have an Apply button that you can click to apply your changes immediately.) As with any other Mac OS X application, you can quit the System Preferences window by pressing ⌘+Q or by choosing System Preferences⇨Quit System Preferences.

### Hey, I got bonus icons in my window!

Some third-party applications can actually install their own groups within your once-pristine System Preferences window. Naturally, I can't document these invited guests in this chapter, but they work the same way as any other group within System Preferences. Click the icon, adjust any settings as necessary, and then close the System Preferences window to save your changes.

# Searching for Specific Settings

Searching for a single button or check box amidst all the settings in System Preferences might seem like hunting for the proverbial needle in a haystack, but your friends at Apple have added a Search box to the right side of the window toolbar. Click in this Search box (or press ⌘+F) and type the setting name, like **screen saver** (or even a word that's generally associated with a setting, like **power** for the Energy Saver settings). Snow Leopard highlights all the icons in System Preferences that have anything to do with the search keywords you entered, as shown in Figure 3-2. You don't even have to press Return!

**Figure 3-2:**
System Preferences highlights the panes that contain your search keywords.

**Book III**
**Chapter 3**

Delving under the
Hood with System
Preferences

To reset the Search field for a different keyword, click the X button that appears at the right of the Search box.

# Getting Personal

The first stop on your tour of the System Preferences window is the Personal section. No singles ads here — this section is devoted to settings that you make to customize the appearance and operation of your Desktop and login account.

## Appearance preferences

The Appearance group appears in Figure 3-3.

**Figure 3-3:**
The
Appearance
pane.

These settings are

✦ **Appearance:** From this pop-up menu, choose a color to be used for buttons, menus, and windows.

✦ **Highlight Color:** From this pop-up menu, choose a color to be used to highlight selected text in fields and pop-up menus.

✦ **Place Scroll Arrows:** Select either radio button here to put the scroll bar arrow buttons together (at the bottom of the scroll bar, in the lower-right corner of the window) or at the top and bottom of the scroll bar.

✦ **Click in the Scroll Bar To:** By default, Mac OS X jumps to the next or previous page when you click in an empty portion of the scroll bar. Select the Jump to the Spot That's Clicked radio button to scroll the document to the approximate position in relation to where you click. (You can also choose smooth scrolling, which looks cool, but many folks think that it's too slow compared with the default scrolling speed.) If you select the Double-Click a Window's Title Bar to Minimize check box, you can minimize a Finder or application window by simply double-clicking the window's title bar.

✦ **Number of Recent Items:** The default number of recent applications, documents, and servers (available from the Recent Items item in the Apple menu, which you can read more about in Book II, Chapter 3) is 10. To change the default, click any of the pop-up menus here and choose up to 50. (Personally, I like 20 or 30 for each.)

✦ **Use LCD Font Smoothing:** By default, this check box is enabled, making the text on your MacBook's LCD display appear more like the printed page.

✦ **Turn Off Text Smoothing for Font Sizes:** Below a certain point size, text smoothing isn't much good for most on-screen fonts. By default, any font displayed at 8 point or smaller isn't smoothed, which is suitable for a high-end video card and monitor. You can speed up the display of text by turning off text smoothing for fonts up to 12 point.

## Desktop and screen saver preferences

Figure 3-4 illustrates the settings in the Desktop & Screen Saver group.

**Figure 3-4:** The Desktop & Screen Saver pane.

The settings on the Desktop tab are

✦ **Current Desktop Picture:** You can click a picture in the thumbnail list at the right half of the screen to use it as your Desktop background. The Desktop is immediately updated, and the thumbnail appears in the *well* (the square box in Figure 3-4). To display a different image collection or open a folder of your own images, click the Add Folder button at the lower left of the window (which carries a plus sign) and browse for your heart's desire; click Choose to select a folder and display the images it contains.

✦ **Layout:** As I explain in Chapter 2 of this minibook, you can tile your background image, center it, fill the screen with it, and stretch it to fill the screen. (Note that filling the screen may distort the image.) The layout control appears only when you're using your own pictures, so you won't see it if you're using a Desktop image supplied by Apple.

✦ **Change Picture:** Select this check box to change the Desktop background automatically after the delay period that you set, including each time you log in and each time your Mac wakes up from sleep mode.

✦ **Random Order:** To display screens randomly, enable the Random Order check box. Otherwise, the backgrounds are displayed in the sequence in which they appear in the thumbnail strip.

✦ **Translucent Menu Bar:** When enabled, this feature turns your Finder and application menu bars semi-opaque, allowing them to blend in somewhat with your Desktop background. If you'd rather have a solid-color menu bar, deselect this check box.

Click the Screen Saver tab to see the following settings:

✦ **Screen Savers:** In the Screen Savers list at the left, click the screen saver that you want to display an animated Preview of on the right. To try out the screen saver in full-screen mode, click the Test button. (You can end the test by moving your finger across the trackpad.) If the screen saver module that you select has any configurable settings, click the Options button to display them. (A screen saver is configurable if the Options button is enabled.)

✦ **Start Screen Saver:** Click and drag the slider here to specify the period of inactivity that triggers the screen saver. To disable the screen saver, choose the Never setting at the far right of the slider.

✦ **Use Random Screen Saver:** Just what it says: If this check box is enabled, a different screen saver module is used each time the screen saver is activated.

✦ **Show with Clock:** If you want your selected screen saver to display the time as well, click this check box to enable it.

✦ **Hot Corners:** Click any of the four pop-up menus at the four corners of the screen to specify that corner as an *activation hot corner* (which immediately activates the screen saver) or as a *disabling hot corner* (which prevents the screen saver from activating). As long as the pointer stays in the disabling hot corner, the screen saver doesn't kick in no matter how long a period of inactivity passes. Note that you can also set the Exposé activation corners from here. (For the scoop on Exposé, see the upcoming section, "Exposé and Spaces preferences.")

## Dock preferences

The Dock group is shown in Figure 3-5.

**Figure 3-5:**
The Dock
preference
pane.

Settings here are

✦ **Size:** Move this slider to change the overall size of the Dock.

✦ **Magnification:** With this check box selected, a Dock icon magically expands, like the national deficit, when you move your pointer over it. You can move the Magnification slider to specify just how much magnification is right for you.

This feature is useful for helping you click a particular Dock icon If you've resized the Dock smaller than its default dimensions or if you have a large number of items in the Dock.

✦ **Position on Screen:** Choose from three radio buttons to make that crazy Dock appear at the left, bottom, or right edge of your Desktop.

✦ **Minimize Windows Using:** By default, Mac OS X animates a window when it's shrunk into the Dock (and when it's expanded back into a full window). From the Minimize Using pop-up menu, you can choose from a genie-in-a-bottle effect or a scale-up-or-down-incrementally effect. To demonstrate, choose an effect and then click the Minimize button (the yellow button in the upper-left corner) on the System Preferences window.

✦ **Minimize windows into application icon:** By default, Snow Leopard minimizes a window as a thumbnail on the right side of the Dock. Select this check box to minimize a window into the icon for the parent application instead.

✦ **Animate Opening Applications:** By default, Mac OS X has that happy, slam-dancing feeling when you launch an application: The application's icon bounces up and down in the Dock two or three times to draw your attention and indicate that the application is loading. If you find this effervescence overly buoyant or distracting, deselect this check box.

**Book III
Chapter 3**

**Delving under the
Hood with System
Preferences**

✦ **Automatically Hide and Show the Dock:** If you like, the Dock can stay hidden until you need it, thus reclaiming a significant amount of Desktop space for your application windows. Select this check box to hide the Dock whenever you're not using it.

To display a hidden Dock, move your pointer over the edge of the Desktop where it's hiding.

You can also change these Dock preference settings from the Apple menu.

## Exposé and Spaces preferences

Figure 3-6 illustrates the Exposé & Spaces settings that you can configure in this group. You can use Exposé to view all the application windows that you're using at one time so that you can select a new active window. Or you can move all windows aside so that you can see your Desktop. Dashboard presents a number of mini-applications (or *widgets*), which you can summon and hide with a single key. Spaces makes it easy to create multiple desktops that you can switch between, each of which has its own set of preloaded applications.

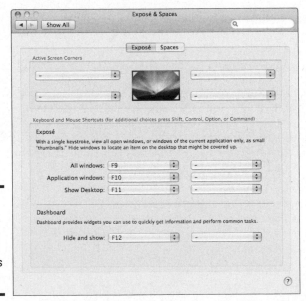

**Figure 3-6:** Set your Dashboard and Exposé preferences here.

On the Exposé pane, the settings are

✦ **Active Screen Corners:** These four pop-up menus operate just like the
Hot Corners/Active Screen Corners in the Desktop & Screen Savers
pane, but they control the operation of the Snow Leopard Dashboard
and Exposé features. Click one to specify that corner as an All Windows
corner (which displays all windows on your Desktop), an Application
Windows corner (which displays only the windows from the active
application), a Desktop corner (which moves all windows to the outside
of the screen to uncover your Desktop), or a Dashboard corner (which
displays your Dashboard widgets). Note that you can also set the Screen
Saver Start and Disable corners from here.

✦ **Keyboard and Mouse Shortcuts:** Click each pop-up menu to set the key
sequences (and mouse button settings) for all three Exposé functions as
well as the Dashboard.

You're not limited to just the keyboard and mouse shortcuts on the
pop-up menus — press the Shift, Control, Option, and ⌘ keys while
a pop-up menu is open, and you see these modifiers appear as menu
choices! (Heck, you can even combine modifiers, such as ⌘+Shift+F9
instead of just F9.)

On the Spaces pane (as shown in Figure 3-7), you find the following settings:

**Book III
Chapter 3**

**Delving under the
Hood with System
Preferences**

**Figure 3-7:**
Configuring
multiple
desktops
from the
Spaces
pane.

✦ **Enable Spaces:** In order to use Spaces, select this check box.

✦ **Show Spaces in Menu Bar:** When this check box is selected, Snow Leopard displays the Spaces desktop number you're currently using in the Finder menu bar. You can click the number in the menu bar to switch to another Spaces desktop or to open the Spaces Preferences pane.

✦ **Rows buttons:** To add a row of Spaces desktops to the Spaces grid, click the Add button with the plus sign. (By default, Spaces starts with two desktops enabled, so new rows and columns are numbered beginning with three.) To delete a row, click the Delete button (which bears a minus sign).

✦ **Columns buttons:** To add a column of Spaces desktops to the Spaces grid, click the Add (plus) button. Click the Delete (minus) button to remove a column from the grid.

If you choose to remove a column or row, Snow Leopard alerts you that the bindings on the deleted desktop(s) will be reassigned.

✦ **Add/Remove Application:** Click the Add Application button (the button with the plus sign under the Application Assignments list) to add an application to one of your Spaces desktops. You can select which desktop should include an application by clicking the up/down arrows next to the Space column for that application's entry. Just click the desired desktop from the pop-up menu that appears. To remove an application, click it in the Application Assignments list to select it and then click the Remove Application button (which sports a minus sign).

Spaces can even add an application to all your desktops — choose Every Space from the pop-up menu.

✦ **Keyboard and Mouse Shortcuts:** Click each pop-up menu to set the key sequences (and mouse button settings) for all three Spaces functions.

As with Dashboard and Exposé keyboard and mouse shortcuts, you can press Shift, Control, Option, and Command keys while the box is open to display modified choices.

✦ **When Switching to an Application:** When selected, this check box allows you to switch applications between Spaces desktops using the ⌘+Tab shortcut. Snow Leopard will jump to the desktop that has an open window for the application you choose, even if that desktop is not currently active.

## Language & Text preferences

The Language & Text group appears in Figure 3-8 with the following tabs:

✦ **Language:** Choose the preferred order for language use in menus and dialogs as well as the standards that Mac OS X will use for each script style.

**Figure 3-8:**
The
Language
& Text pane
in System
Preferences.

✦ **Text:** Specify character combinations that will be automatically replaced with special characters. For example, Snow Leopard will automatically replace the combination **TM** with the special character ™. You can also choose a language for spell-checking and turn on "smart" quotes (where Snow Leopard chooses double or single quotation marks for you).

✦ **Formats:** Find these settings here:

   • *Dates:* You can select a region and use its date conventions (month-day-year versus day-month-year) or you can click the Customize button to build a custom format for both the long date (Saturday, September 24, 2005) and short date (9/24/2005) used throughout Mac OS X. The changes you make are reflected immediately in the sample box at the left.

   • *Times:* Click Customize to select a region to use the preset time conventions. You can choose 12-hour or 24-hour (military) time formats, change the time separator (colons, a period, or a dash), and specify different suffixes for morning (a.m.) and evening (p.m.).

   • *Numbers:* These convention settings determine the separators used for large numbers or numbers with decimals, as well as the currency symbol that you want to use and where it appears in a number. You can also choose between standard (U.S.) and metric measurement systems.

✦ **Input Sources:** Each check box toggles the keyboard layouts available from the Input menu. (To display the Input menu on the Finder menu bar, click the Show Input Menu in Menu Bar check box to select it.) Click the Keyboard Shortcuts button to toggle the shortcuts for switching layouts and input methods.

**Book III
Chapter 3**

**Delving under the
Hood with System
Preferences**

## Security preferences

The Security group is shown in Figure 3-9.

**Figure 3-9:**
Set Security
preferences
here.

Settings here are divided into three tabs:

✦ **General:** To add an extra layer of password security to your laptop (which I recommend if you often work in a public area), select the Require Password after Sleep or Screen Saver Begins check box. Mac OS X then requires that you enter your login password before the system returns from a sleep state or exits a screen saver. Click the pop-up delay menu to specify when the password requirement will kick in (it's immediate by default). If you're an admin-level user, you can set the global security features in the For All Accounts on This Computer section, which affect all user accounts. You can choose to disable the automatic login feature, force Mac OS X to require a login password each time that a System Preferences pane is opened, automatically log off any user after a certain amount of inactivity, or use *secure* (encrypted) virtual memory on your hard drive. You can also mark the Disable Location Services check box to turn off the Location feature, preventing applications from using information based on your MacBook's current location.

Don't want small fingers accidentally controlling your MacBook with the Apple Remote? If you don't need the Remote on a regular basis, click the Disable Remote Control Infrared Receiver check box to select it. (But don't forget to turn your IR receiver back on for your next movie night!)

✦ **FileVault:** These controls allow you to set the master password for FileVault encryption within the current user's Home folder, which makes it virtually impossible for others to access those files. Only an admin-level user can set the master password. After the master password is set, you can click the Turn On FileVault button to enable FileVault encryption for the user who's currently logged in; the user's Login password becomes his FileVault password as well.

✦ **Firewall:** As I discuss in Book VI, Chapter 6, Mac OS X includes a built-in firewall, which you can enable from this pane.

To turn the firewall off entirely, simply click the Stop button. This is the very definition of Not a Good Thing, and I **always** recommend that any MacBook hooked up to a network or the Internet have the system firewall turned **on.** (The only exception is if you're using a network that you *know* to be secure and your access to the Internet is through a router or sharing device with its own built-in firewall.)

When the firewall is enabled, click the Advanced button to set firewall options.

- *To turn the firewall on with only Mac OS X application exclusions,* click Block All Incoming Connections — only the sharing services you select on the Sharing pane in System Preferences are allowed through your firewall.) This is a good choice for the most security-conscious MacBook owner, but your firewall will block third-party applications that try to access your network or the Internet.

- *To turn the firewall on with exclusions,* click Automatically Allow Signed Software to Receive Incoming Connections. (Yep, this is the correct option for just about every MacBook owner.) Any connection to a service (such as Web Sharing) or an application (such as iChat) that isn't listed is blocked, but you can enable access for third-party applications on an as-needed basis.

In firewall-speak, these entries are *rules* because they determine what's allowed to pass through to your MacBook.

It's easy to enable communications with a Mac OS X service: Just use the Sharing pane within System Preferences to turn on a service, and Snow Leopard automatically configures your firewall to allow communications. I describe the Sharing pane in detail later in this chapter.

To add a third-party application, click the Advanced button at the bottom of the Firewall pane, then click the button with the plus sign. Navigate to the application that needs to communicate with the outside world. Click the application to select it and then click Add. To delete an application, select it in the list and click the button with the minus sign. Remember, you don't have to add any of the applications provided by Apple with Snow Leopard, such as Apple Mail, iChat, or Safari; only third-party applications that you install yourself need a firewall rule.

You can edit the rule for a specific service or application by clicking the rule at the right side of the entry. By default, the rule reads Allow Incoming Connections (including both your local network and the Internet); however, when you click the rule, you can also choose Block Incoming Connections to temporarily deny access to that application.

If you suddenly can't connect to other computers or share files that you originally could share, review the rules that you've enabled from this pane. You can also verify that everything's shipshape in the Sharing pane in System Preferences, which I cover later in this chapter.

## Spotlight preferences

The Spotlight group is shown in Figure 3-10.

Settings here are

✦ **Search Results tab:** You can enable or disable the check boxes next to each of the categories to display or hide each category in the Spotlight search menu and dialog. Click and drag the categories to the order that you prefer. For example, I like to see matching documents immediately after matching applications in the Spotlight dialog, so I dragged Documents to the second position in the list. You can also specify a different keyboard shortcut for the Spotlight menu and window.

✦ **Privacy tab:** If you don't want to display the contents of certain folders in the Spotlight — for instance, if you work in a hospital setting and you can't allow access to patient information and medical records — click the Add button (which carries a plus sign) and specify the folder or disk you want to exclude from Spotlight searches. Alternatively, just drag the folders or disks to exclude into the list from a Finder window.

**Figure 3-10:**
Fine-tune
your
Spotlight
search
results here.

# It's All about the Hardware

The next category, Hardware, allows you to specify settings that affect your laptop's hardware.

## CDs and DVDs preferences

The CDs & DVDs group is shown in Figure 3-11.

**Figure 3-11:**
The CD
& DVD
preferences.

Choices here are

✦ **When You Insert a Blank CD:** Click this pop-up menu to specify the action that Mac OS X takes when you load a blank CD-R or CD-RW. You can choose to be prompted or to open the Finder, iTunes, or Disk Copy. Additionally, you can open another application that you select, run an AppleScript that you select, or ignore the disc.

✦ **When You Insert a Blank DVD:** Use this feature to specify the action that your MacBook takes when you load a recordable DVD.

✦ **When You Insert a Music CD:** Choices from this pop-up menu specify what action Mac OS X takes when you load an audio CD. By default, iTunes launches.

✦ **When You Insert a Picture CD:** Choices from this pop-up menu specify what action Mac OS X takes when you load a picture CD. By default, iPhoto launches.

✦ **When You Insert a Video DVD:** Choices from this pop-up menu specify what action Mac OS X takes when you load a DVD movie. By default, DVD Player launches.

## Displays preferences

The Displays group is shown in Figure 3-12.

**Book III
Chapter 3**

**Delving under the
Hood with System
Preferences**

**Figure 3-12:**
Configure
your
MacBook's
display
settings
from this
pane.

The two tabs here are

✦ **Display:** Click the resolution that you want to use from the Resolutions
list on the left and then choose the number of colors (from the Colors
pop-up menu) to display. In most cases, you want to use the highest
resolution and the highest number of colors. You can also choose a
refresh rate (from the, ahem, Refresh Rate pop-up menu). Again, generally,
the higher the refresh rate, the better. Move the Brightness slider to
adjust the brightness level of your display. If you've connected an
external monitor or flat-screen TV to your MacBook, click the Detect
Displays button and Snow Leopard will add them to the list of available
displays, allowing you to redirect your MacBook's video signal.

Enable the Show Displays in Menu Bar check box if you'll be switching
resolutions and color levels often — this means you, Ms. Image Editor
and Mr. Web Designer!

✦ **Color:** Click a display color profile that will control the colors on
your monitor. To load a profile, click the Open Profile button. To
create a custom ColorSync profile and calibrate the colors that you
see on your monitor, click the Calibrate button to launch the Display
Calibrator. (You can also launch it from your Utilities folder within your
Applications folder.) This easy-to-use assistant walks you step-by-step
through the process of creating a ColorSync profile matched to your
monitor's gamma and white-point values.

## Energy Saver preferences

The Energy Saver group is shown in Figure 3-13.

**Figure 3-13:**
The Energy
Saver pane.

Move the Computer Sleep slider to specify when Mac OS X should switch to
sleep mode. The Never setting here disables sleep mode entirely. To choose
a separate delay period for blanking your monitor, drag the Display Sleep
delay slider to the desired period. You can also power down the hard drive
to conserve energy and prevent wear and tear (an especially good feature
for laptop owners).

If you want to start or shut down your laptop at a scheduled time, click the
Schedule button. Mark the desired schedule (the Start Up or Wake check
box and the Shut Down/Sleep check box) to enable them; then click the up
and down arrows next to the time display to set the trigger time. Click OK to
return to the Energy Saver pane.

Some of the settings can toggle events that control Snow Leopard's sleep
mode, including a network connection by the network administrator (Wake
for Network Access). If you want the display to dim before your Mac goes
to sleep, enable the Automatically Reduce Brightness before Display Goes
to Sleep check box. You can also set Mac OS X to restart automatically
after a power failure, which is a good idea if you're sharing music or files
with others. Naturally, MacBook owners will want to click the Show Battery
Status in the Menu Bar check box to select it.

Mac laptop owners can set two separate Energy Saver configurations by
clicking one of the two tabs at the top of the pane:

✦ **Battery Power:** Applies when their MacBook is running on battery
  power)

✦ **Power Adapter:** Kicks in when the laptop is connected to an AC outlet

Your MacBook will automatically switch to the proper configuration when
you plug or unplug your laptop.

**Book III
Chapter 3**

**Delving under the
Hood with System
Preferences**

## Keyboard preferences

The Keyboard group is shown in Figure 3-14.

**Figure 3-14:**
The
Keyboard
preferences
panel.

The two tabs include

✦ **Keyboard:** Move the Key Repeat Rate slider to alter the rate at which a keystroke repeats. You can also adjust the Delay until Repeat slider to alter how long a key must be held down before it repeats. If you change your keyboard, you can always run the Keyboard Setup Assistant by clicking the Change Keyboard Type button — you can also set up a wireless Bluetooth keyboard from this pane.

MacBook owners can set the F1–F12 keys as standard function keys within applications by enabling the Use All F1, F2, Etc. Keys as Standard Function Keys check box. If you enable this feature, you have to hold down the Function (or Fn) key while pressing the F1 through F12 keys to use the regular hardware keys.

If you have a MacBook Pro, you can choose to turn the ambient keyboard lighting on and off from this pane, or turn off keyboard lighting after an inactivity delay that you set.

✦ **Keyboard Shortcuts:** If you're a power user who appreciates the lure of the keyboard shortcut, you can edit your shortcuts here.

Looking for even more keyboard customizing possibilities? Select the All Controls radio button on the Keyboard Shortcuts pane to see additional keys to use.

## Mouse preferences

Figure 3-15 illustrates the Mouse preferences pane.

**Figure 3-15:**
The Mouse preferences pane.

The contents of this pane depend on whether your MacBook has a USB or wireless Bluetooth mouse installed. If you haven't installed a mouse yet, you see a Waiting screen that leads you through the installation process. After you add a mouse, trackball, or other pointing device to your system, you see the settings shown in Figure 3-15.

✦ **Mouse:** Drag the Tracking Speed slider to determine how fast the mouse tracks across your Desktop. You can also drag the Double-Click Speed slider to determine how fast you must click your mouse to cause a double-click. Drag the Scrolling Speed slider to specify the rate at which the contents of windows will scroll. Lefties might want to change the primary mouse button for aftermarket pointing devices. You can also zoom the display with your Mighty Mouse scroll ball while holding down the key of your choice — a great option for image editing. To install a wireless Bluetooth mouse from this pane, click the Set Up Bluetooth Mouse button, which runs the Bluetooth device Set Up assistant.

✦ **(Optional) Bluetooth:** If you're using a wireless Bluetooth mouse or keyboard, you can check the battery level on these devices from this pane. You can also specify whether your Bluetooth keyboard or mouse wakes your Mac from sleep mode. If you don't have a Bluetooth keyboard or mouse, this tab doesn't appear.

**Book III
Chapter 3**

**Delving under the
Hood with System
Preferences**

## Trackpad preferences

Figure 3-16 illustrates the Trackpad preferences pane.

**Figure 3-16:**
The
Trackpad
preferences
pane.

This pane is available only to MacBook owners, allowing this elite crowd to customize the tracking speed and double-click speed for their trackpads. You can also set your MacBook's trackpad for two-fingered scrolling (vertical and horizontal) and zooming. (I imagine both will someday become Olympic events.) If you prefer to zoom by holding down a key, click the pop-up menu to select the key. You can also enable clicking and configure right-clicking by using the trackpad.

I suggest that you leave the Ignore Accidental Trackpad Input check box selected to prevent spurious movements and clicks — and, if you use a mouse with your laptop, you can elect to disable the trackpad while the mouse is connected. This helps to prevent accidental copies or moves within a Finder window!

## Printing and fax preferences

Figure 3-17 illustrates the Print & Fax preferences.

Click the Options & Supplies button to configure the selected printer's features, and click the Open Print Queue button to display the Print Queue window (no great shockers there). To add a new printer or fax connection, click the Add button, which bears a plus sign — Snow Leopard launches the Browser. You can read more about printer and fax setup in Book VIII, Chapter 4.

**Figure 3-17:**
Configure
faxing and
printing
with these
settings.

The other settings here are

✦ **Share This Printer on the Network:** Click this check box to share
this printer with other computers on your network. To specify who
can use your shared printer, click the Set Permissions button. System
Preferences switches to the Sharing pane, where you can add or remove
users from the permission list.

✦ **Default Printer:** Click this pop-up menu to select the installed printer that
acts as the default printer throughout your system. If you choose Last
Printer Used, Mac OS X uses the printer that received the last print job.

✦ **Default Paper Size:** Will that be US Letter or Tabloid? Click this pop-up
menu to specify the default paper size for future print jobs.

If you've added a fax entry to the list, click the entry to set up the fax
send/receive functions built into Snow Leopard. To receive faxes on your
MacBook, you must first set up a fax connection; then, click the Receive
Options button and select the Receive Faxes on This Computer check box.

After faxing is turned on, you can configure the other settings from the Print
& Fax pane and the Receive Options sheet. These settings include

✦ **Fax Number:** Enter the phone number that others call to reach your
MacBook.

✦ **When a Fax Arrives:** You can determine how many times the phone rings before your laptop's external modem answers the incoming call. By default, Mac OS X saves the incoming fax to your Shared Faxes folder, but you can change that location — or you can choose to print the incoming fax on the printer that you specify. Heck, if you like, you can send your fax to both destinations (a disk folder and a printer) or even mail the fax to the e-mail address you specify.

If you send and receive a large number of faxes, make sure you enable the Show Fax Status in Menu Bar check box.

You can also allow other computer users on your local network to send faxes through your MacBook. Enable the Share This Fax on the Network check box, and your laptop's external fax modem appears when the other users add a fax connection.

## Sound preferences

The Sound group is shown in Figure 3-18. To set the overall system audio volume, drag the Output Volume slider. To mute all sound from your MacBook, select the Mute check box. I recommend that you select the Show Volume in Menu Bar check box, which displays a convenient volume slider menu bar icon.

**Figure 3-18:** The Sound preferences pane.

The three tabs here are

✦ **Sound Effects:** From this pane, you can choose the system alert sound and the volume for alerts. You can also choose to mute application and Finder menu sound effects, as well as toggle the sample sound effect when the volume keys are pressed on your MacBook's keyboard (or from the Volume slider). If you use Front Row with your laptop, you can enable or disable the Front Row audio effects from this pane.

✦ **Output:** Use these settings to choose which audio controller your MacBook uses for playing sound. Unless you've installed additional audio hardware, this remains set to Built-in Audio or Internal Speakers. You can adjust the balance between the left and right channels for the selected output controller.

✦ **Input:** These settings allow you to specify an input source. Unless your MacBook includes a Line In input source, leave this set to your Internal Microphone. Drag the Input Volume slider to increase or decrease the input signal volume; the input level display provides you with real-time sound levels. If your MacBook is in a location with a large amount of background noise, click the Use Ambient Noise Reduction check box to improve the quality of your audio input.

# Sharing the Joy: Internet and Network

Your Internet and Network connections are controlled from the settings in this category.

## MobileMe preferences

The MobileMe group is illustrated in Figure 3-19.

**Figure 3-19:** Your MobileMe account is controlled and configured using these settings.

Book III
Chapter 3

Delving under the
Hood with System
Preferences

The four tabs are

✦ **Account:** In the MobileMe Member Name and the Password text boxes, respectively, type your MobileMe member name and password to display the Account tab. If you want to subscribe, click the Learn More button to launch your Web browser and you're whisked to the MobileMe sign-up page. For more information about joining Apple's MobileMe service, see Book VI, Chapter 4.

✦ **Sync:** If you want to synchronize your MacBook (or multiple Macintosh computers) with the personal information and data stored online in your MobileMe account, select the Synchronize with MobileMe check box and click the pop-up menu to specify manual or automatic synchronization. (To manually sync, click Sync Now.) You can also specify which categories of data you want to sync. Naturally, the fewer categories you choose, the less time it takes to sync. To register a computer so that you can sync with it, click the Advanced button and then click Register Computer. Snow Leopard can display your Sync status in the Finder menu bar.

✦ **iDisk:** This pane displays your current iDisk usage and allows you to subscribe for additional space with the Upgrade button. You can set your access privileges for your public folder by selecting or deselecting the Allow Others to Write Files in Your Public Folder check box, and you can add a password that others have to enter before they can access your public folder. For a complete description of iDisk, see Book VI, Chapter 4.

I recommend that you click the iDisk Sync Start button on the iDisk tab to enable the Snow Leopard iDisk syncing function (which creates a local copy of your iDisk on your MacBook). Select the Update Automatically option; this option allows iDisk to run much faster because Mac OS X can read and write by using your local iDisk copy on your hard drive. Your MacBook regularly synchronizes the data on your local hard drive across the Internet with the iDisk on the Apple server. To make sure that you're always using the most recent copy of a file on your iDisk, select the Always Keep the Most Recent Version of a File check box.

✦ **Back to My Mac:** From this list, you can control file and screen sharing across all the computers you use with your MobileMe account. To begin using the Back to My Mac features, click the Start button. (Remember, you'll have to turn on Back to My Mac on all computers that will use this service.)

## Network preferences
The Network group is shown in Figure 3-20.

You can choose an existing Location by clicking the Location pop-up menu at the top of the dialog, or you can create and edit your Locations by choosing Edit Locations from this pop-up menu. (Automatic is the default, and it does a pretty good job of figuring out what settings you need.) As I mention in Book II, Chapter 3, creating Locations makes it easy to completely reconfigure your Network preferences when you connect your computer to other networks — for example, when you take your laptop to a branch office. You can also set up Locations to accommodate different ISP dial-up telephone numbers in different towns.

**Figure 3-20:**
The
Network
pane,
showing
the AirPort
status
information.

If you need to create a new Location that's very similar to an existing Location, click the Location pop-up menu and choose Edit Locations. Then select the Location that you want to copy, click the Action button (bearing the gear symbol), and choose Duplicate Location from the pop-up menu. The new Location that you create contains all the same settings (without several minutes of retyping), so you can easily edit it and make minor changes quickly.

You can choose locations from the Apple menu — a useful trick for laptop road warriors.

### Ethernet network settings

When you select Ethernet from the Services list, the Status pane shows your connection information. Because most networks have a DHCP server to provide automatic settings, you probably don't have to change anything; Snow Leopard does a good job at making introductions automatic between your MacBook and both a local network and the Internet.

Notice the very attractive Assist Me . . . button at the bottom of the Network pane? It's there for a very good reason: Click it, and Snow Leopard launches a network connection and troubleshooting assistant that guides you step-by-step. If your ISP doesn't provide you with instructions on setting up your Internet connection — or that oh-so-smart Mr. Network Administrator is too busy to help connect your MacBook to your office network — use both this book and the network assistant to do the job yourself!

Need to make manual changes to your network settings? Click the Advanced button (it's like opening the hood on your car). The tabs on the Advanced sheet include

✦ **TCP/IP:** These settings are provided either automatically (by using Dynamic Host Configuration Protocol [DHCP]) or manually (by using settings provided by your network administrator).

✦ **DNS:** The settings that you enter here specify the DNS servers and search domains used by your ISP. Typically, any changes you make here are requested by your ISP or your network administrator. Click the Add buttons (with the plus signs) to add a new DNS server address or search domain.

✦ **WINS:** Dating back a few years, WINS is a name server required for computers running NetBIOS (practically dinosaurs in the computer timeline), and likely only those computers running a version of Windows older than Windows 2000. If that sounds like gobbledygook to you, you need to enter something on this tab only if instructed to do so by your network administrator.

✦ **802.1X:** This tab controls which wireless networking security protocols that you may need to connect to a third-party wireless base station or access point. Click the Add Configuration button (with our friend the plus sign) to create a new wireless connection configuration, including your username, password, and the protocols that need to be used. Note that these settings are set automatically when making a wireless connection with an Apple AirPort Extreme base station.

✦ **Proxies:** Network proxy servers are used as part of a firewall configuration to help keep your network secure, but in most cases, changing them can cause you to lose Internet functionality if you enter the wrong settings.

Most folks using a telephone modem, cable modem, or digital subscriber line (DSL) connection should leave these settings alone. Enable and change these settings only at the request of your network administrator, who should supply you the location of a PAC file to automate the process.

If you've enabled your Mac OS X firewall and you use FTP to transfer files, enable the Passive FTP Mode check box on the Proxies pane. I recommend that you enable this setting to allow downloading from some Web pages as well.

✦ **Ethernet:** From this pane, you can configure the settings for your Ethernet network interface card. I *strongly* recommend that you leave the Configure pop-up menu set to Automatically (unless specifically told to set things manually by your system administrator or that nice person from Apple tech support).

## Modem network settings

When you select Modem from the Services list, you can enter the telephone number, account name, and password provided by your ISP. In most cases, that's all the information you need. But if you need to make a manual change, click the Advanced button to display these tabs:

✦ **Modem:** Click the Modem pop-up menu and choose the brand and model of your external modem.

I strongly recommend that you enable the Enable Error Correction and Compression in Modem check box; also select Wait for Dial Tone before Dialing from the Dial Mode pop-up menu. These settings provide you with the best performance and the fastest speeds.

You can also select tone or pulse dialing and whether you want to hear the two modems conversing. (If the caterwauling bothers you, turn off the Sound option.)

✦ **DNS:** These settings are the same as those I cover earlier, in the section "Ethernet network settings."

✦ **WINS:** Again, you're likely to never need these WINS settings, so make changes on this tab only if instructed to do so by your network administrator.

✦ **Proxies:** Some ISPs use proxy servers for their dial-up accounts to maintain security, but changing these settings willy-nilly is inviting disaster. Leave them disabled unless given specific instructions on what to set by your ISP.

✦ **PPP:** These settings are used for a Point-to-Point Protocol connection over a telephone modem. Again, your ISP provides you with the right values to enter here.

If you're concerned about who's using your Internet connection — or you want to add an extra layer of security when you dial out — select the Prompt for Password after Dialing check box on the PPP tab, and Mac OS X prompts you each time for your Internet account password.

I recommend that you select the Show Modem Status in Menu Bar check box on the Modem status pane, which gives you a visual reference on your connection status.

### FireWire and AirPort network settings

The FireWire and AirPort settings on the Advanced sheet are the same as those for Ethernet that I cover earlier in this chapter. However, three settings are on the AirPort status pane that I cover here:

✦ **Network Name:** Snow Leopard handles wireless connections automatically in most cases; if possible, it connects to the last wireless network you joined. If that network isn't available or there are others to choose from, Snow Leopard displays a dialog asking you which available network you want to join. If you want to join only one or more preferred networks (for security or convenience reasons), click the Advanced button and click the Add button (which bears a plus sign) to enter the wireless network name and password.

✦ **Turn AirPort Off:** Okay, here's the honest truth — wireless networking is a significant drain on a laptop battery! If you're sure you're not going to use your MacBook's AirPort network hardware in the near future, you can click this button to activate and deactivate your laptop's network hardware. Turn off AirPort if you don't need it, and your laptop will thank you. (Just turn it back on using this same button when you need it or use the AirPort status menu in the Finder menu bar.)

✦ **Show AirPort Status in Menu Bar:** Hey, speaking of the AirPort Status Menu in the Finder Menu Bar . . . select this check box to display it! You can immediately see the relative signal strength of your connection, switch among available wireless networks, and turn off your AirPort hardware to conserve your battery power (without digging deeply into System Preferences).

## Bluetooth preferences

Since your MacBook has Bluetooth hardware available, the Bluetooth group, as shown in Figure 3-21, appears.

**Figure 3-21:**
The
Bluetooth
pane.

The choices on this pane include

✦ **Device listing:** From this pane, you can opt to allow other Bluetooth devices to discover your MacBook (with the Discoverable check box). All recognized Bluetooth devices in range appear in the list, and you can configure or disconnect them. You can also set up a new Bluetooth device from here by clicking the Set Up New Device button. Also, if you like, Snow Leopard can display a Bluetooth status menu in the Finder menu bar.

MacBook owners who want to conserve power can disable Bluetooth entirely. Just click the Off check box and you save a significant amount of battery time!

✦ **Advanced sheet:** Click the Advanced button to display another group of settings. The Open Bluetooth Setup Assistant check box determines whether Snow Leopard automatically launches the Bluetooth Setup Assistant when no Bluetooth devices are recognized. If you're using a Bluetooth mouse and keyboard, you can wake your MacBook using these devices. You can set Snow Leopard to alert you if an audio request is received from a Bluetooth device, and you can share an Internet connection with connected devices.

You can also edit your Bluetooth Serial Ports from the Advanced sheet, allowing you to use a Bluetooth connection as a virtual serial port. You can add or remove serial services from the Serial Port sheet as well.

## Sharing preferences

Figure 3-22 illustrates the Sharing preferences.

**Figure 3-22:** The Sharing preference settings.

Book III
Chapter 3

Delving under the
Hood with System
Preferences

Click the Edit button to change the default network name assigned to your MacBook during the installation process. Your current network name is listed in the Computer Name text field.

Each entry in the services list controls a specific type of sharing, including DVD or CD Sharing, File Sharing (with other Macs and PCs running Windows), Web Sharing, Screen Sharing, Remote Login, Remote Management (using Apple Remote Desktop), Remote Apple Events, Xgrid Sharing, Internet Sharing, Bluetooth Sharing, Scanner Sharing, and Printer Sharing. To turn on any of these services, select the On check box for that service. To turn off a service, click the corresponding On check box to deselect it.

From a security standpoint, I highly recommend that you enable only those services that you actually use. Each service you enable automatically opens your Snow Leopard firewall for that service. A Mark's Maxim to remember:

**Poking too many holes in your firewall is *not* A Good Thing.**

When you click one of the services in the list, the right side of the Sharing pane changes to display the settings you can specify for that particular service. Note that some services may be disabled, depending on the hardware connected to or installed in your MacBook.

## Tweaking the System

The last section of the System Preferences window covers system-wide settings that affect all users and the overall operation of Mac OS X.

### Accounts preferences

The Accounts group is illustrated in Figure 3-23.

**Figure 3-23:** Configuring accounts is easy from System Preferences.

Each user on your system has an entry in this list. The panes and settings here change, depending on the access level of the selected account. They can include

✦ **Password pane:** Click in these text fields to enter or edit the account name, password (using the Change Password button), and password hint for the selected user.

Click the Address Book Card Open button to edit the card that you mark in the Address Book as My Card. Mac OS X launches the Address Book, and you can edit your card to your heart's content. (For the complete scoop on the Mac OS X Address Book, see Book II, Chapter 6.)

You can set a different MobileMe account name and password for each user account from this pane as well. If you're sharing your Mac with a number of other users, each person can set up his or her own MobileMe account!

If you have administrator access, you can enable Parental Controls for the selected user account or open the Parental Controls pane. (More on Parental Controls later in this section as well as in Chapter 5 of Book III.)

✦ **Picture well:** From the *Picture well* — the square area to the right of the Account list — you can choose one of the thumbnail images provided by Apple to represent you, or drag a photo in from iPhoto. Click the well to display the thumbnails. Click Edit Picture to drag a new image from the Finder or take a video snapshot using your MacBook's iSight camera.

✦ **Login Items pane:** The applications and documents that you add to this list launch automatically each time that the current user logs in to Mac OS X. To add an application, click the Add button (which carries a plus sign), navigate to the desired application and select it, and then click the Add button. (Alternatively, you can simply drag an item from a Finder window into the Login Items list.) To remove an application from the list, click to select it and then click the Remove button (which has a minus sign). Each application can be launched in a *hidden state* — its window doesn't appear on the Desktop. To toggle an item as hidden or visible, enable the Hide check box next to the desired application. The order that Login Items are launched can be changed by dragging entries in the list into the desired sequence.

Note that a user must be logged in to view and change the items on the Login Items pane — even an Administrator-level user can't access another user account's Login items!

You can even set up Login Items directly from the Dock! Control-click (or right-click) the desired Dock icon to display the pop-up menu and then click Open at Login.

✦ **Login Options pane:** Look for the button with the little house icon, lower left. If you're using an admin-level account, click it to set a number of global options that control how users log in. For example, you can choose to display either a Name and Password field on the Login screen (which means that the user must actually type in the correct username) or a list of users, from which a person can select a user ID. (If security is a consideration, use the Name and Password option.) You can also add VoiceOver spoken interface support at the Login screen, making it easier for physically challenged users to log in to this MacBook.

If you choose, you can log in automatically as the selected user by clicking the Automatically Login <*Username*> pop-up menu and choosing your account. (Not a particularly secure feature for MacBook owners, but convenient as all get-out.)

The Login Options pane also allows you to enable or disable Fast User Switching (which I discuss in Book III, Chapter 4), and you can prevent anyone from restarting or shutting down the MacBook from the Login screen by selecting the Hide the Restart and Shut Down Buttons check box.

## Date and time preferences

Click the System Preferences Date & Time icon to display the settings that you see in Figure 3-24.

**Figure 3-24:**
The Date
& Time
preferences
panel.

The three tabs here are

+ **Date & Time:** To set the current date, click the date within the mini-calendar; to set the system time, click in the field above the clock and type the current time.

    You can't set these values manually if you use a network time server. To automatically set your MacBook's system time and date from a network time server, select the Set Date & Time Automatically check box and then choose a server from the pop-up menu that corresponds to your location. (Of course, you need an Internet connection to use a network time server.)

✦ **Time Zone:** Click your approximate location on the world map to choose a time zone or click the Closest City pop-up menu and choose the city that's closest to you (and shares your same time zone). Alternatively, select the Set Time Zone Automatically Using Current Location check box — a real convenience for MacBook owners who are constantly traveling.

✦ **Clock:** If you select the Show the Date and Time in Menu Bar check box, you can choose to view the time in text or icon format. You can also optionally display seconds, the date, AM/PM, and the day of the week; have the time separator characters flash; or use a clock based on 24 hours.

Personally, I get a big kick out of my MacBook announcing the time on the hour . . . plus, it helps pull me back into the real world. (You have to eat sooner or later.) Anyway, if you'd like this helpful reminder as well, select the Announce the Time check box on the Clock pane, and click the pop-up menu to select an hour, half-hour, or quarter-hour announcement.

## Parental Controls preferences

Click a standard level user account in the list to enable or configure Parental Controls for that user. Figure 3-25 shows the Parental Controls settings. (Parental Controls are disabled for administrator accounts and the Guest account.)

**Figure 3-25:**
You can assign Parental Controls to any standard-level user account.

I discuss the Parental Control settings in detail in Chapter 5 of Book III. You can use these settings to restrict a user's access to certain applications, or limit Mail and iChat communications to specific individuals. An administrator can also switch a user account to the Simple Finder, making Snow Leopard much easier to navigate (and limiting the amount of damage a mischievous or malicious user can inflict on your system).

## Software Update preferences

The Software Update settings are shown in Figure 3-26. (Oh, and don't forget that you need an active Internet connection.)

**Figure 3-26:** Keep Snow Leopard up-to-date with the controls in the Software Update group.

The two tabs here are

✦ **Scheduled Check:** I recommend selecting the Check for Updates check box; I also recommend that you choose Daily or Weekly from the pop-up menu. (You can also elect to download critical updates in the background automatically while you continue working.) To check immediately, click the Check Now button.

✦ **Installed Updates:** Click this tab to display a list of the updates you've already applied to Mac OS X and Apple applications. You can open the list as a log file as well, which allows you to cut and paste text.

## Speech preferences

Figure 3-27 illustrates the Speech settings. For a discussion of how these settings are used, visit Book IX, Chapter 3.

**Figure 3-27:**
Snow
Leopard
includes
highly
configurable
Speech
features.

The two tabs here are

✦ **Speech Recognition:** This pane has two tabs of its own: Settings and Commands. With Speakable Items toggled on, you can control Snow Leopard with spoken commands.

  • *Settings tab:* If you have more than one microphone, you can select which one you want to use as well as set the input volume with the Calibrate button. You can change the Listening key (Esc by default) and specify whether your MacBook should listen only while the key is pressed or whether the Listening Key toggles listening on and off. You can also change the name of your computer (using the Keyword box) and whether that name is required before a command. From the Play This Sound pop-up menu, you can indicate what sound effect Mac OS X plays when it recognizes a speech command. (Optionally, Snow Leopard can confirm the command by speaking it if you enable the Speak Command Acknowledgement check box.)

  • *Commands tab:* Here, you can select which types of commands are available as well as whether exact wording of command names is required. Click the self-named button to open the Speakable Items Folder from this pane. Read more about these settings in Book IX, Chapter 3.

✦ **Text to Speech:** Here's a fun pane. Click a voice from the System Voice pop-up menu, and Mac OS X uses that voice to speak to you from dialogs and applications. You can set the Speaking Rate (from Slow to Fast) and play a sample by clicking the Play button. (Try Zarvox, Bubbles, and Pipe Organ.)

**Book III
Chapter 3**

**Delving under the
Hood with System
Preferences**

The Announce When Alerts are Displayed feature actually speaks the text within alert dialogs; to configure spoken alerts, click the Set Alert Options button. You can optionally add a phrase before the text, which you can choose from the Phrase pop-up menu. To add a phrase to the list, like *Don't Panic!,* choose Edit Phrase List from the list. Move the Delay slider to specify how much time your Mac waits before reading the dialog to you.

You can also optionally announce when an application wants your attention, and Snow Leopard can speak the text that's currently selected within an application when you press a key that you specify.

This pane also provides a couple of convenient shortcut buttons that take you to other "speech centers" within System Preferences — specifically, the Date & Time and Universal Access panes.

### Startup Disk preferences

Figure 3-28 illustrates the Startup Disk settings.

**Figure 3-28:** The Startup Disk pane within System Preferences.

To select a startup disk, click the desired startup drive from the scrolling icon list.

Mac OS X displays the version numbers of each system and the physical drives where each system resides. Select the Network Startup icon if you want to boot from a System folder on your local network; typically, such a folder is created by your network administrator. If you've set up a Windows partition on your hard drive using Boot Camp, the folder appears with a Windows logo.

If you're planning on rebooting with an external Universal Serial Bus (USB) or FireWire startup disk, that disk must be connected already, powered on, and recognized by the system before you display these settings.

Click Target Disk Mode to restart your MacBook as a FireWire external hard drive connected to another computer. (This comes in especially handy when you're upgrading to a new Mac and you need to move files between the two computers. I've also used it when the video card in one of my Macs decided to stop working. This allowed me to make an updated backup copy of the ailing Mac's hard drive before I sent it off for repair.) You can also restart your MacBook and hold down the T key to invoke Target Disk Mode.

After you click a disk to select it, click the Restart button. Mac OS X confirms your choice, and your MacBook reboots.

## Time Machine preferences

The Preferences pane shown in Figure 3-29 controls the automatic backups performed by Snow Leopard's Time Machine feature.

**Figure 3-29:** Configure your backups with these Time Machine settings.

To enable Time Machine, click the On toggle switch and then select a disk that will hold your Time Machine backup data on the sheet that appears; click Use for Backup to confirm your choice. If you have an external Time Capsule wireless unit, click Set Up Time Capsule.

By default, Time Machine backs up all the hard drives on your system; however, you may not need to back up some hard drives or folders on your MacBook. To save time and hard drive space, Time Machine allows you to exclude specific drives and folders from the backup process. Click Options and then click the Add button (with the plus sign) to select the drives or folders you want to exclude, and they'll appear in the Do Not Back Up list.

To remove an exclusion, select it in the list and click the Delete button (with the minus sign). Note the Total Included figure increases, and Time Machine adds the item you deleted from the list to the next backup.

By default, Snow Leopard warns you when deleting older backup files, but you can turn this off from the Options sheet as well.

You can elect to back up your MacBook immediately by clicking the Time Machine icon in the Finder menu bar and choosing Back Up Now.

## Universal Access preferences

The final group, Universal Access, is shown in Figure 3-30. These settings modify the display and sound functions within Mac OS X to make them more friendly to physically challenged users. Note that if you select the VoiceOver On radio button, Mac OS X speaks the text for all text and buttons onscreen.

**Figure 3-30:**
The
Universal
Access
pane.

If you have an assistive device that's recognized by Mac OS X, select the Enable Access for Assistive Devices check box to allow it to be used throughout the operating system. You can also elect to display the Universal Access status icon in the Finder menu bar.

The four tabs here are

✦ **Seeing:** These settings make it easier for those with limited vision to use Mac OS X. You can toggle VoiceOver on and off from here; I discuss more on this feature and these settings in Book IX, Chapter 3. To turn on the display Zoom feature, select the Zoom On radio button or press ⌘+Option+8.

To specify how much magnification is used, click the Options button. From the sheet that appears, you can set the minimum and maximum Zoom magnification increments. From the keyboard, use ⌘+Option+= (equal sign) to zoom in and ⌘+Option+– (minus sign) to zoom out. Optionally, you can display a preview rectangle of the area that's included when you zoom. Mac OS X can smooth images to make them look better when zoomed; click the Options button in the Zoom section of the pane and select the Smooth Images check box.

You can also determine how the screen moves in relation to the trackpad pointer from the Zoom Options sheet: By default, the zoomed screen moves with the pointer, but you can set it to move only when the pointer reaches the edge of the screen or maintain the pointer near the center of the zoomed image automatically. If your mouse has a scroll wheel or ball, you can specify a modifier key to activate the Zoom feature.

If you prefer white text on a black background, select the White on Black radio button (or press the ⌘+Option+Control+8 keyboard shortcut). Note that depending on your display settings, it might be easier on the eyes to use grayscale display mode by selecting the Use Grayscale check box. Drag the Enhance Contrast slider to increase the contrast between text and background.

✦ **Hearing:** If you need additional visual cues to supplement the spoken and audio alerts in Mac OS X, click this tab and select the Flash the Screen When an Alert Sound Occurs check box. Two-channel stereo audio can be reduced to single-channel mono audio with the Play Stereo Audio as Mono check box. To raise the overall sound volume in Mac OS X, you can click the Adjust Volume button to display the Sound System Preferences settings, where you can drag the Volume slider to the right.

✦ **Keyboard:** These settings help those who have trouble pressing keyboard shortcuts or those who often trigger keyboard repeats (repetition of the same character) accidentally. If you mark the Sticky Keys On radio button, you can use *modifier keys* individually that are grouped together automatically as a single keyboard shortcut — in other words, you can press the modifier keys in a key sequence one after another instead of all together. Sticky Keys can be toggled on and off from the keyboard by pressing the Shift key five times. (You can optionally specify that Mac OS X sound a beep tone when a modifier key is pressed and whether the modifier keys are displayed onscreen.)

Turn Slow Keys on to add a pause (of the length that you specify) between when a key is pressed and when it's actually acted upon within Mac OS X. You can optionally add a key-click sound each time you press a key. To turn keyboard repeat off entirely, click the Set Key Repeat button, which opens the Keyboard preference settings that I discuss earlier.

Book III
Chapter 3

Delving under the
Hood with System
Preferences

✦ **Mouse & Trackpad:** With Mouse Keys active, you can use the numeric keypad to move the mouse pointer across your screen. Mouse Keys can be toggled on and off by pressing the Option key five times. Drag the Initial Delay and Maximum Speed sliders to specify how long you must hold down a keypad key before the pointer starts to move as well as how fast the pointer should move across the screen. You can also disable the trackpad on your MacBook when using Mouse Keys.

If you prefer a larger pointer, the cursor can be resized to make it easier to spot onscreen. You can also click the Open Keyboard Preferences button to turn on Full Keyboard Access or to remap keyboard shortcuts for both the Finder and many applications.

# Chapter 4: You Mean Others Can Use My MacBook, Too?

## In This Chapter

- Understanding how multiuser systems work
- Configuring login settings
- Changing the appearance of the login screen
- Tightening security during login
- Starting applications automatically when you log in

**W**hether you're setting up Mac OS X for use in a public library or simply allowing your 12-year-old to use your MacBook in your home office, configuring Snow Leopard for multiple users is a simple task. However, you must also consider the possible downsides of a mismanaged multiuser system: files and folders being shared that you didn't want in the public domain, users logging in as one another, and the very real possibility of accidental file deletion (and worse).

Therefore, in this chapter, I show you how to take those first steps before you open Pandora's Box — setting login options, configuring the personal account that you created when you first installed the operating system, and protecting your stuff. (Network administrators call this security check-up *locking things down*. Better start using the terminology now, even before you buy your suspenders and pocket protector.)

## How Multiuser Works on Mac OS X

When you create multiple users in Mac OS X, each person who uses your MacBook — hence the term *user* — has a separate account (much like an account that you might open at a bank). Mac OS X creates a Home folder for each user and saves that user's preferences independently from those of other users. When you log in to Mac OS X, you provide a username and a password, which identifies you. The username/password combination tells Mac OS X which user has logged on — and, therefore, which preferences and Home folder to use.

Each account also carries a specific level, which determines how much control the user has over Mac OS X and the computer itself. Without an account with the proper access level, for example, a user might not be able to display many of the panes in System Preferences.

The three most common account levels are

✦ **Root:** Also called *System Administrator,* this über-account can change *anything* within Mac OS X — and that's usually A *Very* Bad Thing, so it's actually disabled as a default. (This alone should tell you that the Root account shouldn't be toyed with.) For instance, the Root account can seriously screw up the UNIX subsystem within Mac OS X, or a Root user can delete files within the Mac OS X System Folder.

**Enable the System Administrator account and use it only if told to do so by an Apple technical support technician. (And don't forget to disable it immediately afterward!)**

✦ **Administrator:** (Or *admin* for short.) This is the account level that you're assigned when you install Mac OS X. The administrator account should *not* be confused with the System Administrator account!

It's perfectly okay for you or anyone you assign to use an administrator account. An administrator can install applications anywhere on the system, create/edit/delete user accounts, and make changes to all the settings in System Preferences. However, an administrator can't move or delete items from any other user's Home folder within the Finder, and administrators are barred from modifying or deleting files in the Mac OS X System Folder.

A typical multiuser Mac OS X computer has only one administrator — like a teacher in a classroom — but technically, you can create as many administrator accounts as you like. If you do need to give someone else this access level, assign it only to a competent, experienced user whom you trust.

✦ **Standard:** A standard user account is the default in Mac OS X. Standard users can install software and save documents only in their Home folders and the Shared folder (which resides in the Users folder), and they can change only certain settings in System Preferences. Thus, they can do little damage to the system as a whole. For example, each of the students in a classroom should be given a standard-level account for the Mac OS X system that they share.

If Parental Controls are applied to a standard account, it becomes a *managed* account, allowing you to fine-tune what a standard account user can do. (I discuss Parental Controls at length in Book III, Chapter 5.)

Chapter 5 of this minibook covers the entire process of creating and editing a user account.

## Working with the Guest account

The Guest account is a convenient method of granting someone temporary access to your MacBook — in fact, your guest doesn't even need a password to log in! Your Guest account has all the attributes of a standard account, so the visitor has little chance of accidentally (or purposefully) damaging your system. However, after the guest user logs out, the Guest account is "flushed" and all the data and files that that person created using the account and stored in the guest's Home directory are deleted automatically. (This allows the next guest to start with a clean slate.)

By default, the Guest account is disabled. To turn on this feature, open System Preferences, click Accounts, and then click the Guest Account entry in the list. (You may have to click the Lock icon in the lower-left corner of the Accounts pane and provide your admin password before you can continue.) Click the Allow Guests to Log In to This Computer check box to enable it.

Oh, and don't forget that you can enable specific Parental Controls for the Guest account, just as you can for any other account. That should come in handy if your daughter has a slumber party coming up this weekend . . . .

## Configuring Your Login Screen

Book III
Chapter 4

You Mean Others Can Use My MacBook, Too?

Take a look at the changes you can make to the login process. First, Mac OS X provides two methods of displaying the login screen, as well as one automatic method that doesn't display the login screen at all:

✦ **Logging in with a list:** To log in, click your account username in the list, and the login screen displays the password prompt. Type your password — Mac OS X displays bullet characters to ensure security — and press Return (or click the Log In button).

✦ **Logging in with username and password:** Type your account username in the Name field and press Tab. Then type your password and press Return (or click the Log In button).

✦ **Automatic Login:** With Automatic Login set, Mac OS X automatically logs in the specified account when you reboot. In effect, you never see the login screen unless you click Log Out from the Apple menu. (Naturally, this is an attractive option to use if your computer is in a secure location — such as your office — and you'll be the only one using your MacBook. However, if your laptop falls into The Wrong Hands, you're inviting trouble . . . and identity theft.)

To specify which type of login screen you see — if you see one at all — head to System Preferences, click Accounts, and then click the Login Options button. (If the pane is locked, click the Lock icon and supply your admin password.)

✦ To set Automatic Login, display the Login Options settings and click the Automatic Login pop-up menu. Choose the account that automatically logs in from the list. When Mac OS X displays the user Name and Password sheet that you see in Figure 4-1, type the corresponding password and then click OK.

**Figure 4-1:**
Configuring
Automatic
Login
from the
Accounts
pane.

***Never*** **set the Automatic Login feature to an admin-level account unless you're sure to be the only one using your MacBook.** If the computer is rebooted, you're opening the door for anyone to simply sashay in and wreak havoc!

✦ To determine whether Mac OS X uses a list login screen, you must again visit the Login Options settings pane (see Figure 4-2). Select the List of Users radio button for a list login screen or select the Name and Password radio button for a simple login screen where you must type your username and password.

To change settings specific to your account — no matter what your access level — log in with your account, open System Preferences, and click Accounts. From here, you can change your account password and picture, the card marked as yours within the Address Book, and the Login Items launched automatically when you log in. (Peruse more information on the Address Book in Book I, Chapter 6.)

To log out of Mac OS X without restarting or shutting down the computer, choose the Apple menu and then choose Log Out or just press ⌘+Shift+Q. You see the confirmation dialog, as shown in Figure 4-3. Although Mac OS X will display the login screen after two minutes, someone can still saunter up and click the Cancel button, thereby gaining access to your stuff. Therefore, make it a practice to always click the Log Out button on this screen before your hand leaves the mouse, or bypass the confirmation dialog altogether by holding down the Option key as you click Log Out from the menu!

**Figure 4-2:** Will that be a simple or a list login screen?

**Figure 4-3:** Always click Log Out before you leave your MacBook!

You can also enable *Fast User Switching* from the Login Options pane. This feature allows another user to sit down and log in while the previous user's applications are still running in the background. When you enable switching, Snow Leopard displays the currently active user's full name or account icon at the right side of the Finder menu bar. Click the name, and a menu appears; click Login Window, and another user can then log in as usual. (From the Login Options pane, you can also choose to display the current user by the account's short name or the account icon.)

Even though you're playing musical chairs, the Big X remembers what's running and the state of your Desktop when you last left it. (When you decide to switch back, Snow Leopard prompts you for that account's login password for security . . . just in case, you understand.)

## Locking Things Down

If security is a potential problem and you still need to share a Mac between multiple users, lock things down. To protect Mac OS X from unauthorized use, take care of these potential security holes immediately:

✦ **Disable the Sleep, Restart, and Shut Down buttons.** Any computer can be hacked when it's restarted or turned on, so disable the Restart and Shut Down buttons on the login screen. (After a user has successfully logged in, Mac OS X can be shut down normally by using the menu item or the keyboard shortcuts that I cover earlier.) Open the Accounts pane in System Preferences, click the Login Options button, and deselect the Show the Sleep, Restart, and Shut Down Buttons check box. Press ⌘+Q to quit and save your changes. (You can find more about restarting and shutting down in Book II, Chapter 2.)

✦ **Disable list logins.** With a list login, any potential hacker already knows half the information necessary to gain entry to your system — and often the password is easy to guess. Therefore, set Mac OS X to ask for the username and password on the Login screen, as I describe earlier. This way, someone has to guess both the username and the password, which is a much harder proposition.

✦ **Disable Automatic Login.** A true no-brainer. As I mention earlier in the chapter, Automatic Login is indeed very convenient. However, all someone has to do is reboot your MacBook, and the machine automatically logs in one lucky user! To disable Automatic Login, display the Accounts pane in System Preferences and click the Login Options button; then click the Automatic Login pop-up menu and click the Off entry.

✦ **Disable the password hint.** By default, Mac OS X obligingly displays the password hint for an account after three unsuccessful attempts at entering a password. Where security is an issue, this is like serving a hacker a piece of apple pie. Therefore, head to System Preferences, display the Accounts settings, click the Login Options button, and make sure that the Show Password Hints check box is empty.

✦ **Select passwords intelligently.** Although using your mother's maiden name for a password might seem like a great idea, the best method of selecting a password is to use a completely random group of mixed letters and numbers. If you find a random password too hard to remember, at least add a number after your password, like *dietcoke1* — and no, that isn't one of my passwords. (Nice try.) My editor suggests a favorite location spelled backwards, with a number mixed in — easier to remember than a completely random sequence of characters!

For even greater security, make at least one password character uppercase, and use a number at the beginning and ending of the password. Or, do the "c001" thing and replace characters with numbers, like the zero that you insert in dietc0ke.

# Starting Applications Automatically after Login

Here's one other advantage to logins: Each account can have its own selection of applications that run automatically when that user logs in. These applications are *Login Items,* and they appear as a list in the Accounts pane (shown in Figure 4-4). A caveat or two:

✦ **The user setting his or her Login Items must be logged in.** Only the user can modify his or her own Login Items.

✦ **Users must have access to System Preferences.** If the person is using a standard-level account, it must allow access to System Preferences.

**Figure 4-4:** Preparing to launch Address Book every time I log in.

Including an application in your Login Items list is easy: Click the button with the plus sign to navigate to the desired application, select it, and then click Add. (Alternatively, you can just drag items from a Finder window and drop them directly into the list.) Note that items in the list are launched in order — if something needs to run before something else, you can drag the item entries into any sequence.

To launch the application in hidden mode — which might or might not display it in the Dock, depending on the application itself — click the list entry for the desired item and select its Hide check box.

# Chapter 5: Setting Up Multiuser Accounts

## In This Chapter

✔ Adding, modifying, and deleting users

✔ Establishing Parental Controls

✔ Configuring FileVault

✔ Avoiding keychains

*I*n Chapter 4 of this minibook, I introduce you to the different Mac OS X multiuser account levels and the login process. In this chapter, if you're ready to share your MacBook with others, you can discover how to add new accounts and edit existing accounts. Oh, and yes, I also show you how to *frag* — that's multiplayer game-speak for *delete* — accounts that you no longer need. I also demonstrate how to add optional limitations to an individual user account and how to avoid using a *keychain* (which is supposed to make it easier to store that pocketful of passwords that you've created on the Internet).

Yes, you read correctly. By all that's good and righteous, Mac OS X actually has a feature that I *don't* want you to use. Read on to find out more.

## Adding, Editing, and Deleting Users

All multiuser account chores take place in a single System Preferences pane. (Cue James Bond theme song.) The Accounts pane is the star of this chapter, so open System Preferences and click the Accounts icon.

If you haven't added any users to your system yet, the Users list should look like Figure 5-1. You should see your account, which you set up when you installed Mac OS X, set to administrator (admin) level.

 You also have an entry for a *Guest* account, which anyone can use on an as-needed basis. To enable the Guest account, click the Guest entry in the list and click the Allow Guests to Log In to This Computer check box to select it. Note that any files created inside the Guest Home folder or settings changed by the Guest user are automatically deleted when the Guest user logs out (or you restart or reboot your Mac).

**Figure 5-1:**
A typical first look at the Accounts pane.

## Adding a new user account

To add a new user account, follow these steps:

*1.* **In the Accounts pane in System Preferences, click the New User button — which carries a plus sign — to display an empty user record sheet that you see in Figure 5-2.**

**Figure 5-2:**
Setting up a new user account.

TIP

If the New User button is disabled and you can't click it, click the lock at the bottom left of the System Preferences pane and provide your password to unlock the Accounts pane.

2. **Select the access level for this user from the New Account pop-up menu.**

   By default, the user receives a standard level account. You can also choose an Administrator account, a sharing-only account (with access only to shared files), or a Managed standard account with Parental Controls already enabled.

3. **In the Name text box, type the name that you want to display for this account (both in the Accounts list and on the Login screen) and then press Tab to move to the next field.**

   Mac OS X automatically generates an Account (or *short*) name for use as your screen and Buddy name in iChat and various network applications. The short name is also the name of the folder that Mac OS X creates on the computer's hard drive for this user. You can keep the default short name or type a new one, but it must not contain any spaces. Choose the short name carefully, for it can't be changed within the Finder. For more on iChat, jump to Book VI, Chapter 3. (I'll wait for you here.)

4. **Press Tab again.**

5. **In the Password text box, type the password for the new account.**

   Click the button with the key icon next to the Password field, and Snow Leopard is happy to display the Password Assistant, complete with a suggestion. Click the Suggestion pop-up menu to see additional suggestions. You can choose the length of the password and select from several types: letters and numbers, numbers only, memorable, completely random, or even government-quality. The Assistant automatically copies the current password you're considering to the Password text box.

   As always, when you enter a password or its verification, Mac OS X displays bullet characters for security.

6. **Press Tab, type the password in the Verify text box, and press Tab again.**

7. **(Optional) If you decide to use the password hint feature that I describe in Book II, Chapter 4, you can enter a short sentence or question in the Password Hint text box.**

   The hint is displayed after three unsuccessful attempts at entering the account password.

   I recommend that you **do not** *use this option.* Think about it: Any hack could type in anything three times to get your hint to pop up! If you do use this option, at least make sure that the hint is sufficiently vague!

   Press Tab to continue.

8. **To automatically turn on the FileVault encryption feature for this new account, select the Turn On FileVault protection check box.**

   For more information on FileVault, see the sidebar later in this chapter entitled "So you like your privacy . . ."

9. **Click the Create Account button to finish and create the account.**

   The new account shows up in the Accounts list and in the Login screen.

## Editing an existing account

If you have administrator access, it's a cinch to make changes to an existing account from the Accounts pane in System Preferences. (Often, this is to assign a personalized account picture, so I demonstrate that here.) Follow these steps:

1. **Click the account that you want to change in the Accounts list.**

   Don't forget, if the accounts in the list are disabled and you can't select one, you must unlock the Accounts pane. Click the lock at the bottom left of the System Preferences window and type your password.

2. **Edit the settings that you need to change.**

---

# So you like your privacy . . .

These days, everyone's interested in securing his or her personal files from prying eyes. Granted, this isn't a problem if you're the only one using your MacBook. However, if you're sharing a computer in a multiuser environment — or there's even a remote chance your laptop might be lost or stolen — you might want a little more protection than just user permissions for those all-important Fantasy Football formations that you'll unleash next season.

Never fear, Snow Leopard offers a feature called *FileVault,* which provides Home folder encryption that prevents just about anyone except the NSA or FBI from gaining access to the files in your Home folder. (You'll notice that things slow down just a bit when logging in and out or working with files that are several gigabytes in size, but for those of us who need the peace of mind, this minimal performance hit is worth it.) You can enable the FileVault feature from the Security pane in System Preferences. Two passwords control access to your Home folder when FileVault is active:

- The *Master Password* can unlock any Home folder for *any* user. Only someone with an admin account can set the Master Password. The Master Password must be set before you can turn on the FileVault feature for any account on your system.

- Your *Login Password* unlocks your Home folder.

Personally, I love this feature, and I use it on all my Macs running Snow Leopard. Yet, a risk is involved (insert ominous chord here). To wit: *DO NOT* forget your Login Password, and make doggone sure that your Admin user remembers that all-important Master Password! Mac OS X displays a dire warning for anyone who's considering using FileVault: If you forget these passwords, you can't retrieve any data from your Home folder. *Period.* As Jerry Reed says, "It's a gone pecan."

3. **Click the square Picture well to specify the thumbnail image that appears in the Login list next to the account name.**

   Apple provides a number of good images in the preview collection — just click a thumbnail to select it.

4. **To add your own picture, click Edit Picture. You can drag a new image from the Finder or iPhoto into the icon placeholder, or click Choose to select one from an Open File dialog; then click Set.**

   Alternatively, you can click the Take a Video Snapshot button to grab a picture from your MacBook's iSight video camera. *Most* cool.

5. **After you make the changes (and you select just the right image to capture the user's personality — a more difficult task than you might think), press ⌘+Q to save them and close the System Preferences window.**

## Deleting an existing account

To wipe an account from the face of the Earth, follow these steps:

1. **Click the account that you want to delete in the Accounts list.**

2. **Click the Delete User button (which is smartly marked with a minus sign).**

   Mac OS X displays the confirmation sheet that you see in Figure 5-3.

**Figure 5-3:**
Are you
*quite* sure
that you
want to
delete this
genius
composer?

Note that the contents of the user's Home folder can be saved in a disk image in the Deleted Users folder (just in case you need to retrieve something). Alternatively, you can choose to leave the deleted user's home folder as is, without removing it.

If you're absolutely sure you won't be dating that person again, click the Delete the Home Folder option (which doesn't save anything in the Deleted Users folder). You regain all the hard drive space that was being occupied by the contents of the deleted user's home folder.

3. **Click OK to verify and delete the account. Click the Cancel button to abort and return to the Accounts list.**

# Tightening Your Security Belt

Administrators are special people. Just ask one; you'll see. Anyway, when an administrator creates or edits the account for a standard-level user, Mac OS X offers a number of levels of specific rights — *Parental Controls* — that can be assigned on an individual account basis. When an account has Parental Controls assigned, it becomes a *managed* account.

Parental Controls are available only for standard-level users; administrators aren't affected by them because an administrator-level account already has access to everything covered by Parental Controls.

When do you need Parental Controls? Here are three likely scenarios:

✦ You're creating accounts for corporate or educational users, and you want to disable certain features of Mac OS X to prevent those folks from doing something dumb. Just tell 'em you're *streamlining the operating system.* (Yeah, that's it.) For example, you might not want that one particular kid making CD copies of *The Illustrated Anarchist's Cookbook* in the classroom while you're gone. Therefore, you disable the ability for that account to burn CDs or DVDs.

✦ In the same environment, you might want to give a specific standard-level account the ability to administer printers. If Roger in Accounting is both helpful and knowledgeable — oh, and add *trustworthy* in there, too — you might want to give him this capability so that he can handle the print queues while you're on vacation.

✦ You want one or more users to access one — and *only* one — application on the system, or perhaps just two or three applications. To illustrate: In my years as a hospital hardware technician, we had a number of computers that were used solely to display patient records. No Word, no e-mail, nothing but the one program that accessed the medical records database. We called these machines *dumb terminals* although they were actually personal computers. (This trick also works well if you're a parent and you want to give your kids access without endangering your valuable files. Just don't call your computer a *dumb terminal* lest your kids take offense. That's experience talking there.) If you want to allow access to a specified selection of applications, you can set them in that account's Controls.

# Setting Parental Controls

Time to review what each of the settings does. To display the controls for a standard account, click the account in the list and then click the Open Parental Controls button. Click the Enable Parental Controls button, and click the Lock icon in the lower-left corner to confirm your access (if necessary). Snow Leopard includes five different categories of controls, as shown in Figure 5-4:

**Figure 5-4:** You can restrict access to many functions within a Standard account.

Book III
Chapter 5

Setting Up
Multiuser Accounts

✦ **System:** These settings (which I discuss in more detail in a second) affect what the user can do within Snow Leopard as well as what the Finder itself looks like to that user.

✦ **Content:** These settings control the Dictionary and Safari applications. If you prefer that profane terms be hidden within the Dictionary for this user, click the Hide Profanity in Dictionary check box to enable it. Snow Leopard also offers three levels of control for Web sites:

• *Allow Unrestricted Access:* Select this radio button to allow unfettered access for this user.

• *Try to Limit Access:* You can allow Safari to automatically block Web sites it deems adult. To specify particular sites that Snow Leopard should allow or deny, click the Customize button.

• *Allow Access to Only These Websites:* Choose this radio button to specify which Web sites the user can view. To add a Web site, click the Add button (which bears a plus sign) — Snow Leopard prompts you for a title and the Web site address.

✦ **Mail & iChat:** Click the Limit Mail and Limit iChat check boxes to specify the e-mail and instant messaging addresses that this user can communicate with. (Note that this affects only Apple Mail and iChat, so other mail clients, Web-based mail, and instant messaging applications aren't controlled.) To add an address that the user can e-mail or chat with, click the Add button.

Do you want a notification if the user is attempting to send an e-mail to someone not in the list? Click the Send Permission Requests To check box to select it and then type your e-mail address in the text box.

✦ **Time Limits:** Parents, click the Time Limits button, and you'll shout with pure joy — check out the options on this pane in Figure 5-5! You can limit an account to a certain number of hours of usage per weekday (Weekday Time Limits), limit to a specified number of hours of usage per weekend day (Weekend Time Limits), and set a bedtime computer curfew time for both weekdays and weekend days. (Note that vacations and school holidays aren't recognized within Time Limits, so you'll have to manage them manually!)

**Figure 5-5:**
Snow
Leopard
keeps track
of your kid's
computer
usage
so that
you don't
have to.

✦ **Logs:** Snow Leopard keeps a number of different types of *text log files* (which track where the user goes on the Internet, which applications are launched by the account, and the contents of any iChat conversations where the user was a participant). From this central pane, you can monitor all the logs for a particular account. Note that these logs are enabled or disabled from other locations within Snow Leopard: For example, the log showing the Web sites visited and blocked is enabled from the Content pane that I describe a little earlier, whereas the applications log is enabled when on the System pane. iChat logging is turned on from the Preferences dialog within the iChat application.

You can always tell whether an account has been assigned Parental Controls because the account description changes from Standard to Managed in the Accounts list.

Of particular importance are the System controls. Click the System tab to modify these settings:

✦ **Use Simple Finder:** I discuss the Simple Finder in the following section because it's a great idea for families and classrooms with smaller children.

✦ **Only Allow Selected Applications:** When this option is selected, you can select the specific applications that appear to the user. These restrictions are in effect whether the user has access to the Full Finder or just the Simple Finder.

To allow access to all the applications of a specific type — iLife, iWork, Internet, Widgets, Other, and Utilities — click the check box next to the desired group heading to select it. To restrict access to all applications within a group, click the check box next to the heading to deselect it. You can also toggle the restriction on and off for specific applications in these groups; click the triangle icon next to each group heading to expand the list and then either mark or clear the check box next to the desired applications. (If you see a minus sign in the check box, some subordinate items are selected.) To locate a specific application, click in the Search box and type the application name.

To add a new application to the Allow list, drag its icon from the Finder and drop it in the list within the Other group. After you add an application, it appears in the Other group, and you can toggle access to it on and off like the applications in the named groups.

✦ **Can Administer Printers:** With this check box selected, the user can modify the printers and printer queues within the Print & Fax pane in System Preferences. If this option is disabled, the user can still print to the default printer and switch to other assigned printers but can't add or delete printers or manage the Mac OS X print queue.

✦ **Can Burn CDs and DVDs:** Deselect this check box to prevent the user from recording CDs or DVDs via the built-in disc recording features in the Mac OS X Finder. (Note, however, that if you load a third-party recording program, such as Toast, the user can still record discs with it.)

✦ **Can Change Password:** Select this check box to allow the user to change the account password.

If you're creating a single standard-level account for an entire group of people to use — for example, if you want to leave your laptop in kiosk mode in one corner of the office or if everyone in a classroom will use the same account on the machine — I recommend disabling the ability to change the account password. (Oh, and please do me a favor . . . *don't* create a system with just one admin-level account that everyone is supposed to use! Instead, keep your one admin-level account close to your bosom and create a standard-level account for the Unwashed Horde.)

✦ **Can Modify the Dock:** Select this check box, and the user can remove applications, documents, and folders from the Dock in the Full Finder. (If you don't want the contents of the Dock changing according to the whims of other users, it's a good idea to deselect this check box.)

## Assigning the Simple Finder

You can restrict your standard-level users even further by assigning them the Simple Finder set of limitations. The default Simple Finder, as shown in Figure 5-6, is a highly simplified version of the regular Mac OS X Finder. The simplified Dock contains only the Finder icon, the Trash, and the folders for the user's approved applications, documents, and shared files.

**Figure 5-6:**
Whoa! It's the Simple Finder — less filling; still runs great!

This is the network administrator's idea of a foolproof interface for Mac OS X: A user can access only those system files and resources needed to do a job, with no room for tinkering or goofing off.

A Simple Finder user can still make the jump to the full version of the Finder by clicking Finder and choosing Run Full Finder. The user has to enter a correct admin-level username and password.

You can also change the Auto Login account from the Accounts pane. Click the Login Options button under the Accounts list and then click the Automatic Login pop-up menu to choose the account that automatically logs in when Mac OS X starts up. Enter the account password on the confirmation sheet that appears and click OK. Although I've made it clear elsewhere that Automatic Login is not a good security feature in many cases (such as when you're on the road with a laptop), it can be a good feature for those preparing a MacBook for public use. If you set the Automatic Login to your public standard-access account, Mac OS X automatically uses the right account if the MacBook is rebooted or restarted.

Don't forget, you can always choose Log Out from the Apple menu to log in under your own account.

# Using Keychains — NOT

Before I leave this chapter, I want to discuss a Mac OS X feature that's been around since the days of Mac OS 8: the *keychain*. Your account keychain stores all the username/password combinations for Web sites, file servers, File Transfer Protocol (FTP) servers, and the like, allowing you to simply waltz in and start using the service (whatever it is). Sounds handy, doesn't it? And it can be, but you had better watch your step.

I'm perfectly honest here: I **hate** account keychains. With a passion, mind you. As a consultant, Webmaster, and the SYSOP (an ancient Bulletin Board Service acronym meaning *System Operator*) of an Internet-based online system, I know what a hassle it is for users to remember separate passwords, and I feel that pain. (I use separate passwords for everything.) However, three massively big problems are inherent with using keychains:

✦ **Anyone can log on as you.** If your keychain is unlocked, which happens automatically when you log in, all someone has to do is sit at your desk, visit a site or connect with a server, and *bam!* They're on. As *you*. **Think about that.** And then think how many times you get up from your desk, just for a second, to grab another Diet Coke or a doughnut.

✦ **You'll forget your passwords.** If the keychain file is corrupted — and it can happen — your passwords have gone to Detroit without you. Either you've got them on paper hidden somewhere, they're on your recent backup, or it's time to change your online persona.

✦ **Keychains need yet another stinkin' password.** Yep, that's right — your keychain can be locked (either manually or, with the right settings, automatically), and you have to remember yet another password/passphrase to unlock your keychain. "When, oh when will the madness end?"

From a security standpoint, keychains should be **completely off-limits** for anyone who's interested in maintaining a well-locked-down machine. After all, most folks can completely take care of all their Internet and network connections with a handful of passwords, and that's no big deal for anyone to remember. Unfortunately, Snow Leopard creates a keychain automatically for every user, so you have to monitor (and delete) your keychain data manually. (Sigh.)

However, if you're the only person using your MacBook and it resides in your home — personally, I'd prefer a bank vault — and you absolutely *must* use keychains, you can display them all for the current account from the Keychain Access application (see Figure 5-7), conveniently located in Utilities within your Applications folder. Click the Category tab and then click an item in the keychain list to display or edit all its information.

**Figure 5-7:** Take my advice — stay away from the allure of the keychain.

Heck, just think about what I just wrote — anyone can display and *edit* server and site information just by launching this application! That includes your nephew Damien — you know, the one who considers himself the hacker extraordinaire. (While I'm at it, I should mention that it's just as bad to set the Automatic Login feature — which I discuss earlier in this chapter — to an admin-level account. One reboot, and you're rolling out the red carpet for the little rascal. For the inside information on Automatic Login, visit Chapter 4 in this very minibook.)

To help lock things down — at least when it comes to your Internet communications — follow this path:

1. **To display your Internet passwords, click the Passwords category (upper-left).**

2. **Click each Internet password to select it in the list and then click the lowercase *i* button at the bottom of the window to display the information on that password.**

3. **Click the Access Control tab to display the settings that you see in Figure 5-8, one of which I strongly recommend.**

   To minimize the damage that someone can do with this password, you can select the Confirm before Allowing Access radio button. And for yet another level of security, select the Ask for Keychain Password check box.

   Of course, you're probably thinking, "Well, Mark, that pretty much eliminates the purpose of quick, convenient access without passwords, doesn't it?" Yes, indeed it does, but at least your online identity is somewhat safeguarded.

   Click the plus sign button at the bottom of the Keychain Access window to add a new password. Type a name for the item, the username that you typically type to gain access, and the password for that server or site. Then click Add and cross your fingers.

**Figure 5-8:**
Safe-
guarding a
keychain
rather
dilutes its
usefulness,
but I'm
security
conscious.

To display all the keychains you can access, choose Edit⇨Keychain List. To create a brand-new keychain, choose File⇨New Keychain. Mac OS X prompts you for the filename for your new keychain file. In the New Keychain dialog that appears, enter a catchy name in the Save As text box. By default, the keychain file is created in the Keychains folder — a good idea — but if you want to store it elsewhere, click the down-arrow button next to the Where list box and navigate to the desired folder. When you're ready, click the Create button. Now you need to enter yet another password, type it again to verify it, and click OK.

To lock or unlock your login keychain, click the Lock icon at the top-left of the Keychain Access window. (Unlocking your keychain requires you to enter your login password. Go figure.)

You might be saying to yourself, "Geez, this guy is more than a little paranoid." And yes, dear reader, I suppose I am. But then again, who's been uploading all those questionable images and MP3 files to the company server . . . using *your* account?

# Chapter 6: Sharing Documents for Fun and Profit

## In This Chapter

✔ Comparing network sharing with multiuser sharing

✔ Setting and changing permissions

✔ Sharing documents in Microsoft Office 2008 for the Mac

*N*ow here's a topic that MacBook power users can sink their teeth into — the idea that a document on a multiuser system can be *everyone's* property, allowing anyone in your family, workgroup, or highly competitive mob to make whatever changes are necessary, whenever they like.

Of course, potential pitfalls lurk — even in the Apple world, there's no such thing as an operating system that's both powerful *and* perfectly simple. However, I think you'll find that our dear friends from Cupertino have done just about as well as can be expected and that the settings that you use to share documents are fairly easy to understand and use.

Prepare to share!

## Sharing over a Network versus Sharing on a Single Mac

First, allow me to clear up what I've found to be a common misconception by using another of Mark's Maxims.

**Sharing documents on a single computer is fundamentally different from the file sharing that you've used on a network.**

True, multiple users can share a document over a network, which is a topic that I cover in Book VII. But although the results are the same, the way that you share that same document on a single machine betwixt multiple users is a completely different turn of the screw. In this section, I discuss the factoids behind the matter.

## No network is required

Although reiterating that no network is required is seemingly the most obvious of statements, many otherwise knowledgeable Mac OS X power users seem to forget that sharing a document over a network requires an active network connection. (Note the word *active* there.) Unless you physically copy the document to your hard drive — which defeats the purpose of document sharing — any loss of network connectivity or any problem with your network account will result in a brick wall and a brightly painted sign reading, "No luck, Jack." (Or perhaps it's flashing neon.)

On the other hand, a document shared on a multiuser MacBook in the home or classroom is available whenever you need it. As long as the file is located in the Shared folder, the file privileges are set correctly, and you know the password (if one is required by the application, such as a password-protected Word document), then — as they say on "Star Trek" — "You have the conn" whether your network connection is active or not.

## Relying on a guaranteed lock

Sharing documents over a network can get a tad hairy when multiple users open and edit the document simultaneously. Many applications, such as Office 2008 for the Mac, have methods of *locking* the document (giving one person exclusive access) when someone opens it or saves it. However, you always face the possibility that what you're seeing in a shared network document isn't exactly what's in the document at that moment.

A multiuser system doesn't need such exquisite complexity. *You're* the one sitting at the keyboard, and *you* have control: This is what network administrators call a *guaranteed lock* on that document file. Refreshing, isn't it?

But wait! Mac OS X Snow Leopard includes a feature called *Fast User Switching* — I discuss it in Book II, Chapter 2 — that allows other users to remain logged in behind the scenes while another user is at the keyboard. Therefore, if you enable Fast User Switching, two users could have the same document open at the same time. To prevent this, you can simply turn off Fast User Switching from the Accounts pane in System Preferences. (Click Accounts, click Login Options, and clear the Enable Fast User Switching check box.)

It's also possible for someone to use Snow Leopard's Remote Login feature to login to their account across the Internet. You can disable this feature by opening the System Preferences window, clicking the Share icon, and deselecting the Remote Login check box.

## Most places are off-limits

Network users are often confident that they can blithely copy and move a document from one place to another with the greatest of ease, and that's true. Most shared network documents created by an application — such as a project outline created in Word, for example — carry their own sharing information and document settings internally. Thus, you can move that same file to another folder on your hard drive, and the rest of the network team can still open it. (Um, if they have the network rights to access the new folder, of course.)

This isn't the case when it comes to multiuser documents. As you can read in Chapters 4 and 5 of this minibook, Mac OS X places a rather tight fence around a standard-level user, allowing that person to access only the contents of certain folders. In this case, your document must be placed in the Shared folder for every standard-level user to be able to open it. (Alternatively, the document can be stored on an external hard drive, allowing every user account on your system to access it.) If everyone using the document has administrator access, you can store the file in other spots on your system; as long as the permissions are set, you're set. And speaking of permissions . . .

# Permissions: Law Enforcement for Your Files

Files are shared in Mac OS X according to a set of rules called *permissions,* the *ownership* of the file (typically the person who saved the document the first time), and an access level specified as a *group.* The combination of privileges, ownership, and group determines who can do what with the file.

When you (or the person with the administrator account on your MacBook) created your user account, you were automatically granted ownership of your Home folder and everything that it contains as well as any files or folders that you store in the Shared folder or another user's Public folder.

Four possible actions are allowed through permissions:

+ **Read Only:** This action allows the user to open and read the file, which includes copying it to another location.

+ **Read & Write:** This permission grants full access to the file, including opening, reading, editing, saving, and deleting. Read & Write permission also allows the user to copy or move the file to another location.

+ **Write Only (Drop Box):** A neat permission setting that appears only with a folder — it allows access to copy an item to the folder, but not to read any files it contains. (Hence the informal name *Drop Box,* and the + [plus sign] icon added to the folder's icon to identify it.) For example, a drop box is made to order for teachers: Students can submit homework by dragging their work to the teacher's drop box.

+ **No Access:** This is just what it sounds like — the user can't open the file, copy it, or move it.

No matter what permissions you've set, only the System Administrator (or root user) can copy items into another user's Home folder using the Finder. Take my word for it on this one: Simply consider that this can't be done, and **stay as far away from the Root/System Administrator account as possible.** (I repeat: Trust me on this.) Read all about the perils of enabling the System Administrator account in Chapter 4 of this minibook.

These permissions are set in the Info dialog for a file or folder (always accessible by pressing ⌘+I). If you're setting the permissions for a folder, you can also elect to apply those same settings to all the enclosed items within the folder.

To set permissions, follow these steps:

*1.* **Click the item to select it, press ⌘+I (or choose Finder⇨File), and then choose the Get Info menu item.**

   If you have a mouse or trackball with a right button, you can right-click the item and choose Get Info instead. Either way, Mac OS X displays the Info dialog.

*2.* **Click the right-facing arrow next to the Sharing & Permissions heading to expand it, as shown in Figure 6-1.**

   Because I selected a folder, the Apply Enclosed Items button appears at the bottom of the section.

*3.* **To change your own permissions on the item, click the Privilege pop-up menu and choose a new Ownership permissions level.**

   This is likely set to Read & Write, and it's a good idea to leave it alone. If you're the file's owner, you're likely not a security risk.

   Perhaps I should be a little less tactful here: *Never* choose an access level for yourself other than Read & Write without being absolutely sure of what you're doing, because you can potentially prevent yourself from accessing or deleting the file in the future! For example, if you simply want to lock an item to prevent changes being made, **don't** set your Ownership permission to Read Only. (Instead, select the Locked check box in the General section of the Info dialog instead . . . you can easily clear the Locked check box later to make changes to the item.)

*4.* **To change permissions for someone else or a group, click the Privilege value for that user or group and then choose the appropriate value from the pop-up menu.**

   Assigning permissions for an entire group is a good idea for limiting specific files and folders to only Administrator access. (Note, however, that Snow Leopard reserves the group name *wheel* for internal tasks, so *never* alter any permissions for the *wheel* group.)

*5.* **If necessary, set the permission for the Everyone pop-up menu (otherwise known as "I'm going to lump everyone else into this category").**

   If a user isn't the owner of an item and doesn't fit into any group that you've selected, this access permission setting for this file applies to that user.

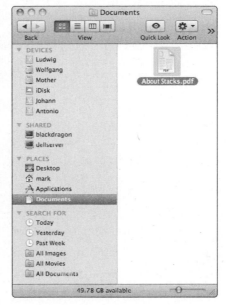

**Figure 6-1:**
The Info dialog, expanded to show Sharing & Permissions.

If you're setting permissions for a folder, Snow Leopard can automatically change the permissions for all the items contained in the folder to the same settings. Click the Action pop-up menu button at the bottom of the Info dialog (which bears a gear symbol) and choose Apply to Enclosed Items. Mac OS X displays a confirmation dialog.

Generally, it's a good idea **not** to override the permissions for all the items in a folder, so use the Apply to Enclosed Items function only when necessary.

6. **After all the permissions are correct, click the Close button to save your changes and return to your friendly Finder.**

If a specific user or group doesn't appear already in the Privilege list, click the Add button (bearing the plus sign) and you can add a specific privilege level for that user or group. You can also delete a privilege level: Click the desired entry to select it and click the Delete button (which bears a minus sign).

## Permission and Sharing Do's and Don'ts

After you get the basics of sharing files and assigning permissions under your belt, you need to master when to change permissions and why you should (and shouldn't) modify them. Follow these common-sense guidelines when saving documents, assigning permissions, and choosing access levels:

✦ **Do use your Shared folder.** The Shared folder is the center of proper document sharing. I know there's a strong urge to create a new document in your Home folder, but you're just making more work for yourself because you'll end up copying that document from your Home folder to the Shared folder. Instead of an extra step, store a document that's intended to be shared in the Shared folder — where it belongs in the first place.

✦ ***Don't* assign permissions just to protect a file from deletion.** Remember, if all you need to do is prevent anyone (including yourself) from deleting an item, you don't need to go to all the trouble of changing permissions. Instead, just display the Info dialog for the item and select the Locked check box to enable it, which prevents the item from being deleted from the Trash until the Lock status is disabled.

✦ ***Do* review the contents of a folder before changing permissions for enclosed items.** That confirmation dialog doesn't appear just for kicks. For example, if you set a highly sensitive, private document with permissions of No Access for everyone but yourself and then you apply less-restrictive permissions globally to the folder that contains the document, you've just removed the No Access permissions, and anyone can open your dirty laundry. (Ouch.) Therefore, make sure that you open the folder and double-check its contents first before applying global permissions to the items it contains.

✦ ***Don't* change permissions in the Applications or Utilities folders.** If you have Administrator-level access, you can actually change the permissions for important applications such as Mail, Address Book, iTunes, and Safari, as well as their support files. This spells havoc for all users assigned to the standard-access level. Be polite and leave the permissions for these files alone.

✦ ***Definitely don't* change System ownership.** Mac OS X is stable and reliable. Part of that stability comes from the protected state of the System folder, as well as a number of other folders on your hard drive. If you displayed the Info dialog for the System folder, you'll see that the Owner is set to *system,* and the Group is set to *wheel* (a term from the UNIX world that encompasses all administrator accounts). Now, promptly close that Info dialog, without making any changes!

✦ ***Never, never,* NEVER change any permissions for any files owned by the System unless specifically told to do so by an Apple support technician. Do NOT monkey with System-owned items.**

This last one is quite striking for a reason, so please heed the warning.

# *Sharing Stuff in Office 2008*

Many Mac OS X applications offer their own built-in document-sharing features. For example, Microsoft Office 2008 for the Mac includes both file-level and document-sharing features. Because Office 2008 is currently the most popular productivity suite available for Mac OS X, I discuss these commands in this final section.

## Document-sharing features

You'll find a number of commands that help multiple users keep track of changes that have been made in a shared Office document. Probably the most familiar is the Word revision tracking features (heavily used during the development of this book), but there are others as well:

✦ **Revision marks:** If several users edit a document, how can you tell who did what? By using *revision marks,* which apply different colors to changes made by different editors, those additions and deletions can be accepted or rejected individually at a later date. If Johnson in Marketing adds incorrect material, you can easily remove just his changes. In a worst-case scenario, you can actually reject all changes and return the document to its pristine condition.

✦ **Compare Documents:** Using this feature allows you to compare a revised document with the original (if, of course, you still have the original file handy). I use Compare Documents only if revision marks weren't turned on before editing began.

✦ **Comments:** Editors can also converse within a document by using embedded Comments. These don't change the contents of the Word file the way revision marks do, but store commentary and notes in a behind-the-scenes kind of way. (Think of a Mac OS X Sticky that appears within a document.) Again, the author of each comment is listed, allowing for (sometimes heated) communication within the body of a document.

✦ **Highlighting:** You've heard the old joke about . . . Well, anyway, a traditional highlighter marker is pretty useless on a computer monitor (leaving a nasty mess for the next user to clean), but Word allows multiple highlighting colors for identifying text. (And for the occasional practical joke — nothing like adding eight different highlighting colors to that important proposal. Just make sure that your résumé is up-to-date.)

## File-level sharing features

Along with the document-level sharing commands, you'll find that Office 2008 applications also offer sharing features that control access to the document file itself.

### Password protection

You can add password protection to any Office 2008 document. Follow these steps with a document created within Word, Excel, or PowerPoint:

1. **Choose File⇨Save As.**

2. **In the Save As dialog that appears, click Options to display the Save Preferences pane.**

3. **Click the Show All toolbar button.**

4. **Click Security to display the Preferences pane that you see in Figure 6-2.**

**Figure 6-2:**
Office 2008 offers two types of document passwords.

5. **To password-protect the document, enter a password in the Password to Open field.**

   This password must be provided when opening the document.

   If you like, you can enter another password in the Password to Modify field. This second password would then also be required to modify the document.

   Both passwords are case sensitive.

6. **Click OK to save the preference changes and return to your document.**

### Document protection

Think of the Protect Document dialog in Word, from which you can effectively write-protect certain elements, as an extra level of security in a multiuser environment. In this Office application, you can protect revision marks, comments, and sections of a document containing forms. A password can be added if desired. To display the Protect Document dialog, click Tools in any of the Office 2008 applications and choose Protect Document from the pop-up menu that appears.

# Chapter 7: Common-Sense Laptop Security

## In This Chapter

✔ Keeping your MacBook off-limits to prying eyes and hands

✔ Using a tracking application to monitor your MacBook

Throughout this minibook, I show you how you can easily share information and files with others — all the while keeping your private files away from prying eyes, safe in your Home folder.

But, good reader, it's time to recognize the unfortunate fact that many Mac owners put *themselves* at risk of identity theft (or loss of their MacBook). Unless you exercise common sense while using your MacBook, you could be the victim, waving goodbye to your personal and financial information.

In this security-conscious chapter, I discuss how to keep your MacBook safe . . . and even how to locate and monitor it remotely in case it *is* lost or stolen!

## MacBook Security 101

Of course, your MacBook is a high-dollar (and highly portable) electronic device, making it a prime target for theft. Don't forget, however, that with a few simple steps, you can also secure the data on your MacBook — both the data displayed on your screen and the information stored in your laptop's hard drive!

In this section, I mention my favorite common-sense MacBook security tips — and yes, I follow every single one of these recommendations with my own MacBook Pro. (Security is King when it comes to my computers!)

### Mark your MacBook

Put your brand on your laptop! Whether you do this using an engraving tool on the bottom of the machine (my personal favorite) or a permanent metal tag, your MacBook deserves some sort of identifying information.

(Forget the old standby, a business card taped to the bottom of the case. Your MacBook needs a more permanent brand.) After all, most of the people in the world are honest, and you might not need that tracking software that I mention later in this chapter. You might leave your laptop somewhere by accident, and someone would like to return it to you. (Don't forget to offer a reward!)

Some laptop owners will want to include their name, address, and other contact information, whereas other Road Warriors might feel more comfortable with just their name and e-mail address. Whatever you choose, branding your laptop is as important as backing it up.

## Use those doggone passwords

This is security at its most basic. Without a strong login password and screen saver password, your MacBook is essentially a sitting duck — and not just to those thieves who would steal your laptop but also to those casual sets of prying eyes that can read an inopportune e-mail or see too much of a private company spreadsheet.

With both a login password in place and FileVault security turned on (which I discuss a bit later in this chapter), you may still lose your MacBook to outright theft, but your personal information and your data will likely *never* be compromised!

## Screen saver hot corners equal instant privacy

Tucked away in the Desktop & Screen Saver pane in System Preferences is the Hot Corners button, which lets you specify a corner of the screen that will immediately activate your screen saver. Using the Hot Corners feature means that just a quick swipe of the finger to the selected corner of your trackpad brings instant security from prying eyes, no matter what application you're using.

I'm reminded of a close friend who once dropped by his manager's office and was asked to report on company sales performance. Through no fault of his own, my friend couldn't help but notice the open memo displayed on the manager's widescreen monitor, which listed co-workers who would be downsized within the month. A fast switch to a screen saver would have preserved the privacy of that memo. (Luckily, my friend wasn't on the list.)

## Buy a security cable, and use it

As a kid, did you lock your bike whenever you left it behind? I certainly didn't — and luckily, my bike was never stolen, but I certainly gave thieves every opportunity to try their luck. Funny thing is, as an adult I lock my bikes religiously! Chalk it up to an enhanced dose of common sense and an adult's appreciation of the cost of a replacement.

Friends, the exact same common-sense rule applies to your MacBook: Buy a security cable and use it to keep your laptop safe from theft. Oh, and you don't have to search for a bike rack to lock down your MacBook — I've used table legs, tree trunks, and wrought-iron fencing to secure my MacBook, depending on how long I'm away. (Of course, if someone's around that you can trust to monitor your laptop, your cable can remain in your backpack. But as long as you're prepared, you'll never have to leave your MacBook unsecured!)

## Avoid the Obvious Laptop Case

Sure, using a laptop case or bag *sounds* like common sense — but MacBooks are so doggone sexy that you'd be surprised how many people carry them around without any protection at all. These Mac owners hear phrases like "rugged aluminum unibody" and "Sudden Motion Sensor hard drive protection" and figure that their laptop can tackle a construction site, a college campus, or a hotel room with impunity.

Part of that is indeed true. Mac laptops are some of the toughest laptops ever made, but they're not immune to bumps, scratches, and the (I hope) rare fall. But if you carry your MacBook from place to place without any protection, it'll soon look like a boxer after a bad fight.

Many folks think that a traditional laptop bag draws too much attention — and to some extent, I agree. (That's one reason no one totes an obvious 15 x 7 bag with a hardware manufacturer's logo emblazoned on the side these days.) If you're a member of this group, consider a *well-padded* laptop sleeve that will allow you to carry your MacBook in your backpack or briefcase; the laptop always goes in on top of those heavy books, of course. Remember, though, that the padding is the important thing. Without that extra cushion, you might as well just toss your unprotected laptop in with the rest of your books and must-have equipment.

## Encryption is your friend

In Book III, Chapter 3, I discuss a number of System Preferences panes. The Security pane is particularly important to laptop users because it allows you to encrypt your Snow Leopard Home folder. Encryption prevents just about anyone from accessing (or even *identifying*) any of the files you've stored in your Home folder. The robust encryption provided by Snow Leopard will certainly stymie just about anyone but the NSA and FBI. (I won't even go there.)

In System Preferences, click Security, click the FileVault tab, and then click Set Master Password to create a backup password that will unlock your Home folder, just in case. (Your login account password is your primary password.) Select Turn On FileVault, and Snow Leopard takes care of automatically encrypting and unencrypting files as necessary.

To take full advantage of an encrypted Home folder, you need the proper login mode (as I discuss in Book III, Chapter 4). Think about this possible security backdoor: From the Accounts pane, you've set your laptop to automatically log you in every time you boot your MacBook. This is the very definition of Not Secure because your login account password automatically bypasses the FileVault encryption! Therefore, make sure that you actually have to log in to access your account. For the full scoop, see Book III, Chapter 5.

## Unsecured Wireless is . . . unsecured

Okay, I like free Internet access as much as the next technology author — it's cool, it's convenient, and public access wireless networks keep popping up more and more all over the world. My favorite example? New Orleans has upgraded to citywide free wireless Internet access, which is perfect for checking your e-mail whilst you're catching beads or listening to jazz. Many more cities are certain to follow in the near future.

However, just because something is *free* doesn't mean that it's *safe*. (Impromptu bungee jumpers, take note.) Unfortunately, the free public wireless access you're likely to encounter is not secure: Anyone can join, and the information you send and receive can be intercepted by any hacker worthy of the name. A public network uses no WEP or WPA key, so no encryption is involved, and therefore no guarantee that your private e-mail, your company's financial spreadsheets, and your Great American Novel aren't being intercepted while you're uploading and downloading them in the airport.

If you *must* use your laptop on an unsecured public network, make sure that the connection itself is secure instead. For example, don't check your e-mail using a Web browser unless your ISP or e-mail service offers an encrypted SSL (Secure Sockets Layer) connection. (Yep, I'm talking again about that little padlock that appears in Safari, which I discuss in Chapter 5 of Book VI. It's not just for ordering things online!)

If you need to establish a secure connection with your home or office network, use an SSL-enabled Virtual Private Network (VPN) client, which allows you to transfer files and remotely operate a host computer with bulletproof security.

# Using a Security Application

The unthinkable happens: Your MacBook is stolen while you're on vacation or on a business trip, and you know that the chances that it will be returned are next to nil. You've resigned yourself to replacing it (and all your data). But wait! What if I told you that you might just receive an e-mail message on your desktop computer that tells you the Internet (IP) address of the thief or perhaps even the address where he or she is staying?

If this scenario sounds a little like a James Bond movie, you'll be surprised to learn that several *tracker applications* are available for Mac OS X that will run invisibly on your laptop. A tracker application can turn your MacBook into a transmitting beacon, broadcasting its current location and all the Internet information it can get to you — allowing you to alert police and apprehend the crook (who might be in the middle of creating an iPhoto library).

For example, MacTrak from GadgetTrak (www.gadgettrak.com) invisibly sends an e-mail to you each time your laptop is connected to the Internet. The e-mail outlines the network environment and physical location of your MacBook, using WiFi positioning. (Heck, your MacBook even takes surveillance photos using its iSight camera and then uploads those images to your Flickr account!)

MacTrak costs about $30 per year, which is pocket change for a corporate Road Warrior or design professional who depends on both the laptop and the irreplaceable data it contains.

**Book III**
**Chapter 7**

**Common-Sense Laptop Security**

# Book IV

# Going Mobile with iLife

# Contents at a Glance

## Chapter 1: The World According to Apple ............ 299

First, Sliced Bread . . . and Now, the Digital Hub ................... 299
What Does Digital Mean, Anyway? ........................... 300
What Can I Digitize? ...................... 301
The Software That Drives the Hub .................................. 302
Can I Use All This Stuff at One Time? ................................ 307

## Chapter 2: Jamming with iTunes and iPod ............ 309

What Can I Play on iTunes? ............ 310
Playing an Audio CD ...................... 311
Playing Digital Audio and Video .... 312
Keeping Slim Whitman and Slim Shady Apart: Organizing with Playlists ............................ 316
And more...

## Chapter 3: Focusing on iPhoto ......... 333

Delving into iPhoto .......................... 333
Working with Images in iPhoto ...... 335
Producing Your Own Coffee-Table Masterpiece ........... 349
You'll Love MobileMe Gallery! ....... 352
Mailing Photos to Aunt Mildred .... 354

## Chapter 4: Making Magic with iMovie ............................. 357

The iMovie Window ......................... 357
A Bird's-Eye View of Moviemaking ............................... 360
Importing the Building Blocks ....... 361
Building the Cinematic Basics ....... 367
Sharing Your Finished Classic with Others ............................... 372

## Chapter 5: Burn Those DVDs! Using iDVD ............................. 375

Introducing Your Mac to iDVD ...... 375
Starting a New DVD Project ........... 378
Creating a DVD from Scratch ......... 380
Giving Your DVD the Personal Touch ............................... 387
And more...

## Chapter 6: Becoming a Superstar with GarageBand ............ 395

Shaking Hands with Your Band ..... 396
Composing and Podcasting Made Easy ................................... 398
Automatic Composition with Magic GarageBand ............. 411
Sharing Your Songs and Podcasts ................................... 413

## Chapter 7: Crafting a Web Site with iWeb ............................. 417

Looking around the iWeb Window ................................... 417
Planning Your Pages ....................... 419
Adding a New Site ........................... 420
Adding a New Page .......................... 421
And more...

## Chapter 8: No, It's Not Called iQuickTime ............................. 429

QuickTime Can Do That? ............... 429
Playing Media with QuickTime ...... 430

## Chapter 9: Turning Your MacBook into a DVD Theater ............................. 435

The DVD Hardware ......................... 435
The DVD Player: It's Truly Shiny ................................... 435
Taking Advantage of Additional DVD Features ............................. 438

# Chapter 1: The World According to Apple

## In This Chapter

✔ Doing things the hub way

✔ Digitizing your life

✔ Making your digital devices work together

**H**uzzah! After years of empty promises of professional-quality media features for home and school — most of them coming from those silly Windows people in Redmond — Apple has developed a recipe for digital success.

By using tightly integrated hardware and software (where everything works smoothly together), Apple gives you the ability to easily organize and produce your own multimedia with the iLife suite of digital tools, which includes iMovie, iDVD, iPhoto, GarageBand, iWeb, and iTunes. That same software also provides fantastic editing capabilities. Finally (and this is very important) — to paraphrase Will Smith in the movie *Men in Black,* "Apple makes these programs look *good.*"

## First, Sliced Bread . . . and Now, the Digital Hub

In today's overloaded world of personal electronic devices, people can try to juggle as many as five or six electronic wonders. Each device typically comes with its own software, power adapter, and connectors to the outside world. Although managing one or two devices isn't terribly difficult, as the number of devices increases, so do the headaches. When you have a half-dozen cables, power adapters, and software to cart around, the digital life can become pretty bleak. (And quite heavy. You'll need more than a back-pack to lug all that gear around.)

To combat this confusion, Apple came up with the idea of a *digital hub,* whereby your MacBook acts as the center of an array of electronic devices. By using standardized cables, power requirements, built-in software, and even wireless connections via *Bluetooth* (the standard for short-range wireless communications between devices) and 802.11x wireless (for connections to your Ethernet network and your Apple TV unit), the MacBook — along with its operating system, Mac OS X — goes a long way toward simplifying your interaction with all the electronic gadgets that you use.

Given the hub terminology, think of the digital hub as a wagon wheel. (See Figure 1-1.) At the center of the wheel is your MacBook. At the end of each spoke is a digital device. Throughout the rest of Book IV, I give you the skinny on each device, but this chapter gives you the overview and tells you how they all work together.

**Figure 1-1:** Hey, look what's in the center of your digital hub!

## What Does Digital Mean, Anyway?

Computers are handy machines. They can process information very quickly and never get bored when asked to do the same task millions of times. The problem is that despite their propensity for reliability and speed, they aren't so hot in the intuition department. You have to tell them how to *do* everything (and most of them talk only to application developers and programmers). Computers know only one thing — numbers — although they do know numbers very, very well.

In fact, *binary* (the language of computers) has only two values — one and zero, which represent *on* and *off*, respectively. (Think of a light switch that toggles: The earliest computers were simply banks of switches that filled up an entire room.) To work with a computer in meaningful ways, you have to describe everything to a computer with numbers — or, if you prefer, *digits*.

By describing audio in numerical digits, you suddenly have something that a computer can work with. Toss a computer as many numbers as you want, and it can handle them. The scientists who figured this out knew that they had a good thing going, so they proceeded to convert anything that they could get their hands on into . . . well, digits. (Sorry about the atrocious pun.) Anyway, this resulted in some interesting technologies, most of which you'll surely recognize:

✦ **Audio CDs:** The music is represented as numbers and is stored on a plastic disc.

✦ **Digital video:** Images and sound are stored together on your hard drive or a DVD as one really, *really* long string of numbers.

✦ **Digital fingerprints:** (No pun intended this time.) Your fingerprint is converted into numerical data, which a computer can use to compare against fingerprint data from other people.

✦ **Automated telephone operators:** When you call a phone operator these days, you often aren't speaking to a real person. Rather, the computer on the other end of the line converts your voice into digits, which it uses to interpret your words. (At other times, I think I'm talking to a real person, but it's hard to tell.)

# What Can I Digitize?

As you've probably guessed by now, practically anything can be digitized. As long as you can represent something as numbers, you can digitize that data. Whether it's photographs, video, or audio, your MacBook is adept at digitizing data and processing it.

## Photographs

Perhaps the most popular of digital devices, the digital camera has transformed photography forever. By using sophisticated electronics, digital cameras convert the image that you see through the camera viewfinder into an image made purely of numbers.

After this numeric information is transferred to your MacBook, your computer can cut, twist, fade, label, and paint your digital images. Because numbers are the only materials involved, you won't need scissors, paint, or adhesive tape to edit images. (Advertising photographers can say good-bye to the old-fashioned airbrush.) Your laptop does it all by manipulating those numbers. It cuts down on the messy art supplies and gives you the comfort of being able to go back in time — something that anyone who's not so handy with scissors can appreciate.

## Music

As I mention earlier in this chapter, audio CDs are one application of music represented as digital data. The physical CD is just a piece of plastic with a metal coating, but you don't even really need CDs any longer. Your MacBook can digitize audio for storage on your hard drive, too, which brings up another important point. Not only is digital information palatable to a computer, it's also very portable. You can store it on any number of storage devices, such as an iPod, a USB flash drive, or an external hard drive. (By the way, if you're a musician, you can use GarageBand and external instruments that will turn your mobile Mac into a combination of synthesizer, amplifier, and backup band. Mozart would've loved this stuff.)

## Video

When you photograph a scene multiple times per second and then replay the sequence, you get (tah-dah!) moving pictures. In the analog (as opposed to digital) world, this would be a strip of celluloid film or magnetic tape. In the digital world, such a sequence of photographs is called *DV,* or *digital video.* After you take your digital video, you can transfer that data to your MacBook to further manipulate it: You can edit it and add transitions, text, and other effects.

## DVD

As is a CD-ROM or a hard drive, a *DVD* is simply a means of storing digital data. Although you can use it to save many different kinds of data, its most common use is for presenting video content. The MacBook digital hub can produce DVDs by using any digital information you give it.

# The Software That Drives the Hub

At the heart of your digital hub is your MacBook. To use and manipulate all the data that arrives at your laptop, your computer needs software, which provides instructions on what to do with the information that you send. Fortunately, Apple has fashioned some of the most attractive and easy-to-use software ever written to help you manipulate and manage your digital lifestyle — and that outstanding software accompanies your new MacBook as part of your purchase! The list of software that belongs to the digital hub includes

✦ **iPhoto:** Use iPhoto to download, manipulate, and organize your favorite digital photographs. After everything is just so, iPhoto can print them, burn them to disc, or even help you design and order a hardbound album! (For way more on iPhoto, go to Book IV, Chapter 3.)

✦ **iTunes:** iTunes offers the ability to create and manage your music and movie collection, along with sundry other media such as podcasts,

Internet radio, audiobooks, and music videos. You can also purchase and download audio tracks and video from Apple's iTunes Store. iTunes can even burn CDs! (Head to Book IV, Chapter 2 for more.)

✦ **iMovie:** Every film director needs a movie-editing suite. iMovie gives you the chance to set up Hollywood in your neighborhood coffee shop with outstanding results. (Just keep that double mocha away from your laptop!) For more, see Book IV, Chapter 4.

✦ **iDVD:** As home video moves toward the digital realm, iDVD becomes an essential tool for authoring your own DVD media. Home movies will never be the same! iDVD is covered in Book IV, Chapter 5.

✦ **GarageBand:** Call it a "music-building" application! Even if you can't play a note, GarageBand makes it easy to create your own original songs — and if you *are* a musician, you can turn your MacBook into a traveling production studio. The latest version can even help you learn how to play an instrument. (Turn to Book IV, Chapter 6 for more.)

✦ **iWeb:** Interested in producing a professional-quality Web site, but afraid that you'll have to give up your personal life to build and maintain it? Never fear; with iWeb you can join the Web publishing crowd the easy Apple way. (I cover iWeb like a blanket in Book IV, Chapter 7.)

✦ **iCal:** To help keep your hectic digital lifestyle in order, iCal (which is included with Snow Leopard) offers complete calendar features. Besides tracking your dates and appointments on your MacBook, you can publish calendars on the Web or share them with different parts of the digital hub. (Or, if you have an iPod, you can even download your appointments and carry 'em with you.)

✦ **iSync:** With so many digital devices at your disposal, it gets hard to keep them all straight. *iSync* is software for automatically synchronizing contact and calendar information between cell phones, your personal digital assistant (PDA), an iPod, the Mac OS X Address Book, and iCal. iSync is included with Snow Leopard.

## iPhoto

What good is a camera without a photo album? *iPhoto,* Apple's photography software, serves as a digital photo album. Use it to help you arrange and manage your digital photos. Beyond its functions as a photo album, iPhoto also gives you the ability to touch up your images through cropping, retouching, scaling, rotating, and red-eye reduction (photographically speaking, not morning-after speaking).

Besides offering editing features, iPhoto also works automatically with your digital camera. Simply plug in the camera to your MacBook's Universal Serial Bus (USB) port, and iPhoto knows it's there. Need to transfer photos from the camera to your photo album? iPhoto can do that, too.

When you complete a collection of photographs that you find interesting, use iPhoto to help you publish them on the Internet or even to create your very own coffee-table book, custom greeting cards, and full-color calendars. (The latest in high-tech: paper products.) And for those of you who still want that nifty wallet print to show off at work or a poster to hang on your wall, you can print them with your own printer or order them online through iPhoto. Orders made with iPhoto show up in your mailbox — the U.S. Postal Service physical one outside your domicile — a few days later.

## iTunes

To help you wrangle your enormous digital music and movie collection, Apple offers iTunes (see Figure 1-2). For starters, iTunes is a sophisticated audio player for all your digital audio files. But iTunes is also handy for converting audio tracks from audio CDs to a number of popular digital audio file formats, such as AAC, MP3, and AIFF. After you import or convert your music into computer files, iTunes helps you manage and maintain your music collection. You can even listen to streaming online "radio stations," 24 hours a day. The latest version of iTunes even allows you to rent or buy videos and movies, either on your MacBook or on your video-capable iPod.

Plus, Apple throws in the iTunes Store, where you can preview hundreds of thousands of songs and videos for up to 30 seconds each without spending a dime. (Podcast subscriptions are usually free, bucko.) If you latch onto something that you'd like to buy, you can use your credit card to purchase and download your media (either as individual tracks for 99 cents each, or as a complete album or movie for a package price). After the media that you've bought is comfortably nestled in iTunes, you can play it on your laptop, burn music to an audio CD, or download it to your iPod.

Why do I keep harping on the iPod? Well, as a proud owner of one, I'm glad you asked: Apple's *iPod* is a versatile, lightweight audio and video player with hidden extras that James Bond would covet. It has enough capacity to store your entire collection of music and several movies, but it's small enough to fit into your shirt pocket. With iTunes, you can instantly exchange media between your MacBook and your iPod. You can also use iTunes to create audio and MP3 CDs for playback elsewhere. And the iPod even works as honest-to-goodness, back-up storage . . . you see, it also functions as a standard external USB 2.0 hard drive. An iPod can display text files and play games; you can even carry your Address Book contacts and iCal appointments with you with aplomb. (For the lowdown on iPod, peruse Book IV, Chapter 2.)

## iMovie

You needn't restrict yourself to still images: Hook up your digital camcorder to your MacBook as well. Use *iMovie,* the easy-to-use video editing application shown in Figure 1-3, to create and edit digital movies.

**Figure 1-2:**
With iTunes, you can buy music and video from the Apple Store.

**Figure 1-3:**
iMovie can turn you into Hollywood material — let's do lunch.

With stunning video-editing candy such as transitions, sound effects, and video effects, iMovie turns your home movies into professional productions that you'll be proud to share with friends and family. Finally, you can have a home-movie night without putting everyone to sleep.

## iDVD

Of course, after you create a video masterpiece, you probably want to save it on a DVD for preservation and future viewing. To help you in your endeavors, use iDVD to create — or, as video professionals call it, *author* — DVD movies. With the preset templates, iDVD will have you cranking out stunning DVDs with interactive menus in no time, ready to use with any DVD player.

## GarageBand

Imagine the freedom to create your own original music by simply dragging "digital instruments" onto a canvas . . . and then adding your own voice as the lead instrument! After the basic melody is in place, you'll be able to edit whatever you like, or even choose different instruments with the click of a mouse. As recently as ten years ago, dear reader, that concept was indeed just a dream. Then, software-based synthesizers and mixing applications brought musicians into the digital age. (The problem was that normal human beings couldn't afford the expensive software or the sample libraries of literally thousands of different instruments.) With the addition of GarageBand, however, the iLife suite provides everything that you need to start making your own music (inexpensively) and then create MP3 files or burn your own audio CDs. And believe me, if I can create a techno track that actually hit the speakers at a local dance club, *you* can, too!

## iWeb

In the days of old — I'm talking five or six years ago here — putting a Web site online meant hours of drudgery, usually with a so-called "what you see is what you get" page creation application. Problem was, "what you saw" was very rarely easy to create, and if you were actually successful in getting the results you wanted, you still had to get all that stuff to appear on a Web server somewhere so that visitors could actually *see* it. With iWeb, the creation of a Web site is intuitive, easy, and downright fun! Click and drag your way to the Web site you want, starting with a number of truly outstanding predesigned templates. Add all sorts of cool pages, such as blogs and automated online photo albums. And the best part? Click a couple of buttons, and your new work of online art appears automatically on your MobileMe Web site, or as a group of files that's ready for uploading to your Web server. Voilà!

# *Can I Use All This Stuff at One Time?*

What makes the digital hub idea even juicier is that it's an *interoperable* model. Let's pause to appreciate that. (What, you don't speak *engineer?* No problem!) In plain English, the digital hub allows you to use digital media from one part of the hub with another part of the hub. Thus, the individual parts of the digital hub can work together to complement each other. To illustrate, consider some digital-sharing scenarios:

✦ **You shoot a great photograph of your kids.** It's so great, in fact, that you'd like to use it as the title screen of your family's home movie. With the digital hub, you can use that same photograph in iMovie to create your home flick. When you're done with that, transfer the whole thing to a DVD by using iDVD, and your masterpiece is safe for decades of viewing. One image just worked its way through three parts of the digital hub.

✦ **You just recorded a catchy song with GarageBand.** You add the song to the soundtrack of the music video that you're creating with iMovie. Then you create a fancy opening menu and burn the finished project to DVD with iDVD to show prospective agents. Again, one piece of media has traveled through three parts of the digital hub!

✦ **Your band becomes popular and starts to play some impressive gigs.** To document your band's rise to stardom, your friend films a concert with a DV camcorder. You use iMovie to transfer the video to your MacBook and create clips of your favorite performances of the concert. The clips are transferred over to the primo Web site you've created with iWeb, and your band's Internet image takes off! After that, it's a simple matter to author to DVD with iDVD, extract the audio from the video for use as an MP3 with iTunes, and grab an image from the video for a band scrapbook that you're creating with iPhoto. Now you've attained honest-to-goodness DHH (shorthand for *Digital Hub Heaven*). You've traversed the entire hub, easily sharing the media along the way.

Lest I forget, I should mention the other advantage of the digital hub: The media that you swap between all your "iApplications" remains in digital form, which is A Good Thing! In the previous example of shooting a concert, for instance, that concert footage remained practically pristine while it was being transferred to DVD, converted to MP3, pasted into your iPhoto album, or uploaded to your iWeb site. (Because some audio and video formats are *compressed* to save space, such as MP3, a purist will argue that you lost a little something. It ain't much.) Unlike with archaic analog VHS tape, you don't have to worry about whether your source is second generation — and you can forget degradation and that silly tracking control.

**Book IV
Chapter 1**

**The World
According to Apple**

# Chapter 2: Jamming with iTunes and iPod

## In This Chapter

✔ Playing music with your MacBook

✔ Arranging and organizing your music collection

✔ Tuning into the world with Internet radio

✔ Sharing your songs across a network

✔ Creating eye candy with the Visualizer

✔ Buying the good stuff from the iTunes Store

Good news! It's time to throw out your Dad's Hi-Fi from the early '70s (you know, the one with the 4-inch speakers that you're embarrassed to show your friends). Every installation of Mac OS X comes with the finest stereophonic gadget in town: a great audio application called *iTunes*. With iTunes, you can listen to your favorite songs and podcasts, organize your music collection, watch a video or a full length movie, listen to radio stations from around the world, buy music and video online, burn CDs and DVDs, and much more! iTunes has so many features that you'll soon find yourself wondering why you even own a stereo at all. In no time, you'll be pondering how much new speakers with a subwoofer will cost for your MacBook.

In this chapter, I show you how to play audio CDs, podcasts, videos, and Internet radio, but that's just the beginning. You discover how to use iTunes' Library to get one-click access to any song in your collection. I even show you how to tune into Internet radio (and share your favorite songs with others on your network), burn audio CDs (if you have the necessary hardware), plug in your iPod, and buy the latest hits from the iTunes Store. Heck, iTunes can even suggest new music for your library based on what you're listening to now. (And I demonstrate how to make your iTunes window look just as good as your music sounds, with visualizations.)

Just in case, though, keep your Dad's Hi-Fi . . . it might fetch a hefty sum as an antique on eBay.

# What Can I Play on iTunes?

Simply put, iTunes is a media player; it plays audio and video files. These files can be in any of many different formats. Some of the more common audio formats that iTunes supports are

✦ **MP3:** The small size of MP3 files has made them popular for file trading on the Internet. You can reduce MP3 files to a ridiculously small size (at the expense of audio fidelity), but a typical CD-quality, three-minute pop song in MP3 format has a size of 3–5MB.

✦ **AAC:** *AAC* (short for Advanced Audio Coding) is an audio format that's very similar to MP3; in fact, AAC files offer better recording quality at the same file sizes. However, this format originally supported a built-in copy protection scheme that prevented AAC music purchased from iTunes from being widely distributed on Macs. (Luckily, this copy protection is no longer applied to iTunes tracks, and you can still burn protected AAC tracks to an audio CD, just as you can MP3 tracks.) The tracks that you download from the iTunes Store are in AAC format.

The iTunes Store's *iTunes Plus* tracks are also in AAC format, but these tracks are not copy-protected, and they're encoded at a higher-quality 256 Kbps rate.

✦ **Apple Lossless:** Another format direct from Apple, *Apple Lossless* format provides the best compromise between file size and sound quality: These tracks are encoded without loss of quality. However, Apple Lossless tracks are somewhat larger than AAC, so it's generally the favorite of the most discerning audiophile for his or her entire music library.

✦ **AIFF:** The standard Macintosh audio format produces sound of the absolute highest quality. This high quality, however, also means that the files are pretty doggone huge. A typical pop song in AIFF format has a size of 30–50MB.

✦ **WAV:** Not to be outdone, Microsoft created its own audio file format (WAV) that works much like AIFF. It can reproduce sound at higher quality than MP3, but the file sizes are very large, very similar in size to AIFF files.

✦ **CD audio:** iTunes can play audio CDs. Because you don't usually store CD audio anywhere but on an audio CD, file size is no big whoop.

✦ **Movies and video:** You can buy and download full-length movies, TV shows, music videos, and movie trailers from the iTunes Store . . . and, with an Apple TV unit connected to your home theater system, you can watch those movies and videos from the comfort of your sofa on the other side of your house.

✦ **Podcasts:** These audio downloads are like radio programs for your iPod — but iTunes can play and organize them, too. Some podcasts also include video and photos to boot.

✦ **Ringtones:** iPhone owners, rejoice! iTunes automatically offers to create ringtones for your iPhone from the tracks you've bought on the iTunes Store. (You can also create ringtones with GarageBand, using songs you've added to your iTunes library.)

✦ **Audiobooks:** No longer do you need cassettes or audio CDs to enjoy your spoken books — iTunes can play them for you, or you can send them to your iPod for listening on the go.

✦ **Streaming Internet radio:** You can listen to a continuous broadcast of songs from one of tens of thousands of Internet radio stations, with quality levels ranging from what you'd expect from FM radio to the full quality of an audio CD. You can't save the music in iTunes, but it's still great fun. (In fact, I run my own station . . . more on MLC Radio later in the chapter.)

# Playing an Audio CD

Playing an audio CD in iTunes is simple. Just insert the CD in your computer's disc tray or disc slot, start iTunes by clicking its icon in the Dock, and click the Play button. (Note that your Mac might be set to automatically launch iTunes when you insert an audio CD.) The iTunes interface resembles that of a traditional cassette or CD player. The main playback controls of the iTunes are Play, Previous Song, Next Song, and the volume slider, as shown in Figure 2-1.

**Figure 2-1:**
The main playback controls:
Play, Previous, and Next.

Book IV
Chapter 2

Jamming with
iTunes and iPod

Click the Play button to begin listening to a song. While a song is playing, the Play button toggles to a Pause button. As you might imagine, clicking that button again pauses the music. If you don't feel like messing around with the trackpad, you can always use the keyboard. The spacebar acts as the Play and Pause buttons. Press the spacebar to begin playback; press it again to stop.

Click the Next Song button to advance to the next song on the CD. The Previous Song button works like the Next Song button but with a slight twist: If a song is currently playing and you click the Previous Song button, iTunes first returns to the beginning of the current song (just like an audio CD player). To advance to the previous song, double-click the Previous Song button. To change the volume of your music, click and drag the volume slider.

As with other Macintosh applications, you can control much of iTunes with the keyboard. Table 2-1 lists some of the more common iTunes keyboard shortcuts.

| Table 2-1 | Common iTunes Keyboard Shortcuts |
| --- | --- |
| *Press This Key Combination* | *To Do This* |
| Spacebar | Play the currently selected song if iTunes is idle. |
| Spacebar | Pause the music if a song is playing. |
| Right-arrow key | Advance to the next song. |
| Left-arrow key | Go back to the beginning of a song. Press a second time to return to the previous song. |
| ⌘+up-arrow key | Increase the volume of the music. |
| ⌘+down-arrow key | Decrease the volume of the music. |
| ⌘+Option+down-arrow key | Mute the audio if any is playing. Press again to play the audio. |

# Playing Digital Audio and Video

In addition to playing audio CDs, iTunes can play the digital audio files that you download from the Internet or obtain from other sources in the WAV, AAC, Apple Lossless, AIFF, and MP3 file formats. Enjoying a digital audio file is just slightly more complicated than playing a CD. After downloading or saving your audio files to your Mac, open the Finder and navigate to wherever you stored the files. Then simply drag the music files (or an entire folder of music) from the Finder into the Music entry in the iTunes Source list. (The added files appear in the Music section of your iTunes Library. Think of the Library as a master list of your digital media. To view the Music Library, select the Music entry in the left-hand column of the iTunes player, as shown in Figure 2-2. Go figure.) Heck, you can also drag a song file from a Finder window and drop it on the iTunes icon in the Dock, which adds it to your Music Library as well.

**Figure 2-2:**
The Music
Library
keeps track
of all your
audio files.

If you drop the file on top of a playlist name in the Source list, iTunes adds it to that particular *playlist* as well as the main Library. (More about playlists in a bit.)

To play a song, just double-click it in the Music list. Alternatively, you can use the playback controls (Play, Previous Song, and Next Song) that I discuss earlier in this chapter (refer to Figure 2-1).

The Source list of iTunes can list up to five possible sources for music:

+ **Library:** This section includes Music, Movies, TV Shows, Podcasts, Audiobooks, iPod Games, and Radio. (Think *Internet radio,* which I discuss further in the section "iTunes Radio.")

+ **Devices:** If an iPod is connected, it appears in the list. (And yes, Virginia, other models of MP3 players from other companies will also appear in the list if they support iTunes.) If you load an audio CD, it appears in the Devices heading . . . anything from the Bee Gees to Fall Out Boy.

+ **Store:** I discuss this later, in the section "Buying Digital Media the Apple Way."

+ **Shared:** If another Mac or PC on your local network is running iTunes and is set to share part or all of its library, you can connect to the other computer for your music. (Shared music on another Mac appears as a separate named folder in the Source list.)

✦ **Playlists:** Think of playlists as folders you use to organize your music. (More on playlists later in this chapter.)

If you've invested in an Apple TV, it will appear in the list as well, allowing iTunes to share media with your Apple TV, which in turn sends it to your ED- or HD-TV.

Notice also that the Library lists information for each song that you add to it, such as

✦ **Song Name:** The title of the song

✦ **Time:** The length of the song

✦ **Artist:** The artist who performs the song

✦ **Album:** The album on which the song appears

If some of the songs that you're adding don't display anything for the title, album, or artist information, don't panic; most MP3 files have embedded data that iTunes can read. If a song doesn't include any data, you can always add the information to these fields manually. I show you how later, in the section "Setting or changing the song information manually."

Clicking any of the column headings in the Library causes iTunes to reorder the Library according to that category. For example, clicking the Song Name column heading alphabetizes your Library by song title. I click the Time heading often to sort my Library according to the length of the songs. Oh, and you can drag column titles to reorder them any way you like (as long as the Name column remains at the far left of the named columns).

iTunes can display your Music Library in three ways: By default, the application uses the *list view* you see in Figure 2-1, where each song is one entry. Click the second View button (at the top of the iTunes window) to group tracks together by album artwork in *grid view*. Click the third View button, and you're browsing by album cover in *cover flow view*, complete with reflective surface!

## Browsing the Library

After you add a few dozen songs to iTunes, viewing the Library can become a task. Although a master list is nice for some purposes, it becomes as cumbersome as an elephant in a subway tunnel if the list is very long. To help out, iTunes can display your Library in another format, too: namely, browsing mode. To view the Library in browsing mode, click the View menu and click the Show Browser item, or press the ⌘+B keyboard shortcut.

The Browse mode of iTunes displays your library in a compact fashion, organizing your tunes into four sections:

✦ **Genre**

✦ **Artist**

✦ **Album**

✦ **Song Name**

Selecting an artist from the Artist list causes iTunes to display that artist's albums in the Album list. Select an album from the Album list, and iTunes displays that album's songs in the bottom section of the Browse window. (Those Apple software designers . . . always thinking of you and me.)

## Finding songs in your Music Library

After your collection of audio files grows large, you might have trouble locating that Swedish remix version of "I'm Your Boogie Man." To help you out, iTunes has a built-in Search function. To find a song, type some text into the search field of the main iTunes window. While you type, iTunes tries to find a selection that matches your search text. The search is quite thorough, showing any matching text from the artist, album, song title, and genre fields in the results. For example, if you type **Electronic** into the field, iTunes might return results for the band named *Electronic* or other tunes that you classified as *electronic* in the Genre field. (The section "Know Your Songs," later in this chapter, tells you how to classify your songs by genre, among other options.) Click the magnifying glass at the left side of the Search field to restrict the search even more: by Artists, Albums, Composers, and Songs.

## Will I trash my Count Basie?

Novice iTunes users, take note: iTunes watches your back when you trash tracks.

To illustrate: Suppose you delete a song from the Library that's located only in the iTunes music folder (which you didn't copy into iTunes from another location on your hard drive). That means you're about to delete the song entirely, and there'll be no copy remaining on your MacBook at all. Rest assured, though, that iTunes prompts you to make sure that you really want to move the file to the Trash.

(I get fearful e-mail messages all the time from readers who are loath to delete anything from iTunes because they're afraid they'll trash their digital music files completely.)

*Remember:* If you delete a song from the Library that *also* exists elsewhere on your hard drive (outside the reach of the iTunes music folder), it isn't deleted from your hard drive. In fact, if you mistakenly remove a song that you meant to keep, just drag it back into iTunes from the Finder, or even from the Trash. 'Nuff said.

**Book IV
Chapter 2**

**Jamming with
iTunes and iPod**

### Removing old music from the Library

After you spend some time playing songs with iTunes, you might decide that you didn't *really* want to add 40 different versions of "Louie Louie" to your Library. (Personally, I prefer either the original or the cast from the movie *Animal House*.) To remove a song from the Library, click the song to select it and then press the Delete key on your keyboard.

You can also remove a song from the Library by dragging it to the Trash in your Dock.

### Watching video

Watching video in iTunes is similar to listening to your music. To view your video collection, click one of these entries in the Source list:

✦ **Movies**

✦ **TV Shows**

If you select Movies or TV Shows, iTunes displays your videos as thumbnails or in cover flow view. Music videos appear as a smart playlist.

From your collection, you can

✦ Double-click a video thumbnail or an entry in the list.

✦ Drag a QuickTime–compatible video clip from the Finder window to the iTunes window. (These typically include video files ending in .mov or .mp4.)

iTunes plays video in the box below the Source list, within the iTunes window, in a separate window, or in full-screen mode, depending on the settings you've chosen on the General pane in the iTunes Preferences window. In full-screen mode, move your pointer to display a control strip at the bottom of the screen, sporting the standard slider bar that you can drag to move through the video (as well as a volume control and Fast Forward/Reverse buttons). You can also pause the video by clicking the Pause button.

## Keeping Slim Whitman and Slim Shady Apart: Organizing with Playlists

As I mention earlier, the iTunes Music Library can quickly become a fearsomely huge beastie. Each Library can contain thousands upon thousands of songs: If your Library grows anywhere near that large, finding all the songs in your lifelong collection of Paul Simon albums is *not* a fun task.

Furthermore, with the Library, you're stuck playing songs in the order that iTunes lists them.

To help you organize your music into groups, use the iTunes playlist feature. A *playlist* is a collection of some of your favorite songs from the Library. You can create as many playlists as you want, and each playlist can contain any number of songs. Whereas the Library lists all available songs, a playlist displays only the songs that you add to it. Further, any changes that you make to a playlist affect only that playlist, leaving the Library intact.

To create a playlist, you can do any of the following:

+ **Choose File➪New Playlist.**

+ **Press ⌘+N.**

+ **Choose File➪New Playlist from Selection.** This creates a new playlist and automatically adds any tracks that are currently selected.

+ **Click a song to select it; then click the Genius button at the lower-right corner of the window.** (The Genius button bears a striking "atom" symbol.) iTunes builds a playlist of songs that are similar in some way (typically by matching the genre of the selection or the beats per minute, but also based on recommendations from other iTunes members). Note that your MacBook needs an Internet connection to create a Genius playlist, and the larger your music library the longer it will take iTunes to build your playlist.

+ **Click the iTunes DJ entry in the Playlist section at the left side of the window.** iTunes delivers a random selection of songs taken from your iTunes Music Library — perfect for your next spontaneous party! You can change the order of the songs in the iTunes DJ playlist (known as Party Shuffle in older versions of iTunes), add songs from your Library, or delete songs that don't fit the scintillating ambience of your gathering. Enjoy!

+ **Click the New Playlist button in the iTunes window** (the plus sign button in the lower-left corner). You get a newly created empty playlist (the toe-tappin' *untitled playlist*).

All playlists appear in the Source list. To help organize your playlists, it's a good idea to . . . well, *name* them. (Aren't you glad now that you have this book?) For example, suppose that you want to plan a party for your polka-loving friends. Instead of running to your computer after each song to change the music, you could create a polka-only playlist. Select and start the playlist at the beginning of the party, and you won't have to worry about changing the music the whole night. (You can concentrate on the accordion.) To load a playlist, select it in the Source list; iTunes displays the songs for that playlist.

**Book IV
Chapter 2**

**Jamming with
iTunes and iPod**

## Some playlists are smarter than others

Click the File menu and you'll see the New Smart Playlist menu command. The contents of a *smart* playlist are automatically created from a specific condition or set of conditions that you set via the Smart Playlist dialog: You can limit the track selection by mundane things, such as album, genre, or artist; or you can get funky and specify songs that were played last, or by the date you added tracks, or even by the sampling rate or total length of the song. For example, iTunes can create a playlist packed with songs that are shorter than three minutes, so you can fill your iPod Shuffle with more stuff! Ah, but wait, you're not limited to a single criterion. If you want to add another criterion, click the plus sign at the right side of the dialog and you get another condition field to refine your selection even further.

You can choose the maximum songs to add to the smart playlist, or limit the size of the playlist by the minutes or hours of play or the number of megabytes or gigabytes the playlist will occupy. (Again, great for automatically gathering as much from your KISS collection as will fit into a specific amount of space on a CD or your iPod.) Mark the Live Updating check box for the ultimate in convenience. iTunes automatically maintains the contents of the smart playlist to keep it current with your conditions at all times in the future. (If you remove tracks manually from a smart playlist, iTunes adds other tracks that match your conditions.)

Now think about what all these settings mean when combined . . . *whoa.* Here's an example yanked directly from my own iTunes library. I created a smart playlist that selects only those songs in the Rock genre. It's limited to 25 songs, selected by least often played, and live updating is turned on. The playlist is named Tracks I've Gotta Hear because it finds the 25 rock songs (from my collection of 1,654 songs) that I've heard least often! After I listen to a song from this smart playlist, iTunes automatically "freshens" it with another song, allowing me to catch up on the tracks I've been ignoring. Completely, unbelievably *sweet* — and another reason that iTunes is the best music player on Planet Earth!

The same song can appear in any number of playlists because the songs in a playlist are simply pointers to songs in your Music Library — not the songs themselves. Add and remove them at will to or from any playlist, secure in the knowledge that the songs remain safe in the Library. Removing a playlist is simple: Select the playlist in the Source list and then press Delete.

Removing a playlist doesn't actually delete any songs from your Library.

## Know Your Songs

Besides organizing your music into Elvis and non-Elvis playlists, iTunes gives you the option to track your music at the song level. Each song that you add to the Music Library has a complete set of information associated with it. iTunes displays this information in the Info dialog, including

+ **Name:** The name of the song

+ **Artist:** The name of the artist who performed the song

+ **Composer:** The name of the astute individual who actually *wrote* the song

+ **Album Artist:** The name of the artist responsible for a compilation or tribute album

+ **Album:** The album where the song appears

+ **Grouping:** A group type that you assign

+ **Year:** The year the artist recorded the song

+ **BPM:** The beats per minute (which indicates the song's tempo)

+ **Track Number:** The position of the song on the original album

+ **Disc Number:** The original disc number in a multi-CD set

+ **Comments:** A text field that can contain any comments on the song

+ **Genre:** The classification of the song (such as rock, jazz, or pop)

You can display this information by clicking a song name and pressing ⌘+I — the fields appear on the Info tab.

## Setting the song information automatically

Each song that you add to the iTunes Music Library might have song information included with it. If you add music from a commercial audio CD, iTunes connects to a server on the Internet and attempts to find the information for each song on the CD. If you download a song from the Internet, it often comes with some information embedded in the file already; the amount of included information depends on what the creator supplied. (And believe me, it's often misspelled as well — think *Leenard Skeenard*.) If you don't have an Internet connection, iTunes can't access the information and displays generic titles instead.

## Setting or changing the song information manually

If iTunes can't find your CD in the online database or someone gives you an MP3 with incomplete or inaccurate information, you can change the information yourself — believe me, you want at least the artist and song name! To view and change the information for a song, perform the following steps:

*1.* **Select the song in either the Music Library list or a Playlist.**

*2.* **Press ⌘+I or choose File⇨Get Info.**

*3.* **Edit the song's information on the Info tab, as shown in Figure 2-3.**

**Figure 2-3:**
View and
edit song
information
here.

Keep in mind that the more work you put into setting the information of the songs in your Music Library, the easier it is to browse and use iTunes. Incomplete song information can make it more difficult to find your songs in a hurry. If you prefer, you don't have to change all information about a song (it just makes life easier later if you do). Normally, you can get away with setting only a song's title, artist, and genre. The more information you put in, however, the faster you can locate songs and the easier they are to arrange. iTunes tries to help by automatically retrieving known song information, but sometimes you have to roll up your sleeves and do a little work. (Sorry, but the DataElves are out to lunch.)

"What about cover art, Mark?" Well, I'm overjoyed that you asked! iTunes can try to locate artwork automatically for the tracks you select. (Note that adding large images can significantly increase the size of the song file.) Follow these steps:

*1.* **Select the desired songs from the track list.**

*2.* **Click Advanced⇨Get Album Artwork.**

You can set iTunes to automatically attempt the addition of album artwork every time you rip tracks from an audio CD, or when you add songs without artwork to your Music Library. Click iTunes and choose Preferences; then click the Store button and click the Automatically Download Missing Album Artwork check box to enable it.

Want to manually add album covers to your song info? Select one (or all) of the songs from a single album in the track list, display the Info dialog, and click the Artwork tab. Now launch Safari, visit Amazon.com, and do a search on the same album. Drag the cover image from the Web page right into the Info dialog, and drop it on top of the "sunken square" image well. When you click OK, the image appears in the Summary pane, and you can display it while your music is playing by pressing ⌘+G, or by pressing the Show or Hide Song Artwork button at the lower left of the iTunes window! (Note that adding large images can significantly increase the size of the song file.)

By the way, if you buy tracks or an album from the iTunes Store, Apple always includes album covers automatically. Thanks, Steve!

## Ripping Audio Files

You don't have to rely on Internet downloads to get audio files: You can create your own MP3, AAC, Apple Lossless, AIFF, and WAV files from your audio CDs with iTunes. The process of converting audio files to different formats is called *ripping*. (Audiophiles with technical teeth also call this process *digital extraction*, but they're usually ignored at parties by the popular crowd.) Depending on what hardware or software you use, each has its own unique format preferences. For example, most iPod owners prefer MP3 or AAC files, but your audio CDs aren't in that format. Being able to convert files from one format to another is like having a personal translator in the digital world. You don't need to worry if you have the wrong format: You can simply convert it to the format that you need.

The most common type of ripping is to convert CD audio to AAC or MP3 format. To rip MP3s from an audio CD, follow these simple steps:

1. **Launch iTunes by clicking its icon in the Dock.**

   Alternatively, you can locate it in your Applications folder.

2. **Choose iTunes➪Preferences.**

3. **In the Preferences window that appears, click the General toolbar button.**

4. **Click the Import Settings button.**

5. **Choose MP3 Encoder from the Import Using pop-up menu.**

6. **Choose High Quality (160 Kbps) from the Setting pop-up menu and then click OK.**

   This bit rate setting provides the best compromise between quality (it gives you better than CD quality, which is 128 Kbps) and file size (tracks you rip will be significantly smaller than "audiophile" bit rates such as 192 Kbps or higher).

7. **Load an audio CD into your MacBook.**

   The CD title shows up in the iTunes Source list (under the Devices heading), which is on the left side of the iTunes window. The CD track listing appears on the right side of the window.

   If iTunes asks you whether you want to import the contents of the CD into your Music Library, you can click Yes and skip the rest of the steps; however, if you've disabled this prompt, just continue with the remaining two steps.

8. **Clear the check box of any song that you don't want to import from the CD.**

   All songs on the CD have a check box next to their title by default. Unmarked songs aren't imported.

   Notice that the Browse button changes to Import CD.

9. **After you select the songs that you want added to the Library, click the Import CD button.**

## Tweaking the Audio for Your Ears

Besides the standard volume controls that I mention earlier in this chapter, iTunes offers a full equalizer. An *equalizer* permits you to alter the volume of various frequencies in your music, allowing you to boost low sounds, lower high sounds, or anything in between. Now you can customize the way your music sounds and adjust it to your liking.

To open the Equalizer (as shown in Figure 2-4), do one of the following:

**Figure 2-4:** Use the Equalizer sliders to tweak the sound of your music.

> ✦ **Choose Window⇨Equalizer.**
>
> ✦ **Press ⌘+Option+2.**

The Equalizer window has an impressive array of 11 sliders. Use the leftmost slider (Preamp) to set the overall level of the Equalizer. The remaining sliders represent various frequencies that the human ear can perceive. Setting a slider to a position in the middle of its travel causes that frequency to play back with no change. Move the slider above the midpoint to boost that frequency; conversely, move the slider below the midpoint to reduce the volume of that frequency.

Continue adjusting the equalizer sliders until your music sounds the way you like it. When you close the Equalizer window, iTunes remembers your settings until you change them again. In case you prefer to leave frequencies to the experts, the iTunes Equalizer has several predefined settings to match most musical styles. Click the pop-up menu at the top of the Equalizer window to select a genre.

After you adjust the sound to your satisfaction, close the Equalizer window to return to the iTunes interface and relax with those funky custom notes from James Brown.

## A New Kind of Radio Station

Besides playing back your favorite audio files, iTunes can also tune in Internet radio stations from around the globe. You can listen to any of a large number of preset stations, seek out lesser-known stations not recognized by iTunes, or even add your favorite stations to your playlists. This section shows you how to do it all.

---

### What's with the numbers next to the station names?

When choosing an Internet radio station, keep your Internet connection speed in mind. If you're using a broadband DSL or cable connection — or if you're listening at work over your company's high-speed network — you can listen to stations broadcasting at 128 Kbps (or even higher). The higher the bit rate, the better the music sounds. At 128 Kbps, for example, you're listening to sound that's as good as an audio CD.

However, if you're listening over a dial-up modem connection, iTunes can't keep up with audio streaming at higher bit rates, so you're limited to stations broadcasting at 56 Kbps or lower.

---

**Book IV
Chapter 2**

**Jamming with
iTunes and iPod**

## iTunes Radio

Although it's not a radio tuner in the strictest sense, iTunes Radio can locate virtual radio stations all over the world that send audio over the Internet — a process usually dubbed *streaming* amongst the "in" Internet crowd. iTunes can track down hundreds of Internet radio stations in a variety of styles with only a few clicks.

To begin listening to Internet radio with iTunes, click the Radio icon located beneath the Library icon in the Source list. The result is a list of more than 20 types of radio stations, organized by genre.

When you expand a Radio category by clicking its triangle, iTunes queries a tuning server and locates the name and address of dozens of radio stations for that category. Whether you like Elvis or not-Elvis (those passing fads, like new wave, classical, or alternative), something's here for everyone. The Radio also offers news, sports, and talk radio.

After iTunes fetches the names and descriptions of radio stations, double-click one that you want to hear. iTunes immediately jumps into action, loads the station, and begins to play it.

## Tuning in your own stations

Although iTunes offers you a large list of popular radio stations on the Web, it's by no means comprehensive. Eventually, you might run across a radio station that you'd like to hear, but it's not listed in iTunes. Luckily, iTunes permits you to listen to other stations, too. To listen to a radio station that iTunes doesn't list, you need the station's Web address.

In iTunes, choose Advanced⇨Open Audio Stream (or press ⌘+U). In the Open Stream dialog that appears (as shown in Figure 2-5), enter the URL of your desired radio station and then click OK. Within seconds, iTunes tunes in your station.

---

### "I have an itch to hear 'Kung Fu Fighting'!"

This particular technology author has a preference for a certain hot Net jam spot: *MLC Radio,* the Internet radio station I've been running for several years now. I call my station a '70s Time Machine because it includes hundreds of classic hits from 1970–1979, inclusive. You hear everything from "Rock and Roll Hoochie Koo" by Rick Derringer to "Moonlight Feels Right" by Starbuck. (Hey, I'm summing up a decade here, so be prepared for both Rush and the Captain and Tennille, too.) The station broadcasts at 128 Kbps (audio CD quality), so you need a broadband connection to listen. For the radio's Internet address or help connecting to MLC Radio, visit my Web site at www.mlcbooks.com — and then follow the steps in the next section to add MLC Radio to your playlists!

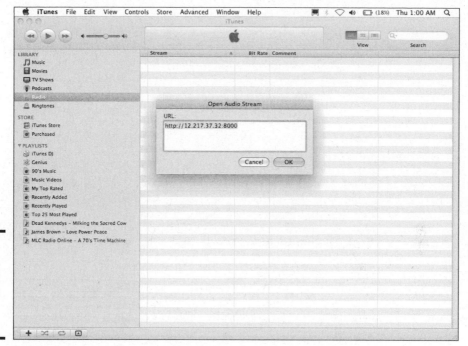

**Figure 2-5:**
Tuning into
MLC Radio,
my Internet
radio
station.

## *Radio stations in your playlists*

If you find yourself visiting an online radio station more than once, you'll be glad to know that iTunes supports radio stations in its playlists. To add a radio station to a playlist from the Radio list, do the following:

1. **Open the category that contains the station you want to add to your playlist.**

2. **Locate the station that you want to add to your playlist and drag it from the Radio list to the desired playlist on the left.**

   If you haven't created any playlists yet, see the section "Keeping Slim Whitman and Slim Shady Apart: Organizing with Playlists" earlier in this chapter to find out how.

Adding a radio station that doesn't appear in the Radio list is a bit trickier but possible nonetheless. Even though iTunes allows you to load a radio station URL manually by using the Open Stream command in the Advanced menu, it doesn't give you an easy way to add it to the playlist. Follow these steps to add a specific radio station to a playlist:

1. **Add any radio station from the Radio list to your desired playlist.**

   Any station in the list will do, as you'll immediately change both the station's URL and name to create your new station entry in the Playlist.

2. **Press ⌘+I or choose File⇨Get Info to bring up the information dialog for that station.**

3. **Click the Summary section and change the URL by clicking the Edit URL button.**

4. **Enter the desired URL and click OK.**

5. **Click the Info tab, type the new station name, and then click OK.**

## iSending iStuff to iPod

If you're lucky enough (like me) to own an iPod, you'll be happy to know that iTunes has features for your personal audio and video jukebox as well. *iPods,* Apple's multimedia players, comprise an entire family of portable devices (ranging from $79 to about $299) that can hold anywhere from about 300 songs to literally thousands of songs, as well as podcasts, photos, and video. This great gadget and those like it have become known worldwide as *the* preferred portable digital media player.

You connect your iPod to any Macintosh or Windows PC with USB 2.0 ports with the included cable. After the iPod's connected, it automatically synchronizes to the playlists in iTunes. The iPod and the iTunes software communicate with each other and figure out what items are in your iTunes Library (as compared with the iPod Library). If they discover songs, podcasts, and video in your iTunes Library that are missing from your iPod, the items automatically transfer to the iPod. Conversely, if the iPod contains stuff that's no longer in iTunes, the iPod automatically removes those files from its drive.

Go back and reread that last sentence above about the iPod **automatically removing** files from its drive. (I'll wait here.) Apple added this feature in an effort to be attentive to copyright concerns. The reasoning is that if you connect your iPod to your friend's computer, you can't transfer songs from the iPod to that computer. Of course, you could always look at it from the marketing perspective as a feature that makes sure your MacBook and iPod are always in total sync. Whatever the case, pay close attention and read all warning dialogs when connecting to a computer other than your own, or you might wipe out your iPod's library.

The best thing I can say about the iPod and iTunes combination is . . . well . . . that there *isn't* anything else to say about them. The auto-sync feature is so easy to use, you forget about it almost immediately. You can, however, auto-sync only selected playlists, or manually sync if you prefer.

This chapter — even as long as it is — just can't explain all the ins and outs of the iTunes/iPod relationship! For a complete look at both iTunes and the iPod, I can heartily recommend a fellow *For Dummies* book, *iPod & iTunes For Dummies,* 7th Edition, by Tony Bove (Wiley Publishing).

# Sharing Your Media across Your Network

Ready to share your music, podcasts, and video — *legally,* mind you — with other folks on your local network? You can offer your digital media to other iTunes users across your home or office. Follow these steps:

1. **Choose iTunes⇨Preferences to open the Preferences dialog.**

2. **Click Sharing.**

3. **Select the Share My Library on My Local Network check box.**

4. **Specify whether you want to share your entire library or only selected playlists and files.**

   Sharing selected playlists is a good idea for those Meatmen and Sex Pistols fans who work at a cubicle farm in a big corporation.

5. **If you want to restrict access to just a few people, select the Require Password check box; then type a password in the text box.**

6. **Click OK.**

Your shared folder appears within the Source list for all iTunes users who enabled the Look for Shared Libraries check box on the same pane of their iTunes Preferences dialog. Note that the music you share with others can't be imported or copied, so everything stays legal.

 Want to change that frumpy default name for your shared media library to something more exotic, like "Dan's Techno Beat Palace"? No problem — display the Preferences dialog again, but this time click the General button and click in the Library Name text box. Edit your network entertainment persona to your heart's content.

---

## Sending music elsewhere with AirTunes

If you're using an AirPort Express portable wireless Base Station, you can ship your songs right to your Base Station from within iTunes, and from there to your home stereo or boom box! (I get into some serious discussion of AirPort Express in Book VII, Chapter 3.)

After your AirPort Express Base Station is plugged in and you connect your home stereo (or a boombox, or a pair of powered stereo speakers) to the stereo minijack on the Base Station, you see a Speakers pop-up list button appear at the bottom of the iTunes window. (If the Speakers button doesn't appear, choose iTunes⇨Preferences to open the Preferences dialog and click the Devices button on the toolbar. Make sure that the Look for Remote Speakers Connected with AirTunes check box is enabled.)

Click the Speakers button, and you can choose to broadcast the music you're playing in iTunes across your wireless network. Ain't technology truly *grand?*

## Burning Music to Shiny Plastic Circles

Besides being a great audio player, iTunes is adept at creating CDs, too. iTunes makes the process of recording songs to a CD as simple as a few clicks. Making the modern version of a compilation (or *mix*) tape is easier than getting a kid to eat ice cream. iTunes lets you burn CDs in one of three formats:

+ **Audio CD:** This is the typical kind of commercial music CD that you buy at a store. Most typical music audio CDs store 700MB of data, which translates into about 80 minutes of music.

+ **Data CD or DVD:** A standard CD-ROM or DVD-ROM is recorded with the audio files. This disc can't be played in any standard audio CD player (even if it supports MP3 CDs, which I discuss next). Therefore, you can listen to these songs only by using your MacBook and an audio player, such as iTunes on a PC running Windows.

+ **MP3 CD:** As does the ordinary computer CD-ROM that I describe, an MP3 CD holds MP3 files in data format. However, the files are arranged in such a way that they can be recognized by audio CD players that support the MP3 CD format (especially boomboxes, DVD players, personal CD players, and car stereos). Because MP3 files are so much smaller than the digital audio tracks found on traditional audio CDs, you can fit as many as 160 typical 4-minute songs on one disc. These discs can also be played on your MacBook via iTunes.

Keep in mind that MP3 CDs aren't the same as the standard audio CDs that you buy at the store, and you can't play them in older audio CD players that don't support the MP3 CD format. Rather, this is the kind of archival disc that you burn at home for your own collection.

To begin the process, build a playlist (or select an existing playlist that you want to record). If necessary, create a new Playlist and add to it whatever songs you would like to have on the CD. (See the earlier section, "Keeping Slim Whitman and Slim Shady Apart: Organizing with Playlists," if you need a refresher.) With the songs in the correct order, select the playlist. Click the Burn Disc button at the bottom of the iTunes window to commence the disc burning process. Click the desired recording format (again, usually Audio CD) in the Burn Settings dialog that appears.

To save yourself from sonic shock, I always recommend that you enable the Sound Check check box before you burn. iTunes will adjust the volume on all the songs on your audio CD so that they'll play at the same volume level.

Ready to go? Click OK, and iTunes lets you know when the recording is complete.

## Backing up within iTunes

iTunes offers a built-in backup feature for your media library — I told you this was the best media player ever designed!

Choose File➪Library➪Back Up to Disc to start the process. You can choose to back up your entire iTunes library and all your playlists (which I recommend) or just the content you've purchased from the iTunes Store. Personally, if I lost everything in my collection except for what I've bought from the iTunes Store, I'd be just as crushed. Back it all up, and you won't be sorry.

Click Back Up, and iTunes will prompt you for blank CDs or DVDs. If you need to restore from your completed backup, just launch iTunes and load the first backup disc into your drive.

How often is often enough when it comes to backing up your content? That depends completely on how often your media library changes. The idea is to back up often enough so that you always have a recent copy of your media files close by.

## Feasting on iTunes Visuals

By now, you know that iTunes is a feast for the ears, but did you know that it can provide you with eye candy as well? With just a click or two, you can view mind-bending graphics that stretch, move, and pulse with your music, as shown in Figure 2-6.

To begin viewing iTunes visuals, choose View➪Show Visualizer (or press ⌘+T). Immediately, most of your iTunes interface disappears and begins displaying groovy lava lamp-style animations (like, *sassy,* man). To stop the visuals, choose View➪Hide Visualizer (or press ⌘+T again). The usual sunny aluminum face of iTunes returns.

You can also change the viewing size of the iTunes visuals in the View menu. From the View menu item, choose Full Screen (or press ⌘+F). To escape from the Full Screen mode, poke the trackpad or press Esc.

You can still control iTunes with the keyboard while the visuals are zooming around your screen. See Table 2-1 earlier in this chapter for a rundown on common keyboard shortcuts.

The iTunes Visualizer has many hidden features. While viewing the Visualizer, press ? to see a list of hidden Visualizer settings.

**Figure 2-6:**
iTunes can
display
some
awesome
patterns!

But wait, more Easter eggs are to be found! Again, while viewing the Visualizer, press one of following keys:

✦ **M:** Changes the Visualizer pattern

✦ **P:** Changes the Visualizer color scheme

Press either of these keys repeatedly to cycle through the various patterns and color schemes lurking deep within the Visualizer. (Personally, I'm a random Visualizer guy . . . there are so many patterns and schemes, I just let my MacBook do all the work.)

Additionally, you'll find third-party Visualizer plug-ins available for downloading on Apple's Web site and other Mac-related download sites — heck, some even display lyrics, karaoke-style! Choose a different Visualizer plug-in from the View➪Visualizer menu item. (Call me old-fashioned, but I like the default, iTunes Visualizer).

## Buying Digital Media the Apple Way

Before we wave goodbye to the happy residents of iTunes iSland, I won't forget to mention the hottest spot on the Internet for buying music and video: the iTunes Store, which you can reach from the cozy confines of iTunes. (That is, as long as you have an Internet connection. If you don't, it's time to turn the page to a different chapter.) If you're not in iTunes, go to www.apple.com/itunes/store.

Click the iTunes Store item in the Source list, and after a few moments you're presented with the latest offerings. Click a link in the store list to browse according to media type, or click the Power Search link to search by song title, artist, album, or composer. The Back/Forward buttons at the top of the iTunes Store window operate much the same as those in Safari, moving you backward or forward in sequence through pages you've already seen. Clicking the Home button (which, through no great coincidence, looks like a miniature house) takes you back to the Store's main page.

To display the details on a specific album, track, video, podcast, or audio-book (whew), just click it. If you're interested in buying just certain tracks (for that perfect road warrior mix), you get to listen to 30 seconds of any track — for free, no less, and at full sound quality. To add an item to your iTunes Store shopping cart, click the Add Song/Movie/Album/Video/Podcast/Audiobook button (sheesh!). When you're ready to buy, click the Shopping Cart item in the Source list and then click the Buy Now button. (At the time of this writing, tracks are usually 99 cents a pop, and an entire album is typically $9.99 . . . what a bargain!

The iTunes Store creates an account for you based on your e-mail address, and it keeps secure track of your credit card information for future purchases. After you use the iTunes Store once, you never have to log in or retype your credit card information again (as long as you're logged in using your account).

The tracks and files that you download are saved to a separate playlist called Purchased. After the download is finished, you can play them, move them to other playlists, burn them to CD or DVD, share 'em over your network, or ship them to your iPod, just as you can any other item in your iTunes Library.

You can also put the Genius button to work for you, in league with the iTunes store. Click the Show Genius Sidebar button at the lower-right corner of the iTunes window — it looks like an arrow inside a square — and iTunes displays the Genius Sidebar, where iTunes recommends music that you can buy on the iTunes Store that's similar to the albums in your Music Library. Click the button again to banish the sidebar.

Remember all those skeptics who claimed that buying digital audio and video could never work over the Internet because of piracy issues and high costs? Well, bunkie, hats off to Apple: Once again, our favorite technology leader has done something the *right* way!

# Chapter 3: Focusing on iPhoto

## In This Chapter

✓ Importing pictures from your hard drive or digital camera

✓ Organizing images with iPhoto

✓ Tweaking the appearance of photographs

✓ Sharing photos with your friends

For years, the Macintosh has been the choice of professional photographers for working with digital images — not surprising, considering the Mac's graphical nature. Apple continues this tradition with *iPhoto,* a photography tool for the home user that can help you organize, edit, and even publish your photographs. (It sports more features than a handful of Swiss army knives.) After you shoot your photos with a digital camera (or even scan images from original film prints), you can import them into iPhoto, edit them, and publish them. You're not limited to photos that you take yourself, either; you can edit, publish, and organize all kinds of digital image files. You can even create a photo album and use the iPhoto interface to order a handsome soft- or hard-bound copy shipped to you.

In this chapter, I walk you through an overview of what iPhoto can do. After that, I give you a brief tour of the controls within iPhoto so that you can see what features are available to you, including features for managing, printing, and publishing your photos.

## Delving into iPhoto

In Figure 3-1, you can see most of the major controls offered in iPhoto '09. (Other controls automatically appear when you enter different modes; I cover them in upcoming sections of this chapter.)

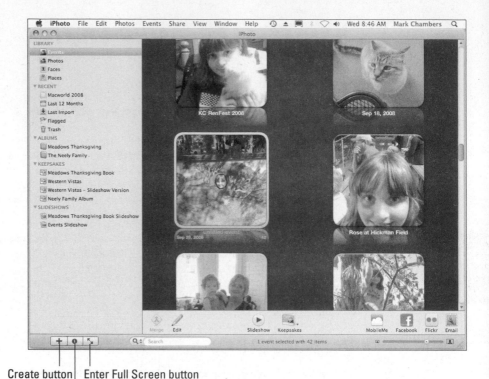

**Figure 3-1:**
iPhoto
greets you
with an
attractive
window.

Create button | Enter Full Screen button

Get Info button

Although these controls and sections of the window are covered in more detail in the following sections, here's a quick rundown of what you're looking at:

✦ **Source list:** This list of image locations determines which photos iPhoto displays.

• You can choose to display either your entire image library or just the last "roll" of digital images that you downloaded from your camera.

• You can create new *albums* of your own that appear in the source list; albums make it much easier to organize your photos.

• Photos can be grouped by *Event* (when they were taken), *Faces* (who appears in the photos), and *Places* (where photos were taken).

• You can create books, calendars, cards, and slideshows.

✦ **Viewer:** This pane displays the images from the currently selected photo source.

You can drag or click to select photos in the Viewer for further tricks, such as assigning keywords and image editing.

✦ **Create button:** Click this button to add a new blank album, smart album, MobileMe gallery, book, calendar, card, or slideshow to your source list.

✦ **Get Info button:** Click this button to display information on the currently selected photos.

✦ **Enter Full Screen button:** Click this button to switch to a full-screen display of your photos. In full-screen mode, the images in the selected album appear in a filmstrip across the top of the screen, and you can click one to view that image using your Mac's entire screen real estate. You can also use the same controls that I discuss later in this chapter for editing and adjusting images; just move the cursor to the top edge of the full-screen display to show the menu or to the bottom edge to show the editing toolbar.

✦ **Play Slideshow:** Select an event, album, book or slideshow in the Source list (or multiple images you've selected in the Viewer) and click this button to start a full-screen slideshow using those images.

✦ **Search box:** Click the button next to the Search text box to locate photos by specific criteria, or just click in the box and start typing to search by description and title.

✦ **Toolbar buttons:** This group of buttons selects an operation you want to perform on the images you've selected in the Viewer. (Note that the toolbar buttons you see may depend on your screen resolution.)

✦ **Thumbnail Resize slider:** Drag this slider to the left to reduce the size of the thumbnails in the Viewer. This allows you to see more thumbnails at one time, which is a great boon for quick visual searches. Drag the slider to the right to expand the size of the thumbnails, which makes it easier to differentiate details between similar photos in the Viewer.

# Working with Images in iPhoto

Even a superbly designed image display and editing application, such as iPhoto '09, would look overwhelming if everything were jammed into one window. Thus, Apple's developers provide different operation modes (such as editing and book creation) that you can use in the one iPhoto window. Each mode allows you to perform different tasks, and you can switch modes at just about any time by clicking the corresponding toolbar button.

In this section, I discuss three of these modes — import, organize, and edit — and what you can do when you're in them. Then I conclude the chapter with sections on publishing and sharing your images.

## Import Images 101

In *import* mode, you're ready to download images directly from your digital camera — as long as your specific camera model is supported in iPhoto. You can find out which cameras are supported by visiting the Apple iPhoto support page at www.apple.com/macosx/upgrade/cameras.html.

Follow these steps to import images:

1. **Connect your digital camera to your MacBook.**

   Plug one end of a USB cable into your camera and the other end into your MacBook's USB port, and prepare your camera to download images.

2. **Launch iPhoto.**

   Your MacBook will probably launch iPhoto automatically when your camera is detected, but you can always launch iPhoto manually by clicking its icon in the Dock (or or double-clicking it in your Applications folder).

3. **Type an event name for the imported photos, such as** Birthday Party **or** Godzilla Ravages Tokyo.

4. **Type a description for the Event.**

5. **To allow iPhoto to automatically separate images into separate events based on the date they were taken, click the Autosplit Events after Importing check box to select it.**

6. **Click the Import All button to import your photographs from the camera.**

   The images are added to your Photo Library, where you can organize them as you wish.

To select specific images to import, hold down the ⌘ key and click each desired photo; then click Import Selected instead of Import All.

---

# Importing images from your hard drive

If you have a folder of images that you've collected already on your hard drive, a CD, a DVD, an external drive, or a USB Flash drive, adding them to your library is easy. Just drag the folder from a Finder window and drop it into the source list in the iPhoto window. iPhoto automatically creates a new album using the folder name, and you can sit back while the images are imported into that new album. iPhoto recognizes images in several formats: JPEG, GIF, RAW, PNG, PICT, PSD, PDF, and TIFF.

If you have individual images, you can drag them as well. Select the images in a Finder window and drag them into the desired album in the source list. To add them to the album currently displayed in the Viewer, drag the selected photos and drop them in the Viewer instead.

If you'd rather import images by using a standard Mac Open dialog, choose File⇨Import to Library. Simplicity strikes again!

7. **Specify whether the images you're importing should be deleted from the camera afterward.**

   If you don't expect to download these images again to another computer or another device, you can choose to delete the photos from your camera automatically. This saves you a step, frees space for new photos and helps eliminate the guilt that can crop up when you nix your pix. (Sorry, I couldn't resist.)

"What's that about an Event, Mark?" After you download the contents of your digital camera, those contents count as a virtual *Event* in iPhoto — based on either the date that you imported them or the date they were taken. For example, you can always display the last images you imported by clicking Last Import. If you want to see photos from your son's graduation, they appear as a separate Event. (Both of these organizational tools will appear in the source list). Think about that . . . it's pretty tough to arrange old-fashioned film prints by the moment in time that they document, but iPhoto makes it easy for you to see just which photos are part of the same group! I explain more about Events in the next section.

There are four methods of organizing photos: the *album*, which you may be familiar with from older versions of iPhoto, *Events*, *Faces,* and *Places*.

## Organize mode: Organizing and sorting your images

In the days of film prints, you could always stuff another shoebox with your latest photos or buy another sticky album to expand your library. Your digital camera, though, stores images as files instead, and many folks don't print their digital photographs. Instead, you can keep your entire collection of digital photographs and scanned images well ordered and easily retrieved by using iPhoto's *organize* mode. Then you can display them as a slideshow, e-mail them, print them to your system printer, use them as Desktop backgrounds, or burn them to an archive disc.

### A new kind of photo album

The most familiar method of organizing images in iPhoto is the *album*. Each album can represent any division you like, be it a year, a vacation, your daughter, or your daughter's ex-boyfriends. Follow these steps:

1. **Create a new album.**

   You can either choose File⇨New Album or click the plus (+) button at the bottom of the source list. Click the Album button at the top of the sheet to display the settings you see in Figure 3-2.

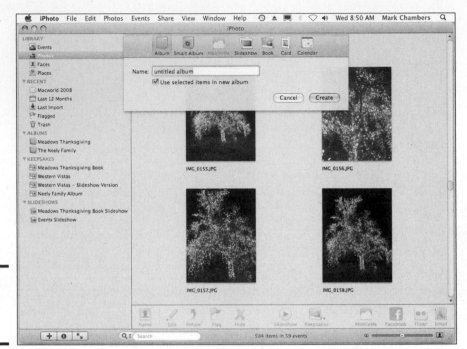

**Figure 3-2:**
Add a new
album in
iPhoto.

## 2. Type the name for your new photo album.

If you want to create an empty album (without automatically including any images that might be selected), make sure you click the Use Selected Items in New Album check box to deselect it.

## 3. Click OK.

iPhoto also offers a special type of album called a *Smart Album,* which you can create from the File menu. (For even faster action, hold down the Option key while you click the Add button.) A Smart Album contains only photos that match certain criteria that you choose, using the keywords and rating that you assign your images. Other criteria text in the photo filenames, dates the images were added to iPhoto, and any comments you might have added. Now here's the really nifty angle: iPhoto *automatically* builds and maintains Smart Albums for you, adding new photos that match the criteria (and deleting those that you remove from your Photo Library)! Smart Albums carry a gear icon in the source list.

You can display information about the currently selected item in the information pane under the source list. Just click the Show Information button at the bottom of the iPhoto window, which sports the familiar "*i*-in-a-circle" logo. You can also type a short note or description in the Description box that appears in the Information pane. For more in-depth information, select the desired item and then press ⌘+I.

You can also change information on an image by selecting it in the Viewer and clicking the Show Information button. Click any of the headings in the pane (Title, Date, Time, and so on) to display a text edit box, and you can simply click in either box to type a new name or alter the photo's date stamp.

You can drag images from the Viewer into any album you choose. For example, you can copy an image to another album by dragging it from the Viewer to the desired album in the Source list.

To remove a photo that has fallen out of favor, follow these steps:

1. **In the source list, select the desired album.**

2. **In the Viewer, select the photo (click it) that you want to remove.**

3. **Press Delete.**

When you remove a photo from an album, you *don't* remove the photo from your collection (which is represented by the Photos entry under the Library heading in the source list). That's because an album is just a group of links to the images in your collection. To completely remove the offending photo from iPhoto, click the Photos entry under the Library heading to display your entire collection of images and delete the picture there, too.

To remove an entire album from the source list, just click it in the source list to select it — in the Viewer, you can see the images that it contains — and then press Delete. (Alternatively, right-click or Control-click the offending album and choose Delete Album from the pop-up menu.)

To rename an album, click the entry under the Albums heading in the Source list to select it and then click again to display a text box. Type the new album name and press Return.

Change your mind? Daughter's ex is back in the picture, so to speak? iPhoto comes complete with a handy-dandy Undo feature. Just press ⌘+Z, and it's as though your last action never happened. (A great trick for those moments when you realize you just deleted your only image of your first car from your Library.)

### Arranging stuff by Events

As I mention earlier, Events are essentially a group of images that you shot or downloaded at the same time — iPhoto figures that those images belong together (which is usually a pretty safe assumption). Figure 3-3 illustrates some of the Events I've created in my iPhoto collection.

As can an album, an Event can be renamed — you just use a different procedure. Click the Events entry under the Library heading in the Source list to display your Events in the Viewer; then click the existing Event name in the caption underneath the thumbnail. A text box appears in which you can type a new name; click Return to update the Event.

Try moving your cursor over an Event thumbnail in the Viewer and you'll see that iPhoto displays the date range when the images were taken, as well as the total number of images in the Event. Ah, but things get *really* cool when you move your cursor back and forth over an Event with many images: The thumbnail animates and displays all the images in the Event, without your using old-fashioned scroll bars or silly arrows! (Why can't I think of this stuff? This is the future, dear readers.)

Notice that "i-in-a-circle" that appears when you hover your cursor over an Event thumbnail? Click it to display the location where the shot was taken, using the Places feature I describe in a page or two.

**Figure 3-3:**
Events help you organize by what happened, not just when it happened!

To display the contents of an Event in the Viewer, just double-click the Event thumbnail. To return to the Events thumbnails, click the All Events button at the top of the Viewer.

Decided to merge those Prom Event pictures with your daughter's Graduation Event? No problem! You could drag one Event thumbnail on top of another, but that's the easy way. Alternatively, click the Events entry under the Library heading in the Source list to display your Events and then hold down ⌘ while you click the Events that you want to merge. Click the Merge button in the toolbar at the bottom of the window, or click Events⇨Merge Events. (Forgot about that menu bar, didn't you?) Click Merge in the confirmation dialog that appears.

Whilst organizing, you can create a brand-new empty Event by clicking Events⇨Create Event. Feel free to drag photos from albums, other Events, or your Photo library into your new Event.

### Working with Faces and Places

iPhoto '09 includes two new organizational tools called Faces and Places. These two categories now appear in the Library section of the Source list.

**Putting names to faces:**

First, let's tackle Faces. This feature is a sophisticated recognition system that automatically recognizes human faces within the photos that you add to your Library. (I don't know whether it works well with pets — but you can try, anyway.) Naturally, you have to identify faces first before iPhoto can recognize them, which it does through a process called *tagging*.

To tag a face, follow these steps:

*1.* **In the Source list, click the Photos item to display your image library.**

*2.* **In the Viewer, click the photo with a person you want to tag.**

The photo is selected, as indicated by the yellow border.

*3.* **Click the Name button in the iPhoto toolbar at the bottom of the window.**

iPhoto displays the tagging pane you see in Figure 3-4. Note that iPhoto has indicated each person's face in the photo with a label.

*4.* **If the face is unrecognized (labeled as unnamed), click the label to open a text box and type the person's name.**

If iPhoto recognizes the face correctly and the name matches the person, click the check mark to confirm the tag. If the face is incorrectly identified, click the X and you can enter a new name.

**Figure 3-4:** Adding another mug to my collection of Faces.

If the name appears on an Address Book contact card, you can click the matching entry that appears to confirm the identity. Wowzers!

If iPhoto doesn't recognize a face at all in the photo (which can happen if the person's face is turned at an angle to the camera, or is in a darker area of the photo), click the Add Missing Face button, and iPhoto places a box in the center of the image. Drag the box over the person's face. If necessary, you can resize the box using the four handles at the corner of the box. Now you can click the label and type the person's name.

5. **Press Return to save the face.**

Notice the expansion button that appears next to the person's name? Click it, and iPhoto displays other photos that likely contain this person's face, allowing you to tag them there as well.

6. **Click Done after you've identified all the faces in the photo.**

After you've tagged an image, it appears in your Faces collection, which you can view by clicking the Faces entry in the Source list. You can click a portrait in your Faces collection to see all the images that contain that person. As you might expect, the more tags you add for a specific person, the better iPhoto gets at recognizing that person!

**Putting photos in their place:**

Places makes it easy to track the location where photos were taken, but it requires a digital camera that includes GPS tracking information in the image metadata. (This is a relatively new feature for digital cameras, so older models aren't likely to support GPS tracking.) Places also requires an Internet connection, because it uses Google Maps.

Click the Places entry in the Source list to display a global map, with push-pins indicating where your photos were taken. You can switch the Places map between terrain and satellite modes, or choose a hybrid display. If you're familiar with Google Maps, these settings are old friends of yours.

Alternatively, click the List View button to display a character-based browser, where you can click on country, state, and city names.

No matter which view mode you choose, clicking a pushpin or location displays the images taken in that area.

## Organizing with keywords

"Okay, Mark, albums, Events, Faces, and Places are great ideas, but there has to be a way to search my collection by category!" Never fear, good MacBook owner. You can also assign descriptive *keywords* to images to help you organize your collection and locate certain pictures fast. iPhoto comes with a number of standard keywords, and you can create your own as well.

To illustrate, suppose you'd like to identify your images according to special events in your family. Birthday photos should have their own keyword, and anniversaries deserve another. By assigning keywords, you can search for Elsie's sixth birthday or your silver wedding anniversary (no matter what Event or album they're in), and all related photos with those keywords appear like magic! (Well, *almost* like magic. You need to choose View➪Keywords, which toggles the Keyword display on and off in the Viewer.)

iPhoto includes a number of keywords that are already available:

✦ **Favorite**

✦ **Family**

✦ **Kids**

✦ **Vacation**

✦ **Birthday**

✦ **Movie**

✦ **Checkmark**

TIP

What's the Checkmark all about, you ask? It's a special case: Adding this keyword displays a tiny check mark icon in the bottom-right corner of the image. The checkmark keyword comes in handy for temporarily identifying specific images because you can search for just your checkmarked photos.

To assign keywords to images (or remove keywords that have already been assigned), select one or more photos in the Viewer. Choose Window⇨ Show Keywords or press ⌘+K to display the Keywords window, as shown in Figure 3-5.

**Figure 3-5:** Time to add keywords to these selected images.

Click the keyword buttons that you want to attach to the selected images to mark them. Or click the highlighted keyword buttons that you want to remove from the selected images to disable them.

### Digging through your library with keywords

Behold the power of keywords! To sift through your entire collection of images by using keywords, click the magnifying glass button next to the Search box at the bottom of the iPhoto window and then choose Keyword from the pop-up menu. iPhoto displays a pop-up Keywords panel, and you can click one or more keyword buttons to display just the photos that carry those keywords.

## You're gonna need your own keywords

I'll bet you take photos of things other than just kids and vacations — and that's why iPhoto allows you to create your own keywords. Display the iPhoto Keywords window by pressing ⌘+K, click the Edit Keywords button, and then click Add (the button with the plus sign). iPhoto adds a new unnamed keyword to the list as an edit box, ready for you to type its name.

You can rename an existing keyword from this same window, too. Click a keyword to select it and then click Rename. Remember, however, that renaming a keyword affects *all the images that were tagged with that keyword.* That might be confusing when, for example, photos originally tagged as Family suddenly appear with the keyword Foodstuffs. To remove an existing keyword from the list, click the keyword to select it and then click the Delete button, which bears a minus sign.

The images that remain in the Viewer after a search must have *all* the keywords that you specified. If an image is identified, for example, by only three of four keywords you chose, it isn't a match and it doesn't appear in the Viewer. (You can create a Smart Album with specific keywords to get around this limitation.)

To search for a photo by words in its description, just click in the Search box and start typing. You can also click that same magnifying glass by the Search box to search through your images by date and rating as well.

*Speaking of ratings . . .*

### Playing favorites by assigning ratings

Be your own critic! iPhoto allows you to assign any photo a rating of anywhere from zero to five stars. I use this system to help me keep track of the images that I feel are the best in my library. Select one (or more) image and then assign a rating using one of the following methods:

✦ Choose Photos⇨My Rating and then choose the desired rating from the pop-up submenu.

✦ Use the ⌘+0 through ⌘+5 shortcuts.

### Sorting your images just so

The View menu provides an easy way to arrange your images in the Viewer by a number of different criteria. Choose View⇨Sort Photos and then click the desired sort criteria from the pop-up submenu. You can arrange the display by date, keyword, title, or rating. If you select an album in the source list, you can also choose to arrange photos manually, which means that you can drag and drop thumbnails in the Viewer to place them in the precise order you want them.

 Naturally, iPhoto allows you to print selected images, but you can also send photos directly to iWeb for use on your MobileMe Web site. Click Share➪Send to iWeb and then choose either Photo Page or Blog from the submenu. iPhoto automatically sends the selected images or album to iWeb and launches the application! You can also use iPhoto's Web Gallery feature to get your photos on the Web. (More on the Web Gallery at the end of this chapter.)

## Edit mode: Removing and fixing stuff the right way

Not every digital image is perfect — just look at my collection if you need proof. For those shots that need a pixel massage, iPhoto includes a number of editing tools that you can use to correct common problems.

The first step in any editing job is to select the image you want to fix in the Viewer. Then click the Edit button on the iPhoto toolbar to switch to the Edit mode controls, as shown in Figure 3-6. Now you're ready to fix problems, using the tools that I discuss in the rest of this section. (If you're editing a photo that's part of an Event, album, Faces, or Places, note the spiffy scrolling photo strip at the top, which allows you to switch to another image to edit from the same grouping.)

When you're done with Edit mode, click the . . . (wait for it) . . . Done button!

### Rotating tipped-over shots

If an image is in the wrong orientation and needs to be turned to display correctly, click the Rotate button to turn it once in a counterclockwise direction. Hold down the Option key while you click the Rotate button to rotate in a clockwise direction.

### Crop 'til you drop

Does that photo have an intruder hovering around the edges of the subject? You can remove some of the border by *cropping* an image, just as folks once did with film prints and a pair of scissors. (We've come a long way.) With iPhoto, you can remove unwanted portions of an image; it's a great way to get Uncle Milton's stray head (complete with toupee) out of an otherwise perfect holiday snapshot.

Follow these steps to crop an image:

*1.* **Click the Crop button in the Edit toolbar.**

**Figure 3-6:**
iPhoto is now in edit mode — watch out, image problems!

2. **Select the portion of the image that you want to keep.**

   In the Viewer, click and drag the handles on the rectangle to outline the part of the image that you want. Remember, whatever's outside this rectangle disappears after the crop is completed.

   When you drag a corner or edge of the outline, a semi-opaque grid (familiar to amateur and professional photographers as the nine squares from the Rule of Three) appears to help you visualize what you're claiming. (Check it out in Figure 3-7.)

3. **(Optional) Choose a preset aspect ratio.**

   If you want to force your cropped selection to a specific aspect ratio — such as 4 x 3 for an iDVD project — click the Constrain check box and select that ratio from the Constrain pop-up menu.

4. **Click the Apply button.**

   Oh, and don't forget that you can use iPhoto's Undo feature if you mess up and need to try again. Just press ⌘+Z.

iPhoto features multiple Undo levels, so you can press ⌘+Z several times to travel back through your last several changes.

**Figure 3-7:**
Select the
stuff that
you want
to keep in
your photo.

### Straightening what's crooked

Was your camera slightly tilted when you took the perfect shot? Never fear!
Click the Straighten button and then drag the slider to tilt the image in the
desired direction. Click the Close button to return to Edit mode.

### Enhancing images to add pizzazz

If a photo looks washed out, click the Enhance button to increase (or
decrease) the color saturation and improve the contrast. Enhance is automatic, so you don't have to set anything.

### Removing rampant red-eye

Unfortunately, today's digital cameras can still produce the same "zombies
with red eyeballs" as traditional film cameras. *Red-eye* is caused by a camera's flash reflecting off the retinas of a subject's eyes, and it can occur with
both humans and animals. (I'm told pets get *green-eye*, but iPhoto can handle
them, too!)

iPhoto can remove that red- and green-eye and turn frightening zombies
back into your family and friends! Click the Red-Eye button and then select
a demonized eyeball by clicking in the center of it. (If the new eyeball is too

small or too large, drag the Size slider to adjust the dimensions.) To complete the process, click the X in the button that appears in the image.

### Retouching like the stars

The iPhoto Retouch feature is perfect for removing minor flecks or lines in an image (especially those you've scanned from prints). Click Retouch and you'll notice that the cursor turns into a crosshair; just drag the cursor across the imperfection.

### Switching to black-and-white or sepia

Ever wonder whether a particular photo in your library would look better as a black-and-white (or *grayscale*) print? Or perhaps an old-fashioned *sepia* tone in shades of copper and brown? Just click the Effects button to display the Effects window, which offers eight different effects you can apply to the photo.

### Adjusting photo properties manually

Click Adjust to perform manual adjustments to brightness and contrast (the light levels in your image), as well as the sharpness, shadow, and highlight levels. To adjust a value, make sure that nothing's selected in the image and then drag the corresponding slider until the image looks the way you want. Click the Close button to return to Edit mode.

While you're editing, you can use the Next and Previous buttons at the lower-right corner of the iPhoto window to move to the next image in the current group (or back to the previous image).

# Producing Your Own Coffee-Table Masterpiece

Book mode unleashes what I think is probably the coolest feature of iPhoto: the chance to design and print a high-quality bound photo book! After you complete an album — all the images have been edited just the way you want, and the album contains all the photos you want to include in your book — iPhoto can send your images as data over the Internet to a company that prints and binds your finished book for you. (No, they don't publish *For Dummies* titles, but then again, I don't get high-resolution color plates in most of my books, either.)

At the time of this writing, you can order many different sizes and bindings, including an 8.5-by-11-inch soft-cover book with 20 double-sided pages for about $20 and a hardbound 8.5-by-11-inch keepsake album with 10 double-sided pages for about $30 (shipping included for both). Extra pages can be added at $0.70 and $1.00 a pop, respectively.

iPhoto '09 can also produce and automatically order calendars and greeting cards, using a process similar to the one I describe in this section for producing a book. Who needs that stationery store in the mall anymore?

If you're going to create a photo book, make sure that the images have the highest quality and highest resolution. The higher the resolution, the better the photos look in the finished book. I personally always try to use images of over 1,000 pixels in both the vertical and horizontal dimensions.

To create a photo book, follow these steps:

1. **Click the desired album in the source list to select it.**

2. **Click the Keepsakes toolbar button and click Book from the pop-up menu.**

   Depending on your screen resolution, iPhoto may have room to display the Book button by itself — no big deal, because things work the same.

3. **Select the size of the book and a theme.**

   Your choices determine the number of pages and layout scheme, as well as the background graphics for each page.

4. **Click Choose.**

   You'll see the controls shown in Figure 3-8.

   In Book mode, the Viewer changes in subtle ways. It displays the current page at the bottom of the display and adds a scrolling row of thumbnail images above it. This row of images represents the remaining images from the selected album that you can add to your book. You can drag any image thumbnail into one of the photo placeholders to add it to the page. You can also click the Page button at the left of the thumbnail strip — it looks like a page with a turned-down corner — to display thumbnails of each page in your book. (To return to the album image strip, click the Photos button under the Page button.)

5. **Rearrange the page order to suit you by dragging the thumbnail of any page from one location to another in the strip.**

6. **In the Book toolbar below the page view, you can adjust a variety of settings for the final book, including the book's theme, background, page numbers, and text fonts.**

   At this point, you can also add captions and short descriptions to the pages of your photo album. Click any one of the text boxes in the page display and begin typing to add text to that page.

Figure 3-8:
Preparing
to publish
my own
coffee-table
masterpiece.

7. **When you're ready to publish your book, click the Buy Book button.**

8. **In a series of dialogs that appears, iPhoto guides you through the final steps to order a bound book.**

   Note that you're asked for credit card information, so have that plastic ready.

I wouldn't attempt to order a book through a dial-up modem connection. The images are likely far too large to be sent successfully. If possible, use a broadband or network connection to the Internet while you're ordering. If your only connection to the Internet is through a dial-up modem, I recommend saving your book in PDF format and having it printed at a copy shop or printing service instead. (Choose File➪Print and then click the Save as PDF button.) Alternatively, pack your MacBook and head to the closest public library or wireless hotspot with Internet access to send the book files wirelessly!

# I really need a slideshow

You can use iPhoto to create slideshows! Click the album or Event you want to display and click the Add button; then choose Slideshow from the toolbar and click Create. Notice that iPhoto adds a Slideshow item in the source list. The same scrolling thumbnail strip appears at the top of the Viewer — this time displaying the images in the album or Event. Click and drag the thumbnails so that they appear in the desired order.

To choose background music for your slideshow, click the Music button in the Slideshow toolbar to display Apple's theme music, as well as the tracks from your iTunes library. To choose a standard theme, click the Source pop-up menu and choose Theme Music; then select that perfect song and click Apply. To choose an iTunes song or playlist, click the Source pop-up menu and choose either the Music item (for your entire library) or a playlist. You can also create a custom playlist by selecting the Custom Playlist for Slideshow check box. Then, drag the individual songs you want to the song list at the bottom of the sheet. (You can drag them to rearrange their order in the list as well.) Click Apply to accept your song list.

To configure your slideshow, click the Settings button in the Slideshow toolbar and click the All Slides tab. In the dialog that appears, you can specify the amount of time that each slide remains on the screen, as well as an optional title and rating displays. You can choose the transition that occurs between photos, too, or specify a random transition each time. MacBook owners appreciate the Aspect Ratio pop-up menu, which allows you to choose a 16:9 widescreen display for your slideshow.

Click the This Slide tab to modify the settings for a specific slide (useful for keeping a slide on-screen for a longer period of time or for setting a different transition than the default transition you choose from the Slideshow toolbar). I can recommend the Automatic Ken Burns effect — yep, the same one in iMovie — which lends an animated movement to the selected image. You can also set the selected photo to display in black and white, sepia, or antique coloring.

To display a preview of a single slide and its transitions, click the desired slide and then click Preview; this is a handy way of determining whether your delay and transition settings are really what you want for a particular slide. When you're ready to play your slideshow, click the Play button, and iPhoto switches to full-screen mode. You can share your completed slideshow by clicking Share in the iPhoto menu, where you can send the slideshow to iDVD (for later burning onto a DVD) or send it through e-mail.

# You'll Love MobileMe Gallery!

iPhoto '09 includes a feature called MobileMe Gallery that does for images what podcasting does for audio: You can share your photos with friends, family, business clients, and anyone else with an Internet connection! (Your adoring public doesn't even require a Mac; it can use That Other Kind of Computer.) iPhoto automatically uploads the selected images and leads you through the process of creating a new Web page to proudly display your photos. However, you *must* be a MobileMe subscriber to use the MobileMe Gallery feature. If you haven't heard the news on Apple's MobileMe service yet, see Chapter 4 of Book VI for the details.

To create a MobileMe Gallery, you designate one or more photos in the Viewer (or even select entire albums or Events in the Source list) and then click the Add button. Click the MobileMe toolbar button in the sheet that appears to display the Web Gallery settings.

Type a name for your new Web Gallery. You can elect to show the title of each photo, allow your visitors to download your images or upload their own, and even allow photos to be uploaded by other computer owners using an e-mail or a Web browser!

 By default, any visitor to your MobileMe Web site can see your gallery. But what if you prefer a little security for those images? In that case, click the Album Viewable By pop-up menu, where you can limit your viewing audience (you can even require that your visitors enter a login name and password before they can receive your photos).

Click Publish, and you'll see that iPhoto indicates that your images are being uploaded with a cool twirling progress icon to the right of the album in the source list. When the process is complete, iPhoto indicates that the photos appear in a MobileMe Gallery with a new heading in the Source list. You're on the air!

Now for the other side of the coin: By selecting your MobileMe Gallery in the Source list and clicking Tell a Friend in the iPhoto toolbar, iPhoto automatically prepares an e-mail message in Apple Mail that announces your new Gallery! Just add the recipient names and click Send. This spiffy message includes instructions for

✦ **Folks using iPhoto '09 on a Mac:** As you can imagine, this is the easiest receive option to configure. After these folks are subscribed, they get an automatically updated album of the same name that appears in their source list, and they can use those images in their own iPhoto projects! From within iPhoto, your visitors can subscribe to your MobileMe Gallery by clicking File⇨Subscribe to Photo Feed and entering the subscription URL.

✦ **Folks using Windows or an older version of iPhoto:** These subscribers can use any Web browser with RSS support (such as the Safari browser that comes with Snow Leopard and is available from Apple for Windows XP or Vista) or any RSS reader. (In effect, your MobileMe Gallery becomes an RSS feed for those without iPhoto '09.)

**Book IV
Chapter 3**

**Focusing on iPhoto**

## Is that Facebook and Flickr I spy?

Indeed it is! iPhoto '09 introduces a direct connection to both your Facebook social networking account (at www.facebook.com) and your Flickr online gallery account (at www.flickr.com), allowing you to simply select one or more photos and send them automatically to either service! These two buttons appear on the toolbar when you're organizing your photos.

The first time you select photos in the Viewer (or an album or Event in the Source list) and click either button, iPhoto prompts you for permission to set up your connection. (Of course, this will require you to enter your Facebook and Flickr account information — hence the confirmation request.) Click Set Up and provide the data that each site requires.

After you've set up your accounts, simply select your photos, albums, or Events and click the toolbar button for the desired service. Apple, you absolutely *rock*!

By default, any changes you make to the contents of your MobileMe Gallery are updated automatically on your MobileMe account, and, in turn, are updated automatically to everyone who receives your images. You can turn this feature off, however, if you have a large number of images and you update often (which can result in your sister's computer downloading a lot of data). To display the Check for New Photos setting for MobileMe Gallery, click iPhoto⇨Preferences and click the Web button on the Preferences window toolbar. (You can also change the title for your Gallery and monitor your iDisk usage from this pane.)

## *Mailing Photos to Aunt Mildred*

iPhoto can help you send your images through e-mail by automating the process. The application can prepare your image and embed it automatically in a new message.

To send an image through e-mail, select it and then click the Email button in the toolbar. The dialog, as shown in Figure 3-9, appears, allowing you to choose the size of the images and whether you want to include their titles, descriptions, and Places location information as well.

Keep in mind that most ISP (Internet service provider) e-mail servers don't accept an e-mail message that's more than 3MB or 4MB, so watch that Size display. If you're trying to send a number of images and the size goes over 2MB, you might have to click the Size pop-up menu and choose a smaller size (reducing the image resolution) to get them all embedded in a single message.

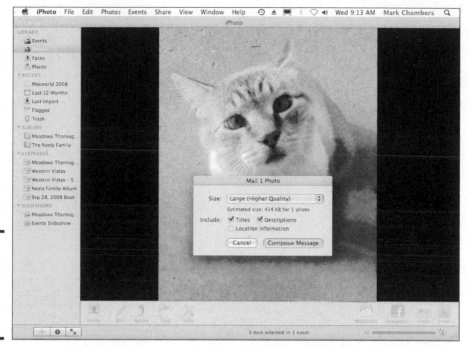

**Figure 3-9:**
Preparing
to send
an image
through
Apple Mail.

When you're satisfied with the total file size and you're ready to create your message, click the Compose button. iPhoto automatically launches Apple Mail (or whatever e-mail application you specify) and creates a new message containing the images, ready for you to click Send!

# Chapter 4: Making Magic with iMovie

## In This Chapter

- ✔ Taking stock of the iMovie window
- ✔ Importing and adding media content
- ✔ Using transitions in your movie
- ✔ Putting text titles to work
- ✔ Sharing your movie with others

Alfred Hitchcock, Stanley Kubrick, George Lucas, and Ridley Scott those guys are amateurs! Welcome to the exciting world of moviemaking on your MacBook, where *you* call the shots. With iMovie, you can try your hand at all aspects of the movie-creating process, including editing and special effects. Built with ease-of-use in mind, iMovie lets you perform full-blown movie production on your Macintosh with a minimum of effort.

Don't let iMovie's fancy buttons and flashing lights fool you: This application is a feature-packed tool for serious movie production. The iMovie controls work the same as many top-notch, movie-editing tools that professionals use. From basic editing to audio and video effects, iMovie has everything that you need to get started creating high-quality movies.

## The iMovie Window

If you've ever tried a professional-level video editing application, you probably felt as though you were suddenly dropped in the cockpit of a jumbo jet. In iMovie, though, all the controls you need are easy to use and logically placed.

Video editing takes up quite a bit of desktop space. In fact, you can't run iMovie at resolutions of less than 1024 x 768, nor would you want to.

To launch iMovie, click the iMovie icon in the Dock. (It looks like a star from the Hollywood Walk of Fame.) You can also click the Application folder in any Finder window sidebar and then double-click the iMovie icon.

To follow the examples I show you here, follow these strenuous steps and create a new movie project:

1. **Click the File menu and choose New Project (or press ⌘+N).**

   iMovie displays the sheet you see in Figure 4-1.

2. **Type a name for your project.**

3. **Select the aspect ratio (or screen dimensions) for your movie.**

   You can select a widescreen display (16:9), a standard display (4:3), or a display especially suited for an iPhone (3:2). If compatibility with the familiar SDTV format is important, I always recommend that you choose standard (4:3) ratio; choosing 16:9 for an SDTV set will result in those familiar black "letterbox" bars at the top and bottom of the screen. On the flip side, choosing 4:3 results in black bars on the left and right when shown on an HD set.

4. **Click a thumbnail to select a theme to apply to your finished movie.**

   If you choose a theme, iMovie automatically adds the transitions and titles that correspond to that theme. (Normally, this is what you want to do. However, if you want to add transitions and titles manually, click the Automatically Add Transitions and Titles check box to deselect it.)

**Figure 4-1:**
Creating a new movie project within iMovie.

If you decide not to use a theme (by selecting the None thumbnail), iMovie can still add an automatic effect between clips. Click the Automatically Add check box and click the pop-up menu to choose the desired effect.

5. **Click Create.**

   You're on your way! Check out Figure 4-2: This is the whole enchilada, in one window.

The controls and displays that you'll use most often follow:

✦ **Monitor:** Think of this as being just like your TV or computer monitor. Your video clips, still images, and finished movie play here. You'll also crop and rotate your video within the monitor.

✦ **Browser toolbar:** This row of buttons allows you to switch between your media clips (video clips, photos, and audio) and the various tools that you use to make your film. The selected items fill the right side of the browser pane below the monitor.

Playhead          Editing toolbar          Project pane          Monitor

**Figure 4-2:**
iMovie
is a lean,
mean video
producing
machine.

Camera Import          Event pane          Browser toolbar

✦ **Event pane:** All the video clips that you use to create your movie are stored in the Event pane. I show you what each of the panes in the iMovie workspace looks like when you tackle different tasks in this chapter.

✦ **Project pane:** iMovie displays the elements that you've added to your movie project in this pane.

✦ **Playhead:** The red vertical line that you see in the Event and Project panes is the *playhead,* which indicates the current editing point while you're creating your movie. When you're playing your movie, the play-head moves to follow your progress through the movie.

✦ **Editing toolbar:** This strip of buttons allows you to control editing functions such as cropping, audio and video adjustments, voiceovers, and selecting items.

✦ **Camera Import window:** Click this switch to import DV clips from your DV camcorder or iSight camera.

Those are the major highlights of the iMovie window. A director's chair and megaphone are optional, of course, but they do add to the mood.

## A Bird's-Eye View of Moviemaking

I don't want to box in your creative skills here — after all, you can attack the moviemaking process from a number of angles. (Pun unfortunately intended.) However, I've found that my movies turn out the best when I follow a linear process, so before I dive into specifics, allow me to provide you with an overview of moviemaking with iMovie.

Here's my take on the process, reduced to seven steps:

1. **Import your video clips either directly from your DV camcorder, iSight camera, or your hard drive.**

2. **Drag your new selection of clips from the Event pane to the Project pane and arrange them in the desired order.**

3. **Import or record audio clips (from iTunes, GarageBand, or external sources, such as audio CDs or audio files, that you've recorded yourself) and add them to your movie.**

4. **Import your photos (directly from iPhoto or from your hard drive) and place them where needed in your movie.**

5. **Add professional niceties, such as voiceovers, transitions, effects, and text to the project.**

6. **Preview your film and edit it further if necessary.**

7. **Share your finished film with others through the Web, e-mail, or a DVD that you create and burn with iDVD.**

That's the first step-by-step procedure in this chapter. I doubt that you'll even need to refer back to it, however, because you'll soon see just how easy it is to use iMovie.

As you might imagine, this chapter simply can't hold a full description of every setting and every procedure within iMovie '09 — but luckily, my good friend Dennis Cohen has done exactly that in his new book *iMovie '09 & iDVD '09 For Dummies* (Wiley Publishing). Dennis will take you from basics to all the in-depth features of these two iLife applications!

# Importing the Building Blocks

Sure, you need video clips to create a movie of your own, but don't panic if you have but a short supply. You can certainly turn to the other iLife applications for additional raw material. (See, I told you that integration thing would come in handy.)

Along with video clips you import from your DV camcorder, built-in iSight camera, and hard drive, you can also call on iPhoto for still images (think credits) and iTunes for background audio and effects. In this section, I show you how.

## Pulling in video clips

Your MacBook is probably equipped already with the two extras that come in handy for video editing — namely, a large hard drive and a FireWire port. Because most mini-DV camcorders today use a FireWire connection to transfer clips, you're all set. (And even if your snazzy new DV camcorder uses a USB 2.0 connection, you're still in the zone, although you will need to modify the steps I provide in this section for your particular device.) Oh, and since your MacBook has an iSight camera on board, you're a self-contained movie studio!

Here's the drill if your clips are on your FireWire-equipped mini-DV camcorder:

1. **Plug the proper cable into your MacBook.**

2. **Set the DV camcorder to VTR (or VCR) mode.**

Some camcorders call this Play mode.

3. **Click the Camera Import button (labeled in Figure 4-2).**

   iMovie opens a new window.

4. **Click the Camera pop-up menu (at the bottom of the Import window) and select your DV camcorder or iSight camera.**

   Playback controls appear under the Camera Import window, mirroring the controls on your DV camcorder. This allows you to control the unit from iMovie. *Keen!*

   To capture video from your iSight camera, click the Video Size pop-up menu to choose the dimensions of the clip; then click Capture. On the sheet that appears, choose the location where the video will be saved, and choose whether to add this video to an existing event or create a new event. Click Capture to start recording, and click Stop when your video is complete. (You can skip the rest of the steps in this section, which deal only with DV camcorders.)

5. **Click the Import button.**

6. **Click the Save To pop-up menu and choose the drive that should store your clips.**

   You can choose to add the new clips to an existing Event or create a new Event. Heck, if the event spanned more than one day, you can create a new Event for each day. (How do they think up these things?)

7. **Click OK and admire your handiwork.**

   iMovie begins transferring the footage to your MacBook and automatically adds the imported clips to your Event Library.

If your clips are already on your hard drive, rest assured that iMovie can import them, including those in *high-definition video* (HDV) format. iMovie also recognizes a number of other video formats, as shown in Table 4-1.

| Table 4-1 | Video Formats Supported by iMovie |
|---|---|
| *File Type* | *Description* |
| DV | Standard 4:3 digital video |
| DV Widescreen | Widescreen 16:9 digital video |
| MOV | QuickTime movies |
| HDV & AVCHD | High-definition (popularly called *widescreen*) digital video, in 720p and 1080i |
| MPEG-2 | Digital video format used for DVD movies |
| MPEG-4 | A popular format for streaming Internet and wireless digital video |

To import a movie file, follow this bouncing ball:

*1.* **Choose File⇨Import and choose Movies from the submenu.**

*2.* **If you're importing 1080i video clips, choose the quality setting.**

   The Large setting will save you a significant amount of hard drive space, but the Full setting preserves the original resolution and detail. (If you're not importing 1080i video, use the default Large setting and click OK. The Full setting demands all the CPU and RAM resources your MacBook can offer, so don't expect to do much else while importing.)

*3.* **Click the drive that should store your clips in the sidebar and then navigate to the desired location.**

*4.* **Specify whether you want to add the imported video to an existing Event or create a new Event.**

   If you choose to add the video to an existing Event, click the pop-up menu and select an Event.

*5.* **Specify whether you want to copy the video (leaving the original movie intact) or have the movie deleted after a successful import.**

*6.* **Click Import.**

   Alternatively, you can also drag a video clip from a Finder window and drop it in the Project pane.

## Making use of still images

Still images come in handy as impressive-looking titles or as ending credits to your movie. (Make sure you list a gaffer and a best boy to be truly professional.) However, you can use still images also to introduce scenes or to separate clips according to your whim. For example, I use stills when delineating the days of a vacation within a movie or different Christmas celebrations over time.

Here are two methods of adding stills to your movie:

✦ **Adding images from iPhoto:** Click the Photo Browser button in the Browser toolbar (or press ⌘+2) and you'll experience the thrill that is your iPhoto Library, right from iMovie (as shown in Figure 4-3). You can elect to display your entire iPhoto Library or more selective picks such as specific albums or Events. When you find the image you want to add, just drag it to the right spot in the Project pane.

✦ **Importing images from your hard drive:** If you're a member of the International Drag-and-Drop Society, you can drag TIFF, JPEG, GIF, PICT, PNG, and PSD images directly from a Finder window and drop them into the Project pane as well.

**Figure 4-3:**
Pulling still
images from
iPhoto is
child's play.

## Importing and adding audio from all sorts of places

You can pull in everything from Wagner to Weezer as both background music and sound effects for your movie. In this section, I focus on how to get those notes into iMovie and then how to add them to your movie by dragging them to the Project pane.

You can add audio from a number of sources:

✦ **Adding songs from iTunes:** Click the Show Music and Sound Effects button in the Browser toolbar (or press ⌘+1) to display the contents of your iTunes Library. Click the desired playlist in the scrolling list box, such as the Dinah Washington playlist I selected in Figure 4-4. (If you've exported any original music you've composed in GarageBand to your iTunes Library, you can use those songs in your own movie!) You can add a track to your movie by dragging the song entry from the Music and Sound Effects list to the desired spot in the Project pane.

✦ **Adding sound effects:** Yep, if you need the sound of a horse galloping for your Rocky Mountain vacation clips, click either iMovie Sound Effects or iLife Sound Effects in the scrolling list box. iMovie includes a number of top-shelf audio effects that you can use in the second audio track on the timeline viewer. This way, you can add sound effects even when you've already added a background song. Again, to add a sound effect, drag it to the perfect spot in the Project pane.

If you have several gigabytes of music in your iTunes Library, it might be more of a challenge to locate "Me and Bobby McGee" by Janis Joplin, especially if she's included in a compilation. Let your MacBook do the digging for you! Click in the Search box below the track list and begin typing a song name. iMovie narrows down the song titles displayed to those that match the characters you type. To reset the search box and display all your songs in the Library or selected playlist, click the X icon that appears to the right of the box.

✦ **Ripping songs from an audio CD:** Load an audio CD and then choose Audio CD from the scrolling list box. iMovie displays the tracks from the CD, and you can add them at the current playhead position the same way as iTunes songs.

✦ **Recording directly from a microphone:** Yep, if you're thinking voiceover narration, you've hit the nail on the head. Check out the sidebar, "Narration the easy way," for the scoop.

**Figure 4-4:** Calling on my iTunes Library to add Dinah Washington to my iMovie.

# Narration the easy way

Ready to create that award-winning nature documentary? You can add voiceover narration to your iMovie project that would make Jacques Cousteau proud. In fact, you can record your voice while you watch your movie playing, allowing perfect synchronization with the action! To add narration, follow these steps:

1. **Click the Voiceover button in the Editing toolbar — it sports a microphone icon — to open the Voiceover window.**

2. **Click the Record From pop-up menu and select the input device.**

   MacBooks sport a decent internal microphone, but you can always add a USB microphone to your system.

3. **Drag the input volume slider to a comfortable level.**

   You can monitor the volume level of your voice with the left and right input meters — try to keep the meters at 50 percent or so for the proper volume level.

4. **To block out ambient noise levels , drag the Noise Reduction slider to the right if necessary.**

If you'd like iMovie to enhance your voice electronically for a more professional sound, click the Voice Enhancement check box to select it. If you need to hear the audio from your movie project while you speak, click the Play Project Audio While Recording check box to select it — note, however, that you'll need to listen to the audio while using a set of headphones (plugged into your Mac's headphone jack) to avoid feedback problems.

5. **Click in the desired spot within a clip in the Project pane where the narration should begin.**

6. **Begin speaking when prompted by iMovie.**

7. **Watch the video while you narrate so that you can coordinate your narration track with the action.**

8. **Click anywhere in the iMovie window to stop recording (or wait until the clip ends).**

   iMovie adds an icon to the Project pane underneath the video with the voiceover.

9. **Click the Close button in the Voiceover window.**

You can fine-tune both the audio within a video clip or the audio clips that you add to your project. With the desired clip selected, click the Inspector button in the Editing toolbar (it bears a proud letter *i*) and click the Audio tab. The Audio Adjustments window that appears includes an array of audio controls that allow you to change the volume of the selected clip, or to give that audio priority over other audio playing simultaneously (such as a sound effect that needs to be clearly heard over background music and the video clip). If your clips dramatically vary in volume, click the Normalize Clip Volume button and then select each clip that you want to set to the same volume; click Normalize Clip Volume again for each clip. You can also set an automatic or manual Fade-in/Fade-out for the audio. When you're done tweaking, click Done. (Oh, and don't forget that you can always return the clip to its original volume; just open this window again and click Revert to Original.)

# Building the Cinematic Basics

Time to dive in and add the building blocks to create your movie. Along with video clips, audio tracks, and still images, you can add Hollywood-quality transitions, optical effects, and animated text titles. In this section, I demonstrate how to elevate your collection of video clips into a real-life furshlugginer *movie*.

## Adding clips to your movie

You can add clips to your movie by using the Project pane and the Event pane. The Dynamic Duo works like this:

✦ **Project pane:** This displays the media you've added to your project so far, allowing you to rearrange the clips, titles, transitions and still images in your movie.

✦ **Event pane:** This displays your video clips arranged by Event (the date they were shot or the date they were imported), acting as the source repository for all your clips. Movies pulled into iMovie, imported into iPhoto, or added manually from the Finder appear here.

To add a clip to your movie, follow these steps:

*1.* **Move your cursor across clips in the Event pane to watch a preview of the video.**

*2.* **When you've decided what to add to your project, you can either add the entire clip or a selection.**

• To select an entire clip, right-click the clip's thumbnail and choose Select Entire Clip from the menu that appears.

• To select a portion of a clip, drag your cursor across the thumbnail. A yellow frame appears around your selection. To change the length of the selected video, drag the handles that appear on either side. If you make a mistake while selecting video, just click any empty space within the Event pane to remove the selection frame and try again.

3. **Drag the selection from the Event pane to the spot where it belongs in the Project pane.**

   Alternatively, you can press the E key or click the Add to Project button (the first button in the Editing toolbar).

Do this several times, and you have a movie, which you've created just as the editors of old used to by working with actual film clips. This is a good point to mention a moviemaking Mark's Maxim:

**Preview your work — and do it often.**

iMovie offers two Play Full screen buttons: one under the Event Library and one under the Project Library. Select the project or Event you want to play and then click the corresponding button (or press ⌘+G). You can also choose View⇨Play Full Screen to watch the selection. Press the spacebar to pause, and press Esc to return to iMovie. You can also move your cursor to display a filmstrip that you can click to skip forward or backward in the project or Event.

To play a selection from the beginning, press \ (the slash that leans to the left). (If you've ever watched directors at work on today's movie sets, you may have noticed that they're constantly watching a monitor to see what things will look like for the audience. You have the same option in iMovie!)

While you're watching video in the Event pane, you may decide that a certain clip has a favorite scene or that another clip has material you don't want, such as Uncle Ed's shadow puppets. (Shudder.) iMovie '09 features *Favorite* and *Rejected* frames, allowing you to view and use your best camera work (and ignore the worst stuff). To mark video, select a range of frames or an entire clip and then click the Mark as Favorite button in the Editing toolbar. Click the Reject button to hide the selected video or frames from view. (You can always unmark a Favorite or Rejected scene using the Unmark button in the Editing toolbar.)

## Removing clips from your movie

Don't like a clip? Bah. To banish a clip from your movie, follow these steps

1. **Click the offending clip in the Project pane to select it.**

2. **Press Delete.**

   Alternatively, you can right-click the clip (or a selection you've made by dragging) and choose either Delete Entire Clip or Delete Selection from the menu that appears.

If you remove the wrong clip, don't panic. Instead, use iMovie's Undo feature (press ⌘+Z) to restore it.

## Reordering clips in your movie

If Day One of your vacation appears after Day Two, you can easily reorder your clips and stills by dragging them to the proper space in the Project pane. When you take your finger off the trackpad, iMovie automatically moves the rest of your movie aside with a minimum of fuss and bother.

## Editing clips in iMovie

If a clip has extra seconds of footage at the beginning or end, you don't want that superfluous stuff in your masterpiece. Our favorite video editor gives you the following functions:

✦ **Crop:** Removes unwanted material from a video clip or still image, allowing you to change the aspect ratio of the media

✦ **Rotate:** Rotates a clip or image on its center axis

✦ **Trim:** Trims frames from a video clip

Before you can edit, however, you have to select a section of a clip:

1. **Click a clip or image in either the Project pane (where changes you make are specific to this project) or the Event pane (where edits you make are reflected in any project using that footage).**

   iMovie displays the clip or image in the monitor.

2. **To select the entire clip or image, simply click it.**

3. **Drag your cursor across the thumbnail to select the section of the media you want to edit. (Note that some editing functions, such as Crop and Rotate, will automatically apply to the entire clip.)**

   The selected region is surrounded by a yellow frame. You're ready to edit that selected part of the clip.

Note the handles that appear at the beginning or ending of the selection. You can make fine changes to the selected section by dragging them.

✦ **To crop:** Click the Crop button in the Edit toolbar to display the frame in the Monitor pane and then click Crop at the top of the Monitor pane. Drag the edges of the frame and the handles to select the section you want to keep. To preview your selection, click the Play button at the top of the monitor. When you're ready, click Done, and everything but the selected region is removed.

✦ **To rotate:** Click the Crop button in the Edit toolbar and then click one of the two rotation buttons (which carry a curved arrow icon). Each click rotates the media 90 degrees in that direction. Click Done when the clip or image is properly oriented.

✦ **To trim:** Choose Edit➪Trim to Selection. iMovie removes the frames from around the selected video.

Edits that you make to one clip or still image can actually be copied to multiple items! Select the edited clip and click Edit➪Copy from the iMovie menu. Now you can select one or more clips and choose Edit➪Paste Adjustments to apply Video, Audio, or Crop edits. (To apply all three types of edits, just choose All.)

## Transitions for the masses

Many iMovie owners approach transitions as *visual bookends:* They merely act as placeholders that appear between video clips. Nothing could be farther from the truth, because judicious use of transitions can make or break a scene. For example, which would you prefer after a wedding ceremony — an abrupt, jarring cut to the reception or a gradual fadeout to the reception?

Today's audiences are sensitive to transitions between scenes. Try not to overuse the same transition. Also weigh the visual impact of a transition carefully.

iMovie includes a surprising array of transitions, including old favorites (such as Fade In and Dissolve) and some nifty stuff you might not be familiar with (such as Cube and Page Curl). To display your transition collection (Figure 4-5), click the Show Transitions button on the Browser toolbar (or press ⌘+4).

To see what a particular transition looks like, move your cursor over the thumbnail to display the transition in miniature.

Adding a transition couldn't be easier: Drag the transition from the list in the Transitions Browser pane and drop it between clips or between a clip and a still image in the Project pane. In iMovie '09, transitions are applied in real time.

## Even Gone with the Wind had titles

The last stop on our iMovie Hollywood Features Tour is the Titles Browser, shown in Figure 4-6. You'll find it by clicking the Title button on the Browser toolbar (which bears a big capital T), or by pressing ⌘+3. You can add a title with a still image, but iMovie also includes everything you need to add basic animated text to your movie.

**Figure 4-5:**
Add
transitions
for flow
between
clips in
iMovie.

**Figure 4-6:**
Add titles
for your next
silent film.

Making Magic
with iMovie

Most of the controls you can adjust are the same for each animation style. You can change the font, the size of the text, and the color of the text.

To add a title manually, follow these steps:

1. **Select an animation thumbnail from the Title Browser pane and drag it to the desired spot in the Project pane.**

2. **Click a background thumbnail to select a background for your title.**

3. **Click the Show Fonts button in the monitor window to make any changes to the fonts or text attributes.**

4. **Click in a text box to type your own line of text.**

5. **Click the Play button to preview your title.**

   iMovie displays a preview of the effect in the monitor with the settings that you choose.

6. **Click Done.**

   The title appears in the Project pane.

## Sharing Your Finished Classic with Others

Your movie is complete, you've saved it to your hard drive, and now you're wondering where to go from here. Click Share on the application menu bar, and you'll see that iMovie can unleash your movie upon your unsuspecting family and friends (and even the entire world) in a number of ways:

✦ **iTunes:** Send your movie to your iTunes Library as a movie.

✦ **Media Browser:** Make your iMovie project available within other iLife '09 applications, in five different sizes suited to different display devices.

✦ **YouTube:** Yep, you read right, you can send your iMovie directly to the YouTube Web site! Can it get more convenient than that? (I think not.)

✦ **MobileMe Gallery:** Share your movie with the world at large by posting it within a Gallery on your MobileMe Web site. (I provide more MobileMe details to chew on in Book VI, Chapter 4.)

✦ **Export Movie:** Create a copy of your movie on your hard drive in one of five different sizes.

✦ **Export using QuickTime:** Create a QuickTime movie with your project using the QuickTime encoding engine (allowing greater control over the export process and the attributes of the finished movie file).

If you use this option, any computer with an installed copy of QuickTime can display your movies, and you can use QuickTime movies in Keynote presentations as well.

✦ **Export to Final Cut XML:** If you'd like to transfer your iMovie '09 project to Final Cut Pro, use this option to create a compatible XML file.

When you choose a sharing option, iMovie displays the video quality for the option and makes automatic changes to the movie attributes. (For example, choosing Tiny reduces the finished movie as far as possible in file size, and the audio is reduced to mono instead of stereo.)

Need to take a movie offline or stop sharing it? You can remove a project from iTunes, your iLife Media Browser, your MobileMe Web site, or the YouTube Web site from the Sharing menu as well. Just click the corresponding Remove menu item. (Of course, you can share the project again at any time.)

If you're worried about permanently reducing the quality of your project by sharing it in a smaller size, fear not! When you choose a sharing option to export your movie, your original project remains on your hard drive, unchanged, so you can share a better-quality version at any time in the future!

After you adjust any settings specific to the desired sharing option, click Publish (or Save) to start the ball rolling.

# Chapter 5: Burn Those DVDs! Using iDVD

## In This Chapter

✔ Traversing the iDVD window

✔ Starting a new iDVD project

✔ Tweaking and adjusting your DVD Menu

✔ Previewing your (nearly) finished DVD

✔ Doing things automatically with OneStep DVD and Magic iDVD

✔ Burning a DVD for your friends and family

A number of years ago, I bore witness to yet another proud moment in Apple history: the arrival of a powerful DVD recorder in an affordable computer. The *SuperDrive* was revolutionary because suddenly folks could create and view their own professional-quality DVDs.

Today the tradition continues: Apple includes iDVD *free* with today's MacBooks as part of iLife '09. With iDVD, you can easily create beautiful presentations with animation and interactive menus that anyone can watch in a standard DVD player or computer DVD drive. And that, friends and neighbors, is the quintessential definition of *cool*.

In this chapter, I show you the basics of creating your first home-cooked DVD movie — and you'll even have fun doing it!

## Introducing Your Mac to iDVD

Figure 5-1 shows iDVD in all its glory. You have to supply your own digital video clips, background audio, and digital photographs, of course.

Menu display

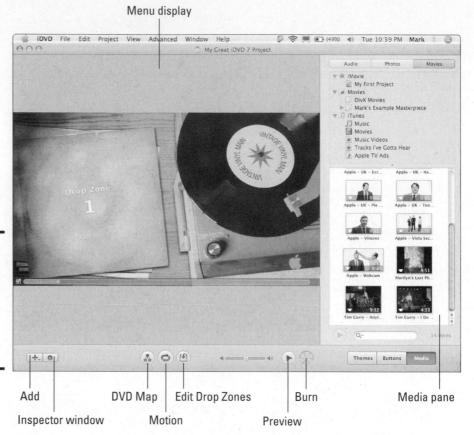

**Figure 5-1:**
iDVD is a
jewel of an
application
— easy to
use and
powerful to
boot.

Add

Inspector window

DVD Map

Motion

Edit Drop Zones

Burn

Preview

Media pane

Take a moment to appreciate iDVD — no secondary windows to fiddle with or silly palettes strung out everywhere. (Can you tell that I've had my fill of old-style DVD authoring applications?) Allow me to list the highlights of the iDVD window:

✦ **Menu display:** This section takes up the largest part of the iDVD window, with good reason. You create your project here. In this case, *Menu* refers to your DVD Menu, not the menu at the top of your MacBook's display.

✦ **Media pane:** You add video, still images, and audio to your project from here, as well as tweak and fine-tune things. The Media pane actually comprises three separate panes. To choose a new pane, click one of these buttons at the bottom of the screen:

- *Themes:* You apply themes (such as Travel Cards, Wedding White, and Baby Mobile) to your DVD Menu to give it a certain look and feel.

- *Buttons:* These options apply to the item currently selected, such as drop shadows on your text titles or the appearance of your Menu buttons.

- *Media:* From here, you can add media items, such as video clips and photos, to your Menu.

✦ **Add button:** From this pop-up menu (which sports a dapper plus sign), you can choose one of three types of buttons to add to a project. The choices are

- *Add Submenu:* Choose this item to add a new submenu button to your DVD Menu. The person using your DVD Menu can click a button to display a new submenu that can include additional movies or slideshows. (If that sounds like ancient Greek, hang on. All becomes clearer later in the chapter, in the section "Adding movies.")

A Menu can hold only a maximum of 12 buttons (depending on the theme you choose), so submenus let you pack more content on your DVD. (Older versions of the application allowed only six buttons, so don't feel too cheated.) Anyway, each submenu you create can hold another 12 buttons.

- *Add Movie:* Yep, this is the most popular button in the whole shooting match. Click this menu item to add a new movie clip to your Menu.

- *Add Slideshow:* If you want to add a slideshow to your DVD — say, using photos from your hard drive or pictures from your iPhoto library — click this menu item.

✦ **Inspector button:** Click this button to display the Inspector window for the current Menu or a highlighted object. From this window, you can change the look of an individual submenu button or an entire Menu.

✦ **DVD Map:** Click the Map button to display the organizational chart for your DVD Menu. Each button and submenu that you add to your top-level DVD Menu is displayed here, and you can jump directly to a particular item by double-clicking it. Use this road map to help design the layout of your DVD Menu system or to get to a particular item quickly. To return to the Menu display, click the Map button again.

✦ **Motion:** Click this button to start or stop the animation cycle used with the current iDVD theme. The animation repeats (just as it will on your finished DVD) until you click the Motion button again.

Need a visual indicator of the length of your Menu's animation cycle? Click View⇨Show Motion Playhead to display the animation *playhead*, which moves below the Menu display to indicate where you are in the animation cycle. As you can with other playheads in the iLife suite, you can click and drag the diamond-shaped playhead button to move anywhere in the animation cycle.

✦ **Edit Drop Zones:** This button allows you to edit the look and contents of a drop zone on your Menu. (Don't worry, I explain more about drop zones in the sidebar titled, "Taking advantage of drop zones," later in this chapter.)

✦ **Preview:** To see how your DVD Menu project looks when burned to a DVD, click Preview. You get a truly nifty on-screen remote control that you can use to navigate your DVD Menu, just as if you were watching your DVD on a standard DVD player. To exit Preview mode, click the Stop button on the remote control.

✦ **Burn:** Oh, yeah, you know what this one is for — recording your completed DVD movie to a blank disc.

That's the lot! Time to get down to the step-by-step business of making movies.

## Starting a New DVD Project

When you launch iDVD for the first time (or if you close all iDVD windows), you get the sporty dialog shown in Figure 5-2. Take a moment to discover more about these four choices.

**Figure 5-2:** Will that be create or edit, manual or automatic?

## Creating a new project

If you choose Create a New Project, iDVD prompts you to type a name for your new DVD project and to set a location where the project files should be saved. By default, the very reasonable choice is your Documents folder. You also get to choose whether your project will display in a Standard (full-screen) aspect ratio of 4:3 or a Widescreen aspect ratio of 16:9. If you've been watching DVD movies for some time, you recognize these two terms.

You'll probably crave Widescreen format if you have a widescreen TV — go figure — but both formats will display on both types of televisions, complete with those black bars we all know and love at the top and bottom (or left and right sides) of the screen.

Click Create, and the iDVD window appears in all its glory.

## Opening an existing project

If you've used iDVD and had a DVD project open the last time you quit the application, iDVD automatically loads the DVD project you were working on. However, you can open any DVD you've created by clicking Open an Existing Project. (To choose a different existing project from the iDVD window, press ⌘+O or choose File➪Open Recent.)

## Automating the whole darn process

If you're a fan of click-it-and-forget-it (or are in a hurry), you can throw caution to the wind and allow iDVD to create your latest epic for you! iDVD offers two automated methods of creating a DVD movie disc.

### Using OneStep DVD

With OneStep, iDVD does almost all of the work automatically, by using the media clips and photos that you specify. To allow iDVD to help you create a movie, click the OneStep DVD button on the top-level menu (refer back to Figure 5-2). If you've already opened a project, choose File➪OneStep DVD from the application's menu bar (to import clips directly from your FireWire mini-DV camera) or OneStep DVD from Movie (to select a clip to import from your hard drive). OneStep DVD does not work with camcorders that use a USB connection to your MacBook. I tell you more about the OneStep DVD feature later, in the section "A Word about Automation."

### Using Magic iDVD

Magic iDVD is the newcomer on the block, and it falls neatly between total automation (with OneStep DVD) and total manual control. Click the Magic iDVD button on the top-level menu (as shown in Figure 5-2). If you've already

**Book IV
Chapter 5**

**Burn Those DVDs!
Using iDVD**

opened a project, you can choose File⇨Magic iDVD from the menu bar to choose a theme, drop specific movies and specific photos into filmstrips, and choose an audio track.

In contrast to OneStep DVD, you get to preview the finished product. If it's to your liking, you can choose to either burn the disc directly or create a full-blown iDVD project with the results. *Sweet.*

You find out more about the new Magic iDVD feature later, in the section "A Word about Automation."

# Creating a DVD from Scratch

Doing things the old-fashioned, creative, and manual way (following the examples in this section) involves four basic steps:

1. **Design the DVD Menu.**

   Choose a theme and any necessary buttons or links.

2. **Add media.**

   You can drag movie files from iMovie, still images from iPhoto, and music from iTunes.

3. **Tweak.**

   Adjust and fine-tune your DVD Menu settings.

4. **Finish things up.**

   Preview and burn your DVD or save it to your hard drive.

## Choosing just the right theme

The first step to take when manually designing a new DVD Menu system is to add a theme. In the iDVD world, a *theme* is a preset package that helps determine the appearance and visual appeal of your DVD Menu, including a background image, Menu animation, an audio track, and a group of settings for text fonts and button styles.

iDVD helps those of us who are graphically challenged by including a wide range of professionally designed themes for all sorts of occasions, ranging from old standbys such as weddings, birthdays, and vacations to more generic themes with the accent on action, friendship, and technology. To view the included themes, click the Themes button in the lower-right corner of the iDVD window (see Figure 5-3).

**Figure 5-3:**
Select a
new theme
from the
Themes
pane.

To choose a theme for your project — or to see what a theme looks like on
your Menu — click any thumbnail and watch iDVD update the Menu display.

If you decide while creating your DVD Menu that you need a different theme,
you can change themes at any time. iDVD won't lose a single button or video
clip that you add to your DVD Menu. You'll be amazed at how the look and
sound of your DVD Menu completely change with just the click of a theme
thumbnail.

## Adding movies

Drop zones and themes are cool, but most folks want to add video to their
DVD. To accomplish this, iDVD uses *buttons* as links to your video clips. In
fact, some iDVD Movie buttons display a preview of the video they'll display!
To play the video on a DVD player, you select the Movie button with the
remote control, just as you do for a commercial DVD.

To add a Movie button, drag a QuickTime movie file from the Finder and
drop it onto your DVD Menu display. (Only MPEG-4 QuickTime movies
and DV streams are supported — MPEG-1 and MPEG-2 movie clips may be

**Book IV
Chapter 5**

**Burn Those DVDs!
Using iDVD**

rejected or converted, or even be added without audio.) Alternatively, click the Add button and choose Add Movie from the pop-up menu.

iDVD and iMovie are soul mates, so you can also display the iDVD Media pane and then click Movies from the pop-up menu. Now you can drag clips from your Movies folder.

No matter the source of the clip, when you drop it onto your DVD Menu, iDVD adds a Movie button, as you can see in Figure 5-4. Note that some buttons appear as text links rather than actual buttons. The appearance of a Movie button in your DVD Menu is determined by the theme you choose.

---

## Taking advantage of drop zones

Most of Apple's animated themes include special bordered areas marked as drop zones. These locations have nothing to do with skydiving; rather, a *drop zone* is a placeholder in the Menu that can hold a single video clip or photograph. When you drag a video clip or an image to a drop zone, that clip or picture is added to the animation in Apple's theme! Think about that for a moment; I know I did. You can actually personalize a Hollywood-quality animated DVD Menu with *your own photos and video!*

Most of the themes included with iDVD include at least one drop zone, and some are practically jam-packed with drop zones. For example, the amazing Forever theme has a whopping six drop zones! If you think a Menu looks just fine without anything in a drop zone, however, you don't have to put anything there. The words *Drop Zone* disappear when you preview or burn your DVD. (Empty frames do tend to look a bit silly in some themes, though.)

To add a video clip or image to a drop zone, simply drag the clip or photo from a Finder window and drop it on the desired drop zone. You can also drag clips or photos from other sources, including the Movies and Photos panes in iDVD's Media pane, the iMovie window, or the iPhoto window. (Remember, Apple is anything but strict on these matters.) Remember, drop zones don't act as links or buttons to other content; the stuff you add to a Menu's drop zones appears only as part of the theme's animation cycle. You can even drag an iPhoto event or album to a drop zone, and it will continuously cycle through the images. *Wowzers!*

To see all the drop zones at one time (without cycling through the animation), click the Edit Drop Zones button at the bottom center of the iDVD window; when you do, you see a thumbnail display of each zone. You can drag items to these thumbnails or jump right to one in the animation by clicking the thumbnail. To delete the contents of a drop zone, click the thumbnail in the editor and press the Delete key.

If you're adding something to a dynamic drop zone (which disappears and reappears during the menu animation cycle), click the Motion button to activate the animation and then click it again to stop the animation cycle. Now click and drag the scrubber bar until the desired drop zone is in view. To delete the contents of a drop zone, Control-click (or right-click) the drop zone and choose Clear.

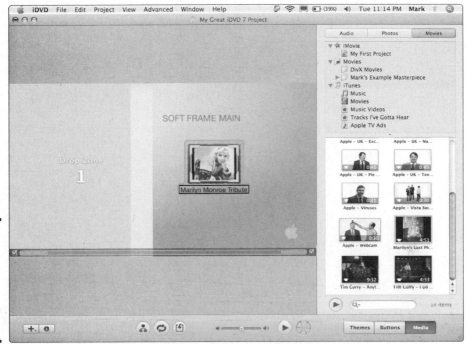

**Figure 5-4:**
A new
Movie
button
appears on
your pristine
DVD Menu.

A Movie button doesn't have to stay where iDVD places it! By default, iDVD aligns buttons and text objects using an invisible grid, but if you don't want such order imposed on your creativity, just drag the object to where you'd like it to be to turn on Free Positioning. (You can also right-click the object and select the Free Positioning item from the menu that appears.) iDVD even provides cool new automatic guides that help you align objects when you're using Free Positioning! You'll see them as yellow lines that appear when objects are aligned along a vertical or horizontal plane.

You can have up to 12 buttons on your iDVD Menu (the theme you choose determines the maximum number of buttons you can add). To add more content than 12 buttons allow, add a submenu by clicking the Add button and choosing Add Submenu from the pop-up menu. Now you can click the submenu button to jump to that screen and drag up to another 12 movie files into it.

Keep your target audience in mind while you create your DVD. Standard TV sets have a different *aspect ratio* (height to width) and *resolution* (number of scan lines on the screen) than a digital video clip, and a standard TV isn't as precise in focusing that image on the tube. If you selected the Standard aspect ratio when you created the project, you can make sure that your DVD content looks great on a standard TV screen by following these steps:

1. **Click View on the old-fashioned iDVD menu (the one at the top of the screen).**

2. **Choose the Show TV Safe Area command.**

   You can also press the convenient ⌘+T shortcut. iDVD adds a smaller rectangle within the iDVD window to mark the screen dimensions of a standard TV.

If you take care that your Menu buttons and (most of) your background image fit within this smaller rectangle, you're assured that folks with a standard television can enjoy your work. To turn off the TV Safe Area rectangle, press ⌘+T again.

If your entire family is blessed with a fleet of HD TVs (or you chose the Widescreen aspect ratio for this project), leave the Show TV Safe Area option off. Today's widescreen displays can handle just about any orientation.

---

# A word on image dimensions

For best playback results on a standard TV, make sure that your background image has the same dimensions as standard digital video — 640 x 480 pixels. If the dimensions of your image don't match the dimensions of digital video, iDVD will stretch or shrink the image to fit, which might have undesirable effects. When your image is stretched and skewed to fit the DVD Menu, Aunt Harriet might end up looking like Shrek.

You can use QuickTime player or iPhoto to change the dimensions of your background image for import into iDVD. For example, you can use the iPhoto crop feature to alter the overall shape of the image and then resize it within iPhoto. Use the Size setting when you export the image from iPhoto and then save the file in the Pictures folder located in your Home folder so that you can find it easily later. (For more on working in iPhoto, see Book IV, Chapter 3.)

If you enjoy a cutting-edge widescreen (16:9) or HD (high-definition) TV display, you won't have the standard TV dimension restriction of 640 x 480 pixels. And because iDVD supports HD video and 16:9 video with a number of widescreen themes, be prepared to kiss the phrases *pan-and-scan* and *full-screen* goodbye and forget about the Show TV Safe Area feature. If your completed DVD projects are purely for your own enjoyment, that's a great idea. However, don't forget that if you distribute your discs to others with old-fashioned TVs dating back to the archaic '80s and '90s, they might not be pleased with what they see!

## Great, now my audience demands a slideshow

Many MacBook owners don't realize that iDVD can use not only video clips but also digital photos as content. In fact, you can add a group of images to your DVD Menu by using Slideshow buttons, which allow the viewer to play back a series of digital photographs. iDVD handles everything for you, so there's no tricky timing to figure out or weird scripts to write. Just click the Add button at the bottom of the iDVD window and choose Add Slideshow. iDVD places a Slideshow button on your DVD Menu.

After the Slideshow button is on tap, add the content — in this case, by choosing the images that iDVD adds to your DVD Menu. Follow these steps to select your slideshow images:

1. **Double-click the Slideshow Menu button — the one you just added to the Menu — to open the Slideshow display (see Figure 5-5).**

2. **Click the Media button (bottom right of the screen).**

3. **Click the Photos tab (top right of the screen) to display your iPhoto library and photo albums.**

**Figure 5-5:** Who needs a projector anymore? iDVD can create a great slideshow!

4. **Drag your favorite image thumbnails from the Photos list and drop them into the My Slideshow window.**

   You can also drag images straight from a Finder window or the iPhoto window itself. (Those Apple folks are sooooo predictable.)

5. **Drag around the photos in the My Slideshow window to set their order of appearance in your slideshow.**

6. **To add audio to these pictures, drag your favorite audio file from the Finder and drop it in the Audio well in the My Slideshow window.**

   The *Audio well* is the box bearing the speaker icon, next to the volume control below the My Slideshow window.

   Alternatively, click the Audio tab to select an audio track from your iTunes library, iTunes playlists, or GarageBand creations.

7. **Click the Return button to return to your DVD Menu.**

If you're using a Menu with animated buttons that display an image (rather than text buttons), you can choose which image you want to appear on the Slideshow button. Click the Slideshow button that you added and see the slider that appears above the Slideshow button. Drag this slider to scroll through the images you added. When you find the image that you want to use for the Slideshow button in the DVD Menu, click the Slideshow button again to save your changes.

## *Now for the music . . .*

Most of the Apple-supplied themes already have their own background music, so you might not even need to add music to your DVD Menu. However, if you want to change the existing background music (or if your DVD Menu currently doesn't have any music), adding your own audio to the current Menu is child's play!

1. **Click the Media button.**

2. **Click the Audio tab to reveal the musical Shangri-La, as shown in Figure 5-6.**

3. **Drag an audio file from the iTunes playlist or GarageBand folder display and drop it on the Menu background.**

   iDVD accepts every sound format that you can use for importing and encoding in iTunes: AIFF, MP3, AAC, Apple Lossless, and WAV audio files.

4. **Click the Motion button (labeled in Figure 5-1) to watch your DVD Menu animation cycle set to the new background audio.**

5. **Click the Motion button again to stop the animation and return to serious work.**

**Figure 5-6:**
You do a lot of fine-tuning from the Audio pane.

# Giving Your DVD the Personal Touch

You can easily make changes to the default settings provided with the theme you chose. iDVD offers all sorts of controls that allow you to change the appearance and behavior of buttons, text, and the presentation of your content. In this section, I show you how to cast out iDVD's (perfectly good) defaults and then tweak things to perfection.

## Using Uncle Morty for your DVD Menu background

Hey, Uncle Morty might not be a supermodel, but he has birthdays and anniversaries, and iDVD is more than happy to accommodate you in documenting those milestones! Follow these steps to change the background of your DVD Menu:

*1.* **Click the Inspector button.**

*2.* **Get an image using one of the following methods:**

- *Drag an image from the Finder* and drop it into the Background well.

- *Drag the image directly into the Menu display.*

- *To use an image from your iPhoto library,* click the Media button and click the Photos tab, and then drag the desired image into the Menu display.

  iDVD updates the DVD Menu to reflect your new background choice.

## Adding your own titles

The one tweak you'll probably have to perform in every iDVD project is changing titles. Unfortunately, the default labels provided by iDVD are pretty lame, and they appear in two important places:

✦ **Menu title:** Your large main title usually appears at the top of the DVD Menu.

✦ **Button captions:** Each Submenu, Movie, and Slideshow button that you add to your Menu has its own title.

To change the text in your Menu title or the titles below your buttons, follow these steps:

1. **Select the text by clicking it.**

2. **Click it again to edit it.**

   A rectangle with a cursor appears to indicate that you can now edit the text.

3. **Type the new text and press Return to save the change.**

## Changing buttons like a highly paid professional

Customizing Movie buttons? You can do it with aplomb! Follow these steps:

1. **Click Buttons.**

2. **Click any Movie button from the DVD Menu to select it.**

   A slider appears above the button, which you can drag to set the thumbnail picture for that button in your DVD Menu. (Naturally, this is only for animated buttons, not text buttons.)

   Enable the Movie check box to animate the button.

3. **To create a Movie button with a still image, drag a picture from a Finder window or the Media pane and drop it on top of the button.**

4. **To adjust the properties for the button, click the Inspector button.**

Table 5-1 describes the button properties — note that some properties won't appear for text buttons.

| Table 5-1 | Button Settings You Can Customize |
|-----------|-----------------------------------|
| *Movie Button Property* | *What It Does* |
| Label Font | Changes the label font, text size, color, and attributes. |
| Label Attributes | Specifies the position of the label and whether it has a shadow. |
| Custom Thumbnail | Drag an image to the Custom Thumbnail well. For Slideshow buttons, drag the Thumbnail slider to select the image that will appear on the button. |
| Transition | Determines the transition that occurs when the button is clicked (before the action occurs). |
| Size | Adjusts the size of the button. Move the slider to the right to increase the button size. |

## *Give my creation motion!*

Earlier in this chapter, you find out how to use a different image for your background, but what about using an animated background? You can use any QuickTime movie from your iMovie library (including those you've taken with your MacBook's iSight camera) to animate your DVD Menu background! Didn't I tell you that this iDVD thing was *huge?*

Keep in mind that your background movie should be a short clip; 20–30 seconds is optimal. A clip with a fade-in at the beginning and a fade-out at the end is the best choice because iDVD loops your background clip continuously, and your animated background flows seamlessly behind your Menu.

I'm not talking drop zones here. (See the sidebar "Taking advantage of drop zones," earlier in this chapter, for an explanation of drop zones.) You can add a movie to a drop zone, of course, but by using a movie clip as a background, you're replacing the entire animation sequence rather than just a single area of the background. Drop zones also don't provide audio, whereas a clip background does include the clip audio.

Follow these steps to add a new animated background:

1. **Click your old friend, the Inspector button.**

   Make sure that no individual objects are highlighted so that the Inspector window displays the Menu properties instead.

2. **Drag a movie from the Finder and drop it into the Background well.**

   You can click the Movies tab in the Media pane to instantly display your iMovie collection.

3. **Click the Motion button in the iDVD window to try out your new background.**

4. **Click the Motion button again to stop the animation cycle.**

## Previewing Your Masterpiece

Figure 5-7 captures the elusive Preview remote control — truly an awesome sight. When you click Preview, the Media pane disappears, and your DVD Menu appears exactly as it will on the finished DVD.

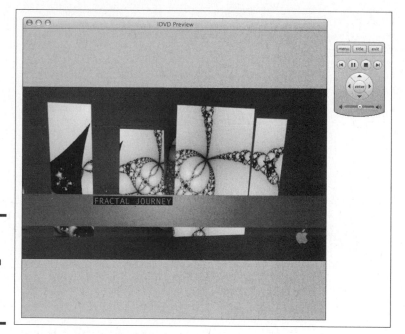

**Figure 5-7:** Preview mode — an incredible simulation indeed.

Ah, but appearances aren't everything: You can also use your DVD Menu! Click the buttons on the remote control to simulate the remote on your DVD player or think outside the box and click a Menu button directly with your mouse pointer. iDVD presents the video clip, runs the slideshow, or jumps to a submenu, just as it will with the completed disc.

This is a great time to test-drive a project before you burn it to disc. To make sure you don't waste a blank DVD, make certain that everything you expect to happen actually happens. Nothing worse than discovering that

Aunt Edna's slideshow from her Hong Kong trip actually displays your family's summer trip to the zoo (whoops). If you made a mistake or something needs tweaking, click the Preview button again, and you're back to the iDVD window proper, where you can edit or fine-tune your project.

iDVD allows you to save your project as a standard Mac OS X *disc image* rather than as a simple project file (or a physical DVD) — you can use Apple's Disk Utility to open and mount the disc image as if it were a burned disc. If you move the disc image to another Mac with a SuperDrive, you can use Disk Utility to burn it on that machine. To save an iDVD project as a disc image, choose File⇨Save as Disc Image (or press ⌘+Shift+R). To save your project as a standard VIDEO_TS folder (suitable for burning with another video-editing or DVD recording application), choose File⇨Save as VIDEO_TS Folder.

Interested in tweaking settings across your entire project? Perhaps you'd like to reduce the time it takes to create and edit your DVD or switch video modes from NTSC to PAL for a DVD that's to be sent overseas. If you'd like to view or change the overall settings for your entire DVD, click Project⇨Project Info to display the Project Info dialog. Heck, you can even switch aspect ratios or change the project name. Thanks, Apple!

# A Word about Automation

At the beginning of the chapter, I mention the easy way to produce an iDVD disc or project, using either OneStep DVD (for complete automation) or Magic iDVD (for partial automation). In this section, I provide you with the details.

## One-click paradise with OneStep DVD

If you're in a hurry to create a DVD from clips on your DV camcorder and you don't mind losing your creative input, OneStep DVD is just the ticket. In short, iDVD allows you to plug in your FireWire-equipped mini-DV camcorder, answer a question or two, and then sit back while the application does *all* the work. iDVD imports the DV clips, creates a basic Menu design, and burns the disc automatically! (Again, note that OneStep DVD doesn't support USB camcorders.)

Using OneStep DVD will appeal to any laptop owner with a SuperDrive. Why not produce a DVD right after a wedding or birthday that you can give as a gift? Photographers who cover those same special events might consider selling a DVD made with OneStep DVD. If you happen to capture something incredibly unique — such as a UFO landing or an honest politician — you can use OneStep DVD to create an instant backup of the clips on your DV camcorder. You could even keep your friends and family up-to-date with the progress of your vacation by sending them a daily DVD of your exploits! (You gotta admit, even Grandma would consider that eminently *sassy!*)

Follow these steps to start the OneStep DVD process:

1. **Click the OneStep DVD button on the iDVD top-level menu (refer to Figure 5-2).**

   Alternatively, choose File⇨OneStep DVD.

   iDVD displays the dialog shown in Figure 5-8.

**Figure 5-8:** Connect your DV camcorder, and OneStep DVD does the rest.

If you want to use OneStep DVD with an existing movie on your MacBook's hard drive, choose File⇨OneStep DVD from Movie instead. iDVD prompts you for the video file to use.

2. **Following the prompts, connect the FireWire cable from your DV camcorder; then turn on the camcorder and set it to VCR mode.**

3. **Click OK.**

4. **Load a blank DVD.**

## Exercising control with Magic iDVD

Got a little extra time? For those who prefer to make just a few choices and let iDVD do the rest, the new Magic iDVD feature just plain rocks! However, you can't import clips directly from your mini-DV camcorder as you can with OneStep DVD; instead, you select one of the following:

✦ **An iDVD theme**

✦ **Video clips** you've already created with iMovie or dragged from the Finder (perfect for use with a USB 2.0 DV camcorder)

+ **Photos** from your iPhoto library or dragged from the Finder

+ **Audio** from your iTunes playlist or dragged from the Finder

Follow these steps to start the OneStep DVD process:

*1.* **Click the Magic iDVD button on the iDVD top-level dialog (refer to Figure 5-2).**

iDVD displays the window you see in Figure 5-9.

**Figure 5-9:** With Magic iDVD, you make some basic choices, and iDVD does the work.

*2.* **Click in the DVD Title box and type a name for your disc (or project).**

*3.* **Click to select a theme from the Theme strip.**

*4.* **Click the Movies tab and drag the desired clips into the Drop Movies Here strip.**

*5.* **To add a slideshow, click the Photos tab and drag the desired photos into the Drop Photos Here strip.**

*6.* **To add audio for your slideshow, click the Audio tab and drag the desired song into the Drop Photos Here strip (a speaker icon appears in the first cell of the strip to indicate that you've added a soundtrack).**

7. **Click Preview to see a preview of the finished project, complete with remote control. To exit Preview mode, click Exit.**

8. **To open the project in its current form in the main iDVD window, click Create Project.**

9. **To record your completed project directly to DVD, load a blank DVD and click Burn.**

To return to the iDVD main window at any time, just click the Close button on the Magic iDVD window.

## Recording a Finished Project to a Shiny Disc

When you're ready to record your next Oscar-winning documentary on family behaviors during vacation, just follow these simple words:

1. **Click the Burn button at the bottom of the iDVD window.**

   I have to admit, the Burn button that appears has to be my favorite single control in all my 20+ years of computing! It looks powerful, it looks sexy . . . it wants to *burn*. (Sorry about that.)

2. **After iDVD asks you to insert a blank DVD-R into the SuperDrive, load a single or dual-layer blank DVD-R, DVD-RW, DVD+R, or DVD+RW (depending on the media your Mac can handle).**

   Your SuperDrive might be able to burn and read a DVD+R, DVD-RW, or DVD+RW, but what about your DVD player? Keep in mind that only DVD-Rs are likely to work in older DVD players. The latest generation of DVD players is likely DVD+R compatible as well, but I've seen only a handful of DVD players that can handle rewriteable media at the time of this writing. Therefore, remember the destination for the discs you burn and choose your media accordingly.

   After a short pause, iDVD begins burning the DVD. The application keeps you updated with a progress bar.

When the disc is finished, you're ready to load it into your favorite local DVD player or back into your MacBook and enjoy your work using Apple's DVD Player.

Either way, it's all good!

# Chapter 6: Becoming a Superstar with GarageBand

## In This Chapter

✔ Navigating the GarageBand window

✔ Adding tracks and loops to your song

✔ Repeating loops and extending your song

✔ Building arrangements

✔ Adding effects to instruments

✔ Exporting your work to iTunes and iWeb

✔ Burning your song to an audio CD

When I was a kid, I always thought that *real* rock stars trashed their instruments after a hard night's worth of jamming — you know, like The Who, Led Zeppelin, KISS, and the Rolling Stones. Guitars got set on fire, or pounded into the stage, or thrown into the crowd like beads during a Mardi Gras parade.

I can make my own music now, but you'll never see me trash my instrument! I compose music on my MacBook with *GarageBand,* Apple's music-making component in the iLife application suite. You can solo on all sorts of instruments, and even add horns, drums, and a funky bass line for backup . . . all with absolutely no musical experience (and, in my case, very little talent, to boot)!

Oh, and did I mention that GarageBand '09 also produces podcasts? That's right, you can record your voice and easily create your own show, and then share it with others from your iWeb site! Heck, add photos and video if you like. You'll be the talk of your family and friends and maybe even your Mac user group.

This chapter explains everything you need to know to create your first song (or your first podcast). I also show you how to import your hit record into iTunes so that you can listen to it on your iPod with a big, silly grin on your face (as I do) or add it to your next iMovie or iDVD project as a royalty-free soundtrack.

# Shaking Hands with Your Band

As you can see in Figure 6-1, the GarageBand window isn't complex at all, and that's good design. In this section, I list the most important controls so that you know your Play button from your Loop Browser button.

Track list    Playhead    Loop    Timeline

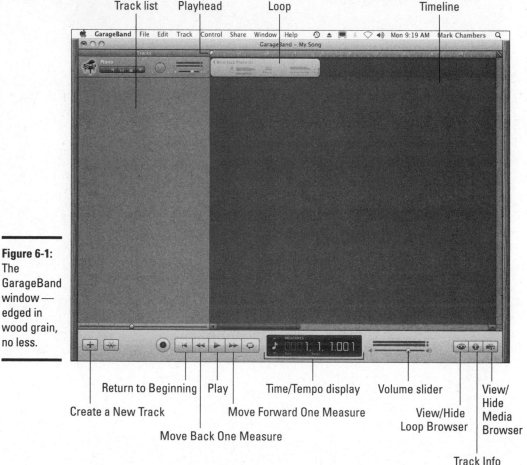

**Figure 6-1:** The GarageBand window — edged in wood grain, no less.

Return to Beginning | Play    Time/Tempo display    Volume slider    View/ Hide Media Browser

Create a New Track    Move Forward One Measure    View/Hide Loop Browser

Move Back One Measure    Track Info

Your music-making machine includes

✦ **Track list:** In GarageBand, a *track* is a discrete instrument that you set up to play one part of your song. For example, a track in a classical piece for string quartet would have four tracks — one each for violin, viola, cello, and bass. This list contains all the tracks in your song arranged so that you can easily see and modify them, like the rows in a spreadsheet. A track begins in the list, stretching out to the right all the way to the end of the song. As you can see in the upper left of Figure 6-1, I already have one track defined — a Grand Piano.

If you're creating a podcast, a *Podcast artwork track* can also appear. Video podcasts can include a movie track as well.

✦ **Timeline:** This scrolling area holds the loops (see the following bullet) that you add or record, allowing you to move and edit them easily. When a song plays, the Timeline scrolls to give you a visual look at your music. (Bear with me; you'll understand that cryptic statement in a page or two.)

✦ **Loop:** This is a prerecorded clip of an instrument being played in a specific style and tempo. Loops are the building blocks of your song. You can drag loops from the Loop Browser to a track and literally build a bass line or a guitar solo. (It's a little like adding video clips in iMovie to build a film.)

✦ **Playhead:** This vertical line is a moving indicator that shows you the current position in your song while it scrolls by in the Timeline. You can drag the playhead to a new location at any time. The playhead also acts like the Insertion cursor in a word processing application: If you insert a section of a song or a loop from the Clipboard, it appears at the current location of the playhead. (More on copying and inserting loops later, so don't panic.)

✦ **Create a New Track button:** Click this button to add a new track to your song.

✦ **Track Info button:** If you need to display the instrument used in a track, click the track to select it and then click this button. You can also control settings, such as Echo and Reverb, from the Edit pane of the Track Info display.

✦ **View/Hide Loop Browser button:** Click the button with the striking eye icon to display the Loop Browser at the bottom of the window; click it again to close it. You can see more of your tracks at a time without scrolling by closing the Loop Browser.

✦ **View/Hide Media Browser button:** Click this button (which bears icons of a filmstrip, slide, and musical note) to display the media browser at the right side of the window; click it again to close it. By closing the media browser, you'll see more of your tracks. If you're already familiar with iDVD, iWeb, or iMovie, you recognize this pane in the GarageBand window; it allows you to add media (in this case, digital song files, still images or video clips) to your GarageBand project for use in a podcast.

✦ **Return to Beginning button:** Clicking this button immediately moves the playhead back to the beginning of the Timeline.

✦ **Move Back/Forward One Measure buttons:** To move quickly through your song by jumping to the previous or next measure, click the corresponding button.

✦ **Play button:** Hey, old friend! At last, a control that you've probably used countless times before — and it works just like the same control on your audio CD player. Click Play, and GarageBand begins playing your entire song. Notice that the Play button turns blue. To stop the music, click Play again; the button loses that sexy blue sheen and the playhead stops immediately. (If playback is paused, it begins again at the playhead position when you click Play.)

✦ **Time/Tempo display:** This cool-looking LCD display shows you the current playhead position in seconds.

You can click the icon at the left of the display to choose other modes, such as

- **Measures** (to display the current measure and mark the beat)
- **Chord** (to display note and chord names)
- **Project** (to show or change the key, tempo, and signature for the song).

✦ **Volume slider:** Here's another familiar face. Just drag the slider to raise or lower the volume.

Of course, more controls are scattered around the GarageBand window, but these are the main controls used to compose a song . . . which is the next stop!

## Composing and Podcasting Made Easy

In this section, I cover the basics of composition in GarageBand, working from the very beginning. Follow along with this running example:

*1.* **Close all existing GarageBand windows.**

GarageBand displays the top-level New Project dialog.

*2.* **Click New Project on the list at the left.**

*3.* **Click the Piano icon and click Choose.**

GarageBand displays the New Project dialog, as shown in Figure 6-2.

By choosing the Piano, my new GarageBand project will have one track already in place — a grand piano. If you choose Electric Guitar or Voice, you'll have a project automatically created with an electric guitar track or male and female voice tracks. To create a completely empty project, choose Loops.

**Figure 6-2:**
Start creating your new song here.

4. **Type a name for your new song and then drag the Tempo slider to select the beats per minute (bpm).**

   A GarageBand song can have only one *tempo* (or speed) throughout, expressed as beats per minute.

5. **If you want to adjust the settings for your song, you can select the**

   - *Time signature (the Time box)*
   - *Key (the Key box)*

   If you're new to music *theory* (the rules and syntax by which music is created and written), just use the defaults. Most of the toe-tappin' tunes that you and I are familiar with fit right in with these settings.

6. **Click the Create button.**

   You see the window shown in Figure 6-1. (The Blues Jazz Piano 01 section in the middle of Figure 6-1 — which I show you how to add in the next section — is an example of a typical loop.)

## Adding tracks

Although I'm not a musician, I am a music lover, and I know that many classical composers approached a new work in the same way you approach a new song in GarageBand: by envisioning the instruments that they wanted to hear. (I imagine Mozart and Beethoven would've been thrilled to use GarageBand, but I think they did a decent job with pen and paper, too.)

**Book IV
Chapter 6**

Becoming a
Superstar with
GarageBand

In fact, GarageBand '09 introduces a *Songwriting* project (also available from the top-level New Project dialog). When you choose the Songwriting project, GarageBand presents you with a full set of four instrument tracks, plus a real instrument track for your voice. (More on software versus real instrument tracks in a page or two.) You're instantly ready to start adding loops and recording your own voice!

If you've followed along to this point, you've noticed two problems with your GarageBand window:

✦ **There's no keyboard.** You can record the contents of a software instrument track by "playing" the keyboard, clicking the keys with your trackpad. (As you might imagine, this isn't the best solution.) If you're a musician, the best method of recording your own notes is with a MIDI instrument, which I discuss later in the chapter. For now, you can display the keyboard window by pressing ⌘+K. If the keyboard window is on the screen and you don't need it, banish the window by clicking the Close button.

Even if you're not interested in the "point-and-click" keyboard, GarageBand offers a musical typing keyboard, where you press the keys on your keyboard to simulate the keys on a musical keyboard. (Hey, if you don't have a MIDI instrument, at least it's better than nothing.) To display the musical typing keyboard window, press Shift+⌘+K.

✦ **The example song has only one track.** If you want to write the next classical masterpiece for Grand Piano, that's fine. Otherwise, on the GarageBand menu bar, choose Track⇨Delete Track to start with a clean slate. (I know, I could have started with a Loops project, but this way you get to see how to delete a track.)

These are the five kinds of tracks you can use in GarageBand '09:

✦ **Software instrument tracks:** These tracks aren't audio recordings. Rather, they're mathematically precise algorithms that your Mac *renders* (or builds) to fit your needs. If you have a MIDI instrument connected to your Mac, you can create your own software instrument tracks. (More on MIDI instruments later in this chapter.)

In this chapter, I focus on software instrument tracks, which are the easiest for a nonmusician to use.

✦ **Real instrument tracks:** A real instrument track is an actual audio recording, such as your voice or a physical instrument without a MIDI connection. (Think microphone.)

✦ **Electric Guitar tracks:** GarageBand includes a real instrument track especially made for an electric guitar, which allows you to use one of five different amplifiers and a number of stompboxes (those effect pedals that guitarists are always poking with their foot to change the sound of their instruments).

✦ **Podcast artwork track:** You get only one of these; they hold photos that will appear on a video iPod (or a window on your iWeb site) when your podcast is playing.

✦ **Movie tracks:** The video sound track appears if you're *scoring* (adding music) to an iMovie movie. Along with the video sound track, you get a cool companion video track that shows the clips in your movie. (More on this in the "Look, I'm John Williams!" sidebar, later in this chapter.)

Time to add a software instrument track of your very own. Follow these steps:

*1.* **Click the Create a New Track button (which carries a plus sign), labeled in Figure 6-1.**

GarageBand displays the New Track dialog.

*2.* **Click the Software Instrument radio button and then click Create.**

See all those great instruments in the Track Info pane on the right?

*3.* **Choose the general instrument category by clicking it.**

I chose Drum Kits.

*4.* **From the right column, choose your specific style of weapon, such as Rock Kit for an arena sound.**

Figure 6-3 illustrates the new track that appears in your list when you follow these steps.

If you're creating a podcast and you want to add a series of still images that will appear on a video iPod's screen (or on your iWeb page), follow these steps:

*1.* **Click the View Media Browser button (labeled in Figure 6-1).**

*2.* **Click the Photos button.**

GarageBand displays all the photos in your iPhoto library and Events.

*3.* **Drag an image from your iPhoto library in the media browser to the Track list.**

The Podcast track appears at the top of the Track list, and you can add and move images in the list at any time, just like the loops that you add to your instrument tracks. (More on adding and rearranging the contents of a track later in this section.)

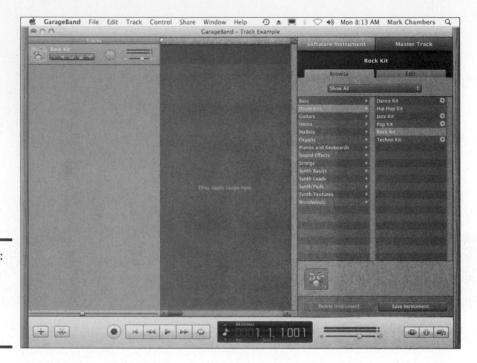

**Figure 6-3:**
The new track appears, ready to rock.

## Choosing loops

When you have a new, empty track, you can add something that you can hear. You do that by adding loops to your track from the Loop Browser — Apple provides you with thousands of loops to choose from — and photos from your media browser. Click the Loop Browser button (which bears the all-seeing eye) to display your collection, as shown in Figure 6-4.

If your browser looks different from what you see in Figure 6-4, that's because of the view mode you're using, just like the different view modes available for a Finder window. The three-icon button in the upper-left corner of the Loop Browser toggles the browser display between column, musical button, and podcast sounds view. Click the middle of the three buttons to switch to button mode.

### Looking for just the right loop

The track in this running example uses a Rock drum kit, but we haven't added a loop yet. (Refer to Figure 6-3.) Follow these steps to search through your loop library for just the right rhythm:

1. **Click the button that corresponds to the instrument you're using.**

   In our example, this is the Kits button in the Loop Browser. Click it, and a list of different beats appears in the pane at the bottom of the Loop Browser window. (Check out Figure 6-4 for a sneak peek.)

**Figure 6-4:**
The Loop
Browser,
shown in
button view.

Search box

2. **Click one of the loops with a green musical-note icon.**

   Go ahead; this is where things get fun! GarageBand begins playing the
   loop nonstop, allowing you to get a feel for how that particular loop
   sounds.

   Because I'm using only software instruments in this track (and throughout
   this chapter), you should choose only software instrument loops, which
   are identified by a green musical-note icon.

3. **Click another entry in the list, and the application switches immediately
   to that loop.**

   Now you're beginning to understand why GarageBand is so cool for both
   musicians and the note-impaired. It's like having your own band, with
   members who never get tired and play whatever you want while you're
   composing. (Mozart would've *loved* this.)

   If you want to search for a particular instrument, click in the Search box
   (labeled in Figure 6-4) and type the text you want to match. GarageBand
   returns the search results in the list.

4. **Scroll down the list and continue to sample the different loops until
   you find one that fits like a glove.**

   For this reporter, it's Southern Rock Drums 01.

**5.** **Drag the entry to your Rock Kit track and drop it at the very beginning of the Timeline (as indicated by the playhead).**

Your window will look like Figure 6-5.

If you want that same beat throughout the song, you don't need to add any more loops to that track. (More on extending that beat in the next section.) However, if you want the drum's beat to change later in the song, you add a second loop after the first one in the *same* track. For now, leave this track as is.

Whoops! Did you do something that you regret? Don't forget that you can undo most actions in GarageBand by pressing the old standby ⌘+Z immediately afterward.

## *Second verse, same as the first*

When you compose, you can add tracks for each instrument that you want in your song:

✦ Each track can have more than one loop.

✦ Loops *don't* have to start at the beginning; you can drop a loop anywhere in the Timeline.

## Look, I'm John Williams!

You, too, can be a famous composer of soundtracks . . . well, perhaps not quite as famous as Mr. Williams, but even he had to start somewhere. To add a GarageBand score to an iMovie, click the Track menu and then click Show Movie Track to display the Movie track. Choose a movie to score from the familiar confines of the Media Browser, and drag it to the Movie Track.

At this point, you add and modify instrument tracks and loops just as you would any other GarageBand project. The existing sound for the iMovie project appears in the Movie Sound

track. A Video Preview pane appears on top of the Track Info pane on the right side of the GarageBand window. When you click the Play button, the video is shown as well so that you can check your work and tweak settings (as described later in the chapter).

After you've finished composing, you can click Share on the menu bar and choose to export your work to iDVD, as a QuickTime movie directly to your hard drive, or to iTunes as a movie. Note that you can't return to iMovie with your project, so scoring should be a final step in the production of your movie.

For example, in Figure 6-6, you can see that my drum kit kicks in first, but my bass line doesn't begin until some time later (for a funkier opening).

**Figure 6-6:**
My Timeline with a synth and an electric bass onboard. Let's rock!

You put loops on separate tracks so that they can play simultaneously on different instruments. If all your loops in a song are added on the same track, you hear only one loop at any one time, and all the loops use the same software instrument. By creating multiple tracks, you give yourself the elbow room to bring in the entire band at the same time. It's uber-convenient to compose your song when you can see each instrument's loops and where they fall in the song.

Click the Reset button in the Loop Browser to choose another instrument or genre category.

## Resizing, repeating, and moving loops

If you haven't already tried listening to your entire song, try it now. You can click Play at any time without wreaking havoc on your carefully created tracks. Sounds pretty good, doesn't it?

But wait: I bet the song stopped after about five seconds, right? (You can watch the passing seconds using either the Time/Tempo display or the second rule that appears at the very top of the Timeline.) I'm sure that you want your song to last more than five seconds! After the playhead moves past the end of the last loop, your song is over. Click Play again to pause the playback; then click the Return to Beginning button (labeled in Figure 6-1) to move the playhead back to the beginning of the song.

The music stops so soon because your loops are only so long. Most are five seconds in length, and others are even shorter. To keep the groove going, you have to do one of three things:

✦ **Resize the loop.** Hover your cursor over either the left or right edge of most loops, and an interesting thing happens: Your cursor changes to a vertical line with an arrow pointing away from the loop. That's your cue to click and drag — and as you drag, most loops expand to fill the space you're making, repeating the beats in perfect time. By resizing a loop, you can literally drag the loop's edge as long as you like.

✦ **Repeat the loop.** Depending on the loop that you chose, you might find that resizing it doesn't repeat the measure. Instead, the new part of the loop is simply dead air. In fact, the length of many loops is limited to anywhere from one to five seconds. However, if you move your cursor over the side of a loop that you want to extend, it turns into a vertical line with a circular arrow, which tells you that you can click and *repeat* the loop. GarageBand actually adds multiple copies of the same loop automatically, for as far as you drag the loop. In Figure 6-7, I've repeated the bass loop that you see in Figure 6-6.

✦ **Add a new loop.** You can switch to a different loop to change the flow of the music. Naturally, the instrument stays the same, but there's no reason you can't use a horn-riff loop in your violin track (as long as it sounds good played by a violin)! To GarageBand, a software instrument track is compatible with *any* software instrument loop that you add from the Loop Browser as long as that loop is marked with our old friend the green musical note.

You can also use the familiar cut (⌘+X), copy (⌘+C), and paste (⌘+V) editing keys to cut, copy, and paste loops from place to place — both on the Timeline and from track to track. And you can click a loop and drag it anywhere. After all, you're working under Mac OS X.

**Figure 6-7:** By repeating the bass loop, you can keep the thump flowing.

Each track can be adjusted so that you can listen to the interplay between two or more tracks or hear how your song sounds without a specific track:

✦ Click the tiny speaker button under the track name in the list, and the button turns blue to indicate that the track is muted. To turn off the mute, click the speaker icon again.

✦ You can change the volume or balance of each individual track by using the mixer that appears next to the track name. This comes in handy if you want an instrument to sound louder or confine that instrument to the left or right speaker.

**Book IV Chapter 6**

**Becoming a Superstar with GarageBand**

A track doesn't have to be filled for every second with one loop or another. Most of my songs have a number of repeating loops with empty space between them as different instruments perform solo.

## Using the Arrange track

GarageBand includes another method you can use to monkey with your music: The *Arrange track* can be used to define specific sections of a song, allowing you to reorganize things by selecting, moving, and copying entire sections. For example, you're probably familiar with the chorus (or refrain) of a song and how often it appears during the course of the tune. With the Arrange track, you can reposition the entire chorus within your song, carrying all the loops and settings within the chorus along with it! If you need another chorus, just copy that arrangement.

To use the Arrange track, display it by clicking Track➪Show Arrange Track. The Arrange track then appears as a thin strip at the top of the track list. Click the Add Region button in the Arrange track (which carries a plus sign) and you'll see a new, untitled region appear (as shown in Figure 6-8). You can drag the right side of the Arrangement region to resize it, or drag it to move it anywhere in the song.

**Figure 6-8:** I've just added a new region in my song's Arrange track.

Who wants an arrangement full of regions named "untitled"? To rename an Arrangement region, click the word *untitled* to select it (the Arrange track turns blue), and then click the title again to display a text box. Type a new name for the region and press Return.

Now, here's where Arrangement regions get *cool*:

✦ To move an entire Arrangement region, click the region's title in the Arrange track and then drag it anywhere you like in the song.

✦ To copy an Arrangement region, hold down the Option key and drag the desired region's title to the spot where you want the copy to appear.

✦ To delete an Arrangement region, select it and press ⌘+Option+Delete.

✦ To replace the contents of an Arrangement region with those of another Arrangement region, hold down the ⌘ key and drag the desired region's title on top of the offending region's title.

✦ To switch two Arrangement regions in your song — swapping the contents completely — drag one of the Arrangement region titles on top of the other and lift your finger from the trackpad.

## Tweaking the settings for a track

You don't think that John Mayer or U2 just "play and walk away," do you? No, they spend hours after the recording session is over, tweaking their music in the studio and on the mixing board until every note sounds just as it should. You can adjust the settings for a track, too. The tweaks that you can perform include adding effects (pull a Hendrix and add echo and reverb to your electric guitar track) and kicking in an equalizer (for fine-tuning the sound of your background horns).

To make adjustments to a track, follow these steps:

*1.* Click the desired track in the track list to select it.

*2.* Click the Track Info button (labeled in Figure 6-1).

*3.* Click the Edit tab to show the settings shown in Figure 6-9.

*4.* Click the button next to each effect you want to enable. (The button glows green when enabled.)

Each of the effects has a modifier setting. For example, you can adjust the amount of echo to add by dragging its slider.

**Figure 6-9:**
Finesse your tune by tweaking the sound of a specific track.

GarageBand offers a Visual Equalizer window that you can use to create a custom equalizer setting for each track. You can display the Visual EQ window by clicking the animated button next to the Visual EQ control on the Edit pane. To change the Bass, Low Mid, High Mid, or Treble setting for a track, click and drag the equalizer waveform in the desired direction. And yep, you can do this while your song is playing, so you can use both your eyes *and* ears to define the perfect settings!

5. **To save the instrument as a new custom instrument — so that you can choose it the next time you add a track — click the Save Instrument button.**

6. **Click the Track Info button again to return to GarageBand.**

Time for a Mark's Maxim:

*Save your work often* **in GarageBand, just as you do in the other iLife applications. One power blackout, and you'll never forgive yourself. Press ⌘+S and enjoy the peace of mind.**

## Join in and jam . . . or talk!

As I mention elsewhere in this chapter, GarageBand is even more fun if you happen to play an instrument! (And yes, I'm envious, no matter how much I enjoy the techno and jazz music that I create. After all, take away my MacBook, and I'm back to playing the kazoo . . . at least until I absorb all the Learn to Play lessons for the guitar.)

Most musicians use MIDI instruments to play music on the computer. That pleasant-sounding acronym stands for *Musical Instrument Digital Interface.* A wide variety of MIDI instruments is available these days, from traditional MIDI keyboards to more exotic fun, such as MIDI saxophones. For example, Apple sells a 49-key MIDI keyboard from M-Audio for around $100; it uses a USB connection to your MacBook.

Most MIDI instruments on the market today use a USB connection. If you have an older instrument with traditional MIDI ports — they're round, so you'll never confuse them with USB connectors — you need a USB-to-MIDI converter. You can find this type of converter on the Apple Web site for around $50. (If you're recording your voice for a podcast, things are easier because you can use your MacBook's built-in microphone; however, most podcasting professionals opt for an external microphone, which offers better fidelity and doesn't force you to sit directly in front of your screen to record.)

After your instrument is connected, you can record tracks using any software instrument. Create a new software instrument track as I demonstrate in this chapter, select it, and then play a few notes. Suddenly you're playing the instrument you chose! (If nothing happens, check the MIDI status light — which appears in the time display — to see whether it blinks with each note you play. If not, check the installation of your MIDI connection and make sure you've loaded any required drivers, as well as your MIDI settings within QuickTime and the input settings in the System Preferences Sound pane.)

Drag the playhead to a beat or two before the spot in the Timeline where you want your recording to start. This gives you time to match the beat. Then click the big red Record button and start jamming or speaking! When you're finished, click the Play button to stop recording.

## *Automatic Composition with Magic GarageBand*

In a hurry? Too rushed to snag loops and tweak effects? Never fear, GarageBand '09 can even compose a song *automatically!* The Magic GarageBand feature provides a wide range of nine different genres of music to choose from — everything from blues to reggae to funk and rock.

To create a song automatically, follow these steps:

1. **Close all GarageBand windows.**

   If you're currently working on a song, GarageBand will prompt you to save it before closing the window.

2. **Click the Magic GarageBand button in the New Project dialog.**

3. **Click the desired genre button and click Choose.**

   Hover your cursor over a genre button to get a preview of the song for that genre.

4. **To hear the entire song with the default instruments, click Entire Song and press the Play button.**

   Alternatively, to hear a short sample of the song, click Snippet and press the Play button.

   As shown in Figure 6-10, you see each instrument on stage. To choose a different musical style for an instrument (or a variation of the instrument), click it and then select the desired sound from the menu below the stage.

   Click My Instrument (the empty space in the middle of the stage) to add your own voice or instrumental using a microphone or MIDI instrument.

**Figure 6-10:** Creating my own arena-rock classic with Magic GarageBand.

5. **When the song fits like a glove, click Create Project to open the song as a project in GarageBand.**

Now you can edit and tweak the song to your heart's delight as you can any other GarageBand project, adding other software or real instrument tracks as necessary.

# Sharing Your Songs and Podcasts

After you finish your song, you can play it whenever you like through GarageBand. But then again, that isn't really what you want, is it? You want to share your music with others with an audio CD or download it to your iPod so that you can enjoy it yourself while walking through the mall!

iTunes to the rescue! As with the other iLife applications that I cover in this book, GarageBand can share the music you make through the digital hub that is your Mac.

## Creating MP3 and AAC files and ringtones

You can create an MP3 or AAC file (or even an iPhone ringtone) from your song or podcast project in just a few simple steps:

1. **Open the song that you want to share.**

2. **Choose Share⇨Send Song to iTunes.**

   GarageBand displays the settings you see in Figure 6-11.

   To create a ringtone and send it to iTunes, choose Share⇨Send Ringtones to iTunes.

3. **Click in each of the four text boxes to type the playlist, artist name, composer name, and album name for the tracks you create.**

   You can leave the defaults as they are, if you prefer. Each track that you export is named after the song's name in GarageBand.

4. **Click the Compress Using pop-up menu and choose the encoder GarageBand should use to compress your song file.**

   The default is AAC, but you can also choose MP3 encoding for greater compatibility.

5. **Click the Audio Settings pop-up menu to select the proper audio quality for the finished file.**

   The higher the quality, the larger the file. GarageBand displays the approximate file size and finished file information in the description box.

6. **Click Share.**

After a second or two of hard work, your Mac opens the iTunes window and highlights the new (or existing) playlist that contains your new song.

**Figure 6-11:**
Tweaking settings for iTunes song files.

# Hey, GarageBand, teach me how to play!

Until the arrival of GarageBand '09, you were limited to creating music — and if you were a nonmusician like yours truly, GarageBand had no practical use as a tool for teaching yourself how to actually *play* an instrument.

Ah, but Apple's introduction of Learn to Play actually turns GarageBand into your private video tutor for basic piano and guitar! From the New Project dialog, click the Learn to Play heading to display your lessons. Right out of the box, you have an Introduction to both instruments, but you can download eight more

free lessons for each instrument from the Lesson Store — and they cover more advanced topics such as fingering and chords. Tim, your on-screen instructor, can even record what you play.

If you find the free Learn to Play lessons valuable, you can move up to the Artist lessons, which are actually taught by famous musicians (including favorites of mine such as John Fogerty and Sting, who actually teaches you how to play "Roxanne")! Each Artist lesson is $4.99 — well worth the price.

## Sending a podcast to iWeb or iTunes

If you've prepared a new podcast episode in GarageBand, you can send it automatically to iWeb or iTunes by following these steps:

*1.* **Open the podcast that you want to export to iWeb.**

   Make sure that the Podcast track is displayed. If necessary, click Track⇨Show Podcast Track to display it.

*2.* **Choose Share⇨Send Podcast to iWeb (or Share⇨Send Podcast to iTunes).**

*3.* **Click the Compress Using pop-up menu and choose the encoder that GarageBand should use to compress your podcast file.**

   Your choices are AAC and MP3 format.

*4.* **Click the Audio Settings pop-up menu to select the proper audio quality for the finished file.**

*5.* **Click Share.**

## Burning an audio CD

Ready to create a demo CD with your latest GarageBand creation? Follow these steps to burn an audio disc from within GarageBand:

*1.* **Open the song that you want to record to disc.**

*2.* **Choose Share⇨Burn Song to CD.**

*3.* **Load a blank disc into your optical drive.**

# Chapter 7: Crafting a Web Site with iWeb

## In This Chapter

✏ **Introducing the iWeb window**

✏ **Planning your site**

✏ **Adding a new site and pages**

✏ **Editing pages**

✏ **Setting site and page attributes with the Inspector**

✏ **Publishing sites to the Internet**

*1* keep telling everyone who'll listen: The Web is *simple.* Or at least it *should* be.

Kids in preschool these days know how to use a browser. Millions of people contribute to FaceBook pages, help to create the dynamic reference wonder that is Wikipedia, and correspond effortlessly through Web-based e-mail. Yet there's one untamed wilderness that many MacBook owners haven't explored — or even set foot in! That's the jungle of *HTML,* the language used to create Web pages. Today's advanced HTML is complex, and it's not particularly fun, either. Have you thrown up your hands and declared, "I guess I'll never get my own Web site on the Internet?"

Forget your Web site envy, fellow Mac enthusiast! With iWeb, Apple has provided a guide through that untamed wilderness . . . and suddenly it's as easy and fun to create a Web site as it is to make a movie or write a song with your MacBook. In this chapter, you discover how to design a site, import your own photos, and add all sorts of different pages.

Soon, you'll proudly hold your head up high and declare to the world, "I am a Webmaster!"

## Looking around the iWeb Window

All of iWeb's major features and controls fit into a single window, naturally, just as it does in iPhoto and iMovie. (I agree with the Apple software designers: *Multiple windows* equals *confusing.*) Figure 7-1 illustrates the iWeb window, complete with a Web site in progress. The stuff to keep your eye on includes:

**Figure 7-1:**
The iWeb
window
holds
everything
you need
to put your
mark on
the Web.

✦ **Toolbar:** Located at the bottom of the window, the iWeb toolbar keeps
all your major controls one or two clicks away.

The iWeb toolbar contains different buttons, depending on the chore
you're handling at the moment. Figure 7-1 shows the set of toolbar buttons that you see when you're editing a page.

✦ **Layout:** You need elbow room to build a Web page, so the Layout section of the iWeb interface dominates the window. You create and edit
your pages in the Layout display and then use it to preview and test-
drive your finished site.

✦ **Site Organizer:** The strip to the left of the layout display is the Site
Organizer, which allows you to organize your Web sites, add new pages
to a site, and select an existing page for editing.

Before we get down to business, it's overview time. You essentially follow
three phases to put your new site on the Web:

*1.* **Decide which pages you need.**

*2.* **Create a new site and build those pages.**

*3.* **Publish your site to your MobileMe account (or to a Web server
using FTP).**

I go over each of these phases in order. (They taught me that in college . . .
along with the history of the Aztecs and the wonders of FIFO accounting.)

# Planning Your Pages

Every properly designed Web site has a purpose: to inform, to entertain, or to provide downloads or contact information. The pages you add to your site should all reflect that common purpose.

iWeb can produce the following types of pages for your site:

✦ **Welcome:** This is the default first page that iWeb adds to a site you create. The Welcome page familiarizes your visitor with the idea behind your site, and perhaps offers a snippet of the latest developments on the site in a "What's New" paragraph.

✦ **About Me:** This page provides a biography of you or another person, listing things like your age, favorite songs, and favorite foods. (After all, that's important stuff.) Links are provided to your photo album pages and other Web sites you want to share.

✦ **Photos:** Oh, this is good stuff here — iWeb makes it easy to add one of those cool online photo galleries for your snapshots, complete with a Web slideshow! You can add Events and albums from iPhoto, too.

✦ **My Albums:** You can organize all your Photos and Movie pages on a single My Albums page. Visitors click a thumbnail to jump to the corresponding Photos page or Movies page — it's a visual index done the *right* way.

✦ **Movie:** Got a QuickTime movie you've created with iMovie to share with others? This is the page that presents it to your adoring fans.

✦ **Blog:** Adding a *Blog* (or personal Web journal) page is a somewhat different beast: iWeb keeps track of each addition you make in an entry list so that you can quickly add or delete entries without requiring tons of scrolling, cutting, and pasting. A Blog page also includes an archive so that deleted entries aren't lost forever.

✦ **Podcast:** Consider a podcast as an audio (or audio/visual) blog — it's designed to be downloaded to a visitor's iPod or computer for later enjoyment. As does the Blog page, a Podcast page has an entry list and an archive list attached to it.

✦ **Blank:** Yep, an old-fashioned blank page, ready for you to fill with whatever you like.

Before you even launch iWeb, jot down on a piece of paper (or put in a Sticky) these important points:

✦ **What message do I want to communicate to visitors?**

✦ **What tone will I use — funny, informal, or businesslike?**

✦ **What stuff do I want to offer: photos, movies, or podcasts?**

Now you have the starting point for your site and you know what you want to include . . . so let's get down with the Web!

# Adding a New Site

When you open iWeb for the first time, the application creates a new site for you, and you can rename and modify this default site to your heart's content. In fact, for many of us, one site is all we ever create — but iWeb can easily handle multiple Web sites, keeping them separate in the Site Organizer.

If there's at least one existing site in your Site Organizer, iWeb automatically displays the last site you were working on. Therefore, if you want to create an entirely new site, you have to perform a little manual labor. Here are a number of different ways to add a site:

✦ **Choose File➪New Site.**

✦ **Press ⌘+Shift+N.**

✦ **Control-click (or right-click) in the Site Organizer and click New Site.**

iWeb leaps into action and displays the template sheet you see in Figure 7-2. Scroll through the template themes in the list at the left of the sheet until you find one that matches the tone you decided on in the previous section. (Informal, formal, or silly, iWeb has templates that match every mood!) Click a template on the left, and the application automatically updates the page type thumbnails on the right.

**Figure 7-2:** Choosing a template for a new site.

When you choose a template, iWeb automatically provides your pages with a common background, color scheme, and fonts so that your finished Web site has a common theme throughout.

After you find the right look and feel, click the desired template in the scrolling list at the left, click the Welcome page thumbnail, and then click the Choose button. iWeb creates a new site heading in the Site Organizer, complete with the default Welcome page. Figure 7-1, shown previously, illustrates the Welcome page from a new site I created with the Main Event template.

## Adding a New Page

Time to add the pages you plan for your site! For example, I've decided to add Photo and About Me pages to the new site I've created. In the following section, I discuss how to edit these pages to personalize them . . . but for now, I just want you to add the pages.

If you have multiple sites in your Site Organizer list, click the top-level heading for the desired site to select it. You can add pages by

+ **Clicking the Add Page button on the toolbar at the bottom of the iWeb window**

+ **Choosing File⇨New Page**

+ **Pressing ⌘+N**

+ **Control-clicking or right-clicking the site header in the Site Organizer and clicking New Page**

Want to start with an existing page as a basis for a new page? Right-click that page entry in the Site Organizer and choose Duplicate. iWeb creates a new page with exactly the same contents and adds it to the site.

Pages are listed under the main site heading in outline format, making it easy to expand or collapse a site by clicking the familiar rotating triangle icon next to the site heading. (Apple calls these *disclosure triangles.* Wowzers!)

Deleting a page — or a whole site, for that matter — is easy in iWeb. Right-click the offending page or site heading in the Site Organizer and choose Delete Page/Delete Site. Note that iWeb doesn't prompt you for confirmation here, so these aren't commands to toy with.

## Editing a Page

If you have your site framework complete, you can actually put your site on the Internet as is! Of course, the photos would all be of good-looking

**Book IV
Chapter 7**

**Crafting a Web Site
with iWeb**

strangers, and most of the text would read like Pig Latin nonsense. (Come to think of it, I've been on some real sites that aren't much better. Go figure.)

I think we both agree, however, that *you* want to personalize your pages with your *own* information. To begin editing a page, click it in the Site Organizer.

## Modifying text

First, update the text with your own information by following these steps:

**1. Click the text you want to replace.**

As do most desktop publishing applications, iWeb uses boxes to enclose text. When you click the text, the box appears, with handles that you can drag to resize the box.

**2. Begin typing your text.**

iWeb replaces the existing template text with the text you type, using the text formatting taken from the template. Don't forget that you can paste text from the Clipboard by pressing ⌘+V. To match the text style of the template, though, press Option+Shift+⌘+V.

Mistakes are *passé* in iWeb. To undo your last action, you can always press the familiar ⌘+Z keyboard shortcut or choose Edit⇨Undo.

**3. Highlight and format your new text as necessary.**

To make changes easier, click the Inspector button in the iWeb toolbar. The window you see in Figure 7-3 appears, allowing you to change text color, alignment, and spacing with aplomb. (You find more about the Inspector later.) You can click the Colors or Fonts buttons on the iWeb toolbar to display a Color Picker or Font Panel for the selected text.

## Don't I have to slave over a hot menu?

You would if you were building a Web site by hand, or if you were using an old-fashioned Web creation application not designed by our favorite company! (Insert smug expression here.)

Let me explain . . . . Every Web site needs a series of links called a *menu* that allows you to jump from one page of the site to another. (For instance, you're probably already familiar with the "tabbed" menu at the top of the Apple Web site that you use to flit from the Mac OS X section to the Support section to the Store section and back again.) In days of old, a site menu was often a nightmare to maintain, especially if your site changed often.

iWeb creates and maintains a menu for each of your sites *automatically* and places it at the top of your pages for you! (You might have noticed that the Welcome menu item already appears in Figure 7-1.) When you add or delete pages, the application updates your menu in the background.

This is the way software is supposed to be designed. Don't you agree?

**Figure 7-3:**
Using the
Inspector
palette to
format text.

**4. Click outside the text box after you're satisfied with the text.**

Because you're likely modifying everything on the template pages from the
title to the last box on the page, repeat Steps 1–4 for each section of text you
want to change.

## Replacing images

If your page includes photographs that you want to change, follow these steps:

**1. Click the image you want to replace.**

As it does with a block of text, iWeb displays a box around the image,
complete with resizing handles.

**2. Drag an image to the image box from a Finder window.**

Alternatively, you can click the Show Media button in the toolbar,
which displays the Media Browser you see in Figure 7-4. From this
window, you can click the Photos tab to choose an image from your
iPhoto library.

You can hide the Media Browser to make more room for your page
layout. Just click the Hide Media button in the toolbar.

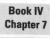

Book IV
Chapter 7

Crafting a Web Site
with iWeb

**Figure 7-4:**
Browsing
my iPhoto
library for
the right
image.

*3.* **Adjust your new image if necessary.**

Click the Adjust button, and iWeb displays a cool, semi-opaque dialog that allows you to tweak image settings, such as tint, brightness, and sharpness (see Figure 7-5). Click Enhance to allow iWeb to choose the settings it considers best for the image or click Reset Image to restore the photo to its original appearance. When you're satisfied with the image, click the Close button on the dialog to return to the image box.

**Figure 7-5:**
Adjusting
an image
in iWeb.

4. **Click outside the image box (usually the page background) after you're satisfied with the photo.**

Again, lather/rinse/repeat for each image you want to change on your page.

## Adding new elements

iWeb also makes it easy to add new items to a page. The list of extras includes

✦ **Audio:** You can add a song (complete with volume control, Play/Pause button, and progress slider) to your page! Either drag an audio file from a Finder window to your page, or click the Audio tab in the Media Browser to select a song from your iTunes or GarageBand collections. You can drag any image to the player that appears. (How about a photo of your daughter instead of album art?)

✦ **Photos:** To add a new image box to your page, drag a photo from a Finder window to the iWeb layout section. Or, click the Photos tab in the Media Browser to choose an image from your iPhoto library, or throw caution to the wind and drag an entire Event or an album to your new page! iWeb takes care of all the details.

✦ **Movies:** Yep, you guessed it. You can drag a movie clip from a Finder window to your page, or click the Movies tab in the Media Browser to choose a movie from iMovie or your Movies folder.

✦ **Text:** Choose Insert⇨Text or click the Text button in the toolbar.

✦ **Shapes:** Click the Shape button in the toolbar to display the pop-up menu and then click the desired shape. (Don't forget to resize it as you desire with the box handles.)

✦ **Widgets:** Click this tab in the Media Browser to insert a *widget* (a Web applet) to your page. For example, HTML Snippet allows you to type HTML code directly into place on the page, or paste HTML code that you've copied from another Web site. You can also insert interactive Google Adsense advertisements or a Google Map. To populate the page with a MobileMe Gallery, choose the MobileMe Gallery widget and select a Gallery you've created using the iPhoto MobileMe Gallery feature. (For the complete scoop on iPhoto, cruise over to Chapter 3 in this mini-book.) Other widgets include a countdown timer and YouTube videos.

You can move a widget anywhere on a page by dragging it, and it can be resized just as a text box can.

✦ **Links:** If you're editing text and you want to insert a Web link, choose Insert⇨Hyperlink and choose from the menu that appears. You can choose to link to another Web page or insert a link that automatically sends an e-mail message to the mail address you provide. You can also offer a file for downloading.

## Doing the slideshow thing

Ready to offer a slideshow on your Web site? Again, we're talking automation here! Add a Photo page to your site and notice that the Start Slideshow button is already in place at the top of the page. All you need to do is add the photos to the page, using the Media Browser or dragging them from a Finder window. When your visitors click the Start Slideshow button, all the photos on the page are displayed in a pop-up window.

It's important to note, however, that some Windows browsers don't support this Slideshow feature. Other Mac and PC owners using Safari can enjoy the show, but don't count on older versions of Internet Explorer (or Firefox) to be able to handle it.

iWeb can automatically detect e-mail and Web addresses that you type in a text box, so you don't have to use the Links menu. To enable this feature, choose iWeb➪Preferences and click the Automatically Detect Email and Web Addresses check box to select it.

✦ **Button:** Your Web page can include buttons that allow your visitors to e-mail you or display the number of hits (visits) your page has received. Choose Insert➪Button and click an option to add or remove a specific button. (If the menu option is selected, the button appears on your page.) Blog and Podcast pages can also offer *RSS feeds* (for automated retrieval of new entries within a Web browser), subscriptions to your podcasts, and slideshows.

With these tools, you can use the Blank page template to create your own new pages. Personally, I prefer to use the professionally designed templates offered by Apple as starting points, removing whatever I don't need and adding new content.

Most Web designers would strongly recommend that you use a common theme for all the pages within a site (to lend continuity). Of course, you can also stick your tongue out at those very same Web designers and select a different theme for every page! To select a different theme for a page, open the page in iWeb and click the Theme button in the toolbar; then click the desired thumbnail from the pop-up menu. Nothing's lost but the old look of the page, so feel free to experiment to your heart's content.

## Tweaking with the Inspector

Earlier, you used the Inspector to change text formatting attributes — but this star performer can do much more than just that! To modify page characteristics, click the page in the Site Organizer, display the Inspector, and click the Page Inspector button, which carries a document icon. These settings allow you to change the name of a page; you can also elect to include or exclude this page from the site menu, or to drop the site menu from this page.

If your site contains a Blog or Podcast page, you can click the RSS button to provide an automated RSS *(RDF Site Summary)* feed to your visitors. (For more information on RSS and how it works in Safari, see Chapter 5 of Book VI.)

## Publishing Your Web Site

After you finish with a new site — or you're satisfied with the edits you make to existing pages — it's time to get your masterpiece on the Web! Even the best Web site design is worth next to nil if it isn't available on the Internet, and in this last section, I demonstrate how to publish your Web site to your MobileMe account or to a separate server maintained by a third party (perhaps your ISP, your company, or Dave down the street).

As I mention in the "Don't forget your site properties!" sidebar, you specify where your iWeb site will be published from the Site Publishing Settings screen. Click the site name in the Site Organizer to display the Publish To pop-up menu (Figure 7-6). iWeb offers the following publishing options:

✦ **Publish to MobileMe:** Your site is hosted by Apple as part of your MobileMe subscription. The application takes care of everything, uploading any changed pages or media.

✦ **Publish to FTP Server:** This publishing option provides you with a completely different collection of settings on the Site Publishing Settings screen. You'll need to furnish iWeb with your Web server's FTP settings (which should be furnished to you by the host) and your site's address (or *URL*).

---

### Don't forget your site properties!

To make global changes to a site, click the site name in the Site Organizer. iWeb switches to the Site Publishing Settings screen (Figure 7-6), where you can change settings such as

✔ The name of the site

✔ Your contact e-mail

✔ Where the site is published (more on this in the next section)

✔ Password protection for MobileMe sites

You can also verify how much space is available on your iDisk, which is where iWeb stores your Web sites if you're a MobileMe member. Heck, iWeb can even update your Facebook profile automatically when you publish your site! What will those Apple designers think of next?

✦ **Publish to a Local Folder:** The final publishing option creates a folder on your hard drive that contains all the files to display your Web site. This is the option to choose if you're not a MobileMe subscriber and you don't use a third-party hosting service. You can add these files directly to your home or business Web server. Once again, you must supply the site URL as it will appear on the Internet after you copy or upload the site files to the server.

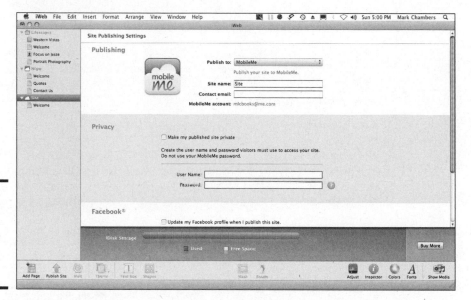

**Figure 7-6:** Setting the publishing method for an iWeb site.

After you've set the type of publishing the site will use, it's time to take care of business! Click the site to select it in the Site Organizer and then click the Publish Site button on the toolbar. The application takes care of everything else, automatically uploading all pages and media (if you choose MobileMe or FTP publishing) or saving them on your hard drive (if you chose the Local Folder option).

In a hurry? You can elect to publish just the changes necessary to update your site: Instead of clicking the Publish Site button on the toolbar, click the File menu and choose Publish Site Changes.

# Chapter 8: No, It's Not Called iQuickTime

## In This Chapter

✔ Viewing movies

✔ Listening to audio

✔ Converting media to different formats

✔ Keeping track of your favorite media

✔ Tweaking QuickTime preferences

QuickTime is a set of exciting technologies that gives you access to the greatest multimedia experience around. Despite its power, don't be surprised if you don't even realize that you're using it sometimes. Built with the average Joe in mind, QuickTime Player takes multimedia to new heights without forcing its users to become rocket scientists in the process.

## QuickTime Can Do That?

QuickTime was created by Apple to perform all sorts of multimedia functions. Although normally associated with movie playback, QuickTime Player can do much more. Whether it's playing movies, audio, animation, or music, QuickTime acts as the main engine that drives all your multimedia needs.

✦ **Media player:** QuickTime Player's main claim to fame is playing all sorts of media — and I do mean *all* sorts. Table 8-1 lists the most popular of the media types that QuickTime can play.

The real beauty of QuickTime Player is that it transparently handles playback of all these media formats and more. You don't even really have to know what each of these formats is to play them. QuickTime Player takes care of that for you.

✦ **Internet media tool:** When it comes to using media from the Internet, QuickTime is in a league all its own. In addition to playing the usual movies and audio files found on the World Wide Web, QuickTime can play (or display) 3-D scenes and animations. As if that weren't enough, QuickTime even lets you interact with some media. For example, with QuickTime, you can navigate within 3-D worlds or play Flash games.

| Table 8-1 | QuickTime Playback Formats |
|---|---|
| *Media Type* | *File Types* |
| Movie | `.mov`*, `.avi`*, `.mpg`, `.dv`, `.mp4`, `3g` (cell phones), `h.263`, `h.264` |
| Audio | `.aiff`, `.wav`, `.mp3`, `.au`, `.sfil`, `.aac`, `.amr` |
| Music | `.mid`, `.kar` |
| 3-D | QTVR (QuickTime Virtual Reality) |
| Animation | `.swf` |

\*Movies in MOV and AVI formats use a wide range of compression schemes, many of them proprietary. For this reason, QuickTime might not be able to play some MOV or AVI movies that you download.

# Playing Media with QuickTime

QuickTime makes a world of movies, audio, graphics, and music instantly available to you. Whether you want to view professional movie trailers or listen to a garage band's new single, QuickTime faithfully reproduces nearly any media format that you feed it.

To launch QuickTime Player, double-click its icon in the Finder. You can also launch QuickTime Player from the Finder by double-clicking a media file that QuickTime can play. (See Table 8-1 earlier in this chapter for a listing of these file types.)

Don't make the mistake of thinking that QuickTime and QuickTime Player are the same thing: *QuickTime* is a technology that hides in the background waiting for instructions to do something with media; *QuickTime Player* is an application that uses the QuickTime technologies. You'll do recording, media conversions, playback, and editing with QuickTime Player. What you won't see is the QuickTime technology in action behind the scenes in applications such as Safari and iTunes.

You can also launch QuickTime Player from its oh-so-convenient Dock icon. For more on the Dock, read Book III, Chapter 2.

## Opening QuickTime movies

To begin viewing and hearing — aw, what the heck, how about *absorbing* — multimedia files, choose File⇨Open File from the QuickTime Player application.

This isn't the only way to open a file with QuickTime Player, though. Some of the other ways to open files with QuickTime Player are

+ **Drag a file to the QuickTime Player icon in the Dock.**

+ **Right-click (or Control-click) a movie and choose Open With; then choose QuickTime Player from the pop-up menu.**

+ **Double-click the media file in the Finder.** If it has a QuickTime-style icon (a blue letter *Q*), it opens automatically in QuickTime Player.

## Operating QuickTime Player

When you open a QuickTime file, QuickTime Player creates a new window to display it. All QuickTime Player windows share some common features:

+ **Close, Minimize, and Zoom controls:** These three controls appear at the top-left corner of most windows in Mac OS X. You probably recognize them by their colors: red, yellow, and green, respectively.

+ **Resize handle:** Drag the lower-right corner of QuickTime Player to resize its movie for playback. Hold Shift while dragging to break free from constrained resizing. If the document contains only sound media, the window grows or shrinks in a horizontal direction when you resize it.

    Any resizing that you perform makes no changes to the original file. QuickTime provides it for your convenience during playback.

Although some window features are common to all QuickTime Player windows, many features depend on the type of media that you wish to play. Table 8-2 lists some of the window features that you might find and the media types associated with those features.

### Table 8-2   QuickTime Player Window Features Based on Media

| Window Feature | Media Type That Uses This Feature |
|---|---|
| Play button | All time-based media: movies, audio, animations, and MIDI |
| Rewind button | All time-based media: movies, audio, animations, and MIDI |
| Fast Forward | All time-based media: movies, audio, animations, and MIDI |
| Timeline | All time-based media: movies, audio, animations, and MIDI |

*(continued)*

**Table 8-2** *(continued)*

| Window Feature | Media Type That Uses This Feature |
|---|---|
| Volume slider | All media with one or more audio tracks |
| Add to iTunes/Share | All media with audio or video |
| Toggle Full Screen | All movies and animations |
| Zoom buttons | QTVR 3-D media |
| Rotate buttons | QTVR 3-D media |
| Mute | All media with one or more audio tracks |

To make your life easier, QuickTime does a lot of work for you behind the scenes each time that it opens a media file. Although you might think that there are different combinations of controls in QuickTime Player, the reality is that the various media windows are more similar than they are different. Figure 8-1 shows the location of various QuickTime Player controls.

**Figure 8-1:** QuickTime Player sports different controls, depending on the media you play.

## Playing media

Playback begins as you might suspect — by clicking the Play button. While a file is playing, the Play button toggles to a Pause button. Click that button to pause playback, which toggles the button back to Play.

Clicking the buttons with double arrows on them advances the playback head at high speed in the direction of the arrows. (Click once to advance at 2x speed; click again to increase the speed.). If the file has audio in it, you hear the playback at high speed, which sounds like an episode of those helium-inhaling Chipmunks. (Remember? *Meee, I waaant a hooola hooop.*) Despite its comical sound, it's helpful for quickly scanning through a file.

You can also advance through the file by dragging the playback head in either direction. This action is permissible while the file is playing or when it's stopped. When you drag the playback head, however, you miss out on the high-speed sound and video that you would get if you used the buttons.

To adjust the volume of a movie, simply move the volume slider left or right. To mute the volume, click the speaker icon to the left of the volume slider.

You can control playback by using the keyboard as well. Table 8-3 summarizes the keyboard shortcuts for playback.

| Table 8-3 | Common Playback Keyboard Shortcuts |
| --- | --- |
| *Keyboard Shortcut* | *What It Does* |
| Spacebar | Starts or stops the player |
| Left/right arrow | Advances the playback head (either one frame at a time or in slow motion) |
| Option+Up/down arrow | Sets the volume to Maximum and Minimum, respectively |
| Up/down arrow | Increases/decreases the volume of the current movie |

Sometimes you might want to play a piece of media more than once. In these situations, you need to loop the playback. To force a movie to loop, choose View⇨Loop or press ⌘+L. Press ⌘+L again to turn off looping.

### Movie info

To see more information about the files that you're playing, ask the expert: QuickTime Player. To view basic information about a movie, choose Window⇨ Show Movie Inspector or press ⌘+I. The resulting window displays the following data:

✦ **Source:** Location of the file

✦ **Format:** Compressor and dimensions of the file

## Recording audio, video, and screens in QuickTime Player

Most folks don't think of QuickTime Player as a recording application. That's because Apple provides applications (such as Photo Booth, iMovie, and GarageBand) that have long been the recording tools of choice in the Mac universe. However, you can indeed record audio, video, and your MacBook's screen display with QuickTime Player, since your laptop is already equipped with the proper hardware (a microphone or line-in device for audio, and an iSight camera or external video camera for video).

When you're ready to record, click File and choose either New Movie Recording, New Audio Recording, or New Screen Recording. You can select your input sources, recording quality, and saved file location by clicking the button with the down arrow. When all the settings are correct, the process itself is a one-click operation: Click the Big Red Button to start and stop recording. QuickTime displays both the recording time and the approximate hard drive space used so far. 'Nuff said.

✦ **FPS:** Preferred rate of playback in frames per second (fps), shown only for video

✦ **Playing FPS:** Actual rate of playback in fps (available during playback only), shown only for video

✦ **Data Size:** Size of the file

✦ **Data Rate:** Preferred rate of playback (in bytes per second)

✦ **Current Time:** Position of the playback head (in units of time)

✦ **Current Size:** Actual movie dimensions (if you've resized the movie since opening the file)

These bits and pieces of information are *read-only* — you can't change them from the Movie Inspector window.

If you'd like to share a multimedia file with others from your MobileMe home page on the Web, choose File⇨Share. After you've typed a name and description for your new file, you can optionally click the Allow Movies to be Downloaded check box to let others download the movie from your MobileMe page. Click Publish, and QuickTime automatically takes care of the rest. Slick as a wet toad!

# Chapter 9: Turning Your MacBook into a DVD Theater

## In This Chapter

✔ Ensuring that you have what you need to watch DVDs on your laptop

✔ Using the DVD Player software

✔ Unearthing the mysteries of the hidden controls

All the creative capabilities of the Mac OS X digital hub are a lot of fun, but at some point, you'll want to take a break from work. In recent years, DVDs have exploded onto the home entertainment scene; because of its high fidelity, convenience, and seemingly limitless storage capacity, the DVD has taken consumers by storm. The idea of an honest-to-goodness theater in your home is now within the grasp of mere mortals (with, coincidentally, merely average budgets). Mac OS X has everything that you'll need to enjoy a night at the movies without ever leaving home. In fact, I highly recommend the 17-inch MacBook Pro for those widescreen classics.

## The DVD Hardware

Before you watch one second of film, get your setup in order. Playing DVDs requires a bit of hardware; fortunately, all recent MacBook models (except the MacBook Air) come equipped with the stuff that's necessary to watch DVDs.

To play DVD movies, you need either an internal DVD-compatible drive in your Macintosh or an external DVD drive with a FireWire or USB 2.0 connection. DVD-ROM drives can only play discs, whereas others, such as the SuperDrive, can both play and record discs. Either type of drive works fine for watching movies on your MacBook.

You can watch any standard DVD that you purchase at your local video store as well as any DVD that you create with iDVD. (For more on iDVD, read Book IV, Chapter 5.)

## The DVD Player: It's Truly Shiny

To watch Frodo Baggins, Don Corleone, or James Bond, you need DVD player software. Mac OS X comes stocked with the perfect tool for the task: DVD Player.

Apple's DVD Player application is included with Mac OS X; you can find it within the confines of your Applications folder. But instead of rooting through the Finder, you can launch DVD Player an even easier way: Simply insert a DVD into the drive. As soon as you do, your MacBook recognizes the disc and launches DVD Player by default for you. (Time for another round of well-deserved gloating about your choice of personal computer.)

This automatic behavior (the DVD playing — not necessarily the gloating) can be curbed, however. You can control what action Snow Leopard takes (if any) when you load a DVD via the CDs & DVDs pane within System Preferences. For all the details, visit Book III, Chapter 3.

However you choose to start DVD Player, you'll notice that it offers two windows:

✦ **Controller:** The small, silver-colored, remote control–looking interface that holds all the controls for the Player

✦ **Viewer:** The large window where you view your DVD movies

In the default Full-Screen mode, of course, you won't see the Viewer window, and the video will take up the entire screen. The controller appears as a floating opaque strip of controls along the bottom of the screen. To display the controls, move your mouse cursor to the bottom of the screen. Move the cursor to the top of the screen and you can switch chapters and jump to bookmarks. (I talk about both later in the chapter.)

If you're already using a traditional DVD player, you'll be right at home with Apple's DVD Player. Even if you've never used a traditional DVD player, you'll find that it's not much different from using a software-based audio player such as iTunes.

## Using the controller

The *controller* is the command center of the DVD Player software. Arranged much the same as a VCR or tape deck's controls, all the familiar controls are present. Check it out in Figure 9-1.

**Figure 9-1:**
Use the controller for mundane playback chores.

## Jumping right to the flying-monkey action

Movies on DVD usually are divided into *chapters* that enable you to jump directly to specific points. That way, you can jump right to the scene, say, where the flying monkey guards march into the Wicked Witch's castle in *The Wizard of Oz*. (Or skip that egg-hatching scene in *Alien* that always makes you nauseated.)

You can navigate to chapters, play the movie from the beginning, or check out special bonus features (such as trailers and documentaries) from the DVD's main menu. To switch to a different chapter in Full-Screen mode, move your mouse to the top of the screen.

Table 9-1 details the fundamental commands present in the DVD Player Controller. Apple software usually has some goodies hidden beneath the surface, and DVD Player is no exception. The controls in DVD Player have a few functions that might not be obvious to the casual user. These are listed in the third column of Table 9-1.

| Table 9-1 | Basic DVD Controls | |
|---|---|---|
| *Control Name* | *What It Does* | *Other Functions* |
| Play | Plays the DVD | Switches into a Pause button anytime a movie is playing. |
| Stop | Stops playback of the DVD | |
| Previous Chapter | Skips to the previous chapter | Click and hold the button to quickly scan through the movie in reverse. |
| Next Chapter | Skips to the next chapter | Click and hold the button to quickly scan forward through the movie. |
| Playback Volume | Adjusts the volume of the DVD audio | |
| Arrow Buttons | Navigates through the menu items of the DVD | |
| Enter | Selects the currently highlighted menu item | |
| Eject | Ejects the DVD from the drive | |
| Title | Jumps immediately to the DVD's title menu | |
| Menu | Displays the menu of the current DVD | |

**Book IV**
**Chapter 9**

Turning Your
MacBook into
a DVD Theater

### Keeping your eyes on the Viewer

As soon as you begin playing with the DVD Player controls, you'll notice activity in the Viewer window, as shown in Figure 9-2.

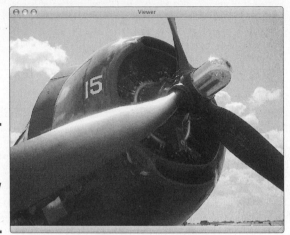

**Figure 9-2:**
The Viewer is the real star of Snow Leopard's DVD Player.

You can think of the Viewer window as a television inside your Macintosh, if it helps, but DVD Player goes one step further. Unlike a television screen, the Viewer has some nice tricks up its sleeve: For example, you can resize the Viewer window by using one of the four sizes listed in the View menu (Half, Actual Size, Double Size, Fit to Screen, and Full-Screen sizes). This is useful for watching a movie in a small window on your Desktop while you work with other applications. You can toggle your Viewer size from the keyboard; for example, select Half Size with ⌘+0 (zero), Actual Size with ⌘+1 (one), and Double Size with ⌘+2 (two).

If you're only in it for the entertainment factor, you'll probably want to resize the Viewer to fill the screen. I like to watch movies in Full-Screen mode, which you can toggle with the ⌘+F keyboard shortcut. If you want to take full advantage of all your screen space yet leave the Viewer window on-screen for occasional resizing, choose Fit to Screen mode with ⌘+3 (three).

## Taking Advantage of Additional DVD Features

As anyone with a little DVD experience knows, DVDs can do a lot more than those archaic tapes that you used to feed your VCR. Apple has included several functions that allow you to explore the extra features and content provided with a DVD movie.

## Controller extras

To use the additional controller features, double-click the small tab at the rightmost (or bottom) edge of the DVD Player Controller. After you do, a trick drawer slides out, displaying the extra controls. (See Figure 9-3.) You can also display or hide the drawer with the Controls⇨Open/Close Control Drawer menu command or by pressing ⌘+] (that's the right bracket key).

**Figure 9-3:**
Expand the controller to view additional controls.

Are you interested in fine-tuning the audio from your DVD movies? If so, choose Window⇨Audio Equalizer, and DVD Player displays a ten-band equalizer. (I often use this feature to add extra bass to a concert DVD.) Click the pop-up menu at the upper right of the Equalizer window, and you can choose a preset (such as Bass Boost or Vocal Boost), or even create your own custom audio presets.

Table 9-2 summarizes the functions that you can perform with these additional controls.

| Table 9-2 | Additional Controller Features |
|-----------|-------------------------------|
| **Control** | **What It Does** |
| Slow Motion (half speed) | Plays a DVD in slow motion at half the original speed |
| Step Button (frame speed) | Steps through a DVD in ultra-slow motion, one frame at a time |
| Return | Navigates to the previous menu |
| Subtitle/Closed Captioning | Displays alternate subtitles and closed captioning on the DVD |
| Audio | Plays alternate audio tracks on the DVD |
| Angle | Displays the current video footage from different camera angles |

**Book IV
Chapter 9**

**Turning Your
MacBook into
a DVD Theater**

Although you won't find a Bookmark button on the controller, DVD Player can set them nonetheless. A *bookmark* is a spot, like a favorite scene, that you specify in a movie so that you can return to it at any time. To set a bookmark at the current spot in the movie, click the Controls menu and choose New Bookmark, or press ⌘+= (the equal sign key). DVD Player even allows you to name the bookmark so that it's easier to remember. To return to a bookmark, choose Go⇨Bookmarks and click the desired bookmark. (If you're enjoying your movie in Full-Screen mode, move your cursor to the top of the screen to use the Bookmarks strip.)

## DVD Player preferences

The DVD Player application has a variety of settings that you can access and adjust via its Preferences window. To open the Preferences window, choose DVD Player⇨Preferences. This brings up the Preferences dialog.

This window consists of six panes:

✦ **Player:** Settings that affect how DVD Player operates

✦ **Disc Setup:** Settings for Audio, Subtitles, Language, and the Web

✦ **Full Screen:** Settings that determine your full-screen viewing configuration

✦ **Windows:** Settings for displaying on-screen information during playback

✦ **Previously Viewed:** Settings that determine what happens when you load a DVD that you watched already

✦ **High Definition:** Settings that specify how high-definition video is displayed on your MacBook

The advantage of these Preference settings is that you can customize your copy of DVD Player to match your needs or desires. (Thanks yet again to the Cupertino Crowd!)

### Player

The Player settings take care of much of the automation within DVD Player.

✦ **When DVD Player Opens:** These two check boxes affect what happens when you launch the DVD Player application. You can force DVD Player to play in Full-Screen mode and automatically begin playback every time you start the application.

✦ **When DVD Player Is Inactive:** If you're multitasking while watching your movie in windowed mode, you can click another window to make it active. This check box determines whether DVD Player will automatically pause while you're working in that other application.

✦ **When a Disc Is Inserted:** Besides automatic playback on startup, you can also make DVD Player start playing a disc automatically when the application is running already. (To illustrate: If this check box is dese-lected, loading a new disc won't automatically start it playing if DVD Player is already running.)

✦ **When Playing Using Battery:** MacBook owners love this feature, since you can conserve power while using DVD Player by selecting this check box. The DVD Player will "spin down" the DVD whenever possible, which may cause a short delay when you fast forward or rewind.

✦ **When Muted:** Do you answer a lot of telephone calls while you sneak a quick DVD movie at work? If so, be sure to enable this option. If you have to press the Mute button on your keyboard while a movie is play-ing, DVD Player automatically adds the subtitles/closed captions so that you can keep up with the dialog. *Super sassy!*

✦ **During iChat with Audio:** Another option for those who like to run mul-tiple applications simultaneously. If you're watching a DVD and start an audio or video chat in iChat AV, you can choose to either mute the DVD audio or pause the DVD playback until you click Play again.

✦ **When Viewer Is Minimized:** Watching a DVD at the office, eh? Enable this check box, and DVD Player automatically pauses the movie when you minimize the DVD Player window; otherwise, the movie continues playing in the tiny Dock icon. (Managers label this feature *downright sneaky*.)

## Disc Setup

The second tab of the Player Preferences window consists of these controls:

✦ **Language:** Sprechen Sie Deutsch? DVDs are designed to be multilanguage-aware. Feel like brushing up on your German, Spanish, or Chinese? You can control the language used for the audio, subtitling, and menus in this section.

✦ **Internet:** Some DVDs with DVD@ccess support can access information on the Internet. Mark this check box to allow that function.

✦ **Audio:** Click this pop-up menu to specify the default audio output signal that you'd like to use. You can also choose to disable the Dolby dynamic range compression feature, which might enhance the sound for two-speaker systems; however, you don't want to damage the lower-output speakers on a MacBook, so I recommend that laptop owners leave dynamic range compression enabled (unless you're using external speakers).

Multiple languages and Web access are not mandatory features of a DVD, so don't be surprised if you see variations of support when it comes to these settings.

## Full Screen

These Preference settings control the default screen display settings within DVD Player.

✦ **Controller:** I generally like to hide the controller after a defined time of inactivity; select the Hide Controller If Inactive for *xx* Seconds check box if you agree. To set the delay period, click in the seconds box and type a new value.

✦ **Displays:** These options specify how DVD Player shares your Desktop with others: politely or downright rudely. You can choose to automatically dim other monitors while a movie is playing (if you have more than one display connected to your Mac), and DVD Player can stay in Full-Screen mode even if another application actually has the active window. Finally, you can choose to remove the menu bar altogether (often called *kiosk mode*), which helps cut down on interruptions and accidents if small hands are nearby — and you can optionally allow Snow Leopard's screen saver to appear on the DVD Menu in kiosk mode.

## Windows

This pane gives you the chance to configure the behavior of the controller and status information for the Viewer window.

✦ **Options:** Mark the Display Status Information check box, and DVD Player adds a small text box at the top-left corner of the Viewer window. In this text box, you see the name of the last task that you performed with DVD Player. For example, click the Stop button to see the word Stop displayed in the Viewer on top of the video beneath it. You can also set the controller to fade away instead of just disappear — it's eye candy, but doggone it, it's *good* eye candy!

✦ **Closed Captioned:** If you do decide to display the closed-caption text from a DVD movie, you can click the color buttons to specify the text color. You can also choose the font for your text.

## Previously Viewed

This pane controls what happens when you load a disc that you've seen already . . . or perhaps your significant other watched it and didn't tell you. (Insert growling noise here.)

✦ **Start Playing Discs From:** If you have to quit DVD Player for some reason, the application is smart enough to remember where you were, and you can choose to begin watching from the beginning, from the last position (where you were when you stopped the last time), or from a default bookmark. Alternatively, just select Always Ask, and DVD Player will prompt you each time this situation crops up.

✦ **Always Use Disc Settings For:** Select these check boxes to specify whether DVD Player should use the same settings you used the last time you watched this disc.

### High Definition

The final DVD Player Preferences pane specifies how both standard DV and high-definition video from a disc you've created in DVD Studio Pro are displayed within the Viewer window. (As I mentioned earlier, the Viewer window size can also be changed from the View menu, but the settings in this pane control what defaults DVD Player uses.)

✦ **For Standard Definition:** You can choose to display the actual video size by default, or to use the default size provided by the DVD.

✦ **For High Definition:** These options affect how a high-definition video signal is displayed. Your choices include the actual video size, a height of 720 pixels, and a height of 1,080 pixels.

Don't forget to click OK to save any changes you make to your DVD Player preferences.

After you have your DVD Player customized to your liking, get out the popcorn, pull up your favorite recliner, and let the movies roll!

# Book V

# iWork for the Road Warrior

The 5th Wave                    By Rich Tennant

"I can be reached at home on my cell phone, I can be reached on the road with my pager and PDA. Soon I'll be reachable on a plane with e-mail. I'm beginning to think identity theft wouldn't be such a bad idea for a while."

# Contents at a Glance

## Chapter 1: Desktop Publishing with Pages.....................447

Creating a New Pages Document................................447
Open an Existing Pages Document..............................448
Saving Your Work...........................................449
Touring the Pages Window....................................449
Entering and Editing Text...................................451
Using Text and Graphics Boxes...............................451
The Three Amigos: Cut, Copy, and Paste......................452
Formatting Text the Easy Way................................453
Adding a Spiffy Table.......................................454
Adding Alluring Photos......................................455
Adding a Background Shape...................................457
Are You Sure about That Spelling?...........................457
Printing Your Pages Documents...............................458
Sharing That Poster with Others.............................459

## Chapter 2: Creating Spreadsheets with Numbers ...............461

Before We Launch Numbers . . ...............................461
Creating a New Numbers Document.............................462
Opening an Existing Spreadsheet File........................462
Save Those Spreadsheets!....................................464
Exploring the Numbers Window................................464
Navigate and Select Cells in a Spreadsheet..................465
Entering and Editing Data in a Spreadsheet..................466
Selecting the Right Number Format...........................467
Aligning Cell Text Just So..................................467
Format with Shading.........................................469
Insert and Delete Rows and Columns..........................470
The Formula Is Your Friend..................................471
Adding Visual Punch with a Chart............................472

## Chapter 3: Building Presentations with Keynote ...............475

Creating a New Keynote Project..............................476
Opening a Keynote Presentation..............................477
Saving Your Presentation....................................477
Putting Keynote to Work.....................................478
Adding Slides...............................................479
Working with Text and Graphics Boxes .......................479
Adding and Editing Slide Text...............................481
Formatting Slide Text for the Perfect Look..................481
Using Presenter's Notes in Your Project.....................482
Every Good Presentation Needs Media.........................482
Adding a Background Shape...................................482
Creating Your Keynote Slideshow.............................483
Printing Your Slides and Notes..............................484

# Chapter 1: Desktop Publishing with Pages

## In This Chapter

✔ **Creating a Pages document**

✔ **Entering and editing text**

✔ **Formatting text**

✔ **Inserting tables and graphics**

✔ **Resizing objects**

✔ **Checking your spelling**

✔ **Printing Pages documents**

✔ **Sharing your work**

**W**hat's the difference between word processing and desktop publishing? In a nutshell, it's in how you *design* your document. Most folks use a word processor like an old-fashioned typewriter. Think Microsoft Word and a typical business letter. (Yawn.)

On the other hand, a desktop publishing application typically allows you far more creativity in choosing where you place your text, how you align graphics, and how you edit formats. I think desktop publishing is more visual and intuitive, allowing your imagination a free hand at creating a document.

In this chapter, I show you how to set your inner designer free from the tedious constraints of word processing! Whether you need a simple letter, a stunning brochure, or a multipage newsletter, Pages '09 can handle the job with ease — and you'll be surprised at how simple it is to use.

## Creating a New Pages Document

Every visual masterpiece starts somewhere, and with Pages, the first stop in creating your document is the Template Chooser window. To create a new Pages document from scratch, follow these steps:

1. **Double-click your hard drive icon and click the Applications entry in the Finder window sidebar. Double-click the iWork folder to open it.**

   The iWork installation program offers to add a Pages icon to your Dock. If you'll be using Pages often, it's a good idea to use this option!

2. **Double-click the Pages icon.**

   Pages displays the Template Chooser window that you see in Figure 1-1.

**Figure 1-1:** Selecting a template from the Template Chooser window.

3. **Click the type of document you want to create in the list to the left. The thumbnails on the right are updated with templates that match your choice.**

4. **Click the template that most closely matches your needs.**

5. **Click Choose to open a new document by using the template you selected.**

## Open an Existing Pages Document

Of course, you can always open a Pages document from a Finder window — just double-click the document icon. However, you can also open a Pages document from within the program. Follow these steps:

*1.* **Double-click the Pages icon to run the program.**

*2.* **Press ⌘+O to display the Open dialog.**

The Open dialog operates much the same as a Finder window in icon, list, or column view mode.

*3.* **Click the desired drive in the Devices list at the left of the dialog and then click folders and subfolders until you've located the Pages document.**

*4.* **Double-click the filename to load it.**

If you want to open a Pages document that you've edited in the recent past, things get even easier! Just click File➪Open Recent, and you can open the document with a single click from the submenu that appears.

## Saving Your Work

To save a Pages document after you finish it (or to take a break while designing), follow these steps:

*1.* **Press ⌘+S.**

If you're saving a document that hasn't yet been saved, the familiar Save As sheet appears.

*2.* **Type a filename for your new document.**

*3.* **Click the Where pop-up menu and choose a location to save the document.**

Alternatively, click the button sporting the down arrow to expand the Save As sheet. This allows you to navigate to a different location, or to create a new folder to store this Pages project.

*4.* **Click Save.**

## Touring the Pages Window

Before we dive into any real work, let me show you around the Pages window! You'll find the following major components and controls, as shown in Figure 1-2:

✦ **Pages list:** This thumbnail list displays all the pages you've created within your document. (For a single-page document, of course, the Page list will contain only a single thumbnail.) You can switch instantly between different pages in your document by clicking the desired thumbnail in the list.

✦ **Layout pane:** This section takes up most of the Pages window — it's where you design and edit each page in your document.

✦ **Toolbar:** Yep, Pages has its own toolbar. The toolbar keeps all the most common application controls within easy, one-click reach.

✦ **Styles Drawer:** This window extension allows you to quickly switch the appearance of selected paragraphs, characters, and lists. You can hide and display the Styles Drawer from the View menu or from the View drop-down menu on the toolbar.

✦ **Format Bar:** This button strip runs underneath the Pages toolbar, allowing you to format selected text, paragraphs, and lists on the fly.

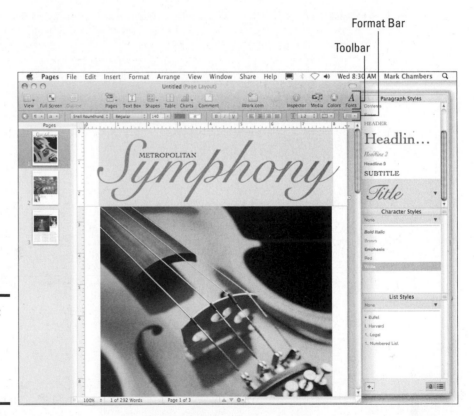

Format Bar

Toolbar

**Figure 1-2:**
The major
points of
interest in
the Pages
window.

# Entering and Editing Text

If you've used a modern word processing program on any computer —
including "freebies" such as TextEdit on a Mac or WordPad on a PC — you'll
feel right at home typing within Pages. Just in case, however, let's review the
high points:

✦ The bar-shaped text cursor, which looks like a capital letter *I*, indicates
  where the text you enter will appear within a Pages document.

✦ To enter text, simply begin typing. Your characters appear at the text
  cursor.

✦ To edit existing text in your Pages document, click the insertion cursor
  at any point in the text and drag the insertion cursor across the characters to highlight them. Type the replacement text, and Pages automatically replaces the existing characters with the ones you type.

✦ To delete text, click and drag across the characters to highlight them;
  then press Delete.

# Using Text and Graphics Boxes

Within Pages, text and graphics appear in *boxes*, which can be resized by
clicking and dragging on one of the handles that appear around the edges of
the box. (Hover your cursor over one of the square handles and you'll see
that it changes to a double-sided arrow, indicating that Pages is ready to
resize the box.)

You can also move a box, including all the stuff it contains, to another location within the Layout pane. Click in the center of the box and drag the box
to the desired spot. Note that Pages displays blue alignment lines to help
you align the box with other elements around it (or with regular divisions
of the page, such as the vertical center of a poster or flyer). Figure 1-3 illustrates a box containing text that I'm moving; note the vertical alignment line
that automatically appears.

To select text or graphics within a box, you must first click the box to select
it and then click again on the line of text or the graphic that you want to
change.

**Figure 1-3:**
Moving a
text box
within the
Layout
pane.

# The Three Amigos: Cut, Copy, and Paste

"Hang on, Mark, you've covered moving stuff, but what if you want to *copy* a block of text or a photo to a second location? Or how about cutting something from a document open in another application?" Good questions, dear reader! That's when you can call on the power of the cut, copy, and paste features within Pages. The next few sections explain how you do these actions.

## Cutting stuff

Cutting selected text or graphics removes it from your Pages document and places that material within your Clipboard. (Think of the Clipboard as a holding area for snippets of text and graphics that you want to manipulate.) To cut text or graphics, select some material and do one of the following:

✦ Choose Edit⇨Cut.

✦ Press ⌘+X.

If you simply want to remove the selected material from your Pages document (and you don't plan to paste it somewhere else), just select the text and press the Delete key.

## Copying text and images

When you copy text or graphics, the original selection remains untouched, but a copy of the selection is placed in the Clipboard. Select some text or graphics and do one of the following:

✦ Choose Edit⇨Copy.

✦ Press ⌘+C.

If you cut or copy a new selection into the Clipboard, it erases what was there. In other words, the Clipboard holds only the latest material you cut or copied.

## Pasting from the Clipboard

Are you wondering what you can do with all that stuff that's accumulating in your Clipboard? Pasting the contents of the Clipboard places the material at the current location of the insertion cursor. You can repeat a paste operation as often as you like because the contents of the Clipboard aren't cleared. However, remember that the Clipboard holds only the contents of your *last* copy or cut operation, so you must paste the contents before you cut or copy again to avoid losing what's in the Clipboard.

To paste the Clipboard contents, click the insertion cursor at the location you want and do one of the following:

✦ Choose Edit⇨Paste.

✦ Press ⌘+V.

# Formatting Text the Easy Way

If you feel that some (or all) of the text in your Pages document needs a face-lift, you can format that text any way you like. Formatting lets you change the color, font family, character size, and attributes as necessary.

After the text is selected, you can apply basic formatting in two ways:

✦ **Use the Format bar.** The Format bar appears directly underneath the Pages toolbar, as shown in Figure 1-2. Click to select a font control to display a pop-up menu and then click your choice. For example, click the Font Family button and you can change the font family from Arial to a more daring font. You can also select characteristics such as the font's background color (perfect for "highlighting" items) or choose italicizing or bolding. The Format Bar also provides buttons for text alignment (Align Left, Center, Align Right, and Justify).

✦ **Use the Format menu.** Most controls on the Format Bar are also available from the Format menu. Click Format and hover the mouse cursor over the Font menu item, and you can then apply bolding, italicizing, and underlining to the selected text. You can also make the text bigger or smaller. To change the alignment from the Format menu, click Format and hover the mouse cursor over the Text menu item.

## Adding a Spiffy Table

In the world of word processing, a *table* is a grid that holds text or graphics for easy comparison. Many computer owners think of a spreadsheet program like Numbers when they think of a table (probably because of the rows and columns layout used in a spreadsheet), but you can create a custom table layout within Pages with a few simple mouse clicks.

Follow these steps:

1. **Click the insertion cursor at the location where you want the table to appear.**

2. **Click the Table button on the Pages toolbar.**

   Pages inserts a simple table and displays the Table Inspector. (Both are visible in Figure 1-4.)

   By default, Pages creates a table with three rows and three columns, with an extra row for headings at the top. You can change this layout from the Table Inspector — just click in the Body Rows or Body Columns box and type a number.

3. **Click within a cell in the table to enter text. The table cell automatically resizes and "wraps" the text you enter to fit.**

   You can paste material from the Clipboard into a table. See the earlier section "Pasting from the Clipboard" for details on pasting.

4. **To change the borders on a cell, click the cell to select it and then click one of the Cell Border buttons to change the border.**

   Select a range of multiple cells in a table by holding down Shift as you click. Hold down ⌘ and click to select multiple cells that aren't contiguous.

5. **To add a background color (or even fill cells with an image for a background), click the Cell Background pop-up menu and choose a type of background.**

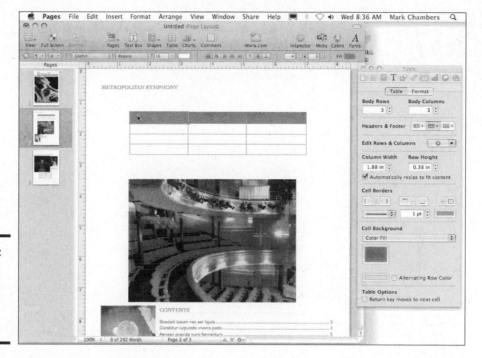

**Figure 1-4:**
Preparing
to tweak
a table in
my Pages
document

# Adding Alluring Photos

You can choose from two methods of adding a picture within your Pages document: as a *floating* object, meaning that you can place the image in a particular spot and it doesn't move, even if you make changes to the text; and as an *inline* object, which flows with the surrounding text as you make layout changes.

✦ **Add a floating object.** Drag an image file from a Finder window and place it at the spot you want within your document. Alternatively, you can click the Media button on the toolbar and click Photos, navigate to the location where the file is saved, and drag the image thumbnail to the spot you want in the document. Figure 1-5 illustrates the Media Browser in action.

Note that a floating object (such as a shape or image) can be sent to the *background*, where text will not wrap around it. To bring a background object back as a regular floating object, click the object to select it and click Arrange⇨Bring Background Objects to Front. (More about background objects later in this chapter.)

**Figure 1-5:**
Hey, isn't
that the
Pages
Media
Browser?

✦ **Add an inline object.** Hold down the ⌘ key as you drag an image file from a Finder window and place it where you want within your document. You can also click the Media toolbar button and click Photos to display the Media Browser. Navigate to the location where the file is saved, hold down the ⌘ key, and drag the image thumbnail to the spot where you want it in the document.

# Manipulating images for fun and profit

If you add an image that appears too large or distorted within your Pages document, you can resize it at any time to correct the problem. To resize an image object, click the image to select it and then drag one of the selection handles that appear along the border of the image. (They look like tiny squares.) The side-selection handles drag only that edge of the frame, whereas the corner-selection handles resize both adjoining edges of the selection frame.

When you hold down the Shift key as you drag, Pages preserves the aspect ratio of the image so that the vertical and horizontal proportions remain fixed.

You can also flip images. Click Arrange on the Pages menu bar to flip the image horizontally or vertically.

# Adding a Background Shape

To add a shape (such as a rectangle or circle) as a background for your text, follow these steps:

*1.* **Click the insertion cursor in the location you want.**

*2.* **Click the Shapes button on the Pages toolbar and choose a shape.**

The shape appears in your document.

*3.* **Click the center of the shape and drag it to a new spot.**

Shapes can be resized or moved in the same manner as image boxes.

*4.* **Before you can type over a shape, remember to select it and choose Arrange⇨Send Object to Background.**

# Are You Sure about That Spelling?

Pages can check spelling as you type (the default setting) or check it after you complete your document. If you find automatic spell-checking distracting, you should definitely pick the latter method.

To check spelling as you type, follow these steps:

*1.* **Click Edit and hover the cursor over the Spelling menu item.**

*2.* **Click Check Spelling As You Type** in the submenu that appears.

If a possible misspelling is found, Pages underlines the word with a red, dashed line.

*3.* **Right-click the word to choose a possible correct spelling from the list, or you can ignore the word if it's spelled correctly.**

To turn off automatic spell checking, click the Check Spelling As You Type menu item again to deselect it.

To check spelling manually, follow these steps:

*1.* **Click within the document to place the text insertion cursor where the spell check should begin.**

*2.* **Click Edit and hover the mouse cursor over the Spelling menu item; then choose Check Spelling** from the submenu that appears.

*3.* **Right-click any possible misspellings and choose the correct spelling, or choose Ignore if the word is spelled correctly.**

## Printing Your Pages Documents

Ready to start the presses? You can print your Pages document on real paper, of course, but don't forget that you can also save a tree by creating an electronic, PDF-format document instead of a printout. (For the lowdown on PDF printing, visit Chapter 4 in Book VIII.)

To print your Pages document on old-fashioned paper, follow these steps:

1.  **Within Pages, click File and choose Print.**

    Pages displays the Print sheet you see in Figure 1-6. (Some settings may vary depending on your printer's specific features.)

2.  **Click in the Copies field and enter the number of copies you need.**

3.  **Select the pages to print.**

    *   To print the entire document, select All.

    *   To print a range of selected pages, select the From radio button and enter the starting and ending pages.

4.  **Click the Print button to send the document to your printer.**

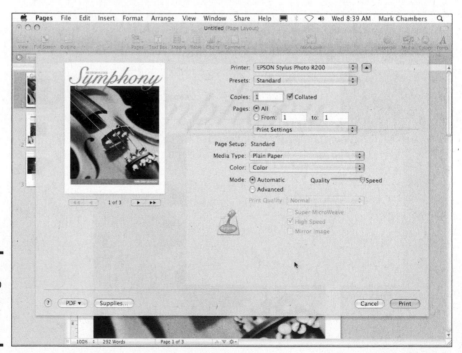

**Figure 1-6:**
Preparing to print a work of art within Pages.

# Sharing That Poster with Others

Besides printing — which is, after all, so passé — you can choose to share your Pages document electronically in a number of ways:

✦ **Sharing on iWork.com.** Apple provides a Web site, `iwork.com`, where you can invite others to view and comment on your Pages document. Click the iWork.com button on the Pages toolbar to get started, and the site will walk you through the rest of the process.

You'll need an Internet connection to use iWork.com (naturally), as well as an Apple ID and a working Apple Mail account. If you didn't create an Apple ID when buying your MacBook or installing Snow Leopard, you can save the day by clicking the Create New Account button on the iWork.com site. If you're not using Apple Mail yet, peruse Book VI, Chapter 2 for all the details.

✦ **Sharing through e-mail.** Click Share⇨Send via Mail, and you can choose to add your Pages document to a Mail message in three different formats: as a native Pages document file, as a Word format document, or as a PDF file. After you've selected a format, Pages obligingly launches Apple Mail for you automatically and creates a new message, ready for you to address and send!

✦ **Sharing through iWeb.** Again, click the Share menu, but this time choose Send to iWeb. Pages automatically opens the iWeb site you last edited and provides your Pages document as a native Pages document file or as a PDF file. (If your visitors may be using PCs or Linux, choose the PDF option.)

✦ **Exporting.** Don't forget that Pages can export your work in one of four different formats: a PDF document; a Word format document; an RTF (Rich Text Format) file; or even plain text. Click Share⇨Export, pick your format, click Next, and then select the location where Pages should save the file. Click Export and sit back while your favorite desktop publishing application does all the work.

To keep your document as close to how it appears in Pages as possible, I recommend either PDF or Word. Your document will retain far more of your original formatting than an RTF or plain-text document would.

# Chapter 2: Creating Spreadsheets with Numbers

## In This Chapter

✓ Opening, saving, and creating spreadsheets

✓ Selecting cells

✓ Entering and editing cell data

✓ Formatting cells

✓ Adding and removing rows and columns

✓ Creating simple calculations

✓ Adding charts to your spreadsheets

✓ Printing a Numbers spreadsheet

A re you downright afraid of spreadsheets? Does the idea of building a budget with charts and all sorts of fancy graphics send you running for the safety of the hall closet? Well, good MacBook owner, Apple has once again taken something that everyone else considers super-complex and turned it into something that normal human beings can use! (Much as Apple did with video editing, songwriting, and Web site creation — heck, is there *any* type of software that Apple designers can't make intuitive and easy to use?)

In this chapter, I get to demonstrate how Numbers can help you organize data, analyze important financial decisions, and yes, even maintain a household budget! You'll soon see why the Numbers spreadsheet program is specifically designed with the home Mac owner in mind.

## Before We Launch Numbers . . .

Just in case you're not familiar with applications like Numbers and Microsoft Excel — and the documents they create — let me provide you with a little background information.

A *spreadsheet* organizes and calculates numbers by using a grid system of rows and columns. The intersection of each row and column is a *cell*, and cells can hold either text or numeric values (along with calculations that are usually linked to the contents of other, surrounding cells).

Spreadsheets are wonderful tools for making decisions and comparisons because they let you "plug in" different numbers — such as interest rates or your monthly insurance premium — and instantly see the results. Some of my favorite spreadsheets that I use regularly include

✦ Car and mortgage loan comparisons

✦ A college planner

✦ My household budget (not that we pay any attention to it)

## Creating a New Numbers Document

As does Pages, the desktop publishing application that's included in iWork '09, Numbers ships with a selection of templates that you can modify quickly to create a new spreadsheet. (For example, after a few modifications, you can easily use the Budget, Loan Comparison, and Mortgage templates to create your own spreadsheets!)

To create a spreadsheet project file, follow these steps:

*1.* **Open your Applications folder and double-click the iWork '09 folder to display its contents.**

*2.* **Double-click the Numbers icon.**

Numbers displays the Template Chooser window you see in Figure 2-1.

If Numbers will be a favorite application on your MacBook, I highly recommend that you allow the iWork '09 installation program to add a Numbers icon to your Dock.

*3.* **Click the type of document you want to create in the list to the left.**

The document thumbnails on the right are updated with templates that match your choice.

*4.* **Click the template that most closely matches your needs.**

*5.* **Click Choose to open a new document using the template you selected.**

## Opening an Existing Spreadsheet File

If a Numbers document appears in a Finder window, you can just double-click the Document icon to open it; Numbers automatically loads and displays the spreadsheet.

**Figure 2-1:**
Hey, these
templates
aren't
frightening
at all!

However, it's equally easy to open a Numbers document from within the program. Follow these steps:

1. **Double-click the Numbers icon to run the program.**

2. **Press ⌘+O to display the Open dialog.**

3. **Click the desired drive in the Devices list at the left of the dialog and then click folders and subfolders until you've located the desired Numbers document.**

4. **Double-click the spreadsheet to load it.**

If you want to open a spreadsheet you've been working on over the last few days, click File➪Open Recent to display Numbers documents that you've worked with recently.

The Template Chooser window also sports both an Open Recent button and an Open Existing File button. Convenience is A Good Thing!

## *Save Those Spreadsheets!*

If you're not a huge fan of retyping data, I always recommend that you save your spreadsheets often (just in case of a power failure or a co-worker's mistake). Follow these steps to save your spreadsheet to your hard drive:

*1.* **Press ⌘+S.**

   If you're saving a document that hasn't yet been saved, the Save As sheet appears.

*2.* **Type a filename for your new spreadsheet.**

*3.* **Click the Where pop-up menu and choose a location to save the file.**

   This allows you to select common locations, such as your desktop, Documents folder, or Home folder.

   If the location you want isn't listed in the Where pop-up menu, you can also click the down-arrow button next to the Save As text box to display the full Save As dialog. Click the desired drive in the Devices list at the left of the dialog and then click folders and subfolders until you reach the desired location. You can also create a new folder in the full Save As dialog.

*4.* **Click Save.**

After you've saved the file the first time, you can simply press ⌘+S in the future and your changes are saved.

## *Exploring the Numbers Window*

Apple has done a great job of minimizing the complexity of the Numbers window. Figure 2-2 illustrates these major points of interest:

✦ **Sheets list:** Because a Numbers project can contain multiple spreadsheets, they're displayed in the Sheets list at the left of the window. To switch between spreadsheets in a project, click the top-level headings (each of which has a spreadsheet icon).

✦ **Sheet canvas:** Numbers displays the rows and columns of your spreadsheet in this section of the window; you enter and edit cell values within the sheet canvas.

✦ **Toolbar:** The Numbers toolbar keeps the most common commands you'll use within easy reach.

✦ **Formula Box:** You'll use the Formula Box to enter formulas into a cell, allowing Numbers to automatically perform calculations based on the contents of other cells.

✦ **Format Bar:** Located directly under the toolbar, the Format Bar displays editing controls for the object that's currently selected. (If you enter an equal sign into the Formula Box, the Format Bar changes into the Formula Bar. No, I'm not making this up.) My goodness, this is starting to sound like that classic movie about the chocolate tycoon and those kids!

**Figure 2-2:**
The
Numbers
window
struts its
stuff.

# Navigate and Select Cells in a Spreadsheet

Before you can enter data into a cell, you need to know how to get to the cell where you want to enter that data. You can use the scroll bars to move around in your spreadsheet, but when you enter data into cells, moving your fingers from the keyboard is a hassle. For this reason, Numbers has various movement shortcut keys that you can use to navigate, and I list them in Table 2-1. After you commit these keys to memory, your productivity shoots straight to the top.

| Table 2-1 | Movement Shortcut Keys in Numbers |
|---|---|
| *Key or Key Combination* | *Where the Cursor Moves* |
| Left arrow (←) | One cell to the left |
| Right arrow (→) | One cell to the right |
| Up arrow (↑) | One cell up |
| Down arrow (↓) | One cell down |
| Home | To the beginning of the active worksheet |
| End | To the end of the active worksheet |
| Page Down | Down one screen |
| Page Up | Up one screen |
| Return | One cell down (also works within a selection) |
| Tab | One cell to the right (also works within a selection) |
| Shift+Enter | One cell up (also works within a selection) |
| Shift+Tab | One cell to the left (also works within a selection) |

You can use the mouse to select cells in a spreadsheet:

✦ To select a *single* cell, click it.

✦ To select a *range* of multiple adjacent cells, click a cell at any corner of the range you want and then drag the mouse in the direction you want.

✦ To select a *column* of cells, click the alphabetic heading button at the top of the column.

✦ To select a *row* of cells, click the numeric heading button on the far left side of the row.

# Entering and Editing Data in a Spreadsheet

After you navigate to the cell in which you want to enter data, you're ready to type your data. Follow these steps to enter That Important Stuff:

*1.* **Either click the cell or press the spacebar.**

A cursor appears, indicating that the cell is ready to hold any data you type.

*2.* **Type in your data.**

Spreadsheets can use both numbers and text within a cell — either type of information is considered data in the Spreadsheet World.

3. **To edit data, click within the cell that contains the data to select it and then click the cell again to display the insertion cursor. Drag the insertion cursor across the characters to highlight them and then type the replacement data.**

4. **To simply delete characters, highlight the characters and press Delete.**

5. **When you're ready to move on, press Return (to save the data and move one cell down) or press Tab (to save the data and move one cell to the right).**

## Selecting the Right Number Format

After your data has been entered into a cell, row, or column, you still might need to format it before it appears correctly. Numbers gives you a healthy selection of formatting possibilities. *Number formatting* determines how a cell displays a number, such as a dollar amount, a percentage, or a date.

Characters and formatting rules, such as decimal places, commas, and dollar and percentage notation, are included in number formatting. So, if your spreadsheet contains units of currency, such as dollars, format it as such. Then all you need to do is type the numbers, and the currency formatting is applied automatically.

To specify a number format, follow these steps:

1. **Select the cells, rows, or columns you want to format.**

2. **Click the Inspector toolbar button.**

3. **Click the Cells Inspector button in the Inspector toolbar to display the settings you see in Figure 2-3.**

4. **Click the Cell Format pop-up menu and click the type of formatting you want to apply.**

## Aligning Cell Text Just So

You can also change the alignment of text in the selected cells. (The default alignment for text is flush left and for numeric data, flush right.) Follow these steps:

1. **Select the cells, rows, or columns you want to format.**

   See "Navigate and Select Cells in a Spreadsheet," earlier in this chapter, for tips on selecting stuff.

**Figure 2-3:**
You can
format the
data you've
entered
from the
Inspector.

2. **Click the Inspector toolbar button.**

3. **Click the Text Inspector button in the Inspector toolbar to display the settings you see in Figure 2-4.**

4. **Click the corresponding alignment button to choose the type of formatting you want to apply.**

   You can choose left, right, center, justified, and text left and numbers right. Text can also be aligned at the top, center, or bottom of a cell.

I would be remiss if I didn't point out that you can also select the cells you want to align and click the appropriate alignment button in the Format Bar. (Leave it to Apple to provide multiple ways of doing the same job!)

Do you need to set apart the contents of some cells? For example, you might need to create text headings for some columns and rows or to highlight the totals in a spreadsheet. To change the formatting of the data displayed within selected cells, select the cells, rows, or columns you want to format and then click the Font Family, Font Size, or Font Color buttons on the Format Bar.

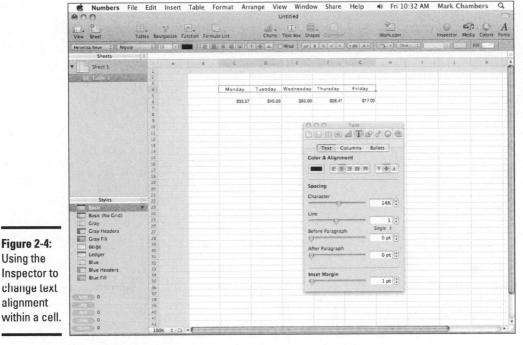

**Figure 2-4:**
Using the
Inspector to
change text
alignment
within a cell.

# Format with Shading

Shading the contents of a cell, row, or column is helpful when your spreadsheet contains subtotals or logical divisions. Follow these steps to shade cells, rows, or columns:

*1.* **Select the cells, rows, or columns you want to format.**

*2.* **Click the Inspector toolbar button.**

*3.* **Click the Graphic Inspector button in the Inspector toolbar.**

Numbers displays the settings you see in Figure 2-5.

*4.* **Click the Fill pop-up menu to select a shading option.**

*5.* **Click the color box to select a color for your shading.**

Numbers displays a color picker (also shown in Figure 2-5).

*6.* **Click to select a color.**

**Figure 2-5:**
Adding
shading
and colors
to cells,
rows, and
columns
is easy in
Numbers.

7. **After you achieve the right effect, click the Close button in the color picker.**

8. **Click the Inspector's Close button to return to your spreadsheet.**

The Fill function is also available on the Format Bar.

## Insert and Delete Rows and Columns

What's that? You forgot to add a row and now you're three pages into your data entry? No problem. You can easily add or delete rows and columns. Really — you can! First, select the row or column that you want to delete or that you want to insert a row or column next to, and do one of the following:

✦ **For a row:** Right-click and choose Add Row Above, Add Row Below, or Delete Row from the shortcut menu that appears.

✦ **For a column:** Right-click and choose Add Columns Before, Add Columns After, or Delete Column from the shortcut menu that appears.

Remember that you can also take care of this business from the Table menu. (Personally, I like to right-click.)

# The Formula Is Your Friend

Sorry, but it's time to talk about *formulas*. These equations calculate values based on the contents of cells you specify in your spreadsheet. For example, if you designate cell A1 (the cell in column A at row 1) to hold your yearly salary and cell B1 to hold the number 12, you can divide the contents of cell A1 by cell B1 (to calculate your monthly salary) by typing this formula into any other cell:

$$=A1/B1$$

By the way, formulas in Numbers always start with an equal sign (=).

"So what's the big deal, Mark? Why not use a calculator?" Sure, but maybe you want to calculate your weekly salary. Rather than grab a pencil and paper, you can simply change the contents of cell B1 to 52, and — boom! — the spreadsheet is updated to display your weekly salary.

That's a simple example, of course, but it demonstrates the basis of using formulas (and the reason that spreadsheets are often used to predict trends and forecast budgets). It's the "what if?" tool of choice for everyone who works with numeric data.

To add a simple formula within your spreadsheet, follow these steps:

1. **Select the cell that will hold the result of your calculation.**

2. **Click inside the Formula Box and type = (the equal sign).**

   The Formula Box appears to the right of the Sheets heading, directly under the Button bar. Note that the Format Bar changes to show a set of formula controls (a.k.a. the Formula Bar).

3. **Click the Function Browser button, which bears the *fx* label. (It appears next to the red Cancel button on the Formula Bar.)**

4. **In the window that appears, as shown in Figure 2-6, click the desired formula and click Insert to add it to the Formula Box.**

5. **Click an argument button in the formula and click the cell that contains the corresponding data.**

   Numbers automatically adds the cell you indicated to the formula. Repeat this for each argument in the formula.

6. **After you finish, click the Accept button to add the formula to the cell.**

That's it! Your formula is now ready to work behind the scenes, doing math for you so that the correct numbers appear in the cell you specified.

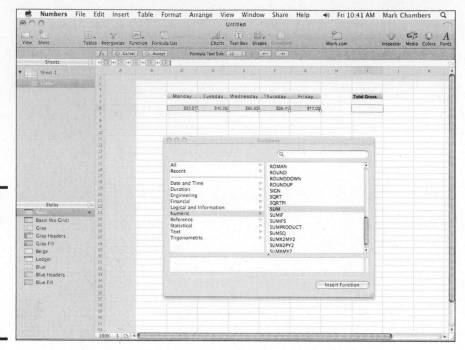

**Figure 2-6:**
If you have
to use
formulas,
at least
Numbers
can enter
them for
you.

To display all the formulas that you've added to a sheet, click the Formula List button in the toolbar.

## Adding Visual Punch with a Chart

Sometimes you just have to see something to believe it — hence the ability to use the data you add to a spreadsheet to generate a professional-looking chart! Follow these steps to create a chart:

1. **Select the adjacent cells you want to chart by dragging the mouse.**

   To choose individual cells that aren't adjacent, you can hold down the ⌘ key as you click.

2. **Click the Charts button on the Numbers toolbar. The Charts button bears the symbol of a bar graph.**

   Numbers displays the thumbnail menu you see in Figure 2-7.

**Figure 2-7:**
Numbers
displays the
range of
chart styles
you can use.

3. **Click the thumbnail for the chart type you want.**

   Numbers inserts the chart as an object within your spreadsheet so that
   you can move the chart. You can drag using the handles that appear on
   the outside of the object box to resize your chart. Figure 2-8 illustrates
   the 3-D chart I generated with just a couple of mouse clicks.

   Click the Inspector toolbar button and you can switch to the Chart
   Inspector dialog, where you can change the colors and add (or remove)
   the chart title and legend.

4. **To change the default title, click the title box once to select it; click it
   again to edit the text.**

After you've added your chart to the sheet, you'll note that it appears in the
Sheets list, as also shown in Figure 2-8. To edit the chart at any time, just
click on the corresponding entry in the Sheets list.

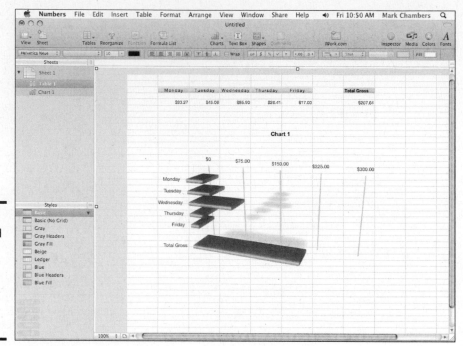

**Figure 2-8:**
My finished
chart
looks like
someone
with talent
drew it
for me!

# Chapter 3: Building Presentations with Keynote

## In This Chapter

- ✔ Creating a new presentation
- ✔ Adding slides
- ✔ Using selection boxes
- ✔ Entering and editing text
- ✔ Formatting text
- ✔ Adding presenter's notes
- ✔ Inserting media and shapes
- ✔ Running a slideshow
- ✔ Printing slides and notes

It seems like only yesterday that I was giving business presentations with a clunky overhead projector and black-and-white acetate transparencies. Fancy color gradients and animation were unheard of, and the only sound my presentations made was the droning of the projector's fan. I might as well have been using tree bark and chalk.

Thank goodness those days are gone forever, because cutting-edge presentation software like Keynote makes slide creation easy and — believe it or not — *fun*! This is the application that Steve Jobs once used for his Macworld keynotes every year, and there's so much visual candy available that you'll never need to shout to wake your audience again. Naturally, Keynote is a perfect match for your MacBook, allowing you to create or edit a presentation while you're on the road.

In this chapter, I demonstrate how simple it is to build a stunning Keynote presentation, and how to start and control your slide display from your keyboard (or even your iPhone or iPod touch). Heck, we'll even print your slides and notes so that your audience can keep a copy of your brilliant work!

# Creating a New Keynote Project

As do the other applications in the iWork '09 suite, Keynote begins the document creation process with a Template Chooser window. To create a new presentation project, follow these steps:

**1. Double-click your hard drive icon and click the Applications entry in the Finder window sidebar. Double-click the iWork folder to open it.**

If presentations are your bread and butter, allow the iWork installation program to add a Keynote icon to your Dock. Your clicking finger will thank you.

**2. Double-click the Keynote icon.**

The Template Chooser window that you see in Figure 3-1 appears. (I have to say that these are probably the most stunning visual building blocks I've ever seen in a presentation application. You should have heard the "oohs" and "ahhs" from the Macworld faithful when Steve Jobs demonstrated Keynote for the first time on the big screen!)

**Figure 3-1:**
Selecting a template from the Template Chooser window.

**3. Click the Slide Size pop-up menu at the bottom of the screen to select the resolution for your completed slides.**

Although you don't necessarily need to select an exact match for the screen resolution of your MacBook, it's a good idea to select the closest value to the maximum resolution of your projector. (If someone else is providing the projector, the default value of 1024 x 768 is a good standard to use.)

4. **Click the template that most closely matches your needs.**

5. **Click Choose to open a new document by using the template you selected.**

## Opening a Keynote Presentation

If an existing Keynote presentation file is visible in a Finder window, you can double-click the document icon to open the project. If Keynote is already running, however, follow these steps to load a project:

1. **Press ⌘+O to display the Open dialog.**

2. **Click the desired drive in the Devices list at the left of the dialog; then click folders and subfolders until you've located the Keynote project.**

3. **Double-click the filename to load it.**

 If you want to open a Keynote document that you've edited in the recent past, things get even easier! Just click File➪Open Recent and you can open the document with a single click from the submenu that appears. (Note that the Template Chooser window has both Open Recent and Open Existing File buttons as well.)

## Saving Your Presentation

When you're done working on a Keynote presentation (or if you'd simply like to safeguard your work in a world of power failures), follow these steps:

1. **Press ⌘+S.**

   If you're saving a document that hasn't yet been saved, the familiar Save As sheet appears.

2. **Type a filename for your new document.**

3. **Click the Where pop-up menu and choose a location to save the document.**

   To select a location not on the Where pop-up menu, click the button with the down arrow symbol to expand the sheet. You can also create a new folder from the expanded sheet.

4. **Click Save.**

## Putting Keynote to Work

Ready for the 5-cent tour of the Keynote window? Launch the application and create or load a project, and you'll see the tourist attractions shown in Figure 3-2:

✦ **Slide list:** Use this thumbnail list of all the slides in your project to help you navigate quickly. Click a thumbnail to switch instantly to that slide.

The Slide list can also display your project in outline format, allowing you to check all your discussion points. (This is a great way to ferret out any "holes" in your presentation's flow.) While in outline mode, you can still jump directly to any slide by clicking the slide's title in the outline. To display the outline, click View➪Outline. You can switch back to the default Navigator Slide list by clicking View➪Navigator.

✦ **Layout pane:** Your slide appears in its entirety in this pane. You can add elements and edit the content of the slide from the Layout pane.

Toolbar

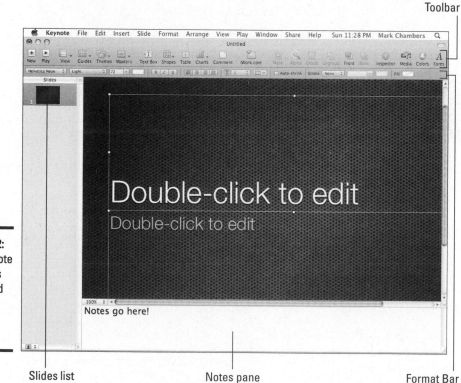

**Figure 3-2:**
The Keynote
window is
dominated
by the
Layout
pane.

Slides list                    Notes pane                    Format Bar

✦ **Toolbar:** As does the toolbar in Pages and Numbers, Keynote's toolbar makes it easy to find the most common controls you'll use while designing and editing your slides. Clicking an icon in the toolbar performs an action, just as selecting a menu item does.

✦ **Notes pane:** If you decide to add notes to one or more slides (either for your own use or to print as additional information for your audience), click View➪Show Presenter Notes to open the Notes pane. This text box appears under the Layout pane.

✦ **Format Bar:** Keynote displays this button strip underneath the Keynote toolbar, allowing you to format selected text, paragraphs and lists on the fly.

## Adding Slides

Sure, Keynote creates a single Title slide when you first create a project, but not many presentations are complete with just a single slide! To add more slides to your project, use one of these methods:

✦ Click the New button on the Keynote toolbar.

✦ Choose New Slide from the Slide menu.

✦ Press ⌘+Shift+N.

✦ Right-click (or Control-click) in the Slides list and choose New Slide from the menu.

Keynote adds the new slide to your Slides list and automatically switches to the new slide in the Layout pane.

Need a slide that's very similar to an existing slide you've already designed? Right-click the existing slide and choose Duplicate to create a new slide just like it. (Consider it cloning without the science.)

To move slides to different positions in the Slides list (and therefore a different order in your Keynote slideshow), drag each slide thumbnail to the desired spot in the list.

## Working with Text and Graphics Boxes

You've probably noticed that all the text within your first Title slide appears within boxes. Keynote uses boxes to manipulate text and graphics. You can resize a box (and its contents) by clicking and dragging one of the handles that appear around the edges of the box. (Your mouse cursor will change into a double-sided arrow when you're "in the zone.") The side-selection handles drag only that edge of the frame, whereas the corner-selection handles resize both adjoining edges of the selection frame.

**TIP**

To keep the proportions of the box constrained, hold down Shift while dragging the corner handles.

Boxes make it easy to move text and graphics together (as a single unit) to another location within the Layout pane. Click in the center of the box and drag the box to the desired spot; Keynote displays alignment lines to help you align the box with other elements around it (or with regular divisions of the slide, like horizontal center). As you can see in Figure 3-3, I'm moving a box on the slide to a new location, and Keynote has supplied alignment lines to help me place it correctly.

**REMEMBER**

To select text or graphics within a box, you should double-click the box.

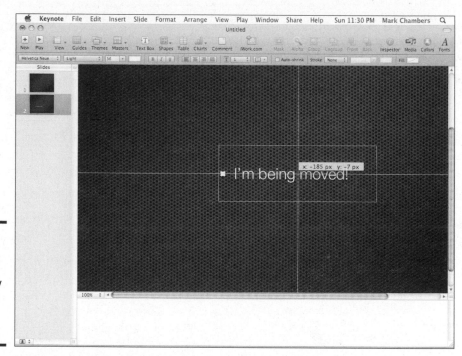

**Figure 3-3:** Alignment lines are provided by Keynote as you move boxes.

**TIP**

If you're resizing a photo in a box, don't forget to hold down the Shift key as you drag the frame. Doing so specifies that Keynote should preserve the aspect ratio of the image so that the vertical and horizontal proportions remain fixed. You can also flip images horizontally or vertically from the Arrange menu.

# Adding and Editing Slide Text

As with Pages and Numbers — which also use boxes for text layout — Keynote allows you to add or edit text with ease. For example, double-click in a box with the text `Double-click to edit`, and the placeholder text disappears, leaving the field ready to accept new text. Any new text you type appears at the blinking cursor within the box.

To edit existing text in your Keynote document, click using the bar-shaped cursor to select just the right spot in the text, and drag the insertion cursor across the characters to highlight them. Type the replacement text, and Keynote obligingly replaces the text that was there with the text you type.

If you want to delete existing text, click and drag across the characters to highlight them; then press Delete. You can also delete an entire box and all its contents: Right-click (or Control-click) the offending box and choose Delete from the menu that appears.

When the contents of a box are just right and you're finished entering or editing text, click anywhere outside the box to hide it from view. You can always click the text again to display the box later.

# Formatting Slide Text for the Perfect Look

Keynote doesn't restrict you to the default fonts for the theme you chose. It's easy to format the text in your slides — you can choose a different font family, font color, text alignment, and text attributes such as bolding and italicizing on the fly, whenever you like.

Select the desired text by double-clicking a box and then dragging the text cursor to highlight the characters. Now apply your formatting using one of these two methods:

✦ **The Format Bar:** The font controls on the Format Bar work just as the controls on the toolbar do: Either click a font control to display a pop-up menu or click a button to immediately perform an action. Clicking the Font Size pop-up menu, for example, displays a range of sizes for the selected text — with a single click on the B (bold) button, you'll add the bold attribute to the highlighted characters.

✦ **The Format menu:** The controls on the Format menu generally mirror those on the Format Bar. To change the alignment from the Format menu, click Format and hover the mouse cursor over the Text menu item. To change text attributes, click Format and hover your mouse over the Font menu.

## Using Presenter's Notes in Your Project

As I mention earlier, you can type text notes in the Notes pane — I use them for displaying alternate topic points while presenting my slide show. However, you can also print the notes for a project along with the slides, so presenter's notes are also great for including reminders and To Do points for your audience in handouts.

To type your notes, just click within the Notes pane; if it's hidden, click View➪Show Presenter Notes. When you're done adding notes, click in the Slide list or the Layout pane to return to editing mode.

To display your notes while practicing, use Keynote's Rehearsal feature. Click Play and choose Rehearse Slideshow, and you can scroll through the notes while the slideshow runs. (More on slideshows in a second.)

## Every Good Presentation Needs Media

Adding audio, photos, and movies to a slide is drag-and-drop easy in Keynote! Simply drag an image, audio, or movie file from a Finder window and place it at the spot you want within your document.

You can also use the Media Browser — click the Media button on the toolbar and click the Audio, Photos, or Movies button to select the desired type. Keynote displays the contents of your various media collections — like your iPhoto and iTunes libraries — or you can also navigate to the file's location on your hard drive, or type in a filename in the Search box at the bottom of the browser. When you've found the file you want to add, drag it to the spot you want in the document. Figure 3-4 illustrates the Media Browser in action.

## Adding a Background Shape

Text often stands out on a slide when it sits on top of a background shape. To add a shape (such as a rectangle or circle) as a background for your text, follow these steps:

1. **Click the insertion cursor in the location you want.**

2. **Click the Shapes button on the Keynote toolbar and choose a shape.**

   The shape appears in your document.

3. **Click the center of the shape and drag it to a new spot.**

   As with image boxes, shapes can be resized or moved.

4. **When the shape is properly positioned and sized, select it and choose Arrange⇨Send to Back.**

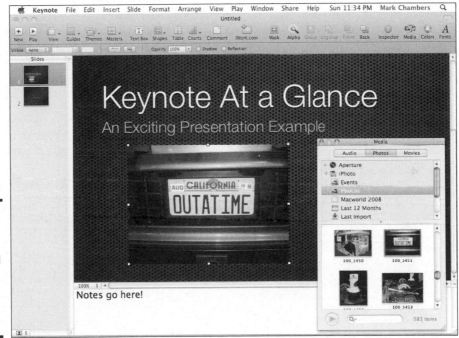

**Figure 3-4:**
It's not just photos — you can add audio and movie clips to a slide, too!

## Creating Your Keynote Slideshow

The heart of a Keynote presentation is the slideshow that you build from the slides you've created. A Keynote slideshow is typically presented full screen, with slides appearing in linear order as they are sorted in the Slides list.

In its simplest form, you can always run a slideshow from a Keynote project by clicking the Play button in the toolbar, or by choosing Play⇨Play Slideshow from the menu. You can advance to the next slide by clicking your mouse, or by pressing the right bracket key, which looks like this: ].

Of course, other controls are available besides just the ones that advance to the next slide! Table 3-1 illustrates the key shortcuts you'll use most often during a slideshow.

| Table 3-1 | Keynote Slideshow Shortcut Keys |
|---|---|
| *Key or Key Combination* | *Action* |
| ] (right bracket) | Next slide |
| P | Previous slide |
| Home | Jump to first slide |
| End | Jump to last slide |
| C | Show or hide the pointer |
| (number) | Jump to the corresponding slide in the Slide list |
| U | Scroll notes up |
| D | Scroll notes down |
| N | Show current slide number |
| H | Hide slideshow and display last application used (the presentation appears as a minimized icon in the Dock) |
| B | Pause slideshow and display a black screen (press any key to resume the slideshow) |
| Esc | Quit |

Keynote offers a number of settings that you can tweak to fine-tune your slideshow. To display these settings, choose Keynote➪Preferences and click the Slideshow button in the Preferences window.

If you have an iPhone or iPod touch handy and you've installed the Apple Keynote Remote application on your device, display the Preferences window and click the Remote button to link your iPhone or iPod touch to your MacBook and Keynote. Now you can use your handheld device as a remote and use it during your slideshow!

## Printing Your Slides and Notes

Okay, I'll be honest: I don't always print handouts for every presentation I give, just because some of the slideshows I run are short introductions to hands-on demonstrations. However, if you're presenting a lengthy slideshow with plenty of information that you'd like your audience to remember, nothing beats handouts that include scaled-down images of your slides (and, optionally, your presenter's notes).

You can also use Keynote to create an electronic PDF-format document instead of a printed handout, which your audience members can download from your Web site. (For the lowdown on PDF printing, visit Chapter 4 in Book VIII.)

To print a hardcopy of your slides and notes, follow these steps:

*1.* **Within Keynote, click File and choose Print.**

Keynote displays the Print sheet you see in Figure 3-5. (Note that some printer-specific features may be different on your screen.)

*2.* **Click the desired format.**

- To print each slide on a separate page at full size, click Individual Slides.

- To print each slide on a separate page with the presenter's notes for that slide, click Slides with Notes.

- To print the contents of your Slides list in Outline view, click Outline.

- To print a handout with multiple slides per page (and, optionally, with presenter's notes), click Handout. Click the Slides per Page pop-up menu to specify the number of slides that Keynote should print on each page.

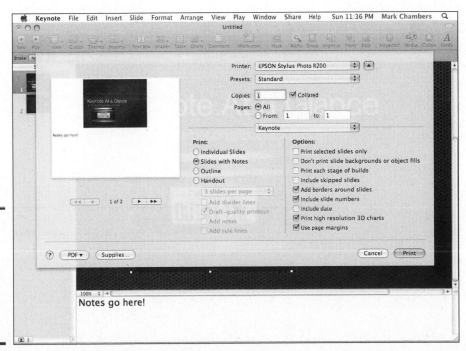

**Figure 3-5:**
Keynote offers a wide range of printing options for your slides and notes.

3. **Select the pages to print.**

   - To print the entire document, select All.

   - To print a range of selected slides, select the From radio button and enter the starting and ending pages.

4. **Select or deselect specific options from the Options column.**

   You can include elements such as the date, borders around each slide, and the slide number as part of each page of the hardcopy.

5. **Click the Print button to send the job to your printer.**

# Book VI

# The Typical Internet Stuff

Add visual impact to an e-mail message with a Photo stationery background.

# Contents at a Glance

**Chapter 1: Getting on the Internet** . . . . . . . . . . . . . . . . . . . . . . . . . . . . . . **489**
- Shopping for an ISP . . . . . . . . . . . . . . . . . . . . . . . . . . . . . . . . . . . . . . . . . . 489
- Investigating Various Types of Connections . . . . . . . . . . . . . . . . . . . . . . 491
- Setting Up Your Internet Connection . . . . . . . . . . . . . . . . . . . . . . . . . . . . 493

**Chapter 2: Using Apple Mail** . . . . . . . . . . . . . . . . . . . . . . . . . . . . . . **497**
- Know Thy Mail Window . . . . . . . . . . . . . . . . . . . . . . . . . . . . . . . . . . . . . . . 497
- Setting Up Your Account . . . . . . . . . . . . . . . . . . . . . . . . . . . . . . . . . . . . . . 499
- Receiving and Reading E-Mail Wisdom . . . . . . . . . . . . . . . . . . . . . . . . . . 503
- Raise the Little Flag: Sending E-Mail . . . . . . . . . . . . . . . . . . . . . . . . . . . . 509
- What? You Get Junk Mail, Too? . . . . . . . . . . . . . . . . . . . . . . . . . . . . . . . . 513
- Attachments on Parade . . . . . . . . . . . . . . . . . . . . . . . . . . . . . . . . . . . . . . . 514
- Fine-Tuning Your Post Office . . . . . . . . . . . . . . . . . . . . . . . . . . . . . . . . . . 515
- Automating Your Mail with Rules . . . . . . . . . . . . . . . . . . . . . . . . . . . . . . 517

**Chapter 3: Staying in Touch with iChat** . . . . . . . . . . . . . . . . . . . . . . . **521**
- Configuring iChat . . . . . . . . . . . . . . . . . . . . . . . . . . . . . . . . . . . . . . . . . . . . 522
- Changing Modes in iChat . . . . . . . . . . . . . . . . . . . . . . . . . . . . . . . . . . . . . 524
- Will You Be My Buddy? . . . . . . . . . . . . . . . . . . . . . . . . . . . . . . . . . . . . . . . 525
- Chat! Chat, I Say! . . . . . . . . . . . . . . . . . . . . . . . . . . . . . . . . . . . . . . . . . . . . 527
- Sharing Screens and iChat Theater . . . . . . . . . . . . . . . . . . . . . . . . . . . . . 530
- Sending Files with iChat . . . . . . . . . . . . . . . . . . . . . . . . . . . . . . . . . . . . . . 531
- Eliminating the Riffraff . . . . . . . . . . . . . . . . . . . . . . . . . . . . . . . . . . . . . . . 532
- Adding Visual Effects . . . . . . . . . . . . . . . . . . . . . . . . . . . . . . . . . . . . . . . . 532

**Chapter 4: Expanding Your Horizons with iDisk** . . . . . . . . . . . . . . . . **535**
- Grabbing Internet Storage for Your MacBook . . . . . . . . . . . . . . . . . . . . 536
- Understanding What's on Your iDisk . . . . . . . . . . . . . . . . . . . . . . . . . . . . 538
- Opening and Using iDisk . . . . . . . . . . . . . . . . . . . . . . . . . . . . . . . . . . . . . . 539

**Chapter 5: Surfing with Safari** . . . . . . . . . . . . . . . . . . . . . . . . . . . . . . **541**
- Pretend You've Never Used This Thing . . . . . . . . . . . . . . . . . . . . . . . . . . 542
- Visiting Web Sites . . . . . . . . . . . . . . . . . . . . . . . . . . . . . . . . . . . . . . . . . . . 543
- Navigating the Web . . . . . . . . . . . . . . . . . . . . . . . . . . . . . . . . . . . . . . . . . . 544
- Setting Up Your Home Page . . . . . . . . . . . . . . . . . . . . . . . . . . . . . . . . . . . 547
- Adding and Using Bookmarks . . . . . . . . . . . . . . . . . . . . . . . . . . . . . . . . . 548
- Downloading Files . . . . . . . . . . . . . . . . . . . . . . . . . . . . . . . . . . . . . . . . . . . 550
- Using Subscriptions and History . . . . . . . . . . . . . . . . . . . . . . . . . . . . . . . 551
- Tabs Are Your Browsing Friends . . . . . . . . . . . . . . . . . . . . . . . . . . . . . . . 552
- Saving Web Pages . . . . . . . . . . . . . . . . . . . . . . . . . . . . . . . . . . . . . . . . . . . 553
- Protecting Your Privacy . . . . . . . . . . . . . . . . . . . . . . . . . . . . . . . . . . . . . . 554

**Chapter 6: Staying Secure Online** . . . . . . . . . . . . . . . . . . . . . . . . . . . . **557**
- What Can Really Happen? . . . . . . . . . . . . . . . . . . . . . . . . . . . . . . . . . . . . . 557
- "Shields Up, Chekov!" . . . . . . . . . . . . . . . . . . . . . . . . . . . . . . . . . . . . . . . . 560
- A Dose of Common Sense: Things Not to Do Online . . . . . . . . . . . . . . . 564

# Chapter 1: Getting on the Internet

## In This Chapter

✔ Selecting an Internet service provider (ISP)

✔ Understanding how your MacBook gets on the Internet

✔ Setting up your Internet connection

*1*'ll be honest — the Internet is a terribly complex monster of a network. If you tried to fathom all the data that's exchanged on the Internet and everything that takes place when you check your e-mail for Aunty Joan's fruitcake recipe, your brain would probably melt like a chocolate bar in the Sahara Desert. A shoebox *full* of arcane things is tucked under the Internet: communications protocols, routing addresses, packets, servers, and other hoo-hah that are beyond the grasp of just about everyone on the planet.

Luckily for regular folks like you and me, Mac OS X Snow Leopard closes the trapdoor on all these details, keeping them hidden (as they *should* be). You don't have to worry about them, and the obscure information that you need to establish an Internet connection is kept to a minimum. In fact, the happiest computer owners I've met think that the Internet is a little blinking light on their DSL or cable modem: If the light blinks in the proper manner, all is well. (I don't argue with them.)

In this chapter, I provide help and advice to those who are searching for an on-ramp to the Information Superhighway — and I lead you through the procedure of adding an Internet connection under Mac OS X. (In other words, you'll get your light blinking properly.)

If you entered your Internet configuration information while you were in the Setup Assistant during the installation of Mac OS X, *you can skip this chapter!* The information contained herein is only for those who add or change their Internet connectivity *after* installing Mac OS X.

## Shopping for an ISP

Before you can connect to the Internet, you must sign up for Internet access. If you already have an ISP (acronym-speak for an *Internet service provider*) or your company provides Internet access, smile quietly to yourself and skip to the next section. Otherwise, hang around while I discuss what to look for in an ISP and how to locate one in your local area.

If you're unfamiliar with the term, an ISP is simply the company you contract with so that you can connect to the Internet. You may be contracting with a cable company, such as Comcast, Bright House, or Mediacom, or you may be using a service such as AOL, Juno, or Earthlink. All these are ISPs.

ISPs are as thick as Louisiana mosquitoes these days, and often they're judged solely by the amount that they charge for basic access. Cost definitely is a factor, but it's not the *only* thing that should determine your choice in a service provider. Consider these guidelines when choosing or switching ISPs:

✦ **Local calling rates:** If you live in a rural area and you're using a dial-up modem, check to make sure that all prospective ISPs offer local calling rates. Believe me, no matter how much fun and how useful the Internet is, it's not worth hours of long-distance charges. (Oh, and don't forget to make sure that your ISP has local access numbers in the cities that you visit regularly.) Since the current MacBook line doesn't include an internal analog modem, you can always add an external USB modem for dial-up Internet access and faxing.

✦ **Broadband service:** Virtually all ISPs now offer digital subscriber line (DSL) or cable modem access. Collectively, these connections are called *broadband* because they offer the fastest method of transferring information to and from the Internet. If you have a home business, a large family, or students — or you telecommute to your office — using broadband can make your life much simpler.

✦ **Quality technical support:** A 24-hour/7-day telephone support line is a godsend for the Internet novice — don't settle for voice support during business hours. Forget e-mail-based support, too; your e-mail application will be dead and gone if your Internet connection gives you problems. (Sound of your palm whacking your forehead.)

✦ **Static IP addresses:** A *static IP address* — the unique number that identifies your computer on the Internet — allows you to set up a professional Web server or File Transfer Protocol (FTP) server. Most ISPs charge an additional amount for a static IP address, so it's not really a good idea for a typical Mac owner at home. Suffice it to say, however, that a business or commercial organization running a Web server or FTP server will benefit from a static IP address.

✦ **E-mail accounts:** Investigate how many individual accounts you receive with various ISPs. Also, find out whether you can maintain them yourself through a Web site. If so, that's a good sign. Additionally, if the prospective ISP provides a Web site where you can read and send e-mail messages, you can stay on top of your e-mail even while you're on the road or vacationing halfway across the globe.

✦ **Web space:** If you want your ISP to host your Web site, this is a no-brainer: The more space you get, the better. A minimum of 1GB is acceptable, but most ISPs provide 3GB or more these days. Also, beware of ISPs that charge you for your Web site if it receives a large amount of traffic: It can be expensive to host a popular Web site if you join one of these ISPs.

✦ **Domain name service:** Finally, the better class of ISP also offers a *domain name service,* which allows you to register something like `your namehere.com`. For the most professional appearance, you can usually pay a yearly fee, and the ISP takes care of all the details in setting up your own `.com` or `.org` domain name.

**Book VI
Chapter 1**

**Getting on the Internet**

Locating an ISP is easy in the modern, Internet-savvy world. In the order that you should try them, here are the tricks that I recommend for finding your local ISPs:

✦ **Check with your cable or telephone companies.** If you're already subscribing to cable service in your area, you're likely to be a candidate for cable Internet access. Also, many local phone companies offer DSL access, but that access area is often limited to certain locations. Call the customer service numbers for these companies and check out what they offer — and don't forget that a broadband cable or DSL connection is always more expensive than an old-fashioned, dial-up connection. ("Maude, did you see the Internet bill this month?")

✦ **Get recommendations from friends and neighbors.** Folks love to give free advice. Ask them how much they're paying, how reliable the connection has been, and how well they rate the ISP's technical support.

✦ **Check your phone directory.** Check the phone book for Internet service.

✦ **Investigate ISP Web sites.** If you have Internet access at work, a friend's house, or your local public library, you can surf to The List (`www.the list.com`), where you can search for ISPs within your area code and location.

# Investigating Various Types of Connections

Consider the types of connections that are available under Snow Leopard to link your MacBook to an ISP (see the previous section for more about ISPs). You can choose from four pathways to digital freedom:

✦ **A dial-up connection:** Old-fashioned, yes. Slow as an arthritic burro, indeed. However, an *analog* (or telephone modem) connection is still a very viable method for reaching the Internet for most computer owners.

It's the cheapest method available, and all you need for this type of connection is a standard telephone jack and a modem. Apple used to include a modem with every computer, but no longer . . . these days, you'll have to buy an external USB modem to make the dial-up connection. (Apple makes one, or any Mac OS X–compatible USB modem will work fine.)

✦ **A broadband connection:** Be it through DSL (which uses a typical telephone line) or cable (which uses your cable TV wiring), broadband Internet access is many times faster than a dial-up connection. Plus, both these technologies are *always on,* meaning that your computer is automatically connected to the Internet when you turn it on and that connection stays active. With DSL or cable, no squeaky whine accompanies your modem while it makes a connection each time you want to check your movie listings Web site. Both DSL and cable require a special piece of hardware (commonly called a *modem,* but it really isn't); this box is usually thrown in as part of your ISP charge. (Note that many cellular providers offer cellular modems for Internet connectivity. Some of these modems use a USB port whereas others use the ExpressCard slot on a MacBook Pro.) DSL or cable broadband connections usually require a professional installation, too.

✦ **A satellite connection:** If you're *really* out there — miles and miles away from any cable or DSL phone service — you can still get high-speed Internet access. The price for a satellite connection is usually much steeper than a standard DSL or cable connection, but it's available anywhere you can plant your antenna dish with a clear view of the sky. Plus, a satellite connection is actually faster than other types of broadband access. Older satellite technologies actually required you to also use a dial-up connection — and the antenna could only receive, not send — but most ISPs that can handle satellite connections now offer satellite systems that both send and receive through the dish.

✦ **A network connection:** The last type of connection concerns those Macs that are part of a local area network (LAN) either at the office or in your home. If your MacBook is connected to a LAN that already has Internet access, you don't need an ISP at all, and no other hardware is required: Simply contact your network administrator, buy that important person a steak dinner, and ask to be connected to the Internet. On the other hand, if your network currently has no Internet access, you're back to Square One: You'll need one of the previous three types of connections.

After you connect one of your computers on your network to the Internet, you can use an Internet sharing device to allow all the computers to share that Internet connection. Book VII, Chapter 4 goes into all the details on sharing an Internet connection on a network.

# Setting Up Your Internet Connection

Okay, so you sign up for Internet access, and your ISP sends you a sheet of paper covered with indecipherable stuff that looks like Egyptian hieroglyphics. Don't worry; those are the settings that you need to connect to your ISP. After you get them in Mac OS X, you should be surfing the Web like an old pro.

Before you jump into this configuration, make sure that you've configured the Internet settings within System Preferences, as I discuss in Book III, Chapter 3. That way, you'll already have entered your default e-mail and Web settings. You'll also need to be logged in using an Administrator account.

## Using an internal or external modem

Follow these steps to set up your Internet connection if you're using your MacBook's external USB modem:

*1.* **Click the System Preferences icon in the Dock and choose Network.**

*2.* **Select External modem from the list at the left side of the pane.**

*3.* **Enter the settings for the type of connection that your ISP provides:**

- *If your ISP tells you to use PPP (Point-to-Point Protocol):* Click the Configure IPv4 pop-up menu and choose Using PPP. If your ISP provided you with DNS Server or Search Domain addresses, type them now in the corresponding boxes.

- *If you're using AOL:* Click the Configure IPv4 pop-up menu and choose AOL Dialup. If AOL provided you with DNS Server or Search Domain addresses, click in the corresponding box and type them now.

- *If you're using a manual connection:* Click the Configure IPv4 pop-up menu and choose Manually. Then click in the IP Address, DNS Servers, and Search Domains fields and enter the respective settings provided by your ISP.

*4.* **If you need to enter PPP settings, click the Advanced button.**

*5.* **In their respective fields, enter the account name, password, telephone number, and (optionally) the service provider name and an alternative telephone number provided by your ISP.**

I always like Mac OS X to connect automatically when I'm using a modem. I hate excess mouse movements, which usually lead to a bad case of Rodent Elbow. To automate your dial-up connection (allowing Snow Leopard to call your ISP whenever your system needs the Internet), click the Connect Automatically When Needed check box to enable it.

*6.* **Press ⌘+Q to exit System Preferences and save your changes.**

## Using Ethernet hardware

Follow these steps to set up your Internet connection if you're using a network, cable modem, or DSL connection:

*1.* **Click the System Preferences icon in the Dock and choose Network.**

*2.* **Select Ethernet from the list on the left of the pane to display the settings that you see in Figure 1-1.**

**Figure 1-1:**
The
Network
settings for
an Ethernet
Internet
connection.

*3.* **Enter the settings for the type of connection that your ISP provides:**

- *If your ISP tells you to use Dynamic Host Configuration Protocol (DHCP):* Choose Using DHCP from the Configure IPv4 pop-up menu, and your ISP can automatically set up virtually all the TCP/IP settings for you! (No wonder DHCP is so popular these days.)

- *If you won't be using DHCP:* Choose Manually from the Configure IPv4 pop-up menu. Then enter the settings provided by your ISP in the IP Address, Subnet Mask, Router, and DNS Servers fields.

*4.* **If your ISP uses PPPoE (Point-to-Point Protocol over Ethernet), click the Configure IPv4 pop-up menu and choose Create PPPoE Service.**

*5.* **Type an identifying name for the PPPoE service.**

*6.* **Click Done.**

7. **Enter the password for your PPPoE connection.**

8. **Press ⌘+Q to exit System Preferences and save your changes.**

Snow Leopard can get down-and-dirty in the configuration trenches as well! To launch an assistant to help with the configuration process, click the Assist Me button and then click Assistant on the Assistant's welcome screen.

**Book VI
Chapter 1**

Getting on
the Internet

# Chapter 2: Using Apple Mail

## In This Chapter

- Adding and configuring Mail accounts
- Receiving, reading, and sending e-mail
- Filtering junk mail
- Opening attachments
- Configuring and automating Apple Mail

*O*kay, how many of you can function without e-mail? Raise your hands. Anyone? Anyone at all?

I suppose that I *can* function without my Internet e-mail, but why should I? Mac OS X includes a very capable and reliable e-mail client, *Apple Mail* (affectionately called *Mail* by everyone but Bill Gates).

In this chapter, I discuss the features of Apple Mail and show you how everything hums at a perfect C pitch. However, you have to sing out, "You've got mail!" yourself. Personally, I think that's a plus, but I show you how you can add any sound you like.

## Know Thy Mail Window

To begin our epic e-mail journey, click the Mail icon in the Dock. Figure 2-1 illustrates the Mail window. Besides the familiar toolbar, which naturally carries buttons specific to Mail, you find the following:

- ✦ **Title bar:** This heading at the top of the Mail window displays information about the current folder — typically, how many messages it contains, but other data can be included as well.

- ✦ **Message list:** This resizable scrolling list box contains all the messages for the folder that you've chosen. To resize the list larger or smaller, drag the handle on the bar that runs across the window. You can also resize the columns in the list by dragging the edges of the column heading buttons.

To specify which columns appear in the message list, choose View⇨ Columns. From the submenu that appears, you can toggle the display of specific columns. You can also sort the messages in the message list from the View menu; by default, messages are sorted by the Date Received. (Alternatively, use Lazy Mark's method: Just click the column that you want to sort by.)

Mailboxes          Message list          Preview box

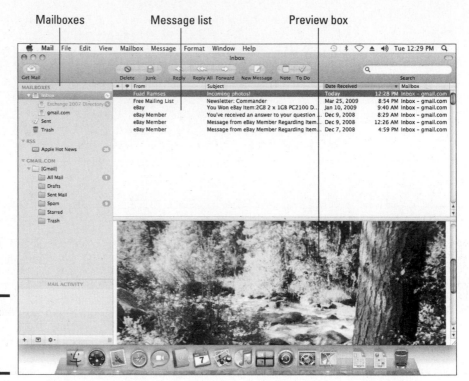

**Figure 2-1:**
The Apple
Mail
window.

✦ **Mailboxes:** The column at the left of the main Mail window is the Mailboxes list. You can click any of the folders to switch the display in the message list. The Mailbox list can be hidden or shown from the View menu by clicking the Show Mailboxes item, or you can press the ⌘+Shift+M keyboard shortcut to hide or show it. To widen or narrow the Mailboxes list, click the divider at the right side of the list. Your mouse cursor turns to a line with double arrows — and drag it in the desired direction.

✦ **Preview box:** This resizable scrolling text box displays the contents of the selected message, including both text and any graphics or attachments that Mail recognizes.

Mail uses the following folders (some of which appear only at certain times):

✦ **Inbox:** Mail you've received already.

✦ **Outbox:** Messages that Mail is waiting to send.

✦ **Drafts:** Draft messages waiting to be completed.

✦ **Sent:** Mail you've sent already.

✦ **Trash:** Deleted mail. As with the Trash in the Dock, you can open this folder and retrieve items that you realize you still need. Alternatively, you can empty the contents of the Trash at any time by pressing the ⌘+K shortcut or by choosing Mailbox➪Erase Deleted Messages.

✦ **Junk:** Junk mail. You can review these messages or retrieve anything you want to keep by choosing Message➪Move To. After you're sure nothing of value is left, you can delete the remaining messages straight to the Trash. (Junk mail filtering must be enabled from the Junk Mail settings in Preferences before you see this box.)

✦ **RSS:** Messages from an RSS news feed that you've subscribed to. You find out more on RSS later in this chapter.

✦ **Notes:** This folder displays notes that you've made. I discuss how to create a new note later in this chapter.

✦ **To Do:** Ah, don't forget those all-important reminders about washing the car, paying taxes, and picking up dog food on the way home. The To Do folder displays your To Do items, which I cover later in the chapter.

You can add new personal folders to the Mailbox list to further organize your messages. Choose Mailbox➪New Mailbox and then type the name for your new folder in the Name box. Click OK to create the new personal folder.

Messages can be dragged from the message list and dropped into the desired folder in the Mailbox list to transfer them. Alternatively, you can move 'em from the Message list by selecting the messages that you want to move, choosing Message➪Move To, and then clicking the desired destination folder.

Also note that Spotlight has staked its claim with the Search box at the upper right in the Mail toolbar.

# Setting Up Your Account

By default, Mail includes one (or more) of these accounts when you first run it:

✦ **The account that you entered when you first installed Mac OS X:** Go to Book II, Chapter 1 to read about the first use assistant that I discuss at the beginning of this book. If you entered the information for an e-mail account, it's available.

✦ **Your MobileMe account:** If you registered for a MobileMe service account, it's included.

✦ **Upgraded accounts:** If you upgraded an existing Mac OS system, your existing Mail accounts are added to the Accounts list in Mail.

# What's a smart mailbox?

Remember the smart folders you can create in the Finder? Well, Apple Mail provides something similar for your e-mail messages: the *smart mailbox.* The contents of a smart mailbox are actually links to messages and To Do items in your Mail folders; these links match the search criteria you specify, such as messages from a specific address or those that contain attachments. Other criteria include the date an item is received, the subject of a message, the mailbox a message is stored in, and so on. You can use smart mailboxes to organize your messages and To Do items in different ways and identify those messages that require special (or **immediate!**) attention.

To set up a smart mailbox, choose Mailbox⇨ New Smart Mailbox, or click the Add button (which carries a plus sign) at the lower-left corner of the Mail window and choose New Smart Mailbox from the drop-down menu. Type a name to identify the mailbox and then click the Contains pop-up menu to choose either

messages or To Do items. Click the Match pop-up menu to specify whether the search should match any one or all of your criteria. Now you can click the pop-up menus to specify what the search should find. To add a new criterion line, click the button with the plus sign. (To delete a criterion line that Should Not Be, click the button with the minus sign next to the offending line.) Note that you can also include messages from Mail's Trash and Sent folders. When you're ready, click OK, and the new smart mailbox appears in the Mailboxes list. It has a cool folder icon with a gear symbol, much like the gear symbol sported by smart folders in a Finder window.

If you've set up your smart folder, it automatically maintains itself when you receive, send, and delete messages and To Do items, always showing whatever matches your criteria. Here's a mind-boggler: Imagine what Ben Franklin could've done if he'd been able to use smart folders!

Speaking of the Accounts list, choose Mail⇨Preferences and click the Accounts button to display the Accounts pane that you see in Figure 2-2. From here, you can add an account, edit an existing account, or remove an account from Mail. Although most folks still have only one e-mail account, you can use a passel of them. For example, you might use one account for your personal e-mail and one account for your business communications. To switch accounts, just click the account that you want to use from this list to make it the active account.

## Adding an account

To add a new account within Mail, choose File⇨Add Account to open an Accounts assistant that leads you through the process. 'Nuff said.

However, I'm a manual kind of guy — at least, that's what I'm told — so I should describe the process. For our demonstration, I'll add a typical ISP POP account from the Preferences dialog, which displays the same Accounts assistant.

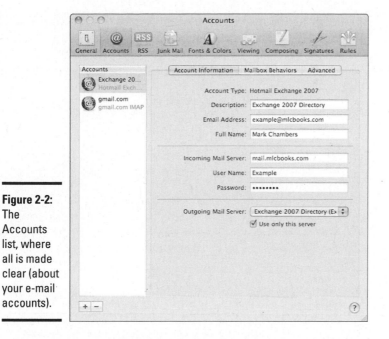

**Figure 2-2:**
The Accounts list, where all is made clear (about your e-mail accounts).

Open the Preferences dialog by clicking Mail and choosing Preferences; then click the Accounts button on the Preferences toolbar. Follow these steps:

*1.* **Click the Add button at the bottom-left corner of the window, which carries a plus sign.**

*2.* **On the General Information pane, type your full name in the Full Name field — or, if this is to be an anonymous account, enter whatever you like as your identity — and then press Tab.**

Messages that you send appear with this name in the From field in the recipient's e-mail application.

*3.* **Type the e-mail address assigned to you by your ISP.**

*4.* **In the Password field, type the password supplied by your ISP for login to your e-mail account.**

*5.* **Click Continue.**

Here's a great feature: If Mail recognizes the type of account you're using, the assistant may offer to automatically complete all the required settings for you! (If the account is recognized, the Continue button switches to a Create button. Smile proudly and click Create, and you're done.) If your account isn't recognized by Mail, it's no big deal — just continue with Step 6.

**6.** **Click the Account Type pop-up menu and choose the protocol type to use for the account.**

You can select an Apple MobileMe account, a Post Office Protocol (POP) account, a Microsoft Exchange 2007 account, an Internet Message Access Protocol (IMAP) account, or a standard Microsoft Exchange IMAP account. If you're adding an account from an Internet service provider (ISP), refer to the set-up information that you received to determine which is right. Most ISP accounts are POP accounts.

When you select an Account Type, the fields may change on the Accounts assistant, but they'll still follow the same general order I give in this POP account demonstration. (In fact, there are fewer fields to fill out for IMAP accounts!) Keep the account information provided by your ISP handy because that data should include everything covered in the assistant.

**7.** **In the Description field, name the account to identify it within Mail and then press Tab to move to the next field.**

For example, *Work* and *Home ISP* are good choices.

**8.** **In the Incoming Mail Server text box, type the incoming mail server address supplied by your ISP.**

If your ISP requires a login for security, you need to enter your server username and password.

**9.** **Click Continue.**

**10.** **On the Incoming Mail Security sheet, click the Authentication pop-up menu and choose the authentication scheme used by your incoming mail server.**

Unless you're told differently by your ISP, the default choice — Password — is very likely correct already.

**11.** **Click Continue.**

**12.** **On the Outgoing Mail Server sheet, type a description for the server and press Tab.**

I typically enter the ISP name.

**13.** **In the Outgoing Mail Server text box, type the outgoing mail server address supplied by your ISP.**

**14.** **If your ISP requires your e-mail application to authenticate the connection, select the Use Authentication check box and type the username and password supplied by your ISP into the corresponding fields.**

**15.** **Click Continue on the Account Summary sheet.**

**16.** **Click Done on the Conclusion sheet.**

You're done! The new account appears in the Accounts list.

You can specify advanced settings for an account. I cover those in the section "Fine-Tuning Your Post Office," later in this chapter.

### Editing an existing account

Need to make changes to an existing account? Choose Mail⇨Preferences and click the account that you want to change. Mail displays the same settings that I explain in the preceding section.

### Deleting an account

If you change ISPs or you decide to drop an e-mail account, you can remove it from your Accounts list. Otherwise, Mail can annoy you with error messages when it can no longer connect to the server for that account. Display the Mail Preferences dialog, select the account that you want to delete, and then click the Remove button (which is graced by a minus sign).

Naturally, Mail requests confirmation before deleting the folders associated with that account. Click OK to verify the deletion or click the Cancel button to prevent accidental catastrophe.

## Receiving and Reading E-Mail Wisdom

The heart and soul of Mail — well, the heart, anyway — is receiving and reading stuff from your friends and family. (Later in this chapter, I show you how to avoid the stuff you get promising free prizes, low mortgage rates, and improved . . . um, performance. This is a family-oriented book, so that's enough of that.)

After you set up an account (or select an account from the Accounts list), it's time to check for mail. Use any of these methods to check for new mail:

✦ **Click the Get Mail button on the toolbar.**

✦ **Right-click the Mail icon in the Dock and choose Get New Mail from the menu that appears.**

✦ **Choose Mailbox⇨Get All New Mail or press ⌘+Shift+N.**

✦ **Choose Mailbox⇨Get New Mail and then choose the specific account to check from the submenu.**

This is a great way to check for new mail in another account without going through the trouble of making it active in the Preferences window.

Mail can also check for new messages automatically; you can find more on this topic in the "Checking Mail automatically" section, later in this chapter.

If you do have new mail in the active account, it appears in the Message list. As you can see in Figure 2-3, new unread messages appear marked with a snazzy blue dot in the first column. The number of unread messages is displayed next to the Inbox folder icon in the Mailboxes list.

**Figure 2-3:**
A new
message
to read. Oh,
joy, and no
spam!

Mail also displays the number of new messages that you've received on its Dock icon. If you've hidden the Mail window or sent it to the Dock, you can perform a quick visual check for new mail just by glancing at the Dock.

## Reading and deleting your messages

To read any message in the message list, you can either click the desired entry (which displays the contents of the message in the preview pane) or you can double-click the entry to open the message in a separate message window, complete with its own toolbar controls.

To quickly scan your mail, click the first message that you want to view in the list and then press the down-arrow key when you're ready to move to the next message. Mail displays the content of each message in the preview pane. To display the previous message in the list, press the up-arrow key.

Mail also allows you to read your messages grouped within threads. A *thread* contains an original message and all related replies, which makes it easy to follow the flow of an e-mail discussion (without bouncing around within your Inbox, searching for the next message in the conversation). Choose View➪Organize by Thread, and the replies in the current folder are all grouped under the original messages and sorted by date. To expand a thread, click the original message to select it; then press the right-arrow key (or choose View➪Expand All Threads). To collapse a thread, select the original message and press the left-arrow key (or choose View➪Collapse All Threads).

Hey, why not let Mail *read* you your mail? (That is, if you can drive and listen to your MacBook speak at the same time!) Simply select one message or a group of messages and then choose Edit⇨Speech⇨Start Speaking. *Wowzers!*

To delete a message from the message list, click the desired entry to select it and then click the Delete button on the toolbar (or press the Del key). To delete a message from within a message window, click the Delete button on the toolbar.

## Replying to mail

What? Aunt Harriet sent you a message because she's forgotten where she parked her car last night? If you happen to know where her priceless '78 Pinto is, you can reply to her and save her the trouble of retracing her steps.

If Aunt Harriet isn't in your Address Book yet, this is a good time to add her. With the message entry selected in the list, choose Message⇨Add Sender to Address Book or just press the convenient ⌘+Shift+Y keyboard shortcut. The person's name and e-mail address are added automatically to your Address Book. To add more information in the Address Book, however, you have to open that application separately. (Read through Book II, Chapter 6 for the skinny on the Address Book.)

To reply to a message in Mail, follow these steps:

*1.* **To respond to a message from the message list, click the desired message entry and then click the Reply button on the toolbar.**

   To respond to a message that you've opened in a message window, click the Reply button on the toolbar for the message window.

   If a message was addressed not just to you but also to a number of different people, you can send your reply to all of them. Instead of clicking the Reply button, click the Reply All button on the Mail window toolbar. (This is a great way to quickly facilitate a festive gathering, if you get my drift.)

   You can also add carbon copies of your message to other new recipients, expanding the party exponentially; more on carbon copies later, in the section "Raise the Little Flag: Sending E-Mail."

   Mail opens the Reply window that you see in Figure 2-4. Note that the address has been added automatically and that the default Subject is Re: <the original subject>. Mail automatically adds a separator line in the message body field that reads On <date>, at <time>, <addressee> wrote:, followed by the text of the original message; this is done so that the addressee can remember what the heck he or she wrote in the first place to get you so happy/sad/angry/indifferent. The original text is indented and prefaced by a vertical line to set it apart. If you like, you can click in the Subject line and change the default subject line; otherwise, the cursor is already sitting on the first line of the text box, so you can simply start typing your reply.

## Displaying all Mail headers

Mail actually hides the majority of the heading lines that help identify and route an e-mail message to its rightful destination. By default, all you'll see is the *filtered heading,* which includes only the From, Date, To, and Subject fields. This is great unless for some reason you need to display the entire message header in all its arcane madness. If you do, press ⌘+Shift+H. You can toggle back to the filtered heading by pressing the same shortcut.

To choose the text from the original message that you want to include in a reply, select the desired text in the original message before you click the Reply button.

2. **After you complete typing your reply, you can select text in the message body and apply different fonts or formats.**

To change your reply's formatting, click the Fonts button on the message window toolbar. From the window that appears, you can choose the font family, the type size, and formatting (such as italic or bold) for the selected text. Click the Close button on the Fonts window to continue. (If you like menus, you can also choose Format from the menu and make changes from there.)

To apply color to the selected text, click the Colors button on the message window toolbar and then click anywhere in the color wheel that appears to select that color. You can also vary the hue by moving the slider bar at the right of the Colors window. After you find the color that expresses your inner passion, click the Close button on the Colors window to continue.

To create a bulleted list in your reply, click Format➪Lists and choose either a bulleted or a numbered list. Mail thoughtfully prepares your first bullet item for you. Press Return to add another bullet item. Click outside the bullet formatting to complete the list.

Care to chat directly with the recipients of your message? Just click the Chat button on the toolbar, and Mail automatically opens iChat and attempts to connect! (Note that this will work only with the recipients who have an instant messaging address in their Address Book card.) This Chat feature also appears on the New Message window toolbar, which I discuss in a page or two.

3. **To add an attachment, click the Attach button on the toolbar.**

Mail displays a familiar Open dialog. Navigate to the to-be-attached file, select it, and click the Open button to add it to the message. (More on attachments in the "Attachments on Parade" section, later in this chapter.) If the recipient is running Windows, make sure the Send Windows-Friendly Attachments check box is enabled — this results in a slightly larger e-mail message size but helps ensure that PC e-mail programs, such as Outlook and Outlook Express, can correctly open your attachments.

Because most folks end up sending photos through e-mail, Apple includes a Photo Browser button on the toolbar. Click this button on the Reply or New Message window toolbars and you can choose a photo from your iPhoto library to insert directly into your message. Heck, you can even take a quick candid shot using Photo Booth and your MacBook's built-in iSight camera.

4. **When you're ready to send your reply, you have two options. You can click the Send button to immediately add the message to your Outbox folder or you can click the Save as Draft button to store it in your Drafts folder for later editing.**

After a message is moved to the Outbox folder, it's sent either immediately or at the next connection time that you specify in Mail Preferences (more on this in the section "Checking Mail automatically," later in the chapter). However, saving the message to your Drafts folder doesn't send it. Read the following section for the skinny on how to send a message stored in your Drafts folder.

**Figure 2-4:**
Replying to an incoming e-mail message.

On Apr 7, 2009, at 12:34 PM, Fuad Ramses wrote:

How about some ocean-front property in Kansas? It's all the rage!

Rediscover Hotmail®: Get e-mail storage that grows with you. Check it out.

## Hey, what does MIME mean?

First, a note of explanation about Internet e-mail. (Don't worry about notes; you won't be tested on this stuff.) Decades back, Internet e-mail messages were pure text, composed only of ASCII characters — that means no fancy fonts, colors, stationery, or text formatting. However, as more and more folks started using e-mail, the clarion call rang forth across the land for more attractive messages (as well as attachments, which I cover in the section "Attachments on Parade"). Therefore, the MIME encoding standard was developed. In case you're interested, MIME stands for *Multipurpose Internet Mail Extensions* — a rather cool (and surprisingly understandable) acronym.

Originally, virtually all e-mail programs recognized MIME, but then the Tower of Babel principle kicked in, and now there are actually multiple versions of MIME. Apple Mail uses the most common variant of MIME, so most folks who receive your e-mail can see them in all their glory (even under Windows).

However, if one of your addressees complains that he got a message containing unrecognizable gobbledygook and a heading that mentions MIME, he's using an e-mail client application that either doesn't support MIME or supports a different version. (Of course, that person could have unknowingly turned off MIME support.) You have two possible solutions: You can ask the addressee to double-check whether MIME is enabled on his end in the e-mail application or you can disable MIME when sending a message to that particular person. When you're composing an original message or a reply, you can use pure text by choosing Format⇨Make Plain Text. (Naturally, this prevents you from doing anything fancy, and files that you attach to a plain-text message might not be delivered correctly.)

---

When you reply to a message, you can also *forward* your reply to another person (instead of the original sender). The new addressee receives a message containing both the text of the original message that you received and your reply. To forward a message, click the Forward button on the Mail toolbar instead of Reply or Reply to All.

If you don't want to include the text of the original message in a reply, choose Mail⇨Preferences. Click the Composing button and disable the Quote the Text of the Original Message check box.

By default, Mail checks your spelling while you type and also underlines any words that it doesn't recognize. (Very Microsoftian.) I personally like this feature, but if you find it irritating, you can turn it off or set Mail to check the spelling just once (when you click Send). Just choose Mail⇨Preferences, click Composing, and click the Check Spelling as I Type pop-up menu to choose the desired option.

# *Raise the Little Flag: Sending E-Mail*

To compose and send a new message to someone, follow these steps:

*1.* **Click the New Message button on the Mail toolbar or choose File⇨New Message (or avail yourself of the handy ⌘+N keyboard shortcut).**

Mail opens the New Message window that you see in Figure 2-5.

*2.* **Enter the recipient's (To) address by**

- *Typing it in directly*
- *Pasting it in after copying it to the Clipboard*
- *Dragging an e-mail address from your Address Book*

or

- *(My favorite) Clicking the Address toolbar button,* which shows you the scaled-down version of the Address Book (the Addresses window) that you see in Figure 2-6.

**Figure 2-5:** An empty Mail message, waiting to be filled.

**Figure 2-6:**
Select
an e-mail
address
from your
Address
Book.

From the Addresses window, click the address that you want to use and then click the To button. To pick multiple recipients, hold down the ⌘ key while you click the multiple addresses. Click the Close button on the Addresses window to close it; then, press Tab.

If you have a huge number of entries in your Address Book, use the Search field on the Addresses window toolbar, which operates just like the Finder window Search box.

3. **When Mail highlights the Cc field (the spot where you can send optional carbon copies of the message to additional recipients), you can type the addresses directly, use the contents of the Clipboard, or display the Addresses window.**

If you use the Addresses window, select the addresses that you want to use and click the Cc button. Then click the Close button on the Addresses window and press Tab.

Looking for the Blind Carbon Copy (Bcc) field? To display it, choose View⇨Bcc Address Field. (A *blind carbon copy* is a message sent to multiple recipients, just like a regular carbon copy, but the recipients aren't listed when the message is displayed — that way, the other recipients don't know who else got a copy of the message.) You can also click the small Field Display pop-up menu at the left side of the Subject field to toggle the display of the Bcc Address Field. Oh, and there's also a Bcc button on the Addresses window — go figure.

**4. In the Subject field, enter the subject of the message and then press Tab.**

Your text cursor now rests in the first line of the message text box — type, my friend, type like the wind! It's considered good form to keep this line short and relatively to the point.

**5. Click the Show Stationery button on the toolbar to display the Stationery strip above the message text box (as shown in Figure 2-7), where you can choose one of many backgrounds that Apple supplies.**

**Figure 2-7:**
Adding visual impact to my e-mail message with a Photo stationery background.

Stationery isn't required, but it really packs a visual wallop! Double-click a thumbnail in the strip to add it to your message; to display a different category of stationery, such as a Greeting or Invitation, click the category buttons on the left side of the Stationery strip.

This one will really knock your socks off: If you choose a Photo stationery background for your new message, you can even drag an image from the Photo Browser, the iPhoto window, or a Finder window to fill the "placeholder" images on the background. (Which, when you think about it, kind of makes sense . . . after all, why send an e-mail from sunny Italy that has stock photos of a strange couple at the top? Add your own travel shots instead!) Figure 2-7 illustrates a Photo stationery background.

Not all e-mail applications on other computers correctly display a message with a stationery background. For the whole scoop, see the "Hey, what does MIME mean?" sidebar, earlier in this chapter. Also, remember that a message with a stationery background is going to be much larger than a simple text message, especially if it contains a number of photos. (And, as you guessed, that also means that it takes longer to send and receive, which is very important for those using a dial-up analog modem connection.) Many Internet service providers limit the size of messages and attachments, so adding a stationery background may render a message undeliverable to some recipients.

6. **After you type your message, select any of the text that you've entered and use the toolbar features I describe in the section "Replying to mail," earlier in this chapter, to apply different fonts or formatting.**

   Click the Fonts button in the message window toolbar to open a window of formatting choices. (Click its Close button to continue.) If you like menus, you can also click Format and make changes from there.

7. **Add color to any selected text, if you like.**

   Just click the Colors button in the message window toolbar and make choices in the Snow Leopard Color Picker that appears; when the hue is perfect, click the Close button on the Color Picker to continue.

8. **To add an attachment, click the Attach button on the toolbar, navigate to the to-be-attached file in the dialog that appears, select the file, and then click Open to add it to the message.**

   Remember, if you'd like to include photos in your message, just click the Photo Browser toolbar button to select images from your iPhoto library, or take a photo with Photo Booth.

9. **When your new message is ready to post, either click the Send button to immediately add the message to your Out folder or click the Save as Draft button to store it in your Drafts folder (without actually sending it).**

To send a message held in your Drafts folder, click the Drafts folder in the Drawer to display all draft messages. Double-click the message that you want to send, which displays the message window (you can make edits at this point, if you like) and then click the Send button on the message window toolbar.

If you don't have access to an Internet connection at the moment, Mail allows you to work offline. This way, you can read your unread messages and compose new ones on the road to send later. After you regain your Internet connection, you might need to choose Mailbox➪Go Online (depending on the connection type).

# What? You Get Junk Mail, Too?

Spam — it's the Crawling Crud of the Internet, and I hereby send out a lifetime of bad karma to those who spew it. However, chucking the First Amendment is *not* an option, so I guess we'll always have junk mail. (Come to think of it, my paper mailbox is just as full of the stuff.)

Thankfully, Apple Mail has a net that you can cast to collect junk mail before you have to read it. The two methods of handling junk mail are

✦ **Manually:** You can mark any message in the message list as Junk Mail. Select the unwanted flotsam in the message list and then click the Junk button on the Mail window toolbar, which marks the message, as shown in Figure 2-8. (Ocean-front property in Kansas . . . yeah, right.) If a message is mistakenly marked as junk but you actually want it, display the message in the preview box and then click the Not Junk button at the top of the preview box.

✦ **Automatically:** Apple Mail has a sophisticated Junk Mail filter that you actually train to better recognize what's junk. (Keep reading to discover how.) After you train Mail to recognize spam with a high degree of accuracy, turn it to full Automatic mode, and it moves all those worthless messages to your Junk folder.

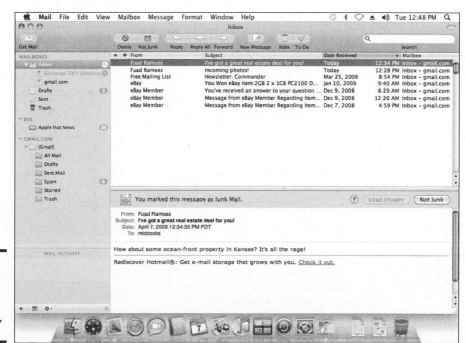

**Figure 2-8:** "Be gone, sludge demons of Junk Mail!"

You customize and train the Junk Mail filter from the Preferences dialog (available from your trusty Mail menu); click Junk Mail to show the settings. I recommend that you first try Mail in Training mode, using the Mark as Junk Mail, But Leave It in My Inbox option. Junk Mail then takes its best shot at determining what's junk. When you receive more mail and mark more messages as junk (or mark them as *not* junk), you're actually teaching the Junk Mail feature how to winnow the wheat from the chaff. In Training mode, junk messages aren't actually moved anywhere — they're just marked with a particularly fitting, grungy brown color.

After you're satisfied that the Junk Mail filter is catching just about everything that it can, display the Mail preferences again and choose the Move It to the Junk Mailbox option. Mail creates a Junk folder and prompts you for permission to move all junk messages to this folder. After you review everything in the Junk folder, you can delete what it contains and send it to the Trash folder. To save a message from junkdom, click the Not Junk button in the preview window and then drag the message from the Junk folder message list to the desired folder in the Drawer.

Finally, you can create a complete set of custom *rules* for your Junk Mail filtering by clicking Perform Custom Actions — the Advanced button displays your Junk Mail rule set and allows you to edit your rules. I explain rules in more depth at the end of this chapter.

If you don't receive a lot of spam — or you want to be absolutely sure that nothing gets labeled as junk until you review it — click the Enable Junk Mail Filtering check box to disable it. (And good luck.)

By default, Mail exempts certain messages from Junk Mail status based on three criteria: if the sender is in your Address Book, if you've sent the sender a message in the past, or if the message is addressed to you with your full name. To tighten up your Junk Mail filtering to the max, you might want to disable these check boxes as well.

To reset the Junk Mail filter and erase any training that you've done, visit the Junk Mail settings in Preferences again and click Reset. Then click the Yes button to confirm your choice.

## Attachments on Parade

Attachments are a fun way to transfer files through e-mail. However, it's imperative that you remember these three very important caveats:

✦ **Attachments can contain viruses.** Even a message attachment that was actually sent by your best friend can contain a virus or malevolent macro — either because your friend unwittingly passed one along or because the virus actually took control of your friend's e-mail application and replicated itself automatically. (Ugh.)

✦ **Corpulent attachments don't make it.** Most corporate and ISP mail servers have a 2–4MB limit for the total size of a message, and the attachments (and any Photo stationery background you might have added) count toward that final message size. Therefore, I recommend sending a file as an attachment only if it's less than 2MB (or perhaps 3MB) in size. If the recipient's e-mail server sends you an automated message saying that the message was refused because it was too big, this is the problem.

✦ **Not all e-mail applications and firewalls accept attachments.** Not all e-mail programs support attachments in the same way, and others are simply set for pure text messages. Some corporate firewalls even reject messages with attachments. If the message recipient gets the message text but not the attachment, these are the likely reasons.

With all that said, it's back to attachments as a beneficial feature. Follow these steps to save an attachment that you receive:

*1.* **Click the message with an attachment in your message list.**

Having trouble determining which messages have attachments? Choose View➪Columns and then click the Attachments item from the submenu that appears to toggle it on. Now messages with attachments appear with a tiny paper-clip icon in the entry.

If Mail recognizes the attachment format, it displays or plays the attachment in the body of the message; if not, the attachment is displayed as a file icon.

*2.* **To open an attachment that's displayed as a file icon, click the file icon and then choose Open Attachment from the pop-up menu that appears.**

If you know what application should be used to open the attachment, click the Open With button and choose the correct application from the submenu that appears.

*3.* **To save an attachment, right-click the attachment (however it appears in the message) and then choose Save Attachment from the pop-up menu.**

In the Save dialog that appears, navigate to the location where you want to save the file and then click Save.

# Fine-Tuning Your Post Office

As is all other Apple software, Mail is easily customized to your liking. In this section, I discuss some of the preferences that you might want to change.

## Adding sound

To choose a sound that plays whenever you receive new mail, choose
Mail⇨Preferences and click the General button. Either click the New
Messages Sound pop-up menu and choose one of the sounds that Apple
provides or choose Add/Remove from the pop-up menu to choose a sound
file from the Sounds folder (which, in turn, is located within your Library
folder). Choose None from the pop-up menu to disable the new mail sound
altogether.

## Checking Mail automatically

By default, Mail automatically checks for new mail (and sends any mail in
your Out folder) every five minutes. To change this delay period, display the
General pane in the Preferences dialog, choose the Check for New Messages
pop-up menu, and then choose one of the time periods. To disable automatic
mail checking, choose Manually; you can click the Get Mail toolbar button to
manually check your mail any time you like. (For example, those folks using
dial-up analog modem connections may not fancy Mail taking control of the
telephone line every 5 minutes.)

## Automating junk mail and message deletion

If you like, Mail can be set to automatically delete sent mail and Junk mes-
sages (as well as permanently erase messages that you relegate to the
Trash). To configure these settings, display the Accounts pane in the
Preferences window, click the desired account, and then click the Mailboxes
Behaviors tab.

To delete Sent messages automatically, click the Delete Sent Messages When
pop-up menu and choose the delay period or action. You can choose to
delete mail after a day, a week, a month, or immediately upon quitting Mail.
Alternatively, you can leave this field set to Never, and Mail never automatically deletes any messages from the Sent folder.

To delete Junk messages automatically, click the Delete Junk Messages
When pop-up menu and choose the delay period or action. (They're the
same as the options available for Sent mail.)

To delete messages from the Trash, click the Permanently Erase Deleted
Messages When pop-up menu and choose the delay period or action —
again, the choices are the same as those for Sent messages.

## Adding signatures

To add a block of text or a graphic to the bottom of your messages as your
personal signature, follow these steps:

1. **Choose Mail⇨Preferences and click the Signatures button.**

2. **From the Signatures pane that appears, click the Add Signature button (which carries a plus sign).**

3. **Click the signature name to open an edit box and then type an identifying name.**

   Press Return to save the new name.

4. **Click inside the text entry box at the right to move the cursor.**

5. **Type the signature itself in the text entry box or copy the signature to the Clipboard and paste it into the text entry box.**

   Because downloading a graphic in a signature takes longer — and because some folks still use plain-text e-mail — avoid the temptation to include graphics in your signature.

6. **If you have multiple signatures, click the Choose Signature pop-up menu to choose which one you want to use or to use them all randomly or in sequence.**

If you prefer the signature to appear above the quoted text in a reply, select the Place Signature above Quoted Text check box.

## Changing the status of an account

Sometimes you can't reach one of your accounts. For example, maybe you're on the road with your laptop and you can't access your office network. Apple Mail allows you to enable and disable specific accounts without the hassle of deleting an account and then having to add it again.

To disable or enable an account, open the Preferences dialog, click the Accounts button, click the desired account, click the Advanced tab, and then select (or deselect) the Enable This Account check box as necessary.

If you disable an account, you should also deselect the Include When Automatically Checking for New Mail check box to make sure that Mail doesn't display an error message. You can always check any account for new mail by choosing Mailbox⇨Get New Mail and then choosing the desired account name from the submenu.

# Automating Your Mail with Rules

Before I leave the beautiful shores of Mail Island, I'd be remiss if I didn't discuss one of its most powerful features: the ability to create *rules,* which are automated actions that Mail can take. With rules, you can specify criteria that can perform actions such as

✦ **Transferring messages from one folder to another**

✦ **Forwarding messages to another address**

✦ **Highlighting or deleting messages**

To set up a rule, follow these steps:

*1.* **Choose Mail⇨Preferences and then click the Rules button on the toolbar.**

   Mail displays the Rules pane.

*2.* **To duplicate an existing rule, highlight it in the list and then click the Duplicate button. (For this demonstration, however, create a rule from scratch by clicking the Add Rule button.)**

*3.* **In the Description field, type a descriptive name for the new rule and then press Tab to move to the next field.**

*4.* **Click the If pop-up menu to specify whether the rule is triggered if any of the conditions are met or if all conditions must be met.**

*5.* **Because each rule requires at least one condition, click the target pop-up menus to set the target for the condition.**

   These include whom the message is from or to, which account received the message, whether the message is marked as junk, and whether the message contains certain content. Select the target for the condition.

*6.* **Click the Criteria pop-up menu to choose the rule's criteria.**

   The contents of this pop-up menu change depending on the condition's target. For example, if you choose From as the target, the criteria include Contains, Does Not Contain, Begins With, and so forth.

*7.* **Click in the expression box and type the text to use for the condition.**

   For example, a completed condition might read

```
Subject Contains Ocean-Front
```

   This particular condition is true if I get an e-mail message with a subject that contains the string Ocean-Front.

*8.* **Add more conditions by clicking the plus sign button at the right of the first condition.**

   To remove any condition from this rule, click the minus sign button next to it. Remember, however, that every rule needs at least one condition.

*9.* **To specify what action is taken after the condition (or conditions) is met, click the first Perform the Following Actions pop-up menu to see the action that this rule should perform. Then click the second pop-up menu and select the action for the rule.**

Choices include transferring a message from one folder to another, playing a sound, automatically forwarding the message, deleting it, and marking it as read.

Each rule requires at least one action.

**10. Depending on the action that you select, specify one or more criteria for the action.**

For instance, if I select Set Color as my action, I must then choose whether to color the text or the background as well as what color to use.

As with the plus button next to the conditions, you can also click the plus button next to the first action to perform more than one action. To remove an action, click the minus button next to it.

**11. When the rule is complete, click OK to save it.**

Here's an example of a complex rule:

If the message was sent by someone in my Address Book *and* the Subject field contains the text FORWARD ME, forward the message to the e-mail address fuadramses@me.com.

This is a good example of an automated forwarding rule. With this rule in place and Mail running on Mac OS X, any of my friends, family, or co-workers can forward urgent e-mail to my MobileMe account while I'm on vacation. To trigger the rule, all the sender has to do is include the words FORWARD ME in the message subject. And if the sender isn't in my Address Book, the rule doesn't trigger, and I can read the message when I get home. Mondo *sassy*.

Each rule in the Rules dialog can be enabled or disabled by toggling the Active check box next to the rule. You can also edit a rule by selecting it in the Rules pane and then clicking the Edit button. To delete a rule completely from the list, select it and then click the Remove button; Mail prompts you for confirmation before the deed is done.

If you decide to create a custom Junk mail processing rule, the process is the same, but you get to it from a different place. Click the Junk Mail button on the Preferences dialog toolbar and click the Perform Custom Actions radio button to select it. You see that the Advanced button is now enabled — click it and you can set up the custom Junk mail rules that handle stuff from any conceivable junk mail source!

# Chapter 3: Staying in Touch with iChat

## In This Chapter

- ✔ Setting up iChat
- ✔ Changing modes in iChat
- ✔ Adding Buddies
- ✔ Inviting a Buddy to chat
- ✔ Sending and receiving files via iChat
- ✔ Sharing screens with another person
- ✔ Ignoring those who deserve to be shunned
- ✔ Adding visual pizzazz with video backgrounds and effects

Throughout humankind's history, our drive has been toward communication — from the earliest cave paintings, through written language, to the telegraph, telephone, and cell phone all-in-one PDA that the guy in the SUV in front of you is using . . . and he's arguing with someone and he's not paying attention and . . . (whump).

So much for the scholarly introduction — anyway, forget that silly cellular phone and your complicated calling plan! As long as you have Mac OS X and an Internet connection, you can instantly chat with your friends and family whether they're across the aisle in another cube or halfway across the world. And, by golly, if your friends have an iSight camera, Web camera, or digital video (DV) camcorder connected to their computer, you'll *see* each other in glorious, full-color video! This modern marvel is *iChat,* and it fulfills the decades-old promise of the video telephone quite well, thank you.

In this chapter, I show you how to gab with the following folks:

- ✦ Others who use iChat (either on your local network or on the Internet)
- ✦ Anyone who uses AIM — that's short for *America Online (AOL) Instant Messaging* — MobileMe, Jabber, or Google Talk
- ✦ Folks who participate in AOL chat rooms

# Configuring iChat

When you first run iChat (by clicking the iChat icon in the Dock), you're prompted to create an iChat account. Type the first name (your name) that you want to use in the First Name field, press Tab, and then type the surname that you want to use. (Yes, you can even use *Bullwinkle Moose* — just leave out the middle initial *J.*)

By default, iChat uses the MobileMe account that you set up when you run Mac OS X for the first time. In this case, your MobileMe account name and password are entered automatically for you, and you're good to go. However, if you're already using AIM, Jabber, or Google Talk and you want to use your existing account, click the Account Type pop-up menu and choose the correct type; then enter your existing account name and password instead.

iChat will also set up Bonjour messaging automatically. Think of *Bonjour* as plug-and-play for your local network. In iChat, Bonjour messaging displays a separate window in which you can see (and yak with) anyone on your local network without having to know his iChat name. That's because Bonjour automatically announces all the iChat users who are available on your network. If you have others using iChat, Jabber, or AIM on your local network, go for this option; if you're not connected to a local network, however, Bonjour messaging isn't necessary. Also, if you're on a public AirPort/ AirPort Extreme network or if you're connecting to the Internet with a modem through dial-up, I recommend disabling Bonjour messaging. (For all that's cool about AirPort and its faster sibling AirPort Extreme, see Book VI, Chapter 3.)

After you finish these configuration necessities, iChat displays the Buddy List window (or, if you're using Bonjour messaging, the two windows) that you see in Figure 3-1. Remember that your Bonjour window displays only those iChat folks on your local network.

A few things to note here about the Buddy List window:

✦ **If you don't like your picture, don't panic.** By default, iChat uses your user account thumbnail image as your visual persona. However, you can add a picture to your iChat iDentity — sorry, I couldn't resist that — by dragging an image to the well next to your name at the top of the Buddy List window. If necessary, iChat asks you to position and size the image so that it fits in the (admittedly limited) space. This picture is then sent along with your words when you chat. In the figures for this chapter, I borrow the smiling face of Wolfgang Amadeus Mozart.

Click your image to display your recent thumbnails. This way, you can even use a different thumbnail image for each of your many moods. (Geez.) Also, you can click Edit Picture from the pop-up menu and capture a new thumbnail with your iSight camera.

**Figure 3-1:**
iChat and
Bonjour
instant
messaging
at its finest!

Add a New Buddy button     Start Screen Sharing button

Start a Text Chat button  |  Start a Video Chat button

Start an Audio Chat button

✦ Check out the buttons along the bottom of the Buddy List window. In order, these buttons are

- *Add a New Buddy* (which I cover in the following section)

- *Start a Text Chat* (plain, old-fashioned chatting via the keyboard)

- *Start an Audio Chat* (chatting with your voice, using microphones)

- *Start a Video Chat* (the ultimate chat, where the parties can both see and hear each other)

- *Start Screen Sharing* (where you can view — or even remotely control — a buddy's computer)

Using these buttons can handle about 90 percent of the commands that you need to give while using iChat, so use 'em! (Note that the Bonjour window doesn't have an Add a New Buddy button because the Buddy list in the Bonjour window is populated automatically by other iChat folks on your local network.)

✦ **Hey, look, there's an iChat menu bar icon!** When you're running iChat, you can choose to add a balloon menu bar icon in the upper-right corner of your screen. Click it to display the options that you see in Figure 3-2. You can change your online/offline status, immediately invite a Buddy for a chat, or display the Buddy list (which I discuss later in the section, "Will You Be My Buddy?"). The menu bar icon appears only if you enable the Show Status in Menu Bar check box. Click iChat in the menu and choose Preferences; then click the General button in the Preferences dialog's toolbar.

**Figure 3-2:**
The iChat Finder menu icon leaps into action.

## Changing Modes in iChat

To launch iChat, you can click its icon from the Dock or launch it from its iChat application icon (which you find in your Applications folder). Or, you can click its menu bar icon, which is grayed out when you're offline. If you're not already familiar with the terms *online* and *offline,* here's the scoop: When you're *online,* folks can invite you to chat and communicate with you. When you're *offline,* you're disconnected: iChat isn't active, you can't be paged, and you can't chat.

Even when you're offline, you can choose Available from the friendly balloon Finder menu bar icon, which automatically switches iChat to online mode. Or you can click a Buddy name directly, which automatically switches iChat to online mode and opens the paging window for that Buddy. (Naturally, you have to have the proper network or Internet connection first.)

You can use another mode, *Away,* whenever iChat is running and you're still online but not available. For example, if I'm away from my MacBook for a few minutes, I leave iChat running but I switch myself to Away mode. My Buddies get a message saying that I'm Away, so they won't bother trying to contact me. When I return to my laptop, I simply swipe my finger across the trackpad, and iChat intelligently inquires as to whether I'd like to return to Available mode. You can also use the menu bar icon to switch from Away to Available (or my other favorite mode, *Twiddling My Thumbs*). Refer to Figure 3-2 to see these choices.

**Book VI
Chapter 3**

**Staying in Touch
with iChat**

iChat can even display the iTunes song you're listening to at the moment. Pick Current iTunes Song from the menu and impress your friends with your digital audio techno-powers.

Speaking of modes, you, too, can create a custom mode — like *Bored stiff!* or *Listening to the Pointy-Haired Boss* — and use it instead of the somewhat mundane choices of *Available* and *Away.* To do this, display the Buddy List window, click the word *Available* beneath your name (refer to Figure 3-2), and a drop-down menu appears. Click Custom Available or Custom Away to create your new mode. An edit box appears, in which you can type the new mode; press Return to automatically add the newcomer to your mode list. You can also switch modes from this pop-up menu.

To choose an existing mode, click it; modes with a green bullet are online modes, and red bullet modes are offline modes. (Apple provides you with some starting choices, like *Surfing the Web* for *Available* and *In a Meeting* for *Away.*) Notice in Figure 3-2 that I created a custom mode called *Getting Another Diet Coke* . . . cAfFeInE fills my life.

## Will You Be My Buddy?

I know that question sounds a little personal, but in iChat, a *Buddy* is anyone whom you want to chat with, whether the topic is work related or your personal life. iChat keeps track of your Buddies in the Buddy list. You can also add them to your Address Book or use the AIM entry in an Address Book contact to generate a new Buddy identity.

To add a new Buddy, follow these steps:

1. **Choose Buddies⇨Add Buddy, or click the Add Buddy button at the bottom of the iChat window and click Add Buddy from the pop-up menu, or press ⌘+Shift+A.**

2. **To create a Buddy entry from an Address Book contact who has an Instant Messaging username, click the down-arrow button next to the Last Name box to display the Address Book list. Click the entry to select it.**

   As a shortcut, you can also click in the First Name box and then type the person's first name, or click in the Account Name box and type the person's Instant Messaging account name.

3. **To add a brand-new person who's not already in your Address Book, type the person's Instant Messaging account name and click the pop-up menu to select the proper account type (either MobileMe or AIM).**

4. **Click Add to save the Buddy information.**

Even when you add a new Buddy and that name appears in the Buddy list, don't be surprised if the name actually fades out after a few seconds — that indicates that the person is offline and unavailable. You can also tell when a person is available if her name appears with a green bullet in the Buddy list.

You can also specify a number of actions that iChat should take if a Buddy logs in or out of Instant Messaging, or if a Buddy changes his or her status to Available. To display these actions, click the desired Buddy's entry in your Buddy list and then press ⌘+Shift+I. Click the Actions button and then choose the event that should trigger the action from the Event pop-up menu. Select the desired check box to specify whether iChat should play the sound that you select, run an AppleScript, or animate the iChat icon by "bouncing" it in the Dock.

Click the Address Card button on the Info dialog to enter or edit the person's

✦ Real name

✦ Nickname

✦ E-mail

✦ Buddy icon

iChat obligingly creates an entry in your Address Book for your new Buddy. (Apple, you truly rock.)

# Chat! Chat, I Say!

Turn your attention to getting the attention of others — through inviting others to chat. Good chatting etiquette implies inviting someone to a conversation rather than barging in unannounced.

If you want to join an AIM chat already in progress, choose File⇨Go to Chat Room (or press ⌘+Control+G). Depending on the service being used, you might have to specify both the type of chat and the specific chat room name.

At this point, it's time to draw your attention to the green phone and video icons next to each person in your Buddy list (as well as next to your own name at the top of the list). If the green phone icon appears next to both your name and your buddy's name, you can enjoy a two-way audio (or voice) chat. If your buddy (or buddies) are lucky enough to have iSight or DV cameras linked over a fast enough broadband connection, you can jump into a real-time, two-way video chat room, complete with audio. (Naturally, your MacBook is already equipped with an iSight camera.) Time for a very important Mark's Maxim that's violated a surprising number of times:

**Always wear a shirt while chatting with video, no matter your impressive physique.** *Always.*

If you don't see these icons, click the Video menu and make sure that the Microphone Enabled and Camera Enabled menu items are selected.

To invite someone, click the desired Buddy from the Buddy list, click Buddies, and then choose Invite to Chat. (Right-click — using two fingers on the trackpad — the Buddy in the list and click Invite to Chat.) You can also click directly on the phone or camera icon next to the person's name in your Buddy list. iChat displays the Group Chat window that you see in Figure 3-3, which also doubles as an Invitation window.

You can invite additional Buddies to enter the chat by clicking the plus button at the bottom left of the Participants list and choosing another Buddy. If the Participants list isn't visible, click the View menu and choose Show Chat Participants.

Type your invitation text into the entry box at the bottom of the window. If you want to use bold or italic text, highlight the text and press ⌘+B for Bold **(B)** or ⌘+I for Italic *(I)*. You can also add a *Smiley* (often called an *emoticon*) to your invitation text: Click in the desired spot in the text, click the Smiley button to the right of the text entry field, and then choose the proper Smiley from the list. To send the invitation text, press Return.

The recipient of your chat invitation can decline or accept your chat invitation. You're notified (as delicately as possible) if the chat has been declined.

**Figure 3-3:**
Inviting
that special
someone.
(Actually,
this guy
owes me
money.)

To invite a Buddy to an audio chat, select that person in the Buddy list, click the Buddies menu, and then choose Invite to Audio Chat (or One-Way Audio Chat, if only one of you has a microphone). A video invitation works in a similar fashion: Click Buddies and choose either Invite to Video Chat or Invite to One-Way Video Chat, depending on the hardware available. (Need I mention that you can just right-click [or Control-click] the person in your Buddy list and choose these commands from the shortcut menu that appears?)

If the chat is accepted, iChat displays a message saying that the Buddy whom you invited has joined the chat, and you now can begin the chat. You don't have to alternate sending messages back and forth between participants — everyone in a chat can compose and send messages at the same time — but I personally like to alternate when I'm chatting one on one. By the way, you might notice that AIM users are represented by the AIM Running Dude icon (unless AOL changes it, or you assign an icon picture of your own, as I describe in the "Configuring iChat" section, earlier in the chapter).

If someone invites you to a chat, you get the opposite side of the coin: A prompt dialog appears, and you can choose to accept or decline the invitation. (If it's a video chat, you even get a video preview of the person inviting you.)

You can resize the Chat window by using the handle at the bottom-right corner, just as you can most other application windows in Mac OS X.

You can also change fonts and colors while composing a line of text. Simply select the text and then choose Format⇨Show Fonts or Format⇨Show Colors (or press ⌘+T or ⌘+Shift+C) to display the Fonts and Colors windows, respectively. These windows can be resized and moved wherever you like.

## Sending SMS messages and e-mail within iChat

iChat doesn't limit you to just a chat between computers! Choose File⇨Send SMS and you can hold an SMS (Short Message Service) conversation with anyone using a digital mobile phone. iChat prompts you for the mobile-phone number, and the connection is made automatically. The SMS chat window looks just like the standard iChat text chat window. (Need I warn you that the charge for text messaging can bankrupt an unsuspecting teenager in an hour?)

You can also choose to ship off an e-mail message from within iChat. Click a person in the Buddy list and click the Buddies menu; then click Send Email to automatically launch Apple Mail.

To save the discussion in a chat, choose File⇨Save a Copy As. In the dialog that appears, type a name for the chat file, select a location where you want to store the file, and then click Save. To automatically save transcripts of all your chats, choose iChat⇨Preferences and click Messages; then select the Automatically Save Chat Transcripts To check box. By default, the transcripts are saved in an iChat folder that's created inside your Documents folder in your Home folder. You can, however, click the pop-up menu to choose another location if you like.

When the iChat window is active, a number of display choices can be made from the View menu. Click the Messages item in the View menu to display these options, including

+ **Show as Text:** Each line that you write and receive in a chat can be displayed in *balloons,* just like your favorite comic — the default — or as simple text. You can also choose to display text lines in the more traditional boxes or as compact text (allowing more room for more characters in the iChat window).

+ **Show Names and Pictures:** Each line can be displayed with the individual's picture, just the name, or both the name and picture.

If you're tired of the default background for the chat window, click View and choose the Set Chat Background menu item to choose a graphic to use for the Chat window. To return to the original appearance, choose the Clear Background menu item.

Click the Buddy list, and the View menu offers a different set of controls: You can sort your Buddy list by first name, last name, or availability; you can also toggle the display of offline Buddies. These options are also available from the Buddy List window toolbar.

Curious about the capabilities of your Mac hardware in iChat? Choose Video⇨Connection Doctor, where you can view statistics and information about your current chat, display the features of iChat that are supported by your Mac, and view any error messages that are generated by iChat during this session.

To close a chat, click the Close button on the Chat window.

## Sharing Screens and iChat Theater

How often have you wanted to show someone a neat new application, or lead your Aunt Mildred through the paces of setting up an Apple TV connection on her system? That's the idea behind the ultimate collaboration tool, *sharing* screens, where you can watch (or even remotely control) the display on another person's Mac — across any broadband Internet or local network connection!

Screen sharing must be turned on for you to send or receive sharing invites. Choose Video⇨Screen Sharing Enabled — a check mark appears next to the menu item when the feature is enabled.

If a buddy invites you to share a screen, you receive a prompt that lets you accept or decline. If you accept the sharing invitation, iChat automatically initiates an audio chat (so that you can gab away to each other while things are happening on-screen). Suddenly, you're seeing the Desktop and applications that your buddy is running, and you can both control the cursor and left- or right-click the mouse.

Throughout the screen-sharing session, iChat maintains a semi-opaque panel on your screen that has three buttons:

✦ **End the Shared Screen Session:** Click this button to exit shared screen mode.

✦ **Switch Desktops:** Click this button to swap between your MacBook's screen and the remote Mac's screen. (Those Mac owners who have enabled Fast User Switching will recognize the cool screen swap animation.)

✦ **Mute Audio:** Click this button to mute the audio during the screen-sharing session.

To invite a buddy to share your screen, choose Buddies⇨Share My Screen.

Okay, if sharing a screen with someone you don't absolutely know and trust doesn't set off alarm bells in your cranium, it **should.** Remember, anyone with shared screen access can perform most of the same actions as you can, just as if that person were sitting in front of your MacBook. Granted, most of the truly devastating things would require you to type your admin password, but a malicious individual could still delete files or wreak havoc any number of ways on your system. **Be careful with whom you share your screen!**

But wait . . . What if you don't *want* to control Aunt Mildred's Mac? Perhaps you just want to share a document instead? For example, you could show off some photos or a movie you've just finished. That's the idea behind iChat Theater, where you can share a document or video and hold a conversation while viewing the content! iChat Theater falls in between Screen Sharing and a simple file download, which I cover in the next section.

**Book VI
Chapter 3**

**Staying in Touch
with iChat**

To select one or more items for your Theater show, choose File⇨Share iPhoto with iChat Theater (to share images from your iPhoto library) or File⇨Share a File with iChat Theater (to share movies and other documents). iChat displays a standard Open dialog, in which you can select one or more items. When you're ready to begin your Theater presentation, click Share. If you're using a video camera, your video appears as a thumbnail, while your content gets center stage.

iChat Theater works with anything that can be displayed in Quick Look or located with Spotlight, including slideshows from iPhoto, a Keynote presentation, or a QuickTime movie.

## Sending Files with iChat

To send a file to a Buddy, click the desired entry in the Buddy list and then choose Buddies⇨Send File. Alternatively, you can use the ⌘+Option+F keyboard shortcut; right-click and choose Send a File; drag the file from a Finder window to the person's entry in the Buddy list; or even drag the file into the text typing window. (How's that for convenience?) A dialog appears to indicate that the recipient is being offered a file transfer request. If the file request is accepted by your Buddy, the transfer begins and is saved where the recipient specifies on her system.

If a Buddy sends you a file, the Incoming File Request pane appears. You can then either click the Decline button (to decline the file transfer) or the Save File button (to save the incoming file to any spot on your system).

Always check any files that you receive from iChat with your antivirus scanning software before you run them!

# Eliminating the Riffraff

Here I need to explain something that I hope you won't have to use — what I like to call the *Turkey Filter*. (iChat is a little more subtle — you just *ignore* people.)

To ignore someone in a chat group, click her name in the list and choose Buddies⇨Ignore *<person>*. When someone is ignored in a chat group, you don't see anything that she types or have to respond to any file transfer requests from that person.

If only it were that easy to ignore someone when he's standing close to you.

Anyway, if the person becomes a royal pain, you can also choose to *block* that person entirely. That way, the offensive cur doesn't even know that you're online, and he can't reach you at all. Click the person in the list and choose Buddies⇨Block *<person>* — the deed is done.

# Adding Visual Effects

Our esteemed Apple software developers decided to bring a little Hollywood special effects "flash" to iChat with video backdrops. You can also use many of the special effects filters provided by Photo Booth to keep your video chat room laughing!

To add a video backdrop to your video feed, choose Video⇨Video Preview to display your stunning self in a live video feed; then choose Video⇨Show Video Effects. Use the scroll buttons to move to the backdrop thumbnails toward the end of the Effects library. When you click one, iChat prompts you to leave the frame for a few seconds so that the plain background behind you can be correctly "masked" (just like those blockbuster special effects used in today's films). When your background has been captured and masked, iChat prompts you to return to your spot, and you'll see that your new static or animated backdrop is in place. *Just plain cool!*

The plainer the background behind you, the better iChat can process and mask your background. A plain wall painted a single color works best.

"But, Mark, I want my *own* movies and photos for backgrounds!" No problem — you'll notice that iChat provides six user-defined backdrop slots for your own selections at the end of the Video Effects collection. (Click the right scroll arrow in the Video Effects window until you reach the last couple of pages.) To add your own visuals, you can:

✦ Drag a video from iMovie to an empty User Backdrop well in the Video Effects window.

✦ Drag a photo from iPhoto to an empty User Backdrop well in the Video Effects window.

✦ Drag a video or photo from a Finder window to an empty User Backdrop well in the Video Effects window.

As long as an item can be displayed in Quick Look, it can be used as a video background. Think of the possibilities!

To try out a Photo Booth effect in iChat, choose Video➪Video Preview to display your live video feed; next, chooseVideo➪Show Video Effects (or press ⌘+Shift+E). Figure 3-4 illustrates the Video Preview and Video Effects windows; click a video effect thumbnail to see how it looks on you in the Preview window! Effects range from simple Black & White to a Thermal Camera look, an Andy Warhol–style Pop Art display, and a number of really cool optical distortions (such as Twirl and Light Tunnel).

**Book VI Chapter 3**

Staying in Touch with iChat

**Figure 3-4:** Andy Warhol would be impressed by my iChat video effect!

After you find just the right video effect, close the two windows and start chatting. If you decide you'd rather return your video persona to something more conventional, display the Video Effects window again and click the Normal thumbnail (which appears in the center of the first screen of thumbnails).

# Chapter 4: Expanding Your Horizons with iDisk

## In This Chapter

✔ **Setting up iDisk**

✔ **Using files and folders on your iDisk**

✔ **Using public files**

**I**f you ask the average MacBook owner about what's available on the Internet, you likely hear benefits, such as e-mail, Web surfing, RSS feeds, Google, and instant communication via iChat. What you may *not* hear is "Convenient, trouble-free storage for my files and folders."

You might have tried to use one of the dozens of storage sites on the Internet that allows you to upload and download files from a personal file area via your Web browser. Unfortunately, these Web-based storage sites are slow in transferring files and lacking in convenience, and they typically offer only a small amount of space. As a result, most computer owners decide that the idea of online storage is neat . . . but impractical.

In this chapter, I show you what *real* online storage is all about. I'm talking about *iDisk,* which is the online storage feature that's integrated into the Mac OS X Finder. No jury-rigged Web site is necessary (although you can use one if you're not on a Mac running Snow Leopard). I admit that online storage doesn't replace the hard drives on your MacBook, but with a MobileMe subscription, you can easily make use of online storage for backups and sharing files with your friends . . . from anywhere on the planet, road warrior!

So how do you actually *use* iDisk? That's the simple part! To use iDisk within Mac OS X, just do what comes naturally — it works the same as any other removable volume's Finder window. You can copy and move files and folders to and from your iDisk, create new subfolders (except in the Backup, Library, and Software root folders, which are read-only), and delete whatever you don't need.

# Grabbing Internet Storage for Your MacBook

To set up iDisk on your Mac OS X system, you need a MobileMe account. You did create one during the installation of the Big X, right? These trial accounts are active for 60 days. To subscribe, visit www.me.com and follow the prompts to join from there. (At the time of this writing, the subscription fee for an individual account is $99 per year from Apple (however, Amazon.com sells MobileMe subscriptions for significantly less). You need a credit card to create a MobileMe account, but you can cancel your trial account at any time.)

Here's a bit of good news: Other than the 60-day limit, there's almost no difference between a MobileMe trial account and a full, $99 yearly subscription, so you can try out all the MobileMe features, exactly as though you were already paying for them. *Sweet!*

With an active MobileMe account, iDisk is available automatically. To see how much storage you're using and to configure access to your Public folder, open System Preferences, click the MobileMe icon, and then click the iDisk button to display the settings that you see in Figure 4-1. (You can also click the Upgrade Storage button on this pane to subscribe to MobileMe, or if you're already a MobileMe subscriber, add storage space.)

**Figure 4-1:** Your iDisk settings are available from System Preferences.

The iDisk Disk Space bar graph illustrates how much of your current iDisk territory you're using.

## Pinning down your iDisk

So where exactly *are* your files kept when you use your iDisk? In earlier versions of Mac OS X, your acre of storage farmland always sat exclusively on one of Apple's iDisk *file servers* — perhaps in Cupertino, perhaps elsewhere. These server computers are especially designed to store terabytes (TB) of information (1TB equals 1,000GB), and they're connected to the Internet via high-speed trunk lines. (And yes, they do have a firewall.) Your Internet copy of your iDisk is still stored on an Apple file server.

However, you can elect to keep a local copy of your iDisk storage area — usually called a *mirror* — on your MacBook's hard drive. Before you scratch your head wondering why you're duplicating your iDisk files on your computer, here's the reason: If you do decide to keep a local copy of your files, you can work on them even when you're not connected to the Internet! Snow Leopard automatically synchronizes any files that you've updated locally with your remote iDisk whenever you connect to the Internet. (If you use multiple Macs at different locations, think about being able to access the latest copies of your files from *any* of them, right from the Finder!)

This nifty mirror also greatly speeds up things when you're browsing the contents of your iDisk or perhaps loading and saving an iDisk document; that's because you're working with your local copy, and Mac OS X updates any changes that you make to the corresponding remote file on the iDisk server. You can tell that things are updating when that funky little yin-yang, circular doodad — the thing next to your iDisk in the Finder window — is rotating in its animated fashion. (And yes, I have it on good authority: That's what the Apple software developers call it, too.)

You're not required to use a mirror, however. To disable the mirroring feature and return to the remote-only operation of old, click the iDisk Syncing Stop button on the iDisk pane in System Preferences to turn it off. Remember, though, that with the mirroring feature turned off, you must have an Internet connection to use iDisk, and things will move more slowly because you're accessing everything across the Internet.

You can specify the access privilege level for other MobileMe users from this pane as well. Select the Read Only radio button to prevent any other MobileMe user from copying files to your Public folder, or select the Read & Write radio button to allow others to save files there.

No matter which privilege level you choose, you can also set a password that other MobileMe users must type before they're allowed access to your Public folder. This is the very definition of *A Truly Good Idea*. (More on the Public folder in the next section.)

If you've already set a password, you can change it by clicking the Set Password button and typing the new word in the Password box. Retype the word in the Confirm box to verify it; then click OK to save the change and return to the MobileMe System Preferences pane.

# Understanding What's on Your iDisk

In contrast to the physical hard drive in your MacBook, your iDisk never needs formatting or defragmenting, and you never have to check it for errors. However, the structure of an iDisk is fixed, so you can't just go crazy creating your own folders. In fact, you can't create new folders at the *root* — the top level — of your iDisk at all, but you can create new folders inside most of the root folders.

Now that you're thoroughly rooterized, here are the folders that you find hanging out in your iDisk:

✦ **Backup:** This is a read-only folder that contains the backup files created with the MobileMe Backup application. You can, however, copy the files in this folder to a removable drive on your system for an additional level of safekeeping.

✦ **Documents:** This folder holds any application documents that you want to store — things like spreadsheets and letters. No one but you can access these items; you can, however, tag items in the Documents folder as *shared*, allowing individuals or groups to download them using an access code sent by MobileMe in an e-mail message. Sharing files is a great way to transfer files too big to send as e-mail attachments.

✦ **Groups:** This folder holds files that you want to share with others in any MobileMe Groups you might have joined.

✦ **Library:** Another read-only folder. This spot contains the configuration data and custom settings that you've created for other MobileMe features.

✦ **Movies:** QuickTime movies go here — again, you can add the movies stored here to your Web pages. (I cover QuickTime like a blanket in Book IV, Chapter 8.)

✦ **Music:** This is the repository for all your iTunes music and playlists, and the contents can be added to your Web pages. (iTunes is the star of Chapter 2 in Book IV.) Mine is stuffed full of Mozart, Scarlatti, and that Bach fellow.

✦ **Pictures:** This folder is the vault for your JPEG and GIF images, including those that you want to use with your Web pages.

✦ **Public:** This is the spot to place files that you specifically want to share with others, either directly through iDisk or with your Web pages. If you've allowed write access, others can copy files to your Public folder as well.

✦ **Sites:** The Web pages that you store here can be created with iWeb, which I cover in Book IV, Chapter 7. In fact, you can even use your own Web page design application and copy the completed site files here.

✦ **Software:** Apple provides this read-only folder as a service to MobileMe members; it contains a selection of the latest freeware, shareware, and commercial demos for you to enjoy. To try something out, open the Software folder and copy whatever you like to your Mac OS X Desktop. Then you can install and run the application from the local copy of the files.

✦ **Web:** This folder holds your MobileMe Galleries created from within iPhoto, as well as other media used by iWeb.

# Opening and Using iDisk

When you're connected to the Internet, you can open your iDisk in one of the following ways:

✦ **From the Finder menu, choose Go⇨iDisk and then choose My iDisk from the submenu or use the ⌘+Shift+I keyboard shortcut.**

✦ **Click the iDisk icon in the Finder Sidebar.**

✦ **Add an iDisk button to your Finder window toolbar by choosing View⇨Customize Toolbar.**

After you add the button, you can click it to connect to your iDisk from anywhere in the Finder.

Your iDisk opens in a new Finder window. After you use one of these methods in a Mac OS X session, your iDisk icon appears on the Mac OS X Desktop; Figure 4-2 shows the iDisk contents in a Finder window. The iDisk volume icon remains until you shut down or restart your MacBook. (Alternatively, you can dismiss the iDisk volume icon from your Desktop using the same method by which you eject an external drive: Click the iDisk icon and press ⌘+E or click the Eject button next to the iDisk icon in the Finder window Sidebar.)

**Figure 4-2:**
The contents of your iDisk — pretty iNeat, I'm thinking.

If you're using a remote PC with an Internet connection, you can log in to the MobileMe page at www.me.com and use your Web browser to access the contents of your iDisk. (Hey, sometimes this is the only choice you have.)

However, you don't actually need to open your iDisk in a Finder window to use it, because you can also load and save files directly to your iDisk from within any application. Simply choose your iDisk as you would any of the hard drives on your system when using the application's Open, Save, or Save As commands.

You can also open an iDisk Public folder — either yours or the Public folder inside another person's iDisk — as if it were an Internet file server. As I explain earlier in the chapter, if that person has set a password, you need to enter that password to gain access to all of his or her iDisk folders. From the Finder menu, choose Go⇨iDisk⇨Other User's iDisk (or, to jump directly to their Public folder, choose Go⇨iDisk⇨Other User's Public Folder). If you choose the former, Snow Leopard prompts you for the other person's member name and password; if you pick the latter, you need only enter the other MobileMe member's account name.

After you enter a valid iDisk member name (and password, if required), you see the MobileMe member's Public folder.

You can also use the server address

```
http://idisk.me.com/username-Public?
```

to connect to an iDisk from computers running Windows and Linux. Check the Help for your operating system to determine how to connect to a WebDAV server (usually called a *Web folder* in the Windows world). When prompted for your access username and password, use your MobileMe account name and password. If you're using Windows XP or Vista, Apple has provided an even easier way to manage your iDisk: Use MobileMe Control Panel for Windows, which you can download from www.me.com.

# Chapter 5: Surfing with Safari

## In This Chapter

✔ **Introducing the Safari window and controls**

✔ **Visiting Web sites with Safari**

✔ **Moving between sites**

✔ **Creating and using bookmarks**

✔ **Receiving files with Safari**

✔ **Surfing with your tabs showing**

✔ **Saving Web pages to disk**

✔ **Protecting your privacy on the Web**

✔ **Blocking those irritating pop-ups**

*W*hen I was designing the Table of Contents for this book, I seriously considered leaving this chapter out. After all, more people use a Web browser now than any other software application. Who really needs a guide to mowing a lawn?

But then again, I suddenly thought of all the hidden features that folks don't know about Apple's Safari browser — for example, the tips and tricks that can help you organize your online visits. It's a little like finding out more about the lawn mower itself: Even though you might not need tips on mowing, many people don't know how to remove the spark plug in the winter or how to sharpen the blade so that you can handle taller grass. To put it another way, *magic is nothing more than technology that someone understands.*

In this chapter, I show you how to use those other controls and toolbar buttons in Safari — you know, the ones in addition to the Forward and Back buttons — and you discover how to keep track of where you've been and where you'd like to go. (Oh, and did I mention that you need an Internet connection?)

***One note:*** Many authors have written entire books on Web browsing. As you might guess, this chapter is far narrower in scope than those books — I have more ground to cover before dinner — and it doesn't include every one of Safari's features. However, I think the coverage that you find here explains all that you're likely to need for most surfing sessions.

# *Pretend You've Never Used This Thing*

Figure 5-1 illustrates the Safari window. You can launch Safari directly from the Dock or you can click the Safari icon within your Applications folder.

Major sections of the Safari window include

✦ **The toolbar:** You'll find the most often used commands on this toolbar — for tasks such as navigation, adding bookmarks, and searching Google. Plus, here you can type or paste the address for Web sites that you'd like to visit. The toolbar can be hidden to provide you with more real estate in your browser window for Web content. To toggle hidden mode, press ⌘+| (the vertical bar right above the backslash) or choose View⇨Hide/Show Toolbar.

✦ **The Bookmarks bar:** Consider this a toolbar that allows you to jump directly to your favorite Web sites with a single click or two. I show you later, in the section "Adding and Using Bookmarks," how to add and remove sites from your Bookmarks bar. For now, remember that you can toggle the display of the Bookmarks bar by choosing View⇨Hide/Show Bookmarks Bar or by pressing ⌘+Shift+B.

Toolbar             Bookmarks bar

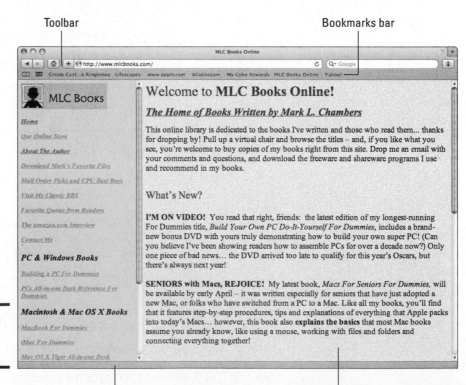

**Figure 5-1:** Safari at a glance.

Status bar             Content window

✦ **The Content window:** Congratulations! At last, you've waded through all the pregame show and you've reached the area where Web pages are actually displayed. As can any other window, the Content window can be scrolled; when you minimize Safari to the Dock, you get a *thumbnail* (minimized) image of the Content window.

The Content window often contains underlined text and graphical icons that transport you to other pages when you click them. These underlined words and icons are *links,* and they make it easy to move from one area of a site to another or to a completely different site.

✦ **The status bar:** The status bar displays information about what the cursor is currently resting upon, such as the address for a link or the name of an image; it also updates you on what's happening while a page is loading. To hide or display the status bar, press ⌘+/ (forward slash) or choose View➪Hide/Show Status Bar.

# Visiting Web Sites

Here's the stuff that virtually everyone over the age of five knows how to do . . . but I get paid by the word, and some folks might not be aware of the myriad ways of visiting a site. You can load a Web page using any of the following methods:

✦ **Type (or paste) a Web site address into the Address box on the toolbar and then press Return.**

If you're typing in an address and Safari recognizes the site as one that you've visited in the past, it helps by completing the address for you. Press Return if you want to accept the suggested site. If this is a new site, just keep typing.

The latest version of Safari includes a *Smart Address* field that displays a new pop-up menu of sites that match the text you've entered. Safari does this by using sites taken from your History file and your bookmarks. If the site you want to visit appears in the list, click it to jump there immediately.

✦ **Click a Bookmarks entry within Safari.**

✦ **Click the Home button, which takes you to the home page that you specify.**

More on this in the section "Setting Up Your Home Page," later in this chapter.

✦ **Click the Show Top Sites button on the toolbar.**

Safari displays a wall of preview thumbnail pages from your most frequently visited sites, and you can jump to a site just by clicking on the preview. Click the Edit button on the Top Sites screen to delete a preview thumbnail — click the X — or you can "anchor" a thumbnail to keep it on the screen permanently by clicking the pin icon next to the desired thumbnail. You can also choose the size of the preview thumbnails in Edit mode.

Because each thumbnail is updated with the most current content, the Top Sites wall makes a great time-saver — you can quickly make a visual check of all your favorite haunts from one screen!

✦ **Click a page link in Apple Mail or another Internet-savvy application.**

Some Mac applications require you to hold down ⌘ while clicking to open a Web page.

✦ **Click a page link within another Web page.**

✦ **Use the Google box in the toolbar.**

Click in the Google box, type the contents that you want to find, and then press Return. Safari presents you with the search results page on Google for the text that you entered. (In case you've been living under the Internet equivalent of a rock for the last couple of years, *Google.com* is the preeminent search site on the Web — people use Google to find everything from used auto parts to ex-spouses.)

✦ **Click a Safari page icon in the Dock or a Finder window.**

For example, Mac OS X already has an icon in the Dock that takes you to the Mac OS X page on the Apple Web site. Drag a site from your Bookmarks bar and drop it on the right side of the Dock. Clicking the icon that you add launches Safari and automatically loads that site.

This trick works only on the side of the Dock to the right of the vertical line.

If you minimize Safari to the Dock, you'll see a thumbnail of the page with the Safari logo superimposed on it. Click this thumbnail in the Dock to restore the page to its full glory.

## Navigating the Web

A typical Web surfing session is a linear experience — you bop from one page to the next, absorbing the information that you want and discarding the rest. However, after you visit a few sites, you might find that you need to return to where you've been or head to the familiar ground of your home page. Safari offers these default navigational controls on the toolbar:

✦ **Back:** Click the Back button (the left-facing arrow) on the toolbar to return to the last page you visited. Additional clicks take you to previous pages, in reverse order. The Back button is disabled if you haven't visited at least two sites.

✦ **Forward:** If you've clicked the Back button at least once, clicking the Forward button (the right-facing arrow) takes you to the next page (or through the pages) where you originally were, in forward order. The Forward button is disabled if you haven't used the Back button.

✦ **Home:** Click this button (look for the little house) to return to your home page.

Not all these buttons and controls must appear on your toolbar. To display or hide toolbar controls, choose View⇨Customize Toolbar. The sheet that appears works just like the Customize Toolbar sheet within a Finder window: Drag the control you want from the sheet to your Safari toolbar or drag a control that you don't want from the toolbar to the sheet.

✦ **AutoFill:** If you fill out a lot of forms online — when you're shopping at Web sites, for example — you can click the AutoFill button (which looks like a little text box and a pen) to complete these forms for you. You can set what information is used for AutoFill by choosing Safari⇨Preferences and clicking the AutoFill toolbar button.

To be honest, I'm not a big fan of releasing *any* of my personal information to *any* Web site, so I don't use AutoFill often. If you do decide to use this feature, make sure that the connection is secure (look for the padlock icon in the upper-right corner of the Safari window) and read the site's Privacy Agreement page first to see how your identity data will be treated.

✦ **Zoom:** Shrinks or expands the size of text on the page, offering smaller, space-saving characters (for the shrinking crowd) or larger, easier-to-read text (for the expanding crowd). Hence the button, which is labeled with a small and large letter *A*.

✦ **Stop/Reload:** Click Reload at the right side of the Address box (look for the circular arrow) to *refresh* (reload) the contents of the current page. Although most pages remain static, some pages change their content at regular intervals or after you fill out a form or click a button. By clicking Reload, you can see what's changed on these pages. (I use Reload every hour or so with CNN.com, for example.) While a page is loading, the Reload button turns into the Stop button — with a little X mark — and you can click it to stop the loading of the content from the current page. This is a real boon when a download takes *foorrevverr,* which can happen when you're trying to visit a very popular or very slow Web site (especially if you're using a dial-up modem connection to the Internet). Using Stop is also handy if a page has a number of very large graphics that are likely to take a long time to load.

✦ **Open in Dashboard:** Click this button to create a Dashboard widget using the contents of the currently displayed Web page. Safari prompts you to choose which clickable section of the page to be included within the widget's borders (such as the local radar map on your favorite weather Web site). Click Add, and Dashboard loads automatically with your new widget. (More on widgets in Book III, Chapter 2.)

**Book VI
Chapter 5**

**Surfing with Safari**

✦ **Add Bookmark:** Click this toolbar button (which carries a plus sign) to add a page to your Bookmarks bar or Bookmarks menu. (More on this in a tad.)

✦ **Google Search:** As I mention earlier, you can click in this box and type text that you want to find on the Web via the Google search engine; press Return to display the results. To repeat a recent search, click the down arrow in the Google Search box and select it from the pop-up menu.

✦ **Print:** Click this convenient button to print the contents of the Safari window. (Dig that crazy printer icon!)

✦ **Report Bug:** A rather strange creature, the Safari Bug button makes it easy to alert Apple when you encounter a page that doesn't display properly in Safari. (Software developers call such glitches *bugs* — hence the name.) When you click the Bug button, you'll see a sheet with the settings shown in Figure 5-2; take time to enter a short description of the problem that you're having. (I also click More Options to enable the Send Screen Shot of Current Page and the Send Source of Current Page check boxes, giving the Apple folks more to work with while they're debugging Safari.) Then click the Submit button to send the bug report to Apple.

**Figure 5-2:**
Have
at thee,
troublesome
buggy page!

# Setting Up Your Home Page

Choosing a home page is one of the easiest methods of speeding up your Web surfing, especially if you're using a dial-up modem connection. However, a large percentage of the Mac owners whom I've talked with have never set their own home page; instead, they simply use the default home page provided by their browser! With Safari running, take a moment to follow these steps to declare your own freedom to choose your own home page:

*1.* **If you want to use a specific Web page as your new home page, display it in Safari.**

I recommend selecting a page with few graphics or a fast-loading popular site.

*2.* **Choose Safari⇨Preferences or press ⌘+, (comma).**

*3.* **Click the General button.**

You see the settings shown in Figure 5-3.

**Book VI
Chapter 5**

**Surfing with Safari**

**Figure 5-3:**
Adding
your own
home page
is an easy
change you
can make.

*4.* **Click the Set to Current Page button.**

# Lean, fast, and mean — that's RSS

Well, maybe not *mean* — after all, I don't want you to be afraid of RSS (RDF Site Summary) pages! RSS Web sites display updated information using a shortened list format, rather like a newspaper headline, without unnecessary graphics or silly advertisements. You can tell when a Web site has RSS pages available because Safari displays an RSS icon at the right side of the Address box on the toolbar. (When you click the RSS icon, the Web address switches to a `feed://` prefix — another indication that you're not in Kansas reading HTML pages anymore.)

To display more information about a news item on an RSS page, click the item headline. Safari opens the corresponding Web page — yep, once again you're back in the world of HTML —

and you can read the full story. To return to the RSS feed, click the Back button on the toolbar. Naturally, RSS feed pages can be bookmarked. In fact, Apple gives you a number of RSS sites that you can explore immediately.

To customize your RSS display, choose Safari➪Preferences and then click the RSS tab. By default, Safari checks for updated RSS headlines every 30 minutes, but you can change this to an hourly or daily check. (Of course, you can also check for updates manually by reloading the RSS page, just as you would any other Web page.) New articles can be assigned a highlighted color, and you can specify the amount of time an item should remain on the RSS page after it's published.

5. **Alternatively, click the New Windows Open With pop-up menu and choose Empty Page if you want Safari to open a new window with a blank page.**

   This is the fastest choice of all for a home page.

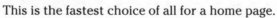

   Choose Top Sites from the New Windows Open With pop-up menu to display the Top Sites screen I described earlier each time you open a new window.

6. **Click the Close button to exit the Preferences dialog.**

   Visit your home page at any time by pressing the Home button on the toolbar.

## Adding and Using Bookmarks

No doubt about it: Bookmarks make the Web a friendly place. As you collect bookmarks in Safari, you're able to immediately jump from one site to another with a single click of the Bookmarks menu or the buttons on the Bookmarks bar.

To add a bookmark, first navigate to the desired page and then do any of the following:

✦ **Choose Bookmarks⇨Add Bookmark.**

✦ **Press the ⌘+D keyboard shortcut.**

   Safari displays a sheet where you can enter the name for the bookmark and also select where it appears (on the Bookmarks bar or the Bookmarks menu).

✦ **Drag the icon next to the Web address from the Address field to the Bookmarks bar.**

**Book VI
Chapter 5**

**Surfing with Safari**

You can also drag a link on the current page to the Bookmarks bar, but note that doing this adds a bookmark only for the page corresponding to the link — not the current page.

To jump to a bookmark

✦ **Choose it from the Bookmarks menu.**

   If the bookmark is contained in a folder, which I discuss later in this section, move your pointer over the folder name to show its contents and then click the bookmark.

✦ **Click the bookmark on the Bookmarks bar.**

   If you've added a large number of items to the Bookmarks bar, click the More icon on the edge of the Bookmarks bar to display the rest of the buttons.

✦ **Click the Show All Bookmarks button (which looks like a small, opened book) on the Bookmarks bar and then click the desired bookmark.**

   The Bookmarks window that you see in Figure 5-4 appears — complete with swank Cover Flow display — where you can review each collection of bookmarks at leisure. As you might expect, Safari's Cover Flow works just as the Cover Flow view does in a Finder window.

   The more bookmarks you add, the more unwieldy the Bookmarks menu and the Bookmarks window become. To keep things organized, choose Bookmarks⇨Add Bookmark Folder and then type a name for the new folder. With folders, you can organize your bookmarks into *collections,* which appear in the column at the left of the Bookmarks window (or as separate submenus within the Bookmarks menu). You can drag bookmarks into the new folder to help reduce the clutter.

To delete a bookmark or a folder from the Bookmarks window, click it and then press Delete.

**Figure 5-4:**
The
Bookmarks
window
puts all your
bookmarks
within easy
reach.

# Downloading Files

A huge chunk of the fun that you'll find on the Web is the ability to download images and files. If you've visited a site that offers files for downloading, typically you just click the Download button or the download file link, and Safari takes care of the rest. You'll see the Downloads status window, which keeps you updated as to the progress of the transfer. While the file is downloading, feel free to continue browsing or even download additional files; the status window helps you keep track of what's going on and when everything will be finished transferring. To display the Download status window from the keyboard, press ⌘+Option+L.

By default, Safari saves any downloaded files to the Downloads folder that appears in your Dock, which I like and use. To specify the location where downloaded files are stored — for example, if you'd like to save them directly to the desktop — follow these steps:

*1.* **Choose Safari⇨Preferences or press ⌘+, (comma).**

*2.* **Click the General tab and then click the Save Downloaded Files To pop-up menu.**

*3.* **Choose Other.**

4. **Navigate to the location where you want the files stored.**

5. **Click the Select button.**

6. **Click the Close button to exit Preferences.**

To download a specific image that appears on a Web page, move your pointer over the image and right-click. Then choose Save Image As from the pop-up menu that appears. Safari prompts you for the location where you want to store the file.

You can choose to automatically open files that Safari considers safe — things like movies, text files, and PDF files that are **very** unlikely to store a virus or a damaging macro. By default, the Open "Safe" Files after Downloading check box is selected on the General pane. However, if you're interested in preventing *anything* you download from running until you've manually checked it with your antivirus application, you can deselect the check box and breathe easy.

Book VI
Chapter 5

Surfing with Safari

 Luckily, Safari has matured to the point that it can seamlessly handle virtually any multimedia file type that It encounters. However, if you've downloaded a multimedia file and Safari doesn't seem to be able to play or display it, try loading the file within QuickTime Player. As you can read in Book IV, Chapter 8, *QuickTime Player* is the Swiss Army knife of multimedia players, and it can recognize a huge number of audio, video, and image formats.

# *Using Subscriptions and History*

To keep track of where you've been, you can display the History list by clicking the History menu. To return to a page in the list, just choose it from the History menu. Note that Safari also arranges older history items by the date you visited the site, so you can easily jump back a couple of days to that page you forgot to bookmark!

In fact, Safari also searches the History list automatically, when it fills in an address that you're typing — that's the feature I mention in the earlier section "Visiting Web Sites."

To view your Top Sites thumbnail screen, press ⌘+Shift+1 or choose Show Top Sites from the History menu.

If you're worried about security and would rather not keep track of where you've been online, I show you how to clear the contents of the History file in the "Handling ancient history" section, later in this chapter.

## Tabs Are Your Browsing Friends

Safari also offers *tabbed browsing,* which many folks use to display (and organize) multiple Web pages at one time. For example, if you're doing a bit of comparison shopping for a new piece of hardware between different online stores, tabs are ideal.

When you hold down the ⌘ key and click a link or bookmark using tabs, a tab representing the new page appears at the top of the Safari window. Just click the tab to switch to that page. (If you don't hold down ⌘, things revert to business as usual, and Safari replaces the contents of the window with the new page.) If you hold down *both* Shift and ⌘ while you click, Safari opens a new tab and automatically switches to the new tab. Figure 5-5 illustrates a number of pages that I've opened in Safari using tabs.

You can also open a new tab by clicking the plus sign that appears at the upper-right corner of the Safari window.

To fine-tune your tabbed browsing experience, choose Safari⇨Preferences to display the Preferences dialog; then click Tabs. From here, you can turn off the confirmation window that normally appears when you close Safari with multiple tabs or windows open. You can also specify whether a new tab or window automatically becomes the active window within Safari.

**Figure 5-5:**
Hang on,
Martha;
we've
struck tabs!

Done with a page? You can remove a tabbed page by clicking the X button next to the tab's title.

## Saving Web Pages

If you've encountered a page that you'd like to load later, you can save it to disk in its entirety. (Just the text, mind you, not the images.) Follow these steps:

*1.* **Display the desired page.**

*2.* **Choose File➪Save As or press ⌘+S.**

*3.* **In the Save As text field, type a name for the saved page.**

*4.* **From the Where pop-up menu, navigate to the location where you want to store the file on your system.**

   To expand the sheet to allow navigation to any location on your system, click the button with the downward arrow.

*5.* **Click the Format pop-up menu to choose the format for the saved page.**

   Usually, you'll want to choose a Web Archive, which saves the entire page and can be displayed just as you see it. However, if you want to save just the HTML source code, choose Page Source.

*6.* **Click Save to begin the download process.**

   After the Save file has been created, double-click it to load it in Safari.

A quick word about printing a page within Safari: Some combinations of background and text colors might conspire together to render your printed copy practically worthless. In a case like that, use your printer's grayscale setting (if it has one) or deselect the Print Backgrounds check box in the Print dialog. Alternatively, you can simply click and drag to select the text on the page, press ⌘+C to copy it, and then paste the text into Word or Pages, where you can print the page on a less offensive background (while still keeping the text formatting largely untouched). You can also save the contents of a page as plain text, as I just demonstrated.

If you'd rather mail the contents of a Web page to a friend — or just a link to the page, which is faster to send over a dial-up Internet connection — choose either File➪Mail Contents of This Page or File➪Mail Link to This Page. (From the keyboard, press ⌘+I to send the contents in an e-mail message or press ⌘+Shift+I to send a link in e-mail.) Mail loads automatically, complete with a prepared e-mail message. Just address it to the recipients and then click Send!

# *Protecting Your Privacy*

No chapter on Safari would be complete without a discussion of security, against both outside intrusion from the Internet and prying eyes around your MacBook. Hence this last section, which covers protecting your privacy.

Although diminutive, the padlock icon that appears at the top of the Safari window when you're connected to a secure Web site means a great deal! A *secure site* encrypts the information that you send and receive, making it much harder for those of unscrupulous ideals to obtain things such as credit card numbers and personal information. You can click the padlock icon (next to the site name) to display the security certificate in use on that particular site.

## *Yes, there are such things as bad cookies*

First, a definition of this ridiculous term: A *cookie,* a small file that a Web site automatically saves on your hard drive, contains information that the site will use on your future visits. For example, a site might save a cookie to preserve your site preferences for the next time or — in the case of a site such as Amazon.com — to identify you automatically and help customize the offerings that you see.

In and of themselves, cookies aren't bad things. Unlike a virus, a cookie file isn't going to replicate itself or wreak havoc on your system, and only the original site can read the cookie that it creates. However, many folks don't appreciate acting as a gracious host for a slew of little snippets of personal information. (Not to mention that some cookies have highly suggestive names, which could lead to all sorts of conclusions. End of story.)

You can choose to accept all cookies — the default — or you can opt to disable cookies altogether. You can also set Safari to accept cookies only from the sites you choose to visit. To change your *Cookie Acceptance Plan* (or CAP, for those who absolutely crave acronyms), follow these steps:

1. **Choose Safari⇨Preferences.**

2. **Click the Security toolbar button.**

   Safari displays the preference settings shown in Figure 5-6.

3. **Choose how to accept cookies via these radio button choices:**

   *Never:* Block cookies entirely.

   *Always:* Accept all cookies.

   *Only from Sites You Navigate To:* Personally, I use this option, which allows sites like Amazon.com to work correctly without allowing a barrage of illicit cookies.

**Figure 5-6:**
Specifying
who's
welcome
in my
cookie jar.

4. **To view the cookies currently on your system, click the Show Cookies button.**

    If a site's cookies are blocked, you might have to take care of things manually, such as by providing a password on the site that used to be read automatically from the cookie.

5. **Click the Close button to save your changes.**

## Cleaning your cache

Safari speeds up the loading of Web sites by storing often-used images and multimedia files in a temporary storage, or *cache,* folder. Naturally, the files in your cache folder can be displayed (hint), which could lead to assumptions (hint, hint) about the sites you've been visiting (hint, hint, hint). (Tactful, ain't I?)

Luckily, Safari makes it easy to dump the contents of your cache file. Just choose Safari➪Empty Cache; then click Empty to confirm that you want to clean up your cache.

## Handling ancient history

As you might imagine, your History file leaves a very clear set of footprints indicating where you've been on the Web. To delete the contents of the History menu, choose History➪Clear History (at the very bottom of the History menu).

Safari also allows you to specify an amount of time to retain entries in your History file. Open the Safari Preferences dialog, click the General tab, and then click the Remove History Items pop-up menu to specify the desired amount of time. Items can be rolled off daily, weekly, biweekly, monthly, or yearly.

## Avoiding those @*!^%$ pop-up ads

I hate pop-up ads, and I'm sure you do, too. To block most of those pop-up windows with advertisements for everything from low-rate mortgages to "sure-thing" Internet casinos, click the Safari menu and verify that Block Pop-Up Windows is selected. (If it's not selected, click the menu item to toggle the menu item on.)

From time to time, you might run across a Web site that actually does something *constructive* with pop-up windows, such as present a download or login prompt. If you need to temporarily deactivate pop-up blocking, press ⌘+Shift+K to toggle it off. Then press ⌘+Shift+K again to turn pop-up blocking back on after you've finished with the site.

# Chapter 6: Staying Secure Online

## In This Chapter

✔ **Understanding the dangers of going online**

✔ **Using a firewall**

✔ **Avoiding trouble online**

*1* know that you've heard horror stories about hacking: Big corporations and big government installations seem to be as open to hackers as a public library. Often, you read that even entire identities are being stolen online. When you consider that your MacBook can contain very sensitive and private information in your life — such as your Social Security number and financial information — it's enough to make you nervous about turning on your computer long enough to check your eBay auctions.

But how much of that is Hollywood? How truly real is the danger, especially to a MacBook owner like yourself? And how can you protect yourself? The good news is that you can *easily* secure your data from all but the most determined hacker — in fact, depending on the hardware that you're using to connect to the Internet, you might be well guarded right now without even knowing it.

In this chapter, I continue a quest that I've pursued for over a decade now — to make my readers feel comfortable and secure in the online world by explaining the truth about what can happen and telling you how you can protect your system from intrusions.

One quick note: This chapter is written with the home and small business MacBook owner in mind. Macs that access the Internet through a larger corporate network are very likely already protected by that knight in shining armor, the network system administrator. (Insert applause here.) Of course, if you're using Mac OS X in your office, you're still welcome to read and follow this material. Check with your system administrator, however, before you attempt to implement any of the recommendations that I make.

## What Can Really Happen?

Before I begin, I want to offer you a moment of reassurance and a little of my personal background to explain that I'm well qualified to be your guide through this online minefield. (After all, you don't want Jerry Lewis lecturing you on how to maintain your Internet security. He's a funny guy, though, *convenez-vous?*)

✦ I've been running and managing all sorts of online systems since the days of the BBS *(Bulletin Board System),* the text-based dinosaurs that used to rule the online world in the early '80s to early '90s. (In fact, my first book was on this very subject — and it contained a chapter on viruses long before they were the darlings of the techno-media.)

✦ As a consultant, I run Web sites and squash virus attacks for a number of companies and organizations.

✦ I run a popular Internet radio station that serves up '70s hits in CD-quality to anyone with a high-speed DSL or cable Internet connection and a copy of iTunes. (More on this broadcasting revolution in Book IV, Chapter 2.)

✦ I keep my own office network of six computers safe from attack while still providing readers all over the world with Web sites and the aforementioned radio station and BBS.

With that understood, here's what can happen to you online *without* the right safeguards, on *any* computer:

✦ **Hackers can access shared information on your network.** If you're running an unguarded network, others can gain access to your documents and applications or wreak havoc on your system.

✦ **Your system could be infected with a virus or dangerous macro.** Left to their own devices, these misbehaving programs and macro commands can delete files or turn your entire hard drive into an empty paperweight. (Although Mac viruses are very rare as I write this, I don't think we'll enjoy such luxury for long. Plus, if you dual-boot your MacBook into Windows XP or Windows Vista, you've suddenly entered a veritable minefield of PC viruses and spyware. More on this in a page or two.)

✦ **Unsavory individuals could attempt to contact members of your family.** This kind of attack may take place through iChat, e-mail, or Web discussion boards, putting your family's safety at risk.

✦ **Hackers can use your system to attack others.** Your laptop can be tricked into helping hackers when they attempt to knock out Web servers and public access File Transfer Protocol (FTP) sites on the Internet. Along the same lines, that innocent Web server you put online can be misused by spam-spewing, online "entrepreneurs." (Cute name, right?)

✦ **Criminals can attempt to con you out of your credit card or personal information.** The Internet is a prime tool used by those trying to steal identities.

## If it smells phishy . . .

Ever heard of the word *phishing?* Con artists and hackers create Web sites that look just like major online stores — including big names such as eBay, PayPal, and Amazon. These turkeys then send out junk e-mail messages that tell you that you must log on to this Web site to refresh or correct your personal information.

As you've no doubt already guessed, that information is siphoned off and sold to the highest bidder. *Your* credit card, *your* password, and *your* address. Luckily, if you follow the tips that I give later in this chapter in the section "A Dose of Common Sense: Things Not to Do Online," you'll avoid these phishing expeditions!

To be absolutely honest, some danger is indeed present every time you or any user of your MacBook connects to the Internet. However, here's the good news. With the right safeguards, it's literally impossible for most of those worst-case scenarios to happen on your MacBook, and what remains would be so difficult that even the most die-hard hacker would throw in the towel long before reaching your computer or network.

Using a Macintosh gives you an advantage: Hackers and virus developers (there's a career for you) are traditionally interested only in "having fun" with PCs running Windows, so the likelihood that Snow Leopard could pick up a virus is far, far less than it would be if you were using Windows XP or Vista. As I mention earlier, if you boot into Windows using Snow Leopard's dual-boot feature on your MacBook, you need to pay heed to Windows XP or Vista security.

Because this is a book that focuses on Mac OS X Snow Leopard, I don't spend much time covering Windows. If you'd like a comprehensive guide to Windows XP, Windows Vista, and the PC world, however, I can heartily recommend the sister volume to this book, *PCs All-in-One Desk Reference For Dummies,* Fourth Edition, published by Wiley. Why the strong recommendation? Well, I wrote that book as well!

Evidently, Apple just doesn't have the numbers to attract the attention of the Bad Guys *yet* . . . yet another reason to enjoy the exclusive nature of the Mac universe (and its UNIX foundation)! (Heck, I even know a couple of fellow Mac owners who feel they just don't need antivirus protection — but believe me, this is *not* an area where you want to be lax and lazy, and you **still need** an antivirus application! More on antivirus software later in this chapter.)

## More of Mark's totally unnecessary computer trivia

The term *hacker* dates far back in the annals of the personal computer — in fact, it originally had nothing to do with networks, the Internet, or illegal activities at all . . . because In The Beginning, there was no public Internet!

"Explain yourself, Chambers!" All right. The original hackers were electronics buffs, ham radio operators, computer hobbyists, and engineers who built (or *hacked*) a working computer out of individual components with a soldering gun and a whole lotta guts. At the time, you didn't simply order a computer from Dell or visit your local Maze o' Wires store in the mall to select your favorite system.

No, I'm talking about the mid-'70s, in the halcyon time before IBM even introduced the IBM PC (and when the only folks using the Internet, which wasn't called that back then,

were military folks and researchers). Even the simplest computer — really nothing more than a glorified calculator by today's standards — had to be lovingly assembled by hand. These early personal computers didn't run software as we know it. Instead, you programmed them manually through a bank of switches on the front, and they responded with codes displayed on a bank of lights. (Think about that the next time you launch Microsoft Word 2008.)

Today, of course, the need to assemble a computer from individual transistors is nonexistent, and the word *hacker* has an entirely different connotation — but don't be surprised if you meet an older member of your Macintosh user's group who's proud to be an old-fashioned hacker! (Look for the soldering gun, usually worn in a holster like a sidearm.)

I also want to point out that virtually everyone reading this book — as well as the guy writing it — really doesn't have anything that's worth a malicious hacking campaign. Things like Quicken data files, saved games of Sims 2, and genealogical data might be priceless to us, of course, but most dedicated hackers are after bigger game. Unfortunately, the coverage that the media and Hollywood give to corporate and government attacks can turn even Aunt Harriet more than a little paranoid. Therefore, time for another of Mark's Maxims:

**It's not really necessary to consider the FBI or Interpol each time you poke your MacBook's power button. A few simple precautions are all that's required.**

## *"Shields Up, Chekov!"*

"Okay, Mark, now I know the real story on what can happen to my computer online. So what do I do to safeguard my MacBook?" You need but two essential tools to protect your hardware (besides a healthy amount of common sense, which I cover in the upcoming section "A Dose of Common Sense: Things Not to Do Online"): a firewall and an antivirus program.

## Firewall basics

First, a definition: a *firewall* is a piece of hardware or software that essentially builds an impermeable barrier between the computers on your side of the wall (meaning your MacBook and any other computers on your network) and all external computers on the other side of the wall (meaning the rest of the Internet).

"But wait a second — if other computers can't reach me and my MacBook can't reach them, how can I use the Internet at all?" Ah, that's the beauty of today's firewalls. By using a series of techniques designed to thwart attacks from the outside, a firewall allows you to communicate safely, even monitoring what you send and what you receive for later examination. Figure 6-1 illustrates the basics of a firewall.

**Figure 6-1:** A firewall, hard at work. (They're not actually made of brick, though.)

A firewall sounds grand and incredibly complex and highly technical — and sometimes it is — but it can also be quite simple. For example:

✦ You can spend anywhere from $50 to thousands of dollars installing sophisticated firewall hardware and/or software.

or

✦ You can activate your firewall by disconnecting your dialup, digital subscriber line (DSL), or cable modem from the wall socket.

Believe it or not, both of those examples technically involve a firewall. In the first case, the firewall is a physical, tangible presence on the network; in the second case, the lack of a connection to the Internet actually acts as a firewall. (Think of it as the Air Firewall . . . no relation to the MacBook Air.) I've spoken to a number of readers who actually do this; however, if you're running a Web site or downloading a file from your company's FTP site, yanking the connection when you head to bed isn't an option. Therefore, most of us will install a physical firewall through hardware or software.

### Do I already have a firewall?

In some cases, you might already be using a hardware firewall and not even know it. For example, many Internet-sharing devices include a built-in NAT firewall. NAT stands for *Network Address Translation,* and it's the most effective and popular hardware firewall standard in use by consumer devices. If you're using an Internet sharing hub or router, check its manual to determine whether it offers NAT as a firewall feature — and if so, turn it on if NAT isn't enabled by default. (See Book VII, Chapter 2 for more on Internet sharing, routers, and firewalls.)

For instance, Figure 6-2 illustrates the configuration screen for my Internet router. Note the options to disable port scanning and ping responses, which are two tricks that hackers often use to detect what's often called a *hot computer* — meaning that the computer can be identified and is accessible to attack. (Wireless networks are notoriously hot — for more information on securing your wireless connections, visit Book VII, Chapter 4.)

### Using the internal Mac OS X firewall

Mac OS X includes a powerful internal firewall, which Snow Leopard makes very simple to use! Most MacBook owners will be perfectly satisfied with this built-in firewall, which is configured through System Preferences — find more information on setting up your firewall in Book VI, Chapter 2.

### Using a commercial software firewall

You'll also find a number of popular alternatives to Snow Leopard's built-in firewall on the market, many of which offer more control over individual applications and more configuration options than your Mac OS X firewall. For example, consider Intego's NetBarrier X5 (www.intego.com), which comes with a number of preset configurations that allow you to choose a basic firewall for your network environment with a single click.

Whether you set up the internal firewall, a shareware firewall, or a commercial firewall, visit a favorite site of mine on the Web: www.grc.com, the home of Gibson Research Corporation. There you'll find the free online utility ShieldsUP!!, which will automatically test just how tight your firewall is and how susceptible your Mac could be to hacker attacks. Visit this site often because this service is updated periodically to reflect new hacking techniques.

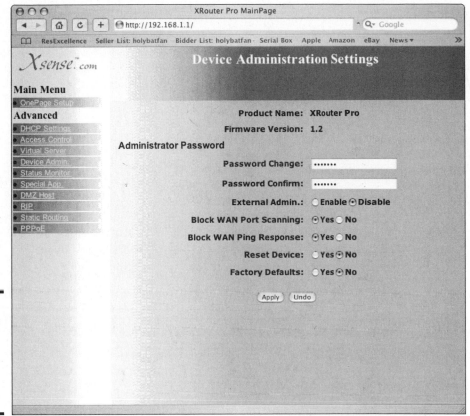

**Figure 6-2:**
My Internet
router is
set to be
downright
rude to
hackers.

## Antivirus basics

Next, consider your antivirus protection (both under Snow Leopard and
Windows XP/Vista, if you're running Boot Camp on your MacBook). *Viruses*
are typically transmitted through applications — you run a program, and
the virus is activated. (Although not the traditional definition of a virus, both
scripts and macros can be used to take control of your system and cause
trouble, as well.) Therefore, you need to closely monitor what I call The Big
Three:

✦ **Web downloads:** Consider every file that you receive from the Internet
  as a possible viral threat.

✦ **Removable media:** Viruses can be stored on everything from CD-ROMs
  and DVD-ROMs to USB flash drives.

✦ **E-mail file attachments:** A "Trojan Horse" or "worm" application sent to
  you as an e-mail attachment is an easy doorway to your system.

Horrors! Mac OS X has no built-in antivirus support. (Then again, neither does Windows.) However, a good antivirus program will take care of any application that's carrying a virus. Some even handle destructive macros within documents. Make sure that the antivirus program you choose offers *real-time scanning,* which operates when you download or open a file. Periodic scanning of your entire system is important, too, but only a real-time scanning application such as Norton AntiVirus can immediately ensure that the documents or the application you just received in your e-mail Inbox is actually free from viruses. (Oh, and don't forget that many of the Software Updates released by Apple for Snow Leopard will plug security holes in our favorite operating system.)

Virus technology continues to evolve over time, just as more beneficial application development does. For example, recently a virus was discovered that's actually contained in a JPEG image file! With a good antivirus application that offers regular updates, you'll continue to keep your system safe from viral attack.

I heartily recommend both Norton AntiVirus from Symantec (available in versions for Snow Leopard and Windows) and Intego's VirusBarrier X5 (available for Snow Leopard only). Both programs include automatic updates delivered while you're online to make sure that you're covered against the latest viruses.

# A Dose of Common Sense: Things Not to Do Online

One more powerful weapon that you can use to make sure that your MacBook stays safe from unlawful intrusion is this: Practicing common sense on the Internet is just as important as adding a firewall and an antivirus application to your laptop.

With this in mind, here's a checklist of things that you should never do while you're online:

✦ **Never download a file from a site you don't trust.** And make sure that your antivirus software is configured to check downloaded files before you open them.

✦ **Never open an e-mail attachment until it has been checked.** Don't give in to temptation, even if the person who sent the message is someone you trust. (Many of today's macro viruses actually replicate themselves by sending copies to the addresses found through the victim's e-mail program. Of course, this problem crops up regularly in the Windows world, but it's been known to happen in the Macintosh community as well.)

✦ **Never enter any personal information in an e-mail message unless you know the recipient.** Sure, I send my mailing address to friends and family, but no one else. In fact, even e-mail can be intercepted by a determined hacker, so if you're sending something truly important, use an encryption application, such as PGP Personal Desktop (www. pgp.com).

✦ **Never enter any personal information on a Web site provided as a link in an e-mail message.** Don't fall prey to phishing expeditions. Some of these e-mail-message/Web-site combinations look authentic enough to fool anyone! No reputable online company or store will demand or solicit your personal information through e-mail or through a linked Web site. In fact, feel free to contact the company through its *real* Web site and report the phishing attempt!

✦ **Never include any personal information in an Internet newsgroup post.** (In case you're not familiar with the term, *newsgroups* are public Internet message bases, often called Usenet groups. Some ISPs offer a selection of newsgroups that you can access.) Newsgroup posts can be viewed by anyone, so there's no such thing as privacy in a newsgroup. (For a glimpse of just how long one of these posts can linger in the great Internet continuum, visit www.google.com, click the Groups button, and search for your name. I can pull up newsgroup messages that I posted back in 1995!)

✦ **Never buy from an online store that doesn't offer a secure, encrypted connection when you're prompted for your personal information and credit card number.** If you're using Apple's Safari browser, the padlock icon appears next to the site name in the title bar. When the padlock icon appears in the title bar, the connection is encrypted and secure.

✦ **Never divulge personal information to others over an iChat connection.**

✦ **Never use the same password for all your electronic business.** Use different passwords that include both letters and numbers, change them often, and never divulge them to anyone else.

✦ **Never give anyone else administrative access to your Web server.**

✦ **Never allow any type of remote access (such as sharing screens) to your MacBook or your network without testing that access first.** It's very important to restrict remote access to visitors whom you trust.

Find more details on securing your network from intrusion — including Internet hacker attacks — in Book VII. I cover System Preferences that can affect the security of your system in Book III.

# Book VII

# Networking in Mac OS X

The 5th Wave                    By Rich Tennant

"Ms. Gretsky, tell the employees they can have
Internet games on their computers again."

# Contents at a Glance

## Chapter 1: Setting Up a Small Network . . . . . . . . . . . . . . . . . . . . . . .569

What Do I Need to Set Up My Network? ....................................................569
Setting Up Your Network.........................................................................573
Understanding the Basics of Network Configuration ...........................574
Configuring Network System Preferences...............................................576
Verifying Connectivity ............................................................................580
Troubleshooting Your New Network ......................................................582

## Chapter 2: Using Your Network . . . . . . . . . . . . . . . . . . . . . . . . . . . . . . .585

It's All about (File) Sharing......................................................................585
Sharing a Connected Printer ...................................................................588
Sharing Files with Windows Computers.................................................588
Accessing File Shares on Windows Computers......................................589
Using FTP to Access Files ........................................................................590
Using the Built-in Firewall......................................................................593
Remote Control of Your MacBook..........................................................595

## Chapter 3: Going Wireless . . . . . . . . . . . . . . . . . . . . . . . . . . . . . . . . . . .599

Speaking the Wireless Lingo ...................................................................599
Figuring Out the Different Flavors of Wireless Ethernet ......................601
Keeping Your Wireless Network Secure..................................................603
Setting Up Your Wireless Network.........................................................606

## Chapter 4: Sharing That Precious Internet Thing . . . . . . . . . . . . . . . .611

Sharing the Internet.................................................................................611
Using Network Address Translation .......................................................612
Ways to Share Your Internet Connection................................................614
Connecting Everything for Wired Sharing..............................................617
Adding Wireless Support .........................................................................620

# Chapter 1: Setting Up a Small Network

## In This Chapter

✔ Finding out what a network is and why you might want one

✔ Setting up the network hardware

✔ Configuring network system preferences

✔ Troubleshooting your network

In the not-so-distant past — I'm talking 15–20 years ago — networks were found only in huge companies that had the money and the workforce to pay for and maintain them. But now, as technology rolls on, a home or small office network is both very affordable and relatively easy to create. In this chapter, I introduce you to this helpful beastie: You discover what networks are, what you can do with them, and how to set up a small network of your own for your home or small business.

Networks can be used for many things. Computers exchange all types of data over a network: files that you want to send between computers or to networked printers, streaming audio or video broadcasts, data for multiplayer computer games, or even a private company Web site (typically called an *intranet*). Anything that you can imagine that would involve moving data between multiple computers can be done by using a network.

## What Do I Need to Set Up My Network?

First, let me define network. In a nutshell, a *network* is a combination of hardware, cables, and software that allows computers and printers to talk to each other. (Heck, you don't even need cables with a wireless network, as I show you in Chapter 3 of this minibook.) To have a network, you need the right hardware and software — and did I mention that all the hardware and software that you need probably came with your MacBook? (Except for those pesky cables, of course.) As you progress through this chapter, you'll discover everything that's required to set up your network so that you can pick up any additional parts you need. Any good-sized computer store (either the brick-and-mortar or online variety) has everything that you need to get up and running.

Now, back to the requirements: You need the right hardware and software to make your network sing. This section covers each component with a description about the role that each part plays on the network and other good stuff you'll want to know to get your network right the first time.

## Something to network

Okay, this might be obvious, but I'm nothing if not thorough. The first thing that you need to build a network is . . . well, *stuff!* That's right, you need to have devices that you want to network. Most times, these are computers (whether Macs or PCs running Windows/Linux/UNIX), printers, personal digital assistants (PDAs), cell phones, and other standalone, network-capable devices (such as file servers and shared tape back-up drives).

## Network interface card (NIC)

A *network interface card,* or NIC, is a hardware device that your computer uses to talk to the rest of the network. The NIC connects to the network cabling, and it speaks the language of electronics, sending data around the network. Nowadays, most networks use the Ethernet networking protocol, and most NICs are Ethernet compatible. All MacBooks have some type of Ethernet NIC hardware built right onto the Mac's main system board. (Note, however, that the MacBook Air offers only wireless hardware built in; you can add a wired Ethernet port to the MacBook Air using an external USB connector.)

## Switch

So you have an assortment of devices in your home or small office that you've decided to network. How do you make them all interconnect? Although you could connect just two computers by using nothing more than a single crossover cable, you need fancier hardware to connect more than two computers: namely, a switch. The switch is used to connect everything, so it's the focal point of the network. Without a switch, you don't have a network.

A *switch* is really just a small box that has a bunch of Ethernet ports on it. A *port* is really just like an Ethernet NIC on your computer, but a switch has lots of them. Inside, all those Ethernet ports are arranged so that the talking (sending) wires from each port connect to the listening (receiving) wires on all other ports. Therefore, when one computer talks, all others listen.

## Thirty-nine flavors of Ethernet . . . but no Rocky Road

Wired Ethernet standards allow for operation at different speeds. Because the Ethernet standard has improved over time, some older Ethernet devices support only the older (slower) speeds. Ethernet's speed is rated by how much data it can transfer in a second — usually in millions of bits per second, or megabits per second (Mbps). Originally, Ethernet was designed to run at 10 Mbps. Now there are different speeds of Ethernet: 10 Mbps, 100 Mbps, 1000 Mbps, and even faster.

The 1000 Mbps Ethernet — also called *Gigabit Ethernet* or just *Gigabit* for short — is still a bit on the expensive side for small home or office networks. All consumer-level Gigabit Ethernet NICs also support running at 10 Mbps or 100 Mbps, so you will hear them called *10/100/1000 Ethernet NICs.* All current MacBook models come with a 10/100/1000 Ethernet NIC built in — except the MacBook Air, which has integrated wireless Ethernet hardware instead.

(Apple offers a USB-to-Ethernet converter for those MacBook Air owners that need a wired connection, but the connection is significantly slower.)

Although Gigabit NICs are now priced under $50, most of the devices that can connect Gigabit NICs still cost significantly more than their 10/100 counterparts. That fact, coupled with the reality that most computer systems can't really even handle or dish out that much data, makes Gigabit Ethernet a choice only for those wanting a high-end network with the best performance.

NICs and other Ethernet equipment that handle only 10 Mbps are rapidly becoming obsolete because virtually all the modern NICs and other Ethernet hardware support both 10 Mbps and 100 Mbps. Most times, you'll see this labeled as *10/100 Ethernet.* For your home networking, you probably want to invest in 10/100 Mbps.

Setting up a switch (and therefore giving birth to your network, which sounds more painful than it is) is usually no more difficult than connecting a power cable to the device and then plugging in your computers with their own Ethernet cables. You'll see various lights on the box — usually a power light indicating that the switch is powered on and operational. You'll also see lights that correspond to each port on the switch; these lights tell you what's going on in the box. For instance, you normally see the following types of lights:

✦ **Link light:** Each port on a switch should have a link light. *Link lights* simply tell you which ports have something alive connected to a given port — that is, a device is connected and powered on.

✦ **Speed light:** Each port on the switch should have a speed light, which tells you the speed of the device at the other end. Some switches have different lights for different speeds, and some use a single light and make it different colors for different speeds.

✦ **Activity light:** When one computer speaks, they all hear it. Typically, an entire switch has only one activity light for the entire network, indicating that someone is speaking. With heavy traffic, the light can appear solid.

Bear with me whilst I spew techno-talk for a paragraph or two. When an Ethernet switch receives a *frame* — that's the name for a standard unit, or packet, of network data — it reads the label on the frame to see the return address of the computer that sent the frame. In a short amount of time (after being turned on and watching the data move around), a switch figures out which computer is located on which port. Then, whenever data comes into the switch, it looks at the *header* (some information on the front of all frames, much like a mailing label on a package that you send) and sees which computer should receive the frame. The switch then sends the frame out the port for that computer only.

This is A Good Thing. Instead of forcing all computers on the network to listen while your MacBook speaks (as antique network hubs did) — known as *half-duplex* — a switch sends the data directly to the only computer that needs to hear it.

## Cables

Cables are the ties that bind . . . literally. *Cables* are used to connect the Ethernet port on each computer to the switch, the central hardware of the network. With a little experience, you'll be a cable-wielding superhero with hundreds of feet of cable draped across every piece of furniture in your place for your first LAN party. (A *LAN party,* by the way, is when way too many techies bring their computers into a very small space, connect them, and play games for 48 hours straight. Oh, and we eat a lot, too. Good stuff!)

Here's the scoop on what kind of cables to use. Technically, you can run 100 Mbps Ethernet over *Cat5* cable (like a super-version of the wire that you use for your telephones).

Although you can do 10/100 Mbps Ethernet over Cat5 cable, any new cables that you buy should be Cat5E or Cat6 — which I talk about in the following section — because these types of cables are specifically meant for use with 1000 Mbps (or Gigabit) Ethernet. I'm sure you noticed that the common denominator here is the Cat5 cable. That's because fiber optic cable, although supporting speeds of 100 Mbps, 1 Gbps, and even 10 Gbps, is much more expensive and more difficult to install.

Hey, did I mention that you can eschew cables entirely? For more information on the lean, mean world of wireless networking, see Chapter 3 of this minibook.

Be sure to buy *straight-through* Cat5E/Cat6 cables (also called *patch* cables) and not *crossover* cables, which are used only in certain circumstances. Crossover cables are mainly used to connect two computers directly (to form a tiny, two-computer network), connect a cable/DSL modem directly to a computer, or connect multiple switches.

Cat5 cable supports speeds of 100 Mbps. 1000 Mbps Ethernet, of course, is designed to run ten times faster than that; luckily enough, it was engineered to be compatible with 90 percent of Cat5 installations. Having said that, I must also point out that some Cat5 cables don't stick to the stringent specifications that 1000 Mbps Ethernet requires. The newer version of Cat5 cable is *Category 5 Enhanced,* or Cat5E for short. Cat5E is recommended for any new installation because it can easily handle 10/100 Mbps Ethernet and yet can handle 1000 Mbps Ethernet as well. Even if you're using 10/100 Mbps Ethernet, you can upgrade someday to 1000 Mbps without having to worry about upgrading your cabling. You may also find Cat6 cabling in your network travels, which can also easily handle 10/100/1000 Mbps speeds.

# Setting Up Your Network

After you collect the hardware components I list earlier in this chapter, you're ready to connect things. Here's a quick list of things to do to get your network fired up:

**1. Find the best location for placing your switch.**

To keep costs down, try to place the switch in a location close to a power outlet that's centrally located so that you can use the least amount of cable. If cost isn't an issue, hide the unit in a closet and just run all the cables along the walls to the hub or switch. And if cost *really* isn't an issue, get your house fully wired with Cat5E cable.

**2. Plug the switch into the power socket.**

Some switches come on automatically when you plug them in and can never be turned off. Others have a power switch that you need to turn on the first time that you plug them in.

**3. Verify that the switch is working by looking at the lights on the front. Check the manual that came with the switch to see what light configuration is normal for that particular unit.**

Until you have computers or printers attached to it, you might just have a status light that shows the switch is powered on. But if the lights on your unit don't match up with what the manual says, you could have a bum unit that you need to return.

4. **Verify that all your devices are near enough to the switch to be connected by your cables; then, turn them all on.**

5. **Get one of your Cat5E or Cat6 cables and connect one cable from the Ethernet jack on your MacBook (on the side) to an open port on the switch.**

You should see a link light or speed light come on that verifies that the two devices sense each other.

6. **Repeat Step 5 until each device is attached to the switch.**

Congratulations, you're a network technician! (Don't forget to call your friends and brag.) The first phase of the network, the physical connection, is complete; the next step is the configuration of Mac OS X.

# Understanding the Basics of Network Configuration

Take a deep breath; there's no need to panic — in fact, configuring your network software basically involves entering a lot of numbers and other stuff in dialogs. (In fact, most folks can just allow Snow Leopard to take care of network settings automatically.) But just so you understand what's involved, this section explains what those numbers are, what they do, and why you ought to know it. Because this is a MacBook book, I stick with configuring Macs running the Big X.

## TCP/IP

First things first: *Protocol* is just the techno-nerd word for a set of rules or a language. A *protocol* is a language that computers use to communicate. Without protocols, the computers on your network would never be able to speak to each other even though you have NICs, cables, and a hub or a switch. The Internet Protocol (IP) part of the TCP/IP suite is what you're really interested in because it's the most important part of your network configuration chore.

### IP addresses

*IP addresses* are like street addresses for computers on a network. Each computer on the network has an IP address, and it needs to be unique because no other computer can share it. When a computer wants to communicate with another computer, it can simply send the data on the network in a nice package that has its address as well as the address of the computer that it's trying to talk to. (Remember frames? If not, take a refresher in the earlier section "Switch.")

An IP address is just a number, but it's written in a strange way. (Go figure.) All IP addresses are written as four sets of numerals between 0 and 255 with a dot (period) between each set. For instance, a common IP address that you might run into is 192.168.0.1. As everyone knows, engineers can't sleep unless they have three or four ways to write the same thing, including IP addresses. The form shown above — which is by far the most common — is *dotted notation.* Each number, such as 192, is an *octet.*

Don't worry too much about this stuff: You don't have to remember terms like *octet* to create your own network. They could be helpful, however, if something goes wrong and you need to place a call to tech support. Plus, you can impress the computer salesperson (gleefully called a *wonk* by Mac power users) at your local Maze 'o Wires store with your mastery of techno-babble.

### IP addresses at home versus on the Internet

One very important thing to keep in mind is that the Almighty IP Address Police — *Internet Assigned Numbers Authority* (www.iana.org) — has broken IP addresses into groups. The two main types of IP addresses are public and private:

✦ **Public IP addresses** can be used on the Internet and are unique throughout the whole world.

✦ **Private IP addresses** are used in homes or businesses and can't be used to talk to the public Internet. Private IP addresses are used over and over by many people and most commonly take the form 192.168.*x.x.* (AirPort Extreme base stations use private IP addresses in the form 10.0.*x.x.*)

You'll almost always get a public IP address from your Internet service provider (ISP), whether you're using a cable modem, digital subscriber line (DSL), or a regular dial-up modem. If you use a cable/DSL router or Snow Leopard's built-in sharing software to share your Internet connection among multiple computers, you'll be using private IP addresses on your network while using a single public IP address to talk to the Internet. (More on that in Chapter 4 of this minibook.)

"Great! I get an IP address, put it into my Network settings in System Preferences, and off I go. Right?" Well, you're close, but here are a few other pieces of information that you might need before you can go surfing around the world:

✦ **Default gateway:** When you send information to other networks — whether in another building or around the world on the Internet — your computer needs to know the IP address of the gateway that will forward your data down the line. The *default gateway* is really just the IP address of a *router,* which is a device that connects multiple networks. A *gateway* gets its name because it really is your gateway to all other networks.

**Book VII Chapter 1**

Setting Up a Small Network

✦ **Subnet mask:** A *subnet mask* is a number that helps your computer know when it needs to send stuff through the router. It's a group of four octets with dots, just like an IP address, but almost always uses 0 or 255 for each of the four octets. Most often, the subnet mask is 255.255.255.0. If the wrong number is entered for the subnet mask, it could keep you from talking to the Internet or even to computers on your own network.

## Software applications

After you have the hardware in place and you've chosen and configured a protocol to allow the computers to all talk to each other, you need software to make use of your new network connections. Time for more good news: A lot of the software that you need to move data on your network is included already in Mac OS X! Here are brief descriptions of some of the network software and protocols already built into Mac OS X and what they're used for:

✦ **FTP:** *File Transfer Protocol* (FTP), part of the TCP/IP protocol suite, allows computers of any type — Mac, PC, Linux, UNIX, mainframe, or whatever — to transfer files back and forth.

✦ **Telnet:** *Telnet* is also part of the TCP/IP suite — you can use it to remotely connect to a computer and execute commands on the remote machine.

✦ **Samba:** *Samba* (or *SMB*) is an open source software suite that enables Mac OS X users to share files with people using Windows computers and allows the Mac users to connect to files that the Windows computers share.

✦ **HTTP:** *HyperText Transfer Protocol* (HTTP), also part of the TCP/IP suite, is used by Web browsers to provide access to all the various pages on the World Wide Web.

# Configuring Network System Preferences

In this section, I show you how to configure your MacBook to communicate with other computers on a local network.

Leave it to Snow Leopard to provide you with assistance — in this case, when you first open the Network pane, you might be greeted with a dialog offering you assistance on setting up the stuff I cover in this section. (Whether you get this *absolutely free* offer of aid depends on whether you upgraded your MacBook from a previous version of Mac OS X or entered your network and Internet settings within the Snow Leopard Setup Assistant.) If you do decide to allow the Snow Leopard Internet/Network assistant to guide you through your network setup, I'll meet back up with you at the next section.

## Using DHCP for automatic IP address assignment

Now I'd like to introduce you to a **very** dear friend of mine — an abbreviation that you will soon grow to love, as does everyone else who's set up a small Mac network. *Dynamic Host Configuration Protocol,* or DHCP for short, is a protocol that enables a computer to automatically get all the information that I've talked about to this point. (Check in your *Webster's* . . . this is the very definition of the word *godsend.*)

You're saying, "Mark, there's gotta be a catch, right?" Well, here's the bad news: Before you can use DHCP, you have to add a *DHCP server,* which provides other computers on the network with their configuration settings. Here's the good news: Most Internet connection-sharing hardware devices (and software-sharing implementations as well) provide a DHCP server as part of the price of admission. (*Internet connection sharing* allows all your networked computers to access the Internet through a single Internet connection. I cover it more in Chapter 4 of this minibook.) Most wired and wireless routers can provide DHCP services these days. Technology marches on.

If you plan to use Internet connection sharing or you know that you have a DHCP server on your network, you can set up your MacBook to automatically obtain the required IP address and information. Open System Preferences from the Dock or the Apple menu and choose Network. From the Network dialog that appears, click the Ethernet entry in the list on the left. Choose Using DHCP from the Configure IPv4 pop-up menu; then click the Apply Now button. Mac OS X contacts the DHCP server to obtain an IP address, a subnet mask, a gateway router IP address, and a Domain Name System (DNS) address. (*DNS servers* convert a human-friendly address, like www.yahoo.com, to a computer-friendly IP address, like 66.218.71.86.)

A few seconds after clicking the Apply Now button, you should see the information come up, as provided by the DHCP server. This lets you know that the process worked and configuration is complete. You might also notice that the DNS Servers information is empty. Fear not: Mac OS X is really using DNS information provided by the DHCP server. Press ⌘+Q to quit System Preferences and save your settings.

If you ever make a network change that screws things up, such as entering the wrong subnet mask or an IP address that isn't in the same range as others on your LAN, you can always click the Revert button to get back your old settings.

One DHCP server on a network is princely, but two or more DHCP servers on a single network will fight like alley cats and grind everything to a halt. Therefore, if you're considering adding a DHCP server to an existing network, make **doggone** sure that you're not treading on another server's toes. (Ask that network administrator person.)

## Manually choosing an IP address range

You say you don't have a DHCP server, and you need to manually assign IP addresses? This configuration also means you need to manually configure the Transmission Control Protocol/Internet Protocol (TCP/IP) Properties. Keep in mind that for now, you're not concerned with the Internet — just computers on the local network.

A result of being on a *local* network — because it's not connected to the Internet, it's also called a *private* network — is that you must use IP addresses that are reserved for private network use. You can use a few different ranges of IP addresses, but I recommend that you choose an address range from the 192.168.*x.x* (or 10.0.*x.x*) networks. In the next section, I show you how.

Down to business: *I recommend that you use IP addresses in the 192.168.x.x range (or the 10.0.x.x range if you're using an AirPort Extreme base station).* What does this mean, exactly? Well, here's the scoop:

✦ **Use IP addresses where the first two octets are 192 and 168 (192.168) or 10 and 0 for AirPort Extreme (10.0).**

Octet numbers are conjoined by periods.

✦ **For the third octet, select any number between 1 and 254.**

It doesn't matter which one you choose as long as you use this same third number on all computers on your network.

✦ **For the fourth octet, select any number between 1 and 254.**

Make sure that every computer on your local network has a different fourth octet number. This is very important; otherwise, your network doesn't work.

✦ **Use 255.255.255.0 as your subnet mask.**

For instance, suppose that you're using three computers on your network. All the IP addresses that you use will start with *192.168.* Next, suppose you choose *123* for the third octet. (Remember that you can choose any number between 1 and 254.) Finally, for the fourth octet, choose the numbers 100, 105, and 110 for the three computers, respectively. (Again, you can choose any numbers between 1 and 254.) The resulting IP addresses used on the three computers are

192.168.123.100

192.168.123.105

192.168.123.110

By the way, I should mention that there are other range possibilities for reserved private networks — AirPort and AirPort Extreme hardware uses a 10.*x.x.x* network range, for example — but the 192.168.*x.x* range is definitely the most popular and the most common default on Ethernet network hardware.

After you know the IP addresses and the subnet mask that you're going to use, start setting up each computer. Being a nice guy, I walk you through the process of configuring Mac OS X with the 192.168.123.105 address as an example.

Be sure that you have all the physical portions of your network powered up and connected as I outline in the earlier section, "Setting Up Your Network."

*1.* **Select any of your Macs to start with and open System Preferences (either from the Apple menu or from the Dock).**

*2.* **From the System Preferences dialog, choose Network.**

The Network pane appears.

*3.* **Click Ethernet in the list.**

*4.* **Click the Configure IPv4 pop-up menu and choose Manually.**

Figure 1-1 shows how things should look.

**Figure 1-1:**
Manually
configuring
TCP/IP
settings.

*5.* **Enter the IP address for this machine (192.168.123.105 in this example) in the IP Address text box.**

6. **Enter the subnet mask of 255.255.255.0 in the Subnet Mask text box.**

7. **If you're using a router or hardware Internet sharing device, enter the IP address used by the router in the Router text box.**

8. **Click the Apply button, and your new network settings take effect.**

9. **Press ⌘+Q to quit System Preferences.**

Repeat this same procedure with the other IP addresses for each of the other Macs that are connected to your network.

Most ISPs also supply DNS server addresses and search domains. If your ISP included DNS server addresses or search domains, don't forget to type them into the corresponding boxes on the TCP/IP panel.

# Verifying Connectivity

After you have your Macs connected and your TCP/IP configuration is done, check to make sure that everything is working. After you have at least two computers on your network, each with a TCP/IP address, you can use a simple little utility called `ping` to test the connection.

`ping` is a very simple, yet extremely helpful, utility that's the first connectivity-testing tool out of the box, even for network professionals. When you use the `ping` utility — referred to as *pinging* something — the application sends out a small packet of data to whatever destination you're trying to reach. When the receiving computer hears the ping, it answers with a ping reply. If the original computer receives the ping reply, you know that the connection between the computers is good.

To ping a computer, you use a little application built in to Mac OS X called *Network Utility,* which allows you to work various network wonders (including checking connectivity, watching the route that your computer takes to get to another computer, and looking up information about Internet domain names). To use Network Utility to check network connectivity, follow these steps:

1. **Open a Finder window, click Applications, and click Utilities.**

2. **Double-click the Network Utility icon to launch the application.**

3. **Click the Ping tab (see Figure 1-2).**

4. **In the Enter the Network Address to Ping text field, enter the IP address of the computer that you want to ping.**

5. **To simply verify connectivity, select the Send Only *x* Pings radio button and enter a low number, such as 5, in the text field.**

   Five or ten pings are plenty to see whether the connection is good.

6. **Click the Ping button.**

Your Mac sends ping packets to the IP address that you entered.

**Figure 1-2:**
Preparing to
ping. (Can
you say
that with
a straight
face?)

**Book VII
Chapter 1**

**Setting Up a Small
Network**

If the pings are successful, text appears in the text box at the bottom of the Ping tab: one line for each ping reply received from the other computer. The end of each line reads `time=` with a number at the end. That number is the amount of time, in 1/1000 of a second (milliseconds [ms]), that it took for the ping packet to go from your computer to the other computer and back.

If your ping is unsuccessful, you see nothing, at least for a little bit. Each ping that you send takes two seconds before it's considered missing in action. So, if you choose five pings, wait ten seconds before you see the results. After all the pings time out — a ping *times out* when it doesn't get returned in the proper amount of time — you see a line of text appear that reads `ping: sendto: No route to host` or `100% packet loss`. Both error messages mean the same thing: All the ping packets that you sent out are now in the packet graveyard, never to be seen again. As you've likely guessed already, this is *not* a good sign for your network connectivity. Look to the following section, "Troubleshooting Your New Network," to find out where to begin troubleshooting this problem.

If you can ping all the other computers on your network from one of the computers, you don't need to go to each computer and ping all the others. You can logically assume that all the computers can communicate. For instance, if you can ping computers B, C, and D from computer A, you don't need to bother with ping tests from computer B, C, or D.

After you have your computers configured and you've verified connectivity among them, start doing the fun stuff that a network allows you to do, such as sharing data, printing, and (most important) playing games with users on other computers.

# Troubleshooting Your New Network

After a network is set up and operating, it rarely has problems — still, Murphy sometimes takes charge, and the darn thing just won't work right. When you do have problems with the network, I recommend using a standard, consistent approach to finding and fixing the problem. This section breaks down troubleshooting into two areas:

✦ **The hardware:** The best place to start troubleshooting a network problem is with the actual equipment, such as the NICs, cables, and hubs/switches. (See earlier sections on each equipment type.)

✦ **The software:** The second place to check for problems is in the configuration of the computers on the network, specifically the configuration on the computer(s) having the problem that you're troubleshooting.

## Physical problems with your network

Although many things on a network can go bad or cause problems, usually network problems are caused by faulty equipment or wiring. Sometimes it's something as simple as a cable not being plugged in snugly. Looking at the physical cables, connections, and equipment is always the best place to start looking for problems. Here is a quick list of physical things to check while trying to fix network problems:

1. **Make sure that both ends of the network cable are firmly connected.**

    First check the end that plugs into the computer and then check the end that connects to the switch.

2. **Turn on the problematic computer to be sure that it's connected to a hub or switch.**

    Check the port on the switch to see whether the link/speed light is lit. (Depending on the switch that you have, you might not have a link light. Many switches use a speed light to indicate a link. Check the manufacturer's manual for your model.) If your computer is on and onnected but no link/speed light is lit, try replacing the network cable.

3. **If you replace the network cable and there still isn't light, try unplugging the cable from the switch and plug it into another port.**

    Choose one of the other computers connected to the switch that works, unplug it, and plug the broken computer into that port for testing. Occasionally, a single port on a switch goes bad; if that happens, just mark it as bad and don't use it anymore. But if all computers connected to the switch stop working, it's probably the switch that's gone south. If the switch is still under warranty, I recommend getting it fixed or replaced.

4. **If you replace the cable, try a different port on the switch, and if other computers work fine on that switch, the NIC inside your computer has possibly gone bad.**

   If you reach this determination, call your local service center to have it looked at and repaired. If you have an older model on which the NIC was added instead of built in, you can simply replace the NIC yourself — MacBook owners, unfortunately, don't have this option.

 The key when troubleshooting physical problems is the link/speed light on the switch. If the link/speed light still doesn't work, the problem likely isn't physical. Start troubleshooting the network configuration on the computer itself.

## Network configuration problems

After checking the hardware, look for problems in the network settings. When using TCP/IP on your network, look for these specific things: the TCP/IP configuration mode, IP address, subnet mask, and router IP address (if you're using a router to connect to the Internet or other networks). To check these settings, open System Preferences and click the Network icon to bring up the Network pane. Click the Ethernet entry in the list and then follow these steps:

1. **Make sure that the Configure IPv4 pop-up menu is set to the appropriate option.**

   - *Using DHCP:* Select the Using DHCP option only if you're using a cable/DSL modem/router or other DHCP server. Otherwise, set this to Manually.

   - *Manually:* If the configuration is set to Manually, check the IP Address, DNS Servers, Router, and Subnet Mask fields to make sure that they're correct. If you're not sure whether your Subnet Mask field entry is correct, you can usually make it the same as other computers on the same network with you. Most times, the subnet mask is 255.255.255.0.

2. **To check your Internet connectivity to the rest of the Internet, try pinging www.apple.com.**

   This checks the router and DNS settings.

3. **If you're set up for DHCP and your TCP/IP settings remain blank, make sure that your DHCP server — which could be your cable/DSL modem/router — is turned on and working properly.**

# Chapter 2: Using Your Network

## In This Chapter

✔ Finding out what you can do with your network

✔ Sharing your files and printers with other Macs

✔ Sharing your files with Windows computers

✔ Accessing files on Windows computers

✔ Configuring the built-in firewall

✔ Remote-controlling your MacBook from afar

Here's one of those incredibly complex concepts that you always find in these computer books: After you have your network all set up and ready to go, you can do all kinds of things with it. (Now wasn't that utterly painless?) You can use your network to share files, share printers, remotely control your MacBook, share music across your network using iTunes, or even play multiuser games against friends. To keep your files safe from unwanted snoops, you can configure the Mac OS X built-in firewall. In this chapter, I cover the basics of file sharing, sharing printers, and using the firewall to protect yourself from intruders.

## It's All about (File) Sharing

One of the main reasons for building a network is sharing files between computers. You might even want to set up a *server,* which is a computer with shared files that are always available to anyone on the network. Think of a server as a common file storage area for the rest of the network. Really, any computer that shares files is technically a server because it's serving, so to speak. But most people use the word *server* only to mean a computer that's dedicated solely to serving files, printers, and so on for the rest of the network.

### Creating an account

Sharing files on your MacBook with other Mac users is a piece of cake. Remember, however, that you need to create an account for anyone whom you want to have access to your files. The accounts that you create can access only three folders, as shown in Figure 2-1:

**Figure 2-1:**
The location
of user
folders and
the Shared
folder on
your hard
drive.

✦ **The account's Home folder:** That specific account's Home folder carries a short version of the username that's in the Users folder on your hard drive. Figure 2-1 shows the Home folder, which is noted with an icon that looks like a house, for the mark account (where *mark* is the short account name for Mark Chambers). The Home folder icon always bears the short account name for the user who's currently logged in.

✦ **The account's Public folder:** Each user account you create also has a Public folder located within its Home folder. Any files you place in the Public folder can be accessed by any user on your Mac.

✦ **The Shared folder:** This folder is also in the Users folder on your hard drive. Anyone with an account on your Mac can access the Shared folder, so it's a great place to keep common files that everyone wants to copy or use.

To create an account, you need to be logged in as an Admin user. Follow these steps:

*1.* **Open System Preferences from the Apple menu (⌘) or the Dock.**

*2.* **Click the Accounts icon.**

*3.* **Click the New Account button, which carries a plus sign.**

*4.* **Fill in the appropriate information, including the name for the account and a password.**

    Note that the name that appears as the short name determines the name of that user's Home folder.

*5.* **Click Create Account.**

*6.* **Press ⌘+Q to exit System Preferences.**

I cover creating accounts in greater detail in Book III, Chapter 5, but that's the short version.

## Enabling file sharing

When you enable file sharing, your files are exchanged over Transmission Control Protocol/Internet Protocol (TCP/IP).

Follow these steps to turn on sharing:

*1.* **Open System Preferences.**

*2.* **Click the Sharing icon to open the Sharing Preferences pane.**

*3.* **Select the File Sharing check box to enable it.**

## Connecting to a shared resource

At the top of the Sharing pane, you can see that other Macintosh users can access your laptop at `afp://<ip address>`, where `ip address` is the IP address for your specific computer. When another Mac user wants to connect to your shared files, that person can do the following:

*1.* **Choose Go⇨Connect to Server from the Finder menu bar.**

*2.* **After the Connect to Server dialog opens, other Mac users can type** afp://*<ip address>* **(where *ip address* is the IP address of your MacBook) and then click the Connect button.**

You can also browse for a shared resource in the Connect to Server dialog. Choose Go⇨Connect to Server or press ⌘+K. Click Browse to locate the shared computer. Note that you might be prompted to choose whether you want to connect as a Guest or a Registered User. To connect to the server as a Registered User, you must supply the right username and password. If you connect as Guest, you don't have to supply a password, but you will have restricted access to only the Public folder for each account on the system that you connect to. If you need to connect as a Registered User, ask an Admin user who controls that Mac to supply you with the correct username and password.

Give the username and password that you created to the person using the other Mac, and he or she can now access files in that account's Home folder as well as any other Public folders on your computer.

The sidebar that appears in Finder windows offers a Shared heading. Click the arrow next to Shared to display other shared resources on your network, just as if you had clicked Browse from the Connect to Server dialog. (I'm starting to think *Snow Leopard* might be a synonym for *convenience*.)

# Sharing a Connected Printer

Sharing your printer for others to use is one of the best reasons to have a network. Setting up your MacBook to share your printer is very easy under Mac OS X. Here's a quick rundown of what you need to do:

1. **Open System Preferences.**

2. **Click the Sharing icon under the Internet & Network section to open the Sharing Preferences pane.**

3. **Click the Printer Sharing check box to enable it.**

By default, when you turn on Printer Sharing, Snow Leopard automatically shares all the current printers connected to your MacBook. To select which printers can be used for shared printing, click the Print & Fax icon in System Preferences. From this pane, you can enable and disable sharing on individual printers.

After Printer Sharing is enabled, follow these steps to connect to that printer from other computers on your network:

1. **Click System Preferences in the Dock.**

2. **Click the Print & Fax icon.**

3. **Click the Add button (which carries a plus sign).**

You might be prompted to add a printer automatically when the Printer Setup Utility opens. Click the Add button to begin the addition. (For more on adding a printer with the Printer Setup Utility, see Book VIII, Chapter 4.)

4. **From the Browser window that opens, click the Default button on the toolbar.**

5. **Click the shared printer you want to use and then click the Add button.**

Already have the Printer Browser open? Then follow the easier path: Clicking the Default toolbar button displays all the available local shared printers. Click the desired printer and then click Add.

# Sharing Files with Windows Computers

If you've deigned to allow PCs running Windows on your network (a generous gesture), you'll probably want to also share files with those computers. Sharing files with a Windows PC — actually a Windows user — is very similar to sharing files with other Mac users.

## Using FTP on the Internet

Because File Transfer Protocol (FTP) is a part of the TCP/IP suite, it works on virtually every type of computer (over both the Internet and your local area network). So, assuming that you have your computer connected to the Internet through a modem or a local area network (LAN) connection, everything that I discuss about FTP and how to use it applies to connecting to FTP servers on the Internet as well. When you connect to FTP servers on the Internet, you can use the Fully Qualified Domain Name (or FQDN for short), such as `ftp.apple.com` instead of an actual IP address. You can also use the FTP server in Mac OS X to make files available to friends on the Internet just as you would to make them available on a LAN.

File sharing must be enabled, as I demonstrate earlier in this chapter. (When you share with other Macs, you're also making those files available to PCs.)

To allow file sharing with Windows computers, follow these steps:

*1.* **Click the System Preferences icon in the Dock.**

*2.* **Click the Sharing icon to open the Sharing Preferences pane.**

*3.* **Click the File Sharing entry.**

*4.* **Click the Options button.**

*5.* **Click the user account (or accounts) that will be accessible by Windows PCs.**

Snow Leopard will growl while you try to enable SMB sharing. That's because you have to enable Windows access on the desired account before it can be used. Snow Leopard prompts you for your password, smugly informing you that the account password will be stored "in a less secure manner." (Take that, Mr. Gates!) Generally, this isn't a problem, but never enable an account for Windows access unless only trusted individuals will use it.

*6.* **Click the Share files and folders using SMB check box to enable it.**

*7.* **Click Done to exit the Advanced dialog, and close the System Preferences window to save the changes.**

**Book VII
Chapter 2**

**Using Your Network**

## *Accessing File Shares on Windows Computers*

If you allow a Windows PC to access your files, you'll also probably want to putter around with files on a Windows PC. Easy!

Accessing files on Windows computers relies on the Samba component (a part of the UNIX foundation of Mac OS X). Follow these steps:

*1.* **Choose Go⇨Connect to Server from the Finder.**

The Connect to Server dialog opens.

*2.* **In the Address box, enter** smb://*<ip address>*, **where *ip address* is the IP address of the Windows computer that you want to connect to.**

*3.* **Click the Connect button.**

Depending on the type of account you have on the Windows PC, Mac OS X might display an SMB (Server Message Block) authentication dialog in which you can enter your username and password. (Think security for the Windows crowd.)

*4.* **Select the desired shared drive to mount from the pop-up menu.**

*5.* **Mount the shared drive according to the Windows version:**

- *If you're accessing a file shared on a Windows 95 or Windows 98 computer:* Simply click OK to mount the share.

- *If you're accessing a file shared on a Windows NT, 2000, XP, or Vista computer:* Click the Authenticate button. Then enter your username and password, click OK, and then click OK again to mount the share.

After you mount the shared drive, you'll see it appear on your Desktop, just as you see a Mac volume. You can use this drive just as you do any other drive on your system. To disconnect from the Windows share, you can

✦ Drag the icon to the Trash in the Dock (which changes to an Eject icon when you start dragging).

✦ Press ⌘+E.

or

✦ Right-click the icon (tap with two fingers on the trackpad) and then choose Eject from the menu that appears.

# Using FTP to Access Files

FTP is part of the TCP/IP protocol suite ( the hoary acronym FTP stands for *File Transfer Protocol.* FTP is one of the oldest methods for sharing files between computers; however, because it's part of the TCP/IP protocol suite, it can be used on many different kinds of computers, including those running just about any type of strange and arcane operating system. You can still manage to exchange files regardless of whether you're using Mac OS X, Windows, Linux, or UNIX. (Heck, even dinosaurs like DOS can join the party.)

FTP is a *client/server* application. In plain English, this means that two pieces make things tick: the *server* (which hosts the connection, rather like a file server) and the *client* (which connects to the server). Mac OS X, thanks to its UNIX foundation, has both an FTP server and client built in. To use FTP, you need a computer running the FTP server software to give others access to files; then the other computer, or client, can connect to the FTP server. After the connection is made, the client can either send files to the server *(uploading)* or get files from the server *(downloading)*. In this section, I cover how to use FTP to give others access to your files as well as talk about the FTP applications that come with Mac OS X.

## Using the Mac OS X built-in FTP to share files

One way to give others access to your files is to run an FTP server on your MacBook. Mac OS X comes with an FTP server built in, so you just have to activate it. You might wonder why you'd use FTP to share files when you can use Personal File Sharing or Windows File Sharing. The main advantage to FTP is compatibility: Not only can people on your LAN access files, but anyone on the Internet can also access your files, regardless of the type of machine they're using.

Just as you do with the other file-sharing methods, you need to create a user account on your computer before someone can connect to and get files from your MacBook. After you have accounts created for the users, you can enable FTP sharing like this:

**Book VII
Chapter 2**

**Using Your Network**

*1.* **Click the System Preferences icon in the Dock.**

*2.* **Click the Sharing icon to open the Sharing Preferences pane.**

*3.* **Click the File Sharing entry.**

*4.* **Click the Options button.**

*5.* **Click the Share Files and Folders Using FTP check box to enable it.**

   Always helpful, Snow Leopard reminds you on the Advanced sheet that people can use `ftp://<ip address>`, where *ip address* is the IP address of your Mac.

*6.* **Click Done to exit the Advanced dialog, and close the System Preferences window to save the changes.**

If you're using an AirPort/AirPort Extreme Base Station or other cable/digital subscriber line (DSL) router to share your Internet connection, place the Mac that you want people on the Internet to access in a *DMZ,* or demilitarized zone. Check your cable/DSL router documentation for more information.

## *Using FTP from Terminal to transfer files*

You can use FTP to transfer files with an FTP server by using the command-line interface (CLI); to use the CLI, open a Terminal, or shell, session. To use a Terminal session, double-click the Terminal icon in the Utilities folder inside the Applications folder. When you open a Terminal session, you're presented with a window that accepts text commands. You'll see a prompt that consists of your computer's name and the folder that you're currently in, followed by your user ID. It's at this prompt where you type various FTP commands.

After you're in the Terminal session, you'll use a series of commands to connect to another computer, move in and out of folders, and transfer files. Following is a list of the basic commands that you need to use FTP as well as a brief description of what each command does.

✦ ftp: This command starts the FTP command-line interface session. You can tell that you're in the FTP client application when you see ftp> as your command prompt. This is where you type all other FTP commands to do things.

✦ open: This command is used to start your connection to another computer. Type this command followed by the IP address of the FTP server that you want to connect to.

✦ ls: Use this command to see a listing of all files and folders in the current folder on the FTP server.

✦ cd: This command allows you to change the folder that you're in. Type **cd** *<folder>* (where *folder* is a specific folder name) to move into a subfolder on the FTP server. Type **cd ..** (that's c, d, space, and two periods) to go back out a folder level.

✦ lcd: This command acts exactly like cd except that it changes the folder that you're currently in on your local system, not the FTP server. Use this command to put yourself in the folder on the local drive that you want to transfer files to and from.

✦ bin: Type this command to get in binary mode to transfer files that aren't plain-text files. (*Always* use binary mode unless you're specifically transferring plain-text files.)

✦ ascii: This command puts you in ASCII mode for transferring text files.

✦ get or mget: To retrieve a single file, use the get command followed by the filename of the file that you want to retrieve. If you want to get multiple files at one time, use the mget command followed by a filename, possibly containing * and/or ? as wildcards.

✦ put or mput: To send a single file, use the put command followed by the filename to send a file to the FTP server. To send multiple files, use the mput command followed by a filename, possibly containing * and/or ? as wildcards.

✦ `quit`: Use the `quit` command to end your FTP session.

To end a Terminal session and exit Terminal at any time, press ⌘+Q. Terminal prompts you for confirmation if necessary.

Many FTP servers will let you send files only to certain folders. Most times this folder is named *Upload, Uploads,* or something similar.

Using these commands will enable you to exchange files with an FTP server. Here's an example of how to use these commands within the Terminal window:

1. **Type** ftp **to get into FTP mode.**

2. **Type** open *<ip address>* **(where** *ip address* **is the server's network IP address) to open your connection to the FTP server.**

3. **At this point, you're asked for a username and password.**

   For many FTP servers, using the username anonymous and your e-mail address as the password is enough to get you logged in. Some sites even allow you to log in without any username or password at all. On secure sites, however, you must use an assigned username and password provided by the administrator of that particular server.

4. **Type** lcd *<folder>* **(where** *folder* **is a specific folder name) to change into the folder on your local drive that you want files to come to or from.**

5. **Type the** ls **and** cd **commands to place yourself into the desired folder on the FTP server.**

6. **Type the** ascii **or** bin **command to set your file transfer mode to ASCII or binary, respectively.**

   This is important because choosing the wrong type will likely cause the transfer to fail. Unless it's a plain-text file, always use binary mode.

7. **Type the** get, mget, put, **and** mput **commands to send or receive the desired files.**

8. **Type the** quit **command to close the connection and exit the FTP session.**

# Using the Built-in Firewall

A *firewall* watches all the network communications coming into your MacBook. It automatically plays the role of security guard, blocking or denying certain network traffic that you want to prevent from reaching your laptop. It acts as another layer of security to help keep you safe from unwanted attacks. That's all well and good, but you must be careful to set up your firewall correctly before you turn it on: A configuration mistake could make your MacBook inaccessible from the network.

**Book VII**
**Chapter 2**

**Using Your Network**

For instance, if you want to enable FTP access on your MacBook but you also want to keep all other traffic from coming into your system, you can tell the built-in firewall to allow only FTP traffic. The firewall on the MacBook will block or allow only TCP/IP traffic — not Bonjour — so Bonjour traffic (which is always from your local network and *not* the Internet, anyway) can always get in.

When enabled, the firewall blocks all traffic that comes into your MacBook. By default, however, the firewall is turned off. So, your first job is to enable the firewall, which you can do by following these steps:

*1.* **Click the System Preferences icon in the Dock.**

*2.* **Click the Security icon.**

*3.* **Click the Firewall tab.**

*4.* **Click the Start button to turn on your firewall.**

*5.* **Click the Advanced button to show the settings that you see in Figure 2-2.**

**Figure 2-2:** You can help protect your MacBook by using Snow Leopard's built-in firewall.

*6.* **Click the Automatically Allow Signed Software to Receive Incoming Connections radio button to select it.**

This enables the firewall. And, by default, virtually all incoming TCP/IP traffic is blocked. You must enable each sharing method that you want to be able to use. When you enable different sharing methods from the Sharing pane in System Preferences (such as File Sharing or FTP Access), you'll notice that those types of traffic now appear in the Firewall list. (In other words, when you turn on a sharing method, the firewall automatically allows traffic for that sharing method, which Snow Leopard calls a *service*. **Most** excellent.)

Click the up/down arrow icon to the right of any service to specify whether the firewall should allow or block connections.

Sometimes, you might want to allow other traffic through your firewall that isn't on the firewall list of recognized services and applications. At that point, you can click the Add button (which bears a plus sign) to specify the application that your firewall should allow. Snow Leopard presents you with the familiar Add dialog, and you can choose the application that needs access.

# Remote Control of Your MacBook

Forgive me whilst I wax techno-nerd here: One of the coolest advantages to a network is the ability to take control of one computer from another computer. For example, sometimes you might need to access files on your Mac Pro desktop while you're on a trip, but you don't have File Sharing enabled. What can you do? You can remotely connect into your Mac Pro and then — just as if you were sitting in front of it — enable File Sharing (as I demonstrate earlier in the chapter). Perhaps you have a file on your computer with someone's phone number that you suddenly need on the road. With remote control, it's at your fingertips! (Sigh . . . ah, technology.)

## Using Screen Sharing

Snow Leopard's Screen Sharing feature, which is available from iChat, can be turned on for individual users from the Sharing pane in System Preferences. You can allow access for all user accounts on your MacBook or limit remote access to selected users. Screen Sharing is Apple's implementation of Virtual Network Computing (VNC) technology.

To set up Screen Sharing, follow these steps:

1. **Click the System Preferences icon in the Dock.**

2. **Click the Sharing icon to open the Sharing Preferences pane.**

3. **Click the Screen Sharing check box to select it.**

4. **To limit remote access for specific accounts, click the Only these users radio button, and click the Add button (which bears a plus sign) to select a user.**

5. **Close the System Preferences window to save the change.**

After you've enabled screen sharing, you can use the Buddies➪Share My Screen menu item in iChat to share your screen with another person. To view another person's screen, use the Buddies➪Share Remote Screen menu item. (For the details on iChat and Screen Sharing, see Book VI, Chapter 3.)

**Book VII
Chapter 2**

**Using Your Network**

## *Remotely control your MacBook (for free, no less!)*

Virtual Network Computing (or VNC, available for many platforms at www.realvnc.com) is a very nice application that enables you to remotely control a computer from pretty much anywhere that has an Internet connection. VNC is easy to install and configure, and it runs on many different platforms, ranging from Windows XP and UNIX on desktop computers and servers to Palm OS and Windows CE on personal digital assistants (PDAs). Wrap your mind around this: You could be at a friend's house on her wireless network and use your PDA to remotely control your MacBook at home over the Internet. Pure, undiluted *sassy!*

Some networks have proxies and firewalls that might interfere with VNC's operation. You can remotely control a computer that's behind a firewall or cable/DSL router, but the firewall/router needs to be configured properly. Because the process varies from one manufacturer to the next, check your cable/DSL router manual for instructions on how to do this.

## *How VNC works*

In a nutshell, VNC takes the graphical interface on your monitor, turns it into data, and sends it to the computer that you're using to remotely control it. The computer that you're using sends keyboard presses, trackpad movements, and clicks to it, acting just the same way as it would if you were sitting right in front of it.

As I mention earlier, you can use Snow Leopard's Screen Sharing feature in iChat to make a remote connection from another Mac to your MacBook. However, you're not limited to using just another Mac using Snow Leopard and Screen Sharing in iChat — you can control your MacBook from a Windows PC, or from an older version of Mac OS X as well! If you've already enabled Screen Sharing (as I demonstrate earlier in this chapter), follow these steps to enable *any* VNC connection:

1. **Click the System Preferences icon in the Dock.**

2. **Click the Sharing icon to open the Sharing Preferences pane.**

3. **Click the Screen Sharing entry.**

4. **Click the Computer Settings button.**

5. **Click the VNC Viewers May Control Screen with Password check box to select it.**

6. **Click within the password text box and enter a password for VNC applications.**

7. **Click OK to exit the Computer Settings sheet, and close the System Preferences window to save the changes.**

Figure 2-3 shows a screenshot of a Mac running Mac OS X Tiger being remotely controlled from a computer running Windows 98. (Yes, I know, it's a travesty, but then again, sometimes you've just gotta use what you've got.)

**Figure 2-3:**
Yes, bucko, that's Mac OS X accessed remotely via Windows!

**Book VII
Chapter 2**

**Using Your Network**

Mr. Paranoia speaks again: **Make doggone sure that you set up the password access correctly for VNC or don't run it!** I can't stress enough how much fun a hacker would have with free remote control over your Mac OS X Desktop.

## Remote control of another computer from your MacBook

A few different VNC viewers exist for Mac OS X. A *VNC viewer* is just an application you use to remotely control another computer running VNC. You can download them at www.realvnc.com/download.html. If you find yourself on a computer without a VNC viewer — heaven forbid — VNC server actually runs over the Web as well! As long as the computer that you're using has a Web browser that supports Java — which Safari does — you can still remotely control your computer.

When you connect to the computer running VNC using a Web browser, the Web server sends a default page that contains a Java applet. That Java applet asks you for the password to connect; upon entering the correct password, it brings up the remote control session right in the Web browser.

# Chapter 3: Going Wireless

## In This Chapter

✔ **Finding out how wireless networking works**

✔ **Discovering wireless security**

✔ **Connecting to other Macs without a wireless access point**

✔ **Connecting to and disconnecting from AirPort networks**

*N*owadays, wireless connectivity is king. For example, wireless phones have gone from being a toy of the technological elite to a permanent fixture on the hip of the common man. The shorts that I'm wearing right now have a special pocket just for a cellphone to ride in; when I'm without my phone, it usually carries a 5th Avenue candy bar. (Perhaps that was too personal . . . sorry.)

Because people have become accustomed to keeping in touch from wherever they are, they also want to have access to their network, at least within their house or workplace, without the hassle of cables. (Which, by the way, are magnets for pets that enjoy a good chew toy.) This desire for convenience and the advances in wireless technology have combined to bring you the concept of the wireless network — as well as wireless coffee shops, wireless access providers, and even wireless gaming centers. (In fact, Apple's iPhone is a wireless Internet marvel, with instant connectivity to any Bluetooth-enabled Mac and full-featured e-mail and browsing that'll knock your socks off.)

Now you can be connected to your home local area network (LAN) and your shared Internet connection (which I cover in Book VII, Chapter 4) from your balcony, deck, lounge chair in the yard, or even your bedroom. In this chapter, I talk about how wireless networks work and then I give you a lot of information to help you get the right pieces to free yourself — *securely,* mind you — from the world of the wired.

# Speaking the Wireless Lingo

Wireless networks aren't all that different from their wired siblings. In this chapter, I discuss some of the features and limitations of wireless networking, but you must first be familiar with a foundation of information.

Because of the technology involved in wireless networks and how things are changing rapidly in this area, you'll find yourself swimming in a sea of acronyms and other techno-babble. Although you don't need to know every little detail to be able to set up your own wireless network, you should know some of these terms so that you can avoid getting stung by hackers or stuck with equipment that's on the verge of obsolescence.

Here's a quick list of terms that you'll see on your road to becoming a wireless network guru:

✦ **WLAN:** WLAN stands for *Wireless LAN.* If you read previous chapters in this minibook, you know that a LAN (local area network) is just a bunch of connected computers and other devices.

✦ **IEEE:** This stands for *Institute of Electrical and Electronics Engineers,* which is an organization that approves standards that allow computers, network equipment, and just about anything else electronic to play nicely together. Sometimes IEEE helps create these standards before approving them, and sometimes it just approves standards that others have produced.

✦ **802.11:** This is the part of the IEEE standards that deals specifically with wireless networking.

Although wireless is usually generically referred to as *wireless networks* (or sometimes even *Wi-Fi*), it's all really a wireless form of Ethernet.

✦ **Wireless access point:** A *wireless access point,* or WAP, is a device that allows wireless network devices to connect to a wired Ethernet network.

✦ **Service Set Identifier:** The *Service Set Identifier,* or SSID, is used to tell your computer the name of the wireless network that you want to use.

✦ **Wired Equivalency Privacy:** *Wired Equivalency Privacy,* or WEP, is an encryption that wireless networks can use to keep your wireless network more secure from snoopers and hackers.

✦ **Wi-Fi Protected Access:** Usually referred to as WPA, this is a security protocol that's more robust and harder to crack than WEP. The latest version, WPA2, is a common security feature on today's wireless hardware.

✦ **Ad Hoc mode:** An *Ad Hoc* wireless network is one in which each wireless device talks directly with all other wireless devices.

Apple calls Ad Hoc mode a *computer-to-computer network.*

✦ **Infrastructure mode:** This is where all wireless devices talk to a WAP, and the WAP then talks to other wireless devices and the wired network.

As I cover the different parts of wireless networking and how to set it up, you'll find yourself using these terms over and over. Before you know it, you'll be spouting these wireless-related acronyms like a pro. (No, really. I'm not kidding.)

# Figuring Out the Different Flavors of Wireless Ethernet

One of the first things that you might notice when you start looking into wireless networking is the existence of different wireless standards. You should at least be aware that these different standards exist: That way, you can be sure to get wireless network components that will work together because *some of the different wireless standards are not compatible.* (Feel free to photocopy this list and stick it on your fridge door.)

## Basic Wi-Fi: 802.11b

IEEE 802.11b has another name that you'll likely see on product advertisements, literature, or boxes in stores: *Wi-Fi,* which stands for Wireless Fidelity. (Kinda like that cutting-edge Hi-Fi stereo from the '60s and '70s, where *Hi-Fi* stands for *High Fidelity.*) Most folks proclaim Wi-Fi as only 802.11b. Wi-Fi was the first version of wireless Ethernet. This version of wireless runs at speeds up to 11 million bits per second, or 11 Mbps. The reason I say that it runs at speeds *up to* 11 Mbps is because the actual speed at which the data is transferred depends on things like signal strength and quality. When the conditions are such that your signal strength or quality is decreased — such as an inconvenient concrete wall between you and your AirPort Base Station — you might find that your wireless connection changes down to 5.5 Mbps, 2 Mbps, or even as slow as 1 Mbps.

802.11b has been largely supplanted in current wireless networking, and almost all the equipment you can buy today is either 802.11g or 802.11n (both of which I cover in a moment). However, if you're working with older computers and existing 802.11b hardware, any networking equipment you buy should be backward compatible with 802.11b.

Apple's AirPort network cards and standard-issue AirPort Base Station used 802.11b. In fact, it's time for Mac owners to swell with pride yet again: Apple was the first computer company to ship 802.11b hardware. (Back then, in 1999, it was the original AirPort Base Station.) Now, of course, Apple has raised the bar with AirPort Extreme, which I discuss later in this chapter, and the AirPort Express mobile Base Station.

In theory, Wi-Fi network cards have the ability to communicate with other Wi-Fi devices and WAPs that are up to 1,000 feet away. Having said that, realize that 1,000 feet is a generous estimate when outdoors on a clear day with no wind blowing — you see what I'm getting at. (You're more likely to see a wildebeest wearing a hula skirt in your living room than see that kind of distance indoors.) In reality, when you set up your wireless network, things such as walls — especially concrete walls, as in basements — and areas with lots of electrical wiring decrease the distance that you can cover. If you use a WAP, plan on no more than 150 feet between wireless computers and the WAP. However, your mileage might vary.

That 11 Mbps bandwidth is shared between all computers using it. Collisions can also occur if more than one computer tries to communicate at the same time. If you have a lot of people on your wireless network, the network will get noticeably slower because of increased collisions. Remember that the total bandwidth is shared among the computers on the wireless network. This applies not only to Wi-Fi but also to the 802.11a (which I cover in the nearby sidebar) and the 802.11g standards.

One last thing about 802.11b networking: Wi-Fi uses the 2.4 GHz frequency range. It actually uses 11 different channels, but they're all around the 2.4 GHz range. If you're using a 2.4 GHz cordless phone or even a microwave, using either device can definitely interfere with or even shut down your wireless network. Keep this in mind when you buy your next phone or wonder why your file transfers stop when you're communing with Orville Redenbacher in the microwave.

## Let's get Extreme: 802.11g

Apple's release of the first generation of AirPort Extreme provided both the speed of 802.11a and the compatibility with Wi-Fi. That's because it used the *802.11g* standard, which operates at speeds up to 54 Mbps (as did 802.11a) but will also operate at the same frequency ranges and play nicely with existing 802.11b equipment. (Notice that we're heading in the right direction again when it comes to naming conventions. Go figure.)

Apple was once again the *first* company to offer 802.11g hardware as standard equipment. Feel free to enjoy the Superiority Dance yet again.

Naturally, there's a downside: 802.11g returned to that pesky 2.4 GHz range, so your cordless phone and microwave can also wreak the same havoc that they did with your original AirPort equipment.

## Raising the bar to 802.11n

I would be remiss if I didn't mention the current wireless standard from IEEE: 802.11n. Most third-party manufacturers (including Apple) now offer only 802.11n wireless equipment. Apple's 802.11n products include the current AirPort Extreme base station, the AirPort Extreme hardware in all of the MacBook line, and the spiffy Apple TV.

Why the hubbub? Oh, I forgot to mention that 802.11n can deliver throughput in excess of 100 Mbps! Don't bet your house that you'll get that kind of speed, though — as with the other members of the 802.11 family, that's likely to be a theoretical maximum speed.

You can't go wrong with the 802.11n standard — think superfast wireless connections in your household or office. Ahh, technology. . . .

# 802.11a networks

*802.11a* was a newer version of wireless Ethernet than 802.11b. 802.11b came out first, and 802.11a came out next. (I guess someone ran into a doorframe.) 802.11a doesn't have a generally recognized handy nickname like Wi-Fi, so just call it 802.11a.

802.11a equipment isn't compatible with Wi-Fi or older 802.11b AirPort Base Stations, so don't make the mistake of buying both 802.11b and 802.11a network equipment. Instead, I strongly recommend that you follow the AirPort Extreme course charted by Apple and use the 802.11g or 802.11n standards (which are backward compatible with Wi-Fi). Just in case, the current AirPort Extreme base station (which uses 802.11n) does support 802.11a — hats off again to the folks in Cupertino!

802.11a can run at speeds up to 54 Mbps — almost *five times* faster than Wi-Fi. This is because 802.11a uses the 5 GHz frequency range instead of the cluttered 2.4 GHz range that Wi-Fi uses. The powers that be set aside the 5 GHz range just for wireless networking, so cordless phones and microwaves (or any other wireless devices, for that matter) can't interfere with the network. The downside to using the higher 5 GHz range, though, is that the distances that can be covered are even less than that of Wi-Fi — no more than about 60 feet to maintain the highest speeds.

Because of the incompatibilities with 802.11b and the arrival of 802.11g and 802.11n, 802.11a equipment has all but disappeared, and you should steer clear of it with a wide berth. (In fact, good luck finding 802.11a hardware anywhere but eBay.)

**Book VII
Chapter 3**

**Going Wireless**

## The guy with the turquoise teeth

I should also mention *Bluetooth* — a strange name for a wireless standard, I admit, but it works like a charm. Bluetooth devices use 2.4 GHz as well, but they're designed only for very short distances . . . up to only about 30 feet. Bluetooth is the future for linking mobile devices (such as personal digital assistants and cell phones) and external peripherals (such as wireless keyboards and mice) to your MacBook. In fact, Bluetooth can turn your MacBook into a completely cordless machine — except for the power cord, of course. Snow Leopard provides built-in support for Bluetooth through the iSync application and the Bluetooth pane in System Preferences.

# Keeping Your Wireless Network Secure

Are you worried about the security of your AirPort wireless network? You *should* be, bunkie. Imagine someone in the next apartment or house — or standing right in your street — intercepting and monitoring your data from your wireless network.

But before you decide to toss the idea of a wireless network, keep this in mind: Even though it *is* technically possible that someone might camp out on your doorstep in order to gain access to your wireless network, for most home networks, this possibility isn't very probable. Even if someone tries to gain access to your wireless network and perhaps even *sniff* your network — a techno-nerd term meaning to record all the data flying around a network — there isn't a whole lot someone can do with that information.

If a friend invites you for an evening of war driving, think "recreational mobile hacking." *War driving* is the act of driving through neighborhoods in a car equipped with a laptop computer and a wireless network card. The payoff? If the hacker is lucky enough to locate a house with an open wireless network, we're talking free wireless Internet access . . . from the comfort of his car! (Not to mention any shared files or information that's available on that network.) Again, keep security in mind when installing wireless hardware, and these bozos will get nothing from your network.

You might say, "But I use my credit card on the Internet to buy stuff." Sure, this is a valid concern; however, if you purchase things on the Internet with your credit card, you should already be using a secure connection provided by the Web site for your personal information so that the data you're sending across your wireless network is already encrypted and relatively safe from thieves. (You can find more on this when I discuss Safari in detail in Book VI, Chapter 5.)

"I have shared my files on my computer. Can the Bad Guys access those shared files?" Another good question, but if you read Book VII, Chapter 2, you know that you have to create an account for those whom you want to access your files. Unless the would-be hacker is very good at guessing usernames and passwords, your files are pretty safe, too.

This is not to say that you bear absolutely no risk of being hacked. If a legitimate user on your wireless network connects to your computer and starts transferring a file, a would-be hacker could potentially record all the traffic and then reconstruct the file that was sent from the data that was recorded. In other words, a hacker could grab that user's username and password. That's where WPA comes in.

## WPA and WPA2

*Wi-Fi Protected Access,* or WPA, is A Good Thing (even if it makes for a silly-sounding acronym). It's currently the standard encryption protocol offered for home wireless networking — WPA2 standard is the latest version, and is even better at defending your wireless network. As you might expect, all of Apple's current AirPort wireless hardware uses WPA2 security, as does most of the wireless hardware you'll find on the shelf at your local Hardware Heaven electronics store. (It's still a good idea to check the specifications on the box, though, to make sure that WPA2 is supported.)

WPA2 works well as a deterrent to keep the wrong people out of your stuff. Although WPA2 isn't going to ward off the spies at the National Security Agency, it's good enough to protect home and small-business networks.

## WEP

WEP is an old friend of mine. Short for *Wired Equivalency Privacy*, it's another ridiculous acronym for another wireless security system. WEP was one of the first widely supported wireless encryption schemes, but in today's world, WEP is now outdated and pretty easy for a hacker to outwit. I strongly recommend that your network use WPA2 whenever possible.

Apple's implementation of WEP comes in two varieties: 40 bit and 128 bit. The more bits used in the encryption, the more secure (and the better) it is.

To use WEP, you need to select a WEP *key,* which is really just a code word:

+ The longer the key, the better.

+ When making a key, use something like *ab8sher7234ksief87* (something that's random with letters and numbers) as opposed to something, like *mykey,* that's easily guessed.

If you're using an Ad Hoc wireless network, all the computers need to have their wireless network card configured with the same WEP key in order to communicate. If you're using a WAP to connect to the rest of the network, you need to use the same key on your computers that you've configured on your WAP.

One thing to note about WEP is that it's been *broken,* meaning that someone has figured out how to undo the encryption that WEP provides. For businesses, especially those with sensitive data, WEP isn't a good security solution.

## The LEAP security standard

*Lightweight Extensible Authentication Protocol* (LEAP) is an encryption protocol developed by Cisco Systems for superior security in the business world. To use LEAP, you need to have a server that's set up to enable users to log in to gain permission to the wireless network. After you initially log in (*authenticate*) to your network, LEAP changes encryption keys on the fly at a time interval that you determine. You could set it so that every 15 minutes your encryption key is changed: Even if someone is in that hypothetical tent on your front lawn, he could never record enough packets to figure out your key because it changes so often.

Setting up a server so that you can use LEAP isn't something for the novice to attempt. I would encourage you to read up on LEAP only if you're very serious about airtight security on your WLAN. The Cisco Web site (www. cisco.com) is a good place to read about LEAP.

**Book VII
Chapter 3**

**Going Wireless**

All current AirPort Extreme wireless network cards and Base Stations are compatible with the Cisco LEAP for higher security.

# Setting Up Your Wireless Network

On to the good stuff. This section describes how to set up an Ad Hoc or infrastructure-based WLAN (wireless LAN).

All of today's MacBooks come with an AirPort Extreme (802.11n) card built in, so you don't have to add or install any wireless hardware to create or use a wireless network!

## Setting up an Ad Hoc wireless network

Using an Ad Hoc network — also called a *computer-to-computer* network — is a fairly easy thing to accomplish in Mac OS X. Plus, you're not limited to just Macs: With an Ad Hoc network, you can also swap niceties with PCs and PDAs that have 802.11b/g/n network interface cards (NICs) installed. This Ad Hoc network is great for setting up an impromptu network in a classroom, exchanging recipes and pictures at a family reunion in a park, or blowing your friend up while gaming across the aisle of a Greyhound bus at 70 mph.

To set up an Ad Hoc network, you first have to create the computer-to-computer network on one of your Macs. This takes advantage of the AirPort Software Base Station that's built into Snow Leopard.

To create a computer-to-computer network, follow these steps:

1. **Click the AirPort status icon on the menu bar.**

   If you haven't set Snow Leopard to display your AirPort status in the Finder menu bar, follow these steps:

   a. *Open the Network pane in System Preferences and choose the AirPort entry in the list at the left of the pane.*

   b. *Enable the Show AirPort Status in Menu Bar check box.*

   c. *Close the System Preferences window to save your changes.*

2. **Click Create Network to display the dialog that you see in Figure 3-1.**

3. **Enter a name for your network.**

4. **Mark the Require Password check box to turn on WEP encryption.**

5. **Enter a password for your network and then enter it again to confirm it.**

## Using non-Apple wireless equipment with AirPort Extreme equipment

Because of Apple's implementation of wireless standards within the AirPort Extreme product line, keep in mind some things when trying to mix Apple wireless equipment with other vendors' 802.11b, 802.11g, or 802.11n equipment. As you discover elsewhere in this chapter, using AirPort wireless networks can require a WPA password that corresponds to the 802.11b/g/n WPA key for encryption. However, the password that you enter for AirPort networks isn't exactly the same as the WEP key for that same network. If you're using an AirPort network card and are trying to connect to a non-Apple WAP, you need to follow a specific procedure. You can find this procedure by going to http://search.info.apple.com and searching on the words *802.11 Compatibility*.

You want my opinion? Because of the issues of using non-AirPort 802.11b/g/n hardware with The Real Thing (AirPort/AirPort Extreme stuff), I recommend that you stick with Apple equipment if possible.

**Figure 3-1:**
Creating a computer-to-computer wireless network through software. *Excellent.*

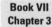

Create a Computer-to-Computer network.

Enter the name of the Computer-to-Computer network you want to create.

Name: Colossus

Channel: Automatic (11)

☑ Require Password

The password must be entered as exactly 5 ASCII characters or 10 hex digits.

Password:

Verify:

Security: 40-bit WEP (more compatible)

Cancel  OK

**Book VII Chapter 3**

Going Wireless

Although you can leave encryption disabled, I highly recommend that you turn it on and choose a password for that extra bit of security. (Just call me Security Man.) Note that the password must be an exact length (which is determined by whether you choose a 40-bit [5-character] key or a 128-bit [13-character] key).

In general, channels 1, 6, and 11 are the only ones that don't overlap other channels — and are therefore the best choices to use. If you're close to other WAPs, AirPort Base Stations, or other Ad Hoc networks, try to find a channel that's not being used, or performance can be degraded. (If you have only one access point, it doesn't matter which channel you select — just allow Snow Leopard to automatically select a channel, which is typically Channel 11.)

6. **Click OK.**

Creating a computer-to-computer network gives the illusion of having an AirPort Base Station. So for people to join your network, they would follow the same steps as those they would use to join any other AirPort network, as I cover in the next section.

## Setting up wireless networks with an AirPort Base Station

After one computer is running a computer-to-computer network or you've set up and configured an AirPort/AirPort Extreme Base Station, you're ready to invite other computers with wireless hardware to the party.

### Joining in an existing AirPort network

After you have a network set up on one of your wireless-enabled computers, you just need to have the other wireless-enabled computers join that network. You can use the same process, as I describe here, to join any wireless network:

1. **Click the AirPort status icon on the menu bar.**

   A list of existing network connections appears in the AirPort menu.

2. **Select an existing network connection that you'd like to join.**

   If you want to join a network whose name doesn't appear in the list — also called a *closed network,* follow these steps:

   a. *Select Join Other Network from the AirPort status menu.*

   b. *Enter the name of the network that you want to join and the password (if any is required).*

   A closed network is another added measure of security — one that's good enough for most people because it's very unlikely that a hacker is going to try to hack a hidden network.

### Disconnecting from an AirPort network

To disconnect from an AirPort/AirPort Extreme network, you can turn off your AirPort card altogether, which I cover in the next section. (Simplicity, they say, is an art.) Another way is to simply connect to another AirPort network — but this option is really only useful if you actually *want* to connect to another network.

### Turning your AirPort hardware on or off

Being able to turn your AirPort/AirPort Extreme hardware on and off actually has its uses:

✦ You might want to use your MacBook in a place where your wireless card shouldn't be used, like

- An airplane (when they tell you to turn off all cell phones)
- A hospital area that doesn't allow cell phones or other wireless devices

✦ Turning off your AirPort/AirPort Extreme hardware conserves your MacBook's battery life.

To turn your AirPort equipment on or off via the AirPort status icon on the menu bar, give it a click and choose Turn AirPort On/Off from the resulting menu.

**Book VII
Chapter 3**

**Going Wireless**

# Chapter 4: Sharing That Precious Internet Thing

## In This Chapter

↙ Finding out how Internet sharing works

↙ Choosing between hardware and software Internet sharing

↙ Connecting your Macs to a cable/DSL router

↙ Adding wireless support to a shared Internet connection

Although I discuss lots of fun stuff that you can do with your network in previous chapters, this has to be my favorite: sharing a single Internet connection between *all* the computers on your network. If you have more than one computer, I'm sure that you've had to deal with the dilemma that pops up whenever more than one person wants or needs to access the Internet at the same time.

Luckily, because small home and office local area networks (LANs) use our old friend TCP/IP for network communications, connecting an entire network to the Internet isn't as troublesome a task as you might think. In this chapter, I talk about different hardware and software options for sharing your MacBook's Internet connection as well as how to include your wireless devices.

## Sharing the Internet

Sharing a single Internet connection among all your computers can be a boon simply because of the reduced chances of random acts of violence. (Internet deprivation can be an ugly thing, you know.) Although I won't claim that Internet sharing will save lives, it can indeed save you from headaches and arguments when more than one person wants to use the Internet at one time.

Throughout this chapter, I talk a lot about *cable* modems and *Asynchronous Digital Subscriber Line* (ADSL) modems. Both of these are high-speed Internet connections — and both are relatively inexpensive — that are offered by your local cable company and your local phone company, respectively. The phone company offers different kinds of digital subscriber line (DSL) connections, the most common of which is ADSL. However, because different kinds of DSL connections exist, in this chapter I refer to them all generically as *DSL*.

To share your Internet connection, you need a few things, so here's a brief checklist:

✦ **An Internet connection:** Typically, this is a cable or DSL modem connection, but older versions of the AirPort Base Station can use a dial-up Internet connection that's accessed via a standard v.90/v.92 analog telephone modem. (Note that recent models of the AirPort Extreme Base Station do not have the capability to use analog dial-up connections.)

✦ **A LAN:** You need a standard LAN (which is connected with cables) or a wireless LAN. (Heck, you can even have a hybrid that has both wired and wireless access.) See Book VII, Chapter 1 for more information about setting up a LAN; see Book VII, Chapter 3 for more on setting up a Wireless LAN (WLAN).

✦ **An Internet-sharing device:** I use the word *device* because the method that you use to share your Internet connection could be through software that you run on one of your computers or hardware that is stand-alone, depending on how you connect to the Internet and what best fits your needs.

When you have these three things ready to go, you can share your Internet connection. However, you need to know some background information to help you choose the right components and get everything up and running.

## Using Network Address Translation

You must determine one thing before you start your Internet sharing quest: the set of network Internet Protocol (IP) addresses that you'll use. If you used Book VII, Chapter 1 to set up and configure your LAN, you might recall that I suggest a specific range of IP addresses to use on your LAN. In case you missed out on Chapter 1 of this minibook, I briefly cover this important topic here so that you can share your Internet connection smoothly. (Forgive me if I wax technical, but 'tis only for the moment.)

When talking about IP addresses, the ruling body that tracks IP addresses and where they're used has broken all IP addresses into two parts:

✦ **Public IP addresses:** *Public* IP addresses are used to communicate on the Internet, and only one device in the entire world can use a given public IP address at any given time.

✦ **Private IP addresses:** *Private* addresses, on the other hand, are supposed to be used only on networks (such as your home LAN) and do *not* connect directly to the Internet. Lots of people can use the same private address because their networks never go public; that is, they never directly access the Internet, so their IP addresses never conflict.

Typically, you'll use private addresses in the form of 192.168.*x.x* on your LAN; however, AirPort Extreme routers use private addresses in the form of 10.0.*x.x* by default. See Book VII, Chapter 1 for an overview of IP addresses and how they work.

You might be wondering to yourself thusly: "If I use private IP addresses on my LAN at home or in the office and I have to use a public IP address to communicate on the Internet, how can my private IP addresses on my LAN communicate with public IP addresses on the Internet?" That is an excellent question, and the answer is *Network Address Translation* (or NAT, for short).

*NAT* acts as a gatekeeper between your private IP addresses on your LAN and the public IP addresses on the Internet. When you connect to the Internet, your Internet service provider (ISP) gives you one — and usually *only* one — public IP address that can be used on the Internet. Instead of one of your computers using that public IP address and depriving all the other computers on the LAN, the hardware or software that you use to share the Internet will take control of that public IP address. Then, when any computer on your LAN tries to communicate on the Internet, your NAT software/ hardware intercepts your communications and readdresses the traffic so that it appears to be coming from your allotted public IP address. (Think of a funnel that collects water from several different sources and then directs all the water into a single stream.)

When the Web site, File Transfer Protocol (FTP) server, or whatever strange Internet intelligence you're using on the Internet replies, it replies to your NAT device. The NAT device remembers which private IP address it should go to on the LAN and sends the information to that computer. See NAT at work in Figure 4-1.

192.168.100.5    192.168.100.10    192.168.100.15

NAT Table
192.168.100.5 = 62.78.147.251 port 15000
192.168.100.10 = 62.78.147.251 port 15001
192.168.100.15 = 62.78.147.251 port 15002

Cable/DSL Router
62.78.147.251

Internet

**Figure 4-1:**
NAT hard at
work —
for the
betterment
of Macs
everywhere.

# Ways to Share Your Internet Connection

After you have an Internet connection and your LAN is set up, you need something to make this NAT thing work. You have two different options to take care of NAT for your shared Internet connection: hardware or software. (Go figure.) Each has pros and cons, so take a look at each option individually.

If you read Chapter 3 of this minibook, you know that Snow Leopard has AirPort software built in. So, since you have AirPort Extreme wireless hardware built-in on your MacBook and you're using Snow Leopard, you can have your MacBook act like an AirPort Extreme Base Station for all the wireless computers on your network, which in turn can use a software NAT.

## Using hardware for sharing an Internet connection

Probably the most popular way to share an Internet connection is to buy a hardware device that connects to your Internet connection, which then connects to your LAN. These devices are referred to as *cable/DSL routers*. The main downside to a hardware Internet connection-sharing device is that it costs more than a software solution.

Cable/DSL routers are nice because they're easy to set up and configure. Too, you can leave them on, which means constant Internet access for those on your LAN. You don't have to worry about turning on another computer to connect to the Internet as you do with a software solution. Sounds like a good spot for a Mark's Maxim:

**Hardware routers are the best choice for sharing your Internet connection, so if you can afford one, you should get one!**

Apple's AirPort Extreme Base Station is not only a *Wireless Access Point* (WAP) for your network, as I discuss in Chapter 3 of this minibook, but also acts as an Internet connection-sharing device. (AirPort Express can't share an Internet connection.) Some older flavors of AirPort Base Station even have a built-in v.90 modem for sharing a single 56 Kbps connection using a dialup account! A base station typically has several Ethernet connections for sharing a high-speed Internet connection, including a dedicated port to connect to a cable/DSL router and two or four ports to connect to other computers on the LAN.

If you think that a cable/DSL router or an AirPort Extreme Base Station could be the karma pathway for you to achieve your goal of sharing your Internet connection, here are some things to consider when deciding which device to buy for your LAN:

✦ **Do you need a switch?** Most cable/DSL routers have a small 3-, 4-, or 5-port switch built in. See Chapter 1 of this minibook to discover more about switches. This multiport capability is nice because the same cable/DSL router that shares your Internet connection is also the centerpiece of your LAN where all your connections meet, thus saving you from having to buy a switch on top of the cost of the cable/DSL router.

Some cable/DSL routers, however, have only a single Ethernet connection to connect to your LAN. So keep in mind that if you choose a device with a single LAN connection, you must supply your own switch that would then connect the cable/DSL router to the rest of your LAN.

✦ **Got modem?** If your only Internet connection is through a dial-up modem account, look for a built-in analog telephone modem on your cable/DSL router. You must have this feature if you want to use a hardware device to share your Internet connection. (Again, older versions of the AirPort Base Station are great for this because the modem is built in, but you'll have to do some shopping on eBay.) Even if you have cable/DSL service, some ISPs also include a dial-up account with your broadband access. With such a bountiful selection of connections, you can plug in your cable or DSL service to the cable/DSL router as well as use the dial-up account as a back-up in case your main service has problems.

**Book VII
Chapter 4**

Sharing That
Precious Internet
Thing

✦ **Want a printer with that?** Some cable/DSL routers also have a port for connecting a printer — a great feature to have because it allows you to leave the printer connected and turned on so that anyone on the network can print to it anytime. (This is much better than connecting the printer to a computer and sharing it because then the computer doing the sharing must always be on in order to make the printer available.) Mac OS X can send a print job to a printer by using Bonjour or TCP/IP, so just make sure that your printer is compatible with TCP/IP printing, also called *LPR* (Line Printer Remote).

## Using software for sharing an Internet connection

As I mention earlier, your MacBook can act like an AirPort/AirPort Extreme Base Station, providing both wireless Ethernet connectivity for other computers on the LAN *and* a shared Internet connection.

Snow Leopard also has built-in software that allows a single computer on your network to share its Internet connection with others on the LAN. To share your Internet connection, follow these quick steps:

*1.* **Click the System Preferences icon in the Dock.**

*2.* **Click the Sharing icon.**

*3.* **Click the Internet Sharing entry in the list on the left side of the pane.**

    This brings up the settings, as shown in Figure 4-2.

*4.* **Click the Share Your Connection From pop-up menu and choose Ethernet.**

*5.* **Select the Ethernet check box (in the To Computers Using list) to enable it.**

    When you do, you're issued a warning that enabling this could affect your ISP or violate your agreement with your ISP. In my experiences, this step has never caused any networking problems. However, if you have any doubts, contact your ISP and verify this.

*6.* **Click OK in the warning dialog to continue.**

    You go back to the Sharing dialog, where you'll notice that the Internet Sharing check box is conveniently ready for you to select it — feel free to click it now.

If you're using a dial-up modem to access the Internet, you need to also make sure that the computer that has the modem also has an Ethernet or wireless LAN connection. Unfortunately, MacBook models don't have a built-in modem, but if you buy an external USB modem from Apple (or a third-party vendor), you can still use this feature.

**Figure 4-2:**
Turning on
Internet
sharing
with Snow
Leopard.

If you're using a cable or DSL modem for your Internet connection, the Mac that you want to run the sharing software on should have two Ethernet connections: one to connect to the cable/DSL modem and one to connect to the rest of the LAN.

The main disadvantage to using a software solution for Internet connection sharing is that the computer that connects to the Internet must be turned on and ready to go all the time so that others on the network can get to the Internet. And although the sharing software operates in the background on the machine it's running on, it still chews up some of the Mac's processing power and memory, so it could slow down other applications that you're running on that computer.

## Connecting Everything for Wired Sharing

After you decide whether to use a software or hardware solution, it's time to get your hands dirty: All the pieces of the puzzle must be set up and connected. In this section, I tell you how to connect things for either the software or hardware method of sharing the Internet connection.

### Using the software method

When you use the software method to share your Internet connection, one of the computers on your network has both the connection to the Internet and a connection to the LAN. Figure 4-3 shows a typical setup for software Internet sharing, whether you're using a dial-up modem account or a cable/DSL modem for your Internet connection.

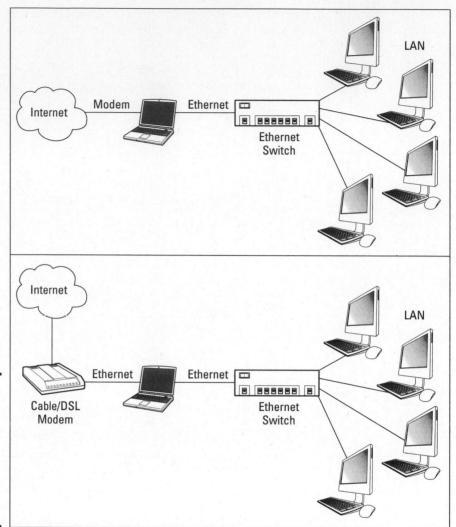

**Figure 4-3:**
Two
different
con-
figurations
for Internet
sharing
through
software.

Keep in mind, though, that when using a cable/DSL modem for your Internet
connection, the computer running the sharing software *must* have two
Ethernet connections.

## Using the hardware method

Not only does using a dedicated piece of hardware free one of the Macs on
your network from the onerous job of hosting the shared connection, but it
also keeps you from having to have more than one Ethernet connection on a
single computer if you're using a cable/DSL modem for your Internet access.
Figure 4-4 shows how you would connect your devices for hardware Internet

sharing by using either a cable/DSL router with a built-in Ethernet switch or a cable/DSL router with a stand-alone Ethernet switch, as you would need to use AirPort or AirPort Extreme.

If you choose to buy a cable/DSL router that has a built-in Ethernet switch, you can simply connect all your computers on the LAN to the built-in switch. However, if you buy a cable/DSL router that has only a single LAN connection, as with older versions of the AirPort Base Station, you must connect that single LAN connection to an external hub or switch in order to get all the computers on the same network.

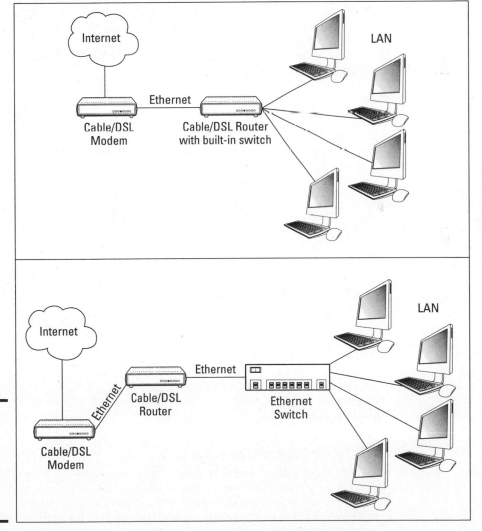

**Book VII**
**Chapter 4**

**Sharing That**
**Precious Internet**
**Thing**

**Figure 4-4:**
A comely
pair of
hardware
Internet
sharing
solutions.

We're talking wired Ethernet here — of course, wireless connections don't require a port on your router or base station. (More on this in the next section.)

Regardless of whether you use the hardware or software method to share your Internet connection, all the computers on your LAN — except the one that's doing the sharing, if you're using software sharing — should be configured to obtain its IP address automatically through our old friend, Dynamic Host Configuration Protocol (DHCP). (See Chapter 1 of this minibook for details on how to do this in Snow Leopard.) Although it's not a requirement that you set up your other devices with DHCP, it's recommended unless you understand the IP addressing scheme required by your cable/DSL router and you're willing to set up the addresses manually. You need to follow the instructions that come with the cable/DSL router or software that you purchase for detailed information on how to configure that.

## Adding Wireless Support

You might have noticed that I mention *wireless* here and there in this chapter. This section covers in a bit more detail how you can add wireless capabilities to your shared Internet party. To discover more about how wireless networks work and how to set up one, see Book VII, Chapter 3.

Basically, you can encounter a couple of situations when trying to add wireless capabilities into the mix. Either you already have an Internet connection-sharing mechanism in place (either hardware or software), or you don't yet have your Internet connection shared.

### If you already have a cable/DSL router or are using software Internet sharing

If you already have a cable/DSL router or if you're using software Internet sharing, like that built into Snow Leopard, you can simply buy a WAP (short for *Wireless Access Point*) and connect it to your LAN. Adding a WAP enables anyone using wireless Ethernet access to your network and thus to your shared Internet connection.

There are many WAPs that you can buy to add wireless to your network. AirPort Extreme is a good example; however, because AirPort Extreme also can do Internet sharing, make sure that you *don't* enable Internet sharing through software on your MacBook! (In this case, you don't want or need this feature because it can conflict with your cable/DSL router operation.)

## *If you do not have a cable/DSL router or an AirPort Extreme Base Station*

If you don't have a cable/DSL router or an AirPort Extreme Base Station for Internet sharing, you have a few options. Each option has an upside and a downside.

One option is to get an AirPort Extreme Base Station, which provides both wireless access for AirPort-enabled wireless computers and Internet sharing for the entire network. Because today's AirPort Extreme Base Stations also feature three built-in Ethernet ports for wired connections, you won't need an additional switch to connect up to three Macs using Ethernet cables.

The other option is to buy a combination cable/DSL router, which has a built-in WAP. Most cable/DSL routers — including the ones that have wireless built in — also have multiple Ethernet ports on them, so connecting computers by using wired Ethernet can be done without buying an external switch.

The final option is that you can use the AirPort software built into Snow Leopard to turn your MacBook into an Airport/AirPort Extreme Base Station, as I discuss earlier. This is a great, low-cost way to add wireless and Internet sharing to your network, but remember that the software will still eat up processor time and memory. For more on wireless networking, read Chapter 3 of this minibook.

**Book VII**
**Chapter 4**

**Sharing That
Precious Internet
Thing**

# Book VIII

# Expanding Your System

The 5th Wave    By Rich Tennant

"Oh, Anthony loves working with AppleScript. He customized all our Word documents with a sound file so they all close with out with a 'Bada Bing!'"

# Contents at a Glance

## Chapter 1: Hardware That Will Make You Giddy . . . . . . . . . . . . . . .625

Parading Pixels: Digital Cameras, DV Camcorders, and Scanners ........ 626
Incredible Input: Keyboards, Trackballs,
  Joysticks, and Drawing Tablets ............................................... 629
Sublime Storage: DVD/Blu-Ray Recorders ................................... 634
Awesome Audio: Subwoofer Systems and MP3 Hardware................... 635

## Chapter 2: Add RAM, Hard Drive Space, and Stir. . . . . . . . . . . . . . .637

Adding Memory: Reasons for More RAM ..................................... 637
Shopping for a RAM Upgrade.................................................. 639
The Tao of Hard Drive Territory .............................................. 641
Internal versus External Storage .............................................. 642
Determining How Much Space You Need.................................... 644
Shopping for a Hard Drive..................................................... 645
Installing Your New Stuff ...................................................... 646

## Chapter 3: Port-o-Rama: Using USB and FireWire. . . . . . . . . . . . . . .649

Appreciating the Advantage of a FireWire Connection ..................... 649
Understanding USB and the Tale of Two Point Oh ......................... 651
Hey, You Need a Hub!........................................................... 652
Uh, It's Just Sitting There....................................................... 652

## Chapter 4: I'm Okay, You're a Printer . . . . . . . . . . . . . . . . . . . . . . . .655

Meet the Printer Browser ...................................................... 655
Adding a Funky Printer ......................................................... 657
Managing Your Printing Jobs ................................................. 659
Sharing a Printer across That There Network................................ 661

## Chapter 5: Applications That You've (Probably) Gotta Have . . . . . . .663

The Trundling Microsoft Mammoth........................................... 664
Your Mac OS X Toolbox: TechTool Pro....................................... 666
Image Editing for the Masses ................................................. 667
The Morass of Digital Video ................................................... 668
Yes, It's Really Called "Toast" ................................................. 669
If You Positively Have to Run Windows . . . ................................ 670
All Hail FileMaker Pro........................................................... 672
Utilities That Rock .............................................................. 673
At Least One Game ............................................................. 676

## Chapter 6: Putting Bluetooth to Work. . . . . . . . . . . . . . . . . . . . . . . .679

Bluetooth: What a Silly Name for Such Cool Technology ................. 679
Adding Wireless Keyboards and Mice to Your MacBook.................... 683
Getting Everything in iSync ................................................... 684
The Magic of Wireless Printing................................................ 685

# Chapter 1: Hardware That Will Make You Giddy

## In This Chapter

✔ Using digital cameras, digital video camcorders, and scanners

✔ Adding keyboards, trackballs, joysticks, and drawing tablets

✔ Using optical recorders

✔ Adding speakers, subwoofers, and an iPod

Hardware. We love it. To a MacBook power user, new hardware holds all the promise of Christmas morning, whether your new toys are used for business or for pleasure. We pore over magazines and visit our favorite Mac Web sites like clockwork to check on new technology.

These hardware devices don't come cheap, however, forcing you to make the painful decision regarding which new hardware you really need in order to accomplish what you want and which hardware is a luxury. Also, if you're a new MacBook owner, you might not know what's available. For example, I constantly get e-mail from readers, asking, "What can I connect to my new computer?" I guess I could reply, "Why, the kitchen sink!" To that end, I decided to add this chapter to the book to let you know how you can expand the hardware for your mobile Mac OS X Snow Leopard powerhouse.

Each section in this chapter provides a description of what a particular device does, an idea of how much it costs, and a set of general guidelines that you can use when shopping. Although this isn't in-depth coverage — after all, the book is supposed to be about your laptop — it will serve to get you started if you've just become a MacBook owner. If you're especially interested in a specific piece of hardware, I recommend other books that you can read for the exhaustive details.

Ready? To quote a great line from the first Batman film: "Alfred, let's go shopping!"

# Parading Pixels: Digital Cameras, DV Camcorders, and Scanners

The first category of hardware toys revolves around images — hardware for creating original images, capturing images in real time, and reading images from hard copy.

## Digital cameras

A digital camera shares most of the characteristics of a traditional film camera. It looks the same, and you use the same techniques while shooting photographs. The difference is in the end result. With a digital camera, instead of a roll of film that has to be developed, you have an image in JPEG, RAW, or TIFF format that's stored on a memory card. The contents of the memory card can be downloaded to your MacBook from within iPhoto (which I discuss with great pleasure in Book IV, Chapter 3) and then the real fun begins. Here are some things that you can do with a digital photograph:

✦ Edit it with an image editor such as Adobe Photoshop Elements

✦ Print it with an inkjet, dye-sublimation, thermal-transfer or color laser printer

✦ Record it to a CD or DVD

✦ Add it to a Web page

✦ Print several of them in a coffee-table book (using iPhoto)

✦ Mail it to friends and family

### What they cost

Consumer-level digital cameras typically sell for anywhere from under $100 (for a 7-megapixel [MP] model) to $300 (for a 10 to 12-MP point-and-shoot camera). *Megapixel* is a general reference to the *resolution* (the size of the image, measured in individual dots called *pixels*) and detail delivered by the camera. Such digital cameras can produce photographs that are well suited for just about any casual shutterbug. Professional digital cameras, which capture far more detail and offer designs that more closely resemble the best SLR film camera, can set you back $600 or more. Because of their cost and complexity, I wouldn't recommend them to someone who's just discovered digital photography.

### What to look for

Here are some general guidelines that I recommend when selecting a digital camera:

✦ **At least a 7MP camera:** As a general rule, the higher the megapixel value, the better the camera.

✦ **At least a 1GB internal memory card:** The *memory card* stores the images that you capture.

✦ **A Universal Serial Bus (USB) 2.0 connection to your MacBook:** I cover USB in all its glory in Chapter 3 of this minibook.

✦ **An optical zoom feature:** *Optical zoom* allows you to draw closer to subjects that are farther away.

Note that I recommended *optical* zoom there and not *digital* zoom. Essentially, digital zoom is a silly feature that simply resizes a portion of your image, providing a blocky close-up. In fact, an image editor like Photoshop Elements can produce exactly the same result as a camera with digital zoom . . . and it looks almost as bad. Only an optical zoom results in a sharper magnification of the subject.

✦ **A self-timer:** With a self-timer, your camera can snap a photo automatically, allowing you to finally be seen in your own pictures!

✦ **A manual flash setting:** Although automatic flash is a good thing most of the time, a manual setting allows you to disable your camera's flash for artistic shots (or just to prevent the glare on subjects with polished surfaces).

## DV camcorders

Like digital cameras, digital video (DV) camcorders are the counterpart to the familiar video camcorder. A *DV camcorder* looks and operates like an analog VHS camcorder, but you can connect it to your laptop via a FireWire (for miniDV-tape camcorders) or USB cable (for mass-storage camcorders) and download your video clips directly into iMovie. Today's crop of DV camcorders can also record in High Definition (HD for short) for your widescreen TV or monitor. (Chapter 4 of Book IV explains all about iMovie, and both FireWire and USB are tackled in Chapter 3 of this minibook.)

Besides the higher quality of digital video, it has a number of other real advantages over analog video:

✦ Digital video can be edited with applications such as iMovie or Final Cut Express.

✦ Digital video can be recorded to a CD or DVD.

✦ Digital video can be posted for downloading on a Web page.

### What they cost

A typical DV camcorder starts at about $200, including camcorders that record directly to a blank DVD and record in HD.

### What to look for

I recommend the following when shopping for a DV camcorder:

+ **The highest optical zoom in your price range:** Again, as with a digital camera, it's important to be able to capture subjects and action when you can't get any closer — think the lion exhibit at the zoo.

+ **Image stabilization:** This helps steady the picture when you're holding the camcorder without a tripod.

+ **Onboard effects:** These effects generally include some snazzy things like black-and-white footage, fades, and wipes.

+ **AV connectors:** Use these to display your video by connecting the camcorder directly to your TV.

+ **Digital still mode:** This enables you to take still photographs if your digital camera isn't handy; however, the image quality isn't as good as a bona fide digital camera.

For an in-depth look at digital video, iMovie and iDVD, check out the brand-new *iMovie '09 and iDVD '09 For Dummies* by Dennis R. Cohen and Michael E. Cohen (Wiley).

## Scanners

Figure 1-1 illustrates a typical flatbed scanner, which is the tool of choice for those Macintosh owners who want to digitize images and text from printed materials. Although you can also connect a sheet-fed scanner, flatbed models are much more versatile and produce better-quality scans.

**Figure 1-1:** The flatbed scanner, King of Digitizing.

Images produced by a scanner can be edited, mailed, displayed on the Web, or added to your own documents, just as the images from a digital camera can be.

### What they cost

A good-quality scanner should cost anywhere from $50–$300, with the best models — featuring the fastest scanning speeds, best color depth, and highest resolutions, or those meant for scanning film negatives — going for around $500.

### What to look for

Try to get the following features in a scanner:

- ✦ **The highest color depth that you can afford:** Get a minimum of 48-bit.

- ✦ **The highest resolution that you can afford:** Get a minimum of 2400 dots per inch (dpi) (optical).

- ✦ **Single-pass scanning:** This feature results in a faster scan with less chance of error.

- ✦ **Transparency adapter for scanning film negatives:** If you're a traditional film photographer, you'll find that a transparency adapter turns a standard flatbed scanner into an acceptable negative scanner.

- ✦ **One-touch buttons for e-mailing your scanned images or uploading them to the Web:** These are controls of convenience — pressing one of these buttons automatically scans the item and prepares the image to be e-mailed or uploaded to a Web site.

- ✦ **USB 2.0 or FireWire connection:** I cover the advantages of both in Chapter 3 of this minibook.

Another shameless (but good-natured) plug: My bestselling book *Scanners For Dummies,* 2nd Edition (Wiley) offers comprehensive coverage of all types of scanners, as well as chapters devoted to advanced features, image editing, and step-by-step projects.

# Incredible Input: Keyboards, Trackballs, Joysticks, and Drawing Tablets

Although your MacBook is already equipped with a keyboard and a trackpad, you can supplement them with enhanced hardware that will add functionality and precision to your work. (Or you can buy a joystick and spend your days wreaking havoc on your enemies.)

## Keyboards

If you want to add an external keyboard to your system, you can take advantage of the convenience of a USB keyboard like the one in Figure 1-2.

**Figure 1-2:** An ergonomic upgrade — the after-market USB keyboard.

### What they cost

Aftermarket (nonstandard-issue) keyboards generally cost anywhere from $30–$100.

### What to look for

Look for the following keyboard features when shopping for a keyboard:

✦ **Programmable buttons:** Configure these to launch applications or run macros.

✦ **Additional USB ports:** Use these to turn your keyboard into a USB hub.

✦ **Numeric keypad:** A true numeric keypad cluster makes entering numbers far faster and more accurate.

✦ **One-touch buttons to launch your browser or e-mail application:** Press one of these buttons to launch your Web browser or Mail.

✦ **Ergonomic wrist pad:** Use these to help prevent wrist strain and repetitive joint injuries.

## Trackballs

Some folks prefer using a trackball, like the one shown in Figure 1-3, over a trackpad any day . . . even the Mighty Mouse that Apple sells separately. Graphic artists find that trackballs are more precise and offer better control, usually including a secondary button to display contextual menus. (One model on the market has eight buttons. Who needs a keyboard?)

**Figure 1-3:**
Many MacBook power users (myself included) favor a trackball over the trackpad.

## What they cost

Trackballs range in price from $20–$90. Most are optical (see the following section), so they need little cleaning, and they'll last for many years of precise pointing at things.

## What to look for

Look for the following features when shopping for a trackball:

✦ **More programmable buttons:** Opt for at least two buttons!

✦ **Optical tracking:** An *optical* trackball — one that doesn't use rollers, instead using a photosensitive sensor to record the movement of the ball — is more precise and easier to keep clean.

✦ **A scroll wheel:** Use this gizmo to scroll documents up and down.

✦ **Ergonomic design:** Look for a wrist pad or slanted buttons.

## Joysticks

Game players, unite! For arcade and sports games, using a joystick results in increased maneuverability, more realistic action, higher scores, less wear and tear on your keyboard . . . and just plain more fun. Joysticks range from the traditional USB aircraft controller, as shown in Figure 1-4, to USB controllers and gamepads that rival anything offered on today's console game machines.

**Figure 1-4:**
The secret weapon of Mac gaming — a joystick.

### What they cost

Joysticks vary in price from $30–$120. At the low end, you'll usually find the gamepad-type controllers, whereas aircraft controllers carry the highest price tag.

### What to look for

Get the following features in a joystick:

✦ **Yet even more programmable buttons.**

✦ **Pitch and yaw controls.** These are for the flight simulator crowd.

✦ **Force feedback.** A *force feedback* joystick or gamepad rumbles and moves in tandem with the action in the game, providing an extra feeling of realism.

## Drawing tablets

A drawing tablet like the one you see in Figure 1-5 might be pricey, but if you're a graphic artist or a designer, using a tablet will revolutionize the way that you work with your MacBook. Rather than using your finger on your trackpad to sketch, you can draw on the tablet freehand, just as you would draw on paper or canvas. Tablets can recognize different levels of pressure, allowing applications, such as Photoshop and Painter, to re-create all sorts of photo-realistic brush effects.

**Figure 1-5:**
Professional
artists and
designers
swear by
the graphics
tablet.

### What they cost

Depending on the size of the tablet and the pressure levels that you need, you'll pay anywhere from just under $100 to a whopping $500 (or even higher).

### What to look for

I recommend the following tablet features:

✦ **Programmable buttons:** See a trend here?

✦ **Accessory mouse:** Some high-end tablets include a mouse that you can use along with the tablet.

✦ **A cordless stylus:** Make sure that it doesn't require batteries.

✦ **The highest number of pressure levels possible:** The more levels that the tablet offers, the more subtle and precise your control is over painting effects.

# Sublime Storage: DVD/Blu-Ray Recorders

Ready to talk storage? Consider a rewriteable DVD-RW drive which can store 4.7GB on a single disc, or dual-layer drives, which can store 8.5GB! (And don't even get me started on the latest generation of optical technology — the Blu-ray recorders — they can store 50GB on a single disc!)

At the time of this writing, adding an external Blu-ray recorder to your MacBook doesn't always mean that you can watch Blu-ray movies, because the digital copyright protection on Blu-ray discs can block playback on many computer graphics cards. Check with the manufacturer of your external drive to see whether it can be used to watch Blu-ray movie discs on your MacBook. Of course, you can always use your Blu-ray drive for recording data discs and backups.

If you'd like to trade data with another Mac or a PC via floppy disks, you can get an external USB floppy drive for under $50; however, I personally eschew floppy disks, which are very unreliable and carry a mere 1.44MB of data. Pick up a USB Flash drive instead.

All recent MacBook models (except the MacBook Air) include a rewriteable DVD-RW SuperDrive — but if your computer is older and didn't come equipped with a recorder (or you want the latest Blu-ray storage capacity), you can always add an external model.

### What they cost

A USB DVD-RW drive averages about $100.

### What to look for

Get the following features in an external DVD recorder:

✦ **An internal buffer of at least 8MB:** The larger the buffer, the less chance that you'll encounter recording errors and the faster your drive will burn.

✦ **At least 16X DVD recording speed:** A no-brainer here. The faster the recording speed, the less time you'll wait for the finished disc.

✦ **AC power through the USB 2.0 or FireWire cable:** This eliminates the need for a separate AC power supply.

✦ **Burn-proof technology:** This virtually eliminates recording errors because of multitasking so that you can continue to work on other applications while you record.

# Awesome Audio: Subwoofer Systems and MP3 Hardware

Although all MacBooks ship with speakers, I'll be honest — the "stock" speakers don't measure up to the standards of a true audiophile. For those who really enjoy their music and their game audio, this last section covers the world of Macintosh aftermarket sonic enjoyment.

## Subwoofer speaker systems

The ever-popular USB port again comes to your rescue. This time, it enables you to connect a more powerful speaker system with a *subwoofer*. In case you've never heard a subwoofer — think chest-rattling *thump, thump, thump* — you should know that they provide the basement-level bass that can add power and punch to both your music and your games. Being hit by an asteroid is a rather flat, tinny experience with a pair of battery-powered speakers that you salvaged from your Walkman years ago. With a new set of speakers and a subwoofer, you'll swear that Han Solo is sitting in the cockpit chair next to you!

With the growing importance of the computer as a replacement for your home entertainment center, investing in a more powerful set of speakers will help you enjoy all those audio CDs and MP3s that you've added to your iTunes Playlists. (Read all about iTunes in Book IV, Chapter 2.)

### What they cost

Most USB-powered speakers with a subwoofer are priced below $100, but true audiophiles looking for surround sound can spring for a better $300 system that includes five satellite speakers and a subwoofer.

### What to look for

Get these features in a subwoofer:

✦ **At least 30 watts of power:** The higher the wattage rating, the more powerful the speakers (and the louder your music can be).

✦ **Additional headphone jacks and stereo mini-plug input jacks:** Use these for connecting your iPod or MP3 player directly to your speaker system. (Read all about iPods in the next section.)

✦ **Magnetic shielding:** This helps prevent your speakers from distorting your monitor display.

## MP3 players (well, actually, just the iPod)

I've lusted after Apple's iPod MP3 player ever since it arrived on campus. Depending on which model you get, this incredible device can hold up to 120GB of digital audio — that's over 30,000 songs — as well as digital photographs and full-length movies! Plus, the iPod also acts as your personal data butler by carrying your files; it's an honest-to-goodness, external USB 2.0 hard drive. In fact, if you pick up an iPod Shuffle, it acts as a USB Flash drive. You can download your contacts and appointments from Mac OS X and view them wherever you go. Just think: Carry your files to and from your office *and* carry DEVO and the Dead Kennedys *and* watch a movie you downloaded as well! Oh, and did I mention that you can play games and use all sorts of applications with the iPod Touch model?

All this fits into a beautiful, stylish package about the size of a pack of cigarettes, with up to a 36-hour lithium rechargeable battery, high-quality earbud headphones, and automatic synchronization with your iTunes music library. (The iPod Shuffle is the smallest member of the iPod family — it's less than 2 inches tall.) Life just doesn't get any better for a technoid like me. If you think that your MacBook is a well-designed piece of equipment, you'll understand why this little box is so alluring. (And why I have one now.)

Sure, other MP3 players are out there, but many of them have the same problems, as follows:

✦ They use digital memory cards, which offer far less capacity than the iPod.

✦ They use standard batteries, or you have to furnish rechargeable batteries (which don't last 36 hours).

✦ They don't operate as an external hard drive, photo slideshow repository, movie theater, or contacts/appointment database.

I say forget 'em. The iPod is worth every cent that you'll pay.

The 4GB iPod Shuffle is less than $80 at the time of this writing, while the 8GB iPod nano runs $149 and the 120GB iPod video model costs $249.

# Chapter 2: Add RAM, Hard Drive Space, and Stir

---

## In This Chapter

- ✔ **Understanding the advantages of extra RAM**
- ✔ **Shopping for a RAM upgrade**
- ✔ **Choosing between internal and external hard drives**
- ✔ **Determining your hard drive needs**
- ✔ **Shopping for a new hard drive**
- ✔ **Installing your upgrades**

**M**ost MacBook owners will make two upgrades — adding more memory (RAM) and additional hard drive space — during the lifetime of their computers. These two improvements have the greatest effect on the overall performance of Mac OS X. By adding RAM and additional hard drive space, not only do you make more elbow room for your applications and documents, but everything runs faster: Think of the Six Million Dollar Man, only a heck of a lot cheaper to operate (and no strange noises accompanying your every move).

In this chapter, I steer you around the hidden potholes along the way for those who aren't well versed in selecting memory modules or weighing the advantages of different types of hard drives. However, if you buy the wrong piece of hardware, remember that using a hammer to make it fit is *not* a workable option.

## Adding Memory: Reasons for More RAM

Of all the possible upgrades that you can make to your MacBook, adding more random access memory (RAM) is the single most cost-effective method of improving the performance of Mac OS X. (In fact, your machine will likely run faster with more memory than a reasonably faster processor!) Here is exactly what Mac OS X uses available RAM for:

- ✦ **Applications:** Naturally, Mac OS X needs system RAM to run the applications that you launch. The more memory in your machine, the larger the applications that you can open and the faster they'll run.

✦ **Overhead:** This includes the operating system itself, as well as various and sundry buffers and memory areas devoted for temporary work. As you would guess, the more memory here, the merrier.

✦ **Virtual memory:** Aha! Now here's something that I mention lightly and politely in Book II but hasn't really amounted to a hill of beans until this moment. (Can you tell I'm a big fan of Bing Crosby?) *Virtual memory* allows Mac OS X to use empty hard drive space as temporary system memory, as shown in Figure 2-1. Data is written to your hard drive instead of being stored in RAM, and then it's erased when it's no longer needed. This is a neat trick that's also used by Windows and Linux. Virtual memory works automatically within Mac OS X.

**Figure 2-1:**
The mysterious beauty of virtual memory — but it still doesn't beat real RAM!

Mac with 2GB of physical RAM

2GB of hard drive space

Mac with 4GB of total memory available, using 2GB of virtual memory

At first, virtual memory sounds like absolute bliss, and it does indeed allow your MacBook to do things that would otherwise be impossible, such as running an application that requires 4GB of RAM in just 2GB of actual physical RAM. However, here come the caveats:

✦ Virtual memory is as slow as molasses in December. Even today's fastest hard drive is many, *many* times slower than real silicon, so any use of virtual memory instead RAM slows down Mac OS X significantly.

✦ Virtual memory abuses your hard drive. If you've ever run Photoshop on a Windows PC with 128MB of RAM, you're having flashbacks right now. Whenever your MacBook is using virtual memory, your hard drive remains almost constantly active. (Hardware types, like myself, call this phenomenon *thrashing* because we know what's happening inside that poor hard drive.) Over time, running any computer with insufficient RAM and behemoth applications will result in a significant increase in hard drive wear and tear.

✦ Virtual memory costs you processing power. With sufficient RAM, Mac OS X gleefully runs as efficiently as it can. When virtual memory kicks in, however, your MacBook has to spend part of its quality time shuttling data to and from the hard drive, which robs your computer of processing power.

The moral of the story is very simple, so it's time for another of Mark's Maxims:

**The less Mac OS X needs to use virtual memory, the better.**

To put it another way, *physical memory* (meaning memory modules) is always a better choice than virtual memory. This is why power users and techno-types crave as much system memory as possible.

A little over five years ago, 256MB of RAM was a quite comfortable figure for most folks, but almost all of today's MacBooks can accept at least a whopping 4GB (that's short for *gigabyte,* or 1,024 megabytes) of system RAM. (The exception to this rule is the MacBook Air, which comes with 2GB of RAM and can't be expanded.)

If you'll be keeping your current MacBook for a few years more, install as much memory as you can afford — you'll thank me every time Mac OS X Snow Leopard boots.

# Shopping for a RAM Upgrade

Before you click some online computer store's Buy button, you need to determine two things that will help you determine which memory module to buy: how much RAM you already have and how much more your system can handle.

## Finding out the current memory in your MacBook

Memory modules are made in standard sizes, so you need to determine how much memory you already have and which of your memory slots are filled. To do this, open the Apple System Profiler by clicking the Apple menu, choosing About This Mac, and then clicking the More Info button.

After you launch this application, it takes a few seconds to scan your laptop and display all sorts of identifying information about the hardware and software that you're using. Check out the Memory item in the Hardware section. Here you can see exactly how many memory modules you have, what type they are, and how much memory each provides. For example, in Figure 2-2, this machine has two memory slots — labeled Bank0/DIMM0 and Bank1/DIMM1. Both those slots are filled to the brim with a 1GB module each, giving me a total physical memory of 2048MB, or 2GB. Jot down the name and contents of each slot on a piece of paper — or, if you're a real Mac OS X power user, add a Sticky to your Desktop with this information. (Stickies are covered in Book III, Chapter 2.)

**Book VIII Chapter 2**

**Add RAM, Hard Drive Space, and Stir**

**Figure 2-2:**
Look under
the hood
with Apple's
System
Profiler.

However, on some machines, only one memory module can be upgraded by a mere mortal. For example, on many older Mac laptops, DIMM0 is an internal module and can be upgraded only by an Apple technician. (Insert sound of harps playing here.)

Unfortunately, this arrangement differs on just about every model of Macintosh ever made — some have more memory slots, and others allow you to upgrade all the system memory instead of just one module. The only way to determine which modules are accessible on your MacBook is to identify the exact model of your laptop.

## Determining the exact model of your laptop

Most folks know the type and model of their computers, but there's a catch here, too: Sometimes the memory that you need varies by the processor in your MacBook. Your eye should be on the actual processor speed and *bus speed* — the transfer speed that data reaches whilst speeding across your motherboard — because they're the identifying factors here.

Again, your salvation turns out to be Apple System Profiler. Just click the Hardware section to display both the machine speed (or *processor speed*) and the bus speed. (For example, my machine has a 1.83 GHz Intel Core Duo CPU running at 667 MHz bus speed.) Grab that same piece of paper (or open that same Sticky) and add these two figures to your list.

Now you're armed with the information that you need to go online and buy the right memory — or, if you'd rather work directly with a human being, you can visit your local Apple dealer, present that most august personage with the list, and have the memory upgrade ordered for you.

Buying memory online is much cheaper. I recommend the following online stores:

- ✦ **MacMall:** www.macmall.com
- ✦ **MacWarehouse:** www.cdw.com
- ✦ **MacConnection:** www.macconnection.com

# The Tao of Hard Drive Territory

Next, turn your attention to the other popular MacBook upgrade — adding extra hard drive space. With today's cutting-edge, 3-D games using a gigabyte of space each and Photoshop CS4 expanding to a minimum of 2GB, IDC (short for *Insidious Data Creep*) is a growing problem. (Bad pun most certainly intended.)

You can save space by deleting those files and folders you don't need, but what fun is that? To reduce your MacBook's waistline before you consider adding more room, I recommend using Spring Cleaning from Smith Micro Software, which you can find at mysmithmicro.com. It's a great tool for locating duplicates, removing empty folders, and uninstalling old programs that you no longer use.

To determine how much free space remains on a hard drive, click the drive's icon on your Desktop and press ⌘+I to display its information, as shown in Figure 2-3. (I'm a major-league Mozart fan-boy, hence the name of my hard drive.)

As a general rule, the following factors indicate that you're ready to upgrade your hard drive territory:

- ✦ You have less than 10GB of space on your current hard drive.
- ✦ You've cleaned *all* unnecessary files, and your MacBook is still lagging behind in storage.
- ✦ You need to share a large amount of data between computers that aren't on the same network. (Read on to discover why.)

**Figure 2-3:**
Checking your drive's free space.

# Internal versus External Storage

Most people who upgrade their existing hard drive do so because they need extra space; however, you might also need to add a hard drive to your system that can go mobile whenever necessary. Unlike an *internal* drive — which resides hidden inside your MacBook's case — an *external* drive is a lean, mean, self-contained traveling storage machine that's perfect for road warriors.

## External drives

External removable cartridge drives, such as a REV drive from Iomega (www.iomega.com), are perfect for folks who have to send cartridges to other locations. Unfortunately, however, the capacities of these drives are rapidly falling behind conventional, nonremovable external hard drives. Also, all MacBooks now have an internal DVD-R drive (except for the MacBook Air), which make it easy to send up to 9GB of data through the mail. Therefore, if you're considering an external unit, go with the most popular pick — a high-capacity nonremovable hard drive, which offers the most storage for your dollar.

Most external drives are *shock-mounted* (meaning that they can take more abuse than an internal hard drive), and they carry their own power supply. In fact, some external drives actually don't need a separate power supply because they draw their power through your MacBook's Universal Serial Bus (USB) or FireWire port. (The next chapter in this minibook tells all about USB and FireWire.) You can also use a superfast external SATA drive with a MacBook Pro if you invest in a SATA card adapter for your laptop's ExpressCard/34 slot.

External drives also have a number of other advantages:

✦ **No installation hassle:** You can easily install a USB or FireWire drive in seconds. Simply plug in the drive to the proper connector on your MacBook, connect the power supply (if necessary), and turn it on. (No software installation necessary. As the folks in Cupertino are fond of saying, "Look, Ma — no drivers!")

✦ **No extra space needed:** Naturally, MacBooks simply don't have the internal space for another drive. Therefore, if you want to keep your existing internal drive as-is while you're adding more storage, an external drive is your only choice.

✦ **File sharing with ease:** With an external drive, you can easily share your data between multiple Macs, even if they're not connected over a network.

✦ **Safe from prying eyes:** Unlike an internal drive, external drives can be secured in a different spot, away from your MacBook. Take your sensitive information home with you or lock it in a safe.

After you plug in an external drive, Mac OS X displays it just like any other hard drive volume. Figure 2-4 illustrates my 60GB FireWire drive in action.

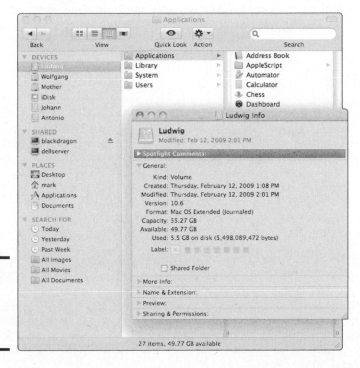

**Figure 2-4:**
A typical
FireWire
external
drive.

**Book VIII
Chapter 2**

Add RAM, Hard
Drive Space, and
Stir

## Internal drives

Your other alternative is to upgrade your internal drive, which can be a hassle. As does a memory upgrade, adding or swapping an internal drive involves opening your MacBook's case. In fact, it's a somewhat more complex procedure than adding memory.

I usually recommend that folks add a second drive rather than swap out their existing drive. You'll avoid the hassle of backing up and restoring your system on a new drive or (even worse) reinstalling Mac OS X and then reinstalling all the applications that you use. (Swapping a hard drive should be the definition of the word *hassle*.) Instead, add a second drive and leave your current hard drive as is (or if you're already using an external drive as a Time Machine backup, add a second external drive).

However, here are a number of very important reasons why many MacBook owners choose updating internal drives, even with the hassle of swapping:

✦ **They're cheaper.** You'll spend significantly less on an internal drive because it doesn't need the case and additional electronics required by an external drive.

✦ **They're faster.** Even a FireWire or USB 2.0 drive isn't as fast as an internal drive.

✦ **They take up less space in your work area.** An internal drive eliminates the space taken by an external drive, which can range anywhere from the size of a paperback to the size of a hardback book.

After you establish that you are in fact ready for more space — and you've decided whether you want to add an internal drive, an external drive, or (if you enjoy punishment) upgrade your existing internal drive — you're ready to consider how big of a drive you need.

# Determining How Much Space You Need

Your next step is to decide just how much hard drive space is enough. I suppose that if your last name is Gates and you had something to do with that Windows thing, you can probably pick just about any drive on the market. However, I have a family, a mortgage, a car payment, and lust in my heart for the latest computer games; therefore, I must be a little more selective.

I have two hard-and-fast rules that I follow when I'm determining the capacity of a new drive:

***1.*** If you're buying a *replacement* for your existing drive, shop for a drive with at least twice the capacity of the existing drive (if possible).

***2.*** If you're buying an *external drive,* shop for a drive with at least the same capacity as your existing internal drive (if possible).

Those rules seem to work pretty doggone well in most circumstances, with these two exceptions: gamers and digital video gurus. These folks need to shoehorn as much space as they possibly can into their systems. If you're a hardcore gamer or if you work primarily with digital video, you need a wheelbarrow's worth of hard drive capacity. Trust me: Buy the biggest hard drive that you can afford.

## Shopping for a Hard Drive

Ready to brave the local Wireless Shed superstore (or perhaps its Web site)? Here's a list of guidelines to keep handy while you're shopping for a new internal or external hard drive:

✦ **Faster is indeed better.** You'll pay more for a 10,000 revolutions per minute (rpm) drive than a slower 5,400 or 7,200 rpm drive, but the extra cash is worth it. Faster drives can transfer more data to your MacBook's processor in less time, especially if you're replacing your MacBook's internal Serial ATA drive.

Faster drives are especially important for storing digital video.

✦ **Serial ATA and EIDE drives are different.** If you're replacing your internal drive, you have to get the same type of drive that you already have: *EIDE* or *Serial ATA*. (EIDE is a common *parallel ATA* standard hard drive used in PCs and older Macs.) Again, System Profiler can tell you which type of drive your MacBook is currently using.

✦ **Avoid used or refurbished drives.** Hard drives are one of the few components in your computer that still have a large number of moving parts. Therefore, buying a used drive isn't a good idea unless it's priced very low.

Because the prices on new hard drives are constantly dropping, make sure that you check on the price for a new, faster drive of the same capacity before you buy that bargain used drive.

✦ **Pick FireWire over USB.** Compared with a FireWire connection, a USB 2.0 external hard drive is less efficient and slightly slower. Because most MacBooks with USB ports also have FireWire ports, make very sure that you buy a FireWire drive! (If your Mac has USB 2.0 ports, which will show up in System Profiler as well, you can buy a USB 2.0 drive without being embarrassed. Or invest in a drive that has both FireWire and USB 2.0 connectors!)

**Book VIII
Chapter 2**

Add RAM, Hard
Drive Space, and
Stir

✦ **Watch the size of the drive when buying internal drives.** Your MacBook's internal drive must fit in a small form factor, so don't invest in a standard half-height 3.5-inch unit!

Do what I do, and call your local Apple certified technician and verify that you're evaluating the right drive before you spend a dime.

# Installing Your New Stuff

After you get your memory modules or hard drive, pick one of two methods of installing them: easy or hard. Guess which method will cost you money?

## The easy way

Your Apple dealer can perform either type of hardware installation for you. You can rest easy knowing that the job will be done right, but money will definitely change hands.

Personally, I always recommend that owners of MacBook and MacBook Pro laptops allow their dealers to install hard drives because these laptops are much more complex than a desktop, and they're much easier to damage.

## The hard way

If you're familiar with the inside of your MacBook, you can install your own upgrade and save that cash. A memory upgrade is one of the simpler chores to perform, but that doesn't mean that everyone feels comfortable taking the cover off and jumping inside a computer; hard drives are a tad more complex.

If you have a knowledgeable friend or family member who can help you install your hardware, buy him the proverbial NSD (short for *Nice Steak Dinner*) and enlist him in your cause. Even if you still do the work yourself, it's always better to have a second pair of experienced eyes watching, especially if you're a little nervous.

Because the installation procedures for both memory modules and hard drives are different for *every* model of MacBook, I can't provide you with any step-by-step procedures in this chapter. Many online stores include installation instructions with their hardware. Other sources for installation instructions include the Apple Web site (www.apple.com) and your Apple dealer. You can use Safari's Google search feature to scan the Internet for installation information for your particular model. However, here are guidelines to follow during the installation:

✦ **Watch out for static electricity.** When opening your MacBook and handling hardware, make certain that you've touched a metal surface beforehand to discharge any static electricity on your body. (You can also buy a static wrist strap that you can wear while working within the bowels of your Mac.)

✦ **Check the notches on memory modules.** Most types of memory modules have notches cut into the connector. These notches make sure that you can install the module only one way, so make certain that they align properly with the slot.

✦ **Make sure you're using the right memory slot.** As I mention earlier in this chapter, MacBooks have multiple memory slots, so check the label on the circuit board to make sure that you're adding the memory to the correct slot. (Naturally, this won't be a problem if you're installing a module into an unoccupied slot.)

✦ **Take good care of older hardware.** If you replace an existing memory module or hard drive with a new one, put the old hardware in the leftover anti-static bag from your new hardware and immediately start thinking of how you'll word your eBay auction . . . *Used 1GB Memory Module for MacBook,* for example.

To determine whether a memory upgrade was successful, you can again turn to the Apple System Profiler. Open the Profiler again and compare the memory overview specifications with the original list that you made earlier. If the total amount of memory has increased and the memory module is recognized, you've done your job well. If not, switch off the MacBook and check the module to make sure it's completely seated in the slot.

# Chapter 3: Port-o-Rama: Using USB and FireWire

## In This Chapter

✔ **Using FireWire under Mac OS X**

✔ **Using USB under Mac OS X**

✔ **Adding a USB or FireWire hub**

✔ **Troubleshooting FireWire and USB connections**

✔ **Adding and updating drivers**

Apple's list of successes continues to grow over the years — hardware, applications, and (of course) Mac OS X — but the FireWire standard for connecting computers to all sorts of different devices is in a class by itself. That's because FireWire has been the port of choice for all sorts of digital devices that need a high-speed connection. Even Windows owners have grudgingly admitted that the latest version, FireWire 800, just plain rocks. Ya gotta love it.

In this chapter, I discuss the importance of FireWire to the digital hub that I discuss in Book III, and I compare it with both version 1.1 and version 2.0 of Intel's Universal Serial Bus (USB) connection technology. I also talk troubleshooting and expansion using a hub.

## Appreciating the Advantage of a FireWire Connection

So what's so special about FireWire, anyway? Why does Apple stuff at least one FireWire port in almost all of its current Macintosh models? (The MacBook Air is an exception.) Heck, even the *iPod* (Apple's MP3 player, which you can read more about in Book III, Chapter 2) originally used only a FireWire connection. (Its *official* name is IEEE 1394, but even the Cupertino crew doesn't call it that — at least not very often.)

First things first. As countless racing fans will tell you, it's all about the *speed,* my friend. The original FireWire 400 port delivers 400 Mbps (megabits per second), which is fast enough for all sorts of peripherals to communicate with your MacBook. The following list includes a number of hardware toys that are well known for transferring prodigious file sizes:

✦ Digital video (DV) camcorders

✦ High-resolution digital cameras

✦ Scanners and some printers

✦ External hard drives and CD/DVD recorders

✦ Networking between computers

For example, consider the sheer size of a typical digital video clip captured by one of today's mini-DV camcorders. DV buffs commonly transfer several hundred megabytes of footage to their computers at one time. Check out the relative speeds of the different types of ports in Table 3-1, and you'll see a big attraction of FireWire and USB 2.0 connections.

| Table 3-1 | Transfer Speeds for Ports through the Ages | |
|---|---|---|
| *Port* | *Appeared on Personal Computer* | *Transfer Speed (in Megabits)* |
| PC Serial | 1981 | Less than 1 Mbps |
| PC Parallel | 1981 | 1 Mbps |
| USB (version 1.1) | 1996 | 12 Mbps |
| FireWire 400 | 1996 | 400 Mbps (version 1) |
| USB (version 2.0) | 2001 | 480 Mbps |
| FireWire 800 | 2002 | 800 Mbps (version 2) |

Ouch! Not too hard to figure that one out. Here are three other important benefits to FireWire:

✦ **Control over connection:** This is a ten-cent term that engineers use, meaning that you can control whatever gadget you've connected using FireWire from your laptop. This is pretty neat when you think about it; for example, you can control your mini-DV camcorder from the comfort of your computer keyboard, just as though you were pressing the buttons on the camcorder.

✦ **Hot-swapped:** You don't have to reboot your MacBook Pro or restart Mac OS X every time that you plug (or unplug) a FireWire device. Instead, the FireWire peripheral is automatically recognized (as long as the operating system has the correct driver) and ready to transfer.

✦ **Power through the port:** FireWire can provide power to a device through the same wire — typically, enough power is available for an external drive or recorder — so you don't need an external AC power cord for some FireWire devices. (Apologies to owners of DV camcorders, but those things eat power like a pig eats slop.)

However, FireWire isn't finished evolving yet — the cleverly named IEEE 1394 B (called *FireWire 800* by anyone with any sense, including the folks at Apple) delivers a whopping 800 Mbps. That, dear reader, oughta be fast enough for both you *and* your loved ones. These ports appear on most of the top-of-the-line Apple desktop and laptop models at the time of this writing.

Oh, and as you would expect from Apple, the new ports will be backward-compatible with older FireWire hardware. However, the ports aren't physically exactly the same, so you'll need a plastic port converter to connect FireWire 400 devices to a FireWire 800 port. (Such important little conversion fixtures are commonly called *dongles*. No, I'm not making that up. Ask your favorite techno-wizard.)

# Understanding USB and the Tale of Two Point Oh

The other resident port on today's MacBooks is the ubiquitous USB, which is short for *Universal Serial Bus*. (By the way, ubiquitous means *ever-present* or *universal,* which I quickly looked up by using my Dictionary widget — read all about widgets in Book III, Chapter 2.) USB has taken the world by storm. It's used for everything from mice to keyboards, speakers, digital cameras, and even external drives and DVD recorders. (A friend of mine never misses the chance to point out that USB — which was originally developed by Intel, the makers of the Core 2 processor — was given its first widespread implementation on the original iMac. *You're welcome,* Intel.)

Unfortunately, those last two are somewhat problematical: Technically, you can add a USB 1.1 external hard drive, but don't expect response times anywhere near what you'd enjoy with an internal hard drive (think more along the lines of a floppy drive). Ditto for a CD recorder — 2X is about the limit for the recording speed with a USB 1.1 connection. (Don't even *think* about recording DVDs over a USB 1.1 connection.) Now, compare this performance with that of similar equipment using a FireWire connection, which provides nearly the speed of an internal hard drive and CD and DVD recording at the fastest pace possible.

As is the case with FireWire, USB connections are hot-swappable and *may* provide power over the connection. (Some USB ports don't supply all the power that devices need — more on this later in this chapter.) A USB port offers a more limited version of Control over Connection as well, making it a good choice for virtually all digital cameras.

Not to be outdone, a USB 2.0 specification arrived several years ago that delivers performance comparable to the original FireWire standard: USB 2.0 can transfer 480 Mbps, although far less efficiently than FireWire, so the FireWire connection is still faster overall. These ports are backward compatible — meaning they work with the original USB 1.1 ports as well. (Don't call Apple a snob . . . at the time of this writing, all the MacBook models in Apple's current stable have USB 2.0 ports.)

Book VIII
Chapter 3

Port-o-Rama: Using
USB and FireWire

# Hey, You Need a Hub!

Suppose that you've embraced FireWire and USB and you now have two USB 2.0 drives hanging off the rear end of your laptop — and suddenly you buy an iPod. (Or you get another USB device that's as much fun as an iPod, if that's actually possible.) Now you're faced with too many devices for too few ports. You *could* eject a drive and unhook it each time that you want to connect your iPod, but there *must* be a more elegant way to connect. Help!

Enter the hub. Both the FireWire and USB specifications allow you to connect a device called a *hub,* which is really nothing more than a glorified splitter adapter that provides you with additional ports. With a FireWire or USB hub at work, you do lose a port; however, most hubs multiply that port into four or eight ports. Again, all this is transparent, and you don't need to hide anything up your sleeve. Adding a hub is just as plug-and-play easy as adding a regular FireWire/USB device.

I should also mention that FireWire supports *daisy-chaining* — a word that stretches all the way back to the days of the Atari and Commodore computers, when devices had extra ports in the back so that additional stuff could be plugged in. However, not every FireWire drive has a daisy-chain port (also called a *passthru port*). With daisy-chaining, you can theoretically add 63 FireWire devices (or 127 USB devices) to your MacBook — talk about impressing them at your next Mac user group meeting!

# Uh, It's Just Sitting There

Man, I *hate* it when FireWire and USB devices act like boat anchors. FireWire and USB peripherals are so doggone simple that when something goes wrong, it really aggravates you. Fortunately, I've been down those roads many a time before, so in this section, I unleash my experience. (That sounds a little frightening, but it's a *good* thing. Really.)

## Common FireWire and USB headaches

Because FireWire and USB are so alike in so many ways, I can handle possible troubleshooting solutions for both types of hardware at one time:

✦ **Problem: Every time I turn off or unplug my external peripheral, Mac OS X gets irritated and displays a nasty message saying that I haven't properly disconnected the device.**

**Solution:** This happens because you haven't *ejected* the peripheral. I know that sounds a little strange for a device like an external hard drive or a digital camera, but it's essentially the same reasoning as ejecting a CD or DVD from your Desktop. When you click your USB or FireWire device and hold the mouse button down, you see that the Trash icon turns into an Eject icon; drag the device icon to the Eject icon and drop it, and the external device disappears from your Desktop. (You can also click the device icon to select it and press ⌘+E. And don't forget the right-click menu . . . right-click the device and choose Eject.) At that point, you're safe to turn it off or unplug the FireWire/USB cable.

If Snow Leopard recognizes the device as an external drive, which is usually the case with a digital camera, external hard drive, or external CD/DVD recorder, you can simply click the Eject button next to the device icon in the Finder window's sidebar.

✦ **Problem: The device doesn't show a power light.**

**Solution:** Check to make sure that the power cable is connected — unless, of course, you have a device that's powered through the connection itself. This can sometimes pose its own share of problems, however, when using USB devices. Not all USB ports provide power to devices because some are designed only for connecting mice, keyboards, and joysticks.

To check whether an unpowered USB port is your problem, either connect the device to a USB port on your MacBook or connect it to a hub or another computer. If the device works when it's connected to another port, you've found the culprit.

✦ **Problem: The device shows a power light but just doesn't work.**

**Solution:** This can be because of problems with your cable or your hub. To check, borrow a friend's cables and test to see whether the device works. If you're testing the hub, try connecting the device directly to your MacBook using the same cable to see whether it works without the hub.

If you're attempting to connect a FireWire device through another FireWire device, try connecting that first device directly to see whether it works. If so, the middleman device either needs to be switched on to pass the data through or it doesn't support daisy-chaining at all — in which case, you may be able to place the "problem" device at the *end* of the chain. Of course, you can always connect both devices directly to your laptop as well.

**Book VIII
Chapter 3**

**Port-o-Rama: Using
USB and FireWire**

✦ **Problem: Mac OS X reports that I have a missing driver.**

**Solution:** Check the manufacturer's Web site and download a new copy of the USB or FireWire drivers for your device because they've been corrupted, overwritten, or erased entirely. Because Mac OS X loads the driver for a USB or FireWire device when it's connected, sometimes just unplugging and reconnecting a peripheral will do the trick.

## Check those drivers

Speaking of drivers . . . old and worn-out drivers are a sore spot with me. *Drivers* are simply programs that tell Mac OS X how to communicate with your external device. Each new version of Mac OS X contains updated drivers, but make certain that you check for new updates on a regular basis. That means using both the Software Update feature in Mac OS X (which I cover in Book II, Chapter 7) *and* going to the Web sites provided by your USB and FireWire hardware manufacturers.

# Chapter 4: I'm Okay, You're a Printer

## In This Chapter

✔ **Adding a local printer**

✔ **Adding a non-USB printer**

✔ **Managing print jobs**

✔ **Sending and receiving faxes**

✔ **Setting up a shared printer**

Of all the improvements made in Mac OS X over Mac OS 9, one of the most important is the simplified printing process — no Chooser, no strange printer ports . . . just a heap of Universal Serial Bus (USB) and network and Bluetooth printing goodness. As I discuss in Book II, Chapter 3, if your USB printer is recognized by Snow Leopard, you can print within seconds of plugging it in, with no muss or fuss. A USB printer is connected physically to your MacBook, but you can also send print jobs over the network to a network printer or even to a wireless printer. (Unfortunately, if that network printer is in another room, you *do* have to get out of your comfortable chair to retrieve your printed document . . . not even Snow Leopard is *that* powerful.)

But what if you want to send documents to a printer over TCP/IP (Transmission Control Protocol/Internet Protocol)? To take care of tasks like that, you need to dig a little further — and I do so in this chapter. You also discover here how to use the features of the System Preferences Print & Fax pane and how to juggle print jobs like a circus performer.

## Meet the Printer Browser

The Printer Browser runs automatically whenever it's needed by Snow Leopard, but you can always summon it at any time by clicking the plus sign (or Add) button on the Print & Fax pane within System Preferences.

If your USB printer is already *natively supported* (has a preloaded driver in Snow Leopard), you might not need to go through the trouble of clicking the Add button on the Print & Fax pane. Mac OS X can add a new USB printer automatically, so don't be surprised if your MacBook swoops in and does it for you as soon as you plug in a new printer. Also, the manufacturer's installation program for your printer might add the printer for you in a behind-the-scenes way, even if Mac OS X lies dormant.

Although the Printer Browser doesn't look like much (as shown in Figure 4-1), power lurks underneath.

**Figure 4-1:** The rather plain-looking Printer Browser is actually a rugged adventurer.

Along the top of the Printer Browser, you'll find four toolbar icons that will display the different types of printer categories possible in Snow Leopard. From the Browser, you can add these printers to your system. The four buttons are

✦ **Default:** Click this button to add or display the entry for the default printer, which always appears in bold type.

To choose a printer you've already added as your default printer, click the Default Printer pop-up menu in the Print & Fax pane and choose that printer. You can also choose the Last Printer Used option, which automatically makes the default printer the last printer you used.

✦ **Fax:** If you have an external USB fax device, click this button to add a fax connection as a printer selection. If you don't want to use Snow Leopard's built-in faxing system, you can print directly to a third-party fax program, such as FAXstf Pro (www.smithmicro.com), which then dials, connects, and sends the document to a fax machine.

✦ **IP:** Click this button to add a remote printer to your Mac through an Internet connection or a local network connection. Sending a job to an Internet Protocol (IP) printer actually shoots the document across a network or Internet connection by using a target IP address or domain name. Generally, it's best to have a *static* (unchanging) IP address for a network printer; if the IP address changes often, for example, you have to reconfigure your connection to your IP printer each time it changes.

## PDF printing for your big cat

Speaking of third-party Mac OS X printer drivers, the most popular example of same is the Adobe Acrobat printer driver, which is installed by Adobe Acrobat and used to create electronic PDF documents. Although you certainly can install Adobe Acrobat under Snow Leopard, I'd be remiss if I didn't mention that you don't *have* to! That's because the operating system provides built-in support for printing documents in Adobe's PDF format (which can then be viewed and printed on any other computer with Acrobat Reader or added

to your Web site for downloading). Acrobat has more features, naturally, but — wait for it — don't pay for Acrobat unless you need it!

In fact, you don't even have to install a PDF print driver or display the Printer Browser! To print a document as a file in PDF format, click the PDF drop-down button in the application's Print dialog, click Save as PDF from the menu, navigate to the desired folder and enter a filename, and then click Save.

✦ **Windows:** Click this button to add a shared printer that's connected to a PC on your local network. "Hey, I get to use the enemy's printers, too?" That's right, as long as a Windows user on your network has shared his printer (via the ubiquitous Windows File and Printer Sharing feature). *Sweet.*

Oh, and there's one additional important control on the toolbar that isn't actually a button: You can click in the Search field and type text to locate a particular printer in any of these dialog lists. (Personally, I don't have that many printers on my network, but in a larger company, this field can save you the trouble of scrolling through several pages of shared printers.)

## Adding a Funky Printer

"And what," you might ask, "is a *funky* printer?" Well, you have a number of possibilities, but they all add up to a non-USB connection. (Remember, I said that USB connections to a printer are generally automatic, or at least handled by the printer's installation software.) Some of the non-USB connections I mention in the previous section include Windows shared printers and IP printers.

No matter which type of funky printer you add, it needs a driver installed in the Printers folder, which resides inside your MacBook's Library folder. (A *driver* is a software program provided by the printer manufacturer that tells Mac OS X how to communicate with your printer.) Also, if the printer is PostScript compatible, it needs a Postscript Printer Description (PPD) file installed in your PPD folder, which also appears in the Printers folder. Luckily, Snow Leopard comes complete with a long list of drivers and PPD files already installed and available — bravo, Apple dudes and dudettes!

**Book VIII**
**Chapter 4**

**I'm Okay, You're a Printer**

To add a funky printer, follow these steps:

*1.* **Launch the manufacturer's installation application, which should copy the driver and PPD files for you.**

If you have to do things the hard way, manually copy the driver file into the Library/Printers folder and then copy the PPD file (if required) into the Library/Printers/PPD folder.

*2.* **If you're adding a physical printer — instead of an application printer driver — verify that the printer is turned on and accessible.**

If you're printing to a shared printer connected to another Mac or PC, that computer has to be on. Luckily, most network printers (and their computer hosts) remain on all the time.

*3.* **Display the Print & Fax pane within System Preferences and click the Add button (with the plus sign) on the Printing pane.**

You see the familiar Printer Browser. Shared printers using Bonjour network technology should show up on the default list, so you can click the printer to select it.

*4.* **To add an IP printer, click the IP Printer button on the browser toolbar.**

Click the Protocol pop-up menu to choose the IP printing protocol (typically either IPP or the manufacturer-specific socket protocol). If you have a choice, it's always a good idea to use the manufacturer-specific socket.

Click in the Address box and type the printer's IP address or Domain Name System (DNS) name, which should be provided by your network administrator or the person running the print server. You can use the default queue on the server by leaving the Queue box blank — which I recommend — or select the Queue text box and type a valid queue name for the server.

If you don't know a valid queue name, you're up a creek — hence, my recommendation to use the default queue.

If you like, you can type a name and location for the remote printer; this is purely for identification purposes. Finally, click the Print Using pop-up menu, choose the brand and model of the remote printer, and then click Add.

*5.* **To add a Windows printer, click the Windows button on the Printer Browser toolbar.**

Click the correct Windows workgroup that includes the printer(s) that you want to use in the left column. After a scan of the specified workgroup,

Printer Browser displays the list of printers that it can access. (Don't forget to thank His Billness later.)

6. **After everything is tuned correctly, click the Print Using pop-up menu and choose the brand and model of the remote printer.**

7. **Click Add to complete the process and admire your new printer on the Print & Fax panel in System Preferences.**

Heck, Snow Leopard even allows you to *order supplies* for many printers from the comfort of System Preferences! Sure, you'll pay a premium price, but think of the techno-nerd bragging rights you'll enjoy at your next Mac user group meeting! Click a printer in the Print & Fax pane and click the Options & Supplies button; then click the Supply Levels tab. When you click the Supplies button, System Preferences automatically launches Safari with the proper Web page from the Apple Store.

## Managing Your Printing Jobs

You can also exercise some control over the documents — or, in technoid, *print jobs* — that you send to your printer. To display the jobs that are *active* (in line and preparing to print), open the Print & Fax pane in System Preferences and click the Open Print Queue button. (Alternatively, click the printer's icon in the Dock to display the same window.)

The actions that you can perform from the Print Queue window (as shown in Figure 4-2) are

**Figure 4-2:**
Monitor your print jobs and control them like puppets.

# Where's the chapter on faxing?

Good question, and here's the answer: Snow Leopard handles faxing so seamlessly that you don't *need* a chapter's worth of instruction! As long as your MacBook has an external analog (dial-up) fax modem connected to a phone line, you're a lean faxing machine.

To fax any open document within an active application, just choose File⇨Print or press ⌘+P. Click the PDF button at the bottom of the Print dialog and click Fax PDF. Either type a telephone number directly in the To field, or click the suave-looking button with the profile next to the field and choose a contact with a telephone number from your Address Book. (Make sure that you type your fax number into the My Fax Number field, just to stay legal.) Next, type a dialing prefix if one is necessary to reach an outside line. If you're going to use your laptop as a fax machine often, I definitely recommend selecting the Show Fax Status in Menu Bar check box. That way, you can monitor what's happening as your Mac sends and receives throughout the day.

If you need a spiffy-looking cover page, select the Use Cover Page check box. Click in the Message box directly below it and type whatever you like. You can optionally type a subject as well. When all is ready, throw caution utterly to the wind and click the Fax button. The Printer Browser treats a fax just as it does any other printed document, so you can cancel it or monitor its progress, as I discuss in the section, "Managing Your Printing Jobs."

Your MacBook can also receive faxes. To enable this feature, open System Preferences and click the Print & Fax icon. Click the entry for your fax in the list, click the Receive Options button, and then select the Receive Faxes on This Computer check box. Set the number of rings Snow Leopard should wait before answering the call. You can save your incoming faxes as files within a folder you specify or e-mail the contents automatically to any e-mail address you like. (Perfect for vacations!) If you like, you can even take the mundane route and print them on your system printer.

✦ **Delete:** When you click a print job in the list and then click the Delete icon, the print job is removed from the queue. You might need to delete a print job if you discover a mistake in the document while printing.

If the job is currently printing, several additional pages might be printed before the job is finally cancelled. In other words, information already sent to the printer might have to be printed before the cancel request can be processed.

✦ **Hold:** Click the Hold toolbar icon to pause printing of the current print job. The status of the print job changes to Hold.

✦ **Resume:** Click a print job in Hold status in the list and then click the Resume icon to resume printing.

✦ **Job Info:** Click this button to display basic information about the selected print job, such as number of pages and page size.

✦ **Pause Printer:** Click this icon to stop all printing to this printer. Note, however, that unlike using the Delete command, Pause Printer doesn't *remove* any print jobs from the list. When jobs are stopped, the Pause Printer icon morphs into Resume Printer — click it to restart all jobs in the queue list.

This is a good feature to use when your printer is about to run out of paper.

✦ **Supply Levels:** If your printer supports remote supply monitoring, you can click this icon to display the current levels of ink and paper in your printer. (Thus saving your feet from the wear and tear of walking.)

✦ **Printer Setup:** Click this icon and Snow Leopard displays the model-specific configuration settings and features (if any) that are available for the selected printer. Of course, these settings vary for every printer produced by the hand of Man — they're actually determined by the manufacturer's printer driver — but they usually include actions (such as cleaning and alignment) and settings (such as print quality).

## Sharing a Printer across That There Network

Before we leave the Island of Big X Printing, I'd like to show you how to share a printer with others on your local network, using Snow Leopard's super-easy Bonjour network sharing feature. (Earlier in this chapter, I show you how to connect to other shared printers around you. Here, you're going to share a printer that's connected directly to your MacBook, like a portable photo printer.)

If you decide to share your printers, don't be surprised if Mac OS X seems to slow down slightly from time to time. This is because of the processing time necessary for your MacBook to store queued documents from other computers. The hard drive activity on your laptop is likely to significantly increase as well.

Once again, turn to System Preferences! Click the Sharing icon; then click the Printer Sharing check box to select it. (When it comes to printing, Snow Leopard gives you more than one way to skin a . . . well, you get the idea, even without the bad pun.) To share a printer, click the check box next to the desired printer (as shown in Figure 4-3) and click the Add button to select which users will have access to the shared printer. (By default, a shared printer can be accessed by everyone.) *Voilà!* You're the guru!

**Book VIII
Chapter 4**

I'm Okay, You're a
Printer

**Figure 4-3:**
Snow
Leopard
takes
care of
everything
when you
want to
share a
printer.

"Hey, what about my firewall?" Perhaps you would worry *if* you were using that Other Operating System — which shall remain nameless here — but you're using Snow Leopard, and everything is set *automatically* for you the moment you click the Printer Sharing check box! Snow Leopard automatically opens the correct port in your firewall to allow printer sharing. (And yes, if you decide not to share your printers and you deselect the Printer Sharing check box later, Snow Leopard cleans up after you. It closes the port in your firewall for you.) Super-flippin' *sweet*.

The printers that you specify are available to other computers within the same IP subnet. In other words, someone in your local network can use your printers, but no one outside your network has access.

If you haven't already assigned a printer a descriptive name, click the desired printer from the list in the Print & Fax pane and then click the Options & Supplies button. Click the General button on the sheet that appears and enter a descriptive name in the Name text field. You can also identify that printer's location in the Location text field. For example, in an office environment, I like to add the room number to a shared printer name (as well as the Location field).

# Chapter 5: Applications That You've (Probably) Gotta Have

## In This Chapter

✔ Using Microsoft Office 2008

✔ Using disk repair applications

✔ Editing images

✔ Editing digital video

✔ Using Internet applications

✔ Burning discs with Toast

✔ Running Windows with Parallels Desktop

✔ Adding third-party utilities

✔ Playing games with Mac OS X

In Chapter 1 of this minibook, I present you with an overview of the most popular hardware that you can add to your MacBook — and where there's hardware, software can't be far behind. (Somebody famous said that — I think it was either Bill Gates or Dennis Miller. I consider both of them famous comedians.)

Anyway, Mac OS X comes with a full suite of software tools right out of the box. You get Internet connectivity, disk repair, a digital audio and video player, basic image editing and cataloging, digital video editing, and — depending on the price that you paid or the MacBook model that you bought — even games and a complete set of productivity applications. However, if you're willing to pay for additional features and a manual (at least what passes for a manual in the manufacturer's opinion), you can make all these tasks easier and accomplish them in even shorter time.

Read on for an overview of the most popular third-party software applications for Mac OS X: what everyone's using, how much they cost, and why they're (usually) better. Before you drop a *wad* of cash on a fancy new application, though, remember yet another of Mark's Maxims:

**If a program you already have does everything you really need — and you like the way it works — you *don't* have to upgrade. Honest and truly.**

# The Trundling Microsoft Mammoth

Yes, I know I've been poking fun at His Gatesness for much of this book — you have to admit, he makes a pretty good target — but he *did* pull PC owners out of the character-based world of DOS, and I'll be the first to say that he does get things right quite often. (Witness my bestselling book *PCs All-in-One Desk Reference For Dummies* [Wiley], recently revised for a fourth edition!)

For example, I've always been more impressed with Microsoft Office than I've been with Microsoft Windows. (At least Windows XP Professional and Windows Vista are steps in the right direction, but they still have a long way to go to match Mac OS X.) Office has long been the productivity suite of choice in the Windows world, and it's also been a popular favorite in years past on the Macintosh side.

A lot of hard work was put into the latest version of Microsoft Office, and it shows. Office 2008 was designed specifically for Mac OS X, using the rules that Apple recommends for the Aqua user interface. As you can see in Figure 5-1, it looks much like a native Mac OS X application (such as Pages from *iWork,* which is Apple's competing office productivity suite).

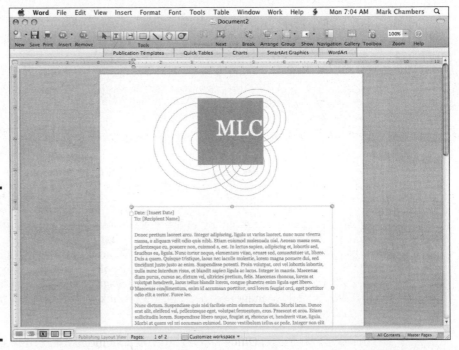

**Figure 5-1:** Man, that is one good-looking Office. Thanks, Microsoft (and I mean that).

However, as with Mac OS X itself, Office 2008 isn't just an attractive exterior. Consider some of the advantages of Office 2008:

## What about iWork?

If you're already using iWork '09, you might have noticed that the Office applications Excel, Word, and PowerPoint provide roughly the same features. Therefore, you might wonder whether you should scrap iWork.

Remember my maxim — if the iWork suite that you're familiar with is doing the job, I recommend that you keep it. After all, iWork is a powerful productivity suite on its own, capable of producing results that are easily as good as or better than Office 2008. Also, Apple provides conversion filters that allow you to open and save Office documents so that you're not isolated from the Office crowd.

On the other side of the coin, I *do* recommend that you buy Office if

✔ You prefer the Office 2008 menu design and features.

✔ You'd like to keep most of the same commands replicated in the same places as the Windows version of Office.

✔ You want to seamlessly share documents with co-workers who use Windows Office on your network or through e-mail.

---

✦ **Perfect document compatibility with the Windows version of Office:** You can both read and write documents with transparent ease, no matter which platform gets the file. Documents can be shared among platforms on the same network.

✦ **Mirrored commands:** Office 2007 and Mac Office 2008 have similar menu items, dialogs, and settings, thus making Mac OS X instantly familiar to anyone who's used Office on a Windows PC.

✦ **Support for native Aqua features:** This includes transparent graphics within your documents, input and confirmation sheets, and palettes for formatting.

✦ **Tons of templates, samples, and support files:** Microsoft doesn't scrimp on ready-to-use documents and templates, as well as additional fonts, clip art, and Web samples.

✦ **Entourage:** *Entourage* is the Macintosh counterpart to Windows Outlook. It combines most of the same features that you'll find in the Apple Mail, iCal, and Address Book applications. (Read about Apple Mail in Book VI, Chapter 2; read about the Address Book in Book II, Chapter 6.) Use Entourage to participate in Internet newsgroups; it also includes a Mailing List Manager to help you keep track of the deluge of list messages that you receive every day.

Besides Entourage, Office 2008 on the Mac includes four other applications:

✦ **Word:** The word processing application that rules the planet

✦ **Excel:** The leading spreadsheet application

  ✦ **Messenger:** Microsoft's answer to iChat, an instant messaging program compatible with the Windows version of Messenger

  ✦ **PowerPoint:** A favorite presentation development application

The Mac Office 2008 Home and Student suite costs about $125 at the time of this writing. You might save a few dollars if you buy it online from a Web store such as MacMall (www.macmall.com).

## Your Mac OS X Toolbox: TechTool Pro

My favorite native Mac OS X disk repair application is TechTool Pro from Micromat (www.micromat.com).

More than just about any other type of application, it's important for a disk maintenance program to be built "from the ground up" for Mac OS X. **Never** attempt to repair a Mac OS X disk using an older repair utility not designed for Snow Leopard.

With TechTool Pro 5 (as shown in Figure 5-2), you can thoroughly check a hard drive for both *physical* errors (such as faulty electronics or a bad sector on the disk surface) and *logical* errors (incorrect folder data and glitches in the file structure). The Disk Utility that's included with Mac OS X does a fine job of checking the latter, but it doesn't perform the physical testing — and TechTool Pro does both.

I should note, however, that TechTool Pro doesn't take care of viruses. Pick up a copy of VirusBarrier X5 (www.intego.com) to protect yourself against viral attack.

TechTool Pro also takes care of disk optimization, which is a feature that's been conspicuously absent from Mac OS X since the beginning. As I explain in Book II, Chapter 7, defragmenting your disk will result in better performance and a faster system overall.

TechTool Pro 5, which will set you back about $80, comes on a self-booting DVD-ROM, so you can easily fix your startup volume by booting your system from the installation disc.

**Figure 5-2:**
Use
TechTool
Pro to check
for all sorts
of hardware
errors.

# *Image Editing for the Masses*

The only one true King of the Retouching Hill in Mac OS X, Adobe Photoshop (www.adobe.com/products/photoshop) has been the digital-image editing favorite of Mac owners for many years now. As does Office 2008, the latest version of Photoshop (CS4) also takes full advantage of the Aqua standard.

You can find more three-pound Photoshop books on the shelf than politicians in trouble, so it's no surprise that I can't provide you with a sweeping list of its features in this section. However, here's a summary of what you can expect from Adobe's crown jewel:

✦ **Superior editing:** The most sophisticated image editing possible for a digital photograph. If you can accomplish an image-editing task in software, it's very likely that Photoshop can do it. You can even combine and splice parts of different images to produce a new work of art or perhaps distort and liquefy an image to produce a new look.

**Book VIII
Chapter 5**

Applications That
You've (Probably)
Gotta Have

✦ **Image retouching tools:** These help you rescue images with problems, such as overexposure and color imbalance. (You can also use tools such as the Healing brush to erase imperfections in the photograph's subject.)

✦ **Plug-ins:** Photoshop has been a standard for plug-in functionality since it first appeared. If you need features that aren't in the application out of the box, you can add them through third-party plug-ins.

✦ **Web posting:** Prepare images for use on the Web.

✦ **Painting tools:** Use these gems to simulate different types of inks, paints, and brushes on different types of media.

Although Photoshop is a hefty $699 for the full package, Adobe has also created a kid brother, Photoshop Elements, which sells for a mere $90. Designed for the novice or intermediate-level photographer, Elements has most of the functionality of the full package that you're likely to need. Elements also provides a number of very helpful assistants to help automate the most common image-editing tasks, as well as one of the most comprehensive Help systems I've ever used.

## The Morass of Digital Video

Two types of applications make up the DV market: *digital video editing* (in which you create a movie) and *DVD mastering* (in which you take that movie and create a DVD movie). You can find a number of great applications on the market in both these categories, all at different price points and different levels of complexity. They include

✦ **iMovie:** I cover this easy-to-use video editing iApp in Book IV, Chapter 4. A good choice for any novice, it's usually bundled for free with today's new Mac models, and you get it as part of the iLife suite.

✦ **iDVD:** This is the DVD mastering counterpart to iMovie. Although it's a snap to use, it doesn't offer a lot of advanced features. (Book IV, Chapter 5 explains iDVD in detail.) Again, you receive it free with your Mac.

✦ **DVD Studio Pro:** Apple's entry into the ranks of DVD mastering can produce a commercial-quality DVD movie disc, but don't expect any hand holding or assistants with this application. This is a serious tool for professionals, and as part of Apple's Final Cut Studio 2, it'll set you back $1,300. With DVD Studio Pro 4 (www.apple.com/finalcut studio/dvdstudiopro), you can add interactive, animated menus, subtitles, multiple audio tracks, and Web interactivity to your DVD projects.

✦ **Final Cut Pro 6:** As another part of that uber $1,300 Final Cut Studio 2 package, you'd assume Final Cut Pro (`www.apple.com/finalcut studio/finalcutpro`) to be the best DV editing package on the market for Mac OS X . . . and you wouldn't get any argument from me. It offers real-time playback with RT Extreme HD — no waiting for rendering — and high-definition support over a FireWire connection. *Sassy.*

# *Yes, It's Really Called "Toast"*

Time to turn your attention to a subject near and dear to my heart: recording data CDs, audio CDs, and DVDs on the Macintosh. Of course, Mac OS X can burn basic data CDs that you can share with your Windows and UNIX friends without any add-on software. If you have a MacBook equipped with a SuperDrive or an external DVD recorder, you can create standard, cross-platform data DVDs, too. But what if you need an exotic format, such as CD Extra, that allows data and digital audio tracks to co-exist peacefully on one disc? Or perhaps you need a self-booting disc, or you just got a Blu-ray external recorder?

There's one clear choice: When you're ready to seriously burn, you're ready for Roxio Toast Titanium (`www.roxio.com`), the CD and DVD recording choice for millions of Mac owners. (No snickering about the name, please.) Figure 5-3 illustrates this powerhouse of an application, which is an elegant design that's both simple to use and perfectly Aqua. Files, folders, and digital audio tracks that you want to record are simply dropped into the application window.

As for exotic formats, here's a list of what types of discs you can record with Toast:

✦ Standard data CDs and DVDs

✦ Standard audio CDs

✦ Video CDs

✦ MP3 discs (which store MP3 audio tracks)

✦ Discs recorded from an image file

✦ Mac volumes

✦ Hybrid PC/Mac discs

✦ ISO 9660 discs

✦ Multisession discs

✦ CD Extra discs

Toast works with both internal and external CD, DVD, and Blu-ray recorders, taking advantage of the latest features on today's drives. You can also copy existing discs, using one or multiple drives.

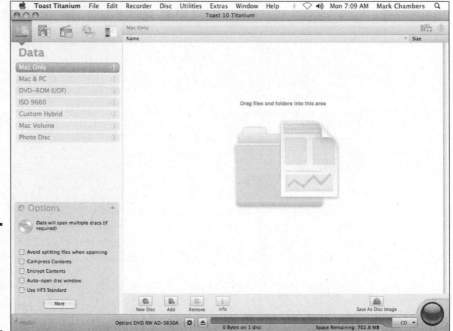

**Figure 5-3:**
Toast is the classic Mac CD and DVD recording application.

Toast is quite affordable at $80. You can buy it directly from the Roxio online store at www.roxio.com.

# If You Positively Have to Run Windows . . .

Here's where Mac power users usually start grinning from ear to ear like Santa's elves on the day after Christmas, because — get this — many of the great Unwashed Windows Horde still actually think that you *can't* run Windows on a Macintosh! Can you believe that? Obviously, they haven't heard of Boot Camp, which is built into Snow Leopard . . . but what if you don't want to reboot to switch operating systems? What if you need to share data between both Mac and PC applications running simultaneously? Well, that's where Parallels Desktop from Parallels (www.parallels.com) comes in, which without a doubt is one of the coolest applications ever written for the Mac.

No, my friend, your eyes aren't deceiving you — you're indeed looking at Windows 2000 running on my MacBook in Figure 5-4. Parallels Desktop (which requires Mac OS X) provides a near-perfect PC environment for any version of Windows from 95 all the way up to Vista; literally, Windows has *no* idea that it's not running on a typical piece of PC iron.

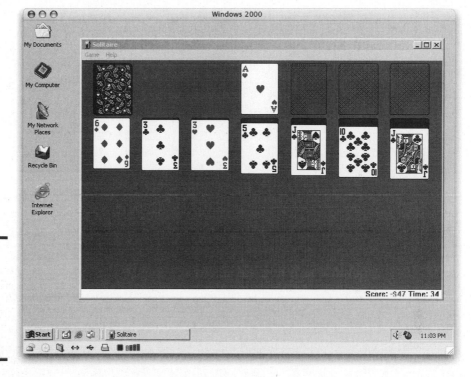

**Figure 5-4:** Take *that*, Bill! I get to play in your pool, without rebooting!

Parallels Desktop simulates everything necessary for you to get the full functionality out of Windows. For example, this jewel automatically (and transparently) handles your Windows Internet connection, network tasks, and CD and DVD access. You can run full-screen or run Windows in a window. (Pun joyfully intended.)

As if that weren't enough, you can also run multiple operating systems. So if you need Linux or Windows 2000 along with your Vista system, no problem — all it takes is the install disc for those operating systems and the hard drive space to hold 'em. Outstanding!

Naturally, performance is an issue — and, to be honest, Parallels Desktop isn't for the PC gamer, even with the newest MacBooks and their super-duper GeForce video cards. Because today's PC games push an actual PC to the limit, they just run too sluggishly on a MacBook emulating a PC — they do run, just slowly. (Also, virtually all of today's blockbuster PC games are also being ported to Mac OS X, so why not just run the Mac version?)

However, when it comes to just about any other type of application, Parallels Desktop running on a late-model Intel-based Mac can deliver performance equal to a typical Pentium 4 PC. The more memory that your MacBook has, the more you can give your virtual PC, so it also pays to have 2GB or more of RAM. I use this application with niche Windows programs that have never appeared on the Mac. (Again, you don't need to use Desktop to run the Windows version of Photoshop CS4 because Photoshop CS4 is also available for the Mac.)

If you're tired of the undeserved taunts from your clueless Windows friends — you know, the ones who say that you can't run both Mac and Windows programs at the same time — head to your browser and order a copy of Parallels Desktop. The program is a very affordable $80 — but don't forget: You have to supply your own copy of Windows. For a free taste of virtual computing, try VirtualBox at www.virtualbox.org.

# All Hail FileMaker Pro

If databases are the name of your game, you've already been using FileMaker Pro for years (on both Mac and Windows, more than likely). For the uninitiated, *FileMaker Pro* (www.filemakerpro.com) is the premier database creation, editing, and maintenance application for Mac OS X. It comes with dozens of ready-made database templates for business, home, and education use, or you can construct your own database in surprisingly short order.

Right out of the box, FileMaker Pro can create

✦ Business databases and forms for inventory, personnel, purchase orders, and product catalogs

✦ Home databases for budgeting, recipes, music CDs, DVD movies, family medical records, and event planning

✦ Education databases for student records, expense reports, field trip planning, book and multimedia libraries, and class scheduling

FileMaker Pro 10 can add images and multimedia to your database, and you can quickly and easily publish your databases on your Web site by using one of the built-in theme designs. (In fact, visitors to your Web site can update your database online, if you like.) FileMaker Pro can also allow multiple users to share data across your network, no matter whether they're running the Mac or Windows version. The latest version even runs scripts automatically based on user input.

At $299, FileMaker Pro 10 is one of the least expensive — and most powerful — applications that you can buy for the Big X.

# Utilities That Rock

The next stop on this Cavalcade of Software is an assortment of the absolute best you've-got-to-get-this utility applications. Sooner or later, you're likely going to buy (or register) these utilities because you'll use them every day.

## StuffIt

In the Windows world, the Zip archive is the king of archiving formats. An *archive* contains one or more compressed files that you can uncompress whenever you need them. Folks store files in archives to save space on their hard drives; archiving is also a neat way to package an entire folder's worth of files in a single convenient file, which you can attach to an e-mail message or send via File Transfer Protocol (FTP). Mac OS X includes built-in support for zip files.

On Planet Macintosh, many folks prefer the StuffIt archiving format. Manage your archives with StuffIt Deluxe 2009, from Smith Micro Software (mysmithmicro.com). StuffIt Deluxe 2009 can both archive and unarchive .sit files (the common name for StuffIt archives) as well as Zip archives from your Windows friends. You can also encrypt the contents of a StuffIt archive for those "sensitive" transfers. The application runs $80 at the Smith Micro Software online Web store.

## QuicKeys X3

QuicKeys X3, from Startly Technologies (www.startly.com), is another example of someone's thinking properly. This time, the idea is to automate repetitive tasks by allowing Mac OS X to memorize what you do. Think of QuicKeys X3 as a system-wide, macro playback application. Unlike AppleScript, however, QuicKeys X3 works within any application and can play back mouse movement and clicks/double-clicks. (And unlike Automator, you can perform *any* action that you could normally perform within an application by typing.)

I've used QuicKeys X3 for a number of different tasks, including

+ Typing a commonly used block of text (such as my address) into applications that don't support macros
+ Launching applications at specific times and dates
+ Operating menus within programs to automate complex tasks
+ Launching Classic or choosing a specific startup disk with a single key sequence

QuicKeys X3 sells for $80 on the Startly Technologies Web site.

## BBEdit

Although we all know and love Mac OS X as a graphical operating system, folks still need a powerful text editor, such as the one shown in Figure 5-5, for creating and modifying text files. For example, software developers and Webmasters still use text editors daily to write applications or apply a quick fix to the HyperText Markup Language (HTML) that makes up a Web page. (I use a text editor to make minor changes to my Web site, MLC Books Online, without firing up a horrendous Web design application. Talk about overkill!)

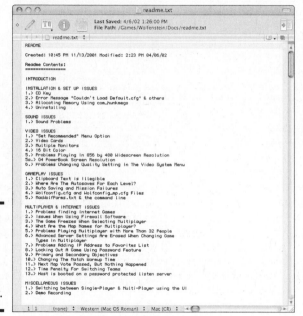

**Figure 5-5:** For editing text, you'll find no better tool than BBEdit.

Bare Bones Software pulls no punches in describing BBEdit — its advertising still proclaims, "It doesn't suck." Gotta give Bare Bones credit; this incredibly popular editor includes features such as

- ✦ **Support for DOS/Windows, Mac, and UNIX text files:** Yes, differences do exist between the platforms, even with a so-called *pure* text file.

- ✦ **Works with text files over 2GB in size:** Try that with TextEdit. Hmm . . . on second thought, please don't.

- ✦ **HTML tools for Web design:** These tools include syntax checking and browser preview.

- ✦ `grep` **pattern-based, multifile search and replace:** In nonprogrammer/ non-UNIX English, that means a very sophisticated search-and-replace function that can span more than one text file.

- ✦ **Syntax coloring:** Use this to help you quickly locate commands and qualifiers in programming languages.

- ✦ **Built-in FTP transfer commands:** No need to launch a separate FTP application: You can send your files right from within BBEdit.

You can even expand the functionality of BBEdit with plug-ins, many of which are free extensions written by programmers and developers specifically for languages such as C/C++, Java/JavaScript, Perl, and Pascal.

BBEdit 9 is available from the Bare Bones Software site for $125.

## REALbasic

The final application that I want to mention really isn't a utility as such; however, you can use it to write your own software, so I guess that it should qualify. As an ex-COBOL programmer, reluctant Visual Basic shareware developer, and recalcitrant dBASE coder, I can tell you that REALbasic (from REAL Software) is definitely the easiest visual drag-and-drop programming environment that I've ever used on a personal computer. If you want to develop your own productivity applications, Mac OS X utilities, or — dare I say it? your own game! — award-winning REALbasic 2009 is the way to go.

Development in REALbasic is as simple as designing the application window by first simply adding controls, text, and multimedia wherever you like. Then just fill in the blanks, such as by setting variables and specifying what happens when the controls are triggered, which you do by using a new implementation of the tried-and-true BASIC language. Of course, some programming knowledge is required, but far less than you'd need with Visual Basic. And the results look as good as anything you can accomplish in those so-called *real* programming languages.

Check out these features:

- ✦ **Cross-platform support so that you can write your program once and compile it for Linux, Mac OS X, *and* Windows.** Code it once; then release three versions with no extra work. This is a *very* Superb Thing.

- ✦ **Support for all sorts of multimedia,** including QuickTime.

- ✦ Ability to **animate and rotate text and objects,** or tap the 3-D power of QuickDraw3D and OpenGL graphics.

- ✦ Capability to **allow printing, network, and Internet communications** within your application.

- ✦ **Automation of Microsoft Office applications** and connection of your REALbasic application to business databases (such as FileMaker Pro).

- ✦ **Completely royalty-free applications,** so you can give them away or release them as shareware.

REALbasic has been such a popular development tool on the Macintosh for so many years that dozens of user-supported Web sites and mailing lists have sprung up, offering all sorts of REALbasic plug-ins, tutorials, and sample code for you to use in your own projects.

REALbasic 2009 comes in two versions: the Personal Edition ($99) and the Professional Edition ($500). You can order either version from the REAL Software site at www.realsoftware.com.

# At Least One Game

To be completely accurate, Mac OS X already comes with at least one game — a very good version of chess, which I cover in the next section — but the Macintosh has never been considered a true gaming platform by most computer owners. Until recently, many popular Windows games were never ported (or converted) for the Mac, and only the most expensive Mac models had the one important component that determines the quality of today's games: a first-rate, 3-D video card.

However, within the last two years or so, all that has changed dramatically. *All* of today's MacBook models feature muscle-car-quality video cards that use the NVIDIA GeForce chipsets; they can handle the most complex 3-D graphics with ease. Match that with the renewed popularity of the Macintosh as a home computer and the performance of the current crop of Intel-based processors, and — wham! Suddenly you've got the best game developers in the business — id Software (www.idsoftware.com) and Blizzard (www.blizzard.com), to name two — releasing Macintosh versions of their newest games concurrently with the Windows version.

For the gamer in you, allow me to take you on a tour of the best of the new generation of entertainment.

## Mac OS X Chess

No mercenaries, no rail guns, and no cities to raze — but chess is still the world's most popular game, and Mac OS X even includes a little 3-D as well. Figure 5-6 illustrates the Chess application at play; you'll find it in your Applications folder.

The game features speech recognition, move hints, take back (or undo) for your last move, and a 2-D or 3-D board. You can also list your games in text form and print them or save games in progress. Maybe it's not a complete set of bells and whistles as commercial chess games offer, but the price is right, and the play can be quite challenging when you set it at the higher skill levels.

Mark Chambers - Computer   (White to Move)

**Figure 5-6:**
Snow
Leopard
says, "How
about a nice
game of
chess?"

## *World of Warcraft*

I end this chapter with Blizzard's best: the online megahit that is World of Warcraft. This MMORPG (short for *massive multiplayer online role-playing game*) is yet another wrinkle in the popular Warcraft game series. World of Warcraft puts the character you create in the boots of human princes, Orc battle generals, undead champions, trolls, gnomes, and elfin lords — in fact, you can create multiple characters and play them as you choose. My recommendation: Stick with the Undead, my friend.

Combat, however, is only half the job. By finishing quests and killing various nasties, you earn experience, upgrade your armor and weapons, and build reputation with various groups throughout the land. You can take to the air, buy goods from mercenaries, and even discover a trade like leatherworking or enchanting. Spells abound, and you can join a guild and chat with the new friends you make online . . . I've played for over two years now, and I'm still excited by this incredible game.

Control is by both keyboard and mouse; the game is easy to understand, but you'll always find someone to kick your posterior in battlegrounds or dungeons over the Internet.

**Book VIII**
**Chapter 5**

Applications That
You've (Probably)
Gotta Have

You'll pay about $50 online for World of Warcraft and then you'll be charged a set fee for each month's subscription . . . and it'll be worth every single penny you spend. (Remember, this is a program you buy on your own; it doesn't come with your Mac or with Snow Leopard.) For all the details and some great desktop backgrounds, check the official site at `www.blizzard.com`.

# Chapter 6: Putting Bluetooth to Work

## In This Chapter

✔ Using Bluetooth for wireless connections

✔ Adding wireless keyboards and mice

✔ Moving data amongst devices with iSync

✔ Adding third-party utilities

✔ Printing over a Bluetooth wireless connection

Time to talk cordless. Your MacBook is already pretty doggone all-inclusive because what most computers string together with cords has been integrated into the laptop's case, including the monitor and speakers. Depending on the connection options that you choose when you buy your laptop (or what you added since), the only cord that you absolutely need might be your AC power cord.

For most of us, this introduces an entirely new realm of possibilities . . . and that results in more questions. Exactly how do other wireless devices communicate with your MacBook? Can you really share the data on your laptop with your cell phone? Can you sit in the comfort of your overstuffed recliner and watch a DVD from 15 feet away?

In this chapter, I describe to you what's cooking in the world of wireless devices. I don't delve into wireless Ethernet networking between your MacBook and other computers; that's covered in depth in the confines of Book VII, Chapter 3. I also don't discuss the Apple Remote in this chapter; that's covered in Book II, Chapter 5. However, I *do* cover the wireless Bluetooth connections that you can make with devices other than computers.

## Bluetooth: What a Silly Name for Such Cool Technology

Originally, wireless computer connections were limited to IR (infrared) and 802.11b (the original Wi-Fi specification for wireless Ethernet networks). This was fine; after all, what were you gonna connect to your Mac besides other computers? Ah, but progress marches on.

## A little Danish history

Enter the explosion in popularity of modern cell phones and personal digital assistants (PDAs). In 1998, a consortium of big-name cell phone, PDA, and computer laptop manufacturers decided that their products needed a method of communicating with each other. This new wireless standard needed to be inexpensive and consume as little battery power as possible, so designers decided to keep the operational distance limited to a maximum of about 30 feet. Plus, the idea was to keep this new wireless system as hassle free as possible: Everyone agreed that when you're using one device, you should simply be able to walk within range of another device for the two to link up immediately and automatically. Thus, Bluetooth was born!

Bluetooth has been incorporated into a range of peripherals and devices, including

✦ Cell phones

✦ Laptops

✦ Wireless computer peripherals, such as keyboards and mice

✦ Printers

✦ Headphones

If the name Bluetooth sounds faintly like Viking-speak to you, it should. For some absolutely ridiculous reason, the companies that developed the Bluetooth standard decided to name their creation after the tenth-century Danish king Harald Blatand, nicknamed Bluetooth, who succeeded in joining Denmark and Norway in a political alliance. Hence the rather Viking and runic-looking Bluetooth symbol. (Geez, these folks need to take a day off. Read comic books or play with a Slinky. *Something.*)

## Is your MacBook Bluetooth-ready?

Danish royalty aside, you still need to know whether your MacBook is ready for a Bluetooth connection. At the time of this writing, all Apple laptops come with internal Bluetooth hardware. If you're using an older Mac laptop without Bluetooth built in, though, you're currently out of the Bluetooth loop.

However, you don't need to pitch your faithful laptop if it doesn't yet talk to the pirate (or if your internal Bluetooth hardware fails)! You can add Bluetooth capability to your computer with a simple USB Bluetooth adapter. The USB Bluetooth adapter from Belkin (www.belkin.com) sells online for about $30. It includes automatic data encryption, which is necessary only if there's a hacker within about 30 to 60 feet of your computer (although in my book, more security is always better). The adaptor can link with up to seven other Bluetooth devices simultaneously. (Come to think of it, there were a lot of people within 30 feet of my MacBook Pro during my last LAN party bash. I guess this stuff really *is* important!)

## Snow Leopard and Bluetooth, together forever

You'd expect a modern, high-tech operating system like Mac OS X to come with Bluetooth drivers. You'd be right, but Apple goes a step further: Snow Leopard comes with a Bluetooth pane in System Preferences and a utility application to help you get your laptop connected with the Bluetooth devices that are likely hanging out in your coat pockets.

Click the System Preferences icon in the Dock. From the Bluetooth pane, you can

✦ **Set up new Bluetooth devices.** Click the Set Up New Device button to run the Bluetooth Setup Assistant, which configures Bluetooth devices for use with Snow Leopard.

Follow the device-specific, on-screen instructions to set up a number of common Bluetooth toys (including keyboards, mice, cell phones, and printers), or you can work with other types of devices by choosing Other. Setup Assistant searches for your Bluetooth device and makes sure that it's ready to party with your MacBook.

Make sure that your Bluetooth device is in range and *discoverable* (available for connections with other Bluetooth devices) before you run the Bluetooth Setup Assistant. Check your user manual to determine how to set your Bluetooth device as discoverable, and make sure that you're about 20 feet (or fewer) away from your MacBook.

✦ **Configure Bluetooth connections.** Click the Advanced button to create, remove, enable, or disable your Bluetooth connections, using them as virtual serial ports (for the simple transfer of data) or virtual modems (for bidirectional transfers, such as using an Internet connection through a Bluetooth cell phone).

These openings to the outside world are presented as individual connections in the Serial Port list, and you can toggle them on and off individually. You can also specify whether a Bluetooth port is encrypted. Figure 6-1 shows an active Bluetooth virtual modem that's set up to allow my MacBook Pro to sync up with my Palm Pilot, using the Bluetooth-PDA-Sync service.

I recommend that you enable the Show Bluetooth Status in the Menu Bar check box. The Bluetooth menu lets you conserve power by turning off your Bluetooth hardware until you need it. You can also conveniently toggle your laptop's discovery status as well as set up a device or send and browse files. (You can even see what devices are connected to your MacBook with the click of a menu icon. 'Nuff said.)

If you know you won't be using Bluetooth devices while you're on the road, disabling a Bluetooth service on a laptop can help conserve battery power.

**Figure 6-1:**
You can
add, delete,
enable,
or disable
Bluetooth
ports
from the
Advanced
sheet.

The other Bluetooth resource that you can use is the stand-alone application Bluetooth File Exchange. (Yes, you can call it BFE if you like. I do whenever possible.) You have to launch BFE the old-fashioned way; it's located in your Utilities folder, inside your Applications folder. As with a traditional FTP (File Transfer Protocol) application, double-clicking the Bluetooth File Exchange icon presents you with a file selection dialog in which you choose the file(s) you want to send to the connected Bluetooth device! You can also elect to browse the files on a networked Bluetooth device so that you can see what the owner of that device is offering.

You can also set up your defaults for file exchanges from the Sharing pane in System Preferences. While you're in the Bluetooth pane, click the File Sharing Setup button, and System Preferences whisks you directly to the Sharing pane. Select the Bluetooth Sharing check box to display the settings shown in Figure 6-2. Here, you can control what Snow Leopard does when you receive files or Personal Information Manager (PIM) data with BFE. For instance, with these settings, Snow Leopard can

✦ Prompt you for permission to receive each file or PIM item

✦ Accept all files and PIM items without restriction or prompting

✦ Save all incoming files and items to the folder that you specify

✦ Offer only the files and items in the folder that you specify when other Bluetooth items browse your MacBook

Personally, I'm all for the defaults in Snow Leopard for file exchanges:

✦ I Want to Know When Someone's Sending Me Something

✦ I Want Anything I Receive to Be Saved in My Downloads Folder

> ✦ If I Turn on File Sharing, I Want to Allow Others to Browse the Contents of My Public Folder

However, feel free to adjust, enable, and disable to your heart's content

**Figure 6-2:**
Configure file exchanges in System Preferences.

# Adding Wireless Keyboards and Mice to Your MacBook

The current crop of Mac laptops arrive at your doorstep in a fully wireless configuration: Apple throws in an internal Bluetooth adapter and an internal AirPort Extreme wireless card. Everything's already included for you. Therefore, you can indeed work keyboard and mouse magic from across the room from your laptop, using a wireless keyboard and mouse that you can buy separately. (Or perhaps you just want a full-size keyboard and external mouse to use when you're working from your home or office.)

A number of wireless Bluetooth keyboard/mouse packages are on the market, and any one of 'em should work fine with your MacBook. In fact, you can buy Apple's wireless Bluetooth keyboard and mouse separately, for a total of about $150. Other offerings from Logitech and our old buddy Microsoft run about the same amount.

When shopping for a Bluetooth keyboard/mouse desktop, keep these facts in mind:

> ✦ **Some keyboards are created more than equal.** Many of today's third-party keyboards are encrusted with extra function buttons that do everything from opening your e-mail application to searching your kitchen cabinets for another can of spray cheese.

I like these programmable function keys — they can bring up your favorite applications with a single keystroke while you're relaxing 20 feet away — so I recommend that you look for the keyboard that offers the most programmable keys in your price range.

✦ **Rodents crave energy.** Does the wireless mouse come with its own recharging stand? If so, that's a big plus. Depending on how much you use your laptop, a mouse that runs on standard batteries can go through a set in as little as a month's time! (Not surprisingly, many computer owners use rechargeable batteries in their wireless mice.) In fact, some wireless mice include an on/off switch to help conserve battery power.

✦ **Wireless doesn't always mean Bluetooth.** Just because a keyboard or mouse is wireless doesn't automatically make it a Bluetooth device. Plenty of wireless RF (radio frequency) devices are out there, too. These toys need their own transmitters, which are usually USB-based as well, so things can get confusing. Therefore, read the box or technical specifications carefully to make sure you're buying Bluetooth.

✦ **Bluetooth stuff isn't self-cleaning.** Sure, your new wireless keyboard and mouse can hang out with you on the sofa, but that doesn't mean they're happy sharing your nacho puffs and grape soda. Look for an optical mouse that doesn't use a ball, and check whether a prospective keyboard can be easily cleaned and maintained before you buy it.

Most Bluetooth devices are installed and controlled through the Bluetooth pane in System Preferences. However, wireless keyboards and mice are a special case because they're installed via the Bluetooth controls in both the Keyboard and Mouse panes. (Geez, those Apple designers give you a dozen roads to the same spot on the map, don't they?)

# Getting Everything in iSync

No jokes about boy bands, please. *iSync* is the data transfer and synchronizing utility application that ships with Snow Leopard, and it works fine with both wired and wireless Bluetooth connections. The difference between Bluetooth File Exchange and iSync is a matter of intelligence:

✦ BFE merely transfers files and dumps them in the folders you specify.

✦ iSync copies and updates your Address Book, Safari, and iCal information between devices. iSync compares the information on both your laptop and your devices and makes sure they end up the same.

iSync also allows you to synchronize data between multiple computers using your MobileMe membership so that the contacts, bookmarks, and calendar data on your MacBook match the data on your Mac Pro. You can control what gets sent from the MobileMe pane in System Preferences.

Just because your phone or PDA supports Bluetooth *doesn't* mean that iSync is guaranteed to work. I know a few Mac owners who are still seething over incompatible devices. For a complete list of the Bluetooth phones, PDAs, and other devices that work with iSync, visit www.apple.com/isync/devices.html.

After your supported Bluetooth device is linked to your MacBook, follow these steps to add the new device to iSync and synchronize your data:

*1.* **Click the Finder icon on the Dock.**

*2.* **Click Applications in the Finder window Sidebar and double-click iSync.**

*3.* **Press ⌘+N.**

iSync displays the Add Device dialog.

*4.* **Click Scan to display any Bluetooth devices in range.**

*5.* **Double-click the device that you want to use.**

The window expands to allow you to specify what data is to be synchronized. (Other settings might appear as well, depending on the device.)

*6.* **Select the check boxes for each data type that you want to exchange.**

*7.* **Click Sync Devices.**

*Never* disconnect a device while a synchronization is in progress. You risk corrupting the data being transferred and locking up your MacBook. Wait until iSync indicates that the synchronization is finished; the application displays a message when the process is complete.

Deleting a calendar event or a contact on either your laptop or the Bluetooth device deletes that same data from the other machine! For example, if you decide that you no longer need your personal contacts on your Mac at work and you delete 'em, *they'll be deleted from your PDA when you synchronize.* When I say that iSync creates a mirror image on both sides of the connection, I'm not lying: Additions appear and deletions disappear.

# *The Magic of Wireless Printing*

To your Mac laptop, a wireless Bluetooth printer is just another Bluetooth connection — but to you, it's the very definition of convenience, especially if desk space is limited next to your Mac. Just set that paper-producing puppy up anywhere in the 30  40 foot range, plug it in, set up the printer in Snow Leopard, and let 'er rip.

Not all printer manufacturers produce Bluetooth models that communicate properly with your MacBook. Make sure that the Bluetooth printer you buy supports HCRP. (Another jawbreaker acronym. This time it stands for *Hardcopy Cable Replacement Protocol.*)

You have two options when installing a Bluetooth printer:

✦ Whenever possible, use the printer manufacturer's software. A printer might require a driver that a typical Bluetooth device doesn't need.

✦ You can usually successfully set up a printer via the Bluetooth Setup Assistant, which you can run from the Bluetooth pane of System Preferences (as I discuss earlier in the chapter):

　a.　*Make sure your printer is set as discoverable.*

　　Check your printer manual to determine how to switch your printer to discoverable mode. This mode allows other Bluetooth devices within range (including your laptop) to recognize and make a connection to your printer.

　b.　*Click the Set Up New Device button.*

　c.　*Choose to install a printer.*

　d.　*Follow the onscreen instructions.*

Luckily, after you successfully set up a Bluetooth printer, you can just press ⌘+P to open the Print dialog box and choose that printer from the Printer pop-up menu. No big whoop . . . and that's the way it *should* be.

# Book IX

# Advanced Mac OS X

You can create simple applications to handle repetitive tasks, such as automatically rotating 10 or even 1,000 images simultaneously.

# Contents at a Glance

## Chapter 1: Using UNIX on Your MacBook . . . . . . . . . . . . . . . . . . . . . . 689

Why Use the Keyboard? . . . . . . . . . . . . . . . . . . . . . . . . . . . . . . . . . . . . . 689
Uncovering the Terminal . . . . . . . . . . . . . . . . . . . . . . . . . . . . . . . . . . . . 693
UNIX Commands 101 . . . . . . . . . . . . . . . . . . . . . . . . . . . . . . . . . . . . . . . 696
Working with Files . . . . . . . . . . . . . . . . . . . . . . . . . . . . . . . . . . . . . . . . . 699
Useful Commands . . . . . . . . . . . . . . . . . . . . . . . . . . . . . . . . . . . . . . . . . 703
UNIX Cadillac Commands . . . . . . . . . . . . . . . . . . . . . . . . . . . . . . . . . . 705
UNIX Programs That Come in Handy . . . . . . . . . . . . . . . . . . . . . . . . . 707

## Chapter 2: AppleScript Just Plain Rocks . . . . . . . . . . . . . . . . . . . . . 711

What's So Great about AppleScript? . . . . . . . . . . . . . . . . . . . . . . . . . . 711
Running a Script . . . . . . . . . . . . . . . . . . . . . . . . . . . . . . . . . . . . . . . . . . 713
Writing Your Own Simple Scripts . . . . . . . . . . . . . . . . . . . . . . . . . . . . 716
One Step Beyond: AppleScript Programming . . . . . . . . . . . . . . . . . . . 718
I Summon Automator — the Silicon Programmer! . . . . . . . . . . . . . . . 721
Help Is at Your Fingertips . . . . . . . . . . . . . . . . . . . . . . . . . . . . . . . . . . . 723

## Chapter 3: Writing and Conversing with Your MacBook . . . . . . . . . 725

Using Ink with a Tablet . . . . . . . . . . . . . . . . . . . . . . . . . . . . . . . . . . . . . 726
Computer, Can You Hear Me? . . . . . . . . . . . . . . . . . . . . . . . . . . . . . . . 727
Your Mac Talks Back! . . . . . . . . . . . . . . . . . . . . . . . . . . . . . . . . . . . . . . 732

# Chapter 1: Using UNIX on Your MacBook

## In This Chapter

- ✔ Why use UNIX?
- ✔ Doing things with the keyboard
- ✔ Introducing UNIX commands
- ✔ Creating text files
- ✔ Exploring deep inside Mac OS X

As I mention in the first chapter of the Book II, UNIX lurks deep beneath the shiny Aqua exterior of Mac OS X. UNIX is a tried-and-true operating system that's been around for decades, since the days when mainframe computers were king. If you don't believe that it's a powerful (and popular) operating system, consider that more than half of all Web servers on the Internet use some variety of UNIX as their operating system of choice.

Besides being battle-tested and having a long history, UNIX offers some fantastic features. Unlike the graphical world of Mac OS X, the keyboard plays an integral role while you're using a UNIX-based operating system. Because UNIX is text based, you'll find that it has evolved with a large set of useful keyboard-driven commands that can perform powerful feats not easily equaled by a mouse user. This chapter examines the role of the keyboard in UNIX operating systems and describes how to execute standard file system commands. You also discover how to use Apple's additional set of commands and install your own commands (and simple programs) from the Internet.

## Why Use the Keyboard?

To begin benefiting from the UNIX underpinnings of Mac OS X, get used to doing things with the keyboard. Although mouse skills can be applied to UNIX, you'll generally find performing UNIX functions faster and easier with the keyboard.

## UNIX keyboarding is fast

Why on Earth would any red-blooded MacBook owner want to leave the comfort of the trackpad to use a keyboard? After all, the graphical user interface is what made the Macintosh great in the first place. With the Finder, you can navigate and manage the various files on your hard drive with a few clicks. This sounds simple enough, but for some tasks, using the keyboard can be just as fast, if not faster.

Suppose, for example, that you need to copy a file from somewhere on your hard drive to somewhere else on that same drive. To do so with the Finder, you must first open a Finder window (by clicking the Finder icon in the Dock or by double-clicking a drive icon on your Desktop). Then, by using a succession of trackpad clicks, you navigate to where the file that you wish to copy resides. Next, you might open another Finder window and navigate to the folder where you wish to copy the file. (Note that opening the second Finder window requires pressing ⌘+N or choosing File➪New Finder Window; clicking the Finder icon in the Dock doesn't open a second Finder window.) Finally, you duplicate the original file and drag that copy to its intended destination.

Comparatively, by using the keyboard and the power of UNIX, you can accomplish the same task with a one-line command. For some tasks, your trackpad (or a USB mouse) is definitely the way to go, but you can perform some other tasks just as quickly, if not faster, with the keyboard. For the skinny on one-line commands, skip down to the upcoming section "Uncovering the Terminal."

## The UNIX keyboard is a powerful beast

So maybe you're not an expert typist, and using the trackpad still sounds inviting. For many scenarios, you'd be correct in assuming that a "pointing thing" can handle the job just as quickly and easily as a bunch of commands that you have to memorize. Using the keyboard, however, offers some other distinct advantages over the trackpad. To allow you to control your computer from the keyboard, all UNIX operating systems offer the *command line tool*. With this tool, you can enter commands one line at a time: hence, its name. Mac OS X ships with the command line application, Terminal. You can find it here:

```
/Applications/Utilities/Terminal
```

One shining feature of the command line is its efficiency. To wit: When you use a trackball or mouse, one click is equal to one command. When you use the command line, on the other hand, you aren't limited to entering one command at a time; rather, you can combine commands into a kind of *super-command* (minus the silly cape, but with bulging muscles intact), with each command performing some action of the combined whole. By using the command line, you can string together a whole bunch of commands to do a very complex task.

For example, consider how many times you'd have to click in the Finder to do the following:

1. **Find all files that begin with the letters *MyDocument*.**
2. **From this list of files, add a number to the beginning of the filename, indicating its size in kilobytes.**
3. **Save the names of all altered files to a text file.**

By using the command line, you could accomplish all these tasks by typing only one *super-command:* that is, a collection of three simple commands combined to form one instruction. The built-in Terminal program that ships with Mac OS X Snow Leopard gives you everything that you need to start using the command line. I show you how in the section "Uncovering the Terminal," later in this chapter.

Delving further into super-commands isn't for the faint-hearted; things get pretty ugly pretty quickly, and this chapter can only show you the very beginning of the UNIX Yellow Brick Road. Therefore, if your thirst for UNIX dominance so compels you, I invite you to do a little independent study to bone up on the operating system. Pick up a copy of the great book of lore entitled *UNIX For Dummies,* 5th Edition, written by John R. Levine and Margaret Levine Young (Wiley).

## Go where no trackpad has gone before

The Finder is generally a helpful thing, but it makes many assumptions about how you work. One of these assumptions is that you don't have any need to handle some of the files on your hard drive. As I mention in Book III, Chapter 6, Mac OS X ships with its system files marked Off Limits, and I generally agree with that policy (which keeps anyone from screwing up the delicate innards of Mac OS X). To secure your system files, Apple purposely hides some files from view.

But what road do you take if you actually need to view or modify those system files? Yep, you guessed it: The command line comes to the rescue! You can use the command line to peer inside every nook and cranny of your MacBook's vast directory structure on your hard drive. It also has the power to edit files that aren't normally accessible to you. With the command line, you can pretend to be other users — even users with more permissions. By temporarily acting as another more powerful user, you can perform actions with the command line that would be impossible in the Finder. (Just remember to make sure that you know *exactly* what you're doing, or you're working with an Apple technical support person — a wrong move, and it'll be time for an Ominous Chord.)

## Automate to elevate

If all these benefits are beginning to excite you, hold on to your socks! Not only can you perform complex commands with the command line, you can go even one step further: *automation.* If you find yourself using the same set of commands more than once, you're a likely candidate for using automation to save time. Instead of typing the list of commands each time, you can save them to a text file and execute the entire file with only one command. Now that's power, right up there with the dynamic duo of AppleScript and Automator!

Of course, you probably don't like doing housekeeping tasks while you're busy on other things, so schedule that list of commands to run in the middle of the night while you're fast asleep. UNIX lets you do that, too, using the `launchd` command.

Note that automation of UNIX commands is totally separate from automation of Mac OS X applications with AppleScript and Automator, which I cover in Book IX, Chapter 2.

## Remote control

"So, Mark, the command line is the cat's meow for efficiently accessing and working with files on my MacBook, and I can use it to automate many operations. Anything else?" I'm glad you asked! By using the command line, you can also send commands to another computer anywhere in the world (as long as you know the right login and password). After you log into another computer, you can use the same commands for the remote computer.

UNIX was created with multiple users in mind. Because computers used to be expensive (and honking huge machines to boot), UNIX was designed so that multiple users could remotely use the same machine simultaneously. In fact, if Mac OS X is your first encounter with UNIX, you might be surprised to know that many UNIX beginners of the past weren't even in the same room, building, state, or even country as the computer that they were using.

Not only can you work with a computer that's in a different physical location, but it's also very fast to do so. Instead of the bandwidth hog that is the Internet, the command line is lean and mean. This permits you to use a remote computer nearly as fast as if it were sitting on the desk in front of you. (This is a great advantage for road warriors who need to tweak a Web or an e-mail server from a continent away.)

# Uncovering the Terminal

The best way to find out how to use command line is to jump right in.
Mac OS X comes stocked with an application named *Terminal.* The Terminal
application is where you enter commands in the command line. It's located
in the Utilities folder within the Applications folder on your hard drive —
choose Applications➪Utilities.

Double-click the icon, as shown in Figure 1-1, to launch Terminal.

**Figure 1-1:**
Find the
Terminal
application
in your
Utilities
folder.

By the way, feel free to make Terminal more accessible by dragging its icon
to the Dock or the toolbar. That way, you won't have to dive this deep into
the Applications folder in the future.

## What's a prompt?

Upon launch of the Terminal application, you'll immediately notice some
text in the window that appears on-screen:

```
Last login: Sun Jun 23 17:51:14 on console
WHITEDRAGON:~ markchambers$
```

As you might guess, this text details the last time that you logged into the
Terminal. The last line, however, is the more important one. It's called the
*prompt.*

The prompt serves some important functions. First, it lists the current directory, which is listed as ~. A tilde character (~) denotes a user's Home directory. By default, you're always in your Home folder each time you begin a new session on the Terminal. After the current directory, the Terminal displays the name of the current user, which is markchambers in this example.

The final character of the prompt is a $. Consider this your cue because immediately after this character is where you enter any command that you wish to execute. Go ahead; don't be shy. Try out your first command by typing **uptime** in the Terminal application. (It's a good idea to type UNIX commands in lowercase.) Your text appears at the location of the cursor, denoted by a small square. If you make a mistake while entering the command, press the Delete key to back up and then type the characters again. (If the typing error is stuck deep in a longer command, press the left- or right-arrow key to move the cursor immediately after the incorrect character and press Delete to back up; then type the correct characters.) After you type the command, press Return to execute it.

```
WHITEDRAGON:~ markchambers$ uptime
6:24PM  up  2:42, 4 users, load averages: 2.44, 2.38, 1.90
WHITEDRAGON:~ markchambers$
```

If all goes well, you should see a listing of how long your Mac has been running since the last reboot or login. In the example listing, the computer has been running for 2 hours and 42 minutes (2:42 in line 2). Simple, eh? Immediately following the listing of the uptime command, the Terminal displays another prompt for you to enter more commands. I examine many more commands later in this chapter.

Prefer a different appearance for the Terminal window? Click the Terminal menu and choose Preferences; then click the Settings toolbar button to choose the color combinations for the Terminal window background and text.

## A few commands to get started

Using the command line is simply a matter of entering simple instructions — or *commands* — into the Terminal application and pressing Return to execute them. It's easy to use the command line to navigate through the various folders on your hard drive. You'll become accustomed to using two vital commands: ls and cd. The ls command is shorthand for *list,* and it does just that: It lists the contents of the current directory. Enter **ls** at your prompt, and you should see a listing of your Home folder.

The complementary cd command (lowercase) — which incidentally stands for *change directory* — opens any folder that you specify. It works much the same as double-clicking a folder in the Finder: The difference is that following the cd command, you don't immediately see all the folder's content. However, the `cd` command requires a *parameter* (extra options or information that appear after the command) so that your Mac knows which folder to open.

For example, to open the Documents folder that resides in your Home directory, type **cd Documents** and press Return. When you do, you might be surprised to see another prompt displayed immediately. So where are all the files in the Documents folder? You must enter another command to see what items are in the folder that you just opened. Type **ls** again to see the contents of the Documents folder.

If you try to open a folder that has a space in its name, make sure to enclose the folder's name in quotation marks, like this:

```
cd "My Picture Folder"
```

Read more about using quotation marks in your commands in the upcoming section "Command-line gotchas."

To return to your Home folder in this example, enter a modified version of the `cd` command:

```
cd ..
```

This causes your MacBook to move back up the folder hierarchy one folder, in this case to your Home directory. By using these three simple commands — `ls`, `cd *foldername*`, and `cd ..` — you can traverse your entire hard drive.

After you successfully enter a command, you can recall it by pressing the up-arrow key. Press the up-arrow key again to see the command prior to that, and so forth. This is an extremely useful trick for retyping extra long file paths.

## Using the skills you already have

Just because the Terminal is text based doesn't mean that it doesn't act like a good Macintosh citizen. All the usual Mac features that you know and love are there for you to use. Copy and Paste functions work as you might expect — but only at the prompt position.

Drag-and-drop is also at your disposal. After you play around with the Terminal for a while, you'll find yourself bored to tears typing the long paths that represent the files on your hard drive. To automatically enter the path of a file or folder to a command, simply drag it to the active Terminal window, as shown in Figure 1-2. The file's full path instantly appears at the location of your cursor. (Thanks, Apple!)

**Figure 1-2:**
Drag a
file from
a Finder
window into
Terminal to
display its
path.

You can even use the mouse while entering commands in the Terminal. Click and drag your mouse over text to select it. From there, you can copy to the Clipboard as you might expect with any other application.

# UNIX Commands 101

To use the command line effectively, familiarize yourself with the commands that are available to you. After all, how can you use a tool without knowing what it can do? Despite having to memorize a few commands, UNIX usually makes it easy on you by abbreviating commands, by following a standard grammar (so to speak), and by providing you with extensive documentation for each command.

## Anatomy of a UNIX command

UNIX commands can perform many amazing feats. Despite their vast abilities, all commands follow a similar structure:

```
command <optional flag(s)> <optional operand(s)>
```

The simplest form of a UNIX command is the command itself. (For a basic discussion on UNIX commands such as `ls`, see the earlier section, "A few commands to get started.") You can expand your use of the `ls` command by appending various *flags*, which are settings that enable or disable optional features for the command. Most flags are preceded by a dash (-) and always follow the command. For instance, you can display the contents of a directory as a column of names (complete with file details) by tacking on a `-l` flag to the `ls` command.

```
ls -l
```

Besides flags, UNIX commands sometimes also have operands. An *operand* is something that is acted upon. For example, instead of just entering the `ls` command, which lists the current directory, you can add an operand to list a specific directory:

```
ls ~/Documents/myProject/
```

The tilde (~) denotes the user's Home directory.

Sometimes a command can take multiple operands, as is the case when you copy a file. The two operands represent the source file and the destination of the file that you want to copy, separated by a space. The following example copies a text file from the Documents folder to the Desktop folder by using the `cp` command (short for *copy*).

```
cp ~/Documents/MyDocument ~/Desktop/MyDocument
```

You can also combine flags and operands in the same command. This example displays the contents of a specific folder in list format:

```
ls -l ~/Documents/myProject/
```

## Command-line gotchas

In earlier sections, I describe a few simple command-line functions. All these commands have something in common: You might not have noticed, but every example thus far involved folder names and filenames that contained only alphanumeric characters. Remember what happens if you have a folder name that has a space in it? Try the following example, but don't worry when it doesn't work.

The `cd` command stands for *change directory*.

```
cd /Desktop Folder
```

The result is an error message:

```
-bash: cd: /Desktop: No such file or directory
```

The problem is that a space character isn't allowed in a path. To get around this problem, simply enclose the path in double quotation marks, like this:

```
cd "/Desktop Folder"
```

Mac OS X lets you use either double *or* single quotation marks to enclose a path with spaces in it. Standard UNIX operating systems, however, use double quotation marks for this purpose.

In a similar vein, you can get the space character to be accepted by a command by adding an escape character. To *escape* a character, add a backslash (\) immediately prior to the character in question. To illustrate, try the last command with an escape character instead. Note that this time, no quotation marks are necessary.

```
cd /Desktop\ Folder
```

You can use either quotation marks or escape characters because they're interchangeable.

## Help is on the way!

By now, you might be wondering how a computer techno-wizard is supposed to keep all these commands straight. Fortunately, you can find generous documentation for nearly every command available to you. To access this built-in help, use the man command. Using the man command (shorthand for *manual*) will display a help file for any command that it knows about. For example, to read the available help information for the ls command, simply type **man ls** at the prompt. Figure 1-3 illustrates the result.

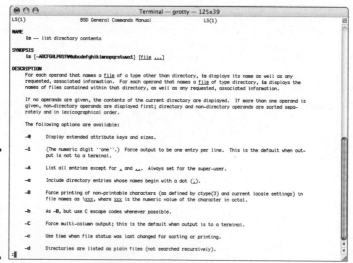

**Figure 1-3:** Use the man command to display help information.

## Autocompletion

To speed things along, the bash shell can automagically complete your input for you while you type. Although the Terminal permits you to enter commands via the keyboard, it is the shell that interprets those commands. Many kinds of shells are available to UNIX users. The shell that Snow Leopard uses by default is bash — another common shell is tcsh. Use the autocompletion features of bash to autocomplete both commands and filenames. To demonstrate, begin by typing the following:

```
cd ~/De
```

Then press the Tab key. The result is that the shell predicts that you will
want to type

```
cd ~/Desktop/
```

Of course, if you have another folder that begins with the letters *De* in the
same folder, you might need to type a few additional characters. This gives
the autocompletion feature more information to help it decide which
characters you want to type. In other words, if you don't type enough
characters, autocompletion ends up like a detective without enough clues to
figure things out.

# Working with Files

If you've used a computer for any time at all, you're no doubt familiar with
the idea of files. Even before the first floppy drive appeared in personal
computers, operating systems have stored data in files . . . they date back to
the days when a mainframe computer occupied an entire floor of an office
building. Mac OS X is no exception, and it's important to understand how
Mac OS X arranges them into folders and how you go about accessing
them via the command line. This section describes the basic file and folder
information that you need to know to tame the beast that is UNIX.

## Paths

Before you dive into UNIX commands, you should first know a few facts . . .
nasty things, facts, but you can't earn your pair of techno-wizard suspenders
without 'em. For starters, as a Mac user, you might not be familiar with how
paths work in UNIX. A *path* is simply a textual representation of a folder or
file. The simplest path is your Home directory, which is denoted by a tilde
character (~) — the tilde character acts as the equivalent of /Users/<your
short account name> (in my case, /Users/markchambers). Any folder
within the Home directory is represented by the folder's name preceded by
a forward slash (/). For example, a document entitled myDoc that resides in
the current user's Documents folder would have a path like this:

```
~/Documents/myDoc
```

Similarly, a folder named *myFolder* that resides in the current user's
Documents folder would have a path like this:

```
~/Documents/myFolder/
```

As you've probably surmised, a *folder* and a *directory* are two different
names for the same thing. *Folder* is the name with which most Mac users are
familiar, and *directory* is a term that UNIX power users prefer. I use the terms
interchangeably throughout the remainder of the chapter.

Because Mac OS X is a multiuser environment — and your applications and files may be located in many different folders across your hard drive — you will want to work with folders or files somewhere other than in your Home folder. Starting from your Home folder, enter the following command:

```
cd ..
```

This moves you to the folder right above your Home folder, which happens to be the Users folder. Using another quick `ls` command will show you all users who are permitted to use the machine. (By the way, Shared isn't a user — it's a folder with privileges set so that any user can access its contents.)

Enter **cd ..** once again, and you find yourself at the root of your main hard drive. The *root directory* is what you see in the Finder when you double-click your hard drive icon on the Desktop. A user's Home directory is represented by a tilde character (~), and the root of the hard drive is denoted by a forward slash (/), as displayed by the prompt:

```
WHITEDRAGON:/ markchambers$
```

It's easy to return to your Home directory by following this sequence:

```
WHITEDRAGON:/ markchambers$ cd Users
WHITEDRAGON:/Users markchambers$ cd markchambers
WHITEDRAGON:~ markchambers$
```

Here's a faster way. Instead of moving through each successive folder until you reach your intended destination, you can specify the path by using just one `cd` command:

```
WHITEDRAGON:/ markchambers$ cd /Users/markchambers
WHITEDRAGON:~ markchambers$
```

Of course, the Home directory is a special folder in that you can also navigate there by simply entering **cd ~**, but the main point here is that you can navigate directly to specific folders by using that folder's path in conjunction with the `cd` command.

Furthermore, when you navigate your hard drive by using paths, you can jump directly to your desired destination from any place. When you enter **cd ..**, it is in relation to your current position, whereas entering

```
cd /Users/markchambers
```

will always take you to the same directory, regardless of your starting point.

## Copying, moving, renaming, and deleting files

After you're comfortable with moving around the hierarchy of your hard drive, it's a cinch to copy, move, and rename files and folders.

To copy files from the command line, use the cp command. Because using the cp command will copy a file from one place to another, it requires two operands: first the source and then the destination. For instance, to copy a file from your Home folder to your Documents folder, use the cp command like this:

```
cp ~/MyDocument ~/Desktop/MyDocument
```

Keep in mind that when you copy files, **you must have proper permissions to do so!** Here's what happens when I try to copy a file from my Desktop to another user's Desktop (strangely named fuadramses):

```
WHITEDRAGON:~ markchambers$ cp ~/Desktop/MyDocument /Users/
    fuadramses/Desktop/MyDocument
```

Denied! Thwarted! Refused!

```
cp: /Users/fuadramses /Desktop/MyDocument: Permission denied
```

If you can't copy to the destination that you desire, you need to precede the cp command with sudo. Using the sudo command allows you to perform functions as another user. The idea here is that the other user whom you're "emulating" has the necessary privileges to execute the desired copy operation. When you execute the command, the command line asks you for a password. If you don't know what the password is, you probably shouldn't be using sudo. Your computer's administrator should have given you an appropriate password to use. After you enter the correct password, the command executes as desired.

In case you're curious, sudo stands for *set user and do.* It sets the user to the one that you specify and performs the command that follows the username.

```
sudo cp ~/Desktop/MyDocument /Users/fuadramses/Desktop/
    MyDocument
Password:
```

A close cousin to the cp (copy) command is the mv (move) command. As you can probably guess, the mv command moves a folder or file from one location to another. (I told you that all this character-based stuff would start to make sense, didn't I?) To demonstrate, this command moves MyDocument from the Desktop folder to the current user's Home folder:

```
mv ~/Desktop/MyDocument ~/MyDocument
```

Ah, but here's the hidden surprise: The mv command also functions as a rename command. For instance, to rename a file MyDocument on the Desktop to MyNewDocument, do this:

```
mv ~/Desktop/MyDocument ~/Desktop/MyNewDocument
```

In this case, you can see that the mv command is really copying the original file to the destination and then deleting the original. Because both folders in this example reside in the same folder (~/Desktop/), it appears as though the mv command has renamed the file.

Again, like the cp command, the mv command requires that you have proper permissions for the action that you want to perform. Use the sudo command to perform any commands that your current user (as displayed in the prompt) isn't allowed to execute. On UNIX systems, not all users are necessarily equal. Some users can perform functions that others can't. This is handy for keeping your child's mitts off important files on your laptop. It also creates a hurdle should you choose to work on files while using your child's restricted user account. The sudo command lets you temporarily become another user — presumably one that has permission to perform some function that the current user can't.

What would file manipulation be without the ability to delete files? Never fear; UNIX can delete anything that you throw at it. Use the rm (short for *remove*) or rmdir (short for *remove directory*) command to delete a folder or file. For example, to delete MyNewDocument from the Desktop folder, execute the rm command like this:

```
rm ~/Desktop/MyNewDocument
```

Once again, deleting files and folders requires that you have permission to do so. In other words, any time that you manipulate files with the command line, you're required to have the proper permission. If your current user lacks these permissions, using sudo helps. You should also check to make sure that your target is correctly spelled and that no pesky spaces that could wreak carnage are lurking in the command.

## Opening documents and launching applications

Launching applications and opening documents is child's play for a UNIX pro like you. The open command does it all. For example, to bring the Finder to the foreground without touching the mouse, use

```
open /System/Library/CoreServices/Finder.app
```

To open a document from the command line, follow a similar scheme. For example, to view an image named myImage.tif that's stored in your Documents folder using the default application (typically Preview), try this:

```
open ~/Documents/myImage.tif
```

# Useful Commands

Manipulating files and viewing folder content is fun, but the command line is capable of so much more! Now I focus your attention on some of the other useful tasks that you can perform with the command line.

Mac OS X comes stocked with a full set of useful commands. You can discover what commands are installed by viewing the files in /usr/bin. Type **cd /usr/bin** to navigate there.

## Calendar

One of my favorite command-line functions is the cal command, which displays a calendar in text form. Simply entering **cal** at the prompt displays a calendar for the current month, as shown in Figure 1-4.

**Figure 1-4:**
Type **cal**
to view a
calendar for
the current
month.

Append a number to the cal command to display a 12-month calendar for that year. The number that follows the cal command is the year for which you'd like to see a calendar. For example, to view a calendar for 1970, type **cal 1970**. The result appears in Figure 1-5.

Append a month number and a year number to display the calendar for that month. For example, to view a calendar for April 2010, type **cal 04 2010**.

Use the –m flag to specify the current year, as in **cal –m 08** for August of this year.

Another useful command that's related to the cal command is date. Type **date** at the command line to display the day, date, time, and year based on your computer's settings.

```
WHITEDRAGON:~ markchambers$ date
Mon Jan 15 11:32:20 CDT 2009
```

```
⊙ ⊙ ⊙                    Terminal — bash — 85x38

WhiteDragon:~ markchambers$ cal 1970
                              1970
        January               February                March
 S  M Tu  W Th  F  S    S  M Tu  W Th  F  S    S  M Tu  W Th  F  S
             1  2  3    1  2  3  4  5  6  7    1  2  3  4  5  6  7
 4  5  6  7  8  9 10    8  9 10 11 12 13 14    8  9 10 11 12 13 14
11 12 13 14 15 16 17   15 16 17 18 19 20 21   15 16 17 18 19 20 21
18 19 20 21 22 23 24   22 23 24 25 26 27 28   22 23 24 25 26 27 28
25 26 27 28 29 30 31                          29 30 31

         April                   May                    June
 S  M Tu  W Th  F  S    S  M Tu  W Th  F  S    S  M Tu  W Th  F  S
             1  2  3  4                1  2    1  2  3  4  5  6
 5  6  7  8  9 10 11    3  4  5  6  7  8  9    7  8  9 10 11 12 13
12 13 14 15 16 17 18   10 11 12 13 14 15 16   14 15 16 17 18 19 20
19 20 21 22 23 24 25   17 18 19 20 21 22 23   21 22 23 24 25 26 27
26 27 28 29 30         24 25 26 27 28 29 30   28 29 30
                       31
         July                 August                September
 S  M Tu  W Th  F  S    S  M Tu  W Th  F  S    S  M Tu  W Th  F  S
             1  2  3  4                   1          1  2  3  4  5
 5  6  7  8  9 10 11    2  3  4  5  6  7  8    6  7  8  9 10 11 12
12 13 14 15 16 17 18    9 10 11 12 13 14 15   13 14 15 16 17 18 19
19 20 21 22 23 24 25   16 17 18 19 20 21 22   20 21 22 23 24 25 26
26 27 28 29 30 31      23 24 25 26 27 28 29   27 28 29 30
                       30 31
        October               November                December
 S  M Tu  W Th  F  S    S  M Tu  W Th  F  S    S  M Tu  W Th  F  S
             1  2  3    1  2  3  4  5  6  7          1  2  3  4  5
 4  5  6  7  8  9 10    8  9 10 11 12 13 14    6  7  8  9 10 11 12
11 12 13 14 15 16 17   15 16 17 18 19 20 21   13 14 15 16 17 18 19
18 19 20 21 22 23 24   22 23 24 25 26 27 28   20 21 22 23 24 25 26
25 26 27 28 29 30 31   29 30                  27 28 29 30 31

WhiteDragon:~ markchambers$ ▮
```

**Figure 1-5:** Type **cal** followed by a year to view the 12 months of that year.

## Processes

Have you ever been curious as to why your hard drive seems to spin and grind on occasion while your system is seemingly inactive? Mac OS X sometimes has a lot of stuff going on behind the scenes. To discover just what your computer is busy doing at any time, use the top command to display all the actions that your computer is currently performing, as shown in Figure 1-6. These activities are called *processes;* some are created when you launch applications, and others are simply tasks that Mac OS X has to take care of to keep things running smoothly.

Besides listing the names of the various processes currently in use, top tells you how much of your CPU is being devoted to each process. This lets you know what process is currently hogging all your computing power.

Sometimes a process stalls, effectively freezing that action. By using the top command to find the Process ID (PID) of the offending process, you can halt the process. Simply use the kill command followed by the PID of the process that you want to stop. (The man help page for the kill command gives more options that may help terminate stubborn processes with prejudice.)

```
 ● ○ ○           Terminal — top — 81×36
Processes:  51 total, 3 running, 1 stuck, 47 sleeping... 211 threads      01:38:31
Load Avg:  0.14,  0.18,  0.16     CPU usage:  2.39% user,  7.66% sys, 89.95% idle
SharedLibs: num =    1, resident =   55M code, 6488K data, 8576K linkedit.
MemRegions: num =  4879, resident =  156M + 128M private,  87M shared.
PhysMem:  219M wired,  617M active,   13M inactive,  849M used,  1190M free.
VM: 7172M + 140M   138581(0) pageins, 0(0) pageouts

  PID COMMAND      %CPU   TIME   #TH #PRTS #MREGS RPRVT  RSHRD  RSIZE  VSIZE
  505 top          3.8% 0:03.90   1    18    29  648K   184K  1132K   74M
  494 bash         0.0% 0:00.00   1    14    19  240K   180K   888K   74M
  493 login        0.0% 0:00.01   1    16    55  240K   224K   716K   75M
  406 Terminal     0.7% 0:05.22   4   104-  123 2832K    11M  8076K  285M
  391 Grab         0.8% 0:26.21   7   193+  251  15M-   23M    23M  327M+
  191 iTunes       6.8% 6:20.46   8   218   415   19M   15M    33M  327M
  188 mdworker     0.0% 0:00.82   4    72    83 1096K  2688K  3004K  120M
  163 launchd      0.0% 0:00.00   3    24    25  112K   276K   436K   74M
  152 smbd         0.0% 0:00.00   1     8    55   64K  3104K   316K   79M
  151 winbindd     0.0% 0:00.01   1    11    46  232K  1752K  1188K   77M
  150 winbindd     0.0% 0:00.00   1     8    37  132K  1748K   636K   77M
  149 winbindd     0.0% 0:00.06   1    14    37  128K  1748K  1292K   77M
  147 cupsd        0.0% 0:07.58   2    32    30  780K   224K  1552K   75M
  146 iChatAgent   0.0% 0:00.27   2    70    56 1236K  2580K  4176K  216M
  141 smbd         0.0% 0:00.16   1    17    55  200K  3104K  1972K   79M
  140 ocspd        0.0% 0:00.02   1    18    21  432K   188K  1004K   74M
  136 usbmuxd      0.0% 0:00.00   2    21    27  208K   180K   596K   75M
  134 iTunesHelp   0.0% 0:00.08   2    59    52  528K  3108K  2440K  219M
  112 ATSServer    0.0% 0:00.65   2    84    70  816K  2352K  2612K  118M
  111 Finder       0.2% 0:25.55   8   431   303   14M    28M    31M  339M
  110 SystemUISe   0.0% 0:02.15   9   261   239 5132K  7392K    10M  284M
  109 Dock         0.0% 0:02.23   5   131   195 2888K   19M  6752K  293M
  108 pboard       0.0% 0:00.00   1    15    23  184K   180K   508K   75M
  105 UserEventA   0.0% 0:00.22   2   141    51  596K   240K  1944K   75M
  104 Spotlight    0.0% 0:04.66   1    59    58 1248K  3764K  4076K  220M
   96 launchd      0.0% 0:00.61   3   133    26  220K   280K   512K   74M
   81 coreaudiod   0.0% 0:00.25   2   161    79 1240K   972K  2180K   77M
   47 WindowServ   0.4% 3:29.65   4   178   631   10M    20M    34M  288M
```

**Figure 1-6:**
The top command displays all running processes.

Do *not* go killing processes with a cavalier attitude! Although Mac OS X is extremely stable, removing the wrong process — such as init or mach_init — is rather like removing a leg from one of those deep-sea drilling platforms: the very *definition* of Not Good. You could lock up your system and lose whatever you're doing in other applications. If you simply want to shut down a misbehaving program, go graphical again (at least for a moment) and use the Force Quit menu command from the Finder menu.

Like top, another handy command for examining process info is ps (short for *process*). Most often, you'll want to append a few flags to the ps command to get the information that you desire. For example, try the following command:

```
ps -aux
```

The man page for ps explains what each flag means. (Read more about using the man command in the earlier section "Help is on the way!")

## UNIX Cadillac Commands

Besides working with files and processes, the command line has all kinds of sophisticated commands. For example, with the command line, you have instant access to a variety of tools for finding files or even stringing together commands.

## Finding files

The command line gives you a number of ways to search for files on your hard drive. The two most commonly used commands are `find` and `locate`.

To use `find`, specify a starting point for the search followed by the name of the file or folder that you want to find. For example, to find the Fonts folder that belongs to your user, enter the command like this:

```
find ~/ -name "Fonts"
```

You should see at least one result of the `find` command.

```
/Users/markchambers//Library/Fonts
```

One great feature of the `find` command is that you can look for a file or folder in more than one location. Suppose you want to find a file named `MyDocument` that you know resides either in your Documents folder or on your Desktop. For this kind of search, use the `find` command like this:

```
find ~/Documents ~/Desktop -name "MyDocument"
```

In this example, you are telling the `find` command which folders it should search when looking for the file named `MyDocument`.

## Using pipes

Nearly all UNIX commands can take on greater abilities by using a construct called the *pipe*. A pipe (|) is represented by that funny little vertical line that shows up when you press Shift+\. The pipe routes data from one command to another one that follows — for example, many UNIX commands produce large amounts of information that can't all fit on one page. (You might have noticed this behavior if you've used the `locate` command.) Joining two commands or functions together with the pipe command is *piping*. To tame the screens full of text, pipe the `find` function to the `less` command. The `less` command provides data one page at a time.

```
find ~/ -name "Fonts" | less
```

When the results fill up one page, the data stops and waits for you to press any key (except the Q key) to continue. When you reach the end of the results, press Q to quit and return to a command-line prompt.

# UNIX Programs That Come in Handy

As a MacBook user, you might be surprised to know that many applications on your hard drive don't reside in one of the typical Applications folders of Mac OS X. These applications, in fact, don't have any graphical user interface like what you're accustomed to. They're accessible only from the command line. The remainder of this chapter covers some of these applications.

## Text editors

UNIX has many text-editing applications for use at the command line. Some of the more popular ones include `pico`, `vi`, and `emacs`. Each of these text editors has its pros and cons — and say thanks to the thorough folks at Apple, because all three are included with Snow Leopard! For my examples here, however, I use `pico` because it's simple to use and sufficient for our needs.

## Creating a new document

To create a text file by using `pico`, simply type **pico** at the command line. The result looks like Figure 1-7.

**Figure 1-7:** The `pico` program is a full-strength text editor, right from the command line.

This is the rough-and-tumble world of UNIX, which preceded the Macintosh by many years. Perhaps this will also help you to appreciate why the Macintosh was so revolutionary when it was introduced. (You can just hear the designers crowing, "We'll call this a *menu!* Yeah, that's the ticket!" The only graphics that you'd see on your monitor were the comics and sticky notes that you stuck to the bottom.)

At the bottom of the screen is a menu of common commands. Above the menu is a large, empty space where you can enter text, much the same as in the word processors that you already know and love. (For those of us that remember the halcyon character-based days of DOS, think older versions of Word and WordPerfect . . . or, if you're a *real* computing dinosaur as I am, consider the original WordStar.) Type some text in that area. Anything will do . . . a letter to a friend, a grocery list, or your school homework.

When you're finished entering your desired text, save the document with the `WriteOut` command in the `pico` menu. Directly next to each command in the `pico` menu is a keyboard sequence used to perform that command. (Refer to the bottom of Figure 1-7.) The ∧ character is shorthand for the Control key on your keyboard. Thus, to save a file, press Control+O. This flies in the face of standard Mac keyboard conventions, where the letter *O* is traditionally used to mean *Open*.

After pressing the Control+O sequence, `pico` prompts you for a filename. Like most UNIX files, you're permitted to enter a simple filename here or a full path to a file. For this example, save the file to your Documents folder, naming it `MyPicoDocument`.

After you've completed and saved the document, pressing Control+X will transport you away from Planet Pico and back to the command line.

## Networking with the Terminal

Because UNIX isn't a new phenomenon, it has many useful networking abilities built into it. In fact, UNIX was instrumental in creating much of what we now take for granted: e-mail, the Internet, and the World Wide Web. Thus, you'll be happy to know that you can communicate over networks with the Terminal in practically any manner that you can dream of . . . and then some!

### WWW and FTP

If you've used the Internet for any time, you're probably familiar with the various means to transport data over a network. From FTP (short for *File Transfer Protocol*) and Telnet to e-mail and the Web, UNIX can handle it all. In fact, UNIX has a command for each of these functions (and many more that have passed into historical obscurity). Rather than use each individual command to send and retrieve data with the Terminal, Apple has conveniently provided a command that can handle them all: `curl`. The `curl` command is competent at all the standard network protocols. To see it in action, pass a Web address (or URL, to The Enlightened) to the `curl` command:

```
curl http://www.mlcbooks.com
```

The result is that you see the HyperText Markup Language (HTML) page that's located at www.mlcbooks.com. Because this isn't particularly useful for most people (it's not very easy to read), you need to add the letter o as a flag. This specifies where you would like to save this file upon download. To save the HTML page to your Home directory, add the –o flag and a path to the destination file.

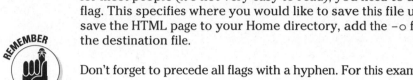

Don't forget to precede all flags with a hyphen. For this example, it would be –o.

```
curl -o ~/mlcbooks.html http://www.mlcbooks.com
```

If you now perform an ls command, you see that curl has, in fact, downloaded the HTML found at www.mlcbooks.com and saved it to a file named mlcbooks.html in your Home directory.

The beauty of curl is that it does much more than just retrieve Web pages: It's equally comfortable with FTP transfers. FTP is used to *download* (or receive) files from a server as well as *upload* (or send) them. Like the previous HyperText Transfer Protocol (HTTP) examples, you only have to provide an FTP address in Uniform Resource Locator (URL) format, and curl will take care of the rest. Of course, most people want to save any files that they download via FTP — not view them in the Terminal as I did the HTML file. Therefore, as in the previous example, you should add the o flag and a path to the destination of your download. This time, I download a README file about curl directly from the makers of curl.

```
curl -o ~/Desktop/README.curl ftp://ftp.sunet.se/pub/www/
    utilities/curl/README.curl
```

If you're familiar with FTP, you might wonder whether curl can upload, too. Yes, indeed! Instead of using the –o flag, you need to use two flags: –T and –u. The –T flag denotes which file you want to upload. The –u flag denotes the username and password. Then, specify the FTP destination address of where you want to upload it. Because this example deals with an upload, the remainder of this example is for an imaginary FTP server. In real life, you'd use the appropriate FTP address, username, and password for an FTP server where you are allowed to upload.

```
curl -T /Desktop/README.curl -u username:passwd ftp://ftp.
    yoursitehere.com
/myfiles/README.curl
```

This example uploads the README.curl file from the Desktop folder that I downloaded earlier to an imaginary FTP server.

### How do you spell success? C-u-r-l!

Sure, HTTP and FTP are handy, but did you know that there are many other protocols for network communications? One of the niftier ones is the *Dictionary protocol.* With it, you can look up words from any server that understands the protocol. Suppose, for example, that you want to know the meaning of the term *DVD.* Enter the following command to find out:

```
curl dict://dict.org/d:DVD
```

With `curl`, Dictionary, and your Dictionary Dashboard widget on the same MacBook, you might never use a "real" paper dictionary again!

# Chapter 2: AppleScript Just Plain Rocks

## In This Chapter

✔ Simplifying your life with AppleScript

✔ Letting AppleScript create scripts for you

✔ Writing scripts on your own

✔ Using Automator to create your own applications

✔ Searching for AppleScript help elsewhere

*U*sing a Macintosh is supposed to make your life easier — and in many ways, it does. But there's a limit to how much your MacBook can do by itself, right? After all, you still have to move your finger on the trackpad, press keys on the keyboard, and read information on the screen to get things done . . . or *do* you? Why not let your computer do the dull chores — such as renaming a thousand digital photographs from your family vacation and organizing them into folders based on the subject of each photo — for you? Although most people are familiar with controlling their MacBooks with the trackpad and keyboard, few realize that they can operate their machines without touching a key or a button, or even glancing at the screen.

## What's So Great about AppleScript?

If one word could describe what AppleScript is all about, it'd be *automation*. *AppleScript* is a technology for automating practically any action that you perform with your MacBook, including both common tasks in the Finder and those that you perform in other applications.

### Automate common tasks in the Finder

If you've ever found yourself repeating some task more than once, you're an ideal candidate for becoming an AppleScript techno-wizard. AppleScript is particularly good at taking the boredom and tedium out of using your laptop by performing all sorts of tasks automatically. To illustrate, consider a few jobs that would take a fair amount of time to do by hand but are a snap with AppleScript:

✦ While writing your next best-selling Great American Novel — or *For Dummies* book on Mac OS X — you make a mistake and misnumber the chapters. All the chapters have a filename bearing the chapter number, but they're all off by one. Sure, you could rename each file by hand, but your book is a large tome and renumbering 42 chapters manually doesn't sound like much fun. (Take my word for it. *Please.*) It'll require several minutes and lots of tedious attention on your part, not to mention introduce the likelihood of human error. But wait, there's another way! When using a simple AppleScript of only a few lines of code, you can rename the chapters in seconds whilst you go grab another Diet Coke.

✦ You're a neat individual and think that your MacBook should reflect your penchant for order — in fact, you like your Desktop icons to be placed just so. Being left-handed, you prefer the icons over on the left side of the Desktop, like some of those *inferior* operating systems. In this situation, an AppleScript can help you do things that aren't humanly possible; not only can you rapidly rearrange the icons on your Desktop, but you can do so with pixel-point accuracy. Without AppleScript, it'd be nearly impossible to precisely align dozens of icons. And if you could, it would take a long time and probably cause you to go blind.

✦ After a font-download binge, you find yourself with hundreds of fonts. You really want to organize them into separate folders based on the date that you downloaded them. AppleScript comes to the rescue again! With a brief script, you could knock out this challenge without ever looking at a single date. Add a couple more lines of code to the script, and AppleScript will take care of creating the folders, too. Right, you know the word: *sassy.*

## Automate tasks in other applications

By using AppleScript, you can also often automate your work from beginning to end, despite the fact that you need multiple applications to do so. Look at a few scenarios, and you'll begin to appreciate why AppleScript is such a powerful technology:

✦ You've just completed creating the ultimate library of bagpipe songs in iTunes — no, really! — and you want to share the list with your friends at the next Bagpipers Anonymous meeting. You could easily send everyone in the group an iTunes Playlist, but not everyone in the club has a Macintosh, let alone a computer. This is going to require creating a hard copy for those members without a computer. Because your bagpipe song list contains thousands of songs, you don't want to retype the name of each song. AppleScript can save the day by extracting the song titles for you and compiling them into a list just in time for your meeting.

✦ AppleScript can take care of your computer-owning bagpipe friends, too. With a few extra steps, you can e-mail all of them the list as well.

✦ Being so doggone fond of bagpipes, you want to send your bagpiping friends a special note during the holidays. To help manage your holiday greeting cards, you can create a record in FileMaker Pro or some other database listing the name and address of each person who should receive a card. If you've entered their street addresses in the Contacts section of your e-mail application, AppleScript can aid in transferring the addresses from your e-mail application to the database. Never again will your bagpiping friends miss a holiday greeting . . . and the world is a much better place.

As you can imagine, there are literally thousands of ways that you can use AppleScript to automate your workflow. (Whoops, I just used a BST, or *Business Software Term*. A *workflow* is a single document or project that one or more people work on using multiple applications. In other words, your document can be automatically manipulated in multiple applications using the same script.)

# Running a Script

The easiest way to get started with AppleScript is to use some scripts that others have written already. *Scripts* are small files that contain a list of commands; this list of commands tells your Mac what function to perform and when to perform it. Fortunately, Apple is kind enough to provide you with several completed scripts with your installation of Snow Leopard. You can find a large cache of scripts in the scripts folder, found in the Library folder, under Scripts.

Many scripts (but not all) end with the extension .scpt. Before you get started running scripts, however, you should know a few things.

## Identifying scripts in the field

Each script that you encounter will be in one of these three formats:

✦ **Script application:** Some AppleScripts act much like an application. To use one, simply double-click it in the Finder, and off it goes to perform whatever tasks it was meant to do. Depending on an internal setting of the script, it might quit when it's finished doing its thing. Most often, the script completes its mission and quits. Scripts are typically identified by the icon that you see in Figure 2-1.

✦ **Compiled script:** You might also encounter AppleScripts that won't run without the aid of another application. Apple calls these *compiled scripts*. Although they can't execute on their own, they do have the abilities of a script built in. They just require a host application to use them.

**Figure 2-1:**
A gaggle
of typical
script icons
caught by
the camera.

✦ **Text file:** In addition to compiled scripts and those that act like applications, a third category of AppleScript that you might encounter is a script stored in a text file. Scripts that are stored in a text file also need a host application before they'll do anything. The main difference between a text file script and a compiled script is that you can read a text file script with any application that can open a text file.

## The AppleScript Editor application

Two of the three possible script types (compiled scripts and text files) require some sort of host application before they'll perform any action. Luckily, Snow Leopard provides you with just such a host: the AppleScript Editor application, which comes with Mac OS X and can execute any AppleScript with ease. With the AppleScript Editor, you can also do much more, including

✦ View or modify an AppleScript

✦ Create a new AppleScript

✦ Check an AppleScript for errors

✦ Save scripts in one of the three possible formats

To launch the AppleScript Editor application, navigate to the Utilities folder (open your Applications folder and then open the Utilities folder) and double-click the AppleScript Editor icon. The AppleScript Editor application displays an empty, script-editing window, as shown in Figure 2-2.

## Executing a script

After you have the AppleScript Editor application running, you can run any AppleScript that you can find. To get you started, Apple has conveniently provided a handful of useful scripts. Navigate to the Scripts folder, which is located in the Library folder.

The scripts are divided into folders based on functionality, such as fonts, mail, and navigation. For example, open the Font Book folder, where you'll find a script named `Delete Empty Collections.scpt`.

**Figure 2-2:**
The
AppleScript
Editor slices
and dices . . .
and even
checks
syntax.
Order now!

Double-click the script to open it. Because it's a compiled script and not an application script, the AppleScript Editor automatically loads the script and comes to the foreground (see Figure 2-3). This particular script opens the Font Book application and checks for empty font collections. If any are found, the script displays a prompt asking for confirmation and then deletes the empty collection if you click the OK button. To see the script in action, click the Run button or press ⌘+R.

**Figure 2-3:**
Click the
Run button
in the Editor
toolbar to
execute
the script
you've
loaded.

# Writing Your Own Simple Scripts

Using someone else's scripts is fun and all, but the real joy of AppleScript comes when you create your own. Not only can you customize a script to your own needs and desires, but saving all those keystrokes can really produce a feeling of euphoria. (Okay, perhaps just Snow Leopard power users will actually experience a heightened sense of existence . . . you'll be there soon.)

## Create a script without touching a key

You needn't wear a pocket protector or tape the bridge of your glasses to become proficient with AppleScript. In fact, the AppleScript Editor can get you up and running with AppleScript in no time at all. The secret weapon of the AppleScript author is the Record function of the AppleScript Editor. You click the Record button, perform one or more actions in a recordable application, and then return to the AppleScript Editor, where you click the Stop button. The AppleScript Editor stores each of your actions and compiles the whole list into an AppleScript.

In *theory*, this is how it should all work, but in reality, finding recordable Macintosh applications isn't always so easy. The Finder is, perhaps, the most recordable application on the MacBook. Although some other applications support recording, so few do that the Finder could be the only recordable application most Mac users ever see.

To try it yourself, take the following steps to automate actions in the Finder:

1. **Bring AppleScript Editor to the foreground.**

   If AppleScript Editor isn't currently running, double-click its icon in a Finder window. If it is running, click its icon in the Dock.

2. **Create a new script by pressing ⌘+N.**

3. **Click the Record button.**

   The Record button is one of four buttons positioned near the top left of a new script window. Refer to Figure 2-3.

4. **Switch to the Finder and perform the actions that you want to automate.**

   When the Finder is active, you can select some icons on the Desktop and move them around, resize any open Finder windows, or navigate to your home directory. Any action that you perform in the Finder should be acceptable fodder for the AppleScript Editor. When you perform tasks in the Finder, the AppleScript Editor automatically generates a script that replicates your actions.

**5.** **Return to the AppleScript Editor and click the Stop button.**

To reactivate the AppleScript Editor, click its icon in the Dock. Click the Stop button to cease the recording of your script.

When you're finished, you should be looking at a complete AppleScript. To test your work, return to the Finder and return any icons or windows that you might have moved or repositioned to their original locations. (You don't want to run a script that doesn't appear to have any effect.) Then return to the AppleScript Editor and click the Run button to watch your automated Finder tasks being performed.

## Building your own scripts

An AppleScript novice can perform all kinds of amazing feats with the recording features of the AppleScript Editor. Because AppleScript uses a kind of pseudo-English language, it's usually pretty easy to figure out what's going on behind the scenes. Consider the following script for an example:

```
tell app "Finder"
   activate
   set windowList to every window -- save list of open
   windows
   repeat with theWindow in windowList
      tell theWindow
         if collapsed is true then
         -- do nothing, because the window is collapsed
         else
            set collapsed to true
         end if
      end tell
   end repeat
end tell
```

(By the way, in the preceding code, I bolded and italicized the commands you'll be working with, but they don't have to be bolded for the script to work.) Anyway, the first thing that you might notice about this script is the first line: the `tell` command, which indicates that this script relates to the Finder. This script activates the Finder, creates a list of open windows, and then examines the state of each window: Is it collapsed or not collapsed? (In Snow Leopard, a *collapsed,* or minimized, window appears in the Dock.)

One of two possible results occurs:

✦ **If the window is already minimized and in the Dock,** nothing happens and the script continues through the list of windows.

✦ **If the window isn't minimized,** the script collapses it.

This continues until the script has examined all open windows. The end result? All open windows end up minimized in the Dock.

Another thing to note about this script is that it has two comments in it (save list and do nothing). Comments can help you remember what you were thinking months later when you open the script again. Although comments help us humans know what's happening, they don't really have any other function. An AppleScript comment begins with two dashes (–).

Here's a big-time Mark's Maxim that every script author should remember:

**Comments are your friend!**

# One Step Beyond: AppleScript Programming

Creating AppleScripts can soon become very involved, bordering on programming. Don't let that term *programming* scare you away, though. You needn't be a software developer to take advantage of AppleScripts. Apple provides a lot of help to get you started along the AppleScript trail.

## Grab the Dictionary

Perhaps the greatest resource for AppleScript novices and experts alike is the AppleScript Dictionary. Although many applications are scriptable, not all are. To be scriptable, an application must contain an AppleScript Dictionary. An AppleScript Dictionary details the various commands and objects of an application that you can access via AppleScript.

The AppleScript Editor application allows you to peer inside an application and view its AppleScript Dictionary. To open an application's Dictionary, choose File➪Open Dictionary. Mac OS X searches through your installed applications and presents you with the Open Dictionary dialog, as shown in Figure 2-4, which lists all applications that have a dictionary and are therefore scriptable.

If you don't see your favorite application in the list, alas, it's probably not scriptable. To make certain, click the Browse button and select the application in question.

After you select an application and click Choose, the AppleScript Editor displays that application's AppleScript Dictionary. An application's dictionary lists all the features of that application that are scriptable.

Scriptable features are divided into categories, called *Suites,* which you can see on the left side of the AppleScript Dictionary. Every Mac application is supposed to support the Standard Suite, which lists common terms that most applications should support.

**Figure 2-4:**
Viewing the
AppleScript
Dictionary
within the
AppleScript
Editor.

Click an item in the Suite on the left side of the Dictionary to view detailed
information about its capabilities, as shown in Figure 2-5.

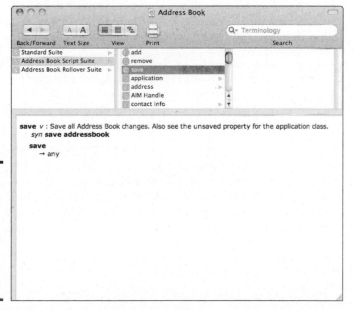

**Figure 2-5:**
Click an
item in a
Suite to
view details
about its
capabilities
and syntax.

By surveying the various Suites of an application, you begin to see what
tasks you can automate. The Finder, with its huge AppleScript Dictionary,
is perhaps the most scriptable of all applications (followed closely by
mammoths like FileMaker Pro).

## *Anatomy of a simple script*

Although a full discussion of AppleScript programming is beyond the scope of this book — after all, we have other things to talk about, too — that doesn't mean that you can't produce some quick and useful scripts. Most AppleScripts begin with a command that addresses the application that you want to automate. Enter this command into a new AppleScript document, which you create by pressing ⌘+N.

```
tell application "Finder"
```

This is like saying, "Hey, Finder, listen up! I'm going to send commands your way!" The double quotation marks surround the application name that you're addressing in the command.

Similarly, after you finish instructing the Finder what tasks you want performed, you must also tell it to stop listening. As such, typical scripts end with

```
end tell
```

With the shell of a script in place, all you have to do is add commands between the `tell` and `end tell` commands of the script. If you want your script to force an application to the foreground, an `activate` command is usually the first line within the shell of your script.

```
tell application "Finder"
  activate
end tell
```

Believe it or not, this is technically a complete and valid script! It doesn't do much, though, so add some more functionality to make it accomplish something worthwhile. For example, suppose you want to perform some housekeeping chores each time you log in to your MacBook. Some desirable tasks might include

✦ Emptying the Trash

✦ Having your laptop say "Hello!" to you

(Okay, I'll grant that hearing your MacBook say "Hello!" isn't a housekeeping chore, but it makes the whole script that much more fun — and really impresses your visitors, too. No one ever said programming had to be boring!)

To add these functions, you can do so by using a language you already know: English. As I mention earlier, Apple tries (and sometimes succeeds) to make AppleScript as English-like as possible. That way, you don't have to know some silly computer language; just use your native tongue. For example, to empty the Trash, tell the Finder to do so.

```
empty trash
```

The trickiest line of code might be the speech, and that's only because you need to remember to add quotation marks. AppleScript thinks that anything without quotation marks is an AppleScript command.

```
say "Hello!"
```

The result is a super-simple script that anyone can read but that performs two powerful functions. The completed script looks like this:

```
tell app "Finder"
  activate
  empty trash
  say "Hello!"
end tell
```

After you complete the script, choose File➪Save to save your script. Because you want the script to execute and then quit, use the File Format field to save it as an Application. Also, make sure that the Stay Open check box and the Startup Screen check box are deselected. And don't forget to name your script in the Save As text field.

To have the script automatically run each time you log in to your MacBook, save the script anywhere you wish. (Assign its location in the Where field of the Save window.) Open System Preferences by clicking its icon in the Dock; then click the Accounts icon. Make sure that your account is selected and then click Login Items. Click the Add button (which proudly bears a plus sign) and navigate to your script in the Open dialog that appears. After you click the Add button of the Open dialog, you see the script in the Login Items window.

# 1 Summon Automator — the Silicon Programmer!

Okay, perhaps I've watched too much "Iron Chef" over the years. Anyway, Snow Leopard features *Automator* (as shown in Figure 2-6) — he's your own personal robotic AppleScript assistant. In fact, Automator can help you create custom applications that can handle your repetitive tasks. Again, you're creating *workflows* here, which are sequential (and repeatable) operations that are performed on the same files or data, and your Automator application can automatically launch whatever applications are necessary to get the job done.

Here's a great example: You work with a service bureau that sends you a CD every week with new product shots for your company's Marketing department. Unfortunately, these images are flat-out *huge* — taken with a 12-megapixel camera — and they're always in the wrong orientation. Before you move them to the Marketing folder on your server, you have to laboriously resize each image and rotate it, and then save the smaller version.

**Figure 2-6:**
Automator
is a dream
come true
for those
who hate
repetitive
tasks.

With Automator's help, you can build a custom application that automatically reads each image in the folder, resizes it, rotates it, and even generates a thumbnail image or prints the image, and then moves the massaged images to the proper folder. You'd normally have to manually launch Preview to perform the image operations and then use a Finder window to move the new files to the right location. But now, with Automator, double-clicking your custom application icon does the trick.

You'll find Automator in your Applications folder. Currently, Automator can handle specific tasks within about 60 applications (including the Finder), but both Apple and third-party developers are busy adding new Automator task support to all sorts of new and existing applications.

To create a simple application using Automator, follow these steps:

1. **Select Custom and click Choose.**

2. **Click the desired application in the Library list.**

   Automator displays the actions available within that application.

3. **Drag the desired action from the Library pane to the workflow pane.**

4. **Modify any specific settings provided for the action you chose.**

5. **Repeat Steps 1–3 to complete the workflow.**

6. **Click Run (upper right) to test your script.**

Use sample files (copies) while you're fine-tuning your application lest you accidentally do something deleterious to an original (and irreplaceable) file!

Figure 2-7 illustrates an application that will take care of the earlier example — resizing and rotating a folder full of images, and then moving them to the Pictures folder.

**Figure 2-7:** Now I'm ready to handle 10 or 1,000 images in a folder — my application does the work!

7. **When the application is working as you like, press ⌘+Shift+S to save it.**

8. **In the Save dialog that appears, type a name for your new application.**

9. **Click the Where pop-up menu and specify a location where the file should be saved.**

10. **Click Save.**

To find all the actions of a certain type within the Library list, click in the Search box at the bottom of the Library pane and type in a keyword, such as **save** or **burn**. You don't even need to press Return!

## Help Is at Your Fingertips

If you want to explore AppleScript further, you have many resources on hand. Sometimes the easiest way to use AppleScript is to copy existing scripts and modify them as necessary; other times, it's a good idea to read the documentation included in Apple's Help system. Whichever approach you use, with a little practice and guidance, you'll soon be doing stupendous tasks with your MacBook.

## Built-in AppleScript Help

The most readily available AppleScript reference is built into Mac OS X. From within Automator, choose Help⇨Automator Help to launch the Automator Help Guide, or choose Help⇨AppleScript Help from the AppleScript Editor. The latter is a great place to begin your AppleScript exploration. It includes detailed documentation about the AppleScript language and loads of demonstration scripts for you to try (or alter) yourself.

## AppleScript on the Web

In addition to the built-in AppleScript help in the Finder, the Internet has much to offer in the way of AppleScript training and examples. As are so many other excellent Web resources, AppleScripts are free!

Not all AppleScripts are created equal: When downloading scripts from the Internet, make sure that they're compatible with Snow Leopard (Mac OS X v. 10.6).

### Apple Computer

The first place on the Web that you should visit for AppleScript help is the Source of All That Is Good, also called the Mother Ship: Apple Computer. Although the built-in OS X help offers a lot, the Apple Web site offers even more scripts, tutorials, and general AppleScript goodness. You can even find a list of all known scriptable applications, which can save you from searching for them with Script Editor. Furthermore, the site maintains an extensive list of links to other useful AppleScript sites.

```
www.apple.com/applescript
```

### Automator World

Automator World devotes its site to all Macintosh scripting. Because AppleScript is such a huge part of scripting the Mac OS, you can be certain that there's something here for you. Besides offering up-to-date news on Automator scripting for the Mac OS, Automator World also gives you access to many scripts, information about scripting books, and details on AppleScripts with interfaces. The sheer volume of information at this site makes it one you shouldn't skip.

```
automatorworld.com
```

# Chapter 3: Writing and Conversing with Your MacBook

## In This Chapter

- ✔ Using handwriting recognition to control Mac OS X
- ✔ Speaking to your MacBook
- ✔ Having your laptop speak back
- ✔ Using VoiceOver to provide feedback in Snow Leopard

If you're a hunt-and-peck typist — leaving you certain that there *must* be some better way to get information into your computer — you'll be happy to know that Apple has you in mind. Since the very first Mac rolled off the assembly line, Apple has had a keen interest in alternative modes of interaction between human and machine. Mac OS X continues in this tradition of alternative computer controls, offering two options for controlling Mac OS X without the keyboard: handwriting and speech.

- ✦ **Handwriting:** By using a pen and computer tablet, you can enter text into your MacBook by simply writing as you would on a sheet of paper.

- ✦ **Speech:** Talk to your MacBook to make it listen and obey your commands. It even talks back!

This chapter guides you through the various options that you have for controlling your laptop without using the keyboard. First, I cover the Mac OS X *Ink* feature, which you use to write on a tablet to enter data into your computer. (Although it sounds a bit ironic, think of Ink as your "digital paper" for the new millennium.) Whatever you write on the tablet appears on the screen as text.

I also give you a look at the more space-age speech capabilities available to you in Mac OS X. With your voice, you can command a Macintosh to perform all sorts of interesting feats. And just so you don't get lonely, the MacBook even talks back to you. (Now you can control your computer just as Spock from "Star Trek" could!) And Snow Leopard's VoiceOver feature makes it easy for your MacBook to read aloud all sorts of text, including Web pages, Mail messages, and word processing documents.

So scoot away from your computer, lean that chair back, and let your laptop take care of the rest.

# Using Ink with a Tablet

Typing on a keyboard can be a tedious and error-prone experience for even the best typists. To help out, Apple added some useful handwriting features to Mac OS X. Based in part on some of Apple's handheld software for the *Newton* (one of the first personal digital assistants [PDAs] and a product released before its time), the handwriting recognition in Mac OS X gives you the ability to write text on a compatible tablet for use in your favorite applications.

The basic process of working with handwriting on Mac OS X goes like this:

*1.* **Attach a tablet to your MacBook.**

   Most tablets use a Universal Serial Bus (USB) connection, so connecting one to your computer is as simple as plugging in the cable from your tablet to a USB port on your MacBook.

*2.* **Write on the tablet with the stylus that accompanies it.**

   A *stylus* is the name given the fake "pen" that accompanies most tablets. A stylus doesn't have any ink in it: It's just a pen-shaped tool with a plastic tip meant for writing on a tablet.

*3.* **Your MacBook interprets your handwriting.**

   After your laptop recognizes the handwriting, it sends that text to the foremost application at the cursor location where you would normally type with the keyboard. You're spared the whole training bit, too.

You aren't restricted to writing just text on the tablet, naturally. You can use it to control the interface of your MacBook as you would a mouse. A tablet also works great for graphics applications, such as Corel Painter and Adobe Photoshop. Many artists are frustrated when drawing with a mouse; when you use a tablet, though, you can feel right at home with the natural pen or brush movements that you've always used, and you can vary the pressure on the pad to control the density and spread of a stroke.

Although Snow Leopard takes care of handwriting recognition, it does offer you a few settings in the Ink pane within System Preferences. To view the System Preferences, click the System Preferences icon in the Dock. From there, click the Ink icon to adjust settings for your tablet.

If you don't have a tablet connected to your MacBook, you can't view the System Preferences pane for Ink. Mac OS X is smart enough to show you only the settings for your current hardware setup.

# Computer, Can You Hear Me?

Remember that classic scene from the movie *Star Trek IV: The Voyage Home* in which Scotty picks up the mouse on a Macintosh and tries to talk directly to the computer? Since the very early days of the Mac OS, Apple has included some form of speech recognition in its computers. Snow Leopard continues to improve on speech recognition by offering a host of tools that let you get more work done in a shorter amount of time. (We're not to that point yet, Scotty, but we're working on it.)

The Speech Recognition features of Mac OS X let you speak a word, phrase, or sentence. After you've spoken, your MacBook goes to work translating what you said — and if it understands the phrase, it then performs an action associated with that phrase. The great part about this system is that you can say any phrase in continuous speech and have your MacBook perform any sort of action that you can imagine. In fact, you aren't limited to just one action: You can perform dozens of actions upon speaking a particular phrase.

Before you get started using Speech Recognition, you need a microphone to get sound into your MacBook. All current MacBook models have a built-in microphone.

If you're looking for the best quality audio input for use with iChat or GarageBand, check out a microphone with a USB connection. You'll get far better sound quality than a microphone that connects to your analog jack.

## The Speech Recognition tab

To get started with Speech Recognition in Mac OS X, open the System Preferences window by clicking its icon in the Dock and then clicking the Speech icon. This brings up the Speech pane, as shown in Figure 3-1.

You'll find that two tabs comprise the speech settings of Mac OS X:

✦ **Speech Recognition**

✦ **Text to Speech**

In this section, I'm concerned only with the Speech Recognition tab. Later, in the "Your Mac Talks Back!" section, I explore the Text to Speech tab.

Esc

**Figure 3-1:**
Hail and
well met,
good
Speech
pane (and
Feedback
window)!

The Speech Recognition pane contains two tabs:

✦ **Settings:** The Settings pane provides a number of settings that control how your MacBook listens to Its Master's Voice. (Meaning you, friend reader.) From here, you can set the sound input, adjust the key on the keyboard that toggles speech recognition on and off, change microphone settings, and name your computer with a keyword. (You *do* want to call your computer by name as any techno-wizard does, don't you?)

✦ **Commands:** When Speech Recognition is active, your MacBook can understand any number of commands. From the Commands tab, you tell the laptop what type of command it should expect you to give. You can also specify whether you'll be giving the commands word for word or your MacBook should be prepared to interpret paraphrasing. A number of specific applications and menus can be configured with speakable items, such as contact names within Snow Leopard's Address Book.

Crowning the Speech Recognition pane are the Speakable Items On and Off radio buttons. You've probably already guessed how to use 'em to switch Speech Recognition features on and off.

When you select the On radio button, the small circular Speech Recognition Feedback window appears on your screen, floating above all other windows. Know this face well because the Feedback window (also shown in Figure 3-1) is your friend and partner. If you use Speech Recognition often, it'll become a constant companion on your Desktop. (More on it in the next section.)

### The Settings pane

At the bottom of the Settings pane is the Upon Recognition section. When your MacBook comprehends one of your stentorian commands, you can set it to respond by playing a sound, speaking a confirmation, or both. This is helpful when you're not sure whether your MacBook understands you. One hundred percent recognition isn't a reality on any computer at this point, so sometimes it helps to have any feedback you can get. Otherwise, you might feel silly shouting at your machine while it sits there doing nothing. (Or perhaps not, if you're into really inexpensive anger management.)

You can choose between two styles of listening with the Listening Method options:

✦ **Listen Only While Key Is Pressed:** Speech Recognition works only while the designated key is held down.

✦ **Listen Continuously with Keyword:** When you speak the keyword, listening turns on and remains on.

To change what key must be toggled or held down, click the Change Key button.

Why change the keyword? Instead of saying, "Computer, empty the Trash!" you might prefer, "Elrond, empty the Trash!" This adds a little bit of personality to the interaction and also gives your computer a slightly longer time to react to your command. (As a general rule, the longer the spoken phrase, the more likely your MacBook will understand it.) If you select the Listen Continuously with Keyword feature, you can change your computer's name via the Keyword text box.

Finally, you can select the microphone that you want to use from the Microphone pop-up menu on the Settings pane — a great feature if you have more than one microphone connected to your MacBook. Click the Calibrate key to adjust the sound volume for better recognition.

### The Commands pane

When Speech Recognition is active, your Mac listens for whatever phrases appear in your Speakable Items folder (a directory on your hard drive that holds a number of scripts). The Commands pane (shown in Figure 3-2) allows you to view the contents of this folder. When you speak a phrase that matches one of these filenames, your Mac automatically executes that script. The script can perform any number of actions, which is what makes Speech Recognition so powerful. Apple includes a large number of scripts with Mac OS X, but you're free to create your own, too.

**Figure 3-2:**
The
Commands
pane
allows you
to specify
which
commands
your Mac
should hear.

To make something speakable, select the item and then speak the command "Make this speakable." The new speakable command is based upon the item's name.

To view the contents of the Speakable Items folder, click the Open Speakable Items Folder button on the Commands pane. The Finder comes to the foreground and navigates to the folder that holds the scripts. This is handy because each item in the Speakable Items folder is speakable.

To the right of the Open Speakable Items Folder button is another button: Helpful Tips. Click it to get some pointers on how to get the best performance from your microphone.

As I mention in the preceding section, the Speech Recognition features of Mac OS X aren't restricted to items in the Speakable Items folder. Any application that supports Speech Recognition is also fair game for your verbal manipulation. To control commands within other applications, use the Commands pane (refer to Figure 3-2). Here you can select the following check boxes:

✦ **Address Book**

✦ **Global Speakable Items**

✦ **Application Specific Items**

✦ **Application Switching**

✦ **Front Window** (requires that you activate assistive devices in the Universal Access pane within System Preferences)

✦ **Menu Bar** (requires that you activate assistive devices in the Universal Access pane within System Preferences)

Mark any one of these options to allow your MacBook to listen to those kinds of commands.

## The Feedback window

After you activate Speech Recognition, you instantly see the Feedback window. You can click and drag the edge of the window to position it anywhere on your Desktop.

The Feedback window includes controls and displays of its own:

✦ **Microphone Level Meter:** The Feedback window displays indicators to let you know how loud the input to your microphone is.

✦ **Visual Indicator:** The Feedback window displays visual feedback to let you know what mode it is in: idle, listening, or hearing a command. When the microphone isn't grayed out but there are no arrows on either side of the microphone, you're in listening mode. When the microphone is flanked by animated arrows, your computer is hearing a command spoken. When Speech Recognition is idle, no arrows are present and the microphone is grayed out.

✦ **Quick-Access Menu:** You can quickly access the Speech preferences for the System or view the Speech Commands window. Just click the downward-pointing arrow at the bottom of the Feedback window, and a menu appears, giving you one-click access to both.

As soon as you disable speech recognition in the System Preferences, the Feedback window disappears.

## The Speech Command window

Because Speech Recognition might be listening for different sets of commands from the Finder or many other applications, Mac OS X provides you with a single listing of all commands that you might speak at any given time: the Speech Commands window. To open the Speech Commands window, click the triangle at the bottom of the Feedback window and choose Open Speech Commands Window from the menu that appears.

The Speech Commands window is a simple one, but it serves an important purpose: to let you know what commands Mac OS X understands. The Speech Commands pane, as shown in Figure 3-3, organizes commands into categories that match the settings in the Speech pane of the System Preferences.

If you launch another application that supports Speech Recognition, Mac OS X adds that application's commands to the Speech Commands window. Speak any of these commands to make your Mac execute that function. For example, Mac OS X ships with speech commands for Address Book, such as Mail To and Video Chat With.

**Figure 3-3:**
The Speech Commands window, hard at work.

If you launch another application that supports Speech Recognition, Mac OS X adds that application's commands to the Speech Commands window. Speak any of these commands to make your Mac execute that function. For example, Mac OS X ships with speech commands for Address Book, such as Mail To and Video Chat With.

*TIP*

Apple might be a big, serious, computer company — yeah, right — but it isn't without a humorous side! With Speech Recognition enabled, say the phrase, "Tell me a joke." Your MacBook replies with a random joke. Say it again, and your MacBook tells you another joke. (Brace yourself, these jokes were likely written by preschoolers . . . they're really, *really* bad.) Oh, and if you get a "Knock, Knock" joke, remember that you have to actually say, "Who's there?"

# *Your Mac Talks Back!*

Mac OS X is great at listening to your speech, but the fun doesn't stop there . . . your MacBook can talk to you, too! By using one of the many available voices — including the default Snow Leopard voice, *Alex* — you can make your computer talk or even sing. (Not as well as Sinatra, but better than Bob Dylan.) And although Speech Recognition lets you speak to your laptop, the VoiceOver feature gives your MacBook the ability to speak text. This is an especially useful feature because it lets you listen to your e-mails, Web pages, or even your homework — sometimes the eyes need a break. The text-to-speech capability gives you the opportunity to lean back in your chair or even get up and walk around while still using your computer.

Text-to-speech settings appear in three places within System Preferences: our old friend, the Speech pane; the Date & Time pane; and the VoiceOver settings within the Universal Access pane.

## The Text to Speech panel

The text-to-speech engine that comes with Snow Leopard has a collection of many different voices from which to choose; some voices are male, some are female, and some aren't human at all. To select your MacBook's voice in Mac OS X, follow these steps:

1. **Click the System Preferences icon in the Dock.**

2. **Click the Speech icon.**

3. **Click the Text to Speech tab, as shown in Figure 3-4.**

**Figure 3-4:** You can select your Mac's voice from the Text to Speech pane.

4. **Click the System Voice pop-up menu to choose a voice for your MacBook.**

   To hear the voice, click Play; Snow Leopard speaks a sentence as a demonstration. To the left of the Play button is a slider for adjusting the speed of the speech. Move the slider to the right to increase the speed at which your MacBook speaks and to the left to slow it down.

Naturally, Alex receives the most attention these days, because he's the default voice for Snow Leopard . . . and Alex definitely provides the most natural-sounding tone and best pacing of the bunch. However, I also think that the old-school voices, like Bruce and Vicki, are still quite intelligible. (I'm a Vicki kinda guy myself.)

### Talking alerts

After you select a voice, you have a variety of ways to make your laptop speak automatically to you, based on some simple rules. For example, every Mac owner has run into an Alert dialog. (*Alert dialogs* are typically accompanied by a select group of words — better left unspoken — from the human behind the keyboard.) An Alert dialog usually displays some kind of icon from the following list:

✦ **Stop sign:** Indicates that something particularly important requires your attention — usually an error or a dire warning.

✦ **Yield sign:** Signals that you should proceed cautiously; not as severe as the Stop sign, but important nonetheless.

✦ **Notification:** Looks like the profile of a person speaking; displays an informative message, but not a warning. You could use this feature, for example, to have a calendar application alert you when you have a meeting or a deadline.

From the Text to Speech pane, you can choose to have your MacBook speak a specific phrase or the contents of the Alert dialog by selecting one of the check boxes at the middle of the pane. If you select the Announce When Alerts Are Displayed check box, click the Set Alert Options button to set alert-specific options:

✦ **Voice:** Choose the voice that should speak alerts. (By default, it's the voice you chose earlier.)

✦ **Phrase:** Click this pop-up menu to choose a "prefix" phrase that's spoken before the actual alert text. By default, Snow Leopard speaks the name of the application that displayed the alert, but you can also choose a phrase from the list or choose to mix up the phrases for a little variety. To add or remove phrases, click the Edit Phrases item.

✦ **Delay:** Drag this slider to control the increment of time that Snow Leopard allows to pass before it speaks.

To hear what your spoken alert settings sound like in use, click the Play button.

If you click the Play button on the Set Alert Options sheet and don't hear anything right away, remember that it doesn't begin speaking until the time has elapsed that you set with the Delay slider. To hear the spoken alerts speak as soon as you click the Play button, move the slider to 0 (zero).

### Other spoken items

In addition to spoken alerts, you can allow your Mac to speak when other actions occur. Again, these settings are found on the Text to Speech pane. Your MacBook can speak in the following circumstances:

✦ **Announce when an application requires your attention:** In case you have your Dock hidden from view, it's not always clear when an application needs your attention. In these instances, Mac OS X grabs your attention via speech.

✦ **Read a selection of text when you press a particular key:** If you have a child who's learning to read, the MacBook can help him or her by reading a selection of text. Kids can figure out how to drag and select text often more quickly than they can read that text.

✦ **Announce the time:** Are you like me, constantly getting lost in time while immersed in your work? (Not to mention your favorite game.) I've set my MacBook Pro to announce the hour, which always keeps my time sense firmly planted.

## The Date & Time pane

There you are, deep in concentration as you finish up the final chapter of your Great American Novel, when you glance at the clock in the Finder menu bar and realize that you were *supposed* to pick up your kids at soccer practice a full hour ago!

You can avoid this shameful lapse of parental responsibility by turning on Snow Leopard's automatic spoken time feature, which is controlled from the Date & Time pane within System Preferences (and is much more effective than a mechanical cuckoo clock). But why go to all the trouble of clicking Show All when you can just click the Open Date & Time Preferences button on the Text to Speech pane? Snow Leopard immediately switches to display the Date & Time pane. You can even click the Clock on the Finder menu bar and click Open Date & Time. (Again, it's all about the convenience when it comes to the geniuses at Apple.)

From the Date & Time pane, click the Clock tab and select the Announce the Time check box to enable your MacBook to speak the time; then use the Period pop-up menu to choose spoken time at the quarter, half, or full hour. You can also customize the voice for spoken time as well.

After you're done, zip back to the Speech pane by clicking the Back button at the top-left corner of the System Preferences window.

## Configuring VoiceOver within the Universal Access pane

With Snow Leopard's VoiceOver utility, your MacBook can provide you with all sorts of verbal feedback, creating a spoken English interface with Snow Leopard — a valuable addition to the operating system for the physically impaired. The feedback includes

✦ **Announcing when certain keys are pressed:** Snow Leopard can tell you when a modifier key (such as Control, Option, or ⌘) is pressed or when the Caps Lock key is pressed.

✦ **Announcing cursor movements:** You hear an audible alert when your mouse cursor switches between windows or when you've clicked a menu.

✦ **Announcing the position of the VoiceOver cursor:** VoiceOver can audibly identify all operating system controls (such as buttons, sliders, and list boxes) by using a special on-screen cursor.

✦ **Reading documents, Web pages, and Mail messages:** VoiceOver can read aloud the contents of all sorts of documents and application windows.

✦ **Speaking the characters you type:** You can set VoiceOver to speak every character or each word you type.

Here is how to enable VoiceOver (or to launch the VoiceOver utility, as shown in Figure 3-5):

**Figure 3-5:**
You can customize the VoiceOver audible feedback with the VoiceOver Utility.

1. **Click the Open Universal Access Preferences button on the Text to Speech pane.**

2. **Select the On radio button (or press ⌘+F5) to enable VoiceOver. (If you're using a current MacBook, MacBook Air or MacBook Pro, or a newer Mac desktop keyboard, press ⌘+Fn+F5 instead.)**

   To customize how VoiceOver operates, click the Open VoiceOver Utility button.

## Speaking text through applications

Although VoiceOver provides a comprehensive text-to-speech interface for Mac OS X, it might be more than you need. If you simply want to hear text spoken within your applications, a number of alternative methods are included in Snow Leopard that don't require VoiceOver.

One of the simplest ways to hear spoken text in Mac OS X is by using the TextEdit application. *TextEdit* is a simple text processor that accompanies every copy of Mac OS X. Besides its handy word processing features,

TextEdit can also speak text. This is good for reviewing a document after you've written it by listening to it. To hear spoken text with TextEdit, follow these steps:

1. **Launch TextEdit from the Applications folder.**

   To open the Applications folder, choose Go⇨Applications from the Finder. In the window that appears, double-click the TextEdit application.

   This launches the TextEdit application and opens a new document.

2. **Enter some text.**

   Either type some text on the keyboard or paste some into the document from the Clipboard. Here's an example:

   ```
   Billy Gates has lots of cash
   Lots of cash
   Lots of cash
   Billy Gates has lots of cash
   I'd like $10 please!
   ```

3. **Choose Edit⇨Speech⇨Start Speaking.**

   Your MacBook begins speaking the text from the document. The speech engine has some intelligence, so you can enter dollar amounts (such as $25,423.12) or Roman numerals (such as Chapter XIV), and the speech engine reads them back in plain English. The result of these two strings would be "twenty-five thousand, four-hundred twenty-three dollars, and twelve cents" and "chapter fourteen."

4. **Choose Edit⇨Speech⇨Stop Speaking.**

   Your MacBook stops speaking. It also stops speaking when it reaches the end of the text.

## Speaking text through services

You can also speak text within most applications by using the Services menu, located under the application's named menu. To speak text from an application, first select that text. Then, choose Application⇨Services⇨ Speech⇨Start Speaking to speak text from many applications (where *Application* is the name of the currently running application). If you don't want to use VoiceOver, this works great for doing things like

✦ **Speaking a Web page aloud**

✦ **Reading your e-mail**

✦ **Listening to a speech you've written in Pages**

As you might expect, choosing Application⇨Services⇨Speech⇨Stop Speaking ceases the banter emanating from your MacBook's speaker.

Alas, not all applications are created equal. Some applications can't access the Services offered in the Services menu. If you don't see Speech in the list of services, you're out of luck.

# Index

## • A •

AAC (Advanced Audio Coding) format, 310, 413–414
About Me page, 419
About This Mac dialog, 102
Abstract folder, Desktop preferences, 209
AC outlet, 30
accessory mouse, tablet, 633
account image, iChat, 522
account keychains, 279–282
Account tab, MobileMe preferences, 243
accounts
  Apple Mail, 499–503, 517
  clean, 176, 180
  file sharing, 585–587
  iChat, 522
  iTunes Store, 331
  MobileMe, 60
  passwords, 60
  vanilla, 176, 180
Accounts pane, Mail preferences, 500
Accounts pane, System Preferences
  adding user accounts, 270–272
  Automatic Login, configuring, 263–264, 266, 279
  deleting user accounts, 273–274
  editing user accounts, 272–273

Guest account, enabling, 263, 269
  Login Items settings, 179–180, 214, 267
  overview, 250–252
Acrobat Portable Document Format (PDF), 51–52
Acrobat printer driver, 657
Action menu, 90, 193
activate command, 720
activation hot corner, 226
Active Screen Corners, 229
Activity Monitor, 148–150
Ad Hoc wireless network, 600, 605–608
Add Account assistant, Address Book, 141
Address Book
  accessing through Spotlight, 116
  adding iChat buddies, 526
  contact cards, arranging, 139–140
  contact information, entering, 135–137
  contact information, using, 137–139
  network directories, using, 140–141
  overview, 41, 133–134
  printing contacts, 142
  vCards, 143
Address box, Safari, 543
address cards, 134–136
Adjust Image dialog, iWeb, 424
Administrator account, 262

Adobe Acrobat Portable Document Format (PDF), 51–52
Adobe Acrobat printer driver, 657
Adobe Photoshop, 667–668
Adobe Photoshop Elements, 668
ADSL (Asynchronous Digital Subscriber Line) modems, 611
Advanced Audio Coding (AAC) format, 310, 413–414
Advanced Bluetooth settings, System preferences, 249
Advanced FireWire and AirPort network settings, System preferences, 247–248
Advanced Modem network settings pane, System Preferences, 246–247
Advanced Network pane, System Preferences, 245–246
Advanced pane, Finder Preferences dialog, 205–206
AIFF format, 310
AirPort Base Station, 601, 608–609
AirPort Express Base Station, 327
AirPort Extreme, 19, 602, 607

AirPort Extreme Base
Station, 614, 621
AirPort network settings,
System Preferences,
247–248
AirPort status menu bar
icon, 106–107
AirTunes, 327
album artwork, 320–321
albums, iPhoto, 337–339,
349–351
Alert dialogs, 733–734
alerts, spoken, 733–734
aliases, 76–77, 98
aligning cell text, Numbers,
467–469
analog connection, 491–492
Angle control, DVD Player,
439
animating, 227, 389–390
Announce the Time feature,
253
Announce When Alerts are
Displayed feature,
256, 734
antivirus software, 178,
563–564
appearance, Mac OS X,
48–52
Appearance pane, System
Preferences, 100, 212,
223–225
Apple Computer Web site,
724
Apple dealer, 176
Apple Lossless format, 310
Apple Mail
adding accounts, 500–502
adding contacts to
Address Book, 136
attachments, 514–515
customizing, 516–517
deleting accounts, 503
editing existing accounts,
503

junk mail, 513–514
overview, 40, 497–499
reading and deleting
messages, 504–505
replying to mail, 505–508
rules, 517–519
sending e-mail, 509–512
Apple menu, 61–63, 98–103
Apple MobileMe, 60
Apple Remote, 16, 81,
129–130
Apple TV, 314
Apple Web site, 170, 183
Apple Web site link, Help
Viewer, 168
AppleCare, 11
AppleScript
automation, 711–713
Automator, 721–723
help, 723–724
overview, 711
programming, 718–721
scripts, 713–718
applets, 218
applications. *See also*
programs; specific
applications by name;
third-party applications
adding to Dock, 215–216
built-in, 40–41
choosing with which to
launch file, 96–97
deleting, 145–146
help system within, 171
icons, 74
Parental Controls, 277
RAM, 637
speaking text through,
736–737
tracker, 295
Applications command, Go
menu, 105
Aqua user interface, 50–51
Arrange track, GarageBand,
408–409

Arrow Buttons control,
DVD Player, 437
Artist lessons, 414
artwork, album, 320–321
ascii command, 592
aspect ratio, 15, 347, 358,
383–384
Asynchronous Digital
Subscriber Line (ADSL)
modems, 611
attachments, Apple Mail,
506, 512, 514–515
audio
digital, playing in iTunes,
312–316
DVD Player, 439, 441
external connections, 18
formats, 310–311, 429–430
importing to iMovie,
364–367
Keynote, adding in, 482
MP3 players, 636
overview, 16, 635
QuickTime Player,
recording in, 434
subwoofer speaker
systems, 635–636
Web pages, adding to, 425
Audio Adjustments
window, iMovie,
366–367
audio CDs, 110, 301,
311–312, 328, 365, 415
audio chat, 527–528
Audio Equalizer, DVD
Player, 439
Audio jacks, MacBook, 22
Audio pane, iDVD, 386–387
Audio well, My Slideshow
window, 386
audiobooks, 311
autocompletion, UNIX
command, 698–699
AutoFill button, Safari, 545

automated telephone operators, 301

Automatic Login, 263–264, 266, 279

automatic spell-checking, 457

automation, 379–380, 391–394, 516, 692, 711–713

Automator, AppleScript, 721–723

Automator World Web site, 724

AV connectors, 628

AVCHD format, 362

away mode, iChat, 525

## • *B* •

Back button
  Finder window toolbar, 192
  Safari, 544
  Setup Assistant, 60

Back command, Go menu, 104

Back to My Mac tab, MobileMe preferences, 244

background
  Desktop, 207–210, 225
  DVD Menu, 389–390
  iChat, 529, 532–533

background music
  DVD Menu, 386
  slideshow, 352

background objects, Pages, 455

Background options, View Options dialog, 200

background shape
  Keynote, 482–483
  Pages, 457

backing up, 58, 161–163, 176, 329

backlit keyboard, 22, 24, 238

Backup folder, iDisk, 538

bash shell, 698

battery, 25, 35–37

battery compartment, 17

Battery Power tab, Energy Saver preferences, 237

BBEdit utility, 674–675

Bcc (Blind Carbon Copy), 510–511

Belkin USB Bluetooth adapter, 680

bin command, 592

binary, 300

bit rate, 323

Black & White folder, Desktop preferences, 209

blank disks, 42

Blank page, 419

Blind Carbon Copy (Bcc), 510–511

blocking
  iChat buddies, 532
  incoming connections, firewall, 233

Blog page, 419

Bluetooth
  iSync, 684–685
  overview, 20, 603, 679–680
  Snow Leopard, 681–683
  wireless keyboards and mice, 683–684
  wireless printing, 685–686

Bluetooth File Exchange, 682

Bluetooth pane, System Preferences, 107, 239, 248–249

Bluetooth Setup Assistant, 249, 681

Blu-Ray recorders, 634–635

Bonjour messaging, 522

Book mode, iPhoto, 349–351

bookmarks, 440, 542, 548–550

Boolean, 119

Boot Camp, 41, 670

booting from CD/DVD, 164

Brightness slider, Displays preferences, 236

broadband connection, 490, 492

Browse mode, iTunes, 315

browser. *See* Safari

Browser toolbar, iMovie, 359

browsing iTunes Library, 314–315

buddies, iChat, 525–526

Buddy List window, iChat, 522–524

buffer, internal, 634

Bug button, Safari, 546

built-in applications, 40–41. *See also* specific applications by name

bulleted lists, 506

burning
  audio CDs from GarageBand, 415
  CDs from iTunes, 328
  data CD, 111
  DVDs from iDVD, 378, 394

burn-proof technology, 635

bus speed, 640

buttons
  adding to Web pages, 426
  captions, DVD, 388
  changing colors, 212
  DVD menu, 377
  programmable keyboard, 630

# • C •

cable Internet connection, 177, 492

cable modem, 611

cable router, 614–615, 617–621

cables
connecting, 31–32
network, 572–573
overview, 43

cache, cleaning Safari, 555

cal command, 702

calendar, UNIX command, 703–704

calibrating
battery, 37
monitor, 236

calling rates, local, 490

camcorder videos, mini-DV, 361

camcorders, DV, 627–628

Camera Import window, iMovie, 360, 362

cameras, 17, 125–128, 626–627

carbon copies (CC), 510

cardboard boxes, 31

cards, contact, 134–136

care, MacBook, 34–37

case, laptop, 293

Category 5 (Cat5) cable, 572

Category 5 Enhanced (Cat5E) cable, 573

CC (carbon copies), 510

cd ... command, 695, 700

CD audio format, 310

cd command, 592, 694–695, 697, 700

CD window, 110

CD/DVD Sharing feature, 27–28

CD-ROM, launching programs from, 81

CDs
adding audio to movies, 365
backups, 163
binary, 301
booting from, 164
burning, 111, 277, 328, 415
importing photos to iPhoto, 336
listening to, 110
ripping tracks, 321–322

CDs & DVDs group, System Preferences, 235

cells, spreadsheet, 461, 465–466

Cells Inspector, 467–468

central processing unit (CPU), 19, 149–150

chapter navigation, DVD, 437

charts, Numbers, 472–474

chat program. *See* iChat

Checkmark keyword, iPhoto, 343–344

Chess game, 41, 676–677

chord mode, GarageBand, 398

Cisco Web site, 605

clean account, 176, 180

Clean Up command, 197–198

cleanliness, 35

client/server application, 591

Clipboard, pasting from in Pages, 453

clips, video, 361–363, 367–370

Clock, 107–108, 253, 735

closed captioning, DVD Player, 439, 442

closed networks, 608

collections
bookmark, 549
font, 110

collisions, 602

color depth, scanner, 629

Color menu, Stickies application, 213

color options, Numbers, 469–470

Color tab, Displays preferences, 236

color-coding files, 93

colors
background, 210
changing, 212
iChat, 528
text, in Apple Mail, 506, 512

ColorSync profile, 236

column view, configuring, 202–203

columns
Numbers spreadsheet, 470
Spaces desktop, 230

command line tool, 690–691

commands, Terminal, 694–695

commands, UNIX
autocompletion, 698–699
calendar, 703–704
escape characters, 698
finding files, 706
help, 698
overview, 696
pipes, 706
processes, 704–705
quotation marks, 697–698
structure of, 696–697

Commands pane, System Preferences, 255, 728, 729–731

comments
AppleScript, 718
Microsoft Word, 289
Spotlight, 95

Compare Documents feature, Microsoft Word, 289

compiled script, 713

composing, with GarageBand, 398–411

Computer command, Go menu, 104

computer mini-vacuum, 35

Computer Sleep slider, Energy Saver preferences, 237

computer-to-computer network, 600, 606

Concatenated RAID Set, 159

configuration
iChat, 522–524
login screen, 263–265
network, 574, 576, 583
view modes, 197–204

confirmation dialog, 90

Connect to Server dialog, 587, 590

Connection Doctor, iChat, 530

connections, Internet, 491–495

connectivity, verifying network, 580–582

contact cards, Address Book, arranging, 139–140

contact information, Address Book, 135–139

content searching, 196

Content tab, Parental Controls preferences, 275

Content window, Safari, 543

contextual menus, 72

controller, DVD Player, 436–437, 439–440

conventions used in book, 3–4

cookies, 554–555

cooling, 29

cooling pad, 37

copying, 453, 701–702

cordless stylus, 633

Core Animation, 52

cover, treatment of, 34

Cover Flow, 204, 314

cp command, 697, 701

CPU (central processing unit), 19, 149–150

CPU History window, 150

CPU Usage window, 150

crashes, 52–54

cropping, 346–348, 369–370

crossover cables, 573

curl command, 708–710

custom folder icons, 75–76

custom modes, iChat, 525

Custom Thumbnails, 389

Customize Toolbar dialog, 194

customizing
Apple Mail, 516–517
Dock, 214–218
Finder toolbar, 192–194
Spotlight, 121–123

cutting, in Pages, 452

**• D •**

daisy-chaining, 652

damage, checking for, 30

Darwin, 53–54

Dashboard, 40, 218–220, 228

data CD, 111, 328

data DVD, 328

data file, antivirus, 178

Date & Time group, System Preferences, 107, 252–253, 735

date command, 703

Dates settings, Language & Text preferences, 231

dead pixels, 33

dealers, Apple, 176, 183

defragmenting hard drive, 164

deleting
Apple Mail accounts, 503
Apple Mail messages, 504–505, 516
applications, 145–146
clips from movies, 368
Dock items, 216
items, 91
iWeb pages, 421
photos from Photo Booth filmstrip, 128
photos in iPhoto, 339
print jobs, 660
protecting files from, 288
rows and columns, in Numbers, 470
songs in iTunes, 315–316
Stickies, 214
system processes, 149
UNIX file, 701–702
user accounts, 273–274

demilitarized zone (DMZ), 591

Description field, Mail preferences, 502

Desktop, 89, 207–220, 225

Desktop & Screen Saver pane, System Preferences, 180, 208–211, 225–226

Desktop command, Go menu, 104

Desktop Pictures folder, Desktop preferences, 208

desktop publishing. *See* Pages

destination drive, formatting, 59

Device listing, Bluetooth preferences, 248

devices, network, 570

Devices heading, iTunes, 313

DHCP (Dynamic Host Configuration Protocol), 577, 620

dial-up connection, 491–492, 615–616

Dictionary, AppleScript, 718–719

Dictionary protocol, 710

Dictionary widget, 15

digital, defined, 300–301

digital audio and video, in iTunes, 312–316

digital cameras, 626–627

digital extraction, 321

digital fingerprints, 301

digital hub. *See also* specific digital hub programs by name
digital, defined, 300–301
digitizing, 301–302
interoperability of, 307
overview, 299–300
software, 302–306

digital still mode, 628

digital subscriber line (DSL), 492, 611, 614–615, 617–621

digital video (DV), 301, 668–669

digital zoom, 627

digitizing, 301–302

dimensions, image, 384

directory, 699

disc image, 391

Disc Setup settings, DVD Player Preferences, 441

disc slot, 15–16

disclosure triangles, 421

disconnecting, from AirPort network, 609

discoverable mode, Bluetooth printer, 686

disk errors, eliminating, 58

disk image, 153, 161

disk optimization, 666

disk repair utilities, 154, 666

Disk Space bar graph, iDisk, 536

Disk Utility
displaying disk information, 151–152
Erase controls, 154–156
First Aid pane, 153–154
overview, 151, 666
partitioning, 156–158
RAID, 158–159
troubleshooting, 178

disks, 42, 154, 155, 158–159

Display Calibrator, 236

display messages, 4

Display options, DVD Player preferences, 442

Displays pane, System Preferences, 105, 235–236

DMZ (demilitarized zone), 591

DNS servers, 577

DNS tab, System Preferences, 246–247

.doc extension, 96

Dock
Apple menu options, 100
CPU usage, monitoring, 150
customizing, 214–218
displaying new emails in, 504
Downloads folder, 550
overview, 51
Parental Controls, setting, 278
restoring windows, 68

switching programs from, 82

Dock group, System Preferences, 226–228

document. *See also* Pages
creating new UNIX, 707–708
multiuser, 284–285
opening, 84–85
protection, Office 2008, 290
saving, 86
sharing, 283–290
sharing features, Office 2008, 289

documentation, application, 146

Documents command, Go menu, 105

Documents folder, iDisk, 538

Documents Stack, Dock, 217

domain name service, 491

dongles, 651

dotted notation, 575

double-click speed, 239

Download Stack, Dock, 217

downloading files, with Safari, 550–551

downloads, 31, 160, 563, 564

Downloads folder, 550

Drafts folder, Mail, 498, 512

drag and drop process, 89–91

drawing tablets, 633–634

Drive Eject key, 63

drivers, 165, 177, 654

Drop Box permission, 285

drop zones, 382

DSL (digital subscriber line), 492, 611, 614–615, 617–621

dumb terminals, 274
duplicating items, 90
DV (digital video), 301,
    668–669
DV camcorders, 627–628
DV format, 362
DV Widescreen format, 362
DVD Map, iDVD, 377
DVD Menu background,
    iDVD, 387–390
DVD Player
  controller, 436–437,
    439–440
  hardware, 435
  overview, 41, 435–436
  Preferences, 440–443
  Viewer, 438
DVD recorders, 634–635
DVD Studio Pro, 668
DVD-R/CD-RW SuperDrive,
    19
DVD-ROM, 81, 435
DVD RW SuperDrive, 634
DVDs. *See also* DVD Player;
    iDVD
  backups, 163
  booting from, 164
  burning, 277
  digitizing, 302
  Front Row, 129
  mastering, 668
DVI connector, 18
Dynamic Host
    Configuration Protocol
    (DHCP), 577, 620

● *E* ●

Edit mode, iPhoto
  adjusting photo
    properties manually,
    349
  cropping, 346–348
  effects, 349
  enhancing images, 348
  overview, 346
  removing red-eye, 348–349
  retouching, 349
  rotating photos, 346
  straightening, 348
editing
  Address Book contact
    cards, 136
  Apple Mail accounts, 503
  drop zones, iDVD, 378, 382
  iWeb page, 421–426
  Keynote slide text, 481
  Numbers data, 466–467
  Sharing preferences, 249
  text, in Pages, 451
  text files, 109
  user accounts, 272–273
  video clips, 369–370
Editing toolbar, iMovie, 360
Editor application,
    AppleScript, 714
effects
  camcorder, 628
  iPhoto, 349
  Photo Booth, 127
EIDE drives, 645
802.11 wireless standard,
    600, 607
802.11a wireless standard,
    603
802.11b wireless standard,
    601–602
802.11g wireless standard,
    602
802.11n wireless standard,
    602
802.1X tab, Advanced
    Network preferences,
    246
Eject control, DVD Player,
    437

ejecting
  discs, 164
  external devices, 653
  removable volumes, 108
Electric Guitar tracks, 401
electricity, static, 647
e-mail. *See also* Apple Mail
  announcing new
    MobileMe Gallery, 353
  within iChat, 529
  sending from Address
    Book, 138
  sending photos through,
    354–355
  sending Web page
    content, 553
  sharing Pages documents,
    459
  Spotlight searches for, 116
  viruses in attachments,
    563–564
e-mail accounts, ISP, 490
embedded Comments, 289
EMC Retrospect
    application, 163
Empty Trash command, 92
emptying Trash, 91–92, 205
Enclosing Folder command,
    Go menu, 104
encryption, 293–294, 554,
    605, 607–608
end tell command, 720
Energy Saver group, System
    Preferences, 236–237
energy saving techniques,
    36
enhancing images, iPhoto,
    348
Enter control, DVD Player,
    437
Entourage, 665
entry-level laptop, 21–22
Equalizer, iTunes, 322–323

Erase controls, Disk Utility, 154–156

escape characters, 697–698

Ethernet
802.11b, 601–602
802.11g, 602
802.11n, 602
Bluetooth, 603
hardware, 494–495
jacks, 30
NICs, 571
overview, 601
port, 18, 32
shared Internet connection, 616
standards, 571
wired, 619–620

Ethernet network settings, System Preferences, 245–246

Event pane, iMovie, 360, 367–368

Events, iPhoto, 337, 340–341

Excel, Microsoft, 665

Exchange 2007 network directories, 141

executing scripts, 714–715

expandability, MacBook, 11

expansion, hardware, 11

exporting
contacts, 138
movies, 372
Pages documents, 459

Exposé & Spaces group, System Preferences, 228–230

Exposé feature, 69, 82–83, 215

ExpressCard slot, 18, 23

extensions, displaying, 95–96

external audio connections, 18

external drives, 642–643

external modem, 493

external USB optical drive, 27

external video connections, 18

extraction, digital, 321

## • F •

Facebook, 354

Faces, iPhoto, 341–342

fan view, Stacks, 216

Fast Forward button, QuickTime Player, 431

Fast User Switching, 63, 265, 284

Favorite frames, iMovie, 368

faxes, 136, 241–242, 656, 660

Feedback window, 731

file attachments, viruses in, 563–564

file management
aliases, creating, 98
Apple menu, 98–103
burning data CD, 111
color-coding, 93
copying files and folders, 89–90
deleting items, 91
duplicating items, 90
editing text files, 109
emptying Trash, 91–92
Finder, 87–88
Go menu, 104–105
Info dialog, 93–97
listening to audio CD, 110
menu bar, 105–108
moving files and folders, 89–90

opening text files, 109
overview, 87
printing, 111–113
recovering items from Trash, 92
renaming items, 93
Services, 103–104

File menu
Address Book, 139, 140
Duplicate option, 90
Make Alias option, 98
Open option, 84–85
Save option, 86

file selection controls, Aqua, 50

file servers, 537, 585

file sharing, 585–590

File Sharing, Spotlight searches, 121

File Transfer Protocol. *See* FTP

file-level sharing features, Office 2008, 289–290

FileMaker Pro, 672

files. *See also* file management
adding to Dock, 215
aliases, 98
color-coding, 93
copying, 89–90
extensions, 95–96
icons, 74–75
locking, 97
moving, 89–90
organizing, 190
protecting from deleting, 288
renaming, 93
restoring with Time Machine, 161–163
sending through iChat, 531

Spotlight Comments, 95
Spotlight searches for, 116–118
UNIX, 699–702
FileVault feature, 272, 293–294
FileVault tab, Security preferences, 232–233
Fill function, Numbers, 469–470
Fill option, Desktop preferences, 209
filmstrip, Photo Booth, 128
filtered heading, 506
filters, search, 120
Final Cut Pro, 373, 669
find command, 706
Find dialog, 195–197
Finder
  automating tasks with AppleScript, 711–712
  icon, 88
  opening new windows, 65
  overview, 87–88, 187
  restarting, 101–102
  setting preferences, 204–206
  toolbar, 191–197
  view modes, 188–191, 197–204
Finder menu, 36, 169
finding files, UNIX, 706. *See also* searching
fingerprints, digital, 301
firewall, 250, 515, 561–562, 593–595, 662
Firewall tab, Security preferences, 233
FireWire, 649–654
FireWire 400 port, 21
FireWire 800, 651
FireWire 800 port, 23
FireWire drive, 643, 645

FireWire network settings, System Preferences, 247–248
FireWire port, 17
FireWire-equipped mini-DV camcorder videos, 361
First Aid pane, Disk Utility, 153–154
flags, 696
flash settings, 627
flatbed scanner, 628
Flickr, 354
Floating CPU window, 150
floating objects, 455
floppy drive, external USB, 634
folders
  color-coding, 93
  copying, 89–90
  deleting applications, 145–146
  icons, 75–76
  iDisk, 538–539
  Mail, 498–499
  moving, 89–90
  organizing files into, 190
  renaming, 93
  restoring with Time Machine, 161–163
  Spotlight searches for, 116–118
  Unix paths, 699
Font Book, 110
fonts, 213, 481, 506, 512, 528
food, 35
footprint, 10
force feedback joystick, 632
Force Quit, 100–102
Format Bar
  Keynote, 479, 481
  Numbers, 465
  Pages, 451, 453
Format Menu
  Keynote, 481
  Pages, 454

formats
  audio, 310
  number, in Numbers spreadsheet, 467
Formats tab, Language & Text preferences, 231
formatting
  Keynote slide text, 481
  text, in Pages, 453–454
Formula Box, Numbers, 464, 471
formulas, Numbers, 471–472
Forward button
  Finder window toolbar, 192
  Safari, 545
Forward command, Go menu, 104
forwards, e-mail, 508, 519
frames, 572
Free Positioning, 383
FreeBSD kernel, 54
Front Row, 40, 129–131
FTP (File Transfer Protocol)
  built-in, 591
  networking with Terminal, 708–709
  overview, 576, 589–591
  servers, publishing Web sites to, 427
  from Terminal, 592–593
ftp command, 592
full screen display, iPhoto, 335
Full Screen mode
  DVD Player, 438, 442
  iTunes, 329

● **G** ●

GadgetTrak MacTrak application, 295
games, 41–42, 56, 676–678

GarageBand
  adding tracks, 399–402
  adjusting settings for
    track, 409–411
  Arrange track, 408–409
  loops, 402–408
  Magic GarageBand,
    411–413
  overview, 303, 306, 395
  sharing songs and
    podcasts, 413–415
gateway, default, 575
General Information pane
  Info dialog, 94–95
  Mail preferences, 501–502
General pane
  Finder Preferences dialog,
    204–205
  Security preferences, 232
generic file icons, 74
Genius button, iTunes, 317
Genius Sidebar, iTunes, 331
get command, 592
Get Info button, iPhoto, 335
Get Mail button, Mail, 503
Gibson Research
    Corporation, 562
Gigabit Ethernet, 21, 571
Go menu, 104–105
Google box, Safari, 544, 546
Google Maps, 343
Grab Service, 103
Graphic Inspector, 469–470
graphics, iTunes, 329–330
graphics boxes, 451–452,
    479–480
graphics card, replacing, 11
graphics engine, Quartz
    Extreme, 51–52
grid, iPhoto, 347–348
Grid Spacing slider, View
    Options dialog, 199
grid view, 216, 314

Group Chat window,
    527–528
Group column, Address
    Book, 134
groups, contact, 139–140
Groups folder, iDisk, 538
guaranteed lock, 284
Guest account, 263, 269

• *H* •

hackers, 558, 560, 604
handling, MacBook, 34–37
handwriting features,
    725–726
hard drive
  adding, 11
  backing up, 161–163
  capacity, 11
  defragmenting, 164
  iDisk, 55–56
  importing images to
    movies, 363
  importing photos to
    iPhoto, 336
  launching programs from,
    80–81
  levelness, 35
  overview, 19
  solid-state drive, 26
  upgrading, 641–647
Hardcopy Cable
    Replacement Protocol
    (HCRP), 686
hardware
  AirPort, 609
  audio, 635–636
  digital cameras, 626–627
  DV camcorders, 627–628
  DVD, 435
  expansion, 11, 30
  icons, 72–73
  input devices, 629–634

Internet sharing, 614–616,
    618–620
  Mac OS X requirements,
    57
  network, troubleshooting,
    582
  overview, 625–626
  removable volumes, 108
  scanners, 628–629
  sound, replacing, 11
  storage, 634–635
  System Profiler, 147–148
Hardware heading, System
    Profiler, 147
Hardware section, System
    Preferences
  CDs & DVDs group, 235
  Displays group, 235–236
  Energy Saver group,
    236–237
  Keyboard group, 238–239
  Mouse group, 239
  Printing & Fax group,
    240–242
  Sound group, 242–243
  Trackpad group, 240
HCRP (Hardcopy Cable
    Replacement Protocol),
    686
HDV (high-definition video)
    format, 362
headphone jacks,
    subwoofer, 635
headphones, 16, 18
Hearing tab, Universal
    Access preferences,
    259
heat, 29, 37
help
  Apple Web site, 170
  AppleScript, 723–724
  within applications, 171

Help Viewer window, 167–168

local Mac outlets and user groups, 173

Mac publications and resource sites, 172

overview, 167

searching, 169–170

UNIX commands, 698

voice technical support, 172

Help Viewer, 167–168, 182

hidden state, 251

hiding

Dock, 100, 228

extensions, 96

Finder status bar, 191–192

Finder toolbar, 191

High Definition settings, DVD Player Preferences, 443

high-definition video (HDV) format, 362

highlighting, 77–78, 289

History, Safari, 551, 555–556

Hold icon, Print Queue window, 660

Home button, Safari, 543, 545

Home command, Go menu, 104

Home folder, 586

home page, 138, 547–548

hot computers, 562

Hot Corners, 226, 292

hot-swappability, 650

.htm extension, 96

.html extension, 96

hubs, 652

hyperlinks, 425–426

HyperText Transfer Protocol (HTTP), 576

## • I •

iBook, 14

iCal, 116, 303

iChat

buddies, 138, 525–526

changing modes in, 524–525

chat process, 527–530

configuring, 522–524

iChat Theater, 530–531

ignoring people, 532

overview, 40, 521

sending files, 531

setting Parental Controls, 276

sharing screens, 530–531

transcript feature, 119

visual effects, 532–533

iChat Theater, 530–531

icon view, configuring, 197–200

icons

aliases, 76–77

Dock, 100–101

files, 74–75

Finder, 88

folders, 75–76

hardware, 72–73

menu bar, 105–107

overview, 72

programs and applications, 74

selecting multiple, 78

selecting single, 77–78

size options, 199, 201

used in book, 6

IDC (Insidious Data Creep), 641

identifying information, laptop, 291–292

identity theft, 558

iDisk, 55–56, 104, 244, 535–540

iDVD

adding movies, 381–384

animating DVD Menu background, 389–390

automation, 379–380, 391–394

burning to DVD, 394

creating new project, 379

DVD Menu background, 387–388

Magic iDVD, 379–380, 392–394

Movie buttons, 388–389

music, 386–387

OneStep DVD, 379, 391–392

opening existing project, 379

overview, 303, 306, 375–378, 668

previewing, 390–391

slideshow, 385–386

theme, 380–381

titles, 388

IEEE (Institute of Electrical and Electronics Engineers), 600

ignoring people, on iChat, 532

iLife '09 suite, 39, 56. *See also* specific iLife applications by name

iMac, 10, 23–24

image, Buddy List window, 522

image editing application, 667–668

image stabilization, 628

images. *See* iPhoto; photos

iMovie
    adding clips, 367–368
    editing clips, 369–370
    importing items to,
        361–367
    moviemaking process,
        360–361
    overview, 128–129,
        303–306, 357–360, 668
    removing clips, 368–369
    reordering clips, 369
    sharing finished movie,
        372–373
    titles, 370–372
    transitions, 370
Import Video mode,
    iMovies, 128
importing
    contact information to
        Address Book, 137
    images to iPhoto, 335–337
    to iMovie, 361–367
    vCards to Address Book,
        143
Inbox folder, Mail, 498
included software, 39–40,
    56
indicator light, iSight
    camera, 126
Info dialog
    choosing application with
        which to launch file,
        96–97
    displaying extensions,
        95–96
    icon information, 72–73
    iTunes, 319–320
    locking files, 97
    Open With options, 96–97
    overview, 93–95
    renaming items, 93
    setting permissions, 286
    Spotlight comments,
        adding, 95
    viewing specifics, 93–95

infrared receiver controls,
    232
infrastructure mode, 600
inline objects, 455–456
input devices, 629–634
Input Sources tab,
    Language & Text
    preferences, 231
Input tab, Sound
    preferences, 243
Input Volume slider, Sound
    preferences, 243
inserting rows and
    columns, Numbers, 470
Insidious Data Creep (IDC),
    641
Inspector, iWeb, 426–427
Inspector button
    iDVD, 377
    iMovie, 366
    iWeb, 422–423
Installation disc, Mac OS X,
    rebooting with, 181
Installed Updates tab,
    Software Update
    preferences, 254
installing upgrades,
    646–647
instant messaging. See
    iChat
Institute of Electrical and
    Electronics Engineers
    (IEEE), 600
Intego NetBarrier X5, 562
Intego VirusBarrier X5, 178,
    564, 666
Intel processors, 19, 24
Intel-based Mac laptops, 14
internal buffer, 634
internal devices, 18–20
internal drives, 644
internal Mac OS X firewall,
    562
internal modem, 493

Internet. *See also* Internet
    sharing; specific
    Internet applications
    by name
    accessing through DVD,
        441
    AppleScript help on, 724
    applications, 56
    connecting cables, 32
    IP addresses, 575–576
    ISP, 489–491
    LDAP directories based
        on, 141
    Mac OS X, 55–56
    newsgroups, 172
    overview, 489
    protocols, 56
    security, 557–565
    Services, 103
    setting up connection,
        493–495
    software, 40
    troubleshooting, 179
    types of connections,
        491–492
Internet & Network section,
    System Preferences,
    243–250
Internet Assigned Numbers
    Authority, 575
Internet media tool,
    QuickTime as, 429
Internet radio, streaming,
    311, 323–325
Internet service provider
    (ISP), 489–491
Internet sharing
    connecting, 617–620
    hardware for, 614–616
    network address
        translation, 612–614
    overview, 577, 611–612
    software for, 616–617
    wireless support, adding,
        620–621

interoperability, of digital hub, 307
invitations, chat, 527–528
invoice, 31
IP address, 574–575, 578–580, 612–613
IP button, Printer Browser, 656
IP printers, 658
iPhoto
  Book mode, 349–351
  dimensions, changing image, 384
  Edit mode, 346–349
  e-mail, sending photos through, 354–355
  Front Row, 129
  importing images, 335–337
  MobileMe Gallery, 352–354
  movies, adding images to, 363–364
  organize mode, 337–346
  overview, 302–304, 333–335
  podcast artwork tracks, creating, 401
iPhoto albums, Desktop preferences, 209
iPod, 304, 326, 636
iSight camera, 17, 24, 125–129, 362
ISP (Internet service provider), 489–491
iSync, 303, 684–685
iTunes
  audio, adding to movies, 364
  audio CD, playing, 311–312
  burning CDs, 328
  digital audio and video, playing, 312–316
  Equalizer, 322–323
  Front Row, 129
  GarageBand projects, 413–415

iPod, 326
iTunes Store, 330–331
listening to CD, 110
overview, 302–304, 309
playlists, 316–318
Radio, 323–326
ripping audio files, 321–322
sharing media across network, 327
sharing movies on, 372
song information, 318–321
supported audio formats, 310–311
visuals, 329–330
iTunes Store, 304–305, 330–331
iWeb
  adding new page, 421
  adding new site, 420–421
  editing page, 421–426
  Inspector, 426–427
  overview, 303, 306, 417–418
  planning pages, 419–420
  publishing site, 427–428
  sending GarageBand projects to, 415
  sending photos from iPhoto to, 346
  sending podcasts to, 415
  sharing Pages documents, 459
iWork, 56, 459, 665

**• J •**

Job Info icon, Print Queue window, 660
joysticks, 632
.jpeg extension, 96
.jpg extension, 96
Junk folder, Mail, 499
junk mail, in Apple Mail, 513–514, 516

**• K •**

kernel panic, 182
.key extension, 96
Key Repeat Rate slider, Keyboard preferences, 238
keyboard
  backlit, 22, 24
  checking function of, 34
  cleaning, 35
  cost, 630
  Dashboard key, 218–219
  deleting items with, 91
  external, 30, 37
  features, 630
  overview, 15, 630
  UNIX, 689–692
  use of, 35
  wireless, 683–684
Keyboard group, System Preferences, 238–239
keyboard shortcuts
  Exposé preferences, 229
  Front Row, 131
  iTunes, 312
  iTunes Visualizer, 330
  Keynote, 484
  Numbers, 465–466
  overview, 79–80
  QuickTime Player, 433
  Spaces preferences, 230
Keyboard Shortcuts tab, Keyboard preferences, 238–239
Keyboard tab
  Keyboard preferences, 238
  Universal Access preferences, 259
keyboard window, musical typing, 400
Keychain Access application, 279–282
keychains, 279–282

Keynote
  background shape,
    482–483
  creating new project,
    476–477
  graphics boxes, 479–480
  media, 482
  opening presentation, 477
  overview, 475, 478–479
  presenter's notes, 482
  printing slides and notes,
    484–486
  saving presentation, 477
  slide text, 481
  slides, adding, 479
  slideshow, creating,
    483–484
  text boxes, 479–480
Keynote Preferences
    window, 484
keypad, numeric, 630
keywords, iPhoto, 343–345
kill command, 704–705
kiosk mode, 442

● *L* ●

Labels pane, Finder
    Preferences dialog, 205
LAN (local area network),
    60, 492, 612
LAN party, 572
Language & Text group,
    System Preferences,
    230–231
Language options, DVD
    Player preferences, 441
laptop cooling pad, 37
laptop security
  case, 293
  encryption, 293–294
  Hot Corners, 292
  marking laptop, 291–292
  overview, 291

passwords, 292
security cable, 292–293
tracker applications, 295
unsecured wireless, 294
laptop shelves, 30
laptop sleeve, 35, 293
laptop stand, 37
launching programs, 80–81,
    702
layout options, Desktop
    preferences, 209, 225
Layout pane
  iWeb, 418
  Keynote, 478
  Pages, 450
lcd command, 592
LCD screens, 15
LDAP (Lightweight
    Directory Access
    Protocol) directories,
    141
LEAP (Lightweight
    Extensible
    Authentication
    Protocol), 605–606
Learn to Play, 414
LED screens, 15
less command, 706
levelness, 35
Library, iTunes, 312–316
Library folder, iDisk, 538
Library heading, iTunes,
    313–314
lighting, 30
lights, external device, 653
Lightweight Directory
    Access Protocol
    (LDAP) directories, 141
Lightweight Extensible
    Authentication
    Protocol (LEAP),
    605–606
Line In jack, 18
Line Out jack, 16

Line Printer Remote (LPR),
    616
link lights, 571
links, Web, 425–426
list login, 263–264, 266
list view, 200–202, 314
The List Web site, 491
Listening Method options,
    Speech preferences,
    729
listening to audio CD, 110
lists, bulleted, 506
local area network (LAN),
    60, 492, 612
local calling rates, 490
local folders, publishing
    Web sites to, 428
local Mac outlets and user
    groups, 173
location
  MacBook, 29–30
  network, 102–103, 244–245
lock, guaranteed, 284
lock slots, 43
locking files, 97, 288
lockups, 52–54
Log Out command, 63
logical errors, 666
Login Items, 179–180,
    216, 267
Login Items tab, Accounts
    preferences, 214,
    251, 267
Login Options tab,
    Accounts preferences,
    251–252, 264–265
Login Password, 272
login screen, configuring,
    263–265
Logs tab, Parental Controls
    preferences, 276–277
Loop Browser, GarageBand,
    402–406

loops, GarageBand, 397, 402–408
LPR (Line Printer Remote), 616
ls command, 592, 694, 700

## • M •

Mac mini, 10
Mac OS X Snow Leopard
  appearance, 48–52
  Bluetooth, 681–683
  Dictionary widget, 15
  firewall, 562
  hardware requirements, 57
  included software, 56
  Installation disc, rebooting with, 181
  Internet, 55–56
  MacBook Air, 24
  multitasking/multithreading, 54–55
  overview, 47–48
  personalizing, 59–60
  stability of, 52–54
  updating, 160
  upgrading to, 58–59
Mac publications and resource sites, 172
MacBook. See also laptop security
  battery, 16
  manual, 31
  models, 21–28
  need for, 12–13
  overview, 1–6, 9–12
  parts of, 13–20
  setup, 29–37
  video card, 20
MacBook Air, 15–20, 23–28
MacBook Pro, 11, 15–16, 18–19, 22–23

MacConnection, 641
MacFixIt Web site, 172
MacGamer, 172
Macintosh user group, 173
MacLife magazine, 172
MacMall, 641
macro commands, 558
MacTrak application, GadgetTrak, 295
MacWarehouse, 641
Macworld magazine, 172
Magic GarageBand, 411–413
Magic iDVD, 379–380, 392–394
magnification, 100–101, 227
MagSafe connector, 16
Mail. See Apple Mail
Mail & iChat tab, Parental Controls preferences, 276
Mail Preferences dialog, 500–503, 508, 514
Mail Service, 103
Mailboxes list, Mail, 498
maintenance
  Activity Monitor, tracking performance with, 148–150
  backing up hard drive, 161–163
  defragmenting, 164
  deleting applications, 145–146
  Disk Utility, 151–159
  drivers, 165
  overview, 145
  special start-up keys, 164
  System Profiler, 147–148
  updating Mac OS X, 160
man command, 698
Manage Widgets dialog, 218
managed account, 216, 262, 274–279
manual, MacBook, 31

manual flash setting, 627
Map button, iDVD, 377
Maps, Google, 343
maps, iPhoto, 343
marking laptop, 291–292
marks, revision, 289
massive multiplayer online role-playing game (MMORPG), 677
Master Password, 272
measures mode, GarageBand, 398
media. See digital hub; specific media programs by name
Media Browser, 372, 423–424, 455–456, 482
Media button, iDVD Slideshow display, 385
media formats, 429–430
media items, DVD menu, 377
Media pane, iDVD, 376
media player. See QuickTime Player
megapixels, 626
memory card, 627
memory module notches, 647
memory slots, 647
menu bar, 105–108
menu bar icon, Buddy List window, 524
menu commands, 3
Menu control, DVD Player, 437
Menu display, iDVD, 376
Menu titles, DVD, 388
menus
  changing colors, 212
  deleting items with, 91
  overview, 71–72
  Web site, 422
Merge button, iPhoto, 341

Message list, Apple Mail, 497

messages, e-mail. *See* Apple Mail

Messenger, Microsoft, 666

metadata, 117

mget command, 592

mice, 633, 683–684

Micromat TechTool Pro, 666–667

microphone, 365–366, 727, 729

Microphone Level Meter, Feedback window, 731

Microsoft Office 2008, 288–290, 664–666

MIDI (Musical Instrument Digital Interface) instruments, 411

MIME (Multipurpose Internet Mail Extensions), 508

mini-DV camcorder videos, 361

Mini-DVI port, 21

Minimize control, QuickTime Player, 431

minimizing windows, 67–68, 227

mini-vacuum, 35

Mirrored RAID Set, 159

mirrors, 537

MLC Radio, 324–325

MMORPG (massive multiplayer online role-playing game), 677

MobileMe account, 60, 427, 499, 536

MobileMe Gallery, 352–354, 372

MobileMe group, System Preferences, 243–244

mobility, need for, 10–11

models, MacBook, 21–28

modem, 106, 493, 615–616

Modem network settings, System Preferences, 246–247

modifier keys, 259

Monitor, iMovie, 359

Motion button, iDVD, 377, 382

mounting, 107–108

mouse, 633, 683–684

Mouse & Trackpad tab, Universal Access preferences, 260

Mouse group, System Preferences, 239

mouse shortcut settings, 229–230

MOV format, 362

Movie buttons, iDVD, 381–383, 388–389

movie formats, 429–430

Movie Inspector, QuickTime Player, 433

Movie page, 419

Movie tracks, 401, 405

movies, 129, 310, 425, 482. *See also* iMovie; QuickTime Player

Movies folder, iDisk, 538

MP3 CD, 328

MP3 files and ringtones, 413–414

MP3 format, 310, 321–322

MP3 players, 636

MPEG-2 format, 362

MPEG-4 format, 362

mput command, 592

multimedia. *See* digital hub; specific media programs by name

multiple icons, selecting, 78

Multipurpose Internet Mail Extensions (MIME), 508

multitasking, 54–55

multithreading, 54–55

Multi-Touch, 64

multiuser documents, 284–285

multiuser systems
  adding new user account, 270–272
  deleting existing account, 273–274
  editing existing account, 272–273
  keychains, 279–282
  Login Items, 267
  login screen, configuring, 263–265
  overview, 261–263, 269
  security, 266, 274–279
  sharing documents, 283–285

music, 129, 302, 352, 386–387. *See also* GarageBand; iTunes

Music folder, iDisk, 538

Music Library, iTunes, 312–316

Musical Instrument Digital Interface (MIDI) instruments, 411

musical typing keyboard window, 400

muting, 242, 407, 432, 530

mv command, 701–702

My Albums page, 419

My Slideshow window, 386

**• N •**

Name column, Address Book, 134

Name text box, Account preferences, 271

named menu, 103–104

names, printer, 662

narration, voiceover, 366

NAT (Network Address Translation), 562, 612–614
Nature folder, Desktop preferences, 208
NetBarrier X5, Intego, 562
NetInfo network, 141
Network Address Translation (NAT), 562, 612–614
Network command, Go menu, 104
network connection, 492
network directories, 140–141
Network heading, System Profiler, 147
network interface card (NIC), 570
Network pane, System Preferences, 106–107, 244–248, 576–580, 583
Network Utility, 580–581
networking, with Terminal, 708–710
networks
  accessing file shares on Windows computers, 589–590
  configuration, 574–576
  file sharing, 585–587
  firewall, using built-in, 593–595
  FTP, using to access files, 590–593
  locations, switching between, 102–103
  network sharing versus multiuser sharing, 283–285
  overview, 569, 585
  remote control, 595–597
  requirements, 569–573
  setting up, 573–574

sharing connected printer, 588
sharing files with Windows computers, 588–589
sharing media across with iTunes, 327
sharing printer across, 661–662
System Preferences, 576–580
troubleshooting, 582–583
verifying connectivity, 580–582
wireless, 599–609, 620–621
newsgroup posts, 565
newsgroups, Internet, 172
NIC (network interface card), 570
No Access permission, 285
Noise Reduction slider, Voiceover window, 366
Norton AntiVirus, Symantec, 564
Note menu, Stickies application, 213
Notes folder, Mail, 499
Notes pane, Keynote, 479, 482
Numbers
  aligning cell text, 467–469
  charts, 472–474
  creating new document, 462
  deleting rows and columns, 470
  editing data, 466–467
  entering data, 466–467
  formulas, 471–472
  inserting rows and columns, 470
  navigating cells, 465–466
  opening existing file, 462–463

overview, 461–462
saving work, 464
selecting cells, 465–466
selecting number format, 467
shading, 469–470
window, 464–465
Numbers settings, Language & Text preferences, 231
numeric keypad, 630

octets, 575, 578–579
Office 2008, 288–290, 664–666
offline mode, iChat, 524–525
OneStep DVD, 379, 391–392
online mode, iChat, 524
online security, 557–565
online storage. *See* iDisk
online stores, 565
online support site, 172
open command, 592, 702
Open dialog, 84–85, 449, 463, 477, 506
Open Dictionary dialog, 718–719
Open Stream dialog, 324–325
OpenGL graphics acceleration standard, 51–52
operand, 697
operating system. *See* Mac OS X Snow Leopard
optical audio Line In jack, 18
optical drive, 15, 19, 25, 27–28, 81
optical output, 18
optical trackball, 631
optical zoom, 627–628

organize mode, iPhoto
  albums, 337–339
  Events, 340–341
  Faces, 341–342
  keywords, 343–345
  overview, 337
  ratings, 345
  sorting images, 345–346
Outbox folder, Mail, 498
Outgoing Mail Server sheet,
    Mail preferences, 502
outlets
  electric, 29–30
  Mac, 173
Output tab, Sound
    preferences, 243
Output Volume slider,
    Sound preferences, 242

### • P •

packing materials, 31
Pages
  background shapes, 457
  copying text and images,
    453
  creating new document,
    447–448
  cutting, 452
  entering and editing text,
    451
  formatting text, 453–454
  opening existing
    document, 448–449
  overview, 447
  pasting from Clipboard,
    453
  photos, 455–456
  printing documents, 458
  saving work, 449
  sharing, 459
  spell-checking, 457
  tables, 454–455

text and graphics boxes,
    451–452
  window, 449–450
.pages extension, 96
painting tools, Photoshop,
    668
Parallels Desktop, 670–672
Parental Controls group,
    System Preferences,
    253–254, 274–278
partitions, 41, 151–152,
    156–158
parts, MacBook, 13–20
passthru port, 652
Password Assistant, 271
Password field, Mail
    preferences, 501
Password Hint text box,
    Account preferences,
    271
password hints, disabling,
    266
password protection, Office
    2008, 289–290
Password tab, Accounts
    preferences, 250–251
Password text box, Account
    preferences, 271
passwords
  account, 60
  account keychains,
    279–282
  iDisk, 537
  iTunes library, 327
  laptop, 292
  logging in, 263
  Login Password, 272
  Master Password, 272
  Parental Controls, 278
  selection of, 266
pasting, in Pages, 453
patch file, 148, 178
paths, UNIX file, 699–700
Pause button, iTunes, 312

Pause Printer icon, Print
    Queue window, 661
PDF (Portable Document
    Format), 51–52,
    142, 657
.pdf extension, 96
performance, tracking
    with Activity Monitor,
    148–150
permissions, 118, 154, 178,
    191–192, 285–288
Personal Information
    Manager (PIM), 137
personal information,
    sharing, 565
Personal section, System
    Preferences, 223–245
personalizing Mac OS
    X, 59–60. *See also*
    customizing
phishing, 559
photo books, 349–351
Photo Booth, 40, 126–128
Photo Booth effect, iChat,
    533
Photo Browser button,
    Mail, 507
photos. *See also* iPhoto;
    Photo Booth
  adding in Keynote, 482
  address card, 136
  for background, 210
  changing in iWeb, 423–424
  digitizing, 301
  DVD Menu backgrounds,
    387–388
  Front Row, 129
  importing to iMovie,
    363–364
  iWeb page, 423–425
  in Pages, 455–456
Photos page, 419
Photos tab, iDVD Slideshow
    display, 385

Photoshop, 667–668
Photoshop Elements, 668
physical errors, 666
physical memory, 639
physical network problems, 582–583
pico text editor, 707–708
Picture well, Accounts preferences, 251
Pictures folder, 209–210, 538
PIM (Personal Information Manager), 137
ping utility, 580–581
pipes, 706
pixels, 33, 626
Plants folder, Desktop preferences, 208
Player settings, DVD Player Preferences, 440–441
playhead, 360, 378, 397
playlists, iTunes, 314, 316–318
podcast artwork track, 397, 401
Podcast page, 419
podcasts, 129, 310. *See also* GarageBand
pointing devices, 66
Point-to-Point over Ethernet (PPoE) menu bar icon, 107
pop-up ads, in Safari, 556
portability, 10
Portable Document Format (PDF), 51–52, 142, 657
ports, 17–18, 21–23, 25, 651–654
Postscript Printer Description (PPD) file, 657–658
Power Adapter tab, Energy Saver preferences, 237
power button, 16, 32–33

power cable, 16, 31
power light, external device, 653
power supply, while upgrading to Mac OS X, 58–59
PowerBook, 14
PowerPoint, Microsoft, 666
PPD (Postscript Printer Description) file, 657–658
PPoE (Point-to-Point over Ethernet) menu bar icon, 107
PPP tab, Advanced Modem network preferences, 247
pre-emptive multitasking, 55
Preferences dialog
  DVD Player, 440–443
  Mail, 500–503, 508, 514
  Safari, 547–548, 550–552, 554–556
presentations. *See* Keynote
presenter's notes, Keynote, 482
pressure levels, tablet, 634
Preview application, 112
Preview box, Mail, 498
previews
  iDVD, 378, 390–391
  iMovie, 368
Previous Chapter control, DVD Player, 437
Previous Song button, iTunes, 312
Previously Viewed settings, DVD Player Preferences, 442–443
Print & Fax pane, System Preferences, 240–242, 658–659
Print button, Safari, 546

Print dialog, 112–113, 142, 553
print jobs, managing, 659–661
Print Queue window, 659–661
Print sheet
  Keynote, 485–486
  Pages, 458
printer
  cable/DSL routers, 616
  managing print jobs, 659–661
  non-USB, 657–659
  overview, 655
  Parental Controls, 277
  Printer Browser, 655–657
  sharing across network, 661–662
  sharing network, 588
Printer Browser, 655–657
printer driver, Adobe Acrobat, 657
printing
  Address Book contacts, 142
  Keynote slides and notes, 484–486
  overview, 111–113
  Pages documents, 458
  Web content, 553
  wireless, 685–686
Privacy tab, Spotlight preferences, 234
Private IP addresses, 575, 613
private networks, 578–579
privileges, 154, 286
processes, 149, 704–705
processor, 11, 19, 22, 24, 640
productivity suite, 41
programmable keyboard buttons, 630

programming, AppleScript, 718–721

programs. *See also* specific programs by name
icons, 74
launching, 80–81
quitting, 86
switching between, 82–84
UNIX, 707–710

Project Info dialog, iDVD, 391

project mode, GarageBand, 398

Project pane, iMovie, 360, 367–368

prompt, defined, 693–694

Protect Document dialog, Microsoft Word, 290

protocol, 56, 574

proxies, 246–247

ps command, 705

.psd extension, 96

Public folder, 538, 540, 586

Public IP address, 575, 613

public wireless network, 294

publications, Mac, 172

publishing iWeb site, 427–428

Purchased playlist, 331

put command, 592

### • *Q* •

Quartz Extreme graphics engine, 51–52

Quick Clicks, Help Viewer, 168

Quick Look, 75, 192–193

QuicKeys X3 utility, 673

QuickTime movies, 372–373

QuickTime Player, 429–434, 551

QuickTime X, 53

quit command, 593

quitting programs, 86

quotation marks, in UNIX commands, 697–698

### • *R* •

Radio, iTunes, 323–326

radio, streaming Internet, 311, 323–325

RAID, 158–159

random access memory (RAM), 22, 57, 637–641, 646–647

random order, displaying Desktop backgrounds in, 210, 226

ratings, iPhoto, 345

RDF Site Summary (RSS) feeds, 427, 548

Read & Write permission, 285

Read Only permission, 285

reading e-mail, 504–505

README file, 146

real instrument tracks, 400

REALbasic utility, 675–676

real-time scanning, 564

rebooting, 177, 181

Recent Folders command, Go menu, 105

Recent Items menu, 98–100

recharging battery, 36

recognition system, iPhoto, 341–342

recording
AppleScript Editor, 716–717
data CD, 111
QuickTime Player, 434
speed, 634
voiceover narration, 366

recovering items from Trash, 92

red-eye, removing, 348–349

regions, Arrange track, 408–409

Rehearsal feature, Keynote, 482

reinstalling Mac OS X, 181–182

Rejected frames, iMovie, 368

Reload button, Safari, 545

Remote, Apple, 16, 81, 129–130

remote control
of another computer, 597
of MacBook, 596
overview, 595
Screen Sharing, 595
UNIX, 692
VNC, 596–597

Remote Disc feature, 25

Remote Login feature, 284

removable volumes, 108, 563

repairs, 12

repeating GarageBand loops, 406–408

replying to e-mail, 505–508

resolution, 236, 626, 629

resources, 172, 182–183

restarting, 61–63, 177

Restore tab, Disk Utility, 161

restoring windows, 67–68

restraining cable, 43

Results window, Spotlight, 120–122

Resume icon, Print Queue window, 660

retouching photos, 349, 668

Retrospect application, EMC, 163

Return control, DVD Player, 439

Return to Beginning button, GarageBand, 397
Revert button, Disk Utility Partitions tab, 158
revision marks, 289
Rewind button, QuickTime Player, 431
ringtones, 311, 413–414
ripping audio files, iTunes, 321–322
rm command, 702
rmdir command, 702
Root account, 262, 286
root directory, 700
Rotate button
  iMovie, 369–370
  iPhoto, 346
  QuickTime Player, 432
rotating trackpad, 64
router, 575, 614–615, 617–621
rows
  Numbers spreadsheet, 470
  Spaces desktop, 230
Roxio Toast Titanium, 669–670
RSS (RDF Site Summary) feeds, 427, 548
RSS folder, Apple Mail, 499
rules, Apple Mail, 517–519
running programs, 80–81

### • S •

Safari
  bookmarks, 548–550
  downloading files, 550–551
  History, 551
  home page, setting up, 547–548
  navigating Web, 544–546
  overview, 40, 541–543
  Safari menu, 71

saving Web pages, 553
security, 554–556
subscriptions, 551
tabs, 552–553
visiting Web sites, 543–544
Samba (SMB), 576
SATA drive, external, 642
satellite connection, 492
Save As dialog, Numbers, 464
Save dialog, 86
Save Preferences pane, Microsoft Word, 289–290
saving
  document, 86
  before force quit, 102
  iDVD movie as disc image, 391
  Keynote presentation, 477
  Numbers spreadsheets, 464
  search criteria, 197
  System Preferences, 222
  Web pages, with Safari, 553
  work in Pages, 449
scanners, 628–629
scanning, real-time, 564
screen, 15
screen saver, 180, 211
Screen Saver tab, Desktop & Screen Saver preferences, 211, 226
Screen Sharing, 595–596
screen size, 11, 22, 24
screen wipes, 42
scripts, 713–718, 720–721
scroll wheel, trackball, 631
Scrolling Speed slider, Mouse preferences, 239
scrolling windows, 66–67
SD memory card slot, 18, 23

Search box
  Address Book, 138–139
  Finder window toolbar, 193
  GarageBand, 403
  iMovie, 365
  iPhoto, 335, 344–345
  Mail, 499
  Printer Browser, 657
  System Preferences, 223
Search function, iTunes, 315
Search in Google Service, 103
Search Results tab, Spotlight preferences, 234
searching
  from Find dialog, 195–197
  from Finder toolbar, 194–195
  help system, 169–170
  iTunes Library, 315
  Spotlight, 115–123
  System Preferences, 223
  Web, 40
Secure Empty Trash method, 92
secure site, 554
Secure Sockets Layer (SSL) connection, 294
security. *See also* laptop security
  account keychains, 279–282
  disk image, 153
  FileVault, 272
  locking files, 97
  multiuser systems, 266, 274–279
  online, 557–565
  restraining cable, 43
  Safari, 554–556

unsecured public network, 294

wireless networks, 603–606

security cable, 292–293

Security Options, Disk Utility Erase Tab, 156

Security pane, System Preferences, 232–234, 290, 293–294, 594

Seeing tab, Universal Access preferences, 258–259

selection box, 78

selection controls, Aqua, 50

selection handles, 456, 479–480

self-timer, 627

sending e-mail, 509–512

Sent folder, Mail, 498

serial ATA drives, 19, 645

Service Set Identifier (SSID), 600

Services, 103–104, 737–738

Settings pane, System Preferences, 255, 728–729

setup, MacBook, 29–37

Setup Assistant, 59–60

shading, Numbers spreadsheet, 469–470

shapes, adding to Web pages, 425

Shapes button, Pages, 457

Share feature, QuickTime Player, 432

Shared folder, 287–288, 586

Shared heading, iTunes, 313–314

shared optical drive, 27–28

sharing. *See also* file sharing; Internet sharing
documents, 283–290

finished movie, iMovie, 372–373

in GarageBand, 413–415

media across network with iTunes, 327

Pages, 459

printer across network, 588, 661–662

screens, with iChat, 530–531

Sharing & Permissions pane, 286–287

Sharing feature, CD/DVD, 27–28

Sharing pane, System Preferences, 121, 249–250, 595, 616–617, 661–662, 682–683

Sheet canvas, Numbers, 464

sheets, Aqua, 50

Sheets list, Numbers, 464

shells, 698–699

shelves, laptop, 30

shock-mounted external drives, 642

shortcuts. *See* keyboard shortcuts

shutdown, 61–63, 177

Sidebar, Finder, 191, 205

signature file, antivirus, 178

signatures, Apple Mail, 516–517

Simple Finder, 277–279

single icon, selecting, 77–78

single-pass scanning, 629

Site Organizer, iWeb, 418, 420–421

Site Publishing Settings screen, iWeb, 427

Sites folder, iDisk, 538

sleeping, 61–63

sleeve, laptop, 35, 293

slides, Keynote, 476–479, 481

slideshows
Front Row, 129
iDVD, 377, 385–386
iPhoto, 352
iWeb, 426
Keynote, creating, 483–484

Slow Motion control, DVD Player, 439

slow motion minimization, 67

Smart Album, 338

Smart Folder, 197

Smart Groups, 140

Smart Mailboxes, 500

smart playlist, 318

SMB (Samba), 576

Smith Micro Spring Cleaning application, 146, 641

SMS messages, iChat, 529

Snow Leopard. *See* Mac OS X Snow Leopard

software
Boot Camp, 41
built-in applications, 40–41
connecting to Internet, 40
digital hub, 302–306
included, 39–40
Internet sharing, 616–618, 620
must-have, 41–42
network, 576
overview, 39
troubleshooting, 178, 582

software firewall, 562

Software folder, iDisk, 539

Software heading, System Profiler, 148

software instrument tracks, 400–401

Software Update pane, System Preferences, 160, 254

Solid Colors folder, Desktop preferences, 209–210
solid-state drive, 19, 26–27
song information, 318–321. *See also* GarageBand; iTunes
Songwriting project, GarageBand, 400
sorting images, iPhoto, 345–346
Sound Check, iTunes, 328
sound effects, iMovie, 364–365
Sound Effects tab, Sound preferences, 242
Sound group, System Preferences, 242–243
Sound Volume menu bar icon, 106
sounds, Apple Mail, 516
soundtracks, movie, 405
Source list, 313, 334
space saving, 10
Spaces, 69, 83–84
speakers, 16, 25, 327, 635–636
special start-up keys, 164
Speech Commands window, 731–732
Speech feature, Mail, 505
Speech group, System Preferences, 254–256
speech recognition, 725, 727–732, 731
Speech Recognition tab, System Preferences, 255, 727–731
speed light, 572
spell-checking, 457, 508
Spotlight
    Address Book, 138
    comments, adding, 95
    customizing, 121–123

expanding search, 120–121
Finder window, 194–195
Help Viewer, 168–169
overview, 115–117
searching for application files for deleting, 146
special features of, 117–119
Spotlight menu, 116, 122
Spotlight pane, System Preferences, 121–123, 234
Spotlight Results window, 120–122
spreadsheets. *See* Numbers
Spring Cleaning application, Smith Micro, 146, 641
spring-loaded folders and windows, 205
SSID (Service Set Identifier), 600
SSL (Secure Sockets Layer) connection, 294
stability, of Mac OS X, 52–54
stabilization
    image, 628
    video, 129
Stacks, 215–217
standard user account, 262
standards, wireless networking, 601–603
start-up applications, 164
startup disk, 153, 256–257
start-up keys, special, 164
static electricity, 647
static IP address, 490
static volume, 108
stationery, 95, 511–512
stations, Internet radio, 323–324
statistics, Finder window status bar, 191

status bar, 191–192, 543
Step Button, DVD Player, 439
stereo mini-plug input jacks, subwoofer, 635
Stickies, 212–214
Sticky Keys, 259
still images. *See* iPhoto; photos
Stop button, Safari, 545
Stop control, DVD Player, 437
storage, online. *See* iDisk
storage capacity, MacBook Pro, 22
storage hardware, 634–635
Store heading, iTunes, 313
straightening photos, 348
straight-through cables, 573
streaming Internet radio, 311, 323–325
Stretch to fit Desktop option, Desktop preferences, 209
Striped RAID Set, 159
structure, UNIX command, 696–697
StuffIt utility, 673
Styles Drawer, Pages, 451
stylus, 633, 726
Subject field, New Message window, 511
submenu button, DVD menu, 377
subnet mask, 576
subscriptions, Safari, 551
Subtitle control, DVD Player, 439
subwoofer speaker systems, 635–636
sudo command, 701–702
Suites, 718–719
super-command, 690–691
SuperDrive, 27, 435, 634

Supply Levels icon, Print
Queue window, 661
surge protector, 30, 42
Switch Desktops button,
iChat, 530
switches, 570–572, 582–583,
615
Sync tab, MobileMe
preferences, 244
System Administrator,
262, 286
system boot menu, 164
System folder, 288
System Preferences
Accounts pane, 179–180,
214, 263–264, 266–267,
269–274, 279
Appearance pane, 100, 212
Bluetooth pane, 107, 681
Date & Time pane,
107, 735
Desktop & Screen Saver
pane, 179–180, 208–211
displaying, 221–222
Displays pane, 105
Hardware section,
235–243
Internet & Network
section, 243–250
Network pane, 106–107,
576–580, 583
overview, 221
Personal section, 223–234
Print & Fax pane, 240–242,
658–659
problems caused by
settings, 178
saving preferences, 222
searching, 223
Security pane, 293–294,
594
setting up Internet
connections, 493–494

Sharing pane, 121, 595,
616–617, 661–662,
682–683
Software Update pane, 160
Speech pane, 733
Speech Recognition tab,
727–731
Spotlight pane, 116–117,
121–123
System section, 250–260
Text to Speech panel,
733–735
Time Machine pane,
107, 161
Trackpad, 64
Universal Access pane,
735–736
System Profiler, 147–148,
181, 639–640
System section, System
Preferences, 250–260
System tab, Parental
Controls preferences,
275, 277
system voice, 733

• *T* •

Table Inspector, 454–455
tables, in Pages, 454–455
tablets, drawing, 633–634
tabs, Safari, 552–553
tagging, 341
Target Disk Mode, 164, 257
TCP/IP, 246, 574
tcsh shell, 698
technical support, 172, 490
TechTool Pro, 666–667
telephone jack, 30
telephone operators,
automated, 301
tell command, 720
Telnet, 576

temperature, 29
Template Chooser window,
447–448, 462–463, 476
templates, iWeb, 420–421
Tempo display,
GarageBand, 398
1080i video clips, 363
10/100 Ethernet, 571
10/100/1000 Ethernet, 571
Terminal, 88, 592–593,
693–696, 708–710
text
adding to Web pages, 425
aligning cell, in Numbers,
467–469
entering and editing in
Pages, 451
formatting, in Pages,
453–454
iWeb page, 422–423
Keynote slide, 481
text boxes, 451–452,
479–480
text editors, UNIX, 707
text file script, 714
text files, 109
Text Inspector, 468–469
Text to Speech panel,
System Preferences,
255–256, 733–735
TextEdit application, 109,
736–737
text-to-speech capability,
732–738
themes
DVD menu, 377
iDVD, 380–381
movie, 358–359
Web site, 426
third-party applications
digital video, 668–669
FileMaker Pro, 672
firewall settings, 233

games, 676–678
Office 2008, 664–666
overview, 663
Parallels Desktop, 670–672
Photoshop, 667–668
System Preferences
    additions, 222
TechTool Pro, 666–667
Toast, 669–670
utilities, 673–676
threads, 504
Thumbnail Resize slider,
    iPhoto, 335
thumbnails, DVD, 389
.tif extension, 96
.tiff extension, 96
tilde (~), 697
Tile option, Desktop
    preferences, 209
Time display, GarageBand,
    398
Time Limits tab, Parental
    Controls preferences,
    276
Time Machine, 161–163
Time Machine pane, System
    Preferences, 107,
    257–258
Time Zone tab, Date & Time
    preferences, 253
timeline, 162, 397, 431
Times settings, Language &
    Text preferences, 231
Title bar, Mail, 497
title bar, window, 69
Title control, DVD Player,
    437
titles
    iDVD, 388
    iMovie, 370–372
To Do folder, Mail, 499
Toast Titanium, Roxio,
    669–670

toggling toolbars, 68–69
toolbar
    Finder, 191–197
    Help Viewer, 167
    iPhoto, 335
    iWeb, 418
    Keynote, 479
    Numbers, 464
    Pages, 451
    Safari, 542
    toggling, 68–69
top command, 704–705
Track Info button,
    GarageBand, 397
Track list, GarageBand,
    396–397
trackballs, 630–631
tracker applications, 295
Tracking Speed slider,
    64, 239
trackpad, 15, 24, 34, 64,
    66, 93
Trackpad group, System
    Preferences, 240
tracks, GarageBand,
    399–402, 409–411
transcripts, iChat, 529
transfer speeds, 650
transitions, 370–371, 389
translucent menu bar,
    210, 226
transparency adapter, 629
Trash, 91–92, 108, 178–179,
    315
Trash folder, Mail, 499
Trim feature, iMovie,
    369–370
troubleshooting, 175–183,
    582–583
turning on MacBook, 32–34
TV Safe Area rectangle,
    iDVD, 384
TV shows, iTunes, 316

• **U** •

undo command, 89, 339,
    347, 422
uninstalling applications,
    145–146
uninterruptible power
    supply (UPS), 30, 42
Universal Access group,
    System Preferences,
    258–260, 735–736
Universal Serial Bus. *See*
    USB
UNIX. *See also* commands,
    UNIX
    files, 699–702
    keyboard, 689–692
    overview, 53–54, 689
    programs, 707–710
    Terminal, 693–696
unmounting, 107–108
unpacking MacBook, 30–31
unsecured wireless
    networks, 294
Update Automatically
    option, MobileMe
    preferences, 244
updates, troubleshooting,
    178
updating Mac OS X, 160
upgrading
    hard drive, 641–646
    installing new items,
        646–647
    limitations to, 11
    to Mac OS X, 58–59
    from older laptops, 14
    overview, 637
    RAM, 637–641
UPS (uninterruptible power
    supply), 30, 42

USB (Universal Serial Bus)
  Bluetooth adapter, 680
  drives, 645
  flash drive, 163, 336
  floppy drive, 634
  keyboard, 630
  keyboard ports, 630
  optical drive, 27
  overview, 18, 651–654
  printer, 112, 655
  SuperDrive, 27
USB 2.0 port, 22–23
user accounts, 270–274
user groups, Mac, 173
user interface, Aqua, 50–51
User Switch menu, 63
username, account, 263
utilities, 42, 673–676
Utilities command, Go
    menu, 105
Utilities folder, 147–159, 161

## • V •

vanilla account, 176, 180
vCards, 137, 143
vents, cleaning, 35
VersionTracker, 172
vertical alignment line,
    Pages, 451–452
VGA connector, 18
video. *See also* iMovie
  adding in Keynote, 482
  binary, 301
  digital, playing in iTunes,
    312–316
  digitizing, 302
  editing, 42
  formats, 362
  Front Row, 129
  iMovie, 128–129
  iTunes, 310
  recording in QuickTime
    Player, 434

video backdrop, iChat,
    532–533
video card, 20
video chat, 527
Video Effects window,
    iChat, 532–533
View menu, Finder window,
    193
view modes, 188–191,
    197–204
View Options, Desktop, 220
View Options dialog,
    198–204
Viewer
  DVD Player, 436, 438
  iPhoto, 334–335, 339
virtual memory, 638–639
Virtual Network Computing
    (VNC), 596–597
Virtual Private Network
    (VPN) client, 294
VirusBarrier X5, Intego,
    178, 564, 666
viruses, 182, 514–515,
    558–559
visual effects, iChat,
    532–533
Visual Equalizer,
    GarageBand, 410
Visual Indicator, Feedback
    window, 731
Visualizer, iTunes, 329–330
VNC (Virtual Network
    Computing), 596–597
voice technical support,
    172
VoiceOver, 735–736
voiceover narration, 366
volume, 106, 366, 398, 407,
    432–433
volume tree structure, Disk
    Utility, 151–152
volumes, 155, 157, 159, 215
VPN (Virtual Private
    Network) client, 294

## • W •

WAP (Wireless Access
    Point), 600, 615, 620
war driving, 604
WAV format, 310
Web browser. *See* Safari
Web folder, iDisk, 539
Web links, 425–426
Web pages. *See* iWeb
Web posting, Photoshop,
    668
Web searches, 40
Web sites. *See also* iWeb
  adding to Dock, 215
  Mac resource, 172
  setting Parental Controls,
    275
  Spotlight searches, 117
web space, ISP, 491
WebClip widget, 219–220
Welcome page, 419
wells, 209
WEP (Wired Equivalency
    Privacy), 600, 605
widescreen aspect ratio,
    15, 24
Widescreen format, iDVD,
    379
widgets, 15, 40, 218–220,
    425
wi-fi, 600–601
Wi-Fi Protected Access
    (WPA/WPA2), 600,
    604–605
window view modes,
    188–191
windows
  changing colors of, 212
  closing, 65–66
  minimizing, 67–68
  moving, 69
  opening, 65–66
  overview, 65

resizing, 69
restoring, 67–68
scrolling, 66–67
switching, 69–70
toggling toolbars, 68–69
zooming, 68
Windows button, Printer
    Browser, 657
Windows computers, 41,
    588–590
Windows printers, 658–659
Windows settings, DVD
    Player Preferences, 442
WINS, 246–247
Wired Equivalency Privacy
    (WEP), 600, 605
wired Ethernet, 571,
    619–620
Wireless Access Point
    (WAP), 600, 615, 620
wireless Ethernet, 19
wireless keyboards,
    683–684
wireless LAN (WLAN), 600
wireless mice, 683–684
wireless networks, 599–609,
    620–621
wireless printing, 685–686
WLAN (wireless LAN), 600
Word, Microsoft, 665
workflow, 713
World of WarCraft game,
    677–678

WPA/WPA2 (Wi-Fi
    Protected Access), 600,
    604–605
wrist rest, 43, 630
Write Only permission, 285
write protection,
    troubleshooting, 180
write-protect icon, Finder
    window status bar,
    191–192
write-protected disks, 154
writing scripts, 716–718

**• X •**

X button, windows, 66

**• Y •**

YouTube Web site, 372

**• Z •**

Zero Out Data option, Disk
    Utility, 156
zip files, 673
zoom, camera, 627–628
Zoom feature, 68, 259,
    431–432, 545
zooming, 64, 68

# Notes

# Notes

# Notes